DIARIES

1946–1949

DIARIES

1946–1949

CAVES OF ICE
&
MIDWAY ON THE WAVES

James Lees-Milne

JOHN MURRAY
Albemarle Street, London

© James Lees-Milne 1983, 1985

First published by Chatto & Windus as
Caves of Ice (1983) and by Faber & Faber as
Midway on the Waves (1985)

Reprinted in 1996
by John Murray (Publishers) Ltd.,
50 Albemarle Street, London W1X 4BD

A catalogue record for this book is available from the British Library

ISBN 0-7195-5591-4

Typeset in 11½pt Bembo by Servis Filmsetting Ltd,
Longsight, Manchester

Printed and bound in Great Britain by
The University Press, Cambridge

Contents

Introduction

In January 1946, when *Caves of Ice* opens, the Second World War had been over for nearly five months. As the title of this volume suggests, domestic conditions in the United Kingdom were bleak, worse in fact than they had been during the war. Rationing seemed more restrictive than ever. And though it is true that exiguous coupons ensured basic provision of food, clothing, petrol and most bare necessities, warmth and light in the home were regarded as luxuries. Without them hardy people were supposed to manage. Electricity was cut off as often as it was left on. An individual's stock of tallow candles soon ran out. It happened that the winter of 1947 was the severest of my lifetime. To keep warm in after-office hours (for in offices during working hours radiators were permitted to function) meant either reading in bed wearing a Balaclava helmet and mittens or sitting on a backless bench in the National Gallery to which few Londoners in those days resorted. In the Gallery both heat and light were available gratis. Of course the summer came in July (to leave in September) but somehow the deprivation of artificial warmth during nine months of the year did not seem to be appreciably alleviated in the interval. By the end of 1949, however, when the diaries close, restrictions on 'luxuries' were generally lessening.

During the years 1946–9 I rented a floor of a friend's house in South Kensington. There I lived when not on the road. This period was probably the busiest of my career as Historic Buildings Secretary to the National Trust. Owners of country houses were adjusting themselves to the dictates of a new society. Several turned to the Trust as a means of assuring the future of their paternal houses, treasures and acres which they dearly loved.

Throughout *Midway on the Waves* my bachelor years were being numbered. The title of this volume denotes a crisis in my career and private life. On approaching the turbulent waters of middle age I sought and found sanctuary in marriage.

In reissuing these two volumes under one cover I feel bound to proffer, if not an excuse, then an explanation of the protean nature of diary keepers. And I don't think I can do better than quote a paragraph I wrote in the 1977 preface of *Prophesying Peace*:

Since, then, a diary is merely a day-to-day chronicle of events, non-events and opinions, it will be full of inconsistencies and contradictions. It reflects the author's shifting moods, tastes, prejudices and even beliefs, to few of which he may remain constant for long. Thus on Sunday he may be wildly in love with life; and on Monday he may be suicidal. On Tuesday he may go to three cocktail parties, and on Wednesday prepare to enter a Trappist monastery. On Thursday he may adore someone whom on Friday he may abhor. On Saturday he may rob a church box, and the same evening give the proceeds to his favourite charity. Unlike the calculating autobiographer and biographer, the candid diarist does not know himself. Nor is he to be known by his diaries, for he is an irrational being, a weathercock, a piece of chaff drifting on every wind of circumstance. And if anyone needs proof of this assertion, he has only to look beneath the mask into his own soul.

J.L.-M.
1995

1946

No one asked me to a party last night, so I dined at home and went to bed early. At midnight heard the sirens and distant cheering. The idiocy of it. Buried my head in the pillow and turned over.

Went to the dentist who said it is trench mouth that I am suffering from. It sounds too disgusting, and I haven't been near a trench. I am destined to suffer from sins uncommitted. Dentist painted the affected area and told me to gargle daily with peroxide. Had tea with dear Lady Throckmorton whose nephew Nicholas Throckmorton, Robert's heir, called. Consequently I couldn't talk with her as intimately about Coughton as I would have liked.

Wednesday, 2nd January

One of the coldest of days. Midi [Gascoigne] lunched, or rather didn't lunch with me. We could not get a table anywhere so finally went to her club where she gave me a scratch meal at 1.45. She says poor Timmie [Buxton, her sister] is fearfully ill and must have another operation to enable her stomach to evacuate through an artificial hole. Ghastly for her; and what is trench mouth compared to this affliction? Drank sherry with old Logan [Pearsall Smith], aged eighty, lying on his bed in his cosy room. He calls it a deathbed cocktail party. He told me a long story of an American cousin of Henry James who stayed with James in Paris. The cousin was known to all as the Sir Galahad of the New World. He invited the novelist to sleep with him. I longed to hear the sequel but Logan was overtaken by a fit of coughing.

Friday, 4th January

Dined with the Moores. Emerald [Cunard] there in bad form. Also present Denis Rickett who after dinner told us that atomic power would not be harnessed to anything useful for years to come and that motors would still be petrol-driven. In other words atomic power is all my eye.

Sunday, 6th January

An explanation is now called for. Why do I resume this diary which three months ago I brought to an end? There is no explanation. I merely missed it like an old friend. It has never intentionally been a confessor, to whom I suppose a good Catholic tells all. And being a bad Catholic I used, when I went to confession, to skate lightly over sins I had a mind to while emphasising those I was less inclined to, and fancied I might with an effort abandon altogether. So too, being cowardly, I treated, and shall continue treating, my diary like an intimate friend who mustn't know everything. If a man has no constant lover who shares his soul as well as his body he must have a diary – a poor substitute, but better than nothing. That is all there is to it in my case.

Monday, 7th January

Began the day in a filthy mood. Was very abrupt with Miss Hall's sister because the spout of the coffee pot was as filthy as my mood. Then I refused to get off a bus when the conductress said, 'No standing'. There were two people standing already. I slipped upstairs where luckily I found an empty seat. When I came down and proffered my 2d., demanding a halfpenny change, I thought she would explode with suppressed rage. Went to the National Gallery which was so full the rooms stank and I thought I should faint. Looked at the Paul Klees. They are pretty designs that would do well for bathroom curtains. Met Kathleen Kennet who invited me to the Priestleys' party on Wed. evening.

Had a talk with the Berwicks over a drink. They were sparring with each other. No wonder she gets irritated by his slowness and prevarications, sweet man though he is. Found myself humming a desperate tune of my own invention out of embarrassment. When the sparring stopped Lady B. said 'Where is that noise coming from?' Then went to Clarissa Churchill's, she prettier than ever. James [Pope-Hennessy] came in fresh from Ireland in a beautiful thick tweed suit made for him over there. He was very proud of it although nearly dying of heat.

Tuesday, 8th January

To Charlecote Park for the day by train. Motored from Banbury station by Stilgoe the temporary agent. I interviewed the new caretaker, Wicker, and his wife. Delightful couple. He has been a gentleman's servant and has good references. So I engaged them straight away at £4 a week, to rise to £4.10.0, which added to two women working three mornings a week at 10s. each is enough for us to pay. Alianore Fairfax-Lucy gave Stilgoe and me luncheon and was most kind. She is a splendid woman, invaluable as a kind of foreman working with the men.

On my return went to a large cocktail party given by Mrs. Hawker and Roger Cary. She, his grandmother, most welcoming. Lady Ravensdale told me how her flat was burgled. While she was out the burglar telephoned asking the maid to meet Lady R. at Paddington and leave the key under the mat. The police know the man to be a certain Kavanagh 'who moves in social circles', but they cannot prove it. A sister of Lord Scarsdale, good-natured but plain, pushed me onto a sofa with her fist, like a pugilist's, so that I sat down heavily. She said, 'I have had three husbands. Now tell me what you have done.' 'Very little,' I answered haltingly.

Wednesday, 9th January

A meeting of the Historic Buildings Committee this morning. The Committee turned down Hever Castle as a gross fake, and it will be interesting to see whether the Executive Committee endorses this. I lunched with Lord Esher and he agreed to support me in appointing Robin Fedden curator of Polesden Lacey; also agreed that I should write the guide book to the place.

Esher spoke most eloquently about the Civil Service mind as we crossed St. James's Park – the foot-bridge is closed for they are digging a bomb from beneath it. Began by saying he never believed in hari-kiri. Many people after 1911 thought the House of Lords was doomed and gave up the struggle, whereas it still survives. He believes it fulfils today another but no less necessary function than it did in 1910. The same could be said of the Monarchy, now that it is constitutional. This is why he believes the National Trust will survive, and profoundly disagrees with [George] Mallaby's, the new Secretary's, memo on the National Parks question. It advocates defeatism in assuming that the Government are bound eventually to take over the Trust's activities. He, Esher, said this attitude was typical of the Civil Service mind, which is perfectionist. He said the aristocratic mind was quite different. It was pragmatical. It made the best out of indifferent materials. He referred to a *parvenu* millionaire's ball he once went to, where banks of flowers were flood-lit in the garden. He touched a lily. It was made of paper; the other flowers were natural. That betrayed the perfectionist mind at work. The aristocracy would never do a thing like that. I was much impressed.

Thursday, 10th January

Professor Richardson entertained me at Brooks's where I ran across him. He gave me names of some young architects suitable for National Trust work. Talked of his visit to Ireland and showed me his sketch-book of various scenes and incidents (sea-sickness on the boat) and elevations of buildings. Said the Irish are the only civilized people left. They evidently enjoyed his jokes. One man said to him over the telephone, 'I cannot dine with you tonight. My horse has a cold.' 'Ah!' said the Professor, 'he has become a little hoarse.' When he left the country the customs asked if he had anything to declare. 'Yes, lots,' said the Professor, 'but you can't get at it. It's all in my head.'

Friday, 11th January

I had a curious luncheon today at Gow's Restaurant with a Mr. Eland, an antiquarian, and three other men who looked like commercial travellers. Eland was my host, to whom I had written asking questions about Shardeloes. He had a shaven black head, no legs, only feet encased in vast boots; aged about seventy; very cultivated, intelligent and modest. He gave me several papers about Shardeloes and Leadbetter's activities there. Has proved to his satisfaction that Leadbetter was the architect. The three commercials never once uttered throughout the meal. Were they a sort of bodyguard?

James dined at Brooks's. He was his enchanting old self, indiscreet and communicative. He is madly in love with a Communist Pole who won't allow J. to go in a taxi because it is patrician. J. being a masochist enjoys this sort of treatment. In his book on Lord Houghton he intends to have a showdown of the upper classes for their cruelty. The Pole's influence of course. J. says he has no manners at all. When bored in other people's houses he takes up a paper and reads. Sounds hell to me.

Saturday, 12th January

Motored in the office Morris to Uppark in Sussex, where [Hubert] Smith and [Ivan] Hills had arrived before me. Lady Meade-Fetherstonhaugh kindly gave me coffee – stone cold – from a pot she held over a log fire. She was welcoming and friendly and most anxious that our scheme should succeed. The country here is heavenly, rolling downs under a pellucid sea-light. Backed by a belt of trees the house commands a panoramic view of sheep-cropped sward and the sea. A romantic house, yet it disappoints me a little. Perhaps because it is so tumbledown, and the slate roof is shiny purple and the elliptical dormers are too spotty. Lady M.-F. showed me all round. She has done wonders repairing the curtains and stuffs and bringing back their old colours by dye from her herb garden. Saponaria is her great secret. She is a first-rate needlewoman and, before the war interrupted her work, spent years labouring away. During the war she had to do her own housework and so the fabric repairs were neglected. She showed me one curtain which was a heap of dull silk tatters, and another, which she has retrieved from a like state. It is a deep, live mulberry colour, minutely hemmed and stitched. The contents of the house are marvellous. She told me that Eddie Winterton was ruled out of inheritance by old Miss Fetherstonhaugh before she died in 1895. He was brought there as a child by his mother and was rather rude; asked his mother why Miss F. dropped her h's, and if he was to own the place one day. The Lady Leconfield of the day was ruled out too. Miss F. asked her what she would do with the silver, if the place were left to her. 'Take it to Petworth of course,' she said. There are no servants in the house now at all. Lady M.-F. and the Admiral gave us luncheon and tea in the basement. Their lives are completely and utterly sacrificed to the house, and they and their son love it. Mr. Cook's agent, Hill, is determined they shall part with *all* the contents for the inclusive offer of £50,000, with which sum they have to endow the house. So they, poor things, will get nothing in cash out of the transaction.

Got back in time to dine with Bridget [Parsons] and Patsy Ward. Very enjoyable evening. Heated arguments after dinner; they both attacking the Catholic Church, and then Bridget and I attacking P's socialism. One uneasy moment when frayed tempers nearly snapped.

Monday, 14th January

Martineau [the N.T. solicitor] ill with mumps and the Secretary cross for reasons unknown. Grandy Jersey lunched but when alone with me is apt to fall asleep like a large and beautiful dormouse. I got back home at 4.30 and there was Lady Esher sitting in my room over a fire so hot that the marble chimneypiece had cracked and was splitting from the wall, and she was trying to screen herself behind the tea table. She had motored all the way from Oxfordshire to meet Doreen [Colston-Baynes] who fortunately remembered to turn up. The three of us munched dainty little cakes provided by Miss Hall. The two ladies liked each other and the meeting was a success. Lady E. brought her copy of *The Regent and His Daughter* from which Doreen transcribed a note that Lady E. had written in pencil at the end. The note was given her by Princess Helena Victoria to the effect that Charlotte Princess of Wales had been poisoned by the Duke of Cumberland. It was a common belief in Queen Victoria's family. Darling Doreen wearing a too short skirt and an old frowsy black hat. She was very forthcoming and communicative.

Went to Cecil Beaton's birthday cocktail party. Talked to Daisy [Fellowes] who had been to Strawberry Hill, and Loelia [Westminster] who introduced me to her beau, Whitney Straight. Talked to a charming young Norwegian over here with his delegation to UNO. Said I would be surprised if I knew how stupid most of the delegates were, especially M. Spaak. I left with Jamesey who was in tears because his Pole has been recalled to Warsaw. J. now hates Stalinism because he says the individual is sacrificed to the Party (i.e. his Pole is recalled by the Comintern). I could have told him that before.

Tuesday, 15th January

Made a regrettable and most extraordinary discovery this morning. *Pediculus pubis* Dr. Black's dictionary calls it, or them, in its genteel phraseology. Now this honestly is not through physical contacts for I have had *none*. I can suggest only the proverbial lavatory seat, perhaps the one in the train last Friday. Public places and conveyances these days are absolutely filthy. I know curates invariably give these reasons and excuses. But I am not a curate with a necessity to lie. Anyway it is a sad record, trench mouth and creepy-crawlies within a fortnight.

Walking down the street I saw my motor driven towards me by that odious Mr. Marcus. He drew up and said, 'You can have the old bus on Friday.' The cheek of it. Instead of saying 'Go to hell and keep it,' I mutely consented. Mustn't become a worm.

Lord Newton lunched at Brooks's to talk about Lyme [Park], for tomorrow he goes to Stockport to consult with the Town Council. I primed the simple man with data. Then went to Hampstead to tea with my lover Lady Binning whose reason for getting me there was to look at her china, now all displayed. But it is nice being loved so much. Then a drink with Pam Chichester because Hamish [St. Clair-Erskine] is in England for a week, returning to Italy on Saturday. Dined with the Subercaseaux's which was a success. Sat next to Emerald, and being rather drunk actually shouted her down. Behaved the same way with Daisy after dinner.

Wednesday, 16th January

God, I am worn out today. Own fault. Mallaby and I had an interview in the morning with Sir Somebody Robinson and Dr. Raby. The first is permanent head of the Ministry of Works. Briefly, he postulated that the Government were just as fit persons to hold country houses as the National Trust, if it was a case of their having to provide funds. Mallaby, being a civil servant, was about to agree, but I gave him no chance to do so, interjecting, 'By heaven, you're not' rather rudely, then explained why. Quite pleased with myself. Michael Rosse, Bridget and Clarissa dined with me at a new restaurant, the Lyric, in Dean Street. No one spoke much. Michael in his table-tapping mood. Clarissa, obviously bored, kept yawning. I was longing to go to bed. A bad host. Before this lamentable meal I went to Uncle Ian Hamilton's ninety-third birthday party at 1 Hyde Park Gardens. When I went to say goodbye he did not recognize me. Watched him sitting amongst the boys of the Gordon Highlanders, as obsessed with the conjuror as they. Several dreary old friends; and poor Bligh, the parlour-maid, in her pale blue uniform, crippled now with arthritis. The ghost of darling Aunt Jean still hovers in that house of Roger Fry's pitch black and green.

Thursday, 17th January

Sir Richard Graham called this morning to discuss Norton Conyers, his house in Yorkshire, which is entailed. The situation is, legally, complicated. Then Michael R. Lunched at Brooks's and we arranged a tour to visit one or two places in Yorkshire, and Little Moreton Hall. I called on Daisy at six and sat on her bed reading to her about Strawberry Hill, eating plum cake and drinking whisky.

Friday, 18th January

A Rolls-Royce is the only car that has aesthetic merits. It has solidity, dignity and beauty even when fifteen years old. It purrs and it glides.

Saturday, 19th January

Bitter cold and frozen snow in patches along the street. Got through very little of my book this weekend. Very dissatisfied with what I have so far written. That intolerably stilted cumbersome style of mine when I try too hard. Motored to lunch with Keith Miller-Jones at his house in Chelsea Square. Just ourselves and Theodora Benson. Who she is I can't make out. Novelist I fancy. Speaks slowly, as though drugged, with eyes shut. I envy Keith this easy, homely, little modern house with its countryfied air.

Sunday, 20th January

Mass. Work at book. Albert Hall concert in Bridget's box. Emerald and foreigners there. Bridget came back to tea, and then Daisy arrived in her black motor with chauffeur.

Tuesday, 22nd January

Lunched with John Wilton at Wilton's. He took me in his luxurious black Rolls to my office, we sitting in the back under rugs, driven by a chauffeur. Surprisingly sybaritic young man. Dined at Sibyl [Colefax]'s Ordinary and sat next to Lady Esher and Daisy. Lady E. said, 'You are sitting next the siren. I shan't be allowed to talk to you, you see.' Only too true. Promptly Daisy ordered champagne for herself and her other neighbour, Lord Hood, who had Barbara Ward on his right. I wish l could have talked to this brilliant young woman. John Russell's new wife, a plain, dark girl there, and John fatter, more prosperous than of yore, the ethereal Shelleyan looks gone already.

Wednesday, 23rd January

Picked up Robin Fedden and Ben Nicolson and motored them down to
Polesden. Fedden serious in his wish to be curator of Polesden. I think he
will do very well. We picknicked in the little room next to the library. I left
them there and went to Worplesdon to collect some books and letters and
a lacquer work-box, Goethe's present to the Carlyles for their wedding.
On my return the telephone rang. It was Rick [Stewart-Jones] back from
Palestine. So I put off my homework, and gave him dinner and Australian
burgundy at Brooks's. Came back here and talked till 12.30.

Friday, 25th January

Set off on tour of the Eastern counties – not perhaps the time of year
most people would choose. I don't choose. Stupidly got lost somewhere
near the Alexandra Palace. Finally reached Hatfield Forest where I ate my
sandwiches under the N.T. symbol, but could not find the Shell Cottage
or my way about. Did my job however and continued to Cambridge. At
3.30 met Lord Fairhaven and a member of the Folk Museum Committee
at the Abbey House off Newmarket road. Lord F. has given the house to
the Museum on condition that the Trust holds covenants over it. Not an
important building, but picturesque; about 1674 of red brick, big
chimney stack and curly gable; some contemporary wainscoting. It will
do for covenants but not for ownership. We should protect all we can in
this negative way, I maintain.

   Walked in the court at King's and got to Anglesey Abbey for tea.
Wonderfully appointed house, soft-treading carpets; full of semi-works of
art, over-heated, over-flowered, and I do not covet it or anything in it. We
had a frugal tea but sumptuous dinner prefaced by whisky and epilogued
by port. Lord F. is precise, complacent and dogmatic. But hospitable and
kind, although aloof and pleased with his noble position. Who is he
anyway? The son of an American oil magnate. We talked till midnight and
groaned delightedly over the way the nation is going to the dogs.

Saturday, 26th January

Woke with slight hangover from whisky and port, and my over-heated
bedroom. I don't like radiators in bedrooms, but like to sleep with the
windows shut in winter. The chauffeur who has two Rolls-Royces here
discovered my clutch was slipping and put it right for me. Very obliging.
Why do clutches always slip?

   I left this hedonistic household and drove to Willingham. Met a Mr.
and Miss Ingle, elderly yeoman type. They took me into their windmill.
Hitherto I have always a little despised windmills, and their whimsy,

flimsy construction. This one, not much to look at outside, a tarred brick base and weatherboarded top, retains its heavy wooden machinery. You climb countless ladders to a great height. There are cogs, wheels, shafts and vents for the grain. The top crowned by a wooden ball, the roof onion-shaped, which should be painted white, revolves with the wind and turns the whole gigantic machinery in rotation. This mill no longer works, alas, and is deteriorating. But the greatness, rudeness and strength of its inside makes me feel proud of my ancestry, for we were yeomen. I suppose it dates from about 1800.

I reached Huntingdon and Hinchingbrooke at one o'c. What a contrast to the Hollywood Anglesey Abbey. No answer from the front door bell, so l drove round to the back. Walked in and wound my way through a labyrinth of passages, finally emerging into the square oak room at the corner where Hinch was squatting over an inadequate fire. He greeted me with, 'My dear Jimmie, has no one helped you find the way in?' He and Rosemary most welcoming. Gave me sherry and a rabbit pie cooked by Rosemary, for the staff consists of army batmen and wives, not trained servants at all, and no cook. The Hinchingbrookes are picnicking in the house, still full of hospital beds and furniture. The hospital has only just vacated. Hinch took me round the outside and inside of the house. The gatehouse and nunnery, with gables, and the large 1602 bay window are the best features. Hinch has contracted for £400 to have the 1880 wing of red brick pulled down; also the ugly pepper-box tower of that date. This will make the house far more manageable and improve its appearance. It will also reveal the nunnery from the gardens, all sloping gently down to a lake with fine elm trees close to the house. The raised terrace overlooking the road is a Jacobean conceit. There is absolutely nothing to see inside the house, apart from the Charles II dado of the staircase.

At 3.30 I found Rosemary on hands and knees scrubbing the kitchen floor, and I helped her swab it over. We went to tea with the Sandwiches, now living in the dower house. Lady S. of enormous girth. Lord S. very distinguished with two prominent wall eyes. He showed me his pictures, ranging from Etty down to present times. Really a superb collection of French Impressionists and English school. We got on well. He rather disapproves of Hinch's intention to make over the place to the N.T. under the 1939 Act.

The kind Hinchingbrookes made me stay the night in the house, so I cancelled my room at the George Inn. Very cold and most primitive bathroom with no bath mat, no soap, etc. Rosemary a true bohemian, untidy and slapdash, and for this reason admirable, and tough. She is like a very jolly able-bodied seaman. Has four children and intends to have lots more. After dinner she showed me the contents of the crops of three pigeons shot that afternoon. Gave a precise anatomical lecture as she tore open

their guts, squeezing out undigested acorns and berries. Then started on
the gizzards and stomachs, by which time I felt rather sick and turned
away. She has studied medicine and wanted to become a qualified doctor,
but Hinch put a stop to that. She is robust, intelligent and affectionate.

Sunday, 27th January

At midday arrived at Woolsthorpe Manor, now empty but left very clean.
The spirit of Isaac Newton still hovers shadowy against the panelled walls
watching for that apple to drop. Met Mr. Smith, a retired electrician who
wishes to rent the house. Then on to Grantham and lunched at The Angel
where I wrote up diary. Today brilliantly sunny, crisp and cold. A lovely day
for my tour. Got to Gunby [Hall] by tea-time. The dear old Field Marshal
[Montgomery-Massingberd] seems older, slower and more ponderous. By
midnight I was worn out by ceaseless talk about Gunby affairs. The Field
Marshal much worried about his health for he has a stoppage. They have
no indoor servants apart from the wonderful Waltons, and old Lady
Massingberd polishes the stairs on hands and knees every morning. She is
seventy-five. Still we had an excellent dinner, waited on by Walton in tail
coat and white tie, I of course in dinner jacket.

Monday, 28th January

Pottered with the Field Marshal this morning round the estate until I
became blue with cold. Left at twelve, always sad to leave Gunby.
Lunched at Tattershall with Mr. Black, Secretary to the Local Committee,
at his villa, a sort of county council cottage, in the village. Mrs. Black gave
a sumptuous luncheon of boiled chicken stuffed with sage – she called
it Irish stuffing. Black and I went to the Castle which the Ministry of
Works have now emptied of their stuffed birds and fossils. They have not
yet removed the wooden hoarding from the chimneypieces. We climbed
to the roof where there is a light on each of the four turrets for the air-
craft, not very sightly things on account of the stays and struts. Left at
3.30 for Womersley [Park] but did not arrive until 7, losing my way after
Doncaster in the dark and rain. Still no signposts on the lesser roads. Only
Michael and Anne, and Susan [Armstrong-Jones] there. Delicious food
and wines as usual.

Tuesday, 29th January

Soon after ten Michael and I set forth, motoring across the Pennines, up
and down little hills through Penistone, Glossop and Macclesfield, in del-
uging rain. At Little Moreton Hall we were given eggs and bacon. I was
cross that nothing which I had recommended during my previous visit
had been done. But the house was clean and well polished.

My petrol allowance falling low, today we got Mr. Woodward to motor us to Steeton. The colliery owners offer us this most interesting late four-teenth-century gatehouse of limestone, with perfect window openings, chimney-shaft and stack. Groined vaulting over main entrance. It is a really remarkable specimen of medieval architecture.

On through Leeds and horrible, lugubrious Airedale, to East Riddlesden Hall, where we met Bruce Thompson. Very cold, snowy day. All agreed this property to be dilapidated, depressing and mismanaged – a discredit to the Trust. Ate sandwiches over a fire. Awful caretaker. On to Kildwick Hall to look at the oak furniture left us by the Briggses. The old brothers have all died and the removal vans were at the door. House on superb site overlooking Airedale. Late seventeenth-century gate-piers and wooden paling across the road, and the seventeenth-century garden house good. House itself Jacobean with some plaster ceilings.

Michael and I set off again in Mr. Woodward's car and drove straight to Clumber. It was a fine crisp morning which turned to raw, drenching rain in the afternoon. Stopped at the main entrance gates which must be by James Paine. Michael took photographs. We noted that the ivy ought to come off the lodges and the heraldic supporters on the piers to be repaired. The long lime avenue is intact; the plantations on either side are devastated. The ornamental trees in the garden untouched, merely neglected like the whole place. Michael had not been here since his great-uncle the Duke's death. There is not one vestige of the house left, nor of the terraces, nor the foundations, so that you can barely tell where the house stood. We walked through the neglected garden down to the lake. Found two garden temples, the one nearer to the house by Paine surviving. The bridge over the lake probably Paine's, and also the charm-ing gate-piers at the Thoresby entrance.

We arrived at Clifton Hall for luncheon which we were given by Mrs. Clifton and her son, Peter, home from Palestine and about to command a battalion of the Grenadier Guards. He was on compassionate leave on account of a threat by the Nottingham Corporation to his property. He told us he had to sell some of the property to pay for death duties. We liked them both and the house enormously. Hardly saw the outside because of the rain. But the inside is very fine. There are rooms of four periods – the Jacobean drawing-room upstairs, 1620, with huge marble chimneypiece of touchstone and deep plaster frieze with heads and masks; and the painted wainscot room of this date, with pilasters gilded and remarkable panels of men doing halberd drill, a room comparable with the one I saw in Holland House: a bedroom ceiling of 1680 with deeply undercut fruits in conventional compartments of the finest description: several chimneypieces of the Kent period, including a panelled room, now painted red and used as another drawing-room: fourthly, John Carr's work, consisting of the octagon hall, one of the finest apartments I have ever seen, the rococo plasterwork of the eight domed ceiling compartments very fine; and two excellent staircases of this period, the crinoline one enchanting.

They gave us chicken, and pancakes filled with treacle and cream; also port wine out of an 1800 port bottle with family crest embossed on it.

We left in the rain at 3.15 for our next destination, Pallis Hall, Norwell, near Newark, which we found in the dark after much searching. It turned out to be a house comprising three tenement hovels. Some half-timbering, but nothing of merit. We never saw the owner, who the villagers assured us was not in her right senses. Michael absolutely refused to look for her or even discuss the proposition. When we got back to Womersley I had to pay £9.10.0. for hire of the car for two days.

Friday, 1st February

Left Womersley for Ripon. On the way stopped at Sharow. A child pointed out to me what was the Sanctuary Cross. All that is visible is a stone plinth and a stump about a foot in height – not a very prepossessing N.T. property. Cathedral at Ripon much restored by Blore and Scott. Splendid monument to William Weddell of Newby with bust by Nollekens; refined, delicate features. At 2.30 reached Norton Conyers, a sunny, pleasant house facing due south across a wide expanse of open park towards Ripon and framed in a broad background of expanding trees. The south front has several curved Jacobean gables and is roughcast, which gives it a somewhat naked appearance. The last Graham baronet stripped off the roughcast to reveal red brick, but soon replaced it when he experienced the damp. Lady Graham, mother of the present baronet, received me. A capable, outspoken and blunt woman, with whom before I left I made friends, but who to start with was hostile. She manages the property of some 18,000 acres for her son who is not agriculturally-minded. At once she made it plain that she did not like her daughter-in-law. Charlotte Brontë stayed here and made it the scene of Rochester's house in *Jane Eyre*. A lunatic Lady Graham was once incarcerated in an attic room which I was shown. The entrance hall is filled with portraits of Grahams. There is a large Ferneley of a meet of the Quorn outside Quenby. The portraits include a Zoffany group, a Battoni, a Hudson, a Romney. There is a wide Jacobean oak staircase. On one tread near the top a large knot of wood is shown. It resembles a horse's hoof, reputedly of the horse which planted it here before collapsing, having borne its master twenty miles home badly wounded after the Battle of Marston Moor. On the stairs a small Zoffany of the housekeeper who was to murder one of the Grahams. Upstairs an oak panelled room with double four-poster bed in which Charles I slept. Lady Graham told me that both James I and Charles I stayed in this room. In the garden are some lead figures and urns of the eighteenth century. Lady Graham had a long talk to me afterwards and said she wanted to endow the house with some private money of her own, but I was not to tell her son this.

At 4.30 I left for Newby [Hall], south of Ripon, for tea. The Comptons are living in the library, a beautiful room like the Kenwood library, only with a flat ceiling and flat soffits to apses. Walls and soffits painted in pale terra cottas, and shades of pink and blue. The quality of the wall decorations and the stairs is splendid. Clare Beck arrived just after me for the weekend.

I left my hat behind at Womersley; also my silver shoehorn.

Saturday, 2nd February

Breakfast at nine in the library, meant by Robert Adam to be the eating-room. Delicious fried eggs and fried fish. Pitch dark and pouring with rain. At eleven the Comptons took me round the garden – rockeries, pergola walks etc. laid out by Captain Compton. Looked at the exterior of the house and the Adam stables. The brick of the house a rosy pink; the dressings of pink sandstone which have badly weathered and are shaling away. Something makes me suspect they have deteriorated, not gradually since they were first put in place, but rapidly within recent years. Taken as a whole the outside of Newby is disappointing. From the present entrance front the two projecting Adam wings look well, but seen from the eastern angles they give the house a lopsided appearance. The servants' wing and billiard-room wing are hideous and make the house far too big and cumbersome. I am sure Wren had nothing to do with the old house for the design is provincial.

The two best rooms are undoubtedly the hall and library. The marble pavement of the hall is exquisite, so too are the white stucco trophies upon the blue walls. The inset framed pictures, the Rosa da Tivoli in particular, impart just the warmth needed. The organ-case was French-polished and varnished about forty years ago. A pity. The Roman columns at the foot of the stairs are of a sea-green tone. There is a handsome Battoni on the stairs of Mr. Weddell as a young man pointing to a recumbent Venus. The library has a fine white statuary marble chimneypiece, of which the face of the right-hand-side term has become green for some reason. The tapestry room was dark because the shutters would not open and the Boucher-Neilson tapestries are covered with cloth to keep off the light and moths. The tapestries, signed and dated, have a grey ground, not pink, like the other Adam sets. The suite of chairs is similarly upholstered. With great difficulty I managed to see the tapestries which Captain Compton showed me by lifting the covers with a long stick. The ceiling of this room is coarse and clumsy.

The famous sculpture gallery looks better in photographs. In reality the decoration is insubstantial. It has also suffered from damp and neglect during the past six years. Stucco paterae have fallen off, showing how shoddy the decoration was. Mrs C. does not like the gallery at all, or the colour of the walls, a faint Pompeian red. The Barberini Venus was unveiled for my benefit. The arms and legs were added. There is a small recumbent hermaphrodite and a smashed group of a satyr rogering a female, which they showed me after some misgiving because of the indelicacy of the subject. I had expected the gallery to be more mausoleum-like, more solid. The oak floor likewise detracts from solidity. The best exhibit is the great green-veined bath with fluted domed lid.

Billiard-room 1900-ish with imitation Spanish leather (really brocatelle) walls and Tudoresque fireplaces. Perfectly beastly.

Sunday, 3rd February

I left at ten in a steady torrential downpour. The chauffeur had washed my car. The Comptons were very kind. He even lent me coupons for 4 gallons of petrol since I was running low. She is totally 1920-ish in appearance and manner, tall with dark glossy hair like Jean Masserene's. In fact she much resembles her. She has a white plastered face, with rouged cheeks and orange lips. Her artificial appearance out of doors is most extraordinary – a sort of affront to nature. I thought Mrs Beck affected. John Wilton says her affectation has become second nature. I had a late luncheon at Grantham and got home at six. After dinner went to see Rick who was painting rooms in No. 102 Cheyne Walk. Had a scratch meal with him in the kitchen of No. 97 and stayed talking till 12.30, then walked home. Felt a slight stiffness in my left cheek.

Monday, 4th February

Woke up with a stiff face. Looked in the glass and saw my face very swollen. Knew at once that I had developed mumps. A doctor called in the evening and confirmed it. At first I was furious because I have so much to do. Then became resigned. London seems to be rife with fell ailments and diseases.

Saturday 8th February

Only on Tuesday did I have a temperature of 101. Have felt quite well and written letters, done N.T. work, telephoned to friends, and slept. Enjoying *Siegfried's Journey*.

I have now been incarcerated a week and had but one visitor in old Clifford Smith. I am not in the least bored for I am a natural recluse. When the sun shines at this time of year in an inviting snowdrop way I feel an urge to go out and snuff the air.

Tuesday, 19th February

Have finished my book, but have much correcting to do. Went this afternoon to see the Constables at the V & A Museum, mostly small sketches for great paintings. Then met Kathleen Kennet in the Park under Watts's statue of Energy. Sunny but cold. We walked round the Serpentine and to the Round Pond. Two old men were sailing toy ships. They followed them earnestly and savagely, poking them with sticks. K. told me that when the weather is warm she hires a rowing-boat for 6d. an hour and rows herself once round the Serpentine.

Wednesday, 20th February

Considering myself free of infection today, I lunch at Sibyl Colefax's house. Violet Trefusis looks like a basilisk, upright in carriage, and very ugly. When we rose after luncheon I noticed a circle of toast round her chair on the carpet, large pieces crescent shaped where her teeth had bitten them. I sat next to Tony Gandarillas, grey and yellow and ill. On my right Mrs Hudson. I remembered how James shocked her at an Ordinary lately. So when she introduced politics I said I was not a Conservative, not a Liberal, not a Socialist. I thought it did not matter what government were in office, and that, if anything, I was an anarchist. I was certainly a Papist and would like to be ruled by the Pope. I heard her asking Raimund von Hofmannsthall afterwards who I was and whether I was a lunatic.

Went to the Greek Exhibition; but all the catalogues were sold and the exhibits numbered only. The crowd was appalling, the smell overpowering.

Dined with Charles Fry [a director of Batsford's], back from the States. He drank seven whiskies and soda while I was with him between 7.30 and 10.30. He is violently pro-American and anti-English. He said he had been away eleven-and-a-half weeks and slept with forty people during that time. From what he told me he must have behaved outrageously through drink. Said the Americans are to a man anti-English (I cannot believe Charles is their single exception); that life there is life, and England so dead that people living here have no idea just how dead. In America you can get up at 3 p.m. if you wish, and lunch at 4.30 a.m. Restaurants are open day and night. I am glad I am English and live in England.

Friday, 22nd February

This afternoon slipped away from the office to see Geoffrey [Houghton-Brown]'s exhibition of paintings in Ebury Street. Sacred abstract art it is entitled. There was one picture of three heads, called the Holy Family, that I liked. Dear Geoffrey, he is peculiarly modest about these works. He has sold none and does not seem in the least surprised. Yet they are not derivative and have a style of their own, and deserve more recognition. Considering how Tory and reactionary his views are it is strange that he puts into his paintings, if not avant-garde, then unorthodox expression.

Johnny Churchill had a small cocktail party of people from his wife's shop. I knew none of them. J. just the same sweet ungrown-up he always will be. John Wilton dined at Brooks's and was gay and charming. One should not see one's friends too often. That is the secret.

Saturday, 23rd February

Lord Crawford came into the office this morning. Only I was on duty. He merely wanted to have a talk, but unfortunately I had a slight hangover from last night and could not make much sense. He said that my mumps had caused more interest in London than the UNO news!

Had tea with Margaret Jourdain and Ivy Compton-Burnett, but really could hardly bear it and left early. These two women do not eat. They stuff. Ivy consumed eight cakes, for I counted, and God knows what besides. Their greed, apart from the indifference if not positive beastliness of their food, has the effect of nauseating me so that I can swallow nothing. They remarked rather pointedly, 'Of course Jim never eats a good tea' – a hint that I don't give them enough to eat when they come to me. They regard a guest not eating a good tea as worse than impolite. One is not paying respect to their way of life, not observing the proprieties, as though, if they were Catholics, one entered their private chapel without genuflecting before the Blessed Sacrament.

Tuesday, 26th February

Old McKechnie, the dentist, warned me that very soon all my back teeth in both rows would have to come out [mercifully he proved wrong]: this on top of incipient baldness is the end itself.

Wednesday, 27th February

To Wildenstein's to look at the Jack Yeats pictures which are a triumph of the rainbow. Eric Newton says they are magic and as such cannot be criticised. Waves of paint stand out a quarter of an inch from the canvas. Dined with Anne Rosse and we cooked woodcock in the basement.

Thursday, 28th February

Motored with Ivan Hills and Hubert Smith to Layer Marney Towers in Essex. Went over the house. Inside there is absolutely nothing that matters save the reverse side of the terracotta window mullions and cills, which like the outside terracotta are in good repair. Climbed on to the roof and noticed two twisted stacks of rubbed brick. The house would do as an institution for there are masses of outbuildings. The owners, nice, dim people, with money and no taste.

Friday, 1st March

Set off with the plasterer from the V & A Museum. It began snowing heavily as we motored out of London. At West Wycombe we looked at the ceiling of the blue drawing-room where a piece of painted blue sky has flaked off. Plasterer says this can easily be repaired. The Museum will do the work for nothing whereas the estimate they gave Grandy Jersey for Osterley came to £80.

Motored to Hartwell [House] and looked at the furniture there. Troops are still in parts of the house. Mr. Cook and Captain Hill have for some reason gutted the place. Both staircases have been taken out and make-shift substitutes put up. All the walls bare to the stone; and floors and ceil-ings gone. I can only suppose there has been bad dry rot. Grounds in a terrible mess, but the equestrian statue of Frederick Prince of Wales well repaired. The avenue is lovely. Went inside the octagonal church. It has a convincingly perpendicular fan-vaulted ceiling with central boss, con-structed by Keene in the 1750s. Owing to the Georgian Group the roof has at last been repaired.

I reached Upton [House, Warwickshire] at 6.30 to stay the night with the Bearsteds. He and Lady B. both charming, with unassuming manners of the well-bred. Hubert Smith arrived just in time for dinner, his car having broken down.

At midnight Lord B. took me round the house. Inside there is nothing of consequence architecturally save a few early eighteenth-century chimneypieces and a beautiful Coleshill-style staircase, rearranged by Lord B. and extended. Morley Horder, architect, built on to the house in the 1920s. But heavens, the contents! There is a lot of good

Chippendale-style furniture and some marvellous Chelsea china of the very best quality. It was badly packed away during the war when the house was occupied by a bank, and some on unpacking found to be damaged. The picture collection superb, as fine as any private collection in England. Many of the pictures are not yet back from the Welsh caves where they were stored with the National Gallery pictures.

Saturday, 2nd March

Very cold, bright, sunny day, snow still lying in patches, which means more to come. This morning we walked round the garden with Lord B. and the agent. It is only the garden he is offering with the house; but he wishes to include all the works of art. So does his son who is to inherit. One side of the house is 1695, the other 1735, but Lord B. has very much enlarged it. The result is pleasing. The grounds are beautiful, a high bank with belt of trees and a steep range of terraces. I am a little doubtful about the propriety of accepting this place, and without contents the offer could not be entertained.

After luncheon drove to Stratford and visited the church where they charge 6d. for entry, which causes resentment. Shakespeare's grave at the altar and its inscription give a tingle down the spine. How can anyone doubt Shakespeare's existence? I had tea with Mrs. Wellstood, a friendly little woman, in her cottage next to Anne Hathaway's at Shottery. She is Secretary of the Shakespeare Trustees. There were two others to meet me. They put me through my paces and criticised the N.T., as well they might, for ineffectual publicity.

Went on to Wickhamford, arriving about seven. Mama well and fatter.

Sunday, 3rd March

Motored to Coughton [Court] to lunch with Sir Robert Throckmorton. Nobody else present. He was disarming. He has no back to his head. He looks very young still. He spoke about Coughton with great sense and intends to live there from time to time.

Mama and I were alone in the evening. We looked through old letters which depressed us very much. They are emblems of mortality. She gave me a beautiful photograph of my grandmother.

Elsie Pethard called this morning and was overjoyed to see me. Talked nineteen to the dozen and kept repeating, 'Isn't he beautiful? Oh, I shouldn't say it, but isn't he beautiful?' For these words I kissed her affectionately when she left. She was my nursemaid when I was two, and sees me at that age today.

Monday, 4th March

Picked up Ben Nicolson at Leamington station and took him to Charlecote. He found nothing of any interest among the pictures, which he dismissed out of hand. These art experts seem to have no regard for family portraits *en masse*, with their historic and social traditions. We left after an early tea for London but on climbing Edgehill ran into fog and snow. Decided to return to Charlecote but the descent was so icy and slippery that we abandoned the car and walked with my suitcase to Edgehill village. There I telephoned Upton. Fortunately, or unfortunately, the Bearsteds had left for London but Dick Samuel said we might stay the night. He welcomed us most warmly and hospitably, gave us wine and dinner and put us both in the big room I had occupied the previous night. Ben is a strange creature. He had no bath and he did not wash. He hardly addressed a word to Dick who cannot have been pleased to have us. Ben is very grubby, but very easy-going and very sweet. I don't think strangers always detect the two virtues. We left the following morning at nine. Ben did not so much as say Thank you to our Good Samaritan host.

Wednesday, 6th March

Went with John MacGregor to inspect the Roman Bath just off the Strand. More interesting than I expected, for there, sunk below the earth in a vast tank lined with Roman bricks, is a bubbling spring. The whole shamefully neglected and choked with dirt and rubbish. I dined with Grandy [Jersey] in his large Victorian-Tudor house in Wimbledon. Inside ugly with shiny mahogany wainscoting. His little touches are 'how', as Harold would say.

Thursday, 7th March

Nancy [Mitford] lunched with me at Wilton's. She is radiant because she has already made £2,000 out of her novel *The Pursuit of Love* and has high hopes of it being filmed in America, where an edition is about to come out. She told me that Tom died intestate and so his estate, quite considerable, was divided between his six sisters. When that fiend Decca was notified she cabled from America, 'Give my one-sixth share to the Communist Party'. Nancy says she is not going to act upon it. She said Michael Duff will almost certainly marry the Duchess of Kent. Peter Rodd thinks her the most beautiful woman, without exception, whom he has ever met. The Duchess very flattering to Nancy about her book.

This evening went to see Doreen, one of my dearest friends. She invariably launches herself on a wave of preciosity. After a couple of glasses of African sherry she, and in consequence I, become acclimatized, and indulge in confidences. She told me she had never been interested in sex, either subjectively or objectively. For example, she cannot bring herself to deal in her book with 'the highly sexed woman' which, she is told, Queen Victoria was. The idea bores as well as repels her.

Friday, 8th March

At luncheon to see the James Ensor collection at the National Gallery. Very interesting this old man's paintings. They are nearly all dated 1881, some even 1879, and he is still alive. I recognize that they are good, but don't much care for his clowns and skeletons wearing hats.

Michael came back from Ireland today, and I dined with him and Anne at the Dorchester in their suite. Bridget and Sachie Sitwell there. He so screws up his face when he laughs that his mouth becomes a tiny triangle.

Had a shock this evening to receive a letter from Stuart, written only a week ago, referring to Logan Pearsall Smith's death. He died after a quick heart attack, his last words being: 'I must telephone to the Pope-Hennessys'. He has made John Russell his literary executor, which will infuriate many older friends.

Sunday, 10th March

James telephoned to explain why he had not been in touch lately. For the past seven weeks he has been madly in love with a French 'cellist. His life has been a turmoil. I drove to lunch with Joan and Garrett [Moore] and there found both James and 'cellist. Both looked very alike, two little black-headed objects, dissipated, green and shagged. James had scratches over his face.

Monday, 11th March

Lunched with James Mann, recently appointed Surveyor of the King's Works of Art. He complained that he had so much work to do reinstating the Tower of London and the Wallace Collection that he had no time for the royal collections. He showed me Sir Edward Barry's deed of covenant which he wants the N. Trust to implement by adding a protective clause covering the heraldic glass in the hall at Ockwells. Before luncheon I went to the V & A Museum with Clifford [Smith] and Leigh Ashton took us into the downstairs basement where there are piles of dusty furniture from which to choose pieces for Montacute. I left at the museum Queen Elizabeth's reputed napkin from Charlecote which Leigh thinks may be sixteenth-century. Also the miniature of Sir Thomas Lucy which may be by Isaac Oliver.

Tuesday, 12th March

This morning the Historic Buildings Committee to my surprise, but pleasure, agreed to recommend acceptance of Upton House on account of the collections, but were very much against acceptance of Hever Castle.

Wednesday, 13th March

At 4.30 Lord Newton called. The silly man was regretting that he had offered the choicest furniture at Lyme to Manchester Art Gallery. Now that the arrangements with Stockport Corporation for the running of Lyme have gone through he realises what a mistake he has made. Of course, he said, they ought to remain in the house, which all along I had begged him to arrange. I was appalled and urged him to write to Manchester asking for them back. He said he did not know how he could. I implored him to put his pride in his pocket and do it.

Thursday, 14th March

Met Michael at Brooks's. He wanted to know whom Grandy Jersey would like the Georgian Group to nominate as an Osterley trustee: not Keeling, not Acworth I said, but I would suggest Michael himself.

Darcy Braddell the architect called and showed me his plans for converting the first floor at Polesden Lacey into flats.

Went to Sibyl's Ordinary. My respect for her gallantry and kindness has developed into true fondness. She is old now and the worldly are always pathetic. Sat next to Joan Oglander who told me that Desmond MacCarthy was trying to persuade John Russell to surrender Logan's literary executorship. Stephen Spender has said that Julia Strachey attended the reading of the will and protested aloud at the fortune having been left to J.R. Spender said it was a real Henry James sequel to Logan's life. Rose Macaulay, with whom I sat after dinner, said she saw J.R. in the London Library looking sheepish and embarrassed. I feel sorry for him. It was not his fault that Logan took a fancy to him.

Saturday, 16th March

Motored to Lacock, having taken my typescript to Batsford's. Lunched at Marlborough at my favourite inn where I was treated as an old, venerated customer. Arrived Lacock Abbey at 2.15, but Miss Talbot in bed with phlebitis. However, a friend deputised for her. Having been asked to come in order to arrange the furniture and expecting it to take the whole of this afternoon and Monday, I was a little annoyed to find there was nothing at all for me to do. Miss Talbot had already done it – and badly. Furthermore, irritated to be given her draft of the guide book to approve, whereas a year ago I at great trouble submitted my own, which was far better then hers, (incidentally based on mine). I was given tea and drove on to Bath, reaching Mrs. Knollys's house, Richmond Lodge, at 6.30.

Sunday, 17th March

Horrible rainy day. Sung Mass in Bath not very inspiring, but the church full. On to Corsham Court in time for luncheon with the Methuens in the Nash library. They believe they have let the Victorian centre part of the house to an art teaching establishment, the state rooms to be used by them only occasionally and shown to the public regularly. Paul and Norah are to live in the north wing which has ten bedrooms. At present the hospital is still in the house. After luncheon I talked to Paul until 5 o'clock tea-time about Corsham and the N.T., and gave him data for his speech to *La Demeure Historique* in Paris in May.

After tea I left Corsham at 6 o'clock. About a mile from the village on the Bath road I saw a small car facing me, up the grass bank as though run into the wall, on its wrong side. I pulled up and was met by a man frantically waving, and holding a handkerchief to his head which was covered with blood. I asked him if he had had an accident. He said he had been assaulted and robbed by two sailors to whom he had given a lift from Bath. I stopped an approaching car and asked for help. They seemed bewildered and did not wish to be involved. So I pushed the man into my car, turned round and drove hell for leather to Corsham again, holding the man's shoulder with my left hand and talking to him without cease. Drove straight to a Maternity Home, which I remembered passing in the morning, rang the bell and handed the man to two nurses, then ran down the street for a doctor. The doctor was off duty and at first reluctant to come. But I made him while I telephoned the police. They came and took all particulars. The man was badly knocked about, but not unconscious. He had complained about his terrible pain all the way in the car and I was afraid he might be going to die. The moral is not to give lifts to more than one person at a time, and then not to let one sit behind you. For it transpired that the sailor in the back seat had biffed the man over the head while the sailor in the passenger seat opened the driver's door and pitched him out. Before doing so he had rifled his pocket of 10s.!

Monday, 18th March

Went down early to Bath to give a statement to the police station. Wandered into the Abbey, the Pump Room and round the Roman baths. The water is extremely warm and steaming. I cannot think why more use is not made of these natural springs and baths and why the people should not be allowed to bathe in them. Instead the water is filthy and full of litter. The ruins are gloomy and ill cared-for. In the Pump room drank half a glass of sulphur water from a dirty tumbler. Pump Room dirty, dingy and neglected.

Left Bath for Great Chalfield Manor. The Fullers away, but his secretary showed me where Major Fuller wanted us to have the drive mended and how they had weeded the moat. On to Trowbridge but Clifford Smith never turned up either there or at Westbury station as arranged. So I went on to Montacute where he arrived soon after me. We stayed this night and the following at The King's Arms.

Tuesday, 19th March

Clifford and I spent the day arranging the few inadequate pieces of furniture so far collected. Did not make much of a show, the only pieces of interest being the Queen Anne chairs given by a Phelips. They originally came from Montacute. Eardley joined us in the evening, and hilarity ensued.

Wednesday, 20th March

Eardley and I took Clifford to Yeovil station and motored to Melbury where we had a quick luncheon with Lord Ilchester, Lady I. being ill in bed. He conducted us round the house, which is huge and in a state of desolation. Lord I. said that unless he could get some more servants he would have to leave the place. Although seven-eighths of the house is unused, little attempt has been made at dust-sheeting. The rooms and furniture are consequently untidy and dreadfully dusty. I understand that Lord Stavordale will pull down the Victorian wing. We did not go inside it. Lord Ilchester's father built it in the 1880s in imitation perpendicular, well designed, well built and not at all to be despised. The library by Salvin, built in the 1870s, is very fine: simple and effective roof, book shelves of pine. Salvin impresses me more and more favourably. The 1690 wing is very beautiful. The material yellow Ham stone, glowing like honey, the columns and dressings of silvery Portland stone, as are the cornices, of which the mouldings have weathered the centuries, for they are still sharp. One contemporary long room has survived, but most of the ceilings are modern and indifferent. One 1690 ceiling, painted with gaily plumed birds, is unusual. Good and indifferent furniture. Interesting collection of family portraits.

Eardley and I visited Barrington Court which is now open once a week and in apple-pie order. Tenants make it clear they resent interference from us. We both disliked the interior, which is merely a museum of bits and pieces brought from demolished houses. The school which has vacated the house did only superficial harm.

Mrs. Knollys, with whom we are staying, is worried to a state border-
ing on hysteria because her cook is leaving. She is a source of much
anxiety to Eardley, with whom she is very proprietary and exacting. She
wishes to be kept informed of his every movement and action. This is a
mistake. She lives only for him. Poor old lady, with her stately Victorian
manner and manners.

Thursday, 21st March

Left Richmond Lodge early for Horton Court on the edge of the
Cotswolds near Old Sodbury. House lies in a cup of hill, steeply wooded,
and overlooking the Severn. It is offered us by a Miss Wills and Tony
Wills, Lord Dulverton's son, is to rent it. It is a manor-house with seven
or eight bedrooms. Miss Wills has spent thousands on it, too many thousands. It has a Norman hall of 1150, perfectly hideous, some interesting
Henry VIII detail, notably carved arabesques; a late Gothic ambulatory
(detached) with Renaissance heads of Emperors, most unusual. Nothing
else inside. The outside was badly restored some sixty years ago and the
stone pointed with black mortar. The walls should be harled all over. I
suppose the house is acceptable on account of its archaeological interest.
The situation is beautiful. The agent whom we took there was a flash-
cad, whom at first I so much disliked that I could not speak to him. In
the end we quite liked him.

Saturday, 23rd March

Bridget dined with me at the Ritz, I having ordered dinner for 9 o'clock.
Found oysters waiting for us on our plates and had a delicious meal. Took
her back to her flat and walked home in the middle of the night.

Monday, 25th March

I motored Gordon Wordsworth in my car to Barnsley Park, four miles
our side of Cirencester, and arrived in time for tea. Lady Violet
Henderson is Gavin Faringdon's mother and the aunt of Gordon's wife,
Doreen. A very friendly woman, nearly seventy, grey haired, wearing
trousers. Unlike Gavin and Roddie she is unsophisticated and direct, and
I would say, uncomplicated. We wandered round the outside. Park naturally pretty but the trees, elms and oaks much decayed. House fascinating,
being of the Vanbrugh school, tall, compact, almost gaunt. Does not stand
well. It wants a forecourt or some more striking external setting. Of
beautiful yellow stone, the capitals of the pilasters, cornices and moulds
sharply defined. The interior extraordinarily baroque, the hall monumental, with bold plaster reliefs, broken pediments, shell-headed alcoves,
statues. Lady Violet is ignorant about houses. She has painted the iron stair

balusters and the oak dado the same green as the walls. The dining-room painted egg blue is of Adam date, with screen at one end. The gilt pier-glasses between the windows belong to the house. The two semi-circular console tables with straight classical legs under them were bought by her at the Bolingbroke sale of Lydiard Tregoze. We had *foie gras* for dinner.

We called at the Wordsworth rectory at Broadwell on our return. Gordon's father greatly resembles the poet, his great-grandfather. He has the only portrait of Dorothy in old age. She is wearing a cap.

Wednesday, 27th March

Grandy Jersey and Leigh Ashton lunched at Wilton's, which cost me £4. Discussed the part the V & A is to play over Osterley. Rather a sticky business, but Grandy wished it. Then to Batsford's for first talk with Charles Fry and Mr. Batsford about the Adam book, for which they will pay me £350.

Thursday, 28th March

Went to Logan Pearsall Smith's memorial service at St. Margaret's Westminster. The Pope-Hennessy family in the front row. The Dame said to me reproachfully, 'I have been in my new flat six months and you have not yet visited me.' The lesson from Ecclesiasticus, beginning 'cast thy bread upon the waters', was read. And what did his bread bring back to Logan? Three volumes of *Trivia*, a reputation of a grammarian, and a sad, lonely and unfulfilled old age. Was struck by one passage in Jeremy Taylor's prayers, 'Accept the stupid and the fools to mercy'. How many did Logan accept? John Russell and wife sat in front of me, he with golden hair like spun treacle.

Sibyl Colefax and Eddie Marsh lunched with me at the Ritz to meet Doreen Baynes, who was the lioness. Doreen seemed happy and was very gay and entertaining. Sibyl amazed me by her memory and apt quotations. Talk was of Maurice Baring, whom Doreen saw much of in Scotland during the war, and loved. I thought Eddie was rather bored.

Friday, 29th March

Trained to Conway. There was a restaurant car again, but the breakfast was so disgusting that I didn't risk luncheon. Attended a meeting with the Town Council in 'Aberconwy'. It was not an easy meeting to start with, for they evidently think, not without reason, that the Trust ought to be more generous with funds and advice. It is a deplorable little property, a neglected and lifeless, unnecessary museum. Stayed two nights with Michael Duff at Vaynol.

Michael has staying a very nice New Zealand boy just back from Germany, by name Dick Wardell, who has intelligence and charm. He contracted pneumonia in a British hospital in Germany through sheer neglect. David Herbert also staying accompanied by his friend Joe, a Glasgow boy with thick black hair like a cedar mop and a baby face – very tiresome and argumentative. Michael can hardly be polite to him.

Thursday, 4th April

To see the collection of Sir Hickman Bacon's watercolours at Agnew's. They now belong to Mindy Bacon of Thonock. Wonderful collection but too large. Charles Brocklehurst came to the office to ask if the NT could offer him a job. Tea party at Doreen's. Arrived at 5.15, brilliant sunlight outside. At first I thought there must be a magic lantern show on, the room plunged in darkness, sunblinds down and curtains drawn. I groped my way across to Doreen who was officiating in a canary-coloured dress. Doreen loathes daylight and out of doors. Her annual agony is having to stay with her brother in the country for a fortnight when the servants have a holiday. Talked to Lady Lovat, now a little, thin, frail old lady. She was wearing a preposterous black pixie hat, with two grey birds' feathers over her temples and a stiff veil that stuck outwards at a crooked angle. On talking about Europe and our destruction of Vienna and German cities she waxed earnest and intelligent. Betty Richards there, very middle-aged and big. I felt like Proust in the last book at the Prince de Guermante's party.

Friday, 5th April

Had to give evidence today in the robbery and assault case at Chippenham. Kind John Wilton called for me at 7.45 in his beautiful Rolls-Royce and motored me down. Weather broke and it rained incessantly. The Chippenham Police Court was Dickensian; a bare Georgian room up a steep staircase. The benches inches thick in dust. John with his broken ankle sat throughout with me. First we listened to a bigamy case. The magistrate, an old fool, might have been John Sutro mimicking. Then our case came on. The two sailors stood handcuffed in the dock. One aged twenty-one, a terrible rough type; the ringleader, aged twenty-two, very small like an eel, very pretty but very wicked, by name Tulip, who in the dock kept winking and giggling with the other, unchecked, which surprised us a lot. We were kept till 3 o'clock, without being allowed a cup of tea and just as though we were the criminals. I was bound over – or whatever it's called – to attend the Salisbury Assizes when the case is referred to them in three weeks time. The whole business a damned nuisance and waste of time.

On our return we went to Lydiard Tregoze. To enter the church one has to get the key from the house. Church has several extremely fine Bolingbroke monuments, some stained glass and rich altar rails in gilded wrought iron that might be by Tijou. A caretaker took us round the house which is empty. It has been bought by Swindon Corporation which does not know what to do with it. It has one w.c., no bathroom, no light and no heating. Until 1942 the Bolingbroke family all lived in the servants' back premises, leaving the front of the house furnished but unattended. Garden elevation typical Palladian, without a perron, the state rooms being on the ground floor. They are very fine. Central hall a high cube with rococo plasterwork. Indeed every room lavishly stuccoed. Small chapel with recess. Remains of old red flock paper on walls. Stairs long and straight, with small balls on the handrail. Condition very poor; some ceilings down and you can see through to the roof timbers. Sad sight.

John dined at Brooks's. Told me he pays his chauffeur £8 a week.

Wednesday, 10th April

At the end of each day I think of what I have accomplished. Today I had tea with Lady Binning in Hampstead. She loves me with the passion of friendship and would lavish costly presents upon me, were I to allow it.

Thursday, 11th April

Today went with one of our new agents to St. John's Institute at Hackney, the first time I have ever visited this property. And what a wretched one! It is no more important than hundreds of other Georgian houses still left in slum areas. Very derelict after the bombing all around it. Tenanted by a number of charitable bodies. It does have one downstair room of linen-fold panelling. I found it terribly depressing and longed to hurry away.

At an SPAB meeting we discussed Chelsea Old Church. As before I was alone in voting against it being rebuilt on the grounds that there is too little of it left. I was in a minority of one – decision taken to rebuild over what rubble remains and to retain absolutely those surviving fragments, but not to reproduce an exact fake. But an exact fake is what they will have to produce, can only produce.

Friday, 12th April

The prevailing anxiety is the threat to surface-mine the actual gardens of Wentworth Woodhouse, up to the back door – a disgraceful business. Shinwell, that wretched man, is bound to allow it.

Dined with Charles Fry at Rules after trying some six restaurants in Soho and not getting a table. Charles far less drunken tonight, but more

sinister. He said I was in bad form, whereas I thought I was in better form
than I had been for days. He took me to task for not being on good terms
with Jamesey. Jamesey told him last night he was very fond of me except
when I was 'diabolically malicious'. Now that is the very expression which
he and I have consistently used in describing Charles. This has given me
something to ponder over. Did he learn it from James? Charles also told
me in a flat sort of voice that I was a great snob. Now if that is not diabolical malice I don't know what is. Of course I am a snob, not a social snob
but an intellectual one. I like the company of my intellectual superiors.

Saturday, 13th April

This afternoon finished off additions to my book and went to tea with
Margaret Jourdain and Ivy. Did not enjoy it at all. How these women eat!
And how horrible their food is! And talking of social snobs, that is what
they are. Their conversation all about the most worthless society people
they have recently met and admired at tea parties. Dined excellently at
the Ritz with John Philipps who leaves tomorrow by air for a hospital in
Switzerland. His blood pressure is too low. Didn't enjoy this either.

Sunday, 14th April

Very virtuously attended 10 o'clock Low Mass and waited till 11.30 all
through the Blessing of the Palms ceremony, and got my palm in the end.
Was amazed by the way elderly well-dressed Pont Street ladies jostled and
fought their way to the altar just as though they were fighting to get the
last packet of spam at Marks & Spencer. Palms this year are the old sort
again, and not that horrid box.
    After midday motored with Rick in his friend Barry Till's car to
Mersham-le-Hatch, the far side of Ashford, Kent. The caretaker, an old
family retainer of the Knatchbulls, took us round the house which is now
empty. Troops have been in it all the war. It is much messed about. There
are few decorated rooms, apart from the Doric hall and the
drawing-room with semi-circular bay. In this room, over the chimneypiece, is an oval inset portrait of Robert Adam. Since Zucchi did the gri-
sailles in the hall I think this portrait is probably by him. The architect is
in his early thirties and very handsome. No one else seems to have
noticed this portrait. The ceiling retains its original colours, but it and the
chimneypiece are much blackened by the banked-up fires of the soldiers.
It is a fine room. The dining-room is disappointing; likewise the library;
bookcases are Regency. The north front is rather too gaunt, but the
brickwork, a beautiful rose, is in perfect English bonding. The stone work
of parapet and comice very clean cut. There is nothing 'ersatz' about this
house. The north view over the water to the chalk downs is splendid. Got

home at 11 o'clock. The caretaker at Mersham made me quite sick by insisting upon showing us the amputated stump of his arm.

Monday, 15th April

Rory Cameron lunched at Brooks's. I ate a fried goose egg which also made me feel as sick as the stump did yesterday. The raw flesh colour of it is nauseating. Left Rory and walked to the Courtauld Institute. Looked at the ceiling of the library and behold! there was a small circular medallion of Adam, also by Zucchi, only ten years older than yesterday. These discoveries are rather interesting. Here Robert Adam is in company with Milton, Newton, Locke, etc., which proves that his contemporaries estimated him, or he estimated himself, highly. This portrait is a small one. Then delivered my typescript to Batsford's again. Mr Harry [Batsford] suggested my editing their new edition of the Methuen guides, which would apparently involve little work and no research.

Tuesday, 16th April

Lunched at Olga Lynn's flat – excellently. Juliet Duff arrived wearing a tall straw top-hat with wide brim, which made her look more than ever like a giant dragoon. But what an outward-giving woman she is. I sat next to Oggy [Lynn] and Mrs. Gilbert Russell. At 2.45 I went to Kenwood where I was shown over the house by the Secretary. It is not yet open to the public, but is very well kept. So too are the grounds, which the public seem to respect, not trampling the grass down or picking flowers. The notices are neat and not over-conspicuous.

To the Piccadilly Theatre, with David Lloyd, his wife and Blanche Lloyd. The latter has mellowed. I think her nice daughter-in-law has humanized her. Blanche spoke with utter contempt of the present Government, and said it was the fault of Mr. Baldwin, which I could not quite understand. The Secretary at Kenwood today also surprised me a little by saying that she considered any infringement of a law passed by this Government was justifiable. We had supper at the Savoy. Blanche so sweet, kind and tolerant that I was much moved. She used to be farouche even when supposedly enjoying herself. I remember when staying with the Lloyds at Lerici in the house they rented from the Lubbocks Blanche would swim with grim determination every morning to a rock. Noël Coward described hers as the face that launched a thousand ships, for we all dived into the sea in order to swim ahead and watch her slow breast-stroke and her fierce demeanour. On her head she carried a book, spectacles, knitting and cigarettes crammed into her bathing cap. Indeed even in pleasure Blanche used to be a forbidding woman.

Wednesday 17th April

Motored Robin Fedden to Polesden, which was looking fresh and beautiful through the sun-tossed rain.

Thursday, 18th April

Bought for Mama a present of a glass paperweight ball with water inside, which when you shake turns into a snow storm. It cost six guineas, an absurd price and I daresay when made cost 5s.

Ivy and Margaret took me to tea with Elizabeth Bowen who lives at No. 2 Clarence Terrace, Regent's Park. She is a very handsome woman only her teeth are rather yellow; she smokes a lot. She stumbles with a slight, breathless stammer over unexpected words. Speaks deliberately, with conviction, and is observant; and sharp as a razor under layers of charm. She said it was more difficult to write a very short short story than a long short story. Said that we must all fight against being state-ridden. She seldom goes out or away for weekends. Besides Ivy and Margaret, Dame Una and James were present. J. came over to talk to me and said that pressure of work alone had prevented him from ringing me up. His Monckton Milnes will not be published until 1948; meanwhile he is trying to finish his book on America. Says he is quite penniless again and has no income. Has £1 to last him till next week. All said with that calculating charm which it is hard to resist. I liked Elizabeth Bowen immensely.

Good Friday, 19th April

Mass of the Pre-Sanctified was at eleven at the Oratory. I had to leave well before the end. Before I left Geoffrey [Houghton-Brown] took me round his Thurloe Square house which is in process of decoration by that horrible H. and his pals. G. wants to move himself and me there in the autumn. The prospect of moving once again appals me. To him it is the breath of life.

Called on Helen [Dashwood] at West Wycombe. She told me that a crowned head, real monarch, might rent the house this summer, and asked what we would do about public opening? Just as I have arranged to open one day a week this is annoying. At Oxford stopped at the Blackfriars church and St. Aloysius church and said a prayer in each. Ate my luncheon just beyond Woodstock. This pretty village is quite spoiled by pylons and thick wires the whole length of the street. The Marlboroughs ought to have stopped it. What are dukes for? The country is looking its very best now, every bush bursting into bud. You can hear them like pistol shots ring out. Stopped at Chipping Norton church and said another prayer.

Called on Deenie at Stow-on-the-Wold and drank coffee with her. Then on to Broadway and said a prayer in that church, making five in all – a small penance for curtailing Mass today – a kind of Stations of the Cross. And what has all this holiness amounted to? Some very reprehensible springtime desires. Devoutness and physical needs have always gone hand in hand with me. They aren't foes, but blood brethren, who refuse to be kept apart.

At Wickhamford they were in the throes of preparation for a cocktail party this evening which they held in the garden. I hardly knew a soul. A few recognizable wizened faces of pre-war good-timers. Nothing but pleasure-seeking and inanities. They having *nothing, nothing* to communicate. The only possibly interesting person present was Pug [Sir Hastings] Ismay, who as Military Adviser to the P.M. during the war, must at least be intelligent. He was being jolly and gay, living down I suspected. He spoke to me most warmly of George Mallaby, towards whom I feel cool.

Saturday, 20th April

I motored to Birtsmorton Court – most luscious, low-lying Worcestershire country, my very favourite – under the lee of the Malvern hills, so long-backed, naked, nobbly and impressive. The dreadful Mr Bradley-Birt received me. House surrounded by a moat and very romantic, were it more genuine. The remains of the gatehouse are thirteenth-cent, the house fifteenth- and sixteenth-cent, I judge, rather like Baddesley Clinton, which is of course the genuine article. But the old boy built just after the last war a wing to the east on the foundations of a wing destroyed by fire a hundred years previously. He did it well outside in half-timber and rosy red brick. Swans swim in the moat, and peacocks preen on the walls. The moated grange (not quite) all right. The interior – two or three rooms of interest, Elizabethan panelled parlour with early Renaissance frieze, plain plaster ceiling. Mullions have been inserted where sash windows were shown in the old *Country Life* article. I could see no contents of quality save a shove-halfpenny table. Most of the furniture heavy black-stained Victorian repros of lodging-house baseness. Brass pots and pans in plenty, table-cloths of plush and doilies. Everlasting flowers in vases of plate. Pretty little church in the garden with two monuments by White of Worcester, one signed, the larger not so, but of a recumbent gentleman. The house is so cluttered with dusty, frowsty things that it appears a mess in spite of four servants, all male, perhaps because all male. Mr. Bradley-Birt spoke almost exclusively of his friendship with Prince Ruprecht of Bavaria and the Kaiser, of whom he has an enormous photograph on the piano.

Monday, 22nd April

Called on poor old Canon Alsebrook in the Evesham hospital. He is a wraith of what he used to be; sitting up beside his bed, looking extremely handsome, but so ill and resigned. He spoke slowly about the Sandys tombs in the church. How often have I listened to this conversation over the years, almost since he christened me? He is an educated but not wise old man. Devoted to the classics, and taught me Latin. Treated abominably by the family who would hide when he called uninvited at the manor, because he, who knew nothing of hunting and shooting, bored them. I can see him retreating shamefacedly and disappointed from the front door down the drive. But I always loved him.

Tuesday, 23rd April

Motored to Wolverhampton and lunched with the Manders. I found Wightwick Manor more interesting than I previously realised. The Kempe stained-glass drawings in a folder more beautiful than the finished things. The Manders' enthusiasm for the Pre-Raphaelites is infectious. He is a very decent, good, thoughtful man. Left-wing. He told me he was sure socialism was right and the rich should be taxed more. But he offers an additional £5000 to the NT so that his house may be maintained out of tax-free money. Is that disingenuous? I think not. Lady Mander talkative and pretty ('Call me Rosalie.' 'Call me Jim.').

   After luncheon I took Lady Mander and her son to Moseley Old Hall. Met old Mr. Wiggin there and spent two-and-a-half hours seeing round. Mr. Wiggin is so slow, mysterious and mystic about Charles II that it is difficult to make headway.

Wednesday, 24th April

Motored to Charlecote where I lunched and spent the afternoon. Back to London. Was just in time to eat a morsel at Sibyl Colefax's Ordinary. Sat next to Ben and after dinner talked to Bogey Harris and Rose Macaulay about Lord Acton the historian. All the time I was only interested in a piece of skin on my index finger that I was trying to twist off.

Thursday, 25th April

Motored the British Legion man and attendant to Cliveden where I installed them. To West Wycombe and back to London. The opening of both these houses is going to be a great problem.

Saturday, 27th April

Thomas Cook advised me it would not be difficult to get a seat to Switzerland provided the visas were first obtained, the French and the

Swiss. This afternoon I trained to Eastbourne where Paul Latham met
me at the station. Just the same in appearance, like a bounding retriever
puppy, hatless, his hair still yellow, clustering and curly. Complexion
slightly sunburned. We had tea at the station buffet. I have not seen him
since my disastrous visit in the summer of 1943. He was giggly and rather
endearing. We dined with his old mother who is staying in Eastbourne
to be near him. She is a dear, ordinary old woman of seventy-nine,
adoring her son. Paul is angelic to her and I have seldom seen any son
treat his mother better. She, he told me, befriended him when he was in
prison, never missed writing, never reproached him, and never has done
since. He says she has always been and always will be his best friend. We
drank South African hock. Paul is living in a different house at
Herstmonceux, on the road: not very comfortable and the ceilings very
low. He is greatly improved. Far less hysterical and more reconciled. Less
sex mad. Seems to take a far saner view of life. He will of course always
be self-centred in that he at once takes it for granted that one is interested in whatever local or domestic matter is absorbing him at the
moment.

Sunday, 28th April

Rained all day as usual. Up very late this morning because I did not get
to sleep till late. I sat on Paul's bed till about 3 a.m. out of affection and
a desire to console. He talked non-stop. We went to Herstmonceux Place,
which is not yet de-requisitioned, and into which he intends to move
next month. It is a beautiful house, not small. Paul plans to do some
unfortunate things, notably alter the entrance hall. The library with
exedrae is a prettily shaped room; the oval stairwell pretty too, but the
troops have smashed several of the balusters. The white panels of Coade
stone on the outside of the house are decorative.

Lady Latham came to luncheon. Paul has a butler who lives out. He,
Paul, not the butler, pays 19s.6d. income tax and all his money is in trust,
so he cannot live on his capital. It is hard for someone in his circumstances, very rich on paper with little money to spend. Went to the Castle
after luncheon and walked round it. Paul has sold it to Greenwich
Observatory. This was my doing for I introduced the Astronomer Royal
to him three years ago when he came to ask for a house from the
National Trust.

Monday, 29th April

Paul says that no one has ever insulted him since he came out of prison,
but I noticed that people in the Eastbourne hotel stared at him. It gives
me a perverse pleasure to be seen with him. All the servants, his own or

other people's, seem devoted to him. He is always doing kindnesses and giving people lifts, and making jokes. Yet he is profoundly unhappy.

This morning I bussed from Hailsham to Uckfield and was met by Mr. Basil Ionides who motored me out to Buxted Park. He is a pleasant, jolly, *bon viveur*, large and well-fed. He told me in confidence that on his wife's death her estate would be worth £2 million. We went all round the house, which was burnt out in 1940. Immediately afterwards they began reconstruction and are still continuing. They took off the top storey altogether so that from the outside the house looks grotesque. Nothing of the inside is left at all except two plaster overmantels of coats of arms and mantling. Everything else is new, or imported. There are chimneypieces from Clumber, overmantels and columns from Kingston House, Felix Hall and so on. Yet the reproduction looks flat and of poor quality. The staircase comes from the Burlington Hotel, General Wade's House. Buxted is full of good things and contains nothing that I would not like to have myself, except the famous scent bottle collection. I cannot recommend the house on its own merits. It is a travesty, a pastiche. And the Ionides do not offer any contents. The park is beautiful, but so are most English parks.

Tuesday, 30th April

This evening went to 41 Yeoman's Row where Geoffrey Lemprière, my Australian friend, is staying. I have not seen him for seven or eight years, perhaps nine. He is exactly the same, like a startled kangaroo, and his age is only betrayed by the tight fold behind the ear, and hair growing from the lobe of the ear. He is no more a ball of fire than he used to be but thoroughly, intrinsically decent. He was in a Japanese prisoner-of-war camp for three years and seven months and spoke of his sufferings quite cheerfully. They were starved and beaten all the time. The Japanese have no redeeming qualities of any kind – not even good looks – and are treacherous, insinuating and cruel. He says he will take me as his guest to Sweden the first week of June by air. This will be a treat.

Wednesday, 1st May

Bridget [Parsons] dined with me here. Anne's son Tony is very ill with meningitis, supposed to be of a fatal kind. At 10.30 Bridget made me accompany her to Emerald Cunard's. Neither of us was changed. We found a dinner party still at the table, all in evening dress: Lord Bruntisfield, Lady Milbanke, Mary Lady Howe, the French Ambassadress and the King of Greece. Ambassadress thanked me for the synopsis of British architecture and furniture I sent her. Was presented to the King as the man who looks after all the public houses of England – Emerald always does this – and shook hands, while bowing slightly. Should one

shake first, or bow first? Or simultaneous? Then B. and I were left talking
to each other and were miserable. We left as soon as we could, long before
the party showed signs of breaking up.

Friday, 3rd May

Dined with Malcolm [Bullock] at the Turf. What is the matter with me
that I find a staleness and futility in those of my friends whose tacit superiority is that they are sophisticated and in the swim? Lord Ilchester joined
us at dinner, telling us how corrupt the police are. He instanced the case
several months ago when he was fined for driving through a military
zone at Wilton. It goes against the grain for me to criticise the police,
naively believing all policemen to be like our dear old Sergeant Haines
at Wickhamford and Badsey who spanked the boys for stealing apples and
succoured old women and lame cats; and, after the Vicar, was the pillar of
village society.

Saturday, 4th May

Alvilde dined. I called for her at Violet Woodhouse's. What a gruff, rude
man Mr. W is. Took Alvilde to the White Tower and gave her a delicious
dinner; then to a news reel. Think A. enjoyed it. I almost loved her this
evening and kissed her affectionately on leaving her at her hotel.

Sunday, 5th May

At last got through to Michael Rosse on the telephone at Caernarvon.
He cannot leave Anne and keep his engagement to address the Wisbech
Society tomorrow. Wants me to be his substitute. Annoyed me a little
by implying that it was my duty to the NT to provide another speaker
at short notice. Not an easy thing to do when I am just off on a number
of engagements in Norfolk, and on a Sunday too. The worry about this
meeting upset me all day. It is a horrid, squally, cold, rainy day too. I
motored after Mass to Bedford and had a look at Willington stables and
dovecote – both well worth holding, and both in tolerable condition.
Stopped at Houghton Mill, rather dilapidated, weatherboarded
construction on river Ouse with distant church spires in the landscape.
Then to Ramsey Abbey gatehouse; very ruinous and in bad state. A
huge crack down the entire side fronting the road. Then across the fens,
the car nearly blown off the straight bank into the drain. One, called
Forty Foot Drain, I followed for nearly eight miles. Bleak and desolate
as in Vita's novel. I approached what I thought was a bad fire. It proved
to be dry black earth driven by the wind. There was a cottage receiving the full brunt of it. It was smothered, almost inundated by a
death-like pall of dust. Had a look at Swanton Morley, where we have

done nothing, and on to Bradenham [Hall] at 6.30. Alec Penrose and his wife out when I called, but returned, and I stayed the night with them. I was so tired that after two cocktails and a bottle of burgundy I hardly knew what I was doing. Nevertheless, after dinner endeavoured to concoct a speech for Alec to deliver in lieu of Michael, he being only too willing and I unwilling.

Monday, 6th May

Alec talked of Christianity of which he is now an enthusiastic supporter. Says this separates him from his family who do not sympathise. Shares with me the recognition of a need to introduce Christian principles into British politics. Thinks a new Christian movement or party must be founded to counter Communism and totalitarianism. Agrees that the next war will be a civil one on a gigantic world scale, not between nations but between these two creeds or issues.

Arrived at Blickling at midday and spent afternoon there with Birkbeck [agent] and Miss O'Sullivan.

Tuesday, 7th May

Dined at Brooks's with Professor Richardson. He said that he reads the Gospel lesson for each day of the year; that age has taught him humility; that never will there be architects until there are patrons again; that without aristocracy of the higher and lower grades there could be no beauty; that consequently it was our duty to oppose this Government at every turn. Yet there is no bitterness in this old man. He is a dear and good man.

Wednesday, 8th May

My Historic Buildings Committee went well. Michael was present. Esher said afterwards that it was the best of all the NT committees. I met Roger Fulford at the bottom of St. James's and he took me to lunch at the Reform. He is as whimsical, teasing and anti-papistical as ever. I like him immensely. He is finishing a book on the Prince Consort. Says that he and John Summerson are both turning their interests from Regency to mid-Victorian. In some measure they have both set a fashion. Says I am always associated in his mind with Christopher Hobhouse and Tom Mitford, both dead.

I motored two of the British Legion attendants back from Cliveden. One of them had a wooden leg and had lost an arm. He was a very nice old fellow. Told me had been a steeplejack and fell ninety feet from a factory chimney. His father and grandfather were jacks, and he loved it. Had climbed Salisbury spire and St. Paul's. Had a photograph of himself

standing on one of the arms of the cross taken by a pal from the other
arm. Four men can sit on each. Yet he fainted with fear when taken down
a mine.

Thursday, 9th May

Called on Harold [Nicolson] at six. He said he would not consider the
National Trust secretaryship because he was intent upon returning to
politics. But advised that the status should be elevated to
Director-General or some such term, and the salary raised. Said James's
'cellist friend was charming. Doreen wrote today that he was 'a wonderful being'.

Friday, 10th May

Meeting day. All the staff made to leave the room while the Secretaryship
was discussed. I learned that the committee agreed to ask Peter Earle to
accept; if he refused, then to advertise. My canvassing had results, so I like
to think, in that the committee scotched a proposal to make the Chief
Agent into the Secretary or to invite Matheson to return.

Saturday, 11th May

After luncheon I called for Keith [Miller Jones] at Sudbrooke and
motored him to the Wick, Richmond Hill. Went over the house opened
to members of the Georgian Group. Then to Riverside House,
Twickenham. Admired the Gibbs Octagon Room and had tea with Mrs.
Ionides. Margaret Jourdain came, wearing a fur wrap. Mrs. Ionides said
peremptorily, 'M.J., take that thing off. You can't be cold.' M.J. had her
revenge when at tea I remarked innocently, 'Dare we cut this beautiful
new chocolate cake?' 'Yes,' she said, 'of course. It will be good for *her.*' She
said Ivy C.-B. has finished her new novel, but none of her novels make
sense. She said she knew little of Ivy's antecedents, but thought her family
had lived in a *substantial* house. She had two sisters living. Her brother
was killed in the 'Little War'. Ivy, she said, had no everyday common
sense. For instance, she never knew in a terminus station which way the
train would leave from.
    We looked at the saloon in Marble Hill. John Fowler thought the
brown veining was original. I am sure it is not.

Sunday, 12th May

Low Mass at ten. Read most of the day the history of Sweden, etc. At tea
Miss Sybil Paley Ashmore came to talk about the Baileys, but was a little
disappointing. She is aged sixty-nine and my second cousin. It is curious
suddenly to meet someone who remembers my grandfather who died

in 1889, and my grandmother in 1896. I had a photograph of the latter on my mantelpiece, and she said, 'There's Christina!' Said she had a beautiful low, Scotch voice, that all the family loved her. That our great-grandfather amassed the family fortune, that his grandson the late Lord was a millionaire, and that in between his two marriages the first baronet led a gay life and begat many illegitimate children. He was perfectly hideous, so there's hope for us all.

Colin Agnew dined. A sweet little man. He said he weighed only eight-and-a-half stone. He is like the White Rabbit in *Alice in Wonderland*.

Monday, 13th May

Alan Lennox-Boyd asked me to luncheon at Chapel Street. There were Princess Natasha Bagration and her husband Charles Johnston, an intelligent, good-looking man, in the F.O., younger than her I should say. She is very nice, with popping eyes and wide teeth. It is ten years since we met. I drank red wine and felt inebriated the rest of the day.

Wednesday, 15th May

Had a long day. Left at 8.30. Trained to Gloucester where I was met by Eardley in his Ford. We lunched at The New Inn. Then drove to Crickley Hill and walked round it. Very beautiful hilltop but we ought to have more of it, right to the edge of the escarpment. Then to Hailes Abbey. I agreed with E. that perhaps after all we should surrender it to the Min. of Works. As it is, it is simply falling down and we have no funds whatever to maintain it. I got to London at ten and had a cold hot dinner – my fault – with the Moores. A French woman and M. Rocher there. He said Anglo-French relations were bad because we imported no French produce. Our Labour Government would not allow it. Joan looked tired. Her beauty shines no less, but it is of a different calibre to what it was when I first met her. It is as though a diamond had turned into a topaz, a no less dazzling jewel, but different.

Thursday, 16th May

Trained this morning to Aylesbury and was motored by Mrs James Rothschild's agent to Waddesdon Manor. What a house! An 1880 pastiche of a François Premier château. Yet it is impressive because it is on the grand scale. There is symmetry and craftsmanship and finish. I suppose most people today would pronounce it hideous. I find it compelling. A nursery school, which was here throughout the war, has just left. It is being scrubbed and cleaned. The Rothschilds are moving back into the whole of it, which is huge. They have been living in the wing. Most of the rooms are panelled with gilded Louis XV *boiserie*. One drawing-room is lined with marble. Furniture French of the highest quality. One room stacked with pictures, taken out of their frames. Could not see them. A hundred acres of grounds offered too. Beautiful trees. In all a better Cliveden. I have written a report, by no means contemptuous, upon it.

Friday, 17th May

A terrific struggle in the Passport Office. They have endorsed my passport which I retrieved from them after being told at first – when my turn in the queue came – that it was not to be found. Then left mine and Geoff Lemprière's at the Swedish Legation for a week. Went to Albert Hall to hear Schnabel but was frankly bored by the thirty-three Beethoven waltz variations.

Saturday, 18th May

Sheila de Rützen lunched at the Ritz but I was obliged to leave in order to pack and start off for the Vyne. Arrived at 5.45. I liked the Chutes much more this time, perhaps because he treated me in a less schoolmastery, more equal-to-equal manner. It is a beautiful house and the garden looking so green and spruce. The wide lawns all mown again. The school has left and they are living in the whole house because she says you cannot shut up part for the moth and general corruption. She is a childlike, almost childish woman, but fundamentally sweet. They live in a Spartan fashion, and their food is not good. Their views are too conservative and unaccommodating. I slept in the Gothic Room above the tomb chapel. We talked for hours and I think they will hand the place over. They know they must be the last of the family to inhabit the whole house and to submit themselves to its exacting demands. A younger generation which has not lived in it as children could not be expected to do the same. They have no servants living in. Four village ladies come during the week.

Sunday, 19th May

Left the Chutes at 10.30. A long sermon delivered at Newbury en route by a very saintly-faced old priest who punched us from the shoulder for not attending the Benediction. He declared that Europe was becoming apathetic to the Real Presence. It was a pity he delivered himself in a style imitative of Mr Churchill making his blood, sweat and tears speech. It hardly came off. This made me late for luncheon at Ted Lister's where I arrived at 1.20, having battled through storm and rain.

Westwood [Manor], Ted and Christo [Bulgarian servant] all looked well. Alex Moulton lunched. He and Ted very thick and see a lot of each other. This through my introduction, and I am pleased. Ted and I drove to Iford [Manor] and had a word with Mike Peto, still on his back with thrombosis, and very bad. He has had three days of injection of penicillin every four hours, deep like a bayonet wound, he says. And he becomes more frightened each time. He was lying on the terrace off the first floor overlooking the garden, even during the rain, which means most of the day, but under a ground sheet. When I saw him, the rain having stopped, he was stripped, wearing a tight pair of blue drawers and a blue silk vest without arms, which made me cold to look at him.

I drove to Bridgewater after tea and stayed alone at the Royal Clarence.

Monday, 20th May

At ten met our Holnicote agent at Nether Stowey. He is the stage pork-pie hat, 'May good fellar' type. I gritted my teeth, determined to be a good fellar myself. Succeeded apparently, for he pressed me to stay with him and wife. I declined. Went all round Coleridge's cottage and decided that Biffens, caretakeress and husband, should stay. Nice people. From Nether Stowey a most beautiful drive to Arlington Court, stormy skies with golden sun, the moors purple, and views distant and clear. Could see right across the Channel to Wales and the houses there. I think Exmoor more appealing than the pent-up lowering Lake District. Arlington Court is plain to ugliness. Of a dark, hard ironstone, the old part is severe Greek Regency, featureless. Unappetising annexe built on c. 1875 by Miss Chichester's father. The park untidy and overrun with rabbits, the whole estate no more remarkable than the country round it. Miss Chichester very old, white haired and dropsical, the last of her line. Looked after by a gentle, fawn-like young man from Shaftesbury Avenue. Her museum, made by herself, is a nightmare of model ships, shells and New Zealand Maori headdresses. She lives and sleeps in her drawing-room which is made into an aviary. Birds fly over her bed and perch on a clutter of bric-à-brac and masses of flowers. In the church is a memorial tablet to Mr. John Meadows, architect from London who died in 1791. The Rectory, which Mr. Meadows may have built (if he was still alive), is a very satisfactory building, with four projecting rounded bays. It has the minimum of ornamentation and relies upon line and curve. A pure architectural abstraction. I was riveted. The Holnicote agent, with the most sympathetic attention, could see nothing in it at all.

Drove over Dunkery to Bradfield [Hall] and stayed the night with the Adamses.

Tuesday, 21st May

Terrible showers all day. Spent the morning with Mrs. Adams in the big house. It is horribly over-restored but the great hall and the Spanish

Room are so good they make the rest worth while. The elaborate interior porch and overmantel in the latter room are superbly grotesque. She talked of Ayrrshire and our mutual relations, all of whose names begin with Glen. She told me her sister, Maud Wellington, had died as a result of 'faithful repression' by the Wellesley family, into whom she had married. Said the aristocracy was played out and that God had arranged for their economic eclipse to coincide with the decline of their morals. This house belongs to her son, Lord Waleran.

Left before tea for Montacute. Found Clifford Smith there. A lovely evening and after dinner we walked round the park, golden with buttercups. Both very depressed by the sad state of the garden, not a whit improved since our last visit. C. says that most of the furniture sent by Mrs. Trafford is the wrong lot, and not what he chose.

Wednesday, 22nd May

Motored to Salisbury to the Assizes. Was not called upon to give evidence for the two sailors pleaded guilty and were given only eighteen months on account of their youth, service and previous good record. The judge was young, about my age, and looked resplendent in his red robes. There was a subsequent case of a man who had raped his daughter, aged fourteen, which I could not wait for and was sorry to miss.

Friday, 24th May

Having spent all yesterday with Clifford arranging to the best of our ability the scanty exhibits we welcomed Sir Geoffrey Hippisley-Cox and Christopher Hussey today. They came from London and made several useful suggestions. Everyone at Montacute is so enthusiastic, the Yates family at the inn and the Shoemarks, a hereditary family of masons in the village, and all helping. At six I motored Sir G. back to London. We dined at The White Hart, Salisbury. He talked the entire way and I was distressed that my car made such a rattle. He told me that the late Sir John French, Lord Ypres, left his whole fortune to Sir Geoffrey with the direction that he should dispose of it as he thought fit. This will caused him enormous worry, trouble and expense. French was one of his greatest friends and a man to whom posterity has yet to do justice. Sir G. is very intelligent, wise and a bonhomme, without being intellectual. The best product of the squirearchy, with no sense of self-importance. Quietly dutiful, self-effacing and human.

Sunday, 26th May

A long day. Left at ten from King's Cross for Doncaster. Michael R. met me and motored me to Wentworth Woodhouse. Had time to walk round the outside and over parts of the inside. It is certainly the most enormous private house I have ever beheld. I could not find my way about the interior and never once knew in what direction I was looking from a window. Strange to think that up till 1939 one man lived in the whole of it. All the contents are put away or stacked in heaps in a few rooms, the pictures taken out of their frames. The dirt is appalling. Everything is pitch black and the boles of the trees like thunder. To my surprise the park is not being worked for surface coal systematically, but in square patches here and there. One of these patches is the walled garden. Right up to the very wall of the Vanbrugh front every tree and shrub has been uprooted, awaiting the onslaught of the bulldozers. Where the surface has been worked is waste chaos and, as Michael said, far worse than anything he saw of French battlefields after D-day. I was surprised too by the very high quality of the pre-Adam rooms and ceilings of Wentworth; by the amount of seventeenth-century work surviving; by the beautiful old wallpapers; and by the vast scale of the lay-out of the park, with ornamental temples sometimes one-and-a-half miles or more away. Lady Fitzwilliam in a pair of slacks, rather dumpy and awkward, came downstairs for a word just before we left. I fancy she is not very sensitive to the tragedy of it all.

We 'entrained' (to use a military term) back to London the same day. On our return Anne gave M. and me a sandwich dinner and a bottle of M.'s best white wine.

Monday, 27th May

To the Albert Hall, Schnabel concert — all Beethoven concertos. S. is indeed a wonderful pianist, sensitive and sure, strong yet not assertive. We dined at the Dorchester at 10 o'clock in Anne and Michael's suite, i.e. the Rosses, Bridget and Christopher Sykes.

Tuesday, 28th May

Ian McCallum lunched. He has pale blue eyes, alert and unforgiving. Spent afternoon at Batsford's. They agreed to give me £50 for the second edition of the National Trust book, and there and then a cheque for £250. Mr. Harry and Charles [Fry] still want me to edit the Methuen guides and also to reduce W.H. Ward's *French Renaissance Architecture* from two volumes to one. I had tea with Lady Esher in the Es' new little house in Chelsea. Lord E. huddled in a chair, wracked by lumbago and not in his usual rumbustious form. Mrs. Oglander and Miss Ethel Sands there, both very chatty.

Thursday, 30th May

Having been to Ascension Day Mass at 8 o'c I left London. Took with
me glass show-cases and the Charlecote Tudor cup. Called at West
Wycombe to glance at the ceilings repaired and repainted. I thought not
too well done considering how the Museum men are experts. Left a small
Staffordshire ornament as a present for Sarah who is to be married on
Saturday. Had a word with Johnnie Dashwood in his office. He was
looking smaller and more mouselike. Then on to Churchill near
Chipping Norton. Had a quick look round the cottage in which Warren
Hastings is supposed to have been born. In itself it is not up to much.
Nothing remains but oak stairs with twisted balusters and some William
and Mary doors. On to Charlecote which looks extremely neat and tidy.
Helped arrange certain rooms. Home for supper at Wickhamford.

Friday, 31st May

A really terrible day spent at Charlecote. It rained cats and dogs and was
bitterly cold. The Lucys all rather overwrought. The guide books have
not come and, worst of all, the British Legion attendants never turned
up. They were expected today in order to learn the history of the house
and be told what to do at the opening tomorrow. Not a sign of them.
There being no telephone I drove to Wellesbourne and rang up the
London office. Dashed back again. Left at 6.30, nothing done. Returned
to Wickhamford almost ill with nerves and anxiety.

Sunday, 2nd June

Woke at seven, finished packing, breakfasted at eight and called at 41
Yeoman's Row. Went with Geoffrey Lemprière to the Imperial Airways
House and were weighed in. Drove in a bus to Northolt Aerodrome,
where we drank coffee and ate a roll. Everything is efficiently done and
the attendants polite. At 10.30 we got into the aeroplane. This was my
first flight since I was sick looping the loop in Captain Butler's Moth over
Broadway Hill in 1925. While the machine was revving up Geoffrey said
I looked scared and started to read to me. This I resented, but I was scared,
and would not look out of the window for quite a time. Then I took
courage and first noticed what I think was Boreham Hall with its canal
in Essex. England looks small, compact and very beautiful from the air.
Most striking features are the fields and hedgerows, chequerboard
fashion, and the number of country houses and demesnes. It was not a
very clear day and at times we were flying blind. I had taken a pill and a
luminol and did not feel ill at all. Only over Denmark was it bumpy. I do
not like it when the machine drops like a stone. Jutland is flat and neat.

It has straight canals and roads with regimented trees. The number of old farmhouses, all in square formation round a courtyard, uniform. Few villages, but the area thickly populated by these scattered homesteads. Reached Copenhagen at 2.15 and bussed to the centre of the town. Walked in the Tivoli Gardens where we had tea. All gay and bright. The sun shining. It is far warmer than in England. It took us precisely a quarter of an hour to fly on to Malmö, which is ugly from the air.

Were met by Geoff's firm's agent who walked us round the town. I was particularly struck by the modern theatre, of simplest lines, too severe and unadorned, faced with a grey-white marble. A pity that the building resolves itself into ugly brick at one extremity. The season is over so we could not enter. The shop windows are *full* of good things. In fact the air of well-being and luxury of the Hotel Kremer where we are staying is wonderful and exhilarating. The shop windows seem replete with everything one could possibly want to buy. The beauty of the boys and girls. Everyone is young. The cream complexion of the men, their blond thick hair. Women with pale blue eyes and bare arms. The standard of good looks immensely high.

We dined in the smart restaurant in the Kungspark, the waiters in trim uniforms, clean as clean can be. Speciality here the hors d'oeuvres which go on and on, accompanied by schnapps.

Monday, 3rd June

I wandered round the town all morning while Geoff and the agent had business appointments. I made notes of the buildings I visited. We lunched with a business man who spoke no English. In the afternoon we were taken by the agent, a nice little man who has lately lost his wife, to the outskirts of Malmö and shown some of the recent suburban development. Extremely impressed by the wholeness, convenience and neatness. Everything is neat here. A garden city of two-storey buildings in rows, each alternate house facing the opposite way so as to ensure privacy. Air of gaiety and happiness. We went into Allström the agent's house, a little, low, long villa, quite prettily furnished with modern birch-wood furniture in traditional eighteenth-century style, but not absurd. A lot to be said for middle-class taste and existence. Complacency breeds content.

Allström took us to dine with a rich merchant's family, by name Mueller. They live well and modishly. Were most hospitable. Meal began with cocktails, then red wine, port wine, and brandy. You must not start drinking until your hostess or host says 'skoll'. Then you wait, or else 'skoll' the other members of the family before drinking yourself. You may never 'skoll' your hostess. Whole paraphernalia a terrible bore. We dined at six, the normal time here, and caught a 9 o'clock train to Göteborg.

You must make a speech before rising from the table and on leaving the dining-room host and hostess shake hands with each guest. I had a third-class sleeper, spotlessly clean with sheets, only a little cramped for there were three of us. The trains are all electric and no dirt. Every carriage scoured by an army of officials on arrival at a large station, and fresh carafes of water provided.

Tuesday, 4th June

Göteborg a charming town of intersecting canals. In the morning I was free to roam around. Examined the Dom, the Museum and all the eighteenth-century houses along the canals, including the Town Hall by Tessin. Bought a few ties and handkerchiefs. We caught a 2.30 train to Stockholm. For six hours the country never varied: fairly flat, heathy, birch woods with green glades of poor grass land, and many lakes. Soil looks thin and the vegetation not as green as in England. On arrival we drove to the Stockholm City Hotel, on the sixth floor of a huge, grim, gaunt building. We had eaten a delicious dinner of grilled salmon on the train. Walked round the town till midnight, wondering open-eyed at the combination of ancient buildings, grand shop windows and brilliant lights.

Wednesday, 5th June

Sweden is a land of lilac, though less of it in Stockholm than in the south. I shall not forget the hedges of lilac, like rhododendrons, at Malmö.

Our guide this morning appeared without his mourning band and tie, and went off to buy flowers for a lady, whom we suspect he is courting. This left Geoff and me free to do shopping. The three of us lunched at the Grand Hotel in a glass shelter overlooking the Palace. In the afternoon Allström conducted us round Skansen in the boiling sun. Looked at primitive Swedish wooden houses, brought from the north and re-assembled here, complete with furniture, utensils, etc. No protection to prevent the public from stealing. They just don't steal in this country, and the stacks of chopped wood for winter fuel lining the side streets are never looted. We drank lemonade to a band. This evening Jane Denham, the Naval Attaché's daughter, dined with us; also Allström's young lady whom we pronounced bossy. We ate at the most expensive restaurant, name of which I forget, and went afterwards to the Tivoli. Went on roundabouts and swings, and I felt ill and was sick. The lights and merriment are something I never remember in England before the war.

Sunday, 9th June

There seems little point in enumerating my doings in Stockholm. Since Geoff left on Thursday I have literally not spoken a sentence to a soul. I have visited the Town Hall, the modern Hagersten Church, the new hospital, the state apartments of the Royal Palace (disappointing), the Palace of Drottningholm (enchanting French formal garden and unique 1760 theatre, complete with contemporary stage equipment), the Hagaslott Pavilion (by far the best rooms I have seen; a veritable Petit Trianon), the National Museum and Northern Museum (the one picture, the other period furnishings). I have also been to the Ballet Joos and two cinemas, one film of *Henry V*. I have eaten in the best restaurants and some of the cheapest, and have bought quantities of clothes, though not as many as I would dare to buy for the risk of paying duties.

Only occasionally in the evenings have I felt lonely. Only once I bought some pleasure. Flat, stale and unprofitable it was too. Talk of cold mutton on Monday. Had there been only some nice hot mutton on Sunday. But no. Experienced little elation and no disgust. On the other hand the sun shone and I am well.

On Monday visited the new cemetery at Eskede suburb by Asplund and was greatly impressed by it. Graves neatly arranged within boskets of birch or pine, all the new tombstones simple and unexceptionable. Did not see one that was offensive. The main chapel and crematorium of white marble; magnificent bronze group within an open temple, and vertical figures aspiring skywards, made more effective by there being no roof over them. The descending ground well laid out in a kind of terrace wall, enclosing little memorial courts, or gardens. Great polished granite Cross standing silhouetted beside the temple. The view from the approach positively welcoming. The whole conception is original, underivative, modern, cheerful. Above all cheerful, as though the Swedes are putting a bold front on death, pretending that darkness is light, corruption is amendment. Death is all for the best in the best of all possible worlds. So contrary to the English approach which is a dismal belief that the trappings of death must be inartistic and rebarbative.

Left by night train, second-class sleeper to Malmö. Met a distinguished Danish count in the next sleeper who spoke of the deplorable condition of Denmark since the war, the workers not working and demanding high wages, just like present-day England.

Tuesday, 11th June

Arrived Malmö at 7.30 just in time for plane to Copenhagen, where I had breakfast. Plane left Copenhagen at 10.45 and reached Northolt at 1.5. It was a large liner, holding forty people, and much larger than the one going out. Consequently it flew higher. Ears started cracking. The higher the more frightening, I think. For some time we were right above the clouds, white like the Alps and dazzling. Watched the shadow of the plane surrounded by an iridescent halo, like a rainbow, chasing below us. Then suddenly a hole made in the clouds and land appeared tiny far underneath. Later we descended and the weather improved. It is strange how flying through clouds shakes the plane and makes it bump. I noticed from the air how sheep and cattle eat their way systematically across a field, keeping to a line, or rather circumference. From a height there is distinct demarcation of colour between the grazed and ungrazed grass.

Wednesday, 12th June

Philip James who lunched with me said that the late Lord Keynes was a man of such superior moral power as well as intellect that in his presence you at once felt elevated to a plane that permitted only the most edifying conversation. He drew the best out of you and his modesty never allowed his intellectual superiority to be overbearing.

John Wilton and I dined at Wilton's, and I suggested our walking across St. James's Park to inspect some photographs at my office. I had not reckoned with the surging crowds of people looking at the illuminated fountains in the lake. We were nearly crushed to death. These fountains are pretty but more suited to the formality of Versailles gardens than the informality of this park.

Friday, 14th June

Meetings today. Our new Secretary, Admiral Bevir, in attendance, although George Mallaby was in the office for the last time. Admiral seems jolly, if too inclined to be facetious. Of course he has been warned by the Chairman that we are not a bureaucratic team of experts, but a dedicated group of happy-go-lucky enthusiasts, who ought not to be bossed about.

Lunched with Harold [Nicolson] at the Travellers'. Lord Crawford pressed me to stay at Haigh Hall next weekend to see his pictures in case a few might do for Montacute. He is packing up and leaving the place for good. I said how sad it must be for him. He looked desperately unhappy for a moment and replied, 'Really, it is just terrible how much I mind.'

Saturday, 15th June

At 10.30 to the Soane Museum and began looking through the Adam drawings. John Summerson came up and said, 'I have not yet studied these in any detail, but a cursory inspection is enough to convince me what a very great man Robert Adam was.' There must be twenty volumes in all and I examined two thoroughly. The coloured drawings are superb. After a quick luncheon went to Batsford's where from two till five went through the illustrations for my book. Made a selection by process of eliminating several hundreds submitted.

At six went to Doreen. She said that when she got going on her writing she became an instrument, a gigantic machine or fountain pen through which outside thoughts and ideas poured, sometimes to the extent of thoroughly alarming her, the *she* remaining such a passive, uncontrolling feature of the process.

Sunday, 16th June

Motored to Polesden Lacey for tea with Robin Fedden who in the face of every domestic adversity has already made a splendid start with the museum. I was very impressed. Midi [Gascoigne] came over afterwards, and I went to sup with her and Derick at their new house nearby. Midi told me that Timmy Buxton is dying of cancer.

Monday, 17th June

Trained with Hubert Smith to Darlington and stayed the night at The Morritt Arms at Rokeby on the Tees. After a late supper we went for a walk to Egglestone Abbey, belonging to the Ministry of Works. Did not like the heavy black pointing of the stonework which they have done there. The situation is very romantic. I disliked the ugly little wooden hut which they have erected just in front of the ruins. The Ministry lacks taste and sensitivity in spite of its academic superiority. Listened to the curlews. Hubert told me that corncrakes are practically extinct in the south.

Tuesday, 18th June

At ten Lord Barnard's agent – very nice man – motored us to Raby Castle. It was pouring torrential rain as it has done every day this season. We had a hurried look round the Castle, of which nothing inside impressed me very favourably. Most of the rooms are heavy 1840. The ball room of that date is enormous. There are vestiges of late seventeenth-century woodwork. Most of the furniture stacked away, but what I saw of it and the pictures at a hasty glance left me cold. The outside is beautiful and 'picturesque'. The park and surrounding country fine and unspoilt. The walled garden is well set out. Of the house the kitchen is the most interesting apartment. Large and square, it is still in use. It has very highly placed windows; a lantern over all and most curious walks, like aisles, through the thickness of the walls. Many old burnished coppers and moulds on shelves. Lord B. is rather severe and practical, and only attractive when he laughs, which is rarely. Lady B. is younger, good-looking, and well dressed in tweeds. A pretty young daughter barely out, and a younger boy, aged about nineteen. They gave us a delicious luncheon of mutton and eclairs filled with real cream; also the richest plum cake stuffed with fruit from New Zealand. Our journey back to London was tedious owing to the train breaking down outside Doncaster station for one-and-a-half hours.

Wednesday, 19th June

I don't think I shall be very happy with the new Secretary, our Vice-Admiral. In his facetiousness there is an underlying disdain which I don't find funny. Lord Rochdale came to see me about his tapestries, a queer, fortyish man with heavy moustache, and rather a zanyish look that people have who are senior wranglers. My telephone never ceased ringing while he was in the office, so that I became frappy, which was rather rude to him.

Charles [Fry] dined at the White Tower. As usual he made me drink. We had a red Greek wine with saffron in it. Charles bores me with his queer talk. It is insensitive of him to suppose that I want to listen to it. He is not a person to see for long. At the St. James's Club Sachie Sitwell joined us. He is going to Holland for a month with Charles and Mr. Batsford. God help him! He talked of Sweden.

Thursday, 20th June

Motored Gwynne Ramsey to Hatchlands. He is a dull, dear little man, down-trodden and shy. Goodhart-Rendel gave us, plus Christopher Gibbs, Acland and May, his agent, an excellent luncheon with sherry and port. There is a happy air about this house, something that may have hung over from the Boscawens' day. Conversation was entirely between G.-R. and me about obscure architects, funny stories about Surrey county families long ago, and his childhood. This embarrassed me a bit because the others sat silently smirking. Christopher said to me afterwards it was a typical Jim conversation. Yet I did not start it, even if I provoked it. We settled several outstanding matters concerning the opening.

To Sibyl Colefax's Ordinary which I did not enjoy. Ben Nicolson, who was present, said to me 'How many marks out of ten do you give this Ordinary?' I said, 'Two.'

Friday, 21st June

The longest day and rather beautiful. This afternoon motored to St. John's Jerusalem for tea to discuss the opening of that house. Walked round the garden with Sir Stephen Tallents, who is a wizened apple. He has the suave, civil servant manner which I don't much trust. His eldest son is a peach – a dark peach, tall and intelligent and sympathetic. As yet untainted by the formalities of Whitehall. I still find this place interesting and desirable. On the way home a torrential downpour obliged me to stop the car for I could not see through the waterfall over the windscreen.

John Wyndham had a drink with me at six to tell me that we must write a letter which he can show his uncle, Lord Leconfield, reassuring him that he may live undisturbed at Petworth during his lifetime. The silly old man. He has been reassured over and over again. After dinner went to the Soane Museum, where John Summerson let me look through the Adam drawings at leisure. One volume of coloured arabesques are by a certain Giuseppe Monochi, whom I have not come across before. John told me that staying with the E......s was squalor indescribable. A friend of his assured him that on coming down to breakfast at what he considered a reasonable hour there was nothing to be seen on the dining-room table but a full, steaming jerry.

Saturday, 22nd June

Took midday train to Wigan and was met by Lord Crawford, hatless, grey and charming. What a nice man he is; what John Wilton calls 'grand', and comparatively young still – say forty-five. He is cultivated, civilized, urbane, polite, industrious on behalf of the arts, dutiful, a patron – in other words an anachronism in this detestable age, fighting a losing battle with no rancour, good-humouredly, agony gnawing at his heart. He took me straight to Winstanly Hall, a large house on the outskirts of Wigan, to deliver a Queen Anne portrait of a mutual ancestress of his and the owner's. While he was delivering I went at his direction to the stable yard, built in 1834 with a terracotta fountain of Father Neptune riding his horses, whose nostrils and ears spout water. Surface mining has just taken place right up to the front door, and the land has not been reinstated. It is the most appalling mess, a wilderness of dead earth in unsightly piles. All the fine trees gone. The house belongs to Squire Bankes – I was introduced to him as such. He is an old, shrivelled man, of great vitality, rather gaga now and inarticulate, a 'character' much beloved. Mrs. Bankes also well-bred and delightful. The ATS have occupied half the house. The whole place is devastation. It has broken the old man's heart and he can talk of nothing else. Yet he shows no bitterness.

The drive of Haigh Hall is entered direct from Wigan. It twirls, twists uphill through massed hedges of rhododendron and laurel. The house lies on a plateau overlooking the chimneys of Wigan, pit heads and hills beyond. It is the house of Mr. Gradgrind, but a well built classical house of 1830, actually designed by Lord C.'s great-great-grandfather, a very pleasing house of local white stone, machine cut. The lines are concise and clean. Compact and symmetrical. Lady Crawford was away, for which he apologised, but his white-haired mother there and a genteel secretary. Hardly any servants. We waited on each other. House in a state of utter muddle for all the furniture and pictures are stacked, and in process of removal. Claret for dinner. He and I talked of all sorts of things, including the NT, until midnight over a rare rum, which is 200 years old. Very strong and we drank it as a liqueur.

Sunday, 23rd June

Lord Crawford took me round the house to look at the stacked pictures of which there are hundreds. I made a list of twenty-five that I thought might be suitable for Montacute. They included several Teniers, a Ruysdael, Ostades, van der Neer, a Pintoricchio, Reynolds of Lady Eglington at the harp, Opie of Dr. Johnson, Romney of the young Pitt, and so forth. Superb collection of pictures, and the Duccio one of the finest pictures in existence. Much of the library has already gone to Balcarres, but he showed me a First Folio Shakespeare rebound, and a Second Folio in original boards. Interior of the house is good of its date. No furniture of much consequence.

Monday, 24th June

Motored to Charlecote for the day and took with me Ramsey and George Dix who liked each other. George a sweet and guileless American, full of enthusiasm for the social life, for which one does not dislike him. The head guide whom I had arranged to meet did not turn up.

Tuesday, 25th June

Today we had a Reports Committee at which the bewildered Admiral was present. He does not know much about the National Trust and is, besides, not an intelligent man. He pierces one with a cold blue eye like a schoolmaster trying desperately to assess a new boy; only he is the new boy. At Batsford's went through illustrations with Fry and made some headway, though not a great deal. Clarissa [Churchill] dined at the White Tower. I tried a technique of rapid talk, which answered well for one hour. After that for lack of collaboration I subsided into an exhausted heap.

Wednesday, 26th June

Arthur Oswald of *Country Life* lunched. He wants to enlist my interest in a new architectural periodical he intends launching, more scholarly than *C. Life* and less precious than the *Architectural Review*. I feel that this gentle and diffident man is under-valued by his colleagues.

Eardley and I went to Salisbury together, and motored to Long Crichel where I stayed two nights. He is, as always, the dearest and best companion on expeditions.

Thursday, 27th June

We spent the day at Montacute arranging the stuff which has come since our last visit. Daylight is beginning to appear on the dusky horizon. On the way back to Long Crichel we stopped at Eastbury Park, now a country club, of which E. is a member. All that is left is one wing of Vanbrugh's house, a fine piece of architecture outside, but after 200 years it still looks the fragment it is. The interior decoration *quelconque*. The Squire's son, Farquharson, runs the club. I thought he and his assistants looked rather louche.

Eddy is unwell with influenza; very low and sepulchral.

Friday, 28th June

Finished our work at Montacute and had tea with Mrs Knollys in Bath. Then called on Mr. Cook the mysterious benefactor's house in Syon Place to see two Raeburns he offers the Trust for Montacute. Before my finger was off the bell he opened the front door himself. Was not the shy, shifty little eccentric I imagined, but a tall, self-possessed man rather like Bogey Harris. Not prepossessing however; cunning I should say. His house is decorator's Georgian; his pictures likewise decorator's, mostly the English school and indifferent specimens at that. He showed us with justifiable pride the façade of the beautiful early Georgian house from Chippenham which he bought when Woolworth's pulled it down. He has re-erected it not – on the whole – too badly. Eardley dropped me at Westwood [Manor]. Alex Moulton dined and on leaving, embraced Ted good-night in the drive, very charmingly, unostentatiously. I was surprised. So too was Ted, but he was delighted.

Saturday, 29th June

This afternoon Ted [Lister] and I motored to Belcombe Court, open to members of the Georgian Group. It was built by Wood of Bath and could be an enchanting house. It belongs to the architect of the new St. George's Hospital, a perky little man called Watkins whom Ted describes as 'off-gent' and his wife as 'comfortable'. They have ghastly taste, and though some of their furniture is good eighteenth-century, yet dull, their colour schemes, light fittings etc. are gruesome. There is also along the whole of one front an unsightly Edwardian conservatory which should be done away with. The octagon room with plaster octagon ceiling and mahogany writing-table built into one wall, noteworthy. The barn, they swear, is fourteenth-century. Ted thinks far later. But architects know nothing of architectural history. If they did they would build better houses. In the evening Ted made me play chess and won every game.

Sunday, 30th June

Lunched at Corsham. Immediately after luncheon Paul said, 'Let's go into the library and sleep.' By the time we followed he was curled up on the sofa under cushions, snoring loudly. He and Norah are worn out, coping with everything themselves. The hospital has gone, leaving a great mess, and the Art School has not arrived. I persuaded Paul to open Montacute on the 20th July.

Monday, 1st July

A most embarrassing press conference was held this morning. G.M. Trevelyan in the chair. The eminent man made a good introductory speech but insisted upon answering most of the questions himself. This he did haltingly and often incorrectly. He is deaf as a post and hardly heard a word. There was an atmosphere of hostility, boredom, and criticism on the part of the Press that we were out of touch with the public.

The Stewart-Joneses had an evening party whither I went after giving John Fowler dinner. Talked to the Eshers; rather drunk, I told him that the new Secretary was a nice philistine – generous of me to add the 'nice'.

Tuesday, 2nd July

Interview at the Treasury over Ham House. After a great deal of manoeuvre I managed to insert a proviso that the NT should be consulted before any removal or even selection of contents was to be undertaken. The Government proposal is that they should keep the contents to be bought, and *hold* them through the V & A Museum. I agreed only if they, and not the Richmond Council, maintained them. Lady Esher had a cocktail party. Terribly hot and sweaty day. After one cocktail I dripped. How horrible. Dined at home and worked at my lecture, but at 9.30 the Dashwoods telephoned and made me go round to them. They poured out their woes re Captain Hill, that monster. I persuaded Johnnie to write a letter of complaint to Esher, and not to involve me.

Wednesday, 3rd July

I lectured to Trinity College of Music: a young, callow audience. No black-out, so the slides were barely visible. The sun streamed in and I sweated and mopped profusely. Again how horrible. I did not lecture well and think I am a bad lecturer. But afterwards the Principal told me the audience were vastly entertained by my frequent asides of understatement and self-depreciation.

Thursday, 4th July

Cooler, thank God. Lunched with George Dix and Malcolm Bullock at the Allies Club. Then got my visa at the French Embassy. Waited one hour in a queue, until I could bear it no longer. My conscience melted away and I exercised my privilege by mentioning M. Rocher's name, and left my passport. Went with Geoffrey Houghton-Brown to the American Ballet at Covent Garden. *Les Sylphides* and two modern ballets, of which *Bluebird* one. Norah Kaye superb dancer. Eglevsky a huge, ungainly, gauche but handsome Anglo-Saxon. Technique excellent but too much Anglo-Saxon stiffness.

Friday, 5th July

Wentworth Day lunched at Brooks's. I plied him with as much propaganda as I could about country houses and donors. He is going to write on the subject for a new Beaverbrook weekly. He is a good Tory and all in sympathy with the abused landowners.

Saturday, 6th July

Motored off at one. Called in Oxford on a Mrs Price for some Jacobean hangings for Montacute. Then to Long Compton where I looked at a Iych-gate. Then Charlecote. Watched and heard the guides in action. They said some awful things: 'This beautiful this and that,' pointing to some hideous furniture. Called the William and Adelaide dining-room William and Mary. I tried to put things right without hurting feelings. Felt like the headmaster, Alington, who used to creep into classrooms and listen to the poor junior beaks making fools of themselves before the boys and head. Got to Wickhamford at seven.

Sunday, 7th July

A heavenly day, hot and mid-summery. Hay smelling. Evening primroses, Canterbury bells, mock orange wafting. Lay about the garden all day with Mama in deck-chairs. The parson's daughters are a help in spite of M. calling them useless, unable to cook, slow and stupid – sometimes to their faces, I fear.

Monday, 8th July

Left Wickhamford at ten and arrived 1.30 at Charlie Brocklehurst's Harebarrow Lodge, three miles north of Macclesfield. Michael Rosse had arrived the night before. After an excellent luncheon we went at 3.30 to Adlington, stopping at Prestbury to see the church. All the churchyards here have flat grave stones made into paths upon which one walks. Adlington is a very fine house. The old part sixteenth-century. Forming a court is a 1757 orange brick wing, built by Carr I should think, with a very tall portico of sandstone columns. A cupola above. Mrs. Legh, the present owner, who has inherited through countless female lines, always retaining the Legh name, has already demolished the end projecting bays so as greatly to spoil the front. She has further horrible plans to demolish the whole of this wing. The condition of the house is deplorable. A hospital has just left. Everything peeling and disintegrating. The great hall has two carved late Gothic 'speres' like the Rufford (Old Hall) ones. Above a gallery an early eighteenth-century organ-case, the organ played upon by Handel. What organ did Handel not play upon, and what bed did Queen Elizabeth not sleep in? On the walls are huge paintings perhaps by Thornhill or Verrio. The other good room is a late seventeenth-cent. oak drawing-room on the first floor with carved limewood à la Grinling Gibbons. The plaster ceiling of this room completely collapsed a month ago, but has been replaced. All the bedrooms in the 1757 wing have 'Chinese' fret ceilings and wooden overmantels holding portraits. Mrs. Legh lives in a lodge by the walled gardens and is going to move into the Brewery over against the big house. She is very unimaginative. In the wilderness garden we counted six temples, all in semi-dereliction. Charlie B. gave us a lot to drink at dinner. Got to bed at midnight.

Tuesday, 9th July

Michael is a delightful companion to travel with, precise, good-tempered, equable. This morning at ten he and I left, calling at Gawsworth Hall, to look at the outside, and the church, which we entered. It has a superb roof. Visited Astbury church again, which has an even finer roof of Jacobean date. Met Pardoe at Little Moreton Hall. Still nothing done since my previous visit, which is worrying, and now the caretaker has died we are faced with a new problem. Had a farm-house lunch there and reached Wolseley Hall at three. This place, the property of Sir Edric Wolseley, has belonged to his family since the Conquest. House has a very fine Charles II staircase, but is much altered since first erected. There is however a Charles II dining-room, the panelling by Pierce but brought from another place. In all other respects the house, gothicised about 1810 and now covered with Virginia creeper, is a poor specimen. Grounds and park likewise indifferent. Whole place disintegrating. They, poor things, rather eccentric and very grubby. We preferred him. Michael was much shocked by the unmade beds and the fuzzy, unbrushed Catholic hair of our hostess. Got to London at 10 o'clock, having eaten in the car a cold collation given us by Charlie.

Wednesday, 10th July

Historic Buildings Committee this morning, after which Michael and I lunched. Called upon Doreen Baynes at six and joined Robin Cornelle at the theatre, a new performance of *Crime and Punishment*, which cast a hopeless Russian gloom, and I did not enjoy it. Considered John Gielgud tonight too mannered. Ate at Pruniers and talked to Robin C. at his house till 2 a.m.

Thursday, 11th July

Lord Bearsted called at 10 o'clock to see the Secretary and me. I did all the talking. He is prepared to endow Upton with £200,000. Patrick O'Donovan lunched. He has a fund of humour which helped me through some miserable months in the Army. Alec Penrose called at tea-time to tell me his aunt has given us £30,000 towards our Jubilee Appeal. Not a bad day for the Trust. At 10.30 went to Oliver Messel's where Anne and Michael and Harold Acton were and a number of Oliver's peculiar friends including a Singhalese captain, whom Anne called a Celanese.

Friday, 12th July

Meeting day. I thought I acquitted myself rather well. Kenneth Rae lunched and I gave him a list of buildings to see in Sweden At 6 left in the car for Montacute where I arrived at 10 o'c, having dined in Basingstoke. I drove with both windows down, and the smell of new-mown hay and hedgerows, of eglantine and elder, was intoxicating. How I love these long, gentle, Shakespearean summer evenings.

Saturday, 13th July

Busy day spent entirely at Montacute. I selected wall space for every single picture and for Lord Rochdale's tapestries. Made progress but there is still much to be done by today next week, when I shall be travelling across France. I found the arrangement of this house so agreeable that I did not want to go abroad, even for a fortnight, while there was still so much to be done.

Sunday, 14th July

Left Montacute this morning early. The weather has changed from the torrid to the cool and showery. I drove to Taunton and went to Low Mass with sermon that seemed endless. But the priest spoke feelingly about loyalty to the Church as a bulwark against vile creeds, whatever these may be. Then to the Somerset garage, where I was met by the coachbuilder, though a Sunday. He explained that he would generally tidy up the coach-work and re-upholster the roof of my car. I left it for at least five weeks.

Bridget dined at the Ritz. We had the nastiest of meals. Drank with her till midnight and she poured out complaints about Anne, with whom a coldness has sprung up. Michael, she complained, did nothing for her as a brother, and was useless. But what on earth does she want that he does not do, I asked. There was no clear reply. Merely a low growl. Poor Bridget, she is what is called her own worst enemy. And yet so beautiful, and proud, and aloof.

Tuesday, 16th July

Lunched with Margaret Jourdain and Ivy at their favourite restaurant, returning to drink coffee at their flat. Humphrey Whitbread joined us for coffee. A timorous, hesitant but nice man.

Thursday and Friday, 18th and 19th July

Spent at Montacute with Eardley and Clifford Smith putting finishing touches to the house, which will not look too bad. They are rather cross with me for leaving them the day before the opening ceremony. It can't be helped for I booked my seat to Switzerland at the beginning of May.

Saturday, 20th July

Up early, having packed last night and fetched some sandwiches from Brooks's which I had the foresight to order during dinner there. At 9.30 my train left London. I had an early luncheon on the channel boat, my last proper meal until late next morning. Reserved a second class seat in the French train, but the seats are narrow. I was very uncomfortable in consequence. Calais is extremely bombed. In fact there are hardly more than a dozen houses standing. At Lille I had some coffee (acorn juice) at the station, but nothing to eat. Indeed there must be very little food in France. The people look shabby, but not so hang-dog, discontented and truculent as the English. I was prepared to sit up all night, but the resolution waned as I got sleepy. By bribing the nice conductor I got a sleeper which I shared, rather oddly, with a pretty, English Mrs Miniver.

Sunday, 21st July

Arrived one-and-a-half hours late – all trains are late except in neutral countries. The Basel customs authorities easy enough. At the station I had a good breakfast, with boiled egg. At 2.30 reached Fribourg. Was greeted by Georges Cattaui – Egyptian Jew turned Christian – who came running up the stairs of the station platform. He is little changed, perhaps greyer, balder, now nearing fifty. He leads an ascetic, holy life, having done his seven years stint of theology at the University here. He at once took me to the new University buildings, having rustled up the architect to meet me. The rooms have many points to recommend them, ingenious mechanisms, a variety of beautiful woods. But there is much that is ugly. I felt very tired at the end of this inspection. At tea Jean de Menasch, Georges's Dominican cousin joined us. A very intelligent and pious man.

Tonight we dined in the hotel with the University architect who is called Denis Honegger, and Monsieur Barraud, who is considered Switzerland's leading artist, a handsome, bluff, pleasant man who smokes a pipe. He speaks no English.

The smell of the lime trees is all pervasive.

Monday, 22nd July

I sleep profoundly and late. Georges goes to bed at 8 o'clock every evening and, rising at 6, attends Mass. These hours would not suit me. Today the sun shone. Greedily I inhaled the strong, dry, torrid southern heat, which I have not experienced for six years. I telephoned Geoffrey's agent at Interlaken about money. To my surprise he was not encouraging so I decided the best thing was to go there immediately. Reached Interlaken at luncheon time. Ate well opposite the station. Then went to the address Geoffrey gave me. Presented my introductory letter, but although they were affable the man concerned was away in Amsterdam. Was advised to send him an air mail letter and wait.

Tuesday, 23rd July

Hotter than yesterday, and cloudless, but by no means too hot. Georges and I went to look at St. Michael's church which is rococo, and the Priests' College attached, founded by St. Canisius. Georges fusses about his health more than anyone I have ever met. Must not get too hot, too cold, wears a muffler and coat, which he puts on and takes off, and talks of his ill health ceaselessly. He also asks after everyone I have ever heard of and never heard of, which is extremely irritating. While we were sitting on a bench, he lamenting his ailments, I rejoicing in my freedom from any, along came a good-looking, sprightly Englishman called Bennet, whom Georges greeted and with whom I shook hands. This man could not linger to gossip because he was in a hurry. He is Professor of English Literature here and aged eighty-five. Georges explained that he had been a pupil of Gerard Manley Hopkins at a Jesuit school. Hopkins used to read fairy stories to him and his other pupils when they became tired of lessons. He is the only person I have met who knew Hopkins personally, unless my old friend Basil Champneys did. But I rather fear he didn't.

Georges left for Berne to lunch at the French Embassy. I, pleased to be left alone, visited the three churches in the middle of the town, looked at the sixteenth-century fountain-heads, and walked across the river over the 1840 suspension bridge, which is of wood. The cables seem most insecure, and when a lorry passed over it full of people the bridge swayed like a ship in a rough sea.

Georges is a cultivated, educated man, but withal a terrible bore. He jumps from one subject to another so that conversation never sustains a level. He never allows me to speak. He is disturbed by what he likes to call my fascist sympathies and remarked tellingly that I was a Catholic rather from political than religious motives. That this was due to my reaching a phase of life where I was neither happy nor unhappy. That later I am almost bound to turn to God. So be it.

This afternoon we went to tea at a château just outside Fribourg called La Poya, belonging to the Comte and Comtesse de Grafenried Villars. It was built in 1701 by an ancestor, and is thoroughly Palladian, and no larger than a villino. The present owner added two 'tourelles' at either end in good taste. In the centre is a high square hall with rococo plaster ceiling and baroque figures in stucco over the doorways. The enrichments are picked out in gold. There are Empire rooms with pink damask walls upstairs, very pretty. Some of the eighteenth-cent. furniture is French, and all exquisite. Oh, the impeccable taste. The Countess was charming (gracious is the word) and gave us tea. There were present the Count, who talked only of *la chasse*, an Italian Marquess who is a fascist, and a daughter and son-in-law, Baron Rambaud, who did the honours and showed me round the house. Balustraded terraces descend in front of the house which has a splendid view over the town and the snow-capped mountains beyond. The trees in the park are ancient and deciduous, and the lawns green and luscious. But on close inspection the grass is very poor, full of dandelions and weeds.

Thursday, 25th July

Georges and I left at nine for Berne, staying at the Hotel Bristol. I telephoned Interlaken, but there is no news of money, and no reply from the hotel at Lugano. Georges is very poor, yet has generously paid for my meals and lent me 50 francs. I don't like owing him money.

Went to the Vuillard exhibition. Indifferent artist, a poor sort of Sickert. It is terribly hot in Berne and we wander about disconsolately, not buying anything. Cannot even afford to buy postcards.

Friday, 26th July

Still no news and no letter from Lugano. Went by myself to the bathing place in the suburbs, called KMV, which was a delirium of excitement. Young and old were there, chiefly the latter, bronzed like niggers, diving and splashing in the blue water, which is constantly changed. Every half hour a bell announces that the waves will begin, whereupon commotion is uproarious and everyone jumps into the pool, shouting. You lie on boards sunbathing and drink tea and lemonade in a gallery overlooking the pool. Never have I felt more carefree, or happier. It didn't seem to matter a scrap whether I had a halfpenny in the world. I knew that something, someone would come to my rescue. The Swiss certainly impress me as a contented people.

Saturday, 27th July

While dressing I was told that the agents were on the telephone. Would I take the 9 o'clock train to Interlaken? This I did and was given 1,000 francs advanced by M. Osterreich who had sent a telegram from Amsterdam. Got back for luncheon rejoicing. In the afternoon went on a shopping spree, feeling like a millionaire. Bought socks and ties and silk handkerchiefs. Wrote to Georges ecstatically, refunding him. At five took a train bound for Lugano. The Grand Palace Hotel stiflingly hot. Slept very badly; restless, almost feverish, diarrhoea.

Sunday, 28th July

Feared I might be ill, but am now inclined to attribute troubles to the height, crossing the Alps. The situation of Lugano is very beautiful, surrounded by close, high mountains. The lake is in a hole. Today the sky is thundery and there is no breath of wind. Wandered in the public gardens along the lake under tall beech and chestnut trees.

Monday, 29th July

Today feel very unwell with violent diarrhoea, but better this evening. I think after all it may be due to slight sunstroke. I overlooked the fact that I am getting bald on the top of my head, damn it. Have a feverish feeling about the eyes. There is not a soul in this hotel to speak to. All dagoes when not English; and when English, dentists. I have a slight headache and am not very happy. Have finished the *Last Chronicle of Barset*.

Tuesday, 30th July

Bought some anti-diarrhoea mixture. Felt better. Saw in *The Times* that poor Timmie Buxton has died, a war victim, though of cancer of the stomach, at the age of forty-three. This has made me wonder if I am suffering from the same complaint. Went this afternoon on a tour of the lake, right round the bend, to the westernmost point.

Wednesday, 31st July

Am still mercifully spared though had a bad night. Took photographs of the Renaissance façade of San Lorenzo early this morning, then did some shopping. Shops not as good as in Sweden: nor is the food. This afternoon crossed the lake to Campione and photographed the baroque front of the little Madonna dei Ghirli, which has flights of steps descending to the water. Campione is by some curious chance an island of Italy in Switzerland. At the south extremity is a rather noble modern Mussolini arch of white and grey striped granite. Some of the fascist architecture is good though abused by all the left-wingers. Walked to the next village, Bissone, with a street of arcaded shops and two dull churches. Then walked across the ugly dam bridge to the far side of the lake. The sun in the full glare of the day was almost too much for me. Even so the heat was dry. I felt myself burning without sweating. Happily found a train back to Lugano in time for a delicious tea. Am reading Shakespeare's sonnets with care. Poetry and architecture are my two great loves. I judge the latter more academically and less subjectively than the former. One should fight with poetry, hammering it, thrashing it with the mind if one is to appreciate it properly.

Thursday, 1st August

Although I have passed my time this week as I had intended and hoped, yet I shall be glad to leave on Sunday. Ten, or rather eleven days of complete solitude are enough. Besides, I am anxious about that accumulating pile of work at home.

Today there is some sort of *festa* and the shops are all shut. I went to church next door (Saint' Angioli) at 9.45. Mass was in progress. I stayed till the end then studied very closely the Bernardo Luini 'Passion', a splendid thing, in excellent preservation. Visited the Museum in the Villa Cacci, a good late classical building of *c.* 1840, but internal decoration poor: stucco and painted ceilings of feeble quality. Museum itself awful, neglected and absolutely lifeless, as I should hate any of mine to be. After luncheon took the steamer to Morcote. Extremely hot and muggy, there being high clouds behind which the sun is sheltering. Climbed the steep eighteenth-century stairs to the S. Sassa church, with splendid square Romanesque campanile, which I photographed.

Friday, 2nd August

Today's jaunt was to walk along a path cut out of the rock, under the roadway, along the northern arm of the lake as far as Gandia. This is an old mediaeval village, the houses tumbling over each other and intersected by labyrinthine passages in the rock. In the evening I bathed in the Lido. I do not stay in the water long, nor do I much care to exhibit my nude body to the public. The corporate diversion of bathing does not appeal. And if I see a beautiful body it merely disturbs me.

Saturday, 3rd August

My last day. Paid my bill at the hotel which amounted to just under 300 francs. I was so horrified that I did not buy the little gold toothpick I had coveted in a jeweller's window all the week. Today I took the funicular up San Salvatore. Less than twenty minutes to climb 3,000 feet. The incline to the summit is 60 in 100 inches, rather frightening. These long established funiculars do not give one confidence. A little too much haze, but the view of the lake in its entirety very lovely.

Two things never cease to astonish me: (1) the hysterical devotion Latin men and women lavish upon male babies, and the consequence that they grow up to be normal extroverts which is not what one would expect – and (2) the English race manages to keep its end up in the world, considering how when confronted with Europeans, of no matter what class, Englishmen never fail to appear to be intellectually inferior.

I rather dread my journey home of two days and one night without a sleeper and without food on the French train, in this torrid heat.

Sunday, 4th August

Left Lugano at nine, having walked to the station in my shirt sleeves, carrying my coat, but slowly, and even so, sweating. Got to Lucerne for luncheon, and went to the exhibition of pictures and tapestries from the Ambrosiana, Milan. Marvellous collection, including some Leonardos. Bought a catalogue to give to Ben Nicolson. Situation of Lucerne less confined than Lugano's with snow-capped mountain range in the distance. Not so sublime. Wandered to the Cathedral and photographed the west end, which is Renaissance. The wooden bridge, covered in, has fifty-two painted panels of the seventeenth century in the spandrels. The fountains here, surrounded with flowers as always in Switzerland, gay and delightful.

Got to Basle at nine. Had rather a rush boarding the train and so too little time to buy food for tomorrow. Did sit up all night.

Monday, 5th August

Two sweet little French boys, aged eight and ten, travelled in my carriage.
They had beautiful manners and offered their food to the other passengers. Were intelligent and capable. They shook hands all round on parting
at Dunkirk. They also had the inestimable advantage of looking clean and
fresh in the early hours of the morning.

On the whole a terrible day. No food but what I had snatched at Basle.
Intolerably hot and the filthiest carriage I have ever travelled in. Half the
glass panes missing and wooden boards substituted. Smuts filtering
through the open window. I have never been dirtier. In the lavatory no
water, no looking-glass, and indescribable caca. The formalities with pass-
ports and luggage at the douane at Calais the worst encountered yet. The
only high light was a delicious tea with eggs and bacon on the English
boat. Still hot on the channel, but the sun has already assumed that
English muslin quality; nothing full-blooded about it. I arrived home
tired out at 10 p.m. Read *Jane Eyre* on the journey.

Saturday, 10th August

All this week in London has been dull. No visits because my car is not
yet ready. Very busy indexing the list of properties for the annual report.
Spent three evenings at the Soane Museum looking through the Robert
Adam drawings. An indescribable number. The versatility of the man.

Sunday, 11th August

There is a serious gas strike. There is now no gas of any kind and grave
difficulties are experienced cooking anything in London.

Tuesday, 13th August

Had a session at Batsford's with Charles Fry and Mr. Batsford. It was
settled that I should add an appendix to the third edition of *The National
Trust*, inclusive of new properties acquired since the first edition was published a year ago; that I should write a guide book of all NT buildings
to be sold at six shillings, this to come out next year; and that I should
write a book on the dawn of English classicism from Henry VIII's reign
down to and including Inigo Jones. We furthermore made some progress
with illustrations for *Adam*, and settled that Batsford's would have photographs taken of a selection of the drawings in the Soane Museum.

At dinner tonight at Brooks's I sat with Eddie Marsh who is selling
many of his books, amongst them twenty presentation copies to him
from Mrs. Belloc Lowndes. He complained that he had to tear out all the
fly-leaf inscriptions. 'Why tear out?' I asked. 'The books will fetch more

if you leave them in.' Eddie frowned, thinking my remark to be in bad taste. Then he told me how Sir James Barrie once sold a number of his books. One day a friend informed him that the shop which had purchased them was displaying them in their window and asking a high price for each copy that contained his name and a dedication. Poor Barrie was obliged to buy back all these books at a higher cost than he had received for them. Silly ass.

Thursday, 15th August

Had a drink with the Terence Maxwells. She is a daughter of Sir Austen Chamberlain. She was rather naively surprised by the high price a copy of Churchill's *Marlborough* fetched when her brother sold it recently. It was given to her father by Winston with an inscription in it.

Friday, 16th August

Ramsey and I motored to Polesden Lacey and saw how Robin [Fedden] has completed the arrangements of the museum. Robin's good manners are more continental than English and, I suspect, actuated by policy rather than warm feeling.

Saturday, 17th August

Arrived at Paddington at 9.10 for the 9.40, but the crowds were so great I could not even reach the platform. Instead waited in a queue until 11.15 for fear of missing the next train. This I caught but was in consequence late at Taunton. Went to the Museum and turned down a sundial offered us. Then collected my car at the garage. The cost was £69, less than I feared. I drove off in a great hurry to Ven, which I found deserted but for Paul Methuen who was sitting in the garden, painting the south front. Sat on the grass talking to him and drinking milk from a mug, for I had had no luncheon or tea. Then went inside the house and looked at the Chippendale armchairs and sofa, which are offered for Montacute. The house seems from outside much larger than it is. The big central hall monumental, the gallery and panelling contemporary. Nothing spectacular in the other downstairs rooms and the bedrooms indifferent. Went on to a charming manor at Horethorne, typical Dorset Jacobean, golden and cobwebbed with silver; shell-headed niches beside the front door. Here offered two rustic 'Chippendale' chairs. On to Sandford Orcas where received most kindly by the Medlycotts and given lemonade and a peach. Got to Montacute for dinner.

Sunday, 18th August

Slept at Mrs. Welsh's cottage, she being away. Her two daughters looked after me. This morning bright sun. Eardley motored over with Eddy

[Sackville-West] and Raymond [Mortimer]. We checked the Montacute inventory room by room. After luncheon motored to Westwood. Called on Ted who gave me tea, and continued to Lacock Abbey. Miss Talbot received me. Looked at her pictures requiring attention, which meant every one, and I made notes. Then back to London, dining at Marlborough.

Wednesday, 21st August

Woke up from another very vivid dream about Tom Mitford who was dressing to go to a luncheon party. He was in his trousers and shirt sleeves and slung round his waist the gold key-chain he always wore, and patted his thighs in self-satisfaction. He was cracking jokes and laughing at himself in his most engaging manner.

Today I motored George Dix on a small NT tour. We went to West Wycombe, Helen accompanying us. After lunching at the Apple Orchard, where I bought for £35 a chest of drawers, we went to the house. Prepared to be angry, I was angry with the guides for not being at their places. They are an inefficient lot. House looking bare but clean and very beautiful. At Cliveden we walked round the grounds and went on to Hatchlands which George liked best of the three houses. We dined late at the Allies Club and there was Malcolm Bullock. Apparently he had invited me to dine and received no reply. He sat with us while we ate and came on to Brooks's where we met Randolph [Churchill] and had drinks. Randolph has a huge belly and is very grey. George could not believe him to be thirty-three and younger than us. Randolph boisterous and argumentative. Talked of Chartwell, wanting to know if there was some snag in the arrangement with the National Trust. He abused Mrs. Greville roundly. Then we all remembered the unwritten law never to discuss women at a club, and laughed.

Thursday, 22nd August

Spent the afternoon at the Soane Museum with Sam Carr from Batsford's. I have looked through the whole fifty-three volumes of Adam drawings and not missed any, although I could well have given more time and attention to them.

Miss Strater, my secretary, left today, with regrets on my part. A sweet girl, aged about twenty.

Friday, 23rd August

Left at six for Wickhamford. Stopped at West Wycombe to look at the Pepper Pots, now practically in ruins, and the Chapel Cottage, the roof of which has collapsed. Called at the house to leave a book for Mrs. Eaton and on leaving saw Helen and Johnnie [Dashwood] on the colonnade.

They were alone and pressed me to dine with them for they had a duck and a bottle of burgundy. They were so friendly that I accepted. Sitting in the dining-room and looking across the table at the north view I thought I had never in my life seen a landscape more idyllic and classical – the lake below, the temple, trees and ducks. Got to Wickhamford by ten. Both parents in bed. I talked at the end of Mama's bed till past midnight.

Saturday, 24th August

Left Wickhamford at eleven and drove to Coughton. Had a word with Wells the old butler and Robert Throckmorton who greeted me at the door. A polite man who does not put me at ease. Then to Warwick and talked to Mr. Hollyoak, the Charlecote agent, suggesting that he might supervise the guides next year. He will submit his terms. Then talked to Quinneys about the Charlecote inventory. Then to Warwick Castle. The guide who conducted my party was an educated man. The banqueting-hall is lamentably restored. The best room is the Red Drawing Room and the adjoining gallery with Charles II ceiling. There is more to see than at Charlecote. The view over the river is romantic, but I don't think the castle from the courtyard very fine. To Charlecote for tea. Brian Lucy and William Buchan there. I like William Buchan although he is rather a precious young man. Left at 7.15 and went to *Measure for Measure* at Stratford. There are some ridiculous scenes, namely the raping of Isabella; and the convenient morality of the Duke is questionable. Bobby Harris acted Angelo, a difficult part. Some of the best acted scenes were the buffoonish ones with Elbow, and the tapster and Froth. These comic pieces seem to make a more convincing picture of Elizabethan everyday life than the serious ones.

Sunday, 25th August

I can easily understand how the very old, in despair, surrender to an easy death with a casual passing of the skeins of life to another generation to unravel. Mass at Broadway.

I fetched poor little Audrey over from Prestbury to Wickhamford for the day. She is much brighter and was very sweet to M. and P. The whole business of A. makes me miserable, and I wonder if a family has the right to cut off a member – which is what it amounts to in this case – who chooses to adopt a life which it disapproves of.

Monday, 26th August

Set off immediately after breakfast for Stourton Castle, near Stourbridge, arriving one hour after time. Was shown round by a rather cross Mrs.

Grazebrook. I had never heard of this house before. Its sole merit lies in a central tower of sandstone. The red brick accretions date from the sixteenth century. On the north side the seventeenth-century casements have survived. Otherwise modern windows put in in 1860 when the house was spoilt. The central court was covered in to form a hall – the usual treatment – and the inside entirely redecorated. A few open stone fireplaces have been left, including that in the bedroom in which Cardinal Pole is supposed to have been born. A few thick brick chimney-breasts survive; all the actual chimneys Victorian. I was in no doubts that the house is unacceptable, and when asked, I told Mrs. G. so. Drove to Dudley to see Mr. Grazebrook in his office. Nice, handsome man of sixty. I repeated to him what I told Mrs. G. Find I have now reached the age when I can say these disagreeable things without causing offence. The authority of years' experience sounds pompous, but it is true.

Next stop Trentham. Had not realised before that the house was demolished in 1905, all but Barry's clock tower and the entrance porch with noble, carved, armorial escutcheons in stone, and the curved, covered colonnade, now very dilapidated and doubtless about to be removed. I prepared to take photographs and to my dismay found my camera glass broken. Very distressing.

Reached Little Moreton Hall at tea-time. The Secretary and Mrs. Bevir arrived a few minutes after. We all had tea together and he and I talked to Bailey, who was disgruntled and opposed to our projected appointment of his wife's cousin, a Dale, in his place. Later I interviewed the Dales and liked them very much. They are descendants of the Richard Dale, 'Carpeder', who 'made thies windovs by the grac of God' in the courtyard in 1559. A lovely thought.

Stayed the night at The Macclesfield Arms in the town of that name, a charming eighteenth-century inn, all newly painted outside, clean and welcoming inside. Food not at all bad. Living in the north is of higher standard than in the south. After dinner strolled in the twilight. Autumn comes earlier here, and there is a faint, misty, burnt-leaf smell in the air. The church has some good seventeenth-century wrought-iron gates with a gilded Fame blowing a trumpet in the overthrow. Someone was practising on the organ. I peeped through the vestry door and saw one of the most beautiful baroque monuments to a Viscount Savage of Rocksavage, dated 1694. The canopy supported by two columns of black touchstone, to which white marble draperies are attached. Below in the valley the trains whistle, shriek and shunt.

Tuesday, 27th August

Drove after breakfast to Lyme the wrong way, over the moors, coming down by Disley. But a beautiful morning and I did not regret it. The large house quite deserted but for one caretaker. I spent two hours going round the inside, checking the fine furniture left – enough to furnish two rooms at most – and the quantity of indifferent family portraits which will serve to decorate. I decided that the house could be used by an institution without harm befalling it, if we kept for show purposes the drawing-room, stag parlour, yellow bedroom and possibly dressing-room (all adjacent), and the saloon (detached). The rest can all be sacrificed. Far the best solution would be to convert the place into flats, if we can't treat Lyme in the Montacute fashion, making Lord Newton's furniture into the nucleus of a regional collection.

I lunched at Macclesfield, called at Moreton and drove back to London, covering 200 miles from Lyme. Dined quite well at Bedford, having had tea at Uttoxeter.

Wednesday, 28th August

Lunched at the Ritz with the Braybrookes and had a useful talk about Audley End. On my return to the office wrote a long letter to the Treasury about it, asking them to help. My new secretary, Miss Kearney, started work today. She is about my age and seems charming. I am sure I shall like her very much. How lucky I am. She told me she was Irish and a Papist.

Sunday, 1st September

Lunched with Dame Una [Pope-Hennessy] in her lovely flat in Lansdown Grove. It consists of one floor of two houses thrown into one, which makes it roomy and convenient. Only her nephew, Simon Birch in the Coldstream, present. Back from Germany. She gave us lamb and apple meringue with real cream; sherry and red wine. Says that her book on Dickens is selling 500 copies a day in the States, but she can get no money from it. She is now writing about Charles Kingsley. James is in Scotland with the 'cellist.

Yesterday saw the Mildenhall silver plate in the British Museum. It is supposed to be decadent. I thought it very fine. Moreover it is absolutely unflawed. Last night K. Kennet came with me to the last performance of the American Ballet. I got two front row seats in the stalls for 18s. each. We had a cold supper at her house afterwards. She considered one dancer, Hugh Laing, in the last ballet, called *Undertow*, the best dancer she had ever seen, better even than Nijinsky.

Monday, 2nd September

Tonight dined at Lady d'Avigdor-Goldsmid's house, 47 Hans Place. She looks just the same, improved if anything in looks, and obviously enjoys her London widowhood. Always hated the country. Harry [d'Avigdor-Goldsmid] joined us at eight, without his wife. He won the M.C. and D.S.O. in the war and was apparently seriously wounded in the face. But he has been well mended and I saw no sign of wounds. His appearance too has improved with age. He is still bombastic, rude and snubbing to his mother, and even to me, but there is great kindliness underneath. He is very happily married and loves his two daughters. He is probably going to give up his bullion broking, for by not earning income he will be better off, he maintains. I don't understand it. I only know that if I gave up work I would starve.

Wednesday, 4th September

My watch stopped again. I was so angry I hit it hard against the table and the winding handle fell out and disappeared. I doubt if it will ever go again. I hope not. I hope it is dead for ever. Rather perturbed this morning by receiving a letter from Lord Esher enclosing a letter to him from Christopher Hussey, complaining about the Trust not giving *Country Life* the *National Trust Guide* to publish – complaining, in fact, about me. But damn it, it is *my* book. To the Treasury and talked with Sir Alan Barlow about Audley End and Ham House.

Saw Osbert Lancaster this evening. He was rather grey, and pustular. Full of gossip about our surviving mutual friends. Says it is all a piece of Nancy's nonsense claiming that she is loved by Palewski who, he maintains, is uninterested (which is absolutely untrue); that Patrick has gone quite queer again; that Joan is divorcing and living with a man, and so on.

Thursday, 5th September

To Knole where met by Cuthbert Acland. The Chief Agent, for whom this appointment was made two months ago, failed to turn up. Acland was splendid. He is very bright and at our interview with Lord Sackville after luncheon dealt excellently with him. Lord S. sits there, very thin, almost tiny, gaunt about the nose and with very gleaming false teeth which he picks, like Eddy. He laughs inwardly, without comment and as though in agreement with us, when we reassure him that the NT will do nothing without his prior sanction. Mason [Lord Sackville's agent] is always deferential to 'his lordship', is the most loyal man in the world, and abounding in humour and common sense. Going round the rooms this morning I was horrified by the piles of dust under the chairs from worm borings. The gesso furniture is in a terrible state. All the picture labels want renewing; the silver furniture cleaning; the window mullions mending.

Friday, 6th September

Lunched alone with M. J. and Ivy C.-B. How they eat! Ivy has a curious habit, when sitting down to a meal, of splaying her legs apart and lifting her skirt above the knees. For an Edwardian spinster it is most indelicate. She attacks the food, literally with venom. They showed me how they were obliged to sprinkle broken glass all over their flower box to prevent a neigh-bour's cat from squatting on it and 'using the earth for its own purposes'. They pick up the glass from the curbs in the square, as though it were cigar-ette ends, and scoop it into newspaper to the surprise of passers-by.

Sunday, 8th September

At Mass it began to pour with equatorial vehemence just as they were praying for fine weather for the harvest. I could not stick the sermon and left. Standing in the portico [of the Oratory] waiting for the storm to abate, a wild figure dashed out of the church, cursing. It was Auberon Herbert, incensed because the priest ought to have been preaching about Poland instead of Love Thy Neighbour.

Visited Sibyl Colefax in University College Hospital, she having broken her hip. There she was in a room darkened by heaps of flowers with one leg above the level of her head and tins of shot, pulleys and weights on strings attached to the other. She looked tiny and lost among it all, yet so gallant, and talking enthusiastically about Lawrie Johnston's garden and the Clarks always falling on their feet, etc.

Dined with the Lancasters. Drank whisky *and* red wine – a mistake. We ate in their kitchen. Karen is so good-hearted and Osbert very amusing and invigorating. Speaking of John Summerson's triplets he said they would of course always be known as the Georgian Group.

Monday, 9th September

By train to Leamington Spa. Colin Jones motored me to Charlecote. Met Hollyoak and discussed various schemes with him and returned to London. Dined with Patrick O'Donovan in a basement in Harley Street, where he lives, off cold turkey and Irish bread and Irish butter. Eamon Fitzgerald, also with me in the Irish Guards, was there. I drank too much cheap wine and port, but the evening was most enjoyable. Patrick has strong political and religious views, but everything is a joke. The other intelligent and donnish.

Tuesday, 10th September

At six went to see the shagreen knife-boxes which came from Montacute and have been bought by a Mr Liddel-Simpson who thinks of giving them back to Montacute. They are very pretty, date about 1730.

Wednesday, 11th September

Lunched with Ian McCallum at Kettner's. Not quite enough to assuage the pangs of hunger. At 6.30 to Sheila de Rützen's and agreed to go to Wales the weekend after next. Johnnie Philipps there with a new Bentley which goes a million miles an hour. Michael says he disgraced himself at Brighton by sliding down the banisters of a rather stuffy hotel at 8.30 a.m., stark naked just as the bishops and schoolmaster guests with their wives were descending to breakfast.

Thursday, 12th September

Michael and I drove to West Wycombe. We looked at all the temples and outdoor frescoes with Johnnie [Dashwood]. Michael agreed that with very little money the temples could be put in order. Lunched at the Apple Orchard and drove to Cliveden. Looked at the furniture which Lord Astor intends giving – what we could find of it, for it was so badly described – and walked round the grounds. Agreed the Blenheim Pavilion needed attention; also that the public ought to be allowed to enter by the Hedsor drive and leave their motors in the back drive. An agreeable and profitable day.

Friday, 13th September

Motored this morning to Gestingthorpe Hall, near Castle Hedingham. Very remote place and rather dilapidated. Poor Miss Oates, the owner, such a nice woman. She is the sister of gallant 'Titus' Oates who deliberately walked out of his tent to die in the Antarctic. She reminded me of K. Kennet by her straightforward manner, robustness and common sense. The exterior is what Sisson calls 'utility Georgian', a little altered by her father who added a pediment, and greatly added to by him at the back so that it is two-thirds larger than originally. It has a simple, stolid Squire Western hall and an astonishing Lord Chesterfield drawing-room of most refined rococo stucco ceiling and walls. She cannot afford to live there or give to the Trust. I really do not know what we can do to help her, poor woman.

I stopped at Bury St. Edmunds and looked inside Angel Corner. Although it stands well it is not good enough for a National Trust property and should never have been accepted. Stayed with the Birkbecks at

Rippon Hall. What an untidy household! Very bad-mannered children who rush at the food and leave their guest unattractive mangled portions. Talked three hours with Birkbeck, whom I much like, about Blickling matters and settled a number of points.

Saturday, 14th September

Spent day at Blickling. There are eight gardeners now and the grounds are greatly tidied up. Miss O'Sullivan is slow and tired, and looks ill. Went on to Felbrigg for dinner. Wyndham Ketton-Cremer's mother staying, a sweet, white-haired old lady. Although physically flaccid he is mentally stimulating. Plenty of serious talk. House huge, but Wyndham is well looked after by his couple. He lives comfortably in the hall. No electric light, and I had to walk miles with a candle from my bedroom to the w.c. at the far end of the Stuart wing.

Sunday, 15th September

Lord and Lady Templewood (Sir Samuel and Lady Maud Hoare that were) came to luncheon, which we had in the Paine rococo dining-room. I sat next to her. She is a big, gauche woman, but easy enough to talk to, and a devoted wife. One is made very conscious of that. He is a small, dapper man, every inch a politician, or rather now a statesman; wearing smartly cut blue serge suit and brown suede shoes, neat shirt and blue tie: silvery hair: very youthful. Spoke of the Government with utmost contempt, particularly of Bevan. Said the Government ought to have evacuated all the military camps for use of civilians, and moved the camps into Germany. Said his book on his Embassy in Spain had proved an unqualified success and even the left-wing papers praised it. They invited me to visit Templewood whenever I liked. They are close friends and neighbours of Wyndham, whom they call Bunny. Wyndham and I went for a long walk in the woods after tea: a gorgeous evening.

Monday, 16th September

I motored to London from Felbrigg, leaving at 9.10, and had luncheon at Brooks's. Dined at Brooks's with Ben and, since I had my car, we met Harold [Nicolson] at Victoria station off the Golden Arrow. He walked briskly up to the gate almost first of the passengers, for he had no luggage at all, only two books. He is here for a week and will broadcast four times. Drove him to Pratts where he gave us two glasses of port. Too much for me. I had had one very large glass with Ben previously and several the night before at Felbrigg. Harold says that each time he eats by himself in Paris the meal costs 25s.

Tuesday, 17th September

A foul day. Poured ceaselessly. I motored Ralph Edwards to Knole and back. Never again. It is a terrible road through south London; endless with trams all the way, and in the wet the road skiddy, as well as hideous. Ralph is extremely entertaining. He has a great sense of humour and is as clever as a monkey. Cocky, peppery and eccentric too. Has a curious rasping, staccato voice, and delicious cynicism. I like cynics. We get on well. At Knole he rushed full speed round the state rooms, but in a few hours had valued all the furniture. Mason had most efficiently prepared an inventory and was very quick jotting down the figures as Edwards rattled them off relentlessly. I followed this performance keenly and was much impressed, for it seemed he never once went wrong, except possibly in under-estimating the tapestries. He missed nothing, giving £20 to one late French table, £15,000 to the James I bed. He pronounced the furniture to be in a shocking state of disrepair, and has already put me on to an old retired craftsman from the V & A who may spend several weeks at Knole douching the furniture with Benzine-Benzol antiworm mixture.

Took Bridget P. to the Cambridge Theatre. *Don Pasquale*, so gay and witty. Superbly done. The baritone was Stabile and Don Pasquale an Englishman, Martin Lawrence, just as good in his way.

Wednesday, 18th September

Charles Fry and Professor Richardson lunched with me. This evening I spent packing up, and moving china and breakable objects to No. 20 Thurloe Square, preparatory to the proper move tomorrow. My rooms in Thurloe Square are not yet finished which is annoying and unsettling.

Saturday, 21st September

Motored to Canterbury and lunched with Christopher Gibbs. Then on to Denton Court, the property of two unmarried sisters of uncertain age, very well-bred and old-fashioned, the Misses Willatt: one wearing skirt to within six inches of the ankles in 1918 style and a large felt hat, turned down, like Vita's. They live in this big house without servants. It is crammed with hot-house flowers and exhales the sour-sweet smell of old women's houses. Denton Court is of little interest. Is built of brick. The garden front has curvilinear gables and late seventeenth-century sash windows. Two ugly Victorian towers have been added. Tappington Hall next door is genuine seventeenth-century, picturesque and 'a wealth of old timbers', where Barham, author of *The Ingoldsby Legends*, lived. There is a fake pedigree of the Ingoldsbys framed and hung here: also fake

Ingoldsby ancestral portraits. There is a Jacobean staircase; otherwise a tiresome old house.

Motored to Stoneacre, and so to Somerhill, arriving dinner time.

Sunday, 22nd September

I like dear old Harry [d'Avigdor Goldsmid] very much. Of course he is not 'dear old' in any sense. He is astringent, disputatious, political. Rosemary I can't make out. They are spending a fortune of capital on the house and horses. Harry's attitude is that the country has gone to the dogs and he may as well spend whatever capital he pleases. I did not enjoy this visit because I do not belong to their plutocratic, bullion-broking, racing, gambling set. Years ago I was very much at home here.

Monday, 23rd September

Motored to Owletts and spent the day checking the contents which belong to the NT. Had an excellent yeoman's luncheon and dear Lady Baker gave me a pound of butter and an egg. The painters are still in my flat and I cannot move in until the end of the week.

Tuesday, 24th September

Paul Hyslop lunched. He is going down to Knole to devise a scheme for the partitions Lord Sackville wants to separate the public from the private visitors. I think he is a good choice as architect for he is known to and liked by Lord S. as a friend of Eddy. Desmond Shawe-Taylor invited me to Covent Garden – *Barber of Seville*, which was very bad. Figaro was such a repellent, facetious old man that he ruined the performance.

Thursday, 26th September

Went to Knole again, this time George Wingfield-Digby accompanying Ralph Edwards and me. Wingfield-Digby pointed out that the best seventeenth-century carpets had silver fish in them and were in just as neglected a condition as the furniture.

Friday, 27th September

To Pendell Court for luncheon and spent the afternoon looking over this horrible house. I did not like the Bell family. The house, originally built in 1624, has been ruined by them: window surrounds new, plate glass inserted, and the whole interior fudged up. Damn this ink, which is intolerable. I cannot write tonight.

Sunday, 29th September

Today I practically finished my new flat, having worked hard at it all the weekend. Last night was my first at no. 20 Thurloe Square.

Jamesey dined at Brooks's. Without any reference being made to our recent estrangement, a *rapprochement* was, I suppose, effected. Our confidences seemed as sincere and easy as of yore. There are certainly enchanting sides to his volatile little character.

Thursday, 3rd October

Eddy Sackville-West lunched at Brooks's. His appearances in London get rarer. He seemed fairly satisfied with the efforts I am now making at Knole. He asked me for a weekend, which surprised me. Then I found it was because he had somebody staying whom no other friend could be persuaded to meet.

Had our Annual General Meeting at the Mansion House. Lord Mountbatten was the chief speaker. He was in Admiral's uniform and is, I think, the handsomest man I have ever seen. At no. 20 Thurloe Square improvements gradually happen.

Friday, 4th October

Motored the Admiral [Bevir] to Polesden Lacey this morning. The meeting between Robin Fedden and Hubert Smith was awkward: awkward for Robin, who was upset, for me, who was embarrassed, but not awkward for the Admiral or Smith, who are both insensitive. Robin was told that he would probably have to move from his quarters, which are the best in the house. He should have been told this before he had made them so nice. We left Robin looking distressed, and I had no opportunity to write him a note of reassurance.

At 2.30 I motored Sir Geoffrey Cox to Montacute. He talked without ceasing but is friendly and simple. We examined some Charles II chairs at Romsey and dined at The White Hart, Salisbury. Thank goodness one can arrive at an hotel again and get dinner without previous booking days beforehand. Drank whisky and port. Sir G. loves his drink. He also loves the great with whom, as Parliamentary Agent, he is constantly in touch. He works terribly hard. He told me that Hartley Shawcross was actually served with a writ for libel by Lord Kemsley the other day. This immensely embarrassed the Prime Minister who had to dictate to Shawcross the grovelling letter of apology which he subsequently issued to the press. Sir G. says Attlee *is* a clever man, namely in steering an even course between the followers of Bevan and Morrison, who detest each other and are the leaders of the two extreme sections of the Labour Party.

We stayed the night at Yeovil where we met Clifford.

Saturday, 5th October

Got to Montacute at 10.30. Rather a rush day. Chris Hussey, Bertie Abdy and Lord Aberconway all came and everyone had his own ideas and talked at variance, except Bertie. The Yateses are installed in their new flat which is very nice except that when anyone uses the w.c. every single sound can be heard, which Mrs. Yates confided to me with a blush was the reason she could not have me to stay. Meeting quite a success, in spite of Bertie's sole comment which electrified the others. He remarked that the public could not of course be admitted to the house because they smelt. There was two minutes dead silence, after which Sir Geoffrey resumed the discussion as though nothing untoward had happened. Afterwards Bertie professed to me to be very pleased with the arrangement of the house. He is so insincere and extravagant with his appreciations and depreciations that he makes little sense.

I motored Christopher home to Froyle and stayed the night with him and Betty. It was fun. She is gay as a cricket, brisk and noisy. Him I got to understand for the first time. He is not censorious or grim as I previously thought, but delightful, with a sardonic humour. How quickly one reverses one's unfavourable opinion of people when one gets to know them. They are leaving their cottage-like house, with its very good furniture, after seven years' stay, for Scotney Castle.

Sunday, 6th October

Motored to Rotherfield Park this morning: Reptonish (actually by Parkinson) house, built about 1820, but added to in the same fashion by the Scott family throughout the last century. It has octagonal towers and pinnacled turrets, a Windsor Castle round tower in stone and flint, a red brick square tower with cupola, and presents a romantic, Germanic air. The park, sloping towards the main road, is an admirable specimen of picturesque layout. There are beech avenues to the north of the house in the form of a cross, dating from the eighteenth century. The Gerald Cokes were lunching.

We motored to tea at Stratfield Saye. Norah Lindsay staying. She says funny things. Took me aside during Gerry's solemn tour of the house and whispered, 'That's where the humble petitioners sit,' pointing to two modest chairs the far side of Gerry's writing-table. The fire seems to have caused but little damage. The house, full of fascinating and historic treasures, is being rearranged with Gerry's unerring taste.

Monday, 7th October

To Knole again with Ralph Edwards to complete his valuation. He is very entertaining with his sardonic, precise speech in a high squeaky voice, and his irascible manner. An awful old scarecrow accompanied us, called Fletcher the craftsman, looking like an undertaker. When we met Lord Sackville he dropped a great brick by saying: 'The condition of the furniture is deplorable, caused by utter neglect,' at which Lord S. bridled. We tried desperately to pick the brick up. For the first time I went into the barracks, or attics, miles of long galleries, with remains of plaster ceilings and some fine Jacobean chimneypieces, under the roofs. Here the visiting retainers used to sleep.

Wednesday, 9th October

Historic Buildings agenda very long. I thought I conducted it well. The Admiral congratulated me afterwards (how unattractively this will read). SPAB meeting after luncheon to discuss the Fountains Abbey question, very fully attended. Esher did not present the case well. I spoke too much in trying to indicate the inconsistency of the Committee's policy in advocating the rebuilding of Holland House and Chelsea Old Church, both of which had been rendered totally ruinous, but not this Abbey. I said that whereas I opposed fake restoration from the foundations I could not on principle oppose making habitable what so largely survived. The vote was succinctly 'for' and 'against'. I and Dame Una voted 'for'; we were in a minority of two. Rick told me on the telephone this evening that I had spoken wisely. He let fall that at the MacGregors' party both Forsyth and Nye (architect members) told him they would like to be offered the chance of rebuilding the Fountains ruins. Yet both spoke and voted against! As Rick said, that Committee can be made to vote in whatever way a clever chairman wants. Dined with the Methuens in their Primrose Hill studio and discussed with them clauses to be imposed upon the Bath Academy in their lease of Corsham to that body.

Thursday, 10th October

Tony Gandarillas dined. Very sweet and eccentric. I asked him how he, aged sixty-two, managed to keep his youthful figure and complexion. He said it was the 'green pipe', explaining that he smoked opium every day of his life.

Saturday, 12th October

Am staying at Wickhamford for a few days. Can hardly speak for laryngitis, so Mama keeps me in bed. I work however. In four days I have written up 25 properties for my Guide, which added to the 30 previously done, brings my total to 55 out of 80.

Monday, 14th October

Papa and I motored to Gaines to tea with the Wrigleys. Kenny and Lucy Lees staying. Kenny told me that as a boy he was brought up at Lower Clarksfield outside Lees. He remembers Higher Clarksfield as a large red brick Georgian house, now long ago destroyed. He said that my great-grandfather Joseph Lees and his brothers John and James, were never educated. Their father spoilt them as children and died when they were young. They were rich. They resolutely refused to go to school. Every morning they were sent off on ponies by their mother, but when out of sight rode away to the hills for the day. They learned nothing. John hated his mother whom, when he grew up, he referred to as 'she', and to James and Joseph as 'your mother'. Kenny remembers John playing billiards with him when he was a tiny boy at Lower Clarksfield. Joseph who managed the colliery came in and said with great excitement: 'John, what do you think? I was offered £500,000 today for the colliery.' John who never interested himself in business, said nothing at all and went on chalking his cue. Coal had been discovered under their land quite by chance in the early eighteenth century. Until then they had been small landowners, not at all important or rich. Not that they ever did become the slightest bit important or very rich.

Friday, 18th October

Called for Michael at 10 o'clock at the Dorchester and motored to Womersley. Stopped at Willington in Bedfordshire and made notes of the condition of the dovecote and stables. On to Hinchingbrooke for luncheon. Rosemary's mother, Ruby Lindsay, wearing an old overall and looking what M. called 'tired and streaky', greeted us. Rosemary Hinchingbrooke, wearing an untidy overall-cum-maternity-gown and sandals down at heel, which outfit likewise shocked M., also greeted us warmly. She was, as always, so welcoming, unaffected and charming. She appears to be going to have her fifth child. They have a manservant whose clothes, for sheer scruffiness, excelled any garments I have ever seen. We looked round the house, now furnished. Family portraits of high quality and interest – a Hogarth of a boy and several Georgian Montagus.

We reached Womersley for dinner. Edward Moulton-Barrett, a great-nephew of the poet, came from London. He had been stationed in the back part of the house during the war.

Saturday, 19th October

Motored Michael to York and spent the morning in the Treasurer's House with the local committee. On the whole a good collection of furniture, well maintained. It is stiffly arranged and the rooms are bare. The Dean took us to the Deanery to show us his collection of modern pottery which we thought very indifferent. He is a friendly, forthcoming cleric. Oliver Sheldon met us and took us to lunch at his house in Bishopthorpe. Gave us a rare meal. Then took us over Lord Burlington's

Mansion House – finer in than out, and the big double cube exquisite.
All the decor in the most splendiferous mayoral taste. The Lord Mayor, a
self-important man, welcomed us. The mayoral silver was spread on the
table for our benefit: some lovely things, notably a 1670 chased chamber
pot, two Queen Anne tankards, and a gold cup, dated 1650, valued at
£5,000. Then to the Merchant Adventurers' Hall, a dull mediaeval structure, with long hall of wooden columns. Sheldon is Governor of this
Company. He is a splendid fellow who runs the York Georgian Society.
He would introduce M. as the Earl of Rosse. Finally, to the Assembly
Rooms, in a truly lamentable condition. Motored back to Bishopthorpe,
the Archbishop's Palace. Archbishop with handsome dark chaplain on the
drive to meet us. He took us hurriedly round but it was too dark to see
much. But a lovely house, especially the Georgian gothick hall by
Atkinson 1769. The gothick façade not really pretty. Wonderful 1680
room with Wren-like ceiling and Renaissance chimneypiece which the
Archbishop, injudiciouly, wants to take away in order to reveal a possible
Tudor fireplace behind. M. and I expressed polite disapproval. He showed
us the icons given him by the Russian bishops on his recent visit to the
Soviet. Says that religion is freely practised and there is no persecution of
priests. I didn't know which to marvel over more, his lack of taste or his
gullibility. Yet we liked him.

Sunday, 20th October

Drove to Mass at Askern, taking Anne's two Irish maids who have bicy-
cled these three miles innumerable times. They allowed me to lose my
way and when I gently reprimanded them remarked that it was quite a
different matter to find the way by car.

We went to tea at Nostell Priory, the Winns. Charles Winn is the
present owner, his father having disinherited the elder son, now Lord St.
Oswald. Winn aged about forty-five, bluff, exquisite manners in that
English natural way, unlike the Frogs. It was foggy as we approached. The
Paine block is too squat for its length and the Adam addition is not in
scale or in proportion. We spent one-and-a-half hours looking over the
inside and even then did not get as far as the Adam block, where I understand the decoration to be nineteenth-century. In the Paine block the
Adam hall is superb and the Adam drawing-room a restrained variant of
the music room at Home House. All these rooms still under dust-sheets
and the furniture piled in heaps. Could not therefore see the famous
Chippendale things. The outside of the house is pitch black, there being
a mine only 100 yards from the house. The park large and not very
beautiful. Lord and Lady Strathallan staying, both very handsome. Mrs.
Winn, the third wife, appeared at tea, a friendly, pretty American. Paine's

few rooms likewise fine, and distinctly rococo. This house, like Wentworth, has a number of lovely eighteenth-century wallpapers. Nothing is shabby and the place is well kept up for the Winns are rich. During the war they put away everything for safety, and all the pictures were taken out of the beautiful inset frames.

Monday, 21st October

Battery completely flat this morning and the car had to be pushed to start it. A horrid, very foggy drive from Womersley to Lyme over the hideous Peaks. We got there at twelve and met Charlie Brocklehurst. Michael most conscientiously went through every room and was vastly impressed by the house, especially the south front and courtyard. We took a lot of photographs. At 2.30 the whole Stockport Corporation arrived in a body. We amicably settled outstanding points.

Michael is so good and they were all impressed by his manner. It is essential that lightweights do not deal with people of this sort. We walked in the sun to Lyme Cage in the late afternoon; then drove to Charlie's lodge where we stayed the night.

Tuesday, 22nd October

Drove to Little Moreton Hall, arriving 9.30 with Charlie where we met Colin Jones, our area agent. The Dales, new tenants, are installed. Already certain improvements have taken place I am glad to say. Michael left at 11 for Clumber. Charlie and I arranged furniture and at 1.30 I drove to London. Arrived without misadventure at 6. Opened the door and there was Stuart Preston. He had arrived from New York yesterday.

Wednesday, 23rd October

Today Professor Richardson lunched with me. We left Brooks's arm in arm, he in a long, thick topcoat, limping now since he broke his ankle and carrying a stout, unfurled umbrella. Slowly we walked up St. James's Street. I imagined the scene to be like William IV and a Cabinet Minister, as might be described by Creevey. The Hanoverian Professor took me to his new offices, above Lenygon's shop in Old Burlington Street. The building is, appropriately, by Kent and his room furnished with incomparable old furniture and a deep Savonnerie carpet. He pointed out with pride and merriment his chair of Queen Anne date, with original covering, and then his gold-headed cane in a corner. 'I like a touch of gold in a room,' he said. He is a darling old man. 'The devil is a real person. You meet him everywhere, James,' he said seriously, shaking his head.

At 6 o'clock had a drink with Bill Astor who talked about Cliveden matters. After a couple of whiskeys I became too confidential. He said that H.S. had no brain and was a lightweight. I agreed, which I should not have done. James dined at Brooks's. His old enchanting self. Told me of his last weekend at West Horsley. Lady Crewe is, he says, the most malignant of women. Of course next week this stricture will be totally reversed.

Thursday, 24th October

Lunched with Midi who said she was dining with Lady Crewe when James was there. Bridget Paget, whom Midi did not know, took Midi up to her bedroom after dinner and said, 'Do you like Peggy?' who is Midi's grandfather's wife. Then she said, 'I hate her. She is inefficient and wicked. All owing to unsatisfactory love life.' Midi concluded that she was doped, but I suggested that it was merely drink.

Friday, 25th October

Lunched with Baron Ash in his rented flat to talk over Packwood affairs. He wants to see Polesden Lacey in order to get ideas for showing Packwood. Then I went to Batsford's to approve the final selection of the illustrations for *Adam* which Sam Carr has made. Sachie [Sitwell] was there and Mr. Batsford showed us amidst guffaws of asthmatic laughter a volume of Gillray cartoons of 1792, all of privies and bums and farts. Too extraordinary, but some very funny indeed. One plate called 'The Blenheim Fart' was, I admit, hilarious. We rocked, as Nancy would say.

Went to Bridget's at seven. Cynthia Jebb was with her, talking rather sweetly about a pinchbeck coronet she had bought for the top of her divan bed, as though the future of the world depended upon it.

Saturday, 26th October

To Wildenstein's to see the exhibition of Sir Harold Wernher's pictures. Not too many, thank goodness. The best I thought was one of a young man with golden beard by Cranach.

Sunday, 27th October

The ridiculous Baron Ash lunched at Brooks's and I took him down to Polesden. It was a dark, drizzly day, but the house was lit up and looked charming. Baron was vastly and genuinely impressed and said that if Packwood could be made to look like this he would be pleased indeed. I refrained from remarking that it never could owing to the inferiority of the contents.

Monday, 28th October

Goodhart-Rendel lunched at Brooks's at his request. He told me he was a little distressed that the agents had decided to cut down some trees in his park contrary to his wishes. He was very nice about it but I was determined that this sort of thing must be put a stop to. The truth is that all aesthetes hate any trees being felled whereas counter-aesthetes love felling as many as they can.

Tonight went to Tony Gandarillas's house at 7.30 to find him and Daisy Fellowes drinking champagne downstairs. So I joined them. Daisy looking younger, thinner and seductive. Her facility for gaiety is infectious. We went to dine at the Savoy in her large Rolls-Royce. It has a glass roof which can be revealed by pushing aside the inner covering; also the glass partition between the back and the driver's seat gently opens or closes by a handle operated by Daisy. I sat next to Carmen Gandarillas, Tony's sad daughter, and to Georgia, whose appearance was lovely. She was wearing little velvet bows in her hair and a heavy gold wrist chain with enormous seals. Sachie and Peter Quennell dining too. Also Daisy's married French daughter, Jacqueline, who has just left a French prison for having betrayed her girl friend to the Gestapo during the war. She is very *mal vue*, and is a silly fat girl. This party such a contrast to my six o'clock talk with darling Doreen, with whom I can communicate for hours on all subjects. This time we discussed the mystery of the 'gentleman'. She said the 'lady' was no mystery. The quality of the first was indefinable, a gift of God; that of the second mundane, and merely a social acquisition.

Tuesday, 29th October

The Eshers motored me down to Polesden. They went round the museum and were delighted with it. Lord E. has approved Michael's memorandum on the proposal that we should have area representatives as well as agents. Lord E. wants to call them area artists, but Lady E. and I think that a bad name which will cause resentment in those who are not artists. I have engineered this little scheme.

Wednesday, 30th October

To Knole again by car. Found a new quick way through Sydenham and Bromley which takes only one hour. Mason and I completed our notes on the condition of the contents. I love working with Mason. The Admiral, Admiraless and Miss P[aterson] came down in the afternoon. I introduced the Admiral to Lord Sackville. Robin who was with me said of the A. and lady: 'They are King and Queen Low-Brow.'

Thursday, 31st October

Cliffy and I met Colonel Horlick at Partridge's and saw eighteen of his Daniel Marot-like chairs, which are ugly yet first-rate. They are valued by Cliffy and Mr Partridge for insurance at £3,500. Colonel Horlick offered to have the seats re-covered. Mr Partridge produced a roll of exquisite green Genoa velvet and Colonel Horlick, without batting an eyelid, agreed to have them covered with this stuff at a cost of £300. The chairs will be loaned to Montacute.

Friday, 1st November

Diane Abdy this evening alone. I was rather apprehensive but it went very well. She is an angel. I took her to Covent Garden to see *Coppélia*, which was gay and extremely pretty. Margaret Dale is a good dancer; Turner an ungainly man. On the whole women excell men at dancing. We dined at the Ivy. This evening cost me all told £5, including taxis.

Saturday, 2nd November

After luncheon motored to Watlington to stay with the Eshers, arriving tea-time. They live in a small house called High Wood, which their son Lionel built for himself before the war as a weekend retreat. They have made over the large house to him and his four sons. Lionel intends to introduce his architect's office there, make flats for the staff out of the back regions and generally contrive a hive of industry. No one in the world is more delicious company than Ld. E. After dinner, and indeed before, and during, he talked incessantly. He is amazing for a man of his age. He honestly thinks the world pleasanter and more interesting than ever before, and that the new post-war life is the most exciting adventure. He sees a resurgence of interest in the arts on a wide basis, and praises this Government for being more progressive in patronising the arts than any former one in history. He dislikes Bevin and Byrnes because he believes that other less intransigent ministers, instead of wrangling with the Soviet, would foster better relations with them. He never fails to be merry and entertaining.

Sunday, 3rd November

Lord E. says he has had a wonderful and enjoyable life. He even sees a great future for the British aristocracy. He possibly overlooks the fact that his life has been a peculiarly easy one, without much hardship and without, I guess, much suffering. We went to lunch at West Wycombe, and afterwards had a conference about particular matters concerning that property, and the awful Captain Hill.

Monday, 4th November

Motored to Hartwell and went round the house. Both Eshers delighted
with it, thought it lovely, and deplored what Hill had done to the interior. He is going to write to Hill expressing his concern, affably he says,
and offering guidance.

Today the loveliest day I ever remember: sun almost burning and no
breath of wind. I went on to Long Crendon and looked at the Court
House. Then lunched excellently in H.J. Massingham's little white house.
His wife did the cooking. Agreeable people, but he did not strike me as
a big man, except physically. He is lame and his hands are feeble. Arthritis
probably. He showed me his collection of bygones; boring things. Old
milk pails and shafts of shepherds' crooks, smocks, etc. Had a look at
Boarstall Tower, and on to Upton for tea.

Tuesday, 5th November

Staying with the Bearsteds. More of his pictures are back from war
storage, including the Italian primitives. The whole makes a superb
private collection. Lord Esher said that B.'s manner is deprecatory. It is.
He speaks in a low voice. He told me that Esher as a boy at Eton was
intellectually pretentious. He wrote poetry which his father published
privately, and this went to his head. I can just imagine this.

An undergraduate from Oxford, named Carris, or something [David
Carritt] came to look at the pictures. Lord B. warned me beforehand to be
kind to him for he would probably be shy. He was by no means shy. A perky
youth of eighteen dashed into the room with abounding self-confidence.
Within minutes he was disputing the entries in Lord B.'s catalogue. I must
say his knowledge of pictures and of everything else touched upon was
astounding. I was amazed. Though polite he is too sure of himself.

Wednesday, 6th November

Diane had a party before dinner. Loelia Westminster looking very handsome in a sensible, pretty little hat, not the enormous cartwheels she
sometimes sports. Diane's brother Newport and his wife. She is new,
young, tall and with the bloom of youth, but nothing more.

Thursday, 7th November

To the Geffrye Museum to look at a table offered us. It was Victorian, *circa*
1850, nice but not important. The museum is housed in a long seventeenth-century range of almshouses in Shoreditch. Very remote. It was
quite well arranged before the war but now has a dusty look. It is on the
shown-to-the-children lines. Dined with Stuart, Ben Nicolson and

Baroness Budberg who was H.G. Wells's mistress until the end. She is a Balt. Has a low, fat, intelligent chuckle. She spoke well of death. Said that H.G. had no belief in an after life, or of God. His faith, or lack of it, never wavered.

Friday, 8th November

Saw Sibyl, still in her hospital. I hate going there and then feel ashamed of myself for so nearly not going. I overheard her telephoning to a friend about Lady Anglesey's death. 'No, no, my dear, it was the left lung; you're quite wrong. She spoke to me herself only four days before she died. The children rang me up at nine that morning, three hours after she had died.' Sibyl, must *be in at* every death, even that of her greatest friend.

Saturday, 9th November

Lunched with Midi and Colin Crewe before the Albert Hall to hear George Chavchavadze play three concertos – a herculean effort, for he had to rehearse all three this morning, owing to some Trades Union condition which I could not understand nor, I think, could poor George. Took Midi to tea with James and then we rushed to a party given by Princess Galitzine for George. He looks much the same, only handsomer. John Wilton dined. Tells me he really is renting Coleshill.

Monday, 11th November

Lunched with Paul Hyslop and Raymond Mortimer, whom do I really like? Not at all sure. Edward le Bas, with black beard, also lunching. He is painting Raymond. Dined with Rory at Claridge's: Alvilde, Tony, Emerald and a beautiful French woman, circa fifty, called Norah Auric, wife of composer. She rolls her lovely eyes and shows the whites, like first quarter moons. After sitting in the lounge (what hell restaurants are) Alvilde and Tony and I went to Angus Menzies's house, where Barbara Ward, Jimmie Smith, Lennox Berkeley and Angus M. were playing and singing. Barbara Ward would sing in a very missish voice which no one applauded. Angus's voice is deep and mellifluous. What a seductive creature he is. Just slightly affected. He has glossy black hair and a Michelangelo mouth and eyes.

Wednesday, 13th November

Motored, a rare sunny day, to near Chaldon. Car broke down. A succession of pings would have revealed to the initiated that a short-circuit was happening. My battery was flat. However a taxi took me on to Tollsworth Manor, a small farmhouse belonging to the Hylton estate which the Youth Hostels Association wants to buy and vest in the Trust. It is of no account at all.

Thursday, 14th November

Jamesey having persuaded me to give a dinner party at home to Harold
Nicolson, Maurice Gendron and himself, chucked this morning because
he had been invited by Clarissa Churchill to dine with the Duchess of
Kent. Can't blame him. So I invited Patrick O'Donovan instead. Harold
talked and talked, chiefly telling funny stories about General de Gaulle's
complete lack of humour. Maurice I liked very much. He is very like
James, but his dark hair curls, not waves.

Saturday, 16th November

Trained to Neath in Glamorganshire. There are restaurant cars again on
the trains, though the food is poor. Was met by an old chauffeur in an old
car and motored to Derwydd in Carmarthenshire, inhabited by Miss
Stepney-Gulston. The outside just like a modern villa, stuccoed over. An
ugly house which in England would be of no account, but here is held
in some esteem. It does contain several chimneypieces and ceilings of
rather remarkable post-Restoration plaster-work in crude, provincial
Inigo Jones style, notably the chimneypiece of the upstairs King's Room,
putti holding swags. Sheila de Rützen came for tea and motored me to
Picton [Castle]. Just she and Johnnie [Philipps, her brother], there. Good
dinner at which we drank hock and a bottle of port.

Sunday, 17th November

This afternoon Johnnie motored me to Manorbier Castle which he
offers to the National Trust. It is very overgrown with ivy and neglected.
J. is totally irresponsible and what the older generation would call a rotter.
But he can be very funny.

Monday, 18th November

Armitage motored me to Tenby this morning. We joined the
Rayner-Woods at the Cobourg Hotel where I stayed the night. Spent a
wretched day looking at the Tudor Merchant's House and then meeting
the Mayor and Councillors of Tenby, endeavouring, without success, to
induce them to be responsible for the house's upkeep. Tenby is a lovely
little town and was beloved by my grandmother who paid it an annual
visit when her servants were on holiday. Lying in bed I almost became
reconciled to the sea, listening to its gentle susurrations.

Thursday, 21st November

Went to Brown's Hotel to tea with Colonel and Mrs. Wingfield Digby
who are very worried about Sherborne Castle. However I much doubt

whether it will come to anything. Their manner not conciliatory and their attitude philistine. He has the typical M.F.H. mentality but, poor man, was today curiously sleepy and, I suspect, ill.

I had a dinner party of Kathleen Kennet, Bridget and Malcolm Bullock, whose wit struck me tonight as the most trenchant and unremitting I had ever listened to.

Saturday, 23rd November

After working in the office this morning went to Agnew's exhibition, one of their all-sorts mixture. After luncheon set off for Moor Place, Much Hadham, for the weekend. This is an interesting house which was built by one Robert Mitchell, a Scot, in 1777 under the full Adam-Wyatt influence. I found the stairwell actually more Wyattish than Adamatic. Mr. Norman is a very charming host with his emphatic utterances. Mark, who is almost as handsome as his extraordinarily handsome father, lives in the house with his wife and five children. Brothers and sisters, all married, live in the village; a most united family. Surprisingly, the house has yellow lincrusta walls.

Sunday, 24th November

It poured all day without cessation. After luncheon Mr. Norman lent me a huge red and blue umbrella and showed me the village of Much Hadham which is truly remarkable for its old cottages with overhangs and substantial red brick Georgian houses. A most élitish village. We had tea at the Hall with the de la Mares. This is a lovely house, red brick again, about 1730, with rectangular entrance hall and splendid wide staircase and contemporary balusters rising in a straight flight. Very fine doorheads and surrounds, particularly those on the first floor landing with the continuation of the cornice over the keys. De la Mare has an unrivalled collection of Japanese porcelain.

Monday, 25th November

Drove to Colchester but my car was going so badly I left it at the inn and continued to Blickling in Carew Wallace's. He is a devastatingly earnest young man. We interviewed candidates for caretakers at Blickling. Found a telegram from Aunt Dorothy and went to tea at Maud Mosley's new house at Aylsham, half a mile from Blickling. Maud M. has become white-haired, crippled with arthritis and an old woman. Aunt D. unchanged I was glad to see.

Tuesday, 26th November

Left Blickling – Wallace and I stayed at the inn – at eleven for Beccles. Looked at Leman House, in deplorable disrepair and not as interesting as

I had expected. Motored to Boxted Hall and inspected a pair of late eighteenth-century library steps, the most exquisite things I have ever seen. They will do admirably for the library at Montacute. Then to Colchester where I picked up my motor, which is still going appallingly.

Thursday, 28th November

Motored the Admiral to Audley End. Every day this month without a single exception it has rained. At eleven we met Lord Braybrooke. Mrs. Hugh Dalton, the Chancellor of the Exchequer's grim-visaged wife, came over from Cambridge, bringing Hickson, secretary to the Cambridge University Extra-Mural Studies people. Went all round the house again and afterwards lunched with Lord and Lady Braybrooke at their nearby villa, and talked. I think Mrs. Dalton was a little impressed by Lord B.'s story of his death duties and appalling financial stringencies since his inheritance, as well as by the importance of Audley End. The purpose of this visit was to solicit her to help the Trust engage the Treasury's interest.

Ate at Brooks's with Ben Nicolson who told me how deeply he regretted not having been more dissolute in his youth.

Friday, 29th November

To Newbury with Eardley where we were met by Mr. Behrend. He took us to see his Memorial Chapel at Burghclere built in 1926 for Stanley Spencer to decorate. This Spencer did over a period of seven years. All the walls are now covered with scenes derived from his experiences in the R.A.M.C. in Salonika. As an achievement it is colossal; as a period piece highly representative. Mr. B. offers it to the Trust. It is, I submit, well worth holding.

Mrs. Hammersley had asked me to her house this evening. But it was raining and I felt too tired to go. Dined with Colin Agnew. Paul Wallraf there. We had a lot to drink, including brandy. Colin became very communicative and persistently upheld the conviction that Hitler had been homosexual.

Monday, 2nd December

Grandy Jersey lunched and we discussed Osterley, still not through yet. I suggested he should agitate his lawyers. I also persuaded him to agree to sell his picture of Upton to Lord Bearsted and let me get an independent dealer's valuation; so I asked Leggatt's to act for him.

Called on Doreen [Baynes] at six. Both agreed how much we disliked, and feared, the *New Statesman* highbrows. When I said to her that among these upstarts, snobs and iconoclasts there were one or two I tolerated as individuals she said, 'That may be, but it is the vapour that arises from them collectively that one disrelishes.' Dined with Malcolm Bullock at the Guards Club and accompanied him to the House of Commons at 10 o'clock for several divisions. I heard no speeches but from the gallery over the Speaker's chair watched the Members dividing, and thought how subfusc, undistinguished and insincere the majority of them looked.

Wednesday, 4th December

At the Estates Committee this morning felt sure that Dr. Trevelyan was the worst chairman I had ever witnessed. Eardley said 'costive' is the adjective for this committee. At luncheon time paid my third visit to the King's Pictures. Thought the Waterloo Lawrences dull, and the Flemish pictures dull. Preferred Charles I's choice of baroque painters. I like the idyllic, pastoral blue garments worn by Bassano's classical shepherds.

Dined with the Eshers, and sat next to Jane Clark who talked of K.'s 'wealth'. When I said he ought to be made a peer she purred. She said it was only peers and their eldest sons who invariably disliked one another, instancing David Crawford's dislike of his father. I thought her rather patronising in her reference to Crawford's poverty. She told me it was my duty to press Sir Alan Barlow to get him paid a salary for his chairman-ship of the NT. She went on about his inability to meet his expenses. My other neighbour was Lady Riddell, oldish, who said she did not believe in the devil and the power of evil. Afterwards talked with Mrs. Lionel Brett, whom I at once found velvety beautiful and adorable – really someone irresistible. She talked of Watlington and their scheme for living in a flat when the rest of the house was divided into offices and flats for his, Lionel's, partners and employees. Esher says Lionel is very much cleverer than himself. This is hard to believe. K. Clark laughed at me because I had never heard of either Itma or Monteverdi. The Eshers' dinner party was in a private room at the Connaught, old-fashioned and cosy.

Thursday, 5th December

Motored this morning to Long Crendon. Visited Mrs. Barry, lady of the Manor. She had asked me tomorrow and I could only manage today. When I arrived a quarter of an hour later than I had stipulated I under-stood why she had been cross on the telephone, for she was dressed for hunting and was waiting for my visit to be over so that she could look for hounds. The Manor is a rather attractive, old-world and completely fake house. Slyly I asked her to lend me photographs of the house before as well as after restoration. This did not make her less cross and she pre-tended she had not restored it. But a great deal of timbering and several stone gothic fireplaces have obviously been inserted. The great hall is quite bogus. I do not think the NT ought to accept covenants over this house. The only good egg is the gate-house on the road. One drives under it. It is of stone, late gothic. She ended in being very sweet to me. I decided that the grounds were worthy of covenants in order to protect the village.

Lunched at the Apple Orchard, West Wycombe. A frightfully cold day and a leaden sky, as though predicting snow. I drove to Hughenden [Manor] at Langley-Taylor's request. The R.A.F. have gone but police still occupy the requisitioned part. They were reluctant to show me over, but ultimately consented. The rooms are empty and, except in Dizzy's library which is quite untouched, all the charming Victorian wallpapers are ruined. I saw no furniture. It is stacked away. Much redecoration is needed. Several chimneypieces are eighteenth-century ones of inlaid marble.

Friday, 6th December

Motored to Salisbury where I lunched. At Exeter I had tea and continued in the moonlight across Dartmoor, which is very beautiful at night, and terrifying – what with escaped prisoners demanding lifts and hounds of the Baskervilles baying at the moon. I reached Tavistock before seven, and had a bath. Stayed at the Bedford Hotel which was full of local diners in pink coats for a Hunt Ball in the town. The ladies I saw were very provincial and un-chic in their home-made, trailing dresses, or 'gowns'.

Saturday, 7th December

Very showery but beautiful day. After breakfast motored across the Tamar into Cornwall, up and down steep hills and descending narrow lanes till I reached Cotehele, which faces east over Calstock and the river. Were it moved just a little further southward the house would be better situated. Then it would overlook the lovely ribbon loop of the river. As it is, the situation is romantic, wild and wooded. The caretaker was away with the key, but the farmer's wife most kindly motored to fetch a daily help from Calstock who has another key. This kind and intelligent woman showed me round the house which is fully furnished. Meanwhile the old coachman, seeing my motor, came and talked. Told me that until 1939 he drove a 1911 Rolls for the late Lord Mount Edgcumbe. He expressed himself very concerned about my 'points'. He left and presently returned, wearing a topcoat with velvet collar and old-fashioned billycock, to present me with the distributor points of his old Rolls. I was charmed by him. Didn't know what to do with object presented.

Cotehele House is not striking from the outside, being squat and spread. It is actually far larger than one is led to suppose from the front, for it has two courtyards. It is uniformly old, late mediaeval with pointed windows, all of granite. The great hall is as fine as any I have seen, with curved windbraces In the roof and plastered whitewashed walls, hung with armour. In the oldest wing all the rooms are panelled, walls plastered and the Stuart furniture upholstered in needlework, none later than the eighteenth century. The contents are untouched, superb. Indeed it is a superb house. Lunched at Tavistock and motored to Pixton [Park, near Dulverton], arriving for tea. Mary Herbert, my hostess, came just before dinner. Only Eddie Grant and an Austrian countess staying.

Sunday, 8th December

Pixton is a little more orderly than usual. The evacuee children have all gone of course, but the house is left rather knocked about. Mary is as majestic as ever, tall, robust, windswept, exceedingly untidy. Her tweed coat and skirt are stained and torn, and the pockets have holes in them. Her breeding and dignity are impeccable; her views are uncompromising, proud and right. Her humour is unimpaired. She is a splendid creature with a massive soul.

Today it poured in cascades from morn till eve, the north wind driving blankets across the valley. So I did not go to Holnicote, but sat indoors all day, talking to Mary and that kindly, silly Eddie Grant.

Monday, 9th December

A better day and at 9.30 drove to Holnicote. By working hard I saw within two-and-a-half hours Luccombe, Horner, Bossington, Allerford and enchanting Selworthy villages, the last up the hill. The view from its church steps superb. What a view! What a church! There is a Jacobean interior porch from the parvise, and some splendid vaulting and fifteenth-century bosses. Lunched at Taunton and reached Montacute at 2.30. Did some good work there with Eardley who joined me. We dined with the Yateses in their new flat (avoiding the w.c.) and stayed at The King's Arms.

Thursday, 12th December

Motored to Knole in Robin Fedden's car, taking Lady Smith-Dorrien of the Royal School of Needlework. Went round all the state rooms, she commenting on the fabrics and we agreeing to send two specimens, one a pillow from the King's bed, for her to repair. She will give us an estimate for having the other things done.

Dined at Lennox Gardens at Mrs. Carnegie's. This interested me historically for here was a pre-Great War upper middle-class regime in full fig. Large, ugly, late-Victorian house. We assembled in capacious drawing-room on first floor. Lots of silver in evidence, silver photograph frames, silver boxes and bric-à-brac displayed on dainty tables. Dining-room table with white brocade cloth and silver candlesticks, spoons and forks shining very bright. Butler and footman both in white ties. Circular metal suspended centre-light with Edwardian electric fitting, called, I think, an electroleer. Sixteen candles burning. Present the Petos and Mrs. Carnegie, whose last husband was Canon Carnegie, Frances Peto's father, and her first Joe Chamberlain, whom she referred to as 'Mr. Chamberlain'. Mrs C., grey, wispy-haired, tall, upright like a ramrod, dressed in black tulle, thin Edwardian waist, low V front, and long grey kid gloves. Opposite me at dinner hung a splendid portrait of her as a young woman by Millais. In the drawing-room is another of her in the early thirties by Sargent, this one full-length depicting a feather plume in her hair. In the Millais the head is close curled, showing delicate ears. Very pretty she must have been. Now be-pince-nezed, severe, correct, but oh such a delightful woman. There is a third portrait of her as a child by William Hunt, American portrait painter. There is one of Joe Chamberlain by Sargent in the dining-room. After dinner she and I talked of Millais, whom she much liked – 'he was so jolly' – and of 'Mr. Sargent' whom she liked too. I wondered how this impeccable, immaculate lady could have allowed herself to have two husbands, even though she was a widow when she married the second, the first being satisfactorily in heaven. Which would she belong to when *she* reached heaven?

Such a flavour of Edwardian London this evening conveyed to me, of hansom cabs and artificial flowers in a long, frilly vase, for a dense yellow fog enveloped us, percolating through the closed windows at the time, and the street outside chill and muffled. Mrs C. is still young in spirit and quick in uptake, with her perfect old-fashioned manners. Speaks with a low, slightly husky, Bostonian voice, very beguiling intonation.

Sunday, 15th December

M. Jourdain and I. Compton-Burnett came to tea at 5 o'clock, which we had before the fire. (I must tell Emily not to put paper mats under the cakes. She must have bought them – with the cakes?) Bought cakes today are detestable, without mats. James and Maurice came in later. They were longing for the ladies to go, and made it plain. But the ladies made it plain that they were not going to leave just to please these two young men, and stayed and stayed till 6.45. Then James and Maurice both leapt to their feet, saying goodbye. So the ladies had to leave whereas the boys stayed behind. I feared this was rather pointed. Maurice spoke not a word until they left, and then asked in his French English, 'Who are these impossible governesses?' J. explained that one of them was the foremost novelist of our time.

Monday, 16th December

Went to Osterley this morning. Perishing. Spoke sharply to the Ministry of Works man who wishes to buy a triangle of the park upon which to erect permanent Government offices. I said the Trust would not stand it for a moment.

Tuesday, 17th December

To tea at Emerald's. Robin Ironside and Lord Tavistock, whom I cut for auld-lang-syne. Horrid party though Emerald was as trilling and funny as I ever heard her. She was very emphatic about men. 'A woman of course can only love a dead man. Why! live men are fickle, inconstant, vain, unreliable, ridiculous. Dead men are none of these things.'

Wednesday, 18th December

To the ballet at Covent Garden with Sheila. *The Fairie Queene*; Purcell music; Shakespeare *Midsummer Night* recitation and singing. Singers awful and Margaret Rawlings a poor sort of Titania. Helpmann a digni-fied Oberon, with very strong character, distinctive face. Scenery and dresses by Michael Ayrton as pretty as could be.

Thursday, 19th December

It was snowing when I left for the office. Was invited to three cocktail parties, and went to one, John Murray's, at delightful No. 50 Albemarle Street, surrounded by Byron relics. Surrounded by old faces. The party was given for Freya Stark. Why? When dozens of the other guests were just as distinguished. I was much moved by Byron's glove in a case, and the shirt worn at his wedding which had been George II's (shirt, not wedding).

Friday, 20th December

Oh, the cold! Motored with the Admiral to Fairford, where we lunched. Had a quick look round Fairford Park, which is flat and dull, with nissen huts all over it. Could not see inside the house which is 1690 outside. It has plain, rambling extensions. At three we reached Buscot. Gavin Faringdon showed us the outside, all kept in apple-pie order. A lovely walled garden in a hollow. The Harold Peto path from the SE angle of the house towards the lake is impressive. The house a well contrived fake.

Paul Hyslop has done very well, I think. Gavin certainly has some first-rate furniture and pictures. House well appointed and heated. The Admiral bewildered by Gavin's socialism-cum-plutocracy, as well he might be. Gavin has a youngish, ogling, rather raddled American staying, or perhaps living with him. For dinner Gerald Berners, Robert Heber-Percy and another young man came over. Rather a sticky meal because of the Admiral being out of things. Poor Admiral more bewildered than ever by the company. His incredulous eyes on stalks. His instincts offended. I did not enhance my credibility by talking too much about art and drama, about which I know little and the Admiral even less. He was well out of his depth and kept trying desperately to surface like a moribund dolphin. When the Faringdon Hall party left Gavin kept us sitting up till long past midnight in spite of poor Admiral's unrepressed yawns.

Saturday, 21st December

A terrible frost in the night. My car could not be started even by Gavin's chauffeur, who actually looks more like a Shaftesbury Avenue cissy than a skilled mechanic. For one hour it was pushed and towed by four gardeners and Gavin's smart Rolls over the icy drive, but it would not budge. So we abandoned it – points again, I suppose – and went by train to London, arriving three hours late, perished, in time for tea.

Monday, 23rd December

Had an awful time trying to do Christmas shopping. Could hardly get into a shop and when in, nothing to buy. Tried five shops for an O.E. tie for my father with no success.

Tuesday, 24th December

Caught the 9.15 to Faringdon. The crowds at Paddington were dense but the queues for each platform were kept in good control. Got to Faringdon at midday, collected car, which started, and drove to Oxford. Lunched at the Randolph vilely and then looked at a portrait by Watts of Mrs. Senior, née Hughes, sister of Tom Hughes, author of *Tom Brown's Schooldays*. A fine full-length, c. 1868. I have written to Sir Geoffrey Mander to ask if he would like it at Wightwick [Manor]. It is enormous. Arrived at Wickhamford for tea to find Deenie staying. No one else of the family.

Friday, 27th December

Papa and I drove to Brockhampton near Bromyard in the morning where we met the Admiral and Mrs. Bevir, Ruby and Christopher

Holland-Martin, and Colin Jones. Lunched in the cold, cold hall and walked round the house where Colonel Lutley's personal belongings are left lying about since the day he died. Something poignant in a house which has suddenly ceased to exist with the last owner. Life arrested in old tobacco jars with the lids off, smelly old pipes, books turned face downwards on tables, the well-worn favourite chair with deep imprint of the late 'behind' and threadbare arms, and the mournful, reproachful gaze of dozens of forgotten ancestors on the walls. Estate, house and contents all left to the National Trust. The house, which has a situation of unparalleled Midlands beauty overlooking valley and woods, could be made decent by the removal of Victorian trimmings round the windows, and the installation of sash-bars. No furniture of museum quality but very nice plain utility Georgian, as genuine as the old squires who for centuries loved it. Two good Georgian bookcases. The Admiral being incredibly muddleheaded and Ruby as friendly as I am sure a swordfish can be. Christopher shocked me deeply by warning me that G., whom I had proposed for election to Brooks's, would be black-balled. What possible reason could there be other than some personal spite? No one is less offensive or more affable to all and sundry. Ruby who drove over in a luxurious Bentley produced a luncheon basket with fittings like a bar, complete with gin and whisky and coffee. Papa and I rather humbly drank our milk. The dear old butler with his sweet, sad smile, is stone deaf and speaks in a whisper. The housekeeper, dignified and courteous like the one at Chesney Wold speaks like a B.B.C. announcer. Papa and I drove down to Lower Brockhampton and examined this little black-and-white manor and gatehouse with enthusiasm. It is just the sort of house my father cares for.

1947

Doreen telephoned and I went to her at six o'clock. She told me that she has a medium who regularly visits her; that she is strictly religious and prays; that she sees visions of the departed, unfortunately too often of the people she most disliked when they were alive; that, notwithstanding, she is eagerly looking forward to death, that her medium tells her it takes the form of life being gently drawn through the fingers. She is not the least melancholy and enjoys *her* life, which is not life as enjoyed by most people. From true life she is too divorced to care whether she exists any longer in this alien world. We all feel like this but most of us cannot withdraw from it in the way she manages to do, i.e. shut herself up in her bedroom and adjoining sitting-room, with curtains tightly drawn, for days on end. I do adore Doreen.

Thursday, 2nd January

Went once again yesterday to the King's Pictures and concentrated on the Primitives which to me are as indistinguishable as one hound in a pack from another. Called on Grandy Jersey in his shop and saw his large picture of Upton that Lord Bearsted wants but won't give £600 for. I hope the shop keeps the wolf from poor Grandy's door.

Friday, 3rd January

Took the manuscript of my Nat. Trust *Guide* to Batsford's. Met Mr Harry who with no explanations put me in a taxi and drove to Marylebone station. There we met Sachie. Mr. Harry produced packets of minute negatives from his capacious pockets. They smelled very strongly of fish which he also keeps in same pockets for his cats. He spread the negatives on the platform, produced a huge magnifying glass and, while spluttering and coughing, examined them on the ground with Sachie. The two made an odd group among the hurrying passengers, Mr. B. wearing a green hat with a huge feather in it.

Sunday, 5th January

Cold, leaden skies. It must snow soon. Left Wickhamford for Mass in Evesham in that hideous church. On to Charlecote for one-and-a-half hours. Alianore Lucy there and Wicker, the caretaker. All is serene. Then to Packwood and lunched with Baron. We had sherry and pâté de foie gras, as good as it used to be; chicken with burgundy; omelette with quince jam and rum blazing; port wine. Baron conducted me over the house which is now in pristine condition. He showed me a Victorian lithograph of the house looking much as it does today. Saw the servants' wing adapted for the caretaker, and discussed this. B. wants a disabled ex-officer, not an artistic person. We don't see eye to eye over this.

Monday, 6th January

Deep snow this morning. At two Emily Empey's [my mother's beloved governess] funeral took place in Wickhamford churchyard. Disagreeable stories current about her death, which was peaceful and fairly sudden, but Mama says the village women would come into her room and discuss her before she was dead and when she may well have been conscious. On Saturday I watched Haines [our chauffeur for sixty years] and Nightingale, the sexton, digging out Molly [Empey]'s grave, for Em's coffin was to rest upon her sister's. It happened that the top of Molly's coffin had quite disintegrated within eight years only, so the two have to be put side by side. The short service with *Abide with Me* and the *Nunc Dimittis* sung in a very high key to the squeaky harmonium, with Tommy Knight playing, moved me deeply. Papa, Mama and I sat in our pew, and nostalgic memories were revived. The beauty and poignancy of this little church amount to the most exquisite thing in the whole world, a sort of sacred island always at the back of my mind which I can retreat to in my thoughts wherever I may be. Mama asked me to compose a short appreciation of Em for the *Evesham Journal* which I did with a great effort this morning. She was I suppose one of the unrecognised saints of this world. After the funeral I motored back to London in the snow. Took me three-and-a-half hours only. I had to drive very cautiously. James dined with me at home.

Tuesday, 7th January

To see Sibyl, now in her own house, but seated in a chair. I believe she hardly walks at all. The Ambassador to Spain there, very annoyed with our Government for having recalled him, entirely owing to pressure by Russia, he says. Mrs. Oglander, wearing a ridiculous, over-smart Parisian hat with vast ostrich feather now the vogue curling under her chin. She is not young or handsome enough for this extravagant bedizenment. Jamesey present, hardly spoke. Told me afterwards how much he disliked her, and Sibyl. Harold also present. Mrs. Oglander talking silly trivialities to Harold, abusing the *New Statesman* and 'Kingsley Wood', meaning thereby Kingsley Martin, foolish female. She never attends either to what she says or one says. But she is good-natured.

Thursday, 9th January

Aunt Katie's funeral at Richmond. Papa could not go and asked me to represent him. She was eighty-eight and died only because ten days ago she broke a leg. She was the last of the Lees great-aunt and -uncle genera-tion, being my grandfather's sister and married to my grandmother's brother, who tippled. Making a great effort to attend her obsequies I nearly missed them because owing to the cold weather I could not make my car start. Just got to the church in time and left car outside the west door, right in the way, as I discovered later, of the hearse and procession. It had to be moved and I did not dare go out and claim ownership. This must have been revealed for, when the procession of four funereal Rolls-Royces drove off to the cemetery, I followed in the rear. Not an unattractive resting-place on a hill above the town. Was invited back to the old lady's house for a large tea at 2.45 . A very old-fashioned sort of Forsyte Saga family gathering. Lots of rather shaming cousins claiming relationship. An un-shaming one was Henry Medd, an architect disciple of Lutyens. Best of the lot was Gladys Lees, Papa's first cousin, a very un-smart, badly dressed, lined old baggage. Distinguished in a well-bred way, clipping her g's, and totally unpretentious unlike some of the younger ones. I gave her a lift but ran out of petrol before I could get to a garage and had to turn her out. I felt a little, and not very, sad about Aunt Katie. I liked her directness.

Friday, 10th January

Meetings today. Lord Esher told the committee that he thought my *Guide* excellent. It isn't of course. Had tea with Harold who has asked the Admiral to send me to the U.S.A. to lecture, and the Admiral replied, 'But I can't spare him.' Harold said a lecture tour was terribly tiring. Dined with Dame Una, James and John. How dismal and carping the Dame can be. James admits she is much on his nerves at present.

Saturday, 11th January

Motored to stay with Maud Russell at Mottisfont [Abbey]. Lunched en route at Winchester and went round the City Mill, our property, a dull little affair. Then to the glorious Cathedral. Particularly admired the fif-teenth-century tombs of Cardinal Beaufort and William Wykeham, with fine, soaring pinnacles of stonework. This is a marvellous century for architecture, notably the nave here. What could be greater than this aspirant, congruous structure, all of a piece? Pouring with rain all day. Stopped at Sparsholt to look at Vaine Cottages, both extremely unim-portant. The Trust does own some low-grade properties. Arrived Mottisfont at four. An oddly assorted party staying: Riette Lamington, who is very beautiful, with fair complexion and hair, agreeable to talk to (Cecil Beaton once called her 'prim and lecherous' to her face) an African woman; Miss Russell, an old sister-in-law; Martin Russell, Mrs R.'s son, dark, Jewish and clever; and Bluey Baker a suave, smooth, elderly Warden of Winchester School, once an admirer of Lady Goonie Churchill, and at New College with my uncle Milne in the nineties.

Sunday, 12th January

At first glance this is a beautiful old house of mellow red brick, the south front having been made symmetrical in George II's reign. The river Test running close beside it, swiftly. A pretty Georgian stable block to the west. Verdant lawns and massive old trees striding to the water's edge. Yet it is not a wholly satisfactory house and is moreover spooky. Built upon and out of the remains of a priory, the house comprises the nave of the church, the north nave wall wholly surviving. This makes me feel slightly uncomfortable. Maud Russell said that in altering floors they dug up several skeletons and reinterred them. (This she whispered to me softly in French while we were looking at a piscina in the larder in the cook's presence.) There are only three living rooms of any size in spite of Mottisfont being a large house. The dining-room is Palladian. The south-east drawing-room has a pretty rococo frieze, now picked out in gold. Mrs. R. ripped out the large hall – it too was Palladian, I see from old photographs – and Rex Whistler perpetrated a ridiculous and flimsy Gothick chiaroscuro trompe l'oeil. It is too slight and too pretty. Mrs. R. has papered all the staircases and the long landing on the first floor in dull marble, rather sombre, but suitable. A curious house because the living-rooms are all on the first floor, and the offices on the ground floor, which is not a basement however.

This morning I walked through the village with Mr. Baker and along the mown grass by the river. He talked of Herbert Baker, no relation, and of Lutyens, both of whom were his friends, chiefly Lutyens. He admitted that Lutyens was always vitriolic about Baker, and Baker Christian-like and charitable about Lutyens.

The furniture in the house is all desirable but gives the impression of having been collected in a hurry. The decoration too seems unfinished. The house has the sparse tidiness of a newcomer, not the cluttered untidiness of accumulated centuries.

Tuesday, 14th January

Went to King's Cross station at 8.45 to find that the train for Gainsborough, scheduled to leave at 9.15, had been cancelled owing to the coal shortage. This put me in ill humour. Went to Brooks's. Returned to catch the 10.10 and reached Gainsborough at 3.43. Was motored to

Thonock Hall. Claud Phillimore was reading in the sitting-room window, overlooking the grey and withered park. A dreary part of the world where grass never looks green and the black trees are stunted.

Mindy Bacon and his wife are delightful, progressive-minded and intelligent, with commendable sense of duty, yet not goody-goody. We had high tea. Captain Crookshank, the M.P. came in – jovial, physically sinister – and at 7.30 we attended a gruesome meeting at the Town Hall with the Town Council. The four of us men, attended by Mindy's agent, swept into a large room where some twenty-seven Councillors were seated round tables. All rose. We established ourselves beside the Chairman, who falteringly read a speech of welcome. Bacon replied, offering the Old Hall to the nation, and then a discussion ensued. The Councillors realised that somehow they must accept the Hall but were obviously embarrassed how to find the means with which to keep it up. I felt rather sorry for them confronted with this white elephant on its last legs. Quite a sticky meeting to start with, but at the finish friendly. The Bacons said the Council were a terrible lot, but Claud and I found them rather nice and fairly enlightened. I spoke from time to time when called upon to answer questions and Claud defended his architectural schemes excellently. At the end speeches were made expressing appreciation of Mindy's public spirit.

Wednesday, 15th January

Pitch dark when called by a dear old man who entered my bedroom and pulled back the heavy curtains. Rats' tails of grey fog swirled across the window panes. Tenderly this old retainer brought into the room a red blanket which he spread before the empty fire grate. Then he trundled a small tin hip-bath on to the red blanket. Then he brought a brass can of tepid water, enough to cover the bottom of the bath. The room must have been several degrees below zero. He might have been a ghost performing the customary function of a hundred years ago. But one hundred years ago there would have been a blazing fire in the grate.

Thursday, 16th January

This evening I went to Sir Ian Hamilton's ninety-fourth birthday party, given for the Gordon Boys' School. Conjuror, ventriloquist. The old gentleman sat huddled in a chair, looking extremely frail and ancient. He was rather pathetic and, I must confess, distasteful. Mama confessed to me the other day that she could not bear the physical proximity of the very old. They made her sick. She felt ashamed. I agree with her, and also feel ashamed, and sick. There was no one at No. 1 Hyde Park Gardens whom I knew, except Charlotte Bonham-Carter, always a faithful friend.

I intend next week to begin my new book.

Saturday, 18th January

Eardley and I left in my car at 10.30, a most lovely morning. We looked for an obelisk near Camberley which has been offered to the NT but could not find it. I stayed the weekend at Long Crichel. Paul Hyslop the other guest. Eardley, Desmond and Eddy lead a highly civilized life here. Comfortable house, pretty things, good food. All the pictures are Eardley's, and a fine collection of modern art too. After dinner Desmond read John Betjeman's poems aloud, and we all agreed they would live.

Sunday, 19th January

A most beautiful day, mild, sunny and blue. Eddy stayed indoors to write an article. We motored to Horton and walked. Admired the tiny church with Queen Anne dormers in the belfry and climbed up to Sturt's Folly which the Shaftesburys offer the NT. A tall, triangular building of brick in English bond. All the interior gone. Only a calcined beam or two left. Shrubs growing out of the broken parapet. The central square tower is rather ugly. E. thinks it best not to accept it.

Monday, 20th January

In the morning E. and I went over Max Gate which was built by Thomas Hardy and his brother in 1885. It is perfectly hideous and shapeless. Of scarlet brick, with two ugly square angle towers. All Hardy's things were long ago removed to Dorchester Museum, so there is little connected with him of interest. Besides the house was shoddily built, with lean-to odds and ends added by him. It will be a constant expense. I shall advise the Historic Buildings Committee to sell it – it is held alienably – and keep the money for buying the birthplace, which is far worthier, one of these days.

We lunched at Judge Jeffrey's house in Dorchester and at 2.30 reached Dillington Park, a delightful Tudor house, almost entirely rebuilt about 1810 in imitation of Barrington Court by Pennethorne. It has a cosy family-house air, most sympathetic. Present owner a young Mrs. Cameron. Her mother, Mrs. Vaughan-Lee, living with her. They offer us practically anything we like for Montacute, and E. and I selected straight away a number of things, including a fine set of ribbon-back eighteenth-century dining-room chairs.

Tuesday, 21st January

I drove from Bath, where we both stayed with E.'s mother, to Brockhampton. A longer journey than I had thought. For one hour I examined the silver there. Nothing rare, but like the furniture in this house, decent country house Georgian. No gold plate or jewellery found. Drove past Ribbesford, which always makes me sad, into Shropshire. Wanted to visit Lilleshall but arrived at four o'clock and thought it too late to call on Mr. Ford. So walked round the ruined Abbey, overgrown with ivy. The whole church survives from west to east end, the huge east window intact except for the tracery. Got to Atcham at 5.30 and stayed at The Mytton and Mermaid, Clough Williams-Ellis's inn, at the gates of Attingham.

Went to Attingham after tea. Lady Berwick rather unhappy and worried about Lord B. who is in bed with a tired heart and has two nurses. I went to see him and was allowed to stay for five minutes. He looks quite a good colour but is even slower of speech than usual. She says he is quite contented and does not want to get up, a bad sign. This sweet man I shall doubtless not see again. Lady B. and I walked round the state rooms, she showing me which pieces of furniture they would like us to take for storage at Lyme.

Wednesday, 22nd January

Cut my mole shaving this morning and thought it would never stop bleeding. T.C.P. finally staunched it. Walked up the drive to Attingham at 10.15 and spent the morning jig-sawing the pictures about, trying with Lady Berwick to see how we could fit the best portraits into the drawing-room, leaving the less good ones in the dining-room which the College is to take over. It is sad for this red room is really the finest of all the rooms, with its deep Pompeian walls. She took my advice about letting the Angelica Kauffmann mythological pictures and mirrors remain in the drawing-room with the third Lord Berwick's furniture. In fact she, usually so positive, is rather pathetically ready to fall in with almost any suggestions, being, I think, in despair. She took me to the cellars and showed me the china stored there. It was made, she feels sure, for Caroline Murat, as indeed was the furniture in the drawing-room.

I motored to Wickhamford. In Kidderminster I noticed that the policemen's helmets still have the old-fashioned spikes which they had when I was a child.

Thursday, 23rd January

Dined with Malcolm Bullock at the Turf off grouse and champagne. The Duke of Devonshire joined us as we were finishing and talked for an hour. He was what is called 'lit up' but by no means drunk. Rather curiously we spoke of old Mr Holmes's association with the National Trust. The Duke said he is known as the chief bugger of the Peak – greatly to my surprise. Next morning a telegram came to the office announcing that Mr. Holmes had died at precisely the moment we were talking about him. I have before been told a story of the Duke of D. killing a man at a public meeting merely by speaking *at* him. The man became apoplectic with rage and died on the spot.

The Duke becoming rather a bore I started fidgeting to induce Malcolm to leave the dining-room and shake him off. The D. repeated the story I had heard from him before that Gerry Wellington wrote complaining that Debo Hartington had christened her son Mornington, which is one of the D. of Wellington's subsidiary titles. The D. of D. replied that she had christened him after her favourite jockey just as she had christened her daughter Emma not after any of the Cavendishes, but after her goat. He said that Princess Elizabeth had been staying with him. She is just like the young Queen Victoria with the old Queen's sagacity. She makes it very plain to the Queen that whereas she, the Queen, is a commoner, she, Princess Elizabeth, is of royal blood. After church in Eastbourne she said to the Vicar, aged seventy-five, 'Your sermon was excellent.' He bridled with pleasure. 'But,' she continued, 'you spoilt it in the last ten minutes.' The Duke says that royalty are always happy if you organise their visits and make them play games, but you must never leave it to them to make suggestions. He is devoted to Mrs. Corrigan, that ridiculous woman, famous for her malapropisms. 'My doctor said to me, if you want to avoid indigestion, you must masturbate, masturbate.'

Saturday, 25th January

Yesterday it began snowing and today doing worse things. It is so extremely cold that even with two fires and a rug over me I was cold sitting at home. I read most of the afternoon and evening. Then dined with the Glenconners in Chester Street, Regent's Park. He has a beaming, smiling face, and yet is inscrutable. Is a very clever business man, not an intellectual. Lady G. is pretty, sympathetic, and intellectual. I drove there in the snow. Dinner was to celebrate the return from the States of Cyril Connolly. Cyril had for him a good colour and behaved less like an inspired oracle, although the star of the evening. He told funny stories of his adventures in America, notably flying experiences and encounters with anti-British feelings. Cyril says our Palestine policy has alienated the American Jews in spite of England having been the asylum of European Jewry for the past ten years. The paper that corresponds with *Horizon* in the States, though far larger, has five editors, all Jews. The Jews' power is out of all proportion to their percentage of the population. Alfred Beit came in after dinner. He said that society in South Africa was less provincial than one might suppose. The English Africans are the more entertaining, the Dutch the more intellectual. The climate is unexceptionable. He invited me to stay. Said Clementine was very happy there. He has sold his Kensington Row house and lent his best pictures to the National Gallery. They are to live out there permanently. That is our loss.

Sunday, 26th January

Today snowing so hard and so cold that John Wilton did not dare motor me to Knole. Instead we lunched at Brooks's and then parted. I dined with James and Maurice who had cooked an all vegetable meal, and for some reason was in a dark humour. People look ugly when in an ill humour.

Monday, 27th January

To Loelia Westminster's cocktail party at 15 Grosvenor Square, very grand flat given her by the Duke whom she divorces tomorrow, I think, for he is to marry a fourth time.

Wednesday, 29th January

Today the cold has been unbelievable. The papers say it is the coldest day for over fifty years. Wearing my snow boots and fur-lined coat I was not once warm. All my pipes, including w.c. pipes, are frozen, so a bath or a wash is out of the question. W.c. at the office frozen likewise. Throughout the country electricity has been cut off and the gas pressure is so low that it is not worth while turning the fire on. And we live in the twentieth century. Even the basic elements of civilization are denied us. Dined with that horror Charles Fry – it is the only word for him – drunken, dissolute and destructive.

Thursday, 30th January

At the King's Pictures today the Dutch paintings literally glowed with warmth and light, like gems. Worldly but infinitely cosy and nostalgic are these little intimate pictures of everyday life, like very accurate dreams. Was especially struck by the small Rembrandt of the Wise Men with a supernatural starlight falling upon the jewels.

Saturday, 1st February

Read *The Age of Erasmus* today. Confirmed in my dislike of the man. These fifteenth- and sixteenth-century scholars were great bores, hardly less so than the 20th-century scholars who write about them. Bridget P. dined. She told me she frankly dislikes her brother for his smug, school-mastery complacency. This remark rather upset me because I love B. and yet I had to refute the charge. She accepted my rebuke in silence.

Monday, 3rd February

Caught the 11.18 to Pulborough where I was met and driven through
slush and snow – then pouring with icy fingers of rain – to Petworth.
Lord Leconfield, now indeed slow, old and blue-faced, waddled to meet
me, clad in yellow gaiters and followed by a black retriever who seems
to be his only friend. He is a pathetic old man, extremely courteous
and over highly bred. Today he was very friendly and not at all
pompous or absurd. Seemed to think it a good idea that I should look
at his furniture, wished me to see it all, and hoped I would be pleased
with its condition. Said in fact he was convinced he was wise in
handing over to the NT. We lunched together (I not sent to the servants' hall). A large meal was left for us on hot stoves in a small
dining-room. His kitchen is in the building over the way and his food
has to pass underground. Promptly at 1.30 he summoned the nice old
housekeeper and Moss, the house-carpenter, to take me round the
house. All the pictures are now re-hung but the state-rooms are still
under dust-sheets. Furniture in splendid condition, smelling of
mansion polish and camphor. The housekeeper has one couple, the
stableman and wife, who work in the house from 6. 30 a.m. to midday.
Lord Leconfield joined us upstairs and waddled around. We made an
odd little party. He is sweet with the servants, jokes with them in his
funny, ponderous way. They however curiously subservient and rather
sycophantic. He explained that his mother cut down all the
four-poster beds because she thought them insanitary, having once
read of a dead bird being discovered in a tester.

He made me walk in the cold, steely hail outside. I don't believe he
was aware of it. The back of the house, with its buttresses, is really very
ugly. I left by bus at four for Pulborough, Lord L. accompanying me
to bus stop. Had tea in train buffet car. Went straight to Doreen in
Ovington Square. She told me I was far too modest, and that was a
mistake. She is always sweet to me. Says she loves Mrs. Trefusis, an
unlikely friend. She has already written half of *The Young Queen
Victoria*.

Tuesday, 4th February

Dined at Barbara Moray's. Her daughter Sarah and Mark Ogilvie-Grant
there, just the four of us. The daughter is a lovely child but at the age of
seventeen is racked with rheumatism and undergoing drastic treatment
by injections. The cause is lack of proper food during the war. Barbara is
avowedly anti-art and is irritated by all the 'culture' seeping down the
classes. Thinks it rot.

Thursday, 6th February

London again blanketed with snow. I stayed at home working at my Lyme Hall guidebook. In the evening to a Catholic semi-society meeting to listen to a Franciscan friar talk on the existence of God. The evening engineered by Dick Girouard. I sat between Pam Chichester and that ape, Lady L. After supper a brains trust – Barbara Ward holding forth in her mincing little voice – which I found wildly irritating.

Friday, 7th February

John Wilton took me in his big, blue Ford car to Knole, in the snow. Bitter cold. I piloted him round the house, like a refrigerator, and the garden where no man had hitherto trod. In our snow boots we crunched over a foot of snow. The new nice housekeeper and Barbara (housemaid, not Ward) already working like Trojans in the Cartoon Gallery.

Loelia dined with me. I took her to *Lady Frederick*, the Somerset Maugham play. Not good. L. told me that the Duke, her husband, was married again this morning. I believe she was feeling rather sad for she said she did not care whether she lived or died. I expect she feels like a dethroned sovereign. She should not seek happiness through pleasure. She is too clever.

Saturday, 8th February

The jolly news today is that all fuel is to be cut off. The cold is appalling. The snow still unmelted. I went to tea at Emerald's in the Dorchester. Tony Gandarillas joined us. We talked of French historians, the Renaissance influence upon France and England, and music. Emerald's knowledge astounds me.

Thursday, 13th February

This week is being a veritable nightmare. On Sunday afternoon it started to thaw and the snow mostly went. On Monday it froze again very hard, so that the slush is like slippery brick. Since Monday we have had no heating in our office apart from one electric fire. And now this is turned off from 9 till 12 and again from 2 till 4 each day. Wrapped in my fur coat with three pullovers underneath, my snowboots kept on, I am still too perished to work properly. The brain becomes atrophied. People are unanimous in blaming the Government for a hideous muddle, yet Mr. Shinwell still remains Minister of Fuel. I seldom stay in the office now but walk, dictate letters, and move away. Have twice been to the National Gallery, which is heated, to look at the Spanish Exhibition of Velasquez, Goya and El Greco. A number of poor old people sit on the benches for hours at a time, their feet wrapped in brown paper, striving to keep warm. At an Historic Buildings Committee meeting yesterday all sat in fur coats, moaning in misery, for no one could concentrate on the Agenda. Lord Esher however as cheerful as ever. He told a member of the Cabinet, 'You Labour people never let us have a dull moment.' Bridget says that if this Govemment goes an extreme left Government will take its place, and that she is quite ready to go to the barricades and shoot. I asked, whom? 'Well, almost anyone,' she replied. Most of the large shops are closed; those that are open have no electricity, and no light except from the odd candle. The streets are blacked out, as in war time, and millions are unemployed for industries have come to a standstill. Food is becoming very short and the situation is as critical and deadly serious as ever it was during the war. The odd thing is apparently that the Government is no more unpopular with the masses than before this *débâcle*.

Friday, 14th February

At 6.15 went to see Kathleen Kennet at Leinster Corner. She is in bed upstairs. I was very shocked and depressed by her condition and feel pretty sure she is dying, and that she knows it. She has pernicious anaemia and has been in bed for three weeks today. and shows no signs of improving in spite of daily injections. Before retiring to bed she had been feeling tired and lifeless, off her food and incapable of rousing herself to make plans for Switzerland in December. I wish I had been financially solvent to make them for her, for she had proposed that we should go together. Now she eats nothing but fruit. The thought of food makes her feel sick. She cannot read for longer than one hour at a time. To get out of bed to go to the bathroom tires her dreadfully. I stayed an hour and when I left she said cheerfully and without emotion: 'If I pass out as a result of this illness, I do not want my friends to mind because I have had a most wonderful innings, a wonderful life. I would rather go than linger decrepit and incurable. The best of this illness is that there is no suffering and I do not become disgusting, at least I don't think I do. I don't decay, become horrible, or smell, for instance. I just linger and gently melt away.' Poor darling, I felt dreadfully moved, yet somehow quite controlled talking to her of such a matter. I tried to make her believe that her time had not come yet, but could not deceive her. When I bent down to kiss her I noticed how soft her face had become, unlike her tough, rugged old skin. It was that of an ancient woman who lived indoors and I noticed a terrible thinness about her neck beneath her nightdress. Her eyes looked dark and shone like coals. This visit has saddened me greatly.

Tuesday, 18th February

Not a sign of thaw. Weather as bitter as ever, and I wear my fur coat and snow boots daily. Still the electricity is cut morning and afternoon. Went to a cocktail party at the Lionel Bretts. Talked to Mark Bonham-Carter, who in conversation becomes alert, whereas in repose his face is dour and disdainful.

Wednesday, 19th February

At midday quitted the office for the rest of the week. Went to Agnew's for the opening by Dr. Trevelyan of the Exhibition of Lord Spencer's pictures from Althorp. Such a crush that I could hardly see a picture, and what I saw did not greatly impress me. Queen Mary was present and each time I wanted to look at a picture I found myself stepping back *on to* her, and had to sidestep. How royalty do get in the way. Nice however to have the old lady about and to see women curtseying to her. She looked very well in a black skin coat, little black hat, not a toque, with blue ostrich feather. Lady Leconfield, enormously tall with a high hat and feather, sought me out, and spoke to me somewhat inconsequentially. I did not realise she had just come out of a home, poor woman. Someone informed me later.

Eardley met me at Salisbury station and motored me to Long Crichel. Eddy S.-W. and Desmond S.-T. there. The house very adequately heated and comfortable. Brilliant fireworks from Desmond who is the gayest, sweetest-tempered, most informative person in the wide world. After dinner a curious discussion ensued about homosexuality. Eddy showed deliberate unreason, and refused to concede a point. He maintained that born homosexuals could never become heterosexuals, whereas I maintained, with no intent to annoy, that this was simply not the case. People were not necessarily born one way or the other; that heterosexuals could become homosexuals, and vice versa; and that there were people capable of falling in love equally deeply with men and women. Eddy stoutly denied the possibility of persons being ambisexual, and with vehemence quoted himself as the over-riding disproof of this notion, assuming that his case was a precedent the world over. He adopted a highly self-pitying attitude, became furious with Desmond and, after much high-pitched, querulous shouting that Desmond always 'attacked' him, left the room. Desmond meant to do nothing of the kind. Afterwards Eardley and Desmond admitted that it was impossible to carry on discussions with Eddy. Indeed they are right. In my hearing Eddy announced that he preferred not to arrive at the truth than to involve himself in controversy, which made him ill. In spite of this I have a great affection for Eddy. He told me the next day that he knew he ought to be contented with his lot but his chronic ill-health and difficult temperament prevented him acknowledging his good fortune. Every day, he said, he was pursued by angst. I understand this because in lesser measure I am too. But not, perhaps, every day.

Thursday, 20th February

Eardley and I motored to Montacute and arranged most of the new consignment of furniture. The house was fairly warm but the Yateses said today was the last day they could keep the boilers alight. I am beginning a cold, for I have a sore throat and am sneezing.

Saturday, 22nd February

Yesterday it snowed so heavily that we had to abandon going to Montacute. I finally decided, after much prevarication, to put off my trip to Herefordshire next week. Came back to London in the afternoon because I detected a *gêne* hovering over Crichel, and was also rather fearful of being stricken with influenza and infecting Eddy.

Wednesday, 26th February

Ever since my Long Crichel visit have felt so rotten with a stuffed cold that today I stayed in bed. I have chosen the first day of sun for a month to incarcerate myself in my gloomy bedroom. Midi came to tea and James dropped in to bring me an expensive illustrated book on Virginian houses which I had told him I coveted. Very sweet of him. He is naturally generous to a fault. I have been reading the diaries of Hugh Dormer with some emotion. He was a young Catholic officer in the Irish Guards whom at Dover I remember for his aloof and reticent manner which distinguished him from the others, and for his – singular and strangely moving in so young a man -- devoutness. He attended Mass every day and, I noticed, always communicated. These diaries are about his courageous exploits after he left the regiment he loved for secret work behind the enemy lines, where he was dropped by parachute. He was finally killed in Normandy. What amazes me is his unshakeable faith, his 1914 ideals and conviction that he was fighting a just war and that death for his ideals would be the crowning reward of his short life.

Thursday, 27th February

This morning went to a very enjoyable performance – the centenary service for Ellen Terry in St. Paul's church, Covent Garden. It was cheerful, and inspiring. Very cold, yellow day in which no woman looked her best. I arrived at 11.30 and had to fight my way in, although I had a reserved seat. I was put in the front of the nave. The Sadler's Wells choir sang anthems; Edith Evans, Sybil Thorndike and Peggy Ashcroft read three Shakespeare sonnets. The lessons were read by Ralph Richardson, Leon Quartermaine and Harcourt Williams. With the exception of the last, who is a handsome elderly man, all the others looked remarkably plain, Richardson a flunkey, Quartermaine a Glasgow thug masquerading as an undertaker, E. Evans as a painted clown (male), and Thorndike as a downtrodden school-teacher. Miss Edith Craig was present and Christopher St. John, wearing a fawn teddy-bear coat, man's porkpie hat, and waving a gigantic bunch of golden daffodils at her friends behind her. The Bishop of London, a mealy-mouthed creature, gave the address.

Saturday, 1st March

I have never been colder. Huddled over a coal fire that gives out an imperceptible flutter of heat I managed to write with great speed an account of Petworth for my National Trust *Guide*.

Sunday, 2nd March

I went to the Cumberland Hotel – a typical hotel for a not very rich foreigner to choose – to meet François Carvalho and Mrs. Dalton who in the Chancellor's car followed us to Osterley. Grandy Jersey was there to receive and conduct us round the house. The visitors were greatly impressed by the quality of Adam's decoration. The state rooms are more or less arranged again and in fairly good repair, but the window frames are all deteriorating. The outside is horribly untidy owing to the brick huts built up to the house by Glyn's Bank, which still occupies most of it. On to West Wycombe. We lunched there and saw village and house – Johnnie had deliberately gone away for the day – which in contrast to Osterley is shabby and of which the quality of the decoration is less fine. Although cold it was a lovely sunny day. At 3.45 the two visitors returned to London in Mrs. Dalton's car. I meant to go westwards but at Stokenchurch the car was going so badly I returned to London. At East Acton it gave out completely, so I pushed the damned thing into a garage and hired a car to transport me and all my luggage back to Thurloe Square. How I abominate cars.

Monday, 3rd March

Stayed in bed all morning for yesterday I felt giddy and odd at times. Rang up Mama who told me to take a train to Evesham and recuperate for a day or two.

Tuesday, 4th March

Stayed in bed reading Henry [Green]'s *Back* this morning. By tea time it started snowing again and blowing a gale.

Wednesday, 5th March

All day it continued to snow. This is the worst storm in these parts ever recorded. A blizzard rages and the snow is piling up. Papa, Mama and I began after luncheon to walk to the Table Land. Bitter wind and twice my hat blew away. Outside the Idions' house and along the Badsey road were drifts six feet deep. One small car managed miraculously to pass. We sent Mama home. The two of us walked on to Badsey to Cull, the baker's to fetch some bread, which, with the milk, had not been delivered today. On the edge of the village we saw Cull's van just about to leave for Wickhamford, so we returned. At the top of the hill over Bully Brook, where a snow drift was rapidly building up, we stopped, and talked to two men. Sure enough the van came and was stuck in the drift. By dint of much pushing the four of us succeeded in extricating it.

Thursday, 6th March

Brilliant sunny day but the snow lying in huge drifts. Haines says no one remembers anything like it before. There are icicles, over three foot long, hanging from the thatch of the cottages. I spent the morning on the roof of the pantry at the Manor shovelling the snow off. It has even blown through the roof of the motor-house loft and is lying in piles on the trunks. My hunting boots were completely buried. In the middle of the squash court was a heap of snow, two foot deep. After luncheon I walked with the Cooks to fetch some milk from the farm at Bower's Hill. There we saw an amusing sight – about twenty men attaching an old cart to a tractor, they following behind and holding the shafts and supporting the milk churns. This curious procession, like a funeral, advanced to Badsey and Wickhamford over snow drifts. A gang of men cleared a passage-way along the road at Pear Tree Corner. Curiously, it is the bits of road running from north to south which are quite impassable. Some drifts are six feet deep. I wished I had a camera. There is something harsh, metallic and savage about the Vale yokels, something extremely primitive, yet unpeasantlike, very material and earthy. Their voices are grating and discordant. When Dick and I were children we spoke broad Worcestershire perfectly. This afternoon they were very good-humoured and though professing to dislike the snow, were enjoying it. Nobody talks of anything but the weather. I had to put off my return to London and my party for Nancy Mitford.

Friday, 7th March

Twenty-nine degrees of frost in the night, and this morning brilliant sun again, what Haines describes as 'a proper bobby-dazzler'. A jeep called for me at nine and took me to Evesham station where I marched up and down the platform waiting for the train. It was an hour late but I got to London for luncheon. A jeep has merits. It is not like a car, but a blue-bottle, for it darts and jumps, buzzes, turns about and practically somersaults from one place to another. It travels as happily over mountains of frozen snow as over the best tarmac road.

Sunday, 9th March

Motored to Chiswick House. Claud Phillimore last night gave me a brochure advancing his theory that the Wyatt wings should be demolished, thus reducing the villa to Lord Burlington's original dimensions. It would be small enough to need comparatively little renovation and upkeep. The place could then be made into a furnished house of the period. We did not go inside but walked round the garden in the snow. At last the thaw has set in with a vengeance, thank God, and the sun is out. J.F. dined with me and we discussed sex problems and how to overcome them by the most practical, mechanical and cynical means.

Tuesday, 11th March

Lunched with Anne Rothermere at Warwick House overlooking the Green Park. Very pre-war, butler and footmen, wines and desserts. A heterogeneous party consisting of Anne (hostess), Bob Boothby, Lady Crewe, James P.-H., Sibyl Colefax, the editor of the *Evening News* and me. Lady Crewe makes no attempt to be friendly or interesting and must, I am sure, be fundamentally a disagreeable woman. Occasionally she melts into a bland cow-like smile, which has one effect – to put her neighbour ill at ease. We necessarily talked politics, and Lady Crewe began by saying she hoped the Liberals would never unite with the Conservatives, whatever else they did. Sibyl and James both agreed in deploring the present Government, yet both voted it into power. Warwick House has little architectural character, but its site, with terrace over park and proximity to St. James's Palace, is enchanting.

Wednesday, 12th March

In the morning met Charles Brocklehurst in Baker Street and looked at some scrappy pieces of Lyme Park tapestry he has taken to be cleaned by Miss Parry who works for Partridges. Her cleaning takes place in a cellar, damp, dark and low, in Dickensian gloom and squalor. Then to St. James's

Street and looked at the picture of Astbury church from Little Moreton Hall which has been cleaned; then to the Pantechnicon and saw and approved Sir Henry Aubrey-Fletcher's chairs and settee, William & Mary, offered for Lyme. The Pantechnicon built in 1830 in neo-Grecian style is purity of architecture, with an old-fashioned air about the interior. It has Doric fluted balusters to the original ramp for horses and vans, original office screen and desk, lamps and stove. Really a lovely and satisfactory building.

After a hurried luncheon I trained to Windsor – raining again – and called at Henry II's Tower. How brash and ugly the Castle is when you get up to it. Miss Hanbury-Williams showed me three pictures she offers for Lyme. The Chapel was locked when I came out but I walked through the Cloisters and down the Hundred Steps and into Eton. At Shefford's bought six green wine glasses to add to my red selection. Bought a tie at New & Lingwood. Eton shops full of attractive clothes and quantities to buy.

On return went to Sibyl's large party in her drawing-room. Gerry Wellington, John Lehmann, Loelia Westminster, Alan Pryce-Jones, Emerald Cunard, Nancy Rodd there. John Lehmann is charming to talk to. Unlike Lady Crewe he makes himself agreeable. Christopher Sykes I find distant. Talk was of Harold Nicolson turning Socialist. Sykes said the reason was that Harold likes to consider himself 'fast'. This is absurd.

Thursday, 13th March

Johnnie lunched with me at Brooks's and said (tongue in cheek, of course) he feared Helen might not be returning at all; she neither wrote to him nor showed signs of coming back to England. He said that he had definitely taken to the bottle – 'baby' he calls it. There is nothing in these times to take to in its place.

Attended a committee meeting of the Georgian Group to discuss Chiswick House. Claud Phillimore's proposal had a lukewarm reception, perhaps rightly. We were told that young Noel-Baker was calling a committee to be held in the House of Commons to investigate the case thoroughly, and be advised by the Georgian Group.

Friday, 14th March

At the Finance Committee this morning the staff were dismissed and salaries were discussed. Mine and Martineau's were raised to £1,000, and Ramsey's to £800. Harold said to me in the afternoon, 'You should have heard the nice things I said about you. They would have made you regret the unkind things you said to me,' referring to my reproofs over his joining the Labour Party.

This evening I had Nancy, Bridget and Tony Gandarillas to dine. At least the food tasted, as Bridget said. They all complimented me over my room [in no. 20 Thurloe Square]. Somehow I did not find the party wholly enjoyable, but Nancy, whom I love, is not always congenial, and her unkind witticisms when first-hand, are often less funny than when repeated.

Saturday, 15th March

On leaving the office at midday I wandered into the Abbey. Walked round the ambulatory and a verger got special permission for me to enter the Queen Elizabeth and Mary Queen of Scots chapel, which I much appreciated. I think the Henry VII vaulting the loveliest thing in English architecture. Nothing raised subsequently strikes the same chords of spirituality. It is the consummation of English gothic architecture. Queen Elizabeth's face must be a portrait from life. Mary's in profile, seen looking towards the light and south, is laden with tragedy. How very moving is the Abbey, especially in winter. It is the silent annals of England. more convincing than any history book, more real than any facts taught in schools.

In the afternoon I drove Rick [Stewart-Jones] and Fred Oppé to Hampton Court. Mr. Rainbow showed us over the Wolsey apartments. They are uninteresting except for the remains of the plaster ceilings of his time, with their definite Italian influence. They are now without colour. Our guide told us that the last resident, a Lady Peel, found them overpowering and induced the Office of Works to demolish half the ceiling of one room. I find it hard to believe the Office would have sanctioned such a thing within recent times. Then we went round the state apartments, most drearily arranged. They fill one with dismay. Arranged sparsely, with little taste and no imagination. It began to snow very heavily again. Rick dined with me at home and stayed till midnight. I reproved him for his sloppy abandon, physical and mental, governess that I am.

Sunday, 16th March

Mama telephoned last night warning me not to motor to Worcester today on account of the bad floods. She said that their cottage was under water and in Oxford the swans were swimming into people's bedrooms, which she thought rather sweet – of the swans presumably. This disturbed me. However I motored Bridget to Kew and we lunched marvellously with Mark. The sun was out and it was warm again. Then I set off for Worcester. Parts of the road I traversed were badly flooded and I had to digress to Gerrard's Cross and join the High Wycombe road. Nothing very bad until the Cotswolds where single traffic because of the heaps of snow still on the verges. At Moreton-in-the-Marsh water was cascading through someone's house into the street. For a moment I thought I would be stuck. Then it started to rain again and a great gale arose so that I feared elm trees would fall across the car. I am now staying in Worcester in a very second-rate hotel, The Crown. There is a musty smell in my tiny bedroom under the eaves. It is so dirty that I do not like to put any of my things in the wardrobe or on the table. All wallpapers peeling. Sluts instead of servants who chatter and giggle behind the screen in the dining-room, and the proprietress in grubby black satin has a cigarette hanging out of her mouth when she speaks. God, I wish these English hotel proprietors could be forced to see what Swiss hotels are like! Food here practically uneatable.

Monday, 17th March

At ten set off for Bromyard, fourteen miles away. Crossed the Severn in Worcester but at Broadway, 7 miles from Brockhampton, I was diverted from my route by a huge tree across the road. The Teme was uncrossable. Motored by devious lanes past Abberley to Chows Top and down to Tenbury. There just managed to cross the Teme and creep down again to Bromyard, arriving at 12.15. Decided to put up at The Hop Pole for two nights, though this is a poor class hotel. At least the people are civil and the bed is comfortable though of the feather variety. One dreads coming across hidden horrors. No bath water here either, just as there was of course none at The Crown. Lunched early at The Hop Pole and arrived Brockhampton at 1.45. Stayed till seven. I had to leave the car at the lodge gate and walk through the snow down the drive. Old Bakewell the butler and Mrs. Hughes the housekeeper very kindly and friendly, and both disappointed that I had not come to stay. He told me a lot about the Colonel [Lutley], how he was a taskmaster of the old school, though just, good-living, God-fearing, and a gentleman. Bakewell's wife lives in one of the lodges and yet for two years this man lived and slept in the big house in order to dress, undress and give the Colonel his bath. He had to sponge him and even clean his feet for he was so crippled with arthritis. Yet Colonel Lutley never left him anything after twelve years service and only paid him £2 a week. Bakewell spoke without resentment and was fond of the old wretch.

I went all round the house with the probate inventory, marking those items I thought might be needed at Montacute, 3 Cheyne Walk or the head office. There is no museum stuff.

Tuesday, 18th March

It poured all night and most of the morning. They say that today there is no possible means of getting to Worcester, not even through Tenbury. I hope to goodness I shall not be stuck at Bromyard for a week. Where the snow has receded and there is not a raging torrent from the high ground over the fields I saw my first snowdrops and aconites, gallantly struggling to brave a perplexing spring. Warmer today, thank God, and beautiful when the sun comes out. I feel miles and miles away from civilization here, cut off from the world. At six when I had finished my day's work I wandered round the grounds and looked at Colonel Lutley's grave. I must see that the NT puts up a gravestone and memorial to him. This sort of thing they are quite capable of overlooking. At least the Trust has something to be grateful to him for.

Wednesday, 19th March

I set off at ten for London. Was advised that at Tenbury the Teme was uncrossable and at Shrewsbury the Severn likewise, but that Worcester was approachable via Malvern. But I found that this was not the case and proceeded to Gloucester. Information was vouchsafed by delighted inhabitants that the river was impassable. Indeed there was a complete halt of traffic near the bridges. Rows of motors stuck in the water. Then some ruffians with a tractor, on seeing that my car was expensive-looking – as they thought – hitched me on to the tail of some lorries, swearing that nowhere was the road deeper than one-and-a-half feet. After we had started two A.A. men in waders warned me that on the contrary the water would be well over the driver's seat and the car would be ruined. By this time the procession was slowly advancing. Nevertheless I induced them to stop the tractor and unhitch me. A small Morris, tied to my tail, was also unhitched. In despair I drove back to Malvern, fifteen miles. Here I was forced to abandon my car in a garage and catch an evening train to Paddington. In Worcester I saw the water in the bedrooms of all the cottages along the river. There has been nothing like these floods since 1770.

Thursday, 20th March

Sheila took me to the first night of *The Magic Flute* at Covent Garden. Oliver Messel's scenery and costumes extremely picturesque, but the singing execrable. The whole performance too long and dragged out by cheap dialogue. In fact it was made into a pantomime.

Friday, 21st March

Jamesey, Maurice and Nigel [Nicolson] dined with me at home here. Enjoyable evening. Nigel remarked that J. and M. were like two little sparrows huddled together on a telephone wire. James said that the Andersons were staying last weekend with Lady Crewe. Sir John's is probably the best brain in England, but J. found him very unsympathetic for all his talk was political. He said the Labour Government would wear themselves out because they could not take politics easily like the Conservatives. Bridget Paget got drunk at dinner and her hair fell in the soup. Sir John Anderson was deeply shocked.

Today I received a letter from Sir Donald Somervell that G. would be blackballed. He advises me to withdraw his candidature. This has incensed me.

Saturday, 22nd March

Worked this morning at Digby Wyatt's address on foreign artists in England in the sixteenth century. Professor Richardson lunched at Brooks's and repeated to me the speech he made yesterday at the R.I.B.A. dinner in the presence of the Archbishop of Canterbury, the French and Chinese Ambassadors, and the Prime Minister. The speech must have been very witty. The Archbishop in replying thanked the Professor for telling him what the Almighty was thinking about current affairs. I showed the Professor Sir Donald Somervell's letter. He said he knew the reason was that G. was considered by staider members of the Election Committee to be a 'pleasurer'; and that they wouldn't have him on account of his treatment of his second wife. He added that twenty years ago such a consideration would not be taken into account, but today the aristocracy were tightening themselves up. He advised me to withdraw his name without ado, and not to resign myself. The Prof. said that after forty no man cherished illusions; that after fifty all he cherished was personal comfort and freedom from agitation. This explained why reforms were carried out by men under that age. He said that Brendan Bracken was undoubtedly Winston Churchill's son; that Dean Swift, after his marriage to Stella, discovered that both she and he were the children of Sir William Temple and his 'incestuous' marriage preyed on his mind. I know that disapproving old prude, Lord Ilchester, is at the back of the blackball affair.

Sunday, 23rd March

After lunching with Sheila I walked to see Kathleen now in the Paddington Hospital. I thought she looked better, but she is very depressed about herself. Says her hair has gone quite white, which is not true. We talked of the purpose of living. I gave her some snowdrops. When I left she said: 'When young men like you come to see me I feel that I shall get well again; that there is still a future for me.' The Gainsboroughs had asked me to tea. But I was feeling so sad I just could not go. Very bad.

Monday, 24th March

A terrible train journey to Aylsham, standing in the corridor. It poured with rain all day. At Blickling met the new caretakers and housemaid who are getting the house straight for the opening in May. In the evening went to Maud Mosley's nice little house, the Dell, where I am staying these two nights. She is very hospitable and solicitous, yet aloof. She talked a lot about the Mosleys and likes Diana at last, but dislikes what she calls her affectations.

Tuesday, 25th March

Spent all day at Blickling. The sun shone and it was beautiful. I adore this place. Did some good work, I think, in helping Miss O'Sullivan to take some tricky decisions. Unfortunately I shall have to return in a month to put the finishing touches, for the furniture is not yet in place, and the dustsheets are still on.

Wednesday, 26th March

Went to a revived Ordinary tonight, the first since Sibyl's restoration to health, and indeed the last I shall attend. The dinner was horrible. Nothing to drink but cider. I sat next to Ben Nicolson and a newly married daughter of Lord De La Warr, a sweet girl. The room in the Dorchester was both hideous and uncomfortable. Kenneth Rae and Ben, with whom I walked away, agreed with me that they too would never go to another.

Thursday, 27th March

Went to the Victoria and Albert at Leigh Ashton's invitation to a buffet luncheon party to see the French tapestries. Met Clarissa [Churchill] and we ate sandwiches together. I only saw the Louis XIV and eigh-teenth-century tapestries, but shall go again tomorrow, for there were no catalogues today. The twentieth-century tapestries are hideous beyond all belief. Sir Eric Maclagan said to me: 'Even if one had one of the least offensive, what would one do with it?' Bertie Abdy told me at Emerald Cunard's this evening that the rise and fall of tapestry weaving coincided with the fluctuation of economy. In what he esteemed the greatest periods, namely the seventeenth and eighteenth centuries, there were 600 different colours available. Today there are less than sixty. Lady Diana Cooper came into Emerald's for tea. She had a streaming cold. I don't care for the insolent way in which she looks through me.

Sunday, 30th March

I have been to the tapestry exhibition again – the formal opening day. But again there were too many people who distracted me by chat. I know nothing more symbolical of pure poetry than the lady outside her tent, 'En toi mon seul désir'. It transcends anything I have ever seen, and makes one want to cry.

Have been thinking a lot over what Professor Richardson said to me. Every man is damned by his own sins in this life at any rate, if not in the next. I am certainly damned here by my defeatism and chronic despair. The outward form my despair takes is a persistent ill-humour and an abandon to selfishness, and hardness of heart, which bespeak a shrivelled soul. I realise that in this life one should love all humanity and care for it. I do not, and so am a dissident. My ill-humour is all-besetting.

Since Friday I have felt very unwell, pains in my stomach and nausea. I hope it may be merely a form of internal chill; but at nights I imagine it to be cancer. I have for weeks past also experienced a curious burning in the legs. This I attribute to phlebitis; and a pounding of the heart, which I suppose to be angina pectoris. In short, something is the matter.

I am staying tonight at Farm Hall, Godmanchester with the Sissons, for he has offered the NT covenants over this house, newly bought, and grounds of twenty acres. He thinks rather too highly of Farm Hall. It is a very, very plain Hanoverian town house, built in 1746 of red brick, with no frills of any kind, a sort of Quaker house. It is too unadorned to be remarkable, but decent nevertheless. One front faces a street of the town. Across the street in a recessed retaining wall, a gate between urned piers affords a view of a small rectangular canal and the Ouse (now flooding every field) beyond. The other front faces an ancient lime avenue, also axial with the front door and canal. Unfortunately the house is not strictly symmetrical on the garden front and was never so, I fancy. Inside there are large rooms, very cold. With my chill I was perished. We sat over a green log fire, the rain battering down outside. Sisson will of course finish decorating very well, but at present the interior is shabby, empty, rather dirty and stinks of cats. The upstairs is filled with odd families which make a noise.

The A.W. Lawrences came to tea at three and stayed till 6.45. He is T.E.L.'s brother, remarkably young-looking, rather earnest, and cracks jokes which are unfunny. He looks at one in that penetrating way that was Matheson's, which I so much dislike. I suppose I have secrets to probe. After they left Sisson and I motored to Hinchingbrooke, the Hs being away, and walked round the outside, examining Sisson's demolitions of the Victorian wing. He has made vast improvements. We agreed that the destroyed wing needed a wall in its place and that the tower should not be totally destroyed, but its top taken off, made lower, so as not to look so thin as it does at present. I was slightly irritated by Sisson's pedantry, and suffered from the cold and discomfort of his house. He now takes snuff in such quantities that the end of his nose and his upper lip are dark orange. So is his handkerchief after incessant blowings.

Monday, 31st March

Loelia took me to the Albert Hall, the two Menuhins playing. Hall far too big for a piano and violin. Then I gave her dinner at Boulestins. We both, without meaning to, cut Mr. Tufnell of Langleys who was sitting at the next table. When I realised what I had done I ran after him to explain. He was quite nice, but said he thought it the rudest, most deliberate insult he had ever received. I am not sure I am glad I ran after him.

Tuesday, 1st April

Went to Knole this afternoon. The state rooms look marvellous and Mason is delighted with the housekeeper and her three women. Everything here promises to run successfully and the women are as happy as larks and proud of the place and their work. The silver in the King's Room all cleaned and shining as though awaiting its royal visitor.

Dined at Cecil Beaton's in Pelham Place. His house in flamboyant Edwardian taste. The three women guests were, I suppose, the three prettiest old-young women in London – Anne Rothermere in sparkling white, a long dress, Diane Abdy and Elizabeth Hofmannsthal, the last by far the most striking of the three. I think she is about the most beautiful woman I have ever seen. I sat next to her and her husband for there was one man too many. Esmond Rothermere was cross and rather pompous; he was suffering from sciatica. Hofmannsthal is a bore, shouting in broken English. He told a terrible story of Lord Anglesey's death which was entirely due to the doctor's negligence and stupidity. Lord A. was perfectly well but because he had nothing to do for two weeks decided to have a simple operation for prostate gland. They put the wrong tubes into him and simply left him to be tortured to death. Cecil was very charming and dulcet. He is a cunning man. His power of observation is acute, and like a gimlet he twists out the inmost dust of the person his steely eye is fixed upon.

Wednesday, 2nd April

Had a good-humoured reply from G. agreeing to withdraw his candidature for Brooks's, but expressing surprise and regret. I shall never feel the same towards Brooks's for this behaviour; shall never forget or forgive.

Took a train to Tenterden and attended the funeral of Edith Craig at Smallhythe. She had been cremated and there was no coffin or urn that I could see. The service was arranged in excellent taste just as Ellen Terry's memorial was. I was impressed by it. The two old women were very upset. I promised to go down and see them in a week's time. Somerset de Chair who was present told me he intended to rent Blickling, come what may. I worked hard in the train, did a long report on the Knole contents and corrected guidebook proofs.

All Easter it was perishingly cold, with relentless rain. Harry Ashwin motored me to Charlecote for tea. I stayed the night with the Lucys. The bedrooms at Charlecote are cosy and Victorian: flowered wallpapers, washstand with pretty flowered china, maplewood furniture, four-poster bed with old chintz hangings, a fire in the grate. Bath with polished wooden rim, brass taps and brass spray on end of a long pipe; deep red, thick, comfortable bath mat.

Thursday, 10th April

Dined with the Johnnie Churchills. It is odd seeing Johnnie so conventionally established in a tidy and well-appointed house. This is entirely his wife, Mary's, beneficent doing. Sarah Churchill was there and I sat next to her. She is beautiful and attractive; physically unlike her father, Winston, and prettier than her sister Diana Sandys. Johnnie described to me his father's death and the keen interest which his uncle Winston took in his brother's illness. He kept telephoning and giving elaborate directions to doctors and nurses as though commanding a battle, using Churchillian phrases like, 'Backs to the Wall!' and 'Certainly Jack must fight to the finish.' On Jack's death he worked himself up to a tremendous emotional pitch and literally shed, or, as Johnnie described it, rained tears around the room. He gave elaborate instructions as to the hymns to be sung at the funeral, quoting dozens of them by heart. Then, Johnnie said, on the very night of his brother's death he read to Johnnie sixty pages of his first book on the South African War, as though to console him, ending with the words, 'I wish I had the power of writing as well as that today.'

Friday, 11th April

A most beautiful day, sunny, clear, balmy. I walked from Queen Anne's Gate to Paddington after six o'clock and all Londoners were singing or whistling with joy over escape from an appalling winter. Spent quarter of an hour with dear Kathleen [Kennet] who is much iller. She looks very tired, her face is softer and her voice perceptibly slower. She admits she is no better and wonders what is the point of surviving, since she can never recover and must always have injections for pernicious anaemia and take insulin for diabetes. Says she has no desire for sweet things. I was mightily depressed by her appearance and languor. As I left I thought the rarity of this woman lies in the fact that I can talk to her as to myself. She is part of me; she understands. She sees the light. She is a darling, although in the past I have in my beastly way been irritated by her. I asked myself as I walked, was my distress selfish. Was it my loss I was lamenting?

Sunday, 13th April

Again a lovely day, clear, yet hazy with heat. There are few birds, sadly enough, left to sing, and only chestnuts in bud. No leaves on the trees yet, though the earth is red as terra cotta. Yesterday Rick motored me to Malvern in his Chevrolet van. A most unfortunate expedition for I allowed my irritation with him to get the better of me and gave vent to odious ill nature. I had breakfast ready for him at eight; he came at nine. At Brockhampton I warned him not to motor down to the old house. He did so and got bogged.

Tuesday, 15th April

I drove down to Kent, singing all the way as loudly as I could, unheard. Passed Knole and lunched at Tenterden. At 2 o'clock called at Smallhythe. The two poor old women remaining were very pathetic. Miss Atwood, eighty-two, is the more spry and affable. Miss St. John, very lame, was wearing brown corduroy trousers, stretched tight over an enormous bum, a yellow scarf round her neck, a magenta beret on her grey hair, shirt and tie. The other one wore a shirt and tie too and is called Tony by her friends; Miss St. J. is called Chris. They showed me over the property and explained its problems. In the Ferry Cottage lives a terrifying woman, Mrs S— who helps them with housework. She wears grey flannel trousers, tight shirt and tie and beret, and is grubby and masculine. She is called Bruce, and refers to Miss St. John as 'Mr Chris'. Really I felt like Alice in Wonderland. I went to tea with darling Vita at Sissinghurst. We discussed Knole. She could not explain how the upholstered Jacobean furniture had survived the eighteenth century. Poor Ben was upstairs with influenza – he sleeps above the dining-room – and before I left Vita came down with his thermometer in her hand. It registered 104 and she was clearly a little alarmed. I went away thinking that the Nicolson family was the most united, luckiest, and happiest I knew. I thought Vita was going to kiss me goodbye. But from shyness

I withdrew, supposing that I did not know her well enough. Vita's brick tower rises gaunt and solemn reflected through the back window of the car as one drives away, along the lane.

Wednesday, 16th April

Had a very long day. Started off in the car at 10 o'c for Caernarvon. When I reached Stafford learned that I had just missed the train to Crewe, so continued by road, and there caught the 4.55, arriving Caernarvon for a late dinner. Met Armitage and walked round the town at dusk. Examined the Castle walls, particularly the grotesques, gargoyles and birds of stone perched upon the ramparts. The Royal Hotel not too bad but nothing to write home about.

Thursday, 17th April

Up here the pussy willows out, also lent lilies and rhododendrons, for it is mild. In the morning Armitage and I met Mr. Evans, the printer and Secretary of the Local Committee of the Segontium Museum. Disappointed to find no improvements yet in hand, and the place in total chaos. Builders apparently about to come at any time. Took a train to Conway where we lunched. Found to our dismay that about half of the contents of 'Aberconwy' do not belong to the NT at all, but to the Council and Museum of Wales. Armitage rather brightly tackled the local antique dealer who may agree to rent this dismal house and move his shop into it. I bought from him a pair of Pontefract bowls on stems for 21s. which is exceedingly cheap. At four left for Crewe, got into my car and drove to Atcham. Stayed the night at The Mytton and Mermaid.

Friday, 18th April

Called on Lady Berwick at 10.30 and rapidly gave her a valuation of those pieces of furniture she is sending to Sotheby's for sale. Then she again offered me her Victorian nursery scrap-screen, which this time I agreed to accept, but on a payment of 10s. 'So,' she said, 'nobody can now say that you accept gifts and bribes from your friends,' which I thought very sweet and generous of her. At 11.30 I was at Lilleshall. Thank goodness the owner, Mr. Ford, was away, and with the agent and his assistant I was able to make a quick scrutiny of two hours. House quite hideous and large, now full of Barnardo children who swarmed like ants round my motor and wrote their names on the dust of the bonnet with their beastly little fingers. I don't know what we could do with this house but the grounds of 600 acres are without question, beautiful. If the Committee refuse it Mr Ford will raise a stink. If they accept, the house will always be an embarrassment.

Called at Letocetum which is a lamentable, tumbledown property. The sheds over the Roman remains have collapsed: the exhibits consist of dusty, broken bits of Roman pottery. The whole place unkempt and uncared for. I would like to blow it up. Then on to Packwood which I walked round with nice Weaver, the gardener, who was really pleased to see me. Now it *is* well cared for. At The King's Head, Aylesbury, drank a heavenly glass of doubtless base port wine and got home after 10 o'c.

Saturday, 19th April

Helen Dashwood dined at the Ritz after my taking her to *Odd Man Out*, a James Mason film (good) and was charming and meltingly sweet. Also looking very pretty in a new Paris hat – not the absurd sort. She expects to be a grandmother any day.

Sunday, 20th April

I motored Charlie Brocklehurst to Montacute. We ate a picnic luncheon which Emily provided. Very good it was too. Filthy weather all this trip and a great gale raging. Charlie made some excellent suggestions which I carried out. We got the gardeners to fetch and carry and re-hang the Pintoricchio in the dining-room where it looked superb. After tea went to Melbury where I stayed the next two nights with the Ilchesters. Charlie stayed with the Stavordales at Evershot. Lady Ilchester is adorable; about seventy, with a blue face and few teeth. Extremely welcoming, she at once puts you at ease. Makes one feel one is a great success. Also is very funny and full of gossip. Drink flowed and John Fox kept plying my glass. Lady I. did not spare hers and a daughter who was staying, was very drunk indeed. After dinner she sat swaying over an old photograph album making no sense at all.

Lady I. told me that her mother Lady Londonderry was a bosom friend of Lady Blanche Hozier, mother of Mrs. Winston Churchill. Lady Blanche confided in Lady Londonderry at Aix just before Mrs. Winston was born that the child's father was Lord Redesdale, her brother-in-law and my Tom's grandfather. This makes Tom and Randolph first cousins as well as second.

I returned from Montacute to London on Tuesday very late, for I was invited by Sibyl Colefax to her box at the opera. I hastily changed and dashed off to Covent Garden in the car. With my bows right across Piccadilly Circus, the car stopped dead, having run completely out of petrol. It was a bad dream come true. Traffic piled up, hooting behind me. I got out, walked up to three policemen on the pavement and begged for help. They pushed and shunted the car to the kerb. Then I walked to three garages before one would sell me petrol in a tin. I missed the first act of

Rosenkavalier, an all-English production, the libretto translation by Alan Pryce-Jones and scenery and décor by Robin Ironside – conventional rococo drawing-room style.

Thursday, 24th April

Joshua Rowley lunched at Brooks's. He is Mindy Bacon's nephew and very like him in looks and manner. Has a quiet, gentle demeanour and sweet expression. He is frightfully keen to become keeper of Packwood and is going to see it next Tuesday.

Friday, 25th April

I lunched with Trenchard Cox at the Athenaeum. He has asked me to stay in Birmingham in June in order to show me Aston Hall which he is resurrecting. A lively, intelligent man with a dry sense of humour. I had tea with Emerald who soon went off to the theatre. She was looking very pretty and in good form. I walked away with Helen Dashwood and Robin Ironside into the sun, across the Park. Charles Fry dined. He promised that Batsford's would pay for my holiday in Rome this autumn and gave me a fine book of coloured reproductions of the U.S.A. National Gallery pictures, which was kind. But he made me drink contrary to my determination to do nothing of the sort, and boasted of his sexual prowess in a way that sickened me. Terrible man, the worst and most depraved I know.

Monday, 28th April

Went to see Kathleen K. still in the Paddington hospital; and took her Ciano's *Diary* which she was delighted to have. She looks terribly tired and definitely older. Complains of fainting and then falling into deep sleeps. There is no sign of improvement. She said she hoped to pass out quietly in her sleep, if she cannot recover, and is going to ask Bill and her doctor to arrange it, if they are convinced there can be no recovery which I now very gravely doubt. 'What is the point of life the moment one cannot live it in a full-blooded manner?' she asked. I left and walked home across the Park sick at heart and again impressed by the realisation that this woman is dear to me because with her I need never dissemble – which is a very rare thing – in mind or spirit; with her there is no call for flattery or insincerity; with her there are no barriers of any kind. Yet I can't determine precisely wherein the intimacy between us lies. This evening, having given me a selection of photographs of Peter's portrait drawings to look through, she remarked: 'You are of course only interested in those of the male. The young women bore you.' 'Oh,' but I said, 'so do the young men very often.'

Tuesday, 29th April

Set off this morning for Norfolk. Lunched at Saffron Walden – a poetic, medieval tapestry, wild-flower name – and looked at the Trust's Sun Inn. Then had the idea of calling on Lord Braybrooke who seemed glad to see me and said he was at the end of his tether. He asked whether we would suggest to the Treasury that they might anticipate his death now by taking Audley End in part payment of estate duties. I don't think they will somehow. Stopped at Cambridge just to visit King's Chapel screen and stalls. I suppose they are the finest specimens of Renaissance work in England. The beauty of this building stirs my very vitals into song. They are cleaning the interior. Men on scaffolding are scouring with simple soap and water the stonework right up to the roof – a vast undertaking and most effective. None of the glass is put back yet. Then stopped at Ely Cathedral and examined Bishop West's chapel, most interesting for its classical detail, notably the vaulting superimposed upon the Gothic. Arrived at Bradenham in time for dinner. Alec Penrose has been ill with blood pressure, but looks well and younger than before, having shaved off his moustache. Frances is very friendly and intelligent, with an attractive languorous, yet determined, manner.

Wednesday, 30th April

To Blickling for the day. Fearfully cold. The ubiquitous, cutting wind persists. I am glad I came. Nothing much has been done. Wallace King's man was waiting for instructions about the posts and ropes. I had to direct him. Also did some rearranging, and put out china, etc. Miss O'Sullivan has no clue how to arrange. She is also understandably reluctant to have any furniture shifted to a different position from where it stood in Lord Lothian's day.

Thursday, 1st May

It is May Day and pouring and blowing icily. Stopped at Cawston Church to gaze my fill at the fourteenth-century roof and painted panels of saints on the screen. At Blickling made my peace with the caretakers and Miss O'Sullivan who is always nice to me. Alec came over and had some useful suggestions for arranging furniture. The rooms now filled do not look any more beautiful because the furniture is on the whole poor. The house was today open for the first time, and only twenty people came. So we need not have fussed ourselves. Alec's second boy lunched. Difficult – and Alec behaved towards him just as my father used to behave towards me. I suppose it is always the parents' fault.

After tea I motored to Holbecks at Hadleigh and stayed the night with

Joshua Rowley. He lives well. I like him very much. He gave me a lot to drink. Already has blue veins pencilling his cheeks. I can't make him out. Why on earth should he want to bury himself in Packwood, in the Midlands, near Birmingham?

Friday, 2nd May

Today my left eyelid has jiggered and throbbed, clear sign of having had too much to drink, for Alec gave me a lot of wine too. After a late break-fast we drove to Stoke-by-Nayland. All this property belongs to the Rowleys, made over to Joshua by his father. We looked at Tendring Hall, the Rowley seat, now occupied by German prisoners and in a sad way. Built by Soane it is severe, if not dull, of yellow brick; but the situation a fine one. At noon I returned alone to London.

Sunday, 4th May

Motored to lunch with Goodhart-Rendel at Hatchlands. His mind bubbles over with information. He never stops talking, imparting know-ledge, but so inarticulately. His step-father, Cooper, was present. He looks like a dormouse that is trying to retreat into his tea-pot and to put, in vain, the lid down upon himself so as to escape drowning in G.-R.'s spate of conversation. I was conducted round the village and the grounds and had a most enjoyable day. G.-R. is very upset by the NT's ridiculous injunctions to cut down the trees at Fuller's Farm. I am entirely in sym-pathy with G.-R. and think it intolerable of the mangel-wurzels to dare dictate to him.

Monday, 5th May

Robin Fedden motored Langley-Taylor and me to Hughenden after lunching at Brooks's. We both thought L.-T. intolerably vulgar and trumpet-blowing. Robin observed at once that we would never get a look-in at Hughenden, and therefore it would be best as well as easiest to leave the whole arrangement of the house to him. It is after all his dis-covery, his waif. Our misgiving was lest too many rooms would be shown with too few contents to fill them. Robin is a sweet fellow and wrote me such a nice letter of gratitude on the completion of his first year at Polesden Lacey.

Wednesday, 7th May

The office puts me into constant rages. The Admiral's incompetence is really reprehensible. How a man like this could be given responsibility for the welfare of a fleet I do not understand. He omitted to forewarn me of the Reports Committee this morning. He went to the Treasury

about Audley End without having read my note to him about Lord
Braybrooke's message. He ignores my advice about the Hatchlands trees.

At midday I left for Cornwall. The luxurious train journey dispersed
my choler, restored my humour, which is bad and uncertain. Read
Ciano's *Diary* which fascinates me. Mussolini was a bore, a philistine, and
played with human lives as with dice. I reached Gunnislake at 7.30 and
Cotehele at 8 for dinner. Lord Mount Edgcumbe is in bed with a temperature, but his Countess, a little, gentle, sweet and pathetic old lady, was
about. Their story is a tragic one. They inherited during the war, and their
only son was killed at Dunkirk. They are now packing up to leave
Cotehele which since the thirteenth century has been in their family. I
am given a bedroom at the top of the entrance gate-tower, approached
by a twisting stone staircase, and in isolation.

Thursday, 8th May

Slept ill: lightning during the night which flashed through my casements
and lit up the great tower and the courtyard. I worked all day in the
state-rooms, listing those contents which the N.T. would like and a few
things to be got rid of. Also noted the condition of the tapestries and furniture, which is bad indeed, rent and worm-eaten. Lady Mount
Edgcumbe asked me whether I thought this and that good or bad, as she
put it, so as to keep or sell. I tried to help to the best of my ability. Most
of the contents are very good indeed, if only they were not so sadly perished. These state-rooms are of the class of the Knole ones and this house
is a miniature Knole of the West. It is so remote that I do not suppose
great numbers will visit it. I hope not. There are two rather bedint, virginal sisters staying to help the poor Mount Edgcumbes pack. At first
their vapid giggling annoyed me, because I don't find Cotehele a joke,
but now I quite like them. Lady Mount E.'s cairn puppy has eaten a
chunk out of the Turkey-work Queen Anne settee, and she thinks it
rather naughty, that's all. There are a butler and some charming servants,
all of the old school. The splendid Mt. Es, having lost their son and heir
are taking to live with them their unknown heir and his wife, who are
New Zealanders.

Friday, 9th May

At 10 o'c Eardley joined me and I spent the morning – pitch dark and
pouring with rain – showing him the house and shifting certain pieces
of heavy furniture, which I had persuaded the family to reject, away from
the state-rooms. At midday we left for Tavistock where we lunched. On
to Buckland Abbey which we looked at from the outside and pronounced ugly and dull, a sort of square pele with desultory wing tacked

on – actually the crossing and nave of the church – but thought the surroundings with distant Tamar very lovely. Had tea at Kingsbridge, and
then to Lady Clementine Waring's, the Moult, Salcombe. It is more fun
being with Eardley than anyone in the world. Lady C. took us to
Overbecks and the museum which contains more shockingly hideous
things than is possible to conceive. E. was loud in his denunciations
which, I saw, were annoying Lady C. So I tried to cheer up Miss
Christian, the woman who in exchange for a free cottage is acting curatrix and was accompanying us. We agreed the butterfly collection might
be quite a good one. It is strange that Lady C., whose own taste is sophisticated, should not be aware of the horrors of Overbecks. She talks so
much that one becomes exhausted. She is bossy and a little dictatorial,
yet intelligent, enthusiastic, forthright, tireless and very kind. Although
she frightens me I like her on the whole, but I think E. does not. After
dinner heard from her the whole saga of Mr Overbeck's love of boys, his
collection of drawings of boys and his having been involved in a police
case, but acquitted. Poor old thing.

Saturday, 10th May

Wonderful day. The Sharpitor and Moult gardens, sloping down to the
sea with no road between, remind me of the French riviera. The blossom
of magnolias, young trees and shrubs against the blue sea was exquisite.
In the morning we motored to Saltram. This was kind of Lady C. because
I had said I was interested in Adam houses. We were received by Captain
'Monty' Parker, tall, handsome brother of Lord Morley, aged about
seventy. He is an old-fashioned man-about-town, Burlington Bertie sort.
He never gets up before eleven and does nothing all day but booze. Lives
here with his brother (away today), both of them bachelors. Had already
been boozing before we arrived and, having ushered us into the hall, clad
in immaculate white ducks, sat by mistake in the coal scuttle.

   This large house, with white painted stucco front, is not very impressive – outside. But cosy. The whole bay of the south wing has had its
stucco removed for repairs from war damage when Plymouth was
bombed. The park is pretty and today at its best. I saw no fine views of
Plymouth Sound and Mount Edgcumbe, but on the contrary one vista
of chimneys and gasometers. The hall and majority of rooms – the library
is Regency – are pre-Adam. Only the saloon and dining-room are
genuine Adam, and marvellous of their sort. The saloon with its coved
ceiling, a double cube, pleased me enormously. The enormous Axminster
carpet was designed by Adam to match the ceiling. The walls are of
striped blue silk, faded to gold. Walls of the velvet room are red, which is
superb. There are numerous Reynolds portraits, for the painter was born

at Plympton and patronised by the Parkers. The family seems rich. Keeble is being employed to repair the great damage caused by dry-rot. The rooms in the east wing are all under dust-sheets, and several walls have had to be stripped to the bare brickwork.

We took Lady Clementine back to the Moult, lunched there, and motored off, to comb some antique shops in Totnes. Had tea at Montacute which is looking fine. E. left me and I took a train from Yeovil to London.

Monday, 12th May

Kathleen [Kennet] said this evening that the effort of keeping alive was ghastly. They make her sit up in her room because she is no worse. But she is no better.

Tuesday, 13th May

To see Lord Wimborne at Wimborne House (Arlington Street) which he says he is leaving soon. He cannot prevent motors parking in his court-yard. He asked many questions about giving Ashby St. Ledgers to the Trust. I went to a party given by Sheila [de Rützen]. The Archduke Robert there like a tall stick, with an agreeable but unintelligent face.

Wednesday, 14th May

Meeting at the House of Commons presided over by Noel-Baker, who has the face of a young angel. He spoke very ably, but it was a terrible meeting, without a purpose. I asked if the meeting could be formulated into a committee, to which other experts might be co-opted, thereby hinting that some of the dead wood present might be eliminated.

Friday, 16th May

Before the Executive Committee Lord Crawford hinted that he might take his pictures away from Montacute for the Travellers' Club. I implored him not to, and made a sudden earnest appeal, telling him how they made Montacute what it now is. 'There you are,' he said to Harold Nicolson, 'that is precisely how he wheedles things out of the old ladies.'

Michael and I drove to Strawberry Hill after six. Wyndham Ketton-Cremer was shyly reading quite a good paper from the chair about Walpole. Professor Richardson spoke after him. Later we were allowed to walk round the house which is kept up better today than when I last visited ten years ago. The Gallery is decidedly pretty; so is the Round Room with the Adam fireplace and ceiling, the only Adam Gothick work I have so far seen. The library could be pretty if painted white and gold instead of brown and gold. We were shown Horace's chapel in the garden, now sadly decaying, the floor fallen in; but a very delicate ceiling of Gothick pendants.

Saturday, 17th May

Bridget and I motored to Drayton House for the day, it being open for members of the Georgian Group. We lunched leisurely en route and found ourselves at a wrong Drayton, a village beyond Rockingham, and had to retrace our steps fifteen or twenty miles. It was well worth the trouble.

Drayton is an exceptionally fine house, more cheerful than Knole which it resembles in some respects, for the spirit of Lady Betty Germain still prevails in both houses. What pleased me most were the Duchess of Norfolk's gates, the ironwork generally, the Talman front, the Grinling Gibbons table in the King's Dining-Room, the tapestries, the great bed of green needlework and velvet, the Webb chimneypiece, the silver-mounted table and silver mirror. The dining-room is in a rather thin Adam style. So is the drawing-room ceiling. What pleased in the garden were the balustrading, the lead urns, the lime avenues and, above all, the secluded luxuriant country around. Bridget and I met Mrs. Stopford-Sackville, the new wife, upstairs. She showed us Lady Betty's two rococo panels of Soho tapestry in her own bedroom. We stopped at Lowick church, with its octagonal tower and numerous weather-vanes, to look at the mediaeval glass and the alabaster Greene monuments. Had a late tea at the inn in Kimbolton by the Castle entrance gates, designed by Adam, dullish work however. We joined the Sachie Sitwells for dinner at an expensive restaurant, Baldwin's, in Dover Street.

Sunday, 18th May

A quiet day to myself. So cold I lit a fire. Went to Mass, read for my new book and visited the National Gallery. The face of the Velasquez Philip IV, about which there has been so much recent dispute, does look a bit white and thin, but I don't know that it is not now as the artist left it. I think people regret the patina of age that pictures, like buildings, acquire. I thought the colours of the cleaned *Chapeau de Paille* looked rather crude. Probably the picture was more pleasing before cleaning, but again I don't think this an argument in favour of letting 'em remain dirty. I think the wholesale onslaught on the Bankside Power Station proposal is stick-in-the-mud nonsense also. What I do object to is the Government's high-handed manner of announcing the *fait accompli*. It is irritating and smacks of totalitarianism. Probably the power station will be a great work of art.

Tuesday, 20th May

Took Miss Kearney to Knole this afternoon. She certainly is the least talkative woman I have ever known. I agreed with Mason at once to raise the wages of our Knole staff who are a little dissatisfied that they receive so few tips because of the large crowds. Saw Lord Sackville who wants the NT to take the North Wing off his shoulders. The public amuse themselves by carving their names on the oak door of the gatehouse on days when they are not admitted to the state-rooms.

The Rosses had a cocktail party in their Park Street house. Talked to Lord Bath about Longleat. He is a handsome and youthful man, with eyes like coals and little white teeth neatly arranged. When he speaks eyes and teeth glisten so that he looks like a fanatic.

Wednesday, 21st May

Motored Eardley to Somerset. We reached Stourhead at 3 o'c. By that time the sun had penetrated the mist, and was gauzy and humid. The air about lake and grounds of a conservatory consistency. Never do I remember such Claude-like, idyllic beauty here. See Stourhead and die. Rhododendrons and azaleas full out. No ponticums, but pink and deep red rhododendrons – not so good – and loveliest of all, the virginal snow white ones, almost too white to be true. Azaleas mostly orange and brimstone. These clothe the banks of the lake. The beech are at their best. We walked leisurely round the lake and amused ourselves in the grot trying to remember Pope's four lines correctly by heart, and forgetting, and running back to memorize. The temples are not in bad order, the Temple of Flora and the Pantheon being particularly well kept. We had tea at the inn at Stourton; then walked rapidly round the first floor of the house, reserving our detailed survey for tomorrow. We were staggered by the amount of first-rate furniture and pictures. There is more than enough upstairs to fill the whole *piano nobile*.

Thursday, 22nd May

I stay at Long Crichel. Both Eddy and Desmond at home; full of affection and gaiety. I greatly enjoy being here. We went off this morning to Stourhead, taking Eddy. He made us stop at Shaftesbury where he and I each bought a pair of blue policeman's trousers which we saw in a shop window going for 12s.6d. each and five coupons. When I tried mine on in the evening they were so stiff they stood up by themselves as though made of three-ply wood, and are quite unwearable. Eddy said the Stourhead gardens were his idea of paradise. We all walked round them once again, discussing how they should be supervised by one person with a landscape eye. We went into the basement and attic floors of the house. They are unfit for human habitation. More and more excellent things reveal themselves in the ground floor rooms. After tea at Long Crichel I motor back to London, picking up a picture for Lyme lent by Lord Newton at Timsbury Manor, a red brick 1880 house he has just bought and where he has reassembled his exquisite Lyme furniture.

Saturday, 24th May

Lunched at the pub at Aylesbury. Was sitting beside a young man who told me he worked at advanced photography with rocket manufacturers. He said there was an Interplanetary Society of six or seven persons, some women, who expect shortly to travel to the moon. They will not be able to return but they will signal back their discoveries, and when their oxygen gives out they will die. Stopped at Charlecote where I had tea. The rooms look quite well, but there are not many visitors. I begin to think visitors will not come here in vast numbers. Got to Wickhamford for supper.

Sunday, 25th May

To Whitsun Mass at Evesham. In the gallery a choir of German prisoners singing, and one read the Gospel and Epistle in German – an excellent idea. Papa and I then went to Hidcote and saw Lawrie Johnston who is old and ill. I walked round the village and assessed the 200-acre property and garden. Cannot see how with five gardeners the NT could hope to maintain the garden with no endowment.

Monday, 26th May

A lovely day. Deenie came in the morning and I drove her and Mama to Brockhampton. They loved old Bakewell and Mrs Hughes and thought how nice it would be to engage them both. We brought a picnic luncheon and ate it in the hall. Mrs Hill ('Stinkie') met me there in the afternoon and discussed various matters, what to throw away and what to keep. I gave her a small chair – not mine to give away – which she coveted. Mrs. Hill is, for someone of eighty-five, spry. She ate three pieces of cake. M. and Deenie thought her hard-boiled because she did not bewail the fate of Brockhampton, they being too inclined to sentimentalise over Brockhampton, whereas they never knew the Lutleys who were of course Mrs. Hill's intimate friends.

Tuesday, 27th May

Left Wickhamford at ten for Coughton Court. Dear Lady Throckmorton welcomed me. A cousin of hers, Miss Hanbury Williams, staying. Lady T.

says she will be seventy next year. She looks remarkably well and strong. I love her quick intelligence. She lives in the whole south wing of Coughton, Sir Robert in the north wing when he is down. Place looks improved and no longer impoverished. We discussed many things. She told me how much she liked Baron Ash and, in a knowing way, how much she disliked Bradley-Birt.

Drove on to Dudley. Looked round the castle in order to study the parts built by Sir William Sharington in 1550. They are much decayed. The Castle grounds are a zoo, teeming with animals and people. A ghastly place. I saw what I wanted and hurried away, sickened by humanity in the gross. The people of the Midlands are incredibly primitive. Then to Wightwick Manor. The Manders conducted me round and dispensed tea. They were kind. I like Rosalie who is highly educated (a woman's college product) and cultivated, which is not the same thing as the first. He is a quiet and wise man. Got to Charlie Brocklehurst's Harebarrow Lodge for dinner.

Wednesday, 28th May

We had a rather wonderful but exhausting day. At the end of it were both absolutely whacked. We got to Lyme at eleven. It was scorching hot. The house full of Corporation electricians, painters and carpenters lying around doing nothing. Charlie was very upset because the Parks Superintendent had the windows painted a pale shit colour without consulting him or even telling him that they intended painting them. He raised a stink and made them repaint the lot a darker shade – all he could do. Both of us very indignant about this. We ran up and down the house deciding where furniture is to go and pictures to be hung. This took hours of time.

On the way back to Harebarrow we visited Bramall, now bought by the Corporation, a much restored black and white house, formerly the Bromley-Davenports'. Quite well maintained outside and in. Conducted round by a vociferous guide who pointed out all the beauties effected by a Mr. Nevile in the 1880s when first bought from the Davenports. Charlie's house is tiny and so congested you can barely move in it. Much sherry and port drinking.

Thursday, 29th May

Today went to Styal village which we liked. It is interesting as an example of an early cotton industrial community, with eighteenth-century mill, master's house, manager's house, apprentices' house and artisans' red brick cottages. Then lunched at Little Moreton Hall which is greatly improved; then visited Mow Cop and Maggoty's Wood. Very hot and thundery day. Called on the Archdeacon at Astbury and saw round his beautiful

Georgian house which he is converting into two and ruining in the process by ripping out all the Georgian fireplaces. It is the most extraordinary thing how holiness and hideousness are compatible. For dinner came Mrs Legh of Adlington and her daughter just married to an American and about to join her husband in Chicago. At 10 o'c we all motored to Alderley Edge and walked along the Edge till caught in a thunderstorm, then drove back through the grounds of Hare Hill, Charlie's place let to the blind for the war. An ugly, shapeless house in pretty situation, the park walks rampaging with rhododendrons and sweet smelling azaleas. I never remember another spring for such galaxies of these plants, or for buttercups. The fields are golden.

Friday, 30th May

Charlie and I motored separately to Attingham from Harebarrow, which took us two hours. We found Attingham a scene of Russian tragedy. Lady Berwick was hollow-eyed and miserable. Once or twice I thought she was in tears. They are fast selling contents and clearing out of the house for the College. They will withdraw into the small east wing. Lord Berwick was wheeled up to us in a chair. He is a shrunken, almost inhuman bundle incapable of moving hand or limb. He speaks lower and slower, and is most piteous. She thinks he may die at any moment. Two nurses are in perpetual attendance and I suspect make the B.s poorer than ever, and this worries her terribly. Charlie looked at the china and bibelots which he thought wonderful but was able only to select a few things for Lyme. He packed them into his car. Lady B. lunched with us at the Inn, poor woman. After tea Charlie and I parted. I drove to Wickhamford, laden with the posts of Caroline Murat's bed which the Berwicks are selling at Sotheby's.

Saturday, 31st May

Sat in the garden at Wickhamford correcting proofs. So hot that I had to be in the shade. Papa went dog-racing at Gloucester. An extraordinary diverson. Mama spent the day watching birds fly in and out of the house, she telling me which each one was, and its habits. When tired of this she looked at caterpillars climbing threads to the tops of trees and wondering, questioning how and why they did it. One of her most endearing qualities is adoration of nature and creatures.

Tuesday, 3rd June

Heat at its height today. I love it, but it is stifling. Everyone else complains. Lunched at the Ritz with Major [Jack] Abbey who gave me a delicious white wine which made me drip like a tap. He invited me in order to grumble about Langley-Taylor whom he hates, and says if we have trouble with him over Hughenden, he will weigh in and help us. After all his father bought Hughenden for the nation, not L.-T. I had a dinner party of Billa Harrod, Puss Milnes-Gaskell and Leigh Ashton. It was so hot that we sat with the windows and door open in a direct draught. Leigh, being very fat, sweated profusely. Food the best I have had here yet: chicken in aspic, strawberries and cream. I am a bad host however, and inattentive. Leigh took us to his Museum across the way where he showed us the Elizabethan miniature collection just opened. They are beautifully displayed behind glass. He is a splendid showman. The V & A was all lit up for us alone, and attendants there in their uniforms. Billa stayed and talked until one o'c, for sleep is out of the question in this heat.

Wednesday, 4th June

The weather has broken and the English summer of one week is over. At Sothebys looked at the settee and two chairs of the famous Dundas suite from Moor Park, designed by Adam in the early 1760s. They had been re-covered in cut velvet and thought the quality of the wood carving none too delicate.

Thursday, 5th June

In the office arranging a tour of the south-west of England in early August for Harold, Vita and myself, which will be fun. Ruby Holland-Martin came to the office to discuss Brockhampton's future, the decision reached being to let Lower Brockhampton to the Youth Hostels.

Friday, 6th June

At Batsford's going through the Adam book illustrations with Sam Carr. He showed me the jacket of my book, taken from an Adam wall design in the St. James's Club. Very pretty. It will be the best part of the book. For £7.10.0. I bought six blue Bristol tumblers this evening with money I haven't got. Now I have blue, green and red for my dinner table.

Saturday, 7th June

Poured all morning. Went to the Hilliard exhibition and saw the last of the French tapestries. Motored Dick Girouard to Claydon after luncheon. We discussed private schools and discovered that we were both at Lockers Park, he rather before me, nearly thirty years ago. So we diverged at Hemel Hempstead and visited the place, which in every respect seemed precisely the same as it was when I left it in 1921, only smaller. There was the very same lilac bush where Matthew my brother-in-law, Peter Coats and I played and made our sanctum. I think the prevailing emotion in those days was fear, and a need for escape.

Claydon most disappointing outside; quite remarkable inside. I have never seen such rococo work elsewhere in England. Gothick Room and above all Chinese Room the most extravagant stuccco- and woodwork imaginable outside Bavaria. The latter room has a Chinese screen recess with nodding mandarins, canopy and bells. Ugly really, but fantastic. Drove Dick as far as Warwick and continued to Birmingham to stay with the Trenchard Coxes.

Sunday, 8th June

This morning Dr. Mary Woodall, Trenchard's keeper (he is not a lunatic) motored us to Aston Hall which is beautifully furnished, better, I thought, than Montacute. All done within one-and-a-half years, like M., and in excellent taste. A minimum of posts and ropes, and better ones than ours. In the afternoon to the Art Gallery which Trenchard took me round showing me the pre-Raphaelite exhibition which is fascinating. He is charming and kind to all, beloved, I guess, by his staff, and she has the same qualities. A *gemütlich* couple. Lord Crawford has just been staying with them and told T. C. that if England were combed no one could be found more suitable for my particular post than myself. I blush, while writing this, with pleasure.

Monday, 9th June

Left the Coxes early for Castle Bromwich Hall and looked at the work in progress. The house much battered about in the war. Then called at Packwood and saw J. Rowley. Lunched at Alcester and arrived at Flaxley Abbey at 3.15. This a very poor house in spite of one gothic refectory and Abbot's guest room with cuspated windbrace roof. Then Matson House, and motored back to London, arriving 11 o'c.

Tuesday, 10th June

Motored Michael and [Angus] Acworth to Chiswick House this morning. With [John] Macgregor, the architect we looked carefully over the rooms. The condition is very bad indeed, but not irreparable. The quality of the Wyatt wings far better than I had supposed, so I hesitated to advocate pulling them down unless the only likelihood of money forthcoming for the repair of the Burlington block were by sacrificing them. Bridget dined with me at the White Tower.

Saturday, 14th June

Harold said yesterday at the General Purposes Committee 'Jim is as sensitive about Charlecote as Lord Tennyson was about *Maud*,' when Esher teased me again about this property, saying, 'You may repair the balustrade in any way you like. It is such a terrible house.' All this week I have been very irritable, having given up smoking. I hope within a month no longer to be tormented.

Lyme Park was opened today, but I did not attend, having done my share, I feel, in compiling the guidebook and arranging the contents. Instead this evening I attended the Polesden Lacey harpsichord concert, taking Rick and Helen Dashwood who, though nice to me, grumbled aloud. The supper was indeed poor, not enough to eat or drink, and 17s.6d. per head is quite expensive. Poor Lord Berwick has now died, and I sent her a telegram and letter. A dear, sweet, and very eccentric man.

Monday, 16th June

Motored after luncheon to Brockhampton, stopping at Wickhamford at 6 o'c. After dining in Worcester, at The Hop Pole, a horrid inn, arrived in the cool of the evening. How beautiful this place is. I walked down to Lower Brockhampton just before dark, the trees dead quiet, not even whispering, and the undergrowth steaming. Two enormous black and white bulls gave me a fright by noiselessly poking their great faces over a gate and peering at me in a meditative manner. This evening the whole tragedy of England impressed itself upon me. This small, not very important seat in the heart of our secluded country, is now deprived of its last squire. A whole social system has broken down. What will replace it beyond government by the masses, uncultivated, rancorous, savage, philistine, the enemies of all things beautiful? How I detest democracy. More and more I believe in benevolent autocracy.

Tuesday, 17th June

Up early. Visited the chapel, making notes. At eleven Eardley came and then the van to take things to Montacute, chiefly books. Thus do we despoil the Lutleys' ancient heritage. The three van men all came into the house smoking. No manners. Bakewell was sweet to them. A delicious old creature. He does not seem to repine. It was a heavenly day. I motored back in the afternoon, calling on Mama, and consuming a piece of cake and some milk. Arrived in London simultaneously with my father who is to stay three nights here, he having my room, I sleeping in Geoffrey's at the very top of the house, in G.'s absence. I gave a dinner party of Lady de Vesci, Bridget Parsons, Charlie Brocklehurst and my father, five being the largest number I have yet had round my small table. It was a good meal and they all said they enjoyed it. We had lobster to begin with. Papa stayed behind and the four of us went to the Georgian Group reception at the Soane Museum. Thousands of people I knew. I was so tired that I could not sleep in Geoffrey's room.

Wednesday, 18th June

To the exhibition of the Great Duke of Wellington's silver plate, porcelain and pictures at the V & A. The quality of the silver gilt seems poor when you look into it; much of the design coarse. Yet fascinating. The plate too realistic to be great art surely. Of all the objects the diamond that had belonged to the Duke of Marlborough and was given by the Prince Regent to the Iron Duke was the beautifullest. Professor Geoffrey Webb called this morning to tell me he has succeeded Clapham as Editor of the Royal Commission's volumes and to exhort me to provide proper catalogues of the National Trust's collections.

Thursday, 19th June

I left Papa who is going to Ascot today and staying on here tonight. At 10.30 I picked up Michael Rosse and motored to Norfolk. We lunched at Bury St. Edmund's. A lovely hot day. Our first call was Yarmouth where we studied the Trust's building, No. 4 South Quay. We both came to the same conclusion that the NT should press for the preservation of the façades of the whole block of which No. 4 is a part; that it would not matter sacrificing the rear portion, so much of which has been devastated by bombing; that the Elizabethan rooms of our house must at all costs be preserved; and that new buildings must not show above the skyline of the Quay when looked at from the river. We suspect that much of the wainscot of the dining-room is made up. We continued to Burnham Market where we had a drink with Silvia Combe. We stayed the night at the Moorings Hotel, opposite Scolt Head, and dined at Holkham.

I would definitely put Holkham among the first twenty great houses of England. With its collections it forms one very great work of art indeed. Lord Leicester is a charming and cultivated man. There were, besides Michael and me, Silvia, Lord L. and his son, Tommy Coke, a nice, weak person, and my contemporary. Delicious dinner of cold venison eaten in the low-ceilinged, long room on the ground floor between the family and the strangers' wings. I sat next to Lord Leicester who said how disappointed he was that the family entail prevented him handing over Holkham. His last words to me were: 'If you can find any means whereby the Trust can take over this house and its contents, I shall be prepared to leave it, should my not staying on make the transfer easier.' After dinner we walked all round the house. The high quality of the architecture and contents takes the breath away. The planning too is astonishingly convenient. There are four complete wings detached from the centre block. Yet when inside the house you get the impression that there are no breaks and the five entities make one house, huge though it be. You get vistas from one wing through the centre block into another wing, conveying a surprising effect of grandeur. The other impression made upon me was the marmoreal, classical simplicity of unadorned wall spaces contrasting with the rich ornamentation of ceilings and doorways and fireplaces. The sculpture gallery in particular struck me in this way – so pure, correct, and serene. We spent some little time at the end of the tour in the library where I was chiefly interested in the detailed account book kept by the first Lord Leicester who amassed his collections before the age of twenty-five. Lady Leicester is away, staying in Silvia's house, with a nervous breakdown brought about by anxiety and the worry of keeping up Holkham with practically no servants. What these wretched landowners have to go through! Yet Holkham is superbly kept up, all the steel grates, for instance, shining brightly, the work of one devoted daily.

Friday, 20th June

This morning we visited the Mill at Burnham Overy and were shocked by its condition. We drove on to Blickling. Michael pleased by excellent condition of the house inside and the garden, but not by the house outside, or the temples. Looked at the Swanton Morley property on our way to Bradenham. Motored to Wisbech where Michael addressed that Society and spoke very well. He has a good delivery and a good vocabulary. I was impressed. We returned to Bradenham at 11.30 and only within the last three miles did I need to put on my side-lights. I love the extreme limits of days and nights. Now the chirpings of midnight delight the ear.

Saturday, 21st June

This motoring – today's is the third 200-mile drive – nearly kills me. By the end of the day I feel sick with tiredness. Yet each night I have slept well which makes amends. We left Bradenham at 10.30 and reached St. Osyth's Priory at one o'c. General Kincaid-Smith the owner, a bad seventy-seven, is slow and at times quite inarticulate, but an old dear. He gave us an old man's luncheon, ending with plum cake and port wine, a funny midsummer's day meal. The house inside is uniformly drab, but outside very remarkable, being chiefly of chequer-work grey and brown stone. There is an entrance gateway of flint, knapped within panels formed of dressed stone with quatrefoil heads. The garden is attractive. It is walled, with occasional views of the gatehouse, the octagonal tower with cupola and vane, and the large tower. We were conducted round the outside slowly, painfully. How the old do tire one. The General offers the property and investments to yield £1000 per annum. There are 350 acres of *in*fertile ground, 'with walls and towers girdled round'.

Tuesday, 24th June

To see poor Kathleen K., still in hospital although she has been taken in a chair by car to visit her exhibition of sculpture. It exhausted her. Her voice is noticeably feebler. I foolishly brought her a large book of U.S.A. works of art. At once I saw that it was too big and heavy for her to lift, but she said she would manage somehow to get it propped up. She told me not to give it to her for soon she would be in her grave. I am afraid she is much weaker. I did not stay long. Dined with Johnnie Churchill and wife, but was thinking of K.

Thursday, 26th June

Saw the Dulwich Gallery pictures at the National Gallery. How lovely are the Nicolas Poussins, those idyllic yet passionless blues and greens. What a world one enters of piping and bleating.

Friday, 27th June

Motored from Long Crichel to Montacute with Eardley. We worked like blacks carrying carpets and books brought from Brockhampton. Happy beasts of burden we were. It was great fun. In consequence we made the library the best room in the house, the polished brown spines the colour of fresh conkers looming through the gilded trellis of the shelves; and the very special light which filters through the heraldic glass, splodges of azure and gules and vert on the Savonnerie carpet.

Sibyl Colefax stays tonight at Long Crichel. She has just returned from Italy where she went and whence she travelled by herself. She actually spent Tuesday night sitting in the waiting-room of Milan station because she had lost a visa or something. This is gallantry as well as muddle.

Saturday, 28th June

I motored away early and called upon Sir Walter Jenner at Lytes Cary, near Kingsdon, an old late gothic manor-house to be left to the Nat. Trust by him. He is eighty-seven this year. He received me lying in a four-poster bed and wearing a night-cap with a bobble. A gloomy house, but with a fine open hall with braced rafters and carved frieze. Sir Walter has added a whole wing and made the house too large, out of scale. Christopher Hussey at Montacute later said it was a good example of the development of taste, Sir Walter's 'William and Mary' additions, done in the first decade of this century, and not what we would do today. The south front with chapel is very unspoilt and delightful. Got to Montacute at luncheon time. Sir Geoffrey Cox, Lord Aberconway and Hussey came to the meeting. We agreed to sack Scotts', the gardening firm, and to employ our own gardeners. The three of them very pleased with the house. Wilson, the head adviser to the Royal Horticultural Society, came down. He and Lord A. conferred. I motored Lord A. and Sir G. back to London in under four hours. Lord A. refused to stop en route for dinner.

Sunday, 29th June

At Brooks's at luncheon sat with Eddy, up for his second broadcast on Knole. So I asked him to dine. Jamesey came too and we enjoyed ourselves. Eddy said the sort of people he was disposed to dislike were those who seemed to him second-rate editions of himself, and those who excelled in certain professions (i.e. museum experts) in which he could have excelled if he had tried.

James and I walked to Ladbroke Grove to listen-in to Eddy. On the way J. told me how two weeks ago he found himself engaged to Ann Ebury and how to his infinite relief he just managed to scrape out of it. She was very determined and even threatened to adopt Ann Pope-Hennessy as her pen name. Eddy's voice came very clearly over the air: just a little plaintive but without affectation or over-emphasis. Moreover it was poetical.

Tuesday, 1st July

Took a morning train to Appledore in Kent and walked to the village in warm, drizzling rain which made the hedgerows and hay smell like amber. Perhaps my renunciation of cigarettes has restored my sense of smell, or made it acuter. Miss Johnston's furniture was of no account. A wasted visit, except that I read and slept in the train. It was a rest after motoring. The rhythm of carriage wheels over the track induces delicious fantasies sacred and profane. Sometimes I am in the arms of God, and sometimes of Satan, as a priest once described one of the loveliest lovers I ever enjoyed. There is romance in the queer, flat marshland in these parts, where the sea has receded within history and left low, flat pasture and elevated, straight roads.

Wednesday, 2nd July

Tony Wills, Lord Dulverton's eldest, wrote today telling me that for over a year he has been installed at Horton Court, our property, left us by Miss Wills a year ago, without our ever knowing it! He has asked me to dine at Boodle's. He is about thirty-one, slight, fair, with a prominent nose between twinkling eyes. The eyes melt into smiles in a benevolent but cautious manner. He tells me he has three children. We talked about the Pilgrim Trust. He is thinking of persuading his father to endow a similar Wills trust.

Thursday, 3rd July

I motored to Great Hampden, arriving 11.30. Was met by Parker-Jervis and Lord [Bertie] Buckinghamshire, aged about forty-one, whom I now remember at Eton as Hobart. He is single, reserved, and rather charming, ugly, with a turned-up nose and moustache. He seems very much older than me I am pleased to say. I liked him for his forthrightness and excellent manners. He offers Hampden House and about 100 acres to the Trust. The house is let to a girls' school who pay a rent of £800 a year. It is really not first-rate. The property was granted to the Hampdens by Edward the Confessor. The house dates from every period, from King John even, having two arches of his reign. The great hall with roof was brought from an old barn on the estate, the late seventeenth-century balustrade being original to the gallery. A suite of rooms in the south wing decorated *c.* 1740 in Palladian style is handsome, but, if not ruined, spoilt by use as girls' class-rooms. The staircase is Jacobean and painted with arcaded panels on the dado to give a perspective effect. The south façade is symmetrical with escutcheons in stone on the roof. The windows tame Vanbrughian. The demesne now much gone to seed. I think it is a borderline case. John Hampden of course lived and died here.

Lunched most excellently at The Hampden Arms, a tiny pub. Under the inn's name is inscribed on a board, 'The Earl of Buckinghamshire licenced to sell beer and tobacco'. I reached Fenton House by four and had tea with Lady Binning, who was rather fatter than hitherto, a little deafer and very 'malade imaginaire'. She is an odd woman, ridiculous and very nice. We strolled and sat about the garden which is one of the prettiest in London. She now thinks she should make more provision for maintenance of the garden. Then I had a drink with Terence Maxwell who, as one of Mrs. Greville's trustees, complained about the NT's waiving all responsibility for the upkeep of Mrs. G.'s father's and husband's graves in Bookham churchyard. He begged me to investigate the matter. I think this is the least we can do after accepting such a great benefaction as Polesden and Charles Street. This evening the Maxwells' house was burgled while they were in bed. Terence chased the burglar downstairs. Diana telephoned the police who arrived in one-and-a-half minutes and caught him hiding behind a door.

Friday, 4th July

Went to Covent Garden to see the last performance of Oliver [Messel]'s production of *The Magic Flute*. It was the Rosses' party, Mrs. Messel, Oliver and his court there. Afterwards we dined at the Savoy, and watched the dancing. I disliked this part of the evening, drinking all the time and being bored stiff. Anne looked pretty as a picture, wearing a dress and lace shawl in Winterhalter style.

Saturday, 5th July

The Georgian Group had a meeting at Somerset House, preceded by a talk by John Summerson in St. Mary-le-Strand church, hideously decorated. Then a tour round the principal apartments of Somerset House, much cut up by offices and likewise hideously decorated. The door-locks with royal crowns and medallions of George III on key-escutcheons most beautifully chased. Clifford Smith introduced me to Banister Fletcher, that great man, aged only seventy-five. He said the vaulting by Chambers over the Strand entrance was the best work of its kind in Europe; and I had never noticed it before in my life.

Bridget and I motored to Polesden Lacey for the second concert. This time it was horrible: beastly little quaint and dainty airs, and an affected soprano warbling. Supper filthy. My car emitted appalling fumes from the back where a floor board had become detached. Bridget calls the car the Belsen Gas Van.

Monday, 7th July

To the theatre – *Annie Get Your Gun* – with Bridget and Lady de Vesci; other guests being Countess Borromeo and her son Carlo. She is Lady de V.'s first cousin, their mothers being sisters and daughters of the Duke of Newcastle. We sat in a box. Bridget and I called for the Borromeos and motored them to the theatre. After the first interval Lady de V., accompanied by Mark Ogilvie-Grant, swept in, in one regal gesture, embraced Countess Borromeo first on one, then the other cheek, and took her front seat as of right. It was a sudden movement, full of grace and dignity, such as I imagine the Empress Eugenie practised. I enjoyed the performance more than the first time. We dined at the Savoy – Alsatian wine – and I motored them home. Then took Mark to Kew. We walked in his garden, smelling the strong lilies and sipping brandy. I warmed to him. How easy, cosy, sympathetic he is, like all my old friends of that generation.

Tuesday, 8th July

Had my hair cut and look shorn and v. ugly. However I feel in good form and none the worse for last night's lateness and drink. I feel unaccount-

ably social and gay so unlike me. I am in a 'swimgloat'* and don't want
to be out of it so long as the season lasts. There is still a flavour of season
in London, even now, with all the exhibitions and theatres in full swing.
I called for Sibyl and motored her to Wyndham's theatre where she was
given two stalls by Binkie Beaumont for *Deep are the Roots*. Sibyl climbs
nimbly into my car which at least has leg room (although she hardly has
any legs to speak of), and then scurries through the crowds, head down.
I follow behind keeping a protective finger upon her rounded back,
rather like bowling a hoop. Our seats were behind the Eshers. It was a
most enjoyable play, beautifully acted. Deals with the Negro problem in
the Southern States. Sibyl took me to Binkie B.'s party in Lord North
Street afterwards. All the cast came in. I talked to the Negro and his
mother who were sweet and as earnest off the stage as on. Both looked
darker and more natural than on stage where, I suppose, they were light-
ened so as to engage our sympathies. The Carisbrookes were there and I
was caught by him in a corner where he talked for hours about Mrs.
Greville. He said she never minded about people's morals or what they
did. That was their concern. He said he was cross with someone or other
because that person had expressed disapproval of Ivor Novello's 'nancy
manner'. Oh gosh! Lady Carisbrooke is thin and pretty; also rather tired
and embittered. They both pressed me to luncheon at Kew next Sunday,
or rather he pressed and she politely acquiesced. Then I went up to Noël
Coward and said to him, 'You and I have two great friends, both dead, in
common. George Lloyd and Mrs. Cooper, Aunt Eva.' He recalled who I
was and made me promise I would ring him up when he returned from
the States and we would dine and have a long talk about both of them.
His white teeth flash when he smiles, but his smile is unconvincing. He
is a very ugly man with rather bloated, sagging, red cheeks and hollow
eyes. He has moreover a thin, flat behind which implies shallowness of
character.

Thursday, 10th July

Anne [Rosse] telephoned at 7.30 asking me to dine, so weakly I accepted,
and went. Michael's mother, Countess Borromeo and son Carlo, there.
All Borromeo sons are called Carlo after the Saint. When Michael and
Anne went to the Plunkett ball, to which I did not go, we stayed behind
and talked of Fascist Italy. The Borromeos have little opinion of the King
of Italy who, they argue, should have abdicated as soon as Mussolini fell,
and then Prince Umberto would have stood a chance of remaining. She
said a neo-Fascist party is forming itself in Italy today.

*An expression used by the Souls and taught me by Logan Pearsall-Smith.

Friday, 11th July

Walked with Lord Esher across the Park. We lunched together. He said
Lord Crawford told him that Mrs. Dalton reminded him of a certain
rabbit-trap which was so cruel it had to be discarded. He, Esher, whenever he saw her thought of the wolf dressed up as Red Riding-Hood's
grandmother. At Brooks's we sat at John Christie's table. Christie said it
was time that bad productions ceased to be commercially profitable.
Esher said that good productions were not allowed to have long runs
because they were sponsored by the Government, and so were not supposed to make a return. He said to me afterwards that, whereas undoubtedly Christie had great genius, he was impossible to work with. No team
spirit. If he, Esher, were made chairman of the Covent Garden trustees,
he would appoint Christie because he was the only Englishman to have
a practical understanding of opera, and then give him absolute control.

After dinner I helped Rick arrange No. 3 Cheyne Walk into the late
hours of tomorrow morning.

Saturday, 12th July

Motored Michael Rosse to Knole. Fedden joined us late in the morning,
haggard and white with a hang-over. My puritanical reaction was distaste. Bridget assured me that she found him wet. He certainly is not this,
I retorted. We witnessed the crowds arriving at the house and talked to
the women guides. The arrangements seem to be working smoothly.
They get 400 to 500 visitors every Saturday.

I dined with Colin Agnew and motored a guest back to Cardinal's
Wharf on the right bank of the river. A most romantic view of the river
with moonlight on the swirling surface and St. Paul's silhouetted against
the northern sky, the dome seeming spherical rather than circular in the
semi-darkness.

Sunday, 13th July

Lunched with the Carisbrookes. Drove to Mark's house and walked
across Kew Green to the King's Cottage where they live. It is a shapeless
house with little character. Just the Carisbrookes, Mark and a fat, middle-
aged woman in gloves, a sort of fortune-teller. Lord C. dispensed very
strong martinis before luncheon (which was excellent) running around,
helping us to potatoes like any little waiter. He was immaculately dressed
in a well-pressed check suit, padded shoulders, and jangling with gold
bracelets and rings. He reminded me of an old, spruce hen, cackling and
scratching the dust in a chicken-run – really, a typical old queen. He
jabbers away, yet is not altogether stupid; has good taste, and is sophisti-

cated. Lady Carisbrooke is very sweet and has a langorous charm. We talked about brain. She said it was possible for a man to lose a third of his physical brain and yet for his mind to be unimpaired. We conjectured from this that the mind was not a physical attribute nor even dependent upon a physical structure for its being. It might in consequence well be immortal. After luncheon Lord C. took me all round the house, even into the cellars and attics, complaining how inadequate was the house, which the King has given him. He showed me portraits of his mother, Princess Beatrice, and his sister, Queen Ena of Spain. No talk however of the present royal family or the young betrothed couple, for which good marks. He said that Queen Alexandra was the most beautiful woman he had ever seen. All her limbs were of a like excellence to her face. However he did vouchsafe that Queen Mary hates wearing black. He likes bringing the topic of conversation to venereal disease and unnatural vice; and he chases one into a corner and talks so close that one expects him to pounce at any moment. 'And if one resisted,' Mark said, 'would it be lèse-majesté?'

Thursday, 17th July

Mama has stayed with me this week. She came on Monday and left today. I think she enjoyed herself, and I am very sorry that I was not nicer to her. I am sadly aware of Eddy's remark that one is irritated most by those people who share one's own faults to an enhanced degree; and by faults I mean venial failings, because my mother has none of my major failings. Sheila de R. thought her attractive and her figure that of a girl.

Friday, 18th July

Dined last night at Wilton's with John Fowler and Hardy Amies, a good-looking dress designer, who is thirty-eight, but so youthful in face and figure as to be mistaken for twenty-eight. Today I motored to Petworth, calling for Robin Fedden at Polesden. We stopped at Juniper Hall to see the 'Adam' room buried in that otherwise frightful house. The plaster panel reliefs of the Four Seasons on the walls are of excellent quality.

Sunday, 20th July

Worked quite hard this weekend and was happy in consequence.

This afternoon I motored James and the 'cellist's fiancée to Greenwich. Saw over the Queen's House, which escaped the bombs but shows signs of suffering from concussion. The rest of the Palace is sad and inaccessible. A tennis court in the centre open courtyard and canvas hangings. We agreed the people looked drab, infinitely boorish, bored and dirty. James said that of course they are all on the downward grade. People *are hell*! J. and the fiancée came back for tea. I dined in and read more.

Monday, 21st July

Dear Alan Pryce-Jones lunched, but I was a frost. His brilliance simply enhances my dimness. He says he is to become editor of the *Times Literary Supplement*, and hopes to make it cover pictures, music and drama. He wants long reviews to be signed by the contributors. If he succeeds the *T.L.S.* will become the most important cultural organ in England. He says James has failed to change the *Spectator* reviews for the better.

Called on Doreen Baynes. She admitted that at times James hurt her grievously by his thoughtlessness. But she said, 'I do not reproach him, for in return for my patience he gives me his youth.' Then I called for Alvilde Chaplin and took her to Paz Subercaseaux's where we dined. I enjoyed this party, and would have enjoyed it more could I have left earlier. Instead we sat till midnight. Even so I was the first to rise and leave. The Robertis from the Italian Embassy present, and Madame Auric and Robin Ironside. Contessa Roberti, an American, is quite pretty but dresses her hair in that hideous skinned fashion, rolled at the sides and on top. Alvilde agreed with me that it was a mistake. A. looking very handsome in black.

Tuesday, 22nd July

Mrs. Hugh Dalton called for me at the office punctually at 11.30 in a large Daimler limousine, driven by the Chancellor's becoming and respectful chauffeur. With her a French boy, Marc Viénot. We drove to Queen's Gate and picked up the Iraqi Ambassadress, Princess Zeid, whose husband is uncle of the present King, and their daughter. The Princess is middle-aged, rather big with handsome, beaming lacquer face and two pairs of eyebrows: her natural brows still freely visible and the pair pencilled over them forming Moorish arches. She has dark, frizzly hair in curls kept together precariously under a web of hairpins. Fat, friendly, and an artist. The daughter, who is on holiday from a college in the States where she has led an independent sort of existence, has ugly oriental lips, like Georges Cattaui's, and spots. But she is an exceedingly well educated girl. We motored to Sevenoaks where we lunched. At luncheon the girl told me that when she returns to Iraq she will have to retire into purdah, and this prospect appals her. No wonder.

At The Royal Oak I forestalled criticism by offering Mrs Dalton some bread, already placed on the table, by saying, 'Come along. We are breaking the law but next year we won't have this golden opportunity.' She made a wry face, and took a piece. The two Iraqis made intellectual observations throughout the visit and, I think, enjoyed themselves hugely. The Princess pointed out that the carnation and tulip embroidered on the Elizabethan chairs at Knole were of Arabian origin; likewise the Jacobean strapwork ceilings. The early rugs impressed her favourably. On the way home the daughter sang songs from *Annie Get Your Gun*. She is what you might call a forward miss for she takes on whatever subject is broached; and the arts and English literature are her passion. She is going to have a rude shock when she gets back to the harem.

Today I understood the qualities of Mrs. Dalton without liking her. She is very intelligent indeed. She has a clear, practical mind. Her interest in culture is sincere. Her sense of historic tradition is genuine and I believe that she does not mean to break with it. Yet one cannot forget the diabolical venom poured out by the husband whom she undoubtedly loves and reveres. How this man can care for tradition, as he protests, is beyond my comprehension. Mrs. Dalton has, needless to say, no charm whatever, and she petrifies.

Wednesday, 23rd July

Lady Crewe came up to me at the Allies Club and asked me to speak on her behalf to the Ministry of Planning. She says she opened the local newspaper last week to read that West Horsley was to be made a satellite town and a main road was to be driven through her garden. But her house would be saved by serving as the centrepiece of a round-about. I went to Tony Gandarillas's party, meeting Lord and Lady Greville as I left and talking about Ronnie whom she worships. I did not enjoy this party. I should not go to these parties if I do not enjoy them. Unfortunately I do not know for sure that I won't in advance.

Thursday, 24th July

Oh Lord, I lunched at Wilton's with Oggy Lynn, whom to meet like this I do like. She is shaped like a small egg and it is far easier to talk to her when she is sitting down, provided one is too. Tony Pawson and Madam Auric there. Conversation was frivolous, Parisian and about dress designers. Oggy sensed that I was out of my depth, for which I gave her good marks for kindness. She exudes sympathy and understanding. She says the Government are going to exact a capital levy in the autumn.

At the Rosses, saying goodbye to them, in came Bridget and Sachie. Sachie confirms the gloomy prognostication about the impending capital levy. I hurried away to change into another suit for dinner with the Lennox-Boyds. Found Alan and Patsy drinking champagne with Prince Bernhard of the Netherlands. The latter is better looking than his photo-

graphs imply. Has a good complexion and figure, and not the Harold
Lloyd face I imagined. He was dressed in a black tie with sparkling
diamond links in his soft white cuffs. Was speaking volubly in slightly
American English, and intelligently about the Dutch Indonesian situation. He shakes one's hand in a firm, 'manly' grip. Alan was so tired after
the Baths' ball and a House of Commons sitting until 7 a.m. today that
he fell asleep after dinner. I discreetly left at 10.45.

Friday, 25th July

At breakfast I opened a letter from Wayland Hilton Young saying his
mother's state had rapidly worsened in the last few days and was now very
grave. He went on: 'She is not well enough to understand that I have
written to you, but if she were, I think she would be glad that you should
know.' Nothing further. I was miserable but of course not surprised.
Remorseful too because I was thinking only last night that I must ring
up and go to see her again, dreading to be told she was not well enough.
I telephoned Keith who had been trying to get me at my office. He said
that Kathleen died early this morning.

I motored to Cranbury Park, the other side of Winchester, by appointment. It was the best thing I could do. A glorious day and very hot. I was
alone with my thoughts. I wept as I drove along. Not since Tom's death
do I remember weeping for the loss of a friend.

I reached Cranbury Park at 1.15 to be told that Mrs. Tankerville
Chamberlayne was in London. She had forgotten all about my visit, and I
was cross. I went off to lunch at an hotel, returned at 2.30, and insisted on
seeing Miss T.C., her sister-in-law. This curious woman, looking like a cook
and speaking like one, showed me the ground floor rooms, at first suspiciously, then more agreeably. The outside of this house of scarlet brick is
good imitation Georgian and I suppose *c.*1840. A few of the rooms, notably
hall with barrel ceiling and the ballroom, are magnificent, perhaps by Wyatt.
I noticed a lot of good furniture and Romneys of Lady Hamilton, and large
oils by Thomson of the same date. I spent exactly an hour there. Then drove
to Winchester. For the first time in my life I saw the school and Herbert
Baker's cloisters which excite such undiscriminating admiration. I do not
think they are a masterpiece, but rather chichi plagiarism. The large expanses
of mown lawn are very beautiful. I had tea and attended divine service in
the Cathedral. Looked at Bishop Gardner's Chantry Chapel, 1555, with its
classical work. Interesting for Queen Mary was still on the throne and the
Catholic Italians — or could they be Spaniards? presumably worked this.
Drove on slowly to Montacute, dining at Shaftesbury under the bogus
Chevy Chase sideboard. I thought of K. and how she might have admired
it, and I would have been angry with her.

I don't yet know at what hour K. died this morning, but I suddenly woke up about 4.45 and remained awake for three-quarters of an hour. It is most unusual for me to do this once I have fallen asleep. I experienced a strange heaviness and depression.

Saturday, 26th July

Grief is an odd emotion. How much of it is self-indulgence? Today I have been very cheerful. Yesterday I was genuinely sad and yet never felt more tormented by sex. Perhaps the two conflicts have some association. I left Montacute at 10.30, having slept at Mrs. Welsh's cottage in the village – comfortable enough in the summer. Got to Westwood for luncheon.

Ted Lister is no older and, surprisingly, less deaf. Norah Methuen brought Austin Hall, the architect, to tea. In going round the house he slipped on a loose rug in the porch room and fell, crash, in a horizontal position on the floor. I saw the whole accident happen and thought he must have broken his back, but not at all. He is a handsome, healthy man of about sixty. He told us at tea that Lutyens was the greatest architect of the past 100 years; that Gerry Wellesley and Goodhart-Rendel never rose to greatness because, being rich men, they did not trouble to learn. I don't altogether agree with this. Hall said they were both better interior decorators than Lutyens, Baker or Giles Scott. The old professional architects are always contemptuous of amateurs.

Ted and I dined at Greenhill with John Leslie. John talked about K. Kennet's obituary and remarked how curiously phrased was one passage. Now I had read the obituary this afternoon. I wrote it at K.'s instigation ten years ago and on reading it today was appalled, for *The Times* have cut it by half and mangled it. In truth I admit it was badly written by me in the first instance.

Sunday, 27th July

The weather is sublime. It is toasting hot. Ted does not get up till after twelve when we have 'brunch'. It is an experience to stay in this extraordinary ancient house like a museum, with Christo the Bulgarian who does everything down to managing Ted, the quirkiest old Conservative ever known. 'Stinking Government!' is the phrase for ever on his lips. Alex Moulton came to dine, reserved, intelligent, yet curiously young and unsophisticated. He is re-introducing the steam motor-car into general use, so Ted claims. We sat in the garden in shirt sleeves till after midnight, under the stars, gossiping and laughing. These are life's moments. Suddenly Alex rose to his feet, embraced his host, jumped into his car, and was gone. Ted fumbled for the silver chamber-candlesticks, lit them and we separated for the night.

Monday, 28th July

I drove to Wickhamford, had a quick luncheon and fetched my Vi-spring mattress from the manor, which was sold last week. I did not want to go into the house again yet could not avoid doing so because my father came with me to help carry the mattress. Luckily the new owners were out. I tried not to look but could not help noticing how beautiful the garden was in spite of the fearful desolation. A horrible land-girl, cigarette dangling from lower lip, showed us where the mattress was in the hall. I hurried away to Brockhampton for the night.

Wednesday, 30th July

Lunched today at Sibyl Colefax's. Other guests were the Eshers, the Chancellor of the Exchequer and Mrs. Dalton, Malcolm Sargent, Barbara Ward, Binkie Beaumont and the Chancellor's P.P.S., a smug young Labour M.P., by name Christopher Mayhew, I think. I being the least important guest sat between Binkie Beaumont, to whom I have little to say and for whom I have little sympathy, and the young M.P., whom I cordially disliked. Consequently was not entirely happy until the end of the meal when conversation became general and spirited. I overheard Barbara Ward say in her genteel little manner to the Chancellor that a capital levy was quite workable, and just the ticket. How dare she on such an occasion! She was at great pains to sell the idea to Dalton and demonstrate how it could be done. Mr. Dalton fulfilled all my pre-conceived ideas of him. He is affable, bombastic and diabolically clever. I am sure he is also dishonest and evil. He is a big, tall man, bald with pointed skull – Mephistophelean. He has an insinuating, ingratiating manner. He thumped the table when speaking about the editor of the *Economist*, saying: 'He persistently misrepresents all my endeavours and I damned well won't be interfered with. He will get nothing out of me and [curiously enough] he won't get anything out of me socially.' Speaking of the Land Fund he said, 'Fifty million pounds are to me what a halfpenny is to a millionaire. I can spend what I like internally. Money spent in the country bears no relation to money spent outside it.' He flattered himself that he had spent money on patronage of the arts and amenities and jeered at Snowden, his predecessor, for having declined the offer from the Duke of Montrose's executors of Glencoe, which Snowden described as 'waste land. What use could it be to the Exchequer?' He said how surprised he was that, when his proposed gift of lands to the National Trust was made at the Annual Meeting of the Trust last year through Lord Esher, it was greeted by the members in stony silence. Had Lord Esher announced that some millionaire had made a fraction of such an offer, it

would have evoked loud applause. So I piped up: 'I quite understand, Mr.
Chancellor. Why should the announcement be greeted with applause
when the members learnt that *you* were prepared to make the National
Trust a present of their own money and lands?' At this Mr. D. rubbed his
hands and guffawed with hideous laughter. Malcolm Sargent and
Beaumont then severally complained to the Chancellor that Board of
Trade regulations prevented foreign artists being employed here, with the
consequence that the standard of opera and theatre must remain low.
Dalton very obligingly asked us all to brief him with our complaints.
After the meal he came up and thanked me for acting cicerone to his
beastly wife. My neighbour Mayhew, the young M.P., infuriated me by
his condescending manner, denying that there was any financial crisis. It
was all a newspaper ramp. He asked me if I was 'one of us.' I replied, 'By
this I infer that you ask, am I a Socialist. Look again.' Then he said, 'You
are a Tory?' 'No,' I said, 'I am far too right wing.' 'Just a reactionary then?'
he said. 'Yes, against your Government.'

Thursday, 31st July

I motored to Quidenham in Norfolk for the day; through Breckland,
which is intriguing no-man's land. Michael Rosse hates it. I looked at the
outside of Euston and photographed it. Since I created a bad impression
the only time I ever met Lady Albemarle I put myself out to please, and
think I succeeded. She and Lord A. were both charming and begged me
to stay as long as I wished. It is a stern house, not of great importance.
Almost entirely rebuilt in 1815 by an architect called Latham, in fine
rose-red brick with neat pointing. Pictures, portraits and furniture good,
notably large mahogany Regency sideboards with stout brass rings and
mountings. Lady A. is pretty and intelligent. He very distinguished. She
told me how she became a Papist after her marriage, and so did her
daughter, a lively, pretty amusing girl. I liked her a lot. Then Lord A.'s
youngest son by his first wife was converted to the consternation of the
Keppel family. Doubtless they detest Lady A. She is head of the W.V.S. I
left after tea, they all waving me off at the door. It was a happy summer
outing.

Friday, 1st August

Had a conference in the City about Osterley. Grandy there. I find I am
apt to dictate at the meetings I attend now; a sign of confidence, perhaps
over-confidence. Motored after tea to Packwood, arriving late for dinner.
Joshua Rowley only just recovering from scalding his leg badly. I thought
Packwood had lost its garnished appearance. Joshua pointed out how
ugly the flower border scheme is; all the flowers are yellow which must

indicate some odd trait in Baron Ash's character. Joshua still mystifies me. Why does he want to be isolated in this lonely place?

Saturday, 2nd August

Got to Charlecote at 10.30 and met Dr. Shaw and the brewing expert who says the brew-house here is complete, rare and important. I went round the house listening to the guides who all said their piece well. It is impossible to prevent them lapsing into occasional inanities. I wonder how much the substance of what they say matters. On my return to London I visited Sulgrave Manor. It is the best arranged and best kept of any show house I have been to. For this Clifford Smith is responsible. The old man does have his good points.

At dinner at Brooks's got into conversation with a young man, Ian Anstruther, just returned from Washington where he was secretary to Lord Inverchapel, whom he greatly admires. He is shocked by this country and says for the first time in its history the upper classes are not wanted. A nice, old-fashioned young man. 'To be a gentleman today,' he says, 'is a disadvantage.'

Monday, 4th August

Geoffrey [Houghton Brown] lunched to meet Ivy and Margaret. Ivy told a sudden, irrelevant story of their war days in a cottage near Newbury: how they kept poultry from York*sheer*. One died. The others were so little moved by its death that they walked on it. They then looked at Geoffrey's furniture upstairs, and his bed by Jacob. When Margaret does not think a piece of furniture good she says, 'I would get rid of that if I were you.'

Tuesday, 5th August

I got to West Wycombe after one o'c just before Harold Nicolson and Vita Sackville-West arrived. We lunched at the Apple Orchard and walked round the village; drove up to the church on the hill and looked at the Mausoleum. Then to the house. Helen [Dashwood] welcomed us. She was pretty but tired, and seemed sad. Johnnie has already moved into Chips Manor and Helen is obviously reluctant to follow. W.W. is tottering on its last legs. Harold made little effort to be forthcoming. We left at four, drove through the Hambleden Valley. The Nicolsons have a habit I like of driving up to houses. This we did at Fawley Court. The house has been refaced with very ugly scarlet brick. We had tea at The Red Lion Henley, Vita drinking water. Then on to Newbury. I pointed out the gates of Shaw House, so up that drive we went. Walked round the house which we greatly admired, only deploring the Crittall windows and corridor annexe stuck on to the back. Then to the Sandham Memorial Chapel, which they did not much like and thought should not have been accepted. Stayed at the Chequers Hotel, Newbury. We pool our money and I am made treasurer and pay the bills. Vita went to bed early and H. sat up reading a book on Lenin for a review. At dinner we guessed what awful impositions Attlee would announce tomorrow. Harold admits that he foresees no solution to the predicament we are in, and his reason for becoming a socialist is that socialism is inevitable. By joining he feels he may help by tempering it; by remaining outside he can do nothing. He says the sad thing is that no one dislikes the lower orders more than he does. Vita keeps saying how hungry she is. It is true that in hotels one does not get enough to eat.

Wednesday, 6th August

At 8.30 walking to buy a newspaper I met Vita who said she had just sent a telegram to Ben whose birthday it is today. I said, 'Oh, and not to me? for it is mine too.' So she bought me some lavender-water as a present. A very full day. We drove to Avebury and diverged to see the isolated gate-piers in the field at Hampstead Marshall, for they move me strangely. Then to see Inkpen Rectory. The gardener let us in for the owner was away. H. and V. were delighted with the little formal Le Nôtre layout and H. made drawings of it in his pocket-book. We drove up to Littlecote and the gardener said Sir E. Wills was away, so we walked round this house. Large; I did not like the orangery additions to the main front. The place was purring with gardeners. Long herbaceous borders, vast lawns admirably kept, but very much the rich man's garden, tastelessly laid out. I liked the bit where the Kennet tributary flows through a narrow lawny enclave. Emboldened by these adventures we overreached ourselves and met our Waterloo at Ramsbury Manor. Vita drove straight up the drive and stopped before the front door. We admired the house when, lo! the owner, Sir Francis Burdett, wearing yachting jacket, with bibulous face and the very incarnation of Colonel Blimp, descended the steps. He was waving a newspaper. Vita said, 'Shall we drive off?' but it was too late. Colonel Blimp angrily asked us what we wanted. Vita said we had made a mistake and turned to me. I said, 'Littlecote'. After an uncomfortable half-minute we left. Harold squared his shoulders and sat dumb and miserable, trying not to be seen. At Avebury we looked at the stones and went into the museum, very well arranged, and saw the manor and church from the outside. Lunched at Marlborough and drove through Amesbury to Dinton. Were shown over Little Clarendon by Miss Engleheart and pursued by the old mother, aged ninety-two and without memory. The daughter was so sweet to her, and so humble and nice that Vita was much impressed. We walked round Hyde's House and the chauffeur told us about Mr. Philipps will faked by a strange valet in the hotel at Mentone where he died. The valet added a codicil purporting to leave all Mr. Philipps' property to him. Went to Dinton House and were given tea by the Y.W.C.A. lady warden. The Nicolsons did not much care for this house, nor Hyde's, preferring Little Clarendon of the three. Piggle Dene sarsen stones property they thought ill-kempt and a discredit to the Trust.

We finally drove to Wilton to have a drink with David Herbert in his strange little garden temple, the front decorated with lavish stone carving. Here we were told that Attlee's news was not at all drastic or disagreeable. From there to Long Crichel, arriving 7.30. Eddy greeted us, Eardley and Desmond being abroad. After dinner a long, interesting conversation after listening to a resumé of Attlee's speech at 9 o'c. Again Harold talked of his political belief that only the Labour Party can save us from the terrible situation we are in. He says all the factories are controlled by Communist shop stewards.

Thursday, 7th August

Extremely tired today. At twelve we left with Eddy for Amesbury where V. and H. parted from us to lunch with Stephen Tennant. E. and I walked into Amesbury Park which is still full of soldiers who have destroyed the entrance gates and one of John Webb's gate-piers. Park overgrown and desolate. House Victorian, the portico impressive. On the Nicolsons returning we drove to Stourhead. While the others walked round the lake I went to the house and talked to Rennie Hoare. He doesn't know what he wants and is already shifting our things about. When they met him V. and H. thought him sinister. They did not like the house.

Friday, 8th August

Harold worked till eleven when we left. We agreed that Eddy had been the perfect host. Drove to Ven and straight up the drive to the house in Vita's usual abrupt fashion that upsets Harold and now alarms me. There was a woman at the door whom I asked if Sir Hubert Medlycott were about. I thought she was the housekeeper. She took me all round the garden to look for him and failing to find him disclosed that she was the tenant. So I explained who we were and asked if we might see the garden by ourselves. She readily consented and showed us inside the house as well. Then we drove to Montacute where we lunched and walked round the garden, V. and H. telling me what flowers to plant in the forecourt borders. They were not as enthusiastic over the interior as I had hoped. Harold had to write his *Spectator* article so V. and I left him alone in one of the empty rooms. We drove to Ilchester where I bought a Lowestoft jug from an antique dealer. Had tea at an inn; and on to

North Cadbury Court. I prevented Vita driving up to the front door. She does this thing not as a tripper but as an eighteenth-century aristocrat who has a right. We went to the church, and she walked straight from the churchyard into the garden. I rang the bell and Sir Somebody, the owner, a nice old buffer, appeared, munching his tea. He let us in. The entrance front is grey-cold stone, late Elizabethan; the garden front Regency with central semi-circular bay and iron balcony, a surprising contrast. The front hall was done by Avray Tipping very well. A Regency ball-room behind. Drove past Maperton which turned out not to be the house we expected, and quite dull. Vita drove straight through the gate and round the sweep in her inimitable manner. Then back to Montacute, where I am staying in the bedroom Eardley arranged for the public. The Nicolsons stay in Yeovil.

Saturday, 9th August

This morning brought the first signs of autumn. Montacute was silvery with faint dew in the early light. H. and V. called at 9.45 and walked round the outside. They were much moved by the silent beauty of the house. We drove straight to Stoke-sub-Ham and looked at the Little Priory. To my surprise they thought this might prove a worthy property. The little 'great hall' can undoubtedly be made very attractive. Then to Barrington Court which they also found beautiful; and were struck by the Lyles' modern buildings and layout. The gardens have got back to their pre-war standard, the borders ablaze, and only six gardeners. The Lyles, who were away, are living in the red brick wing, the Court proper being empty. At one o'c we reached Knightstones, one mile south of Ottery St. Mary, belonging to Colonel Reggie Cooper, a funny old thing who was at school with Harold, is round as Humpty Dumpty, and wears an eyeglass. He bought this house just before the war. It is a plain, granity, Cornish-looking house with carved 'Jacobean' barge-boards, *c.* 1820. He has made a pretty little garden with fountains, and has sumptuous farm buildings for his Guernsey cows. There is a large great hall with open roof and wide frieze with dolphins. He gave us a superlative luncheon of chicken Maryland with fried bananas, mangoes, junket and Devonshire cream. Cocktails and white wine. He is thinking of re-buying Cothay and wants us to see it on Monday. Then on to Killerton where we had tea with Sir Richard and Lady Acland. We all disliked this property, the garden, the ugly shrubs, the house, the ménage, the dogmatic owners, and two little plain boys. She drove us round the estate after tea. In the house is established the Workers' Transport Company, people smelling of disinfectant, a working woman singing out of tune. We saw no point in this property which is no more beautiful than the surrounding country. The Adam ceilings and marble fireplaces, if they are by Adam, are thin and poor. The Aclands live in a part of the house.

We stayed at the Royal Clarence Hotel, Exeter, and walked through the Cathedral. Fine roof. I liked a tablet in the north aisle to a young organist, dated 1586, the carved marble organ-case of remarkably modern design.

Sunday, 10th August

We had an extra hour's sleep and I went to Mass at eight behind the Cathedral. The priest scolded the congregation fiercely for coming in late. At Forde House Vita bought a silhouette picture for Eddy. Then to Bradley Manor which the Ns thought shockingly neglected: the entrance unkempt, fields a forest of thistles and the paths choked with weeds. Mrs. Woolner's husband, an ungracious, ugly man, showed us round rapidly. The house swarming with babies. We then continued to Saltash Ferry, having driven miles out of our way because Harold ventured upon map-reading which was disastrous. He has no geography sense whatever. We crossed the Tamar in the ferry and drove round Saltash to Trematon Castle. Lunched there with the Claud Russells (*fraises des bois*). All of us disappointed with this plain Regency house within the curtilage of an old castle, where the Black Prince is said to have lodged. The view towards Devonport and *Vanguard* moored there, impressive. Sir Claud is a bit of a stick, distinguished and aloof like most Russells, so Harold says. He enunciates each vowel like Mr. Gladstone masticating. She, half Greek, is pretty but whiney. Thence to Cotehele where the Mount Edgcumbes were assembled to greet us and give us tea. The Ns slightly disappointed with this house too, V. finding it inferior (which it is) to Knole. But that is no disparagement in my eyes. I stayed alone at the Bedford, Tavistock, the Ns going to H.'s brother for the night.

Today gloriously sunny and hot. The Nicolsons do not really care for classical buildings, only liking the Gothic or Elizabethan. Harold is wonderfully untidy. Dust, ash all over his hat and clothes. Vita wears one terra cotta dress, very shiny and long in the skirt, and brown espadrilles, yet is always distinguished and 'grande dame'. We all agreed the Mount Edgcumbes were charming with the most unaffected good manners – 'because they are gentlemen,' Vita added.

At 9.15 I heard Mr. Attlee's speech broadcast in my hotel. In the crowded lounge it was received in grim silence. When over not a soul spoke or made a single comment. Instead, he and she went on with their reading, so typically English. A sign of native phlegm or stupid indifference, who can tell?

Monday, 11th August

Yesterday I felt quite ill. Today better, perhaps because we leave this relaxing climate. At ten the others called for me. I took Vita to a shop I had found and for two guineas bought her a small bag she liked, made of *ersatz* leather. Then we drove over Dartmoor in steamy heat. A cloudless horizon. The police warned us that two convicts had escaped from the prison. This thrilled us. Some of the ponies on the moor have become piebald. At Bradfield [Hall] we drove to the front door. I found Mrs Adams in the garden wearing a large straw hat, beneficent and *jolie-laide*. She showed us the principal rooms and the Ns thought that, although over-restored, the house was worth the Trust holding. Having lunched at a wayside café we eventually found Cothay down devious lanes. I had always heard so much praise of this house that I was disappointed. Since Colonel Cooper's day Sir F. Cook has done atrocious things to it, viz: taking off the crenellation from the gatehouse, chopping the great room into a series of little ones, putting in a hideous window on the garden side and making ridiculous ogival door-heads in the great hall. The beautiful garden laid out by Col. Cooper has sadly gone to seed, but could be reinstated. A great deal of over-restoration has happened inside and out. Inside the only good features left are the great hall and the frescoes.

From Cothay we drove to Coleridge Cottage, Nether Stowey, which interested Harold. Here we met the Agent. Then to East Quantoxhead which from the outside looks like Princetown, Vita said. To her chagrin H. and I were pusillanimous, and refused to go in. The vulgarity of Glastonbury so disappointed and disgusted H. who expected it to be like Tintern Abbey that he would not look at the ruins. We reached Wells for dinner and stayed at The Swan. After dinner we walked to the Bishop's Palace, the Cathedral and Vicar's Close. We were shocked to find the Bishop's moat a clutter of waste paper. From a distance we thought it was white water lilies.

Tuesday, 12th August

Left The Swan Inn where we had been treated with kindness. The food in this and all the hotels however is infamous. We looked at Tor Hill in good trim. Drove to Nunney and admired the Castle. It is a darling. Struck by the batter of the drum towers. Batter always conveys strength. Then to Mells, spending some time in the church and churchyard. Moved by the sad end of the Horner family with the death of Edward in the first war, and impressed by his equestrian statue by Munnings, the Eric Gill lettering, and the inscription of Raymond Asquith's tablet on the plain wall within the tower. We felt that this family had had something to contribute to life and art until the end. I did not admire Lutyens's tomb for the McKennas although nothing he did is ignoble. Drove on to Lacock and lunched at the Red Lion, badly. Then went round the monastic remains of the Abbey with a guide who was good. Remarked on the unkempt condition of the cloister garth, and the cobwebs and untidiness of the walks. Miss Talbot showed us round the house. The Ns were pleased with Lacock, though not with its condition. Then to Great Chalfield where the Fullers showed us round the Manor. Place very spick and span. Then to Corsham to tea with Norah Methuen, Paul being away painting. She took infinite pains and was most kind. Vita never drinks tea and has lemon squash and soda water whenever she can. The ceilings of the state rooms have all been re-whitened by Holborough of Tetbury and the damask curtains in the Saloon and covers of the Chippendale chairs beautifully repaired by Norah's own fingers. She has covered them with a fine net, dyed the same red as the damask beneath. The Nicolsons did not even pretend to be interested in these eighteenth-century rooms.

At Bath we stay at the Lansdown Grove Hotel, very comfortably. After dinner walked up the hill to call on Mrs. Knollys, whose complaints and too evident possessiveness of Eardley horrified V.

Wednesday, 13th August

We were treated with almost nauseating respect by the proprietress of this hotel who thanked the Nicolsons for their patronage and even me for my 'graciousness in saying I had slept well'. Harold is childishly embarrassed by this sort of remark; hates it and blushes with rage.

This morning we sauntered in Bath and were revolted by the drabness of the Pump Room where there should have been gay music and inviting coffee and biscuits. Instead no efforts made of any kind. The Ns pronounced the sulphur water horrid. Vita liked the Circus best of all the Bath sites. After luncheon we drove past Solsbury Hill to Dyrham and looked at the church. Then called on Lady Islington who showed us the house. She was very active and bustling. A 'Soul', she is outspoken, amusing, hard and thoroughly Edwardian. I quite see how Stuart is fascinated by her. She is leaving Dyrham because the Blathwayts are returning. She says she hates them and is going to take away everything that she put into the house, even the baths. She said casting an eye at me, 'He looks disapproving. Is he hostile?' Next we drove to Iron Acton, and Thornbury and Berkeley Castles, which last H. and V. raved about. Me it does not move. I like castles to have emphasis, verticality which this dumpy structure lacks. Then to Horton Court for tea with the Wills's who did not seem prepared for us. They are a sweet couple and were both bewildered. The Ns were not greatly taken with this house. Then after several misadventures in the Stroud Valley we reached Nether Lypiatt at 7.45, and quickly saw over. Mrs. Woodhouse away, dying in Brighton. I think this is one of, if not *the* most covetable house in England. It combines the classical with the picturesque. The garden layout is perfect. We dined in Stroud late but rather well, for a change, and stayed tonight at The New Inn Gloucester. After ten when the non-residents left, we sat drinking in the courtyard under the stars. At eleven Vita began to write an article for the *Observer*.

Thursday, 14th August

The New *is* pretty. The galleries are overhung with weeping creeper, and the walls behind the galleries have been successfully painted a deep, bold red. Vita, having finished her article, was down for breakfast before me. Harold likewise had read books for his reviews before breakfast. We all put the Cathedral very high on our list – the stout round piers are asking to be embraced. Some of the Jacobean monuments are painted. We liked the lady leaning on her arm in the Lady Chapel with her blue eyes, and the incomparably beautiful effigy of Edward II. Oh, why do they not remove the opaque Milanese glass from the cloisters? We set off for Hailes Abbey and Harold was appalled by the condition of this property. Then to Stanway where Vita demanded to see the house. We walked straight through the house to the garden beyond. Stanton we saw and Chipping Campden where we had the nastiest of all luncheons at the smart hotel. It being one of the hottest days we were given hot soup from a tin, stringy steaks, uncooked vegetables, trifle. Of all this V. and I hardly ate anything, neither of us indeed having eaten much at Gloucester, not being inclined to face the sausages. At 2.30 we arrived at Hidcote. To our dismay we saw the table laid for four. Lawrie Johnston had expected us and said rather tartly that he had provided a succulent meal. This blow was almost more than we could bear. Vita was given innumerable cuttings, Lawrie J. having relented. Garden pronounced lovely. We arrived at Charlecote at four. I warned the Ns that Brian Fairfax-Lucy was a dress reformer. Behold, he appeared in a pair of tight little white shorts, white sandshoes, a white satin shirt open at the neck, and a blue ribbon tied in a bow at his navel. The Ns decided that of all the people we had so far met the Lucys were the nicest. They considered the gardens here a disgrace. At six we listened to the repeat broadcast about the National Trust which we had missed on Sunday. The best part was the feature about Charlecote and Brian's admirable speech, he sitting with us in the room listening. This is curious and to me still a bit uncanny.

We stayed at The Falcon Inn, Stratford-on-Avon, a good olde-worlde hostelry and went to the *Merchant of Venice* which was atrocious.

Beatrix Lehmann a poor Portia, Shylock not too bad, but the young men all mannered and chi-chi, the décor shoddy modern.

Friday, 15th August

So hot under the eaves that I slept badly. Vita was asked for her autograph on leaving the hotel. We drove to Packwood. The weather overcast and almost drizzling. On arrival the sun came out and the day turned into the hottest of all. The Ns rather liked this place and its contents and admired the scrupulous way it is kept up. They liked Joshua Rowley but thought he looked unhealthy. They shook hands and talked to Weaver the gardener, who said he was a wireless fan of Harold's. V. and I scolded Harold afterwards for not relishing this reference. They greatly admired the way Weaver arranged the flowers and decided that, so long as we could afford the bedding out and had so good a gardener, we should leave the garden as it is. We lunched at Banbury and spent the last money from the pool. Looked at Boarstall Tower and Long Crendon. At Slough I was dropped, and we said goodbye. They were sweet and kind in saying I had been a good guide. I kissed Vita on the cheek. I have grown to love her. She is an adorable woman. I have enjoyed this tour immensely.

Found a charming letter at home from Peter Scott telling me about the way Kathleen's remains were dealt with. She was cremated and the three of them took the ashes and scattered them, Lord K. reading Wordsworth. The sun was bright. There were few people bathing from the beach. This was at Sandwich. It was a pagan, idyllic and appropriate ceremony, just what she would have liked.

Sunday, 17th August

Stayed at home for the weekend happily, working on a review for the *Spectator*. Saw James this evening. He tells me he is in love with a paragon of a girl aged twenty-two. I am not sure that I believe him, but I daresay he may marry quite soon, but disastrously. This is my jolly little forecast. Then Henry Reed dined with me at Brooks's. His too fulsome praise of my book of which he has read the proofs, makes me question his intelligence.

Tuesday, 19th August

Travel agents telephoned that they have booked me a seat in an aeroplane to Milan on the 25th September. Dr. Pevsner lunched at Brooks's. He gave me four alternative subjects about Robert Adam to write for the *Architectural Review*. This man, whom hitherto I have pictured as dry, pedantic and rather carping, proved to be friendly, eager to assist, and encouraging .

Wednesday, 20th August

Went to Hampstead in the afternoon to call on Mrs. Angeli, the daughter of William, niece of Dante Gabriel and Christina Rossetti and grand-
daughter of Ford Madox Brown. She suffers from heart, is about seventy,
very frail and ill. She lives with a daughter, very Italian in looks. Mrs
Angeli is surrounded with heaps of books, piles of furniture, china and
framed drawings by Dante Gabriel, in confusion indescribable, her house
having been destroyed by a bomb, and she and her daughter now lodging
in a clergyman's house. She offers to lend us a quantity of pictures for
Wightwick Manor. She told me she owned Shelley's sofa, bought by him
in Pisa and slept on by him the night before he died (why and how?).
After his death Mary gave it to Leigh Hunt, who gave it to Trelawny, who
gave it to William Rossetti.

Went this evening to Westminster Abbey to see Henry VII's tomb. The
burnished bronze pilasters at the four corners, the angels, the bronze –
or are they black marble? – wreaths. How strange too are the Darnley
and Buckingham tombs on either side, both so proud, extravagant and
meant to endure. And so they have by a miracle survived the war. Yet 'not
marble, nor the gilded monuments of princes shall outlive this powerful
rhyme'. And Shakespeare will be read when they are reduced to molten
sludge and slime. I looked too at Hugh Easton's R.A.F. window. It is true
the colours glow and give promise of eternal life, but the design is somewhat banal, confused and laboured in a neo-Pre-Raphaelitish sort of
way. I like the silver altar rails and two candelabra. These are the dear
Professor [Richardson]'s work.

Thursday, 21st August

Today is my Uncle Robert's birthday; and he died thirty years ago,
cannon-fodder he was, and his name is known to a very few. Yet I shall
remember him.

Friday, 22nd August

Motored home this afternoon. It was fine, warm and sunny. My parents
were sitting under the apple tree drinking gin and orange. Then Deenie
came and we dined at the long teak table on the west side of the cottage
watching the sunset. My father declared he had never been happier in his
life.

Saturday, 23rd August

Went to Overbury Court. I was late and Ruby Holland-Martin had gone
out riding. His mother showed me the collection, formed by the father,

of old brass which might do for East Riddlesden Hall. Some of the ink pots are almost elegant. Old Mrs. Holland-Martin deplored the moral decadence of the English people. How could I respond but by sighing sympathetically? Called at Harvington Hall, Little Moreton Hall and slept at The Macclesfield Arms Hotel, where I was given four courses of which lobster was one.

Sunday, 24th August

At Lyme [Park] was conducted round the house by the Town Clerk of Stockport, by name Morgan. Considering the vast hordes of visitors who come here – 45,000 into the house alone since mid-June – it looks fairly well, and there is not much that jars. I lunched with the Morgans in their house, Belmount, a large substantial villa, the rooms painted diarrhoea, stippled walls, lincrusta ceilings; furniture wicker and leatherette. 'Tasty' and comfortable. Huge luncheon, badly cooked. An important alderman and wife to meet me. All very polite, kind and dull, *dull*. Weak coffee in the 'lounge' and dreary platitudes about cricket and sport. Yet I liked Mrs. Morgan, a sweet, bright, pretty woman and keen housewife, aged fifty, with grey hair, permed. The alderman and wife have just been to Switzerland for a holiday and were full of complaints that they were not allowed to spend more than £75. Ten years ago they had never heard of Switzerland or £75.

At last, party over, they drove me back to Lyme, and I was entreated to witness the scene at the height of its numbers on a beautiful summer day. It was a nightmare of crawling, shirt-sleeved, smelly, happy people. All behaving extremely well. There was one moment only when I hated them, seeing and hearing them stamping up the grand staircase like a herd of untameable buffaloes. The furniture looks drear enough behind the ropes, but what can we do when there are such crowds? I left at four and stopped at Wythenshawe Hall. This small park likewise crawling with and trampled thin by people. A melancholy, over-restored, black-and-white house, with a red brick Georgian far side. But shut up and empty. Then drove to Hale Manor, near Widnes, to stay with Peter and Monica Fleetwood-Hesketh in a very pretty 1700 red brick house. We walked to the ruins of Hale Hall, the 1806 façade by Nash standing alone, gaunt above a flat stretch of land to the Mersey, the starkness spoilt by a row of strident red-roofed villas on the skyline.

Monday, 25th August

This morning walked with Peter down to the Mersey, gazing across at the chimneys of Runcorn and the great iron bridge-conveyance, called a transporter, of Widnes. There are a pretty white lighthouse and cottage on the shore below Hale where the coast runs towards Liverpool. After luncheon I drove the Heskeths to Speke Hall where we were met by the Town Clerk, the City Engineer and a member of the Finance Committee, all smelling strongly of drink. I was not at all satisfied that this house was being looked after by the right committee, and gathered that the inside of the house comes exclusively within the control of the City Engineer. At present all the contents of Miss Watts' trustees are still in the house waiting to be sold. There is much that is really horrid, oak furniture black as pitch. But Peter rightly remarked, the point about these old Lancashire houses is that the rooms should be filled with black oak and be 'rather terrifying'. I think it would be a mistake entirely to replant the wood between the house and sea. There is still a definite country house flavour about Speke, marooned though it be, for it is wonderfully sheltered from the aeroplane factories and housing estates around it. After tea we motored in Peter's Dodgem, made in 1929, to Ince Blundell Hall, the home of Mrs Weld Blundell. It is lived in by her husband and daughter, whose name is Montagu, and the brother-in-law, also Weld Blundell, born Weld, and his children, called Weld. It is a romantic Papist establishment. The Pantheon, built *circa* 1810, is marvellous, filled with Roman statuary collected by a Mr. Blundell of the day. It must be one of the finest statuary collections left in private hands. The acoustics in the Pantheon are so bad that you cannot hear a word distinctly. The picture-gallery and dining-room, added *circa* 1850, are in the eighteenth-century style. The main portion of the house is George I, and might be by Talman. Unfortunately the windows have plate glass. We were given cocktails before leaving.

Some of the new Liverpool houses being built are admirable, of decent materials, neat designs, especially those near Knowsley.

Tuesday, 26th August

The Heskeths are very late people They dine at nine, and there is lots to drink. Last night two bottles of champagne and bed after one. Even then I had to insist upon retiring, contrary to Peter's inclination, I think. His ideas about N. Trust properties are absolutely right, just as his taste is faultless. He is an escapist from realities, a civilized being. At 10.45 we left for Rufford Old Hall where we were met by the chairman of the local committee, the architect, the curator Ashcroft, and old Jarrett, who spoke to me about his book on Shakespeare which is still unpublished. Rufford looked well kept and tidy. The armour needed cleaning, and the varnish removing. We went on to the roof and examined the leads and stone tiles. Peter and I lunched with the chairman, Mr. Gosselin, and the architect at the Park Hotel, Preston.

After luncheon we motored to Ribchester, up the Ribble valley. Here the country at once improves and Lancashire ceases to be industrial, and becomes rural. The mountains are in the background. The new curator, installed in the dismal Museum, grumbled about the conditions. Considering that she has one small room to keep tidy I was not very sympathetic. The state of the ruins is poor indeed, but work on them is to start in the autumn. From here we drove to Parrox Hall, across the Fylde of Lancashire, a district distinguished by the trimness of its coverts and its white-washed houses. Parrox Hall has great charm. It too is white-washed; stands in a miniature park with, alas, some nasty development close to. It is a typical small squire's homestead. Probably late Elizabethan, or Jacobean, with low, latticed windows, and a stone Gothic portico added to the front *circa* 1820. It is cheerful and homely. The hall has a flagged floor, dark panelling with lozenge pattern panels, a stairway leading directly off it, and much dark oak furniture. Among the furniture in this room are several late seventeenth-century chairs with original leather seats and backs inscribed with a crown, brass studs and finials, said to have come from Portugal. Several fourpost beds, one very fine Jacobean bed in which Cromwell is said to have slept before Prestonpans. Each bedroom leads to the next, for there are no passageways. Much of the oak is made up and heavily varnished in the Lancashire fashion. Mrs. Elletson, mother of the owner, lives here with her unmarried sister, a Miss Philipps. The owner was abroad. There are two bachelor cousins, aged seventy-six and eighty-five, staying. They have stayed here every summer since they were boys. Mrs. Elletson is nervous about the Trust and asked sad little questions, like: 'Would her sister still be allowed to paint in the garden studio?' 'Would the servants be allowed to stay on?' Would they not? One feels that the mode of life at Parrox Hall has not changed since the house was built.

After tea we left at 6.30. I dropped Peter at Lancaster station and drove through the romantic Lune valley, past Hornby Castle, Melling, Thurland and Kirkby. Stayed the night at Barbon Manor, a large, baronial, 1870 house high above the village, remotely and beautifully situated. Roger Fulford lives here with his wife and step-son, Lord Shuttleworth. The house teems with sons and daughters. After dinner we talked politics. Roger told his experiences as a Liberal candidate at the last election and in 1931, both times unsuccessful. When I gave vent to my right-wing views they were horrified, but amused. Mrs F. said she admired my honesty. Barbon is a Liberal stronghold.

Wednesday, 27th August

I wrote letters this morning in Roger's eyrie at the top of the house overlooking the Lune valley, where he works. Then he took me in his car to

Dent, a perfect, small mediaeval village or townlet. Roger drives as slowly and carefully as he speaks. He recounted the Shuttleworth story: how the old Lord died during the war; his two sons were both killed in the 1914–18 war. The elder son's two sons were killed in the last war. The present Lord's younger half-brother, Mrs. Fulford's son, a Lyttleton, was also killed in the last war. The present Lord himself lost both his legs in battle. He lives here and at Gawthorpe, crippled by death duties.

We lunched at The Sun Inn, Dent, which is still governed by twenty-four 'Statesmen'. Its streets are cobbled, its cottages all of cob, painted white. It has a large church and a fountain. Open country runs up to it from all sides. It seems to be the end of the world. We approached it by a rough lane along Barbon Beck, over the mountains. On my return I packed and left. I enjoyed this visit immensely. Mrs. F. pressed me to come again – very kind considering the polarity of our political views. She is intelligent, vivacious, handsome and some years older than Roger.

I stay tonight with the Bruce Thompsons at Troutbeck.

Thursday, 28th August

I wrote many letters this morning. Bruce motored me on a tour of NT properties in the Lake District. Cartmel Gate House was first on the list. In the church is a 1620 rood screen with classical entablature and baroque pillars with vine leaves entwined. Then Hawkshead, where we lunched. Then Hill Top, Beatrix Potter's house, with all her personal belongings lying around loose, the prey to any thief. Yet it is the best showhouse of an eminent person I have seen, still of course fresh and new. But what will it be like when Beatrix Potter is no longer revered and the little cottage is worn out, and the carpets and rugs threadbare? And on we went to Borran's Field, Ambleside, Town End. Bruce, who is a master of showmanship, the most meticulous of guardians and the oldest member of the staff, took my criticisms, such as they were, with amused tolerance.

We dined at Windermere and called at Sir Samuel Scott's after dinner. He is a snobbish little man speaking with disapproval of so common a man as Lord Woolton being elected to Brooks's club.

Terribly upset by the announcement that the basic petrol ration is to be cut off and all foreign travel to cease.

Friday, 29th August

Sent Mama a birthday telegram from Northumberland. Went over to Huntingstile, the Wordsworths' house on the west side of Grasmere. This is a Victorian stone-built house, ugly and large, which looks north-east and gets little sun in the summer and none in the winter. I left my car, and Gordon and Doreen Wordsworth drove me to Hotbanks Farm and

Housesteads on the Roman Wall, and a wonderful drive it was, up to
Thirlmere past Saddleback, to Penrith, over the moors towards Hexham
and the Allen Valley to Hotbanks. Here we lunched under a wall. Gordon
had business at the Farm and Doreen and I walked upon the Roman Wall
to Housesteads Camp. It was superb tracing the undulating line of the
wall along the ridge of the wild rolling country, now a thick raised
embankment with a flat path-like top, now a thin snake. The Fort is one
of the most evocative Roman remains in England, for vast excavated
foundations survive, gate-piers and two water tanks, their stone sides
worn from the women washing and scrubbing linen, their lead joints, the
runnels of the latrines. The Fort stands on a sloping hill and is impressive
seen from the road. There are likewise remains of terraces on the opposite slope, seen from the Camp.

It was so hot we stopped for bottles of mineral lemonade, drinking in
the car in shirt sleeves. We visited Allen Banks and walked through the
wooded ravine. There were people picnicking on the rocks in the
middle of the river, which is so dry. Drove back through Ullswater,
looking at the new property at Glencoyne, and dining at Huntingstile. I
went back to Troutbeck at ten. Received a letter from my bank that I was
overdrawn £400 which depressed me very much indeed, for I thought I
had been reducing, not increasing my overdraft.

Saturday, 30th August

Bruce Thompson and I motored in my car to Armathwaite Hall Hotel
where he had a directors' meeting. I went on alone to Cockermouth to
see Wordsworth's House. It is let as an antique shop of a superior sort,
and so is well furnished. Apart from its association it is a good house built
in 1745. Plain outside but untouched. Interior unaltered too. A particularly good drawing-room upstairs with pedimented doorcases. To think
of the Wordsworth family living here in a room which to their simple
taste must have been ornate and ostentatious. The garden with raised
terrace is as the poet knew it. I bought for £3 a set of steel fireplace
implements, date about 1800. Condition perfect. Felt impelled to spend
because of the bank's letter. Bruce and I motored in the afternoon to
Keswick and at Stable Point on Derwentwater took the Trust's boat from
the woodman and rowed to Kempsholme Island and Lord's Island, where
we landed. Then to St. Nichol's landing-point. Here we picked up two
spinster girl friends of Bruce's and rowed to another small island and ate
sandwiches for tea. We left them there and I rowed from St. Nichol's back
to Stable Point. I can think of nothing more sublime than this lake, surrounded by steep mountains, lawns sloping to the shore, Derwent Isle
woods and St. Herbert's Isle Woods. We motored to the Druids Circle.

This miniature Stonehenge is not only romantic but 'aweful' in the eighteenth-century meaning of the word. On a small, flat plateau it seems to
be the centre of the universe, for it forms the hub of a vast circumference
of mountain tops and is solemn and sanctified by the ancient folk who
frequented it, not knowing anything of the world beyond their horizon,
across the barrier that encircled them. I stay tonight and the following
night with the Wordsworths at Huntingstile.

After dinner Gordon read, extremely well, Canon Rawnsley's
conversations with old peasants and Wordsworth's butler, all of whom had
known the poet. He pronounced very skilfully their own words in
dialect, which he can speak. They conveyed a convincing picture of the
old poet, gruff, aloof, moody, and mumbling and bumbling to himself as
he roamed the dales by lamplight. Gordon told me that, when as children he and his brother and sisters lived with their parents at Whitemoss,
American visitors used to beg his father, who was a parson, to be allowed
to shake hands with him as Wordsworth's great-grandson, for a fee. The
father hated these attentions and would dismiss the officious Americans
with distaste. But the children, whenever they had the chance, used to
indulge in these little transactions themselves, receiving small tips for the
privilege of allowing a pat on the head.

Sunday, 31st August

Motored to Ambleside for Mass. The young priest gave us a wigging for
not turning to God in our present extremities. How did he know that I
don't? Gordon and I went to Allan Bank at 12.30 and Mrs. Rawnsley,
widow of Canon R., one of the co-founders of the Trust, showed me
the house. The Wordsworths lived here before moving to Rydal Mount.
It is a plain house, modernised, ugly and spoilt. Mrs. R. has a collection
of Wordsworth manuscripts, and portraits of him and Southey. She is
about seventy-five, very intelligent, talkative and well informed. I liked
her. She came to lunch at Hungtingstile and then took me to Grasmere
churchyard. She told me the yews were planted by Wordsworth. Showed
me the Greens' grave, but would not go up to the Wordsworths' because,
I suppose, of the trippers. Took me inside the church with its curious
arches and superimposed arcades which divide the two aisles. All but one
old pew have gone. The poet's mural tablet is by Woolner. She then took
me to Dove Cottage, quite a humble little place with a tiny garden. As
she says, the vast numbers of visitors have dispelled much of the sanctity
of the place. There is little inside, except the wainscoting and doors, that
is original. The kitchen is minute and pitch dark. How they all, with children, squeezed in is difficult to imagine. Then she showed me the
museum, but one must be alone to study the letters. Mrs. Rawnsley has

a dark, swarthy face with suspicion of a moustache. She thinks highly of Gordon.

After tea we walked round the lake by Loughrigg Terrace. The shadows began to lengthen, the bells of Grasmere church to ring. It was very still and beautiful; but there were too many people on the hills and the road. Rydal Water has tall rushes at the shore's edge. Gordon loves this district passionately, but Doreen hates it, and this is very distressing for him. It does not predict domestic content.

Monday, 1st September

I left Grasmere at 9.30 on as beautiful a morning as I could wish for: the lake absolutely glassy, a faint mist obscuring the far shore. I motored through Lancashire, diverging just a little to have a look at Borwick Hall, near Carnforth, happily inhabited and cared for, and stopping at Lancaster, of which the bridge is by Carr. Lunched at Wigan where I left my camera in the hotel, only remembering it when I got to Wellington at tea time. Before Wigan at the approach of the dreadful industrial country, the sky darkened. I thought storm clouds portended much-needed rain, but not a bit of it, only the filthy smoke which gathers in the sky here every day of the year, fair or foul. However before Wigan I diverged to Chorley to see Astley Hall, a truly remarkable house, Jacobean but altered in 1666. Very well kept up, both grounds and house. My only adverse comment the turnstiles at the front door into the hall. The astounding features are the ceiling and frieze of the high hall, and the ceiling of the adjacent drawing-room. These ceilings in Wren-style compartments have stucco foliage in the very highest relief, and putti dangling from them in the round. The putti are of large size bearing arrows, and slung, as it were, invisibly from the soffits. The drawing-room ceiling is low and these heavy ornamentations are quite oppressive, although so beautifully fashioned. It is remarkable to find this gem of a house in such lugubrious and polluted surroundings. The country south of Lancashire is in colour burnt straw. I got to Wickhamford at seven to find the garden, dry, parched and sad. Mama was in the orchard watering the beds.

Tuesday, 2nd September

I left at eleven and after Chipping Norton drove straight to North Crawley where Mr. Chester now lives in the Old Rectory. He has let Chicheley to a school. He and his wife showed me ten chairs of walnut, parcel gilt in a rich manner, *temp.* 1730 with original gros-point backs and seats. The needlework is in excellent condition and the colours are unfaded. It must have been kept covered all these years when not in use.

I have never seen chairs so lovely. There is likewise one gilt console table of Kent style, which is very fine. Afterwards I motored to Chicheley and looking at the outside met the headmaster. I said, 'I am afraid I am trespassing.' He was in his shirt-sleeves about to garden. Nevertheless he showed me all round, taking me into the house. There is an entrance hall with marble arcade, a ceiling canvas supposedly painted by Kent, and a wide staircase leading from the hall. Many of the Chester looking-glasses and pictures are left in the room. For a boys' preparatory school the house is exceptionally clean and well kept. I congratulated the master like anything.

Wednesday, 3rd September

Found at the office a parcel from darling Vita, containing present of a silver pencil with engraved inscription, ' J. from V. August 5–15 1947', a souvenir of our tour. Nothing could have given me more delight. Dined at Sibyl's. Not much fun. Jamesey walked into the flat while I was in the bath to say goodbye for he is off to France tomorrow morning for three weeks. He said with a wry look that Maurice had married on the 1st and now it had happened, in spite of his having engineered it, he rather regretted it.

Friday, 5th September

At 11.30 I went to see Lady Astor in Hill Street at her request. Although over sixty she is a great beauty. White hair, healthy complexion and vital movements. She has dignity and deportment, in spite of her vulgarisms . She wanted to impress upon me the necessity of keeping Miss O'Sullivan at Blickling. As she advanced into the room she said, 'Why are you a convert to that awful Catholicism? Do you not bitterly regret it?' I replied, 'Not in the very least.' She said, 'My greatest fear and horror is Communism. Roman Catholicism breeds it.' I replied, 'Roman Catholicism is the only hope left in the world of combating Communism which I too abominate.' She said, 'It is only Catholic countries that go Communist because of the poverty and discontent fostered by the priests. No Protestant countries become dictatorships.' I protested vigorously, and she hissed, 'How dare you say so? You wicked child. Philip Lothian left them. He saw how evil they were.' All this was delivered with vehemence and good humour. She said we must meet again and have a proper battle. Then she said, 'You are in earnest and you feel passionately, and I like that.' As I said goodbye I replied, 'And you care passionately, and that is why I have always admired you.' It was a curious little encounter.

I bought six plates and dishes and went on a shopping spree in spite of my terrible financial straits. Perhaps because of them. Also returned to Mama the £100 she had generously lent me.

Monday, 8th September

Gerald du Gouray invited me to a cocktail party at Claridge's given by the Regent of Iraq in his sumptuous suite. The Regent and Queen Mother want to buy a house in the country, but near London, for the minority of the young King, now at school in England. The Regent with whom I spoke for some time – painfully – is rather short, well-built, fairly handsome, with pleasant brown eyes. He has a roundish face and is neatly dressed in a smart brown suit, very western. I could of course think of nowhere for him off the cuff, but promised that, if given full particulars of his needs, would look around. A stiff sort of function, like all royal occasions.

Tuesday, 9th September

Had planned to dine at home and work. But a young man, by the name of Peter Tunnard, rang up asking to see me. He wants a job with the NT I asked him for a drink and he came at 6.30. He is about twenty-six, dark, personable. He stayed till eight so I asked him to dine. He knows Rome and was able to give me information and advice. Result: work went by the board. After dinner I walked with him to Dickie Buckle's house where he is staying, and I did not get back till midnight. Enjoyable evening. Oh, the weakness of my resolutions.

Friday, 12th September

Feeling unaccountably – on the other hand perhaps accountably – depressed; toothache at nights, fear of the aeroplane and fear, just a slight one, that if not careful I may never fall in love again. Mindy Bacon lunched. He is enormous in size, a head taller than me and doubly broad. We talked of Gainsborough Old Hall. During the evening, dining alone I became very sad and unhappy, a rare thing to happen to me these days. All this weekend I have worked at a beastly article for the *Architectural Review*, which bores me stiff.

Sunday, 14th September

At tea time Peter Tunnard came and we drove to Polesden Lacey, then on to Midi's. She has just come out of a nursing home, and is very thin but pretty, and rather shaky on her feet, poor dear. Peter and I dined at home. I feel guilty that someone as young as he and with a splendid war record should be without a job. Although worried he is very cheerful about it.

Thursday, 18th September

Old Mrs. George Keppel has died. It was curious to see that little, bent old woman scuttling about the Ritz this year, with the white face of a grey mare, and to know that she was King Edward VII's magnificent, upstanding, beautiful, powerful mistress. A ghost from a past more remote from today than the day of Marie Antoinette from hers.

I motored Eardley to Stourhead where we spent the afternoon. Mrs. Hoare at home, looking extremely lost and harrassed, arranging dahlias in servants'-hall pots. She has no taste. At least E. and I decided upon a plan of campaign: we would get the experts, Professor Waterhouse, Leigh Ashton, Mrs. Esdaile, Margaret Jourdain, to go through all the contents. When we had their advice then we would do the arranging of the state-rooms ourselves, which will, I think, be great fun, provided Rennie Hoare leaves us alone.

We drove on to Taunton where I left my car to be repainted. I chose dark blue with black wings which sounds chic enough. Returned to London with E., had a delicious supper in his flat at eleven and walked home.

Saturday, 20th September

To the office and then lunched with Margaret and Ivy alone. Talking of Charlotte Bonham-Carter, with whom they had just stayed, they remarked: 'She never will say a single disagreeable thing about anyone. A most tiresome woman to be with.' Ivy has found an American publisher whose agent over here treats her just as if she were one of her own characters of fifty years ago. 'Of course there will be no drink if you come to my flat.' And, 'If you lunch at this restaurant you can be sure no one will speak to you.' But, Ivy says, the trouble is that she has no biographical material. 'There just is none.'

Sunday, 21st September

This weekend I have read a second book by Stratton on the Italian Renaissance. Spoke to Joan and Garrett Moore who are flying to Rome the same day as I leave, but by a different plane, they flying direct. It is very disappointing. A girl came to tea called K. Hopkins. She rang me up yesterday having seen a letter by me in *The Times* and remembering me from Grenoble days where, she says, we were great friends. She came, and still I could not remember her at all. This, she complained, was no compliment. I am suffering from toothache, and will have to lose two teeth, so Mr Boutwood informs me with glee in his eye.

Monday, 22nd September

Bridget dines with me at home. It is the first time I have seen her for weeks. When I do see her after an interval I realise how devoted I am to her, in spite of her incessant grumbles. She started off with complaints against Michael for preferring the Messel family to his own. 'Well, perhaps he does,' I said.

Tuesday, 23rd September

Sibyl lunched alone with me at the Ritz. She had thought she might be staying in Rome too but, rather to my relief, the project is off. She is difficult to hear. Her voice is indistinct and her poor head is bent downwards. She has given me an introduction to Berenson in Florence, and says I must go and see him. She told me that before the war the Ritz management called her in to redecorate the hotel, but she gave them a straight talk and made them promise they would never touch the interior which had more distinction than any other hotel in London. If they did, she would make life hideous for them by ventilating their philistinism in the press, the House of Lords and Commons and over the wireless. We owe her a great debt.

John Wilton dined with me at Brooks's. He was very charming but has grown stout. I gave him warning to take heed or his jaw would become as pronounced as Lord Fairhaven's. He thinks he will not rent Coleshill after all and wishes to buy Trafalgar.

Wednesday, 24th September

Lunched at the Ritz with the Pryce-Joneses. Sat between Poppy P.-J. and Karen Lancaster, and had nothing to say to either. Osbert L. was present and Princess Marthe Bibesco, dressed very oddly, her flat hat entwined in a green veil which issued therefrom and like a waterfall enveloped the rest of her person. Her thick legs were encased in black stockings over which she wore bottines. She has an intelligent, whimsical face and talks learnedly of French literature. I went to the dentist again. Mr. Boutwood is busy viciously killing two nerves in two teeth.

Charles Fry, with whom I had a date to dine last night but who was delayed by the *Queen Elizabeth*, made me go to his flat at seven for a drink. He is back from the States for three weeks, then returns for good. I thought it politic to see him. He was exactly the same as before, drunken and boastful. He says I must stay with him next year in New York – I would sooner die than do such a thing – and write a book on America. Why not on the world? I have spent little time in packing, hoping to supplement a scanty wardrobe in Rome.

At 4.40 Emily, good soul, called me to say my bath was ready. It was pitch dark but a hired Rolls came punctually. I picked up a dear old lady, but at Terminal House discovered that we were on different aeroplanes. Mine did not leave the airport till eight. A sunny morning. From the air one sees that London is sprinkled with reservoirs, as though the metropolis were in flood. The fields and hills of Kent are wreathed in mist like dirty snow, but I watch the sun literally scoop the mist away. Over Deal we run through a dark storm and there are splashes of rain against the glass windows. I think how lumbering and slow aeroplanes are, like old buses. I wonder they do not take longer than they do. Apart from the clicking of ears I am unaffected by change of altitude. In an hour and a quarter we circle over Brussels and land. And there is Geoff Lemprière, with whom I have barely time to exchange greetings and be handed by him two yellow pills to take over the Alps. There is no time for breakfast, and I have coffee and an apple at a bar. We immediately change into another Sabena, rather an old machine, and in no time are off. The journey is foolproof, yet there is much hanging about. I am writing this in the air over France, at a great altitude, rising every minute over dense forests. It is getting cold. In spite of the height we are not in the sun, and there is a leaden canopy overhead. I wish they would bring me something to eat.

We find ourselves over the Rhône because they say the weather is too bad to risk the Alps. Here it is clouding over and becoming misty. How long the Rhône is. We follow it for quite three-quarters of an hour, and as there are hills on either side it is not very agreeable. We seem to be on a level with the tops of them. Passing Marseilles and over the sea it becomes stormy. Angry purple clouds gather. It is becoming bumpy. Many passengers are sick, and it is considered a bad journey. Somehow I don't feel at all sick. After the bumps it is smooth again. There is not the horrid rhythmical roughness of the sea. Then we turn back and there is some difficulty landing at Marseilles at 2.45. We stay at the airport till 6.30. Every kind of inanity takes place. All our luggage from the aeroplane is taken to the *douane* and the French go through our bags, which are then returned to the plane. At last rooms are found for us at Cassis, fifty kilometres away. The bus driver loses the way, and we do not arrive till nine. We dine and are sent to a tiny lodgement to sleep. A terrible storm gets up in the night and at 6 a.m. we are woken up with a bowl of nasty acorn coffee and hard black pellets of bread.

All the telephone wires are on the ground and the battery of the bus has been allowed to run down. We cannot therefore go to Marseilles to catch a train, and the weather is too bad to fly, so we may have to stay here another night. At seven I walk into the town. All the fishermen's boats in the quay are smashed by the storm. It is a nice little old town, endurable no doubt in sunny weather, but with no buildings of any distinction. There is hopelessness, inefficiency and depravity in the faces and mien of the French here. Many of my fellow passengers say they will never again travel by air.

This unexpected visit to Cassis is like a story by Rose Macaulay. We are cooped up in a horrid hotel, cut off from the world. Inevitably the party separates into little groups of companionable malcontents. The nun, to whom our misfortunes are attributed, is left severely alone. So is the Roumanian suffering from asthma. My group, which is by far the best, consists of an American of Italian extraction who speaks indifferent English, is President of some international company, cashes cheques and drinks steadily; an English-born girl, Mrs Gregory, married to an American pilot, and a Russian lady, age about fifty, who lives in Milan. We become intimate friends and are quickly on Christian name terms. With one it looks as though I shall be on still more intimate terms before another twelve hours have elapsed.

In the afternoon we hire a taxi to Marseilles and at the Air France office discover that our aeroplane was damaged on the ground during the storm last night and we certainly cannot leave before tomorrow. We despatch cables and telegrams and drink dubonnet and eat good cakes at a café, watching the crowds of ugly, shoddy, sullen, hard-faced, hostile Frenchmen and women. When we communicate with them they are unsympathetic, un-cooperative and prone to cheat us. We dislike them. On our return to the hotel at Cassis there is a fearful row with the taxi-driver who, supported by the proprietor and his wife, certainly would cheat us, did we not prevail. The consequence is that the hotel staff is uniformly unpleasant for the rest of our stay. But we are the enforced guests of Sabena Air Line. During dinner my group becomes still more intimate: the Russian confesses that she has loved her husband consistently for thirty years; the American that he has loved his wife for six months and now has mistresses whenever they are available; Mrs. Gregory that she has had two husbands, plans to have a third, and, looking me straight between the eyes, indicates that she intends to have me tonight as a sort of supplementary. I have nothing to confess, at least in this company.

Saturday, 27th September

To my horror, we were called this morning at 4.45, in fact just after I had got back to my own bedroom, like a thief in the night. Consequently I am dog tired all day. We are given a horrid breakfast at the big hotel. The black bread is barely eatable, the acorn coffee barely drinkable. There is no butter and no milk. Poor Mrs G., having as I alone know had no more sleep than I had, is in despair how to feed her baby of under two. I do not know how babies in this country are able to survive. We drive in the charabanc to Marseilles airport and leave at nine. We fly over huge, ugly Marseilles, and over that sink of iniquity Cassis, and Toulon where the sunk battleships in the harbour are clearly visible, just as I recollect having seen an aerial photograph taken of them after the sinking during the war. There are still clouds and lightning storms, and over Lombardy there are low, fleecy white clouds, pierced by shafts of sun like sharp lances. The fields are inundated by the torrential rain of the past days. We make for Bergamo but turn back because they tell us we may land at Milan after all. We are the first plane to do so for three days. Here we wait four hours. I decide not to stay in Milan after all since there is a spare seat on the plane to Rome. So at the risk of incurring further expense I, with the kind assistance of the officials and a friendly Italian traveller, book the seat, for which I am to pay at the other end. There are only coffee and biscuits to drink and eat here, but both taste delicious, and the Italians are politer, just as they are cleaner than the Frogs.

At 2.30 Mrs. G., her child and I, the 'incommunicada' nun and the kind, silly Italian traveller get into a Lai plane and fly for Rome. We are the only passengers from the lot who started from London. The weather over the plain of Lombardy is clear. The country looks incredibly neat, smiling and gracious. The Po is yellow as ochre. I suppose there are few sights more beautiful than the country between Milan and Rome on a fine day with intermittent clouds, seen from 9,000 feet. Stepping out in Rome one is struck as by the air of a conservatory. An American friend greets Mrs. G. and by some extraordinary act of generosity which I do not understand settles my extra fare, plus 700 lire for excess luggage, as though I had been a guardian angel and not a wicked seducer. Simply do not understand. Yet I cannot like this tall, middle-aged, slouching, oh-yahing and utterly philistine American friend. Nor do I care for the husband, when we meet him, nor the newly-furnished flat with its ferns, laced window curtains, spanking walnut dining-room suite, and plethora of silver mugs. They are all very kind to me however, and even send me in their car, after profuse goodbyes (Mrs. G.'s slightly guarded perhaps) to the Hotel de Ville where I am staying. Here I wash and try to undeafen myself before calling on the Moores at the Hassler next door. Joan welcomes me with an embrace and Garrett orders himself a drink which he has in his dressing-gown on the terrace of their room overlooking the Spanish Steps. I dine alone in my hotel for 1170 lire, a fearful price.

Sunday, 28th September

Sleep soundly after my debauch and succession of early rises. It is terribly hot all day and I have brought the wrong clothes. Garrett calls me and I go round to the Hassler where poor Joan is in bed with a bad stomach-ache and cannot get up. So Garrett and I walk to the Villa Medici, but cannot see inside it. Then we walk down the Via Sistina to the Baths of Diocletian. Here Garrett with great efficiency engages a guide who turns out to be educated and knowledgeable. For an hour and a half he conducts us round the sculpture gallery. I like the mosaics, particularly the Grecian one of a skeleton and the tag, 'Know Thyself'. I lunch with the Moores in their bedroom, then have a siesta till four, sleeping soundly. Garrett wakes me up rudely by walking into my room. We go off to Santa Maria Maggiore. The Sangallo ceiling in gold, the eighth-century mosaics, which almost make me sick with excitement. Then we walk to San Pietro in Vincoli to look at the Moses, as colossal in aggression as in conception. Here there is a tomb, no, it is in San Clemente, of Cardinal Roverella dated 1476 which is pure Renaissance. Such a thing I have never seen in my life before. In another church immediately beneath this one are the remains of a Roman plaster ceiling in square panels and one long panel of arabesques very similar to the tomb which unconsciously followed it hundreds of years later. These underground basilicas are immensely impressive and moving. I dined at a *trattoria* very well. With wine it cost me 800 lire. Then sat and talked to Joan.

Monday, 29th September

It is a step to the Pincio gardens where I walked in the early morning – holm oaks, statuary, fountains and horse-drawn *carozze*. I looked at the Pantheon, the prototype of so much I love and endeavour to preserve. The most complete Roman building, I suppose in the world – the interior a cosmos in miniature like something pendant from the heavens, columns of *giallo antico* and *pavonezzetta* and porphyry floor. The emptiness, the solemnity of this extraordinary globe. Then I looked at the Cancelleria Palace, the church in it by Bramante, the *cortile* of the palace so chaste and beautiful. Lunched alone at another *trattoria* and after a siesta met Garrett and Sarah Churchill. We looked at Santa Maria della Pace, the cloisters there by Bramante, likewise austere, and within the church Raphael walls and a chapel with 'overladen reliefs' – according to my Murray – by Simone Mosca. We then drove to the Capitol where Sarah left us. She, an intelligent girl, has lived in Rome six months and yet has never been to the Pantheon, or St. Peter's. Her skin is translucent like alabaster. Garrett and I looked at the outside of Michelangelo's piazza and palaces, Marcus Aurelius's equestrian statue (traces of gold paint still visible on the horse's head) and the Forum, and the Mamertine prison in which St. Peter was incarcerated. I never need go to the last place again.

Tuesday, 30th September

So hot that I bitterly regret not having brought more suitable clothes, but this afternoon walked in my shirt and a pull-over without a jacket. Found Peter Tunnard's tailor, Ciro, who will make me a suit for the equivalent of £30, which I am to pay in England. Walked to St. Peter's. I think Mussolini was right to pull down the old buildings in the Borgo for now one can for the first time see the basilica, dome and all, from the Ponte Sant' Angelo. What a mistake the Latin cross was, and how angry Bramante and Michelangelo would have been. I was too tired to join Garrett and Joan this afternoon and, after a siesta, walked to San Pietro in Montorio. The best evening view of Rome is from the Janiculum; the best morning view from the Pincio, with the sun behind one. I walked along the Tiber, looking at six or seven palaces.

Wednesday, 1st October

Walked to the Palazzo Doria, stopping at the Trevi Fountain, that rococo delight, on the way. At ten o'clock Prince Doria greeted me. He is so exceedingly polite and smiling that I deduce he shuns intimacies. He is rather bent from the waist like an old apple tree. He has had tuberculosis of the spine, poor man, and was tortured by Mussolini, I believe. His Princess, with broad Scotch accent, like a comfortable nanny, is an angel. To my surprise we were joined by Garrett and Barbara Rothschild, brought by the friendly Italian father of Yvonne Hamilton, whom they call Papageno. For two hours we were shown round the *piano nobile* of this gigantic and gloomy palace. Pictures v. important. Memling and Lippi and to crown all the Velasquez of Pope Innocent X. Beautiful rich Genoese velvet stuffs, curtains and chair covers. Some curtains of a Neapolitan yellow ground. Some terra cotta wall hangings, others crimson and brown. The grisaille ceilings in arabesques poor. In one room stands the Pope's velvet covered throne turned to the wall, a customary protest among the Roman nobility against the Pope's incarceration within the Vatican city in 1870. A few princes only have the right to invite the Pope to their palaces. Another princely privilege among the Black Nobility is the Baldacchino (the Doria one sheltering the portrait of Innocent X) on either side of which repose the velvet cushion and umbrella carried in the Prince's carriage in case he meets the Pope's equipage in the street. In which event he is obliged to descend and kneel, if needs be, in the rain and mud. Nearly all the gilded furniture in the Palace is swathed with thick leather case covers. Prince Doria says that only the Palazzo Colonna is still inhabited as a private dwelling by the family, in addition to his own.

At 12.15 we parted and I looked at the Palazzo Vidoni, Palazzo Linotte and Palazzo Lante. Then went to the flat the Moores have been lent for two days in the via Margutta. Sir D'Arcy Osborne and Barbara Rothschild were there. After luncheon we questioned Sir D'Arcy about the Vatican. He said he had the highest opinion of Vatican diplomacy although the Vatican was not as well informed on foreign affairs as might be expected. The Pope [Pius XII] was a saint, and had the charm of our Queen Elizabeth. He was now launching into unequivocal condemnation of Communism. He had hated the war and went to every endeavour to end it. But so rigidly did he maintain his neutrality that he pleased no one. Far from being Machiavellian the Cardinals were the kindest of men. Sir D'Arcy ought to know, having spent the whole war shut up in the Vatican, and being an unprejudiced Protestant to boot.

This evening I walked miles, past the Quirinale and the Colosseum to the Tiber, finding myself beside the temples of Fortuna Virile and Vesta, two of the best preserved in Rome. I walk everywhere, intending to know every street and square inch of the old city before I leave. Dining with the Moores Barbara Rothschild said that Garrett and I made the oddest spectacle walking the streets on Sunday, two of the tallest, slimmest and seemingly most disdainful men who could not be anything but English. The Moores and Barbara all leave tomorrow, and I shall miss them.

Thursday, 2nd October

A rather lonely day. Not one of the seven people to whom I have posted letters of introduction has so far replied. The only letter I get is one from Sibyl Colefax asking me to bring her back a pair of shoes. I spent the whole morning in S. Maria del Popolo. A treasure house for the student of the Renaissance. Then walked through Vignola's gate up the straight drive of the Villa Borghese to the Casino. I believe that the balustrade still in the forefront of the house is the original one and that Lord Astor took away the other balustrade on the garden side, without replacing it. At any rate the brick fillings at Cliveden should not be left in their nakedness but be plastered and washed over.

In the evening I walked miles again to the Baths of Caracalla where Shelley wrote *Prometheus Unbound*. Was disgusted by its condition. It has become a dump for old war *matériel* and barbed wire. There is no romance about it, no vegetation, no clinging vine or trailing ivy.

Inelegant, naked brick ruins bore me. I continued to the Porta Latina, looking at the tiny chapel, reputedly by Bramante, of S. Giovanni in Oleo, octagonal, brick-filled, dated 1509, with a wide terra cotta frieze of large honeysuckles and a stone finial capping the whole. There were motor-bicycle trials in progress, and discords rent the air.

At Rampoldi's this evening for a drink I was introduced to Prince Wolkonsky, a middle-aged silly, who said he would cash my travellers' cheques at the black market rate which is far more favourable than the bank rate.

Friday, 3rd October

All night it poured with rain. This morning the rain fell in hard, straight prongs. I got up late, for where could I go? Also I am suffering from slight diarrhoea, a common complaint here. Barbara R. and Joan M. have both been victims. So I took a taxi to the Vatican Museum. On my return found an invitation to the Legation for luncheon tomorrow and another from Roger Hinks. At 9.30 Guy Ferrari came, but an interruption at the door frightened him. It turned out to be merely a telegram, not a police-man which G. for some extraordinary reason feared. He said he had momentarily forgotten that the Occupation was a thing of the past.

Saturday, 4th October

I was conducted by a guide with an inadequate electric torch down to the enormous Golden House of Nero below the Baths of Titus. It is dark, gloomy, muddy, full of rubbish, and sinister. But I was fascinated by the remains of Roman paintings, the arabesques which Raphael copied in the Loggie and which Adam studied when in Rome. He must have been let down through a hole on the end of a rope, with a candle in a lantern. My guide, an old ruffian, smelling of drink, was very informative in bad French. These arabesque fragments date from the first century AD. They represent birds, flowers, foliage. The Throne Room is barrel-vaulted and divided into squares, painted. There is no stucco.

At luncheon time I went to the Chancellery where I met Victor Perowne, the Minister to the Vatican, who motored me and Roger Hinks to luncheon in his house near the Baths of Caracalla. He is tall, languid, cultivated, slightly cynical, a typical British diplomat. His wife is a sad little thing, with a peaky face. After luncheon Perowne motored me to the Villa Madama, which is not open to the public but is being prepared for the head of the State. Saw the famous loggie begun by Raphael and Giulio Romano for Cardinal Giulio de Medici. The loggie are now glazed. They remind me of Adam's or rather Rose's stucco in the rotunda at Kedleston. They are unpainted and white. There is one deeply coved room painted in arabesques and two wooden panelled ceilings with Medici arms. Victor Perowne confirmed that the Pope's charm was overwhelming. His manner was affectionate. Unfortunately he seldom saw him. Dined with Sarah Churchill and the Duchess of Marlborough, a typical English lady, conventional, limited and hard, with large feet.

Sunday, 5th October

Sarah dined with me in a *trattoria*. Her beauty is of a very frail sort, her hair Botticelli gold. She is of a romantic disposition. There is something guileless about her, like Johnnie, and she will be the victim of disillusions. She says that Randolph, to whom she is devoted, is most unhappy. But then it is his own fault for being so objectionable to everyone he meets.

Monday, 6th October

A most glorious, translucent day, and hot again. I met Ruth Lowinsky at the Chancellery and we drove to S. Maria del Popolo. I have never seen a woman sweat so much, but she was wearing a thick tweed coat and skirt. Guy Ferrari came to see me in the evening and very nearly cried when I told him I was leaving on Friday. He said he wanted to become an 'English' architect, did not like Italians. But since he is one, was born and has always lived here and must go on living with his compatriots, I told him he could not be silly and must try to like them.

Tuesday, 7th October

Early this morning I walked very slowly through the Pincio and the Porta del Popolo to the Villa Papa Giulio. What a glorious surprise it was. It is a museum of Tuscan figurines, rather dreary and even ugly artefacts, but some fine Greek and Etruscan vases, amphora, kraters. The garden is laid out with stone screens. Arabesque stucco panels, steps leading down to a sunk water basin – alas, the fountains are dry – and caryatides upholding arches, too heavy for them. Stage scenery of rococo delights. Few people there at this early hour. On the garden side of the casino is a hemicycle colonnade, decorated with painted *treillage* work of vines, cupids, peacocks, storks – what James Adam, I believe, condescendingly described in his diary as 'vastly well for the country'. It is one of the prettiest scenes of fantasy I have seen in Rome.

Alice Gainsborough and her son, Gerry, turned up this morning and I got rooms for them in my hotel. We walked to the Pincio for tea. I dined with Roger Hinks at an extremely good restaurant where we were given lots of butter. Apropos of contemporary art books he complained that it was considered fashionable and gentlemanlike to be inaccurate, and this drives him mad. He was full of complaints and, like Guy, dislikes the Italians.

Wednesday, 8th October

Tried again to leave my note on Sarah, but at 9.30 got no answer when I rang at her door high up on the topmost floor of the Palazzo Buonaparte – I had tried with Roger Hinks last night with no success. So I proceeded rather unhappily to the Capitoline and entered the museums. Looked idly at the sculpture, but not seriously. It is foolish to go to galleries on the mere chance of finding something that may interest one. One should go with a definite quarry in view, and then allow one's interests to be distracted, provided one returns to pursuit of said quarry afterwards. Then I ate three delicious iced cakes and drank orange juice, and visited my tailor. Lady Gainsborough and Gerry lunched at a *trattoria*. They have no interest in profane Rome whatsoever, only in sacred Rome. They have fixed up an audience with the Pope for themselves and for me on Saturday, but I cannot stay till then.

After a happy siesta, induced by copious white wine, I walked to the Protestant Cemetery. I have a sore throat today and am starting a cold. Damn! The lovely sad spot has horrid blocks of flats built up to its walls. From within one can hear the squeal of trams like the shrieks of the damned from inside the gates of paradise. For the Cemetery is enclosed within a barren, soulless, squalid suburb. Nevertheless it retains its special peace, serenity and poignancy. I picked a shred of box from Keats's grave and of lonicera (inappropriate shrub) from Shelley's. This was the only way I could pay my respects. I had nothing to give them. So I took from them, as I have taken all my life. There is something presumptuous in Trelawny's officious proximity to Shelley's remains; but Severn's to Keats's is touching, and well earned.

Then I rang up Sarah, and hurray! she said she would dine. After a cocktail at the hotel we dined at Nino's. How good it all was. She has a way with her which melts the susceptible hearts of Italians. We ordered prosciutto and salami, and her favourite dish of grilled turkey, wrapped in bacon, with cheese over it. We drank much red wine. It was a successful evening. She is bright, independent, bohemian, yet elegant, which is a welcome contradiction. She has a sense of humour and poise, awful word, but what other is there? She is quite uneducated, which is strange considering who she is. She is dedicated to her own art however. She explained to me why she loved Rome. She does no sightseeing and has no understanding of architecture. She says it is the movements of the city which she relishes: movements of the statues, the fountains, the bridges, the curves of façades of churches, the actions of

the Romans in the streets, and even the mudguards of the *carozze*. I
really am intrigued by her. I walked her home and was amused by the
impression this blond beauty, apparently unnoticing, makes upon the
staring, lascivious Italians.

Thursday, 9th October

My cold is worse. I had a night of fever and sweated like Mrs. Lowinsky.
It thundered and today is raining intermittently. I have done little, feeling
ill. I called on Sarah in her garret at the Palazzo Buonaparte, just to see
how she lives. It is charming, right under the eaves: only two little rooms.
Then she dropped me at the Palazzo Rospigliosi where I lunched with
Sir D'Arcy Osborne. There were Monsignor Hemmick and Count Eddie
Bismarck. The first is a worldly prelate, cackling and gossiping like an old
woman, yet just avoiding scandalous talk; the other a middle-aged sissy,
the younger brother of Prince Otto who figures so prominently in
Ciano's *Diary*. Sir D.'s apartments are spacious, dark and cool, his *salone*
dating from the seventeenth century. Amused I listened with flapping ears
but closed mouth to the gush of gossip about people of whom I knew
nothing. Harold Acton has arrived in Rome today by air from Ireland.
He left Birr yesterday evening. He and I and Roger Hinks dined in the
restaurant in the Palazzo Colonna.

Friday, 10th October

All day it poured with rain and my cold was at its height. Harold walked
up to the hotel at 10.30 and we went to the American Express. He then
lunched with me at the hotel. What exquisite manners he has, never
intruding, deferring to women with charm and attention. And what is
going on in his mind all the while? He lives for literature, the arts and
things of the mind. At 1.30 I left for Florence. Sarah telephoned before
my departure.

   At the Grand Hotel I have a luxurious room with bath, overlooking
the Arno and Bellosguardo. Geoff Lemprière and his Italian business
agent, boring man, met me. We dined and walked round the Duomo and
down the Arno in the lamp-light. I was horrified by the amount of bomb
damage around the Ponte Vecchio, of which the houses in the middle
have been destroyed. Geoffrey, who is a good fellow but by no means a
highbrow, has the irritating qualities of the perpetual schoolboy. He will
be facetious without ever being witty.

Saturday, 11th October

In the morning visited the Duomo and San Lorenzo. The first cold and
brown, almost ugly inside. Donatello figure on south wall of Joshua

redeems all. Dome pineapple shape. The second so full of treasures that a
cursory visit leaves the mind in turmoil, not to be expressed.

The last time I was in Florence was 1937. The first time 1927. I was
with Hoel Llewellyn, fresh from Eton. We drove from the station to a
remote and squalid door which was opened by a sinister gentleman in
dirty pyjamas. We instantly decided the address we had been given was a
house of ill fame and terrified, silly little fools, turned on our heels dragging our luggage, having dismissed the taxi.

Most of this afternoon I slept, feeling rotten. In the evening met
Hamish [St. Clair-Erskine] in the Grand Hotel and had drinks with him.
As he was going to stay at Berenson's I gave him my letter of introduc-
tion. He returns on Tuesday to Venice where he too is staying with the
Chavchavadzes, so I was able to give him a letter to George likewise.

Sunday, 12th October

A lovely, clear, keen autumnal day, in so far as there is any sense of the
seasons here. I am feeling better. Drove to San Miniato, listened to a Mass
and sat for an hour ensconced in one of the deep walnut choirstalls.
Seldom have I seen a more exquisite church, eleventh-century;
Byzantine mosaics in the apse; tabernacle by Michelozzo, soffit of glazed
terracotta, sea-blue ground with white rosettes by Della Robbia. Marble
pulpit Romanesque. Then drove with Geoff to Fiesole duomo; afternoon
the Bardia, Fiesole.

Geoffrey and the business man left early, to my intense relief. Once
more I am on my own. At 12.40 the Berenson car called to take me to I
Tatti to lunch with this grand old man, of whom I am mortally frightened. I found Raymond Mortimer there, very friendly. He told Berenson
that we had known each other for twenty years and he hoped I valued
his friendship. Signorina Mariano lives here as hostess. Sweet woman
who relieves tension and makes one happy. She said she had received six
letters from Sibyl about me. l apologised. Then in came the great man.
The great man is a tiny man, white-bearded and eighty. Looks frail and
tired, and is neat. When he speaks he speaks to the point. No irrelevan-
cies, no pleasantries. I felt very shy and was tongue-tied. He saw at once
that I had nothing to communicate to him. But I was fascinated by listening to his talk to others. My fellow guest was Mrs. Bliss, a grand Henry
Jamesian lady, old, and described as a wise goose. Berenson is tiresome in
that he is very conscious of being the famous art-dictator and sage, surrounded by applauding disciples. This expectancy of deference does not
make for ease. And no small talk is allowed. After all a modicum of small
talk does oil the wheels. In stony silence he dismisses a conventional
advance as a triviality, which it doubtless is. When he talks he demands

attention, and is not the least averse to obsequious confirmation of his utterances. He speaks scoffingly of religion and observers of the Christian principles, like T.S. Eliot. In the late afternoon while the others were having siestas I wandered into the library. I have never seen a larger private library. Every art book published must be here. And portfolios of every known work of art recorded. I took out a book about the Villa Madama, Rome, and read it on the terrace. Probably this was against the rules. Before tea Raymond and I strolled up the hill, he expatiating upon the beauty of the grey-green landscape. I thought the little brown farm-houses, villas and villinos dotted upon the hills were what constituted the Italian landscape, which is essentially suburban, the very quality which in England we consider an affront to our landscape.

During tea in the loggia Berenson sat in the full sun, talking of London. I asked him if he had not thought London beautiful before 1914. He said No, the mews were filthy slums, the fogs were stifling, and the number of drunk women and their smell overpowering. Talked about the Italian temperament. When Italians complained to him that the Americans were plutocrats, he told them they were heliocrats. He is a little deaf. He conveyed to me the impression of a great man striving to be something which he isn't. Perhaps he wishes he were an aristocratic connoisseur, and not a self-made professional expert.

Tuesday, 14th October

This morning Santa Croce. Ugly 1860 marble front. Wonderful things within an unsympathetic building – Giotto frescoes, door by Michelozzo into the corridor, and the Pazzi Chapel surpassing words. To the Bargello. By noon everything shut, virtually for the rest of the daylight.

At 4.30 Peter Rodd and Adelaide Lubbock, who are staying at the Grand because their car has broken its axle, shared a taxi with me to the Villa Pietra. For the first time I met old Mr. and Mrs. Acton, he very English, she very American, with white hair, pretty, pencilled eyebrows, and bearing no resemblance to Harold either in looks or speech. They nag at Harold and ask him to fetch the ash-trays, to ring the bell, to turn on and off lights and generally fag. All this he does with good humour as a matter of course. The garden, entirely made by Mr. Acton out of nothing, is ideal, straight walks between evergreen trees, with copious statuary, some very good, and stone gateways. In many respects the love-liest garden I have ever seen. The villa is sixteenth-century, compact, large, stuccoed and washed a pale lemon. It is so full of works of art and primitives that it gives you a headache. It is splendid, but not cosy. Dined tonight with Peter and Adelaide Lubbock. They were gay and entertain-ing. I had thought I disliked Peter, but I now discern a latent charm. His

knowledge of Roman and mediaeval history is stupendous, but his delivery is relentless and boring. He has inspired me to devote myself to a
course of Gibbon and Gregorovius.

Wednesday, 15th October

Cold over except for catarrh which vitiates taste and makes smells of
tobacco and petrol like hell's sulphur. Walked this morning to Santo
Spirito, the purest Renaissance church in Florence after San Miniato. The
continuous arcade of Corinthian columns at the crossing really is like a
forest of smooth tree trunks. Met Peter and Mrs. L. at a small *trattoria*. She
said she was suffering from Primitive indigestion. Ate succulent chicken
breasts.

Every Englishman seems to come to this hotel at some time or
another. This afternoon I met David Horner with Osbert Sitwell. The
latter walks with a stick like Malcolm Bullock. His voice resembles
Sachie's, low and modulated. He is of heavy build, with a strong
Hanoverian face, straight grey hair running back from the forehead. He
shakes hands with a large, soft, yet firm grip. I dined with the Moores at
their little house in Costa di San Giorgio, rented from Mrs. Leith. Besides
Barbara Rothschild (impossible not to love) there were Una Lady
Trowbridge and Julian Amery, who sat next to each other. I, being short-
sighted, was surprised when approaching Lady T. to shake hands, to discover she was not a man. She wears close-cropped, straight white hair;
small earrings it is true, but a man's dinner jacket and black bow tie. She
lives entirely in the past and talks of Miss Radclyffe Hall as 'John'. 'John'
and I did this and that. She told Garrett all about the prosecution case
over *The Well of Loneliness* and the way the two of them had been per-
secuted. She spoke intelligently of D'Annunzio. She is a devout Papist
and believes in miracles. Said she was now always lonely and unhappy,
yet preferred a good climate without friends to a bad one, like England,
with them. To my embarrassment I saw her turn to Amery and heard her
ask, 'Are you the brother of the boy they hanged?' Then she expressed to
him her feelings on that subject. I walked her back to her very small
albergo on the Lung 'Arno.

Thursday, 16th October

The Pitti Palace is full of middle-aged spinsters making miniature copies
of the Raphael Madonnas and, if one so much as looks over their shoulders, trying to sell them to one. Like Hampton Court there are too many
state rooms in a line, broken by no passages. Found Prodd and Mrs. L.
still in the hotel awaiting a new axle; we lunched again at our cheap and
good *trattoria* where the charming waiter looks like Oliver Messel and

runs up to our table with a skip and a jump, showing very white teeth. I saw them off in their car and went and read *The Moonstone* in the Cascine, very uncomfortably, for in Italy there seem to be no benches with backs to them, only cold marble slabs at the best.

Harold gave me dinner tonight. He walked all the way from his parents' villa, carrying a large stick with a knob in case of trouble late at night. An excellent dinner; felt rather sick through over-eating. We walked down the Via Tornabuoni along the Arno, through the Palazzo Uffizi arcade and past the Palazzo Vecchio. Harold taught me to appreciate the enduring monumentality of this building. We walked down the Via San Gallo and after admiring the Palazzo Pandolfini, parted there.

Observations on Florence. (1) Walks at night, when the main streets are empty and quiet. Narrow, tortuous streets are mysterious and forbidding by lamp- and particularly by moon-light. Then you can appreciate the vast, rugged, abstract beauty of the palaces in the sharp shadows of semi-darkness. Things not noticeable by day loom into sight. Here a window pediment, there an armorial escutcheon suspended over a doorway. (2) Although mercifully the chief monuments have escaped the fighting the spirit of Florence has been very seriously impaired by the destruction of the bridges and houses along the Arno. (3) The Florentines are not quite so beautiful, nor so lively, as the Romans. (4) A Vespa (motor scooter) would be an ideal vehicle in London, nipping in and out of the lumbering traffic and the queues.

On my return on foot along the Arno I met the handsome young Italian who had been in the hotel with a party of tiresome English people last night. He was sitting on the embankment wall tapping the stone with his heels. Very sweet he was. He took me in a taxi to the Porta Latina where we got out and walked arm-in-arm towards the pitch darkness of the Boboli Gardens, which were shut now. 'But I know a way in,' he said, 'and we shall have it entirely to ourselves.' We did. When we parted I walked home under the stars. I salute his evanescent youth and beauty.

Observation (5) Berenson is a vain, blasphemous, tricky Jew. (6) Made before: the Italians don't like sitting down, nor do they mind about comfort.

Friday, 17th October

I write this on my bed at the Hotel Touring, Milan, waiting for Geoff to turn up. I hope he does soon for I hate this soulless commercial hotel and this vast, evil and ugly city. Instead of stopping at Bologna on my way I took the eleven o'clock *rapido* straight here, an easy journey, having paid a last visit to San Lorenzo and that lovely sacristy with the 'intarsia' wooden pews, and the very dull Duomo interior and the supercilious

Joshua by Donatello. For five shillings I bought en route a carton of spaghetti, not very good, roast chicken still warm, chip potatoes, half a bottle of Chianti and an apple, and was happy. Why the hell can one not do this on an English train journey?

I walked to the Milan Duomo: the vertical perspective seen from the north-west striking; the west façade unsuccessful. Entering is like plunging into a very dense forest. Always dark, now that so much of the stained glass has gone it is darker still because the missing windows are boarded up. People move about mysteriously, but one can study nothing in detail. I strained my eyes at the St. Bartholomew flayed, carrying his own skin over one arm and looking perfectly nonchalant and composed, like Anthony Eden.

(7) The Italians are working like blacks rebuilding their bridges and small towns, badly destroyed between Florence and here. They are a nation of stonemasons. The new houses are mostly traditional and decent, if plain.

Geoffrey arrived at eight having been delayed by fog. I was as glad to see him today as I was glad to see him depart from Florence. We went straight to the Galleria, dined and listened to the band who were all enjoying themselves, singing and playing and singing in turns. We looked at the spot in the Duomo square where Mussolini and La Petacci's bodies were ignominiously exposed. But no sign of the petrol-filling station.

Saturday, 18th October

This morning we went to Santa Maria delle Grazie which has been fearfully bombed, but is in process of restoration. So well done that you can barely tell which parts are new. Interesting to compare the terra cotta work on the apse by Bramante with our similar and almost coeval stuff in England, such as the tombs and screen in Oxburgh church, which derives from it. The Cenacola, badly damaged, was not visible. Then to Sant'Ambrogio to see the atrium, an interesting survival of the old basilica. Detail here very Byzantine. I insisted upon visiting Sant 'Eustorgio to see the Portinari chapel by Michelozzo. It is as gracious and sweet as all his tabernacles and chapels, but has been altered to some extent since built. The plaster decorations down the piers and the reliefs upon the frieze of angels with bells, all coloured. The sacristan showed us with relish the grizzled black head of St. Peter the Martyr, much decomposed, the flesh like old, hard, untreated leather. It occurred to me that Guy's comely black head might resemble the Martyr's in 400 years' time. Geoff left for Rome at 1 o'clock and I for Venice at 2.45. Had a horrid journey standing much of the time, or diving into the restaurant car for drinks, chiefly to get a temporary rest on a seat.

Reached Venice at 8.10. Already dark. To my great relief was met by the Chavchavadze's gondolier at the station, who said, 'La Principessa ha detto che Lei era grand' uomo.' This made me happy, not because I was a tall man, but because I was recognised. What a lovely gondola! Jet black and sumptuously upholstered with brass figureheads at either side, brightly polished, crests and a coronet and black silk ropes and tassels. There is etiquette about gondolas too. The gondolier sees that you sit in the proper seat. When you accompany the Princess, her seat is on the right, yours on the left; and you, the man, must get out first. The first gondolier, wearing livery with wide sailor's collar, brass buttons, striped waistcoat, knee breeches, a beretta with big, black pom, takes the prow. Behind him stands Mario, the second gondolier. There can be few things more romantic, more transporting from this dismal modern age, than to find yourself at dead of night, under the stars and dim spangled lamps, skimming down the small canals, the gondoliers shouting, 'Hoih! hoih!' as you approach a corner. Rhythmically, swiftly you glide, your wake gently lapping the palaces, faster seemingly down the narrow canals, slower into the Grand Canal, where indeed the romance is not lessened, if anything intensified at this hour by the noisy *vaporetti*, whose rough wake rocks the gondola and rudely smacks against the prow. Never once do the *gondolieri* pause. We reached the Palazzo Polignac, very sombre in the darkness, its great striped *pali* rising from the water at the steps. This is a fine Lombardi palace and the Chavchavadzes rent the second and top floors, which are splendid and high. There are many servants, all male, silent and respectful.

We dined at 9 o'c, the Cs' usual hour. George delighted to see me and as charming as ever. Elizabeth, bigger than before. Hamish and a young 'cellist staying. A brigadier and wife, a daughter of Bourne & Hollingsworth, dreary folk, came to dinner. When they left we talked till two.

Sunday, 19th October

I woke at 9.30 and rang for coffee and fruit. My room is large, with a floor of scagliola, a large bed with white and gold posts, raised on a dais, the windows looking up the Grand Canal through the high-arched Accademia bridge to the Palazzo Fornari, and down the Canal towards the Salute. Elizabeth says Venice is so fragile that each time she returns, it is with relief that she finds it still there, and not dissolved. How long can it survive, its huge palaces supported on wooden piles? She and I went to the steps of the Piazzetta in the gondola, and walked to High Mass in St. Mark's, standing tightly wedged, for Mass was said by the Patriarch himself on account of the visit of St. Somebody from Hungary, his 700th anniversary. He was behind us in a glass case, embalmed and wearing red gloves and slippers. I did not feel in the least devout. There is a cold wind blowing through the *calle*. But we were sheltered and warm, drinking coffee in the Piazza.

Monday, 20th October

It is distinctly cold. In the Palazzo large wood fires are lit, and the stoves are being cleaned out. Walking in Venice today I caught, mingling with the smell of fruit and the moist, excretal smell of the lesser canals which I love, a scent of firewood that is faintly English and preposterous. I am not taking my sight-seeing very seriously here. I did too much of it in Rome and Florence. Furthermore, I am luxuriating in the comfort and superb meals of the palazzo, the flow of wine and the late hours. The first night at dinner there were, after martinis with fresh lemon peel in them, white and red wine and two sorts of champagne. After soup there is invariably a fish or some such course before the meat. After tea I sit upstairs in George's attic while he practises the piano. Then at eight have a bath. This afternoon Hamish with the 'cellist, Dimitri Marcovitch, who is twenty-five and of some renown, went by gondola to look for Tiepolos in the Madonna del Orto and San Giovanni in Bragora. Hamish says that Mario, who stands at the helm of the gondola, looks as proud and beautiful as Michelangelo's Adam.

Wednesday, 22nd October

Today George motored Hamish and me to the Villa Maser. George's car would not start and a typical Russian scene ensued for an hour, of George shouting, his Mexican valet, the two gondoliers, five garage men and ten small boys pushing and offering advice. The battery was flat. Finally we got off. The car is an enormous American Cadillac. On arrival we were told that our hostess was away with her father, Count Volpi, who is dying. Her daughter, Esmeralda, acted hostess. She is a lovely girl of twenty, with black hair piled on the top of her head, olive complexion, the reddest lips, and prune dark eyes with velvety lashes. We arrived at 2.15 for luncheon. I had heard so much about the Villa Maser that I was disappointed. I know it to be one of the great dwellings of the world, the work of three outstanding artists, Palladio, Veronese, Vittoria. But it presents a cardboardy appearance and is over-restored. The Veronese rooms are approached upstairs, on the *piano nobile*, which at the rear leads straight to a little enclosed court, with central pool, semi-circular arcade with statues in niches, grotto and a maiden spouting water into the pool through her breasts. The villa is built on a steep slope. Vittoria's stuccowork inside has lost its crisp mouldings because too often repainted or lime-washed. The Veronese rooms are of course superb in conception, but the execution is not entirely satisfactory. Nevertheless they are extremely pretty. The colours vary in a dozen shades of green and yellow. The whole is light and cheerful.

The landscape in front of the villa is rather dull, but the little church is delightful. A rotunda, with two projecting square towers, a round, stepped dome with cupola, and a Corinthian portico of marble columns, the capitals connected by stone swags of carved foliage. The interior is circular with balustraded gallery running just under the dome. The quality of Vittoria's stucco here is far better than in the villa. George was a trifle upset that I was not more enthusiastic about Maser.

Friday, 24th October

The sun has gone. It is grey and cold. Paid a visit to the Biblioteca Marciana. Palladio called it Sansovino's masterpiece. Vittoria's stuccowork is by no means as refined as that of the Adam brothers. No wonder they despised Palladio's interiors. Visited the inside of San Francesco della Vigna. One chapel decorated by Vittoria shows that he could be less of an artist than Oliver Messel. In the afternoon the gondola took me and the Mexican to see the two Palladio churches across the water. In the niches of Il Redentore are painted wooden silhouettes of saints, rather like the Jacobean figure doorstops at Knole, a form of statuary I have not seen elsewhere in Italy.

Many, too many people came to the Palazzo this evening. I remained silent. I do not find Elizabeth Chavchavadze very sympathetic, and polite and kind though she is to me, I think I bore her.

Saturday, 25th October

I left for England today. It was raining hard in Venice, and was cold. Hamish, Dimitri and Elizabeth accompanied me to the station in the gondola under the *felze*, which was put up. It was like riding in a sedan chair. They left for their tour to Bologna.

Thursday, 30th October

An American girl in the train between Dover and Victoria, her first sight of England, said to me, 'My, what a number of chimneys! In our country we may have one chimney to each house; here it must be one chimney to each room.' That is one manifestation of England's cosiness before the war when every chimney would be smoking. Now the grates are empty, or nearly so. Tonight I went to the Albert Hall in the Rosses' box to hear Bruno Walter conduct the London Philharmonic – three glorious symphonies of Beethoven. The Eshers entered, and he said to me, 'You are to go to Harewood at once. The Princess Royal has been on tenterhooks, awaiting your return from Italy.' Then, 'You will have to treat her with less of your usual easy-go-lucky manner, my lad.'

Sunday, 2nd November

In the train to Evesham I talked to an old English woman just returned from Germany where she had been staying with her sister, married to a German landowner outside Cologne. She was still in a state of shock from what she had seen and enraged against the Allies for keeping the Germans starved. Where, she kept saying, does the food go to? Her sister's family eat day after day boiled carrots and potatoes at every meal, served on silver plates by footmen in white gloves. They have no tea, coffee, butter, bread or meat. The Germans are utterly done for, and in despair. Her sister's son, born and bred in England, was killed on the Russian front. The tragedy of Germany, she says, haunts her.

James lunched with me on Friday. He looked thin and ill. I was almost worried about him, and at once was made to understand that something dramatic had happened to him. He told me over coffee that E.P. was engaged, and that was the cause of his distress. He is so upset that he begs me to make no reference to it again. It is a little difficult to sympathise because, when she was disengaged, Jamesey made no endeavours to marry her. He refuses to go out in the evenings and has to complete the first volume of Lord Houghton by the end of the year.

Everyone I meet complains of distended stomach and attributes it to the starchy food. The food in England is worse than during the war, dry and tasteless, even at Brooks's.

Monday, 3rd November

Motored to Brockhampton. In the afternoon members of the Barneby family arrived and by a sort of muddled arrangement we distributed to them certain things they severally wanted, for which they paid probate figures. The Admiral, who was present, behaved very well, and saw the point of the Trust behaving like gents and not bureaucrats. Now the Ministry of Works would never have allowed these poor people to have a few family trinkets, which have little monetary value and mean all the world to them.

Wednesday, 5th November

John Rothenstein showed Sir Geoffrey and Lady Mander and me all the Pre-Raphaelite things of Mrs. Angeli's which he is storing and agreed to exhibit them first of all at the Tate. This will give us good publicity and furthermore the Tate will clean up and catalogue them for us, for nothing.

I dined with Barbara Moray who arrived very late having been at a cocktail party at which the King and Queen were guests. The K. and Q. did not leave till nearly 8 o'c, so no one else could go before them. Barbara said the King remarked to her naively, 'We keep wondering whether Philip realises what he is in for.' The Queen loves informal parties where she meets people who are doing interesting things in the world, and she hates leaving. At dinner tonight were Mr. Clare and Lady Doris Vyner. They spoke of Fountains Abbey and said the deal with the Roman Catholics was off, much to their disappointment. Tonight Barbara was very sparkling and witty. She is sharp and intelligent. But is there softness underneath? She has taken up weaving.

Thursday, 6th November

Another conference in the City over Osterley. I made them deal with points in which the Trust was interested, and then left for tea at Old Battersea House. This time poor old Mrs Stirling was less irritating and spoke sensibly of her wishes concerning the future of this house. She also showed me the twenty-four pieces of de Morgan pottery which Miss Stopford-Brook has bequeathed to the Trust. This house is a muddle. Again I was impressed by the Botticelli-like portrait painted by Mrs. de Morgan. The technique and the lavish gold are deliberately Botticellian. Very beautiful one must admit, and little the worse for being derivative.

Walked home in the fog, and then to the Albert Hall for the Bruno Walter concert in Bridget's box. The Mahler First Symphony nostalgic, moving, dreamy, but too long drawn out. Could not make up its mind to come to an end. The Albert Hall beautiful in the fog. You could not see the roof. Only the outline of the arcades, the capitals faintly lit, were visible on the opposite side of the hall. We walked to Adelaide Lubbock's afterwards, cars crawling, their drivers leaning out of open windows, buses guided by conductors holding flares. Very *gemütlich*, and general anxiety making people friendly, not irritable. I am the only person who loves the cosy, muffled mystery of London fogs. Poor Oggy Lynn had to walk miles guided by Christopher Sykes. A. Lubbock a very sympathetic woman. Whimsical too.

Friday, 7th November

At noon went to Lord Lytton's Memorial Service in Westminster Abbey. The largest attendance I have ever seen at a memorial. It was very beautiful indeed. I represented the National Trust and went in at 11.50 to find the Abbey already full. I sat in the north aisle close to Asquith's memorial, which his daughter, Lady Violet Bonham-Carter went up to after the service and scanned minutely. Mrs. Churchill facing me sitting in the end canopied stall, marked Lector. The sun streamed in strong gushes through those windows which are still filled with glass. It is so difficult to dis-associate the monuments from the architecture that one can overlook the arresting beauty of the vertical, aspirant piers, arches and vaults. It is one of the most noble buildings in the world. A long procession of deans and acolytes. A hymn to the airmen composed by Lord Lytton, in honour of 'Anthony' I suppose, and set to music by Vaughan Williams, was sung. I had grown to like it by the time the third verse was reached. I looked at these hundreds of eminent and intelligent people, the élite of English brain and breeding, all of whom were for this half hour concentrating their thoughts on one thing, their own impending deaths, their near conviction of annihilation and desperate hope of an unlikely survival.

Walked in the sun across St. James's Park to the Allies Club where Barbara Moray and her youngest daughter, Arabella Stuart, who was on half-term leave from school, lunched with me. Mark [Ogilvie-Grant] came too. We had a tolerable meal. Barbara touchingly kind, Arabella frail and pretty. May become a beauty.

At 6.30 I went to 55 Park Lane to see Sarah Churchill, a meeting I have been much looking forward to. She distressed me by explaining that she was not at all well, not having slept for three nights owing to some worry, which she would not divulge. She looked extremely thin. Was wearing a long flying-fox fur wrap. She walks with a brave, galleon-like, thrusting movement that is not inelegant, but attractive and characteristic, as though always in a hurry and breasting the storms of life. We went to the Italian film at the Curzon Cinema, *To Live in Peace*. Returned to Thurloe Square to dinner, and the fire. S warned me that she might fall asleep at any moment, she felt so unwell. Consequently, although she chatted away, she did not make the evening exhilarating.

She told me that her father was very elated by the municipal election results, and was now confident that his party had a following in the country. Already people in the streets were more respectful to him.

Saturday, 8th November

Wrote another contribution to my NT *Guide*. I sold 120 books for £6 to a shop in the Fulham Road, which I happened to pass by; and finished reading Coryat's *Crudities*. Also went to the National Gallery to see the pictures which have been recently cleaned. The exhibition is the ultimate vindication of cleaning. I do not think any reasonable man could still object to it being done by an expert with the scientific care that the Gallery undoubtedly takes. I am inclined to think that the photographs taken after cleaning make the originals look more scraped and chalky than in fact they do look. I reached this conclusion after comparing the

detailed photograph of a satyr's face in Rubens's *Silenus* with the painted
face on the canvas.

Sunday, 9th November

On the whole a satisfactory weekend. I wrote a section on Attingham for
the *Guide*. Dined with the Chaplins at the Allies Club. Ti Cholmondley
joined us. She now wears her white hair scraped back and a crimson
wreath stuck on the back of it. Instead of looking younger she looks 102.
She told us in a disingenuous way how spiritual she had become and
divorced from the physical. What an absurd woman. Anthony always
amuses me. We talk arrant nonsense together, having got on to that beam.
How does one get off it?

Monday, 10th November

To Knole for the day. Had quite a profitable time with Robin and Mason
settling opening hours for next season. In the afternoon I talked with
Lord Sackville who seems happy, apart from a complaint that the Trust
do not pay their bills and have owed him money for nine months. I said
to Robin as we left: 'It is odd but I have little affection for Knole, although
I know it so well.' He replied that the only quality it has which appeals
to him is atmosphere. But I am normally very responsive to atmosphere.
Here I don't seem even to catch that.

Tuesday, 11th November

Lady Crewe has invited me to serve on the Keats-Shelley Memorial
Committee, and the Princess Royal has asked me to stay at Harewood on
the 26th. I dined with Dame Una Pope-Hennessy and James. Carmen
Gandarillas was there. She said her father, Tony, rushed into the house today
with a rumour that the Queen was about to have a baby, and if it were a
boy, what would become of Princess Elizabeth? On the way home
Carmen said that Dame Una's erudition and aggressive lack of small talk
alarmed and upset her. How could one be at ease with a bluestocking like
that? When I am sitting next to her now I just give up and make no attempt
at conversation. This evening she spoke of Queen Victoria's wickedness in
shaping the twentieth-century European disasters by her Bismarckian
alliances and dynastic ambitions; then about Lamartine, on whom she is
very set, Madame de Staël, Kingsley and her son, John's superior knowledge of Nicholas Hilliard to any living person's on God's earth.

Wednesday, 12th November

Historic Buildings Committee this morning. Eardley, who attended, said
at luncheon afterwards that the meeting was the most entertaining two

hours he had ever spent. It consisted of a public flirtation between Esher
and me and the two of us Gerry-baiting. Esher said, 'I know no man, but
the Duke of Wellington, who says "No" more often than Mr. Molotov.'
He made Eardley purr by telling him that he always liked his ideas, E.
having submitted a scheme that the Trust should put its country house
libraries to public use.

Thursday, 13th November

Clifford Smith lunched at Brooks's. I wish this man were not so kind and
fundamentally good-hearted, for then I really could dislike him. He
pressed me to see that Margaret Jourdain was paid for any little jobs she
undertook for the Trust, since she was so hard up.

Again I went to the Albert Hall in Michael's box to see – or is it to
hear? – Bruno Walter conduct the London Symphony Orchestra. Superb
– Bruckner's Te Deum and Beethoven's Ninth Symphony. Charlie
Brocklehurst said to me, 'This would tame even a Bolshevik.' X., and I
suppose his wife, were in the box. His proximity made me feel self-conscious. I must have been no more than fifteen – if that – when I met my
'undoing' from his hands twenty-three years ago. I rather enjoyed it,
although of course pretending not to. I still remember the smell of the
soap he used. Cyril Connolly was in the box, looking like Rubens's
Silenus.

Friday, 14th November

Immensely surprised to read in the paper at breakfast that Dr. Dalton had
resigned on account of having given away to the press the headings of
his Budget speech before delivery. There was much speculation in my
office this morning whether Mrs. Dalton would come to the Executive
Committee. She did come, not punctually as she normally does to discuss
with the staff before the meeting points of interest to her but, wisely, just
after the meeting had begun so as to avoid general conversation. She was
rather more truculent and talkative than usual, doubtless trying to maintain her *sang-froid*, yet I have seldom seen any woman so betray her true
feelings by her looks. Her face when in repose was drawn, mauve and
sagging. She was far from tearful, or abashed, just downright broken. I felt
sorry for her. It shows how ambitious she is, how much she relished her
horrible husband's position. It is interesting that humans, when deeply
moved, cannot disguise their expressions, however successful they may be
in disguising their manner of speaking and their gestures.

Harold Nicolson told me that John Sparrow has given him for his
birthday present a letter to Byron from Lord Clare written at Harrow,
telling B. how unhappy B. had made him and admitting his love for him.

On the letter in B.'s handwriting was jotted in later years, 'Just a foolish schoolboy's quarrel'.

After the Executive Committee I took the 6.30 to Taunton. There was a hideous scramble for seats in the restaurant car. I failed to get one, and dinner. The discomfort of travel by train in England is unsurpassed. The Castle Hotel, Taunton, were kind. As a concession they gave me, tired and ravenous, a whisky and soda and three ginger biscuits.

Saturday, 15th November

Fetched my car from the Taunton garage. It looks very smart, painted dark blue with black wings. The roof has been mended to prevent leaks. Other small improvements. My bill will probably amount to £60.

I lunched at Montacute with the Yateses. The house looking very spruce and the garden far tidier, now that we have our own regular gardeners. Drove back to London and dined late at Brooks's. Sat with John Walter who tells me he is a Liberal. He claims that the Liberals, if they were less ambitious and abandoned their silly pretence of winning elections, could in fact become a power in Parliament, for they would hold the balance in every debate and turn out whichever Government became unpopular. As a director of *The Times* he receives £250 p.a. but as a Walter wields little authority today. He says Colonel Astor's views are very limited now, but he is very powerful. Barrington-Ward is a rebel by nature and will always support the underdog; and Carr, the Foreign Correspondent, has to Walter's great relief, retired. It was he who made *The Times*'s foreign policy so pro-Russian and foolish.

Rick S.-J. told me on the telephone that he met Ruth Draper yesterday. She said that during her English tour she has earned £38,000. What with American and British taxes she is £1,000 to the bad, after payment of her expenses. What a commentary!

Monday, 17th November

Joshua, in whose parents' house, Holbecks near Hadleigh I am staying, drove me to Colchester where we picked up Major Parker, who lives in a villa in this town. We went on to Faulkbourne Hall, which he owns. His mother, aged ninety, lives there. I had heard much of this house, but it is disappointing and even ugly. The park and landscape featureless. Witham town is creeping perilously close. It, the house, centres on a square red brick tower, fifteenth-century I suppose, or early sixteenth-, like Hadleigh Deanery and Layer Mamey. It is built of small Tudor bricks. It has crenellations and delicate, degenerate – from the military standpoint, which was its purpose – machicolations. But the house has been extended from time to time, culminating in nineteenth-century make-shift corridors over back courts, most haphazard and untidy. Apart from an oak seventeenth-century staircase, somewhat altered, and a few William and Mary pine-panelled rooms, stripped, the interior is equally unsatisfactory. The surroundings make the outside even duller than it need be. I thought Major Parker a stupid man for offering the house and no land, apart from three or four fields, and no other endowment. I mean, he could not expect us to accept such a proposition. He says his son, just married, wishes to live here but will probably abandon it after a few years' attempt. Then what? A school, I suppose.

We dropped Major Parker at Colchester and went to Fingringhoe Hall to lunch with the Furneaux, he a brother of Lady Birkenhead. A nice couple with good taste. She is tall, handsome, outspoken, the type I like. This James I brick house is far nicer than Faulkbourne. She offers to lend the Trust two portraits of ancestors by Hoppner. The one of the wife in old age appears in the Hoppner book.

Tuesday, 18th November

Joshua left early for Packwood. I had to take out all the plugs of my car, blow on and wipe the bloody things before the engine would start, which it finally did with the utmost reluctance. I visited the Deanery, Hadleigh. The gatehouse of rich brickwork overlooks the churchyard, and is similar in type to Faulkbourne. Reached Blickling at 1.30 and lunched at the Buckinghamshire Arms with the de Chairs who motored down from London. Went round the house with them and Carew Wallace, they deciding what colours they want for decorating. As C.W. says, we shall never get a licence to repaint all the rooms, and the de Chairs seem intent upon living in every room of this vast palace. After tea went to the Dell to stay with Maud Mosley. She in bed with a bad attack of bronchitis. Her grandson, Simon Mosley, Johnnie's boy, came to dinner. He is in the Coldstream and says he wants to be an opera singer – tenor. He is taking lessons in London. Says that fifty per cent of the guardsmen in his company refused to contribute towards a present for Princess Elizabeth. The dissentients came to him in a body and, quite pleasantly, gave him their reasons. *One*, they said the Royal Family did nothing for anybody, and *two*, the Royal Family would not contribute towards a present for their weddings. When Simon Mosley said that without the Royal Family the Brigade of Guards, with its privileges and traditions would cease to exist, they replied, 'Good! Let them both cease to exist.'

Wednesday, 19th November

Aunt Maud is much better today. She is distressed that the Sunday papers announced that she was sitting in the front row of Tom Mosley's political meeting last Saturday, when all the time she was ill in bed here in Aylsham. Already local Aylsham people have criticized her for being a fascist whereas she has in fact joined the Conservative Party in Norfolk. They conclude that she is a fascist in disguise.

Friday, 21st November

My three days at Blickling have been profitable. Have shifted a great deal of furniture about. Drove to Wymondham church to see the terra cotta tomb of the last Abbot of the Minster, a sort of canopied sedilia at the right of the great reredos by Comper. Arrived at Wingfield Castle to stay the night with Baron Ash. A lovely place it is. From 1 p.m. until 12.30 after midnight I was with Baron who did not once stop talking, fishing for compliments for his generous gift of Packwood to the Trust and praising himself. But his food was good.

The Castle dates from the 1380s. Retains its wide moat all round. You enter by the gate-tower of knapped flint work and dressed stone. You pass over the bridge – Baron longs to substitute a real drawbridge – into the inner court which, apart from the south-west wing where he lives, is now a shell. There are hefty chimney breasts and brick stacks. The wing drops sheer into the moat. We walked in the dusk to Wingfield church to see the de la Pole tomb made of wood. Baron is allowed no petrol for his car and is very isolated. But he does not mind. He sees himself as a mediaeval baron marooned and defensive within his castle, a happy isolationist.

Saturday, 22nd November

After climbing to the gate-tower roof, from which there is a wide all-round view of this singularly flat, yet not hideous country, and listening to the eerie screams of the wind whistling through the lead pipe in the gargoyle's mouth, I left at ten. The East Anglian wind kept me awake last night. It delighted Baron in making him feel more than ever marooned as though on board ship, himself the captain, nice Miss Eden his faithful crew and very efficient and solicitous cook-housekeeper. I drove to Framlingham and looked at the four well-known monuments in the church, dating from Henry VIII's reign. They are among the best examples in England of Italian Renaissance copyists' work. Tentative work, and unfortunately in bad condition. They are made of a coarse white stone which has cracked and is crumbling.

Rick dined with me at home, arriving late as usual, at nine. My relations with him are of the strangest. Charmed and irritated by turns.

Sunday, 23rd November

Collected and catalogued my photographs bought in Italy. Gave an enjoyable luncheon party of Doreen Colston-Baynes, Roger Fulford and Ivy Compton-Burnett. Doreen wanted to talk to Roger about Queen Victoria whose young life she is writing. Roger is now publishing a life of the Prince Consort. I could see how happy Doreen was. They all stayed till twenty to four. Roger said to me afterwards, for we walked together to St. James's, that he feared from what Doreen had told him the Royal Family were not opening their records to her, and questioned whether it was not because of the trouble he has got into from Queen Mary who gravely resented Roger's imputations that Prince Albert interfered in British politics. Ivy was very characteristic, speaking volubly in her breathless, sharp manner, and often being very amusing. She began by saying she never read the sort of books Roger and Doreen wrote and knew nothing of the subjects, implying that she cared less. Then she repeatedly interjected observations which were very much to the point, while they were confabulating, which they did at length over coffee. The four of us then discussed how we wrote: Doreen never at a writing-table, which gives her claustrophobia, but preferably in bed or sitting on a stool at the fire, or in a field on the grass, a pad and paper on her knee; Ivy always at her table at the window with an electric fire the other side of her; Roger always at his writing-table, with piles of notes, carefully dock-eted around him, and several bottles of differently coloured inks; I at my little Empire bureau, if the weather is warm, or in my armchair as close to the fire as possible, if the weather is cold, papers balancing on the arms of my chair, a small table, a bookstand and the floor.

Roger was in the Abbey during the Wedding, out of sight in the tri-forium, watching the scene through field-glasses. He said the Princess looked pretty, as well as enchanting. He favours Prince Philip, as I do. Doreen does not. Doreen says she has been steeped so long in Queen Victoria that she knows her far better than her best friend. And who is that? She would not say.

Monday, 24th November

Mr. Elletson called this morning to say he had quite decided to hand over Parrox Hall and could provide an endowment producing £500 p.a. and a further £250 p.a. after his or his mother's death, whichever might die last. I lunched at the Écu de France with Mr. Sedgewick who had invited Jock Murray to meet me. Jock remains a boy, gay and simple, giggling and popping lumps of sugar out of his coffee cup into mine and back again. Correct Mr. Sedgewick was rather shocked by this odd behaviour until we explained that we had been at Eton together. 'Oh, Eton! That explains it,' he said ambivalently.

Tuesday, 25th November

A meeting in the office summoned by Lord Aberconway, at which he, Dr. Taylor and Major Bowes-Lyon, the Queen's brother, a genial man, represented the Royal Horticultural Society. They raised a matter long overdue that a Gardens Committee of the National Trust and the R.H.S. should be formed in order to raise money and to administer a select few of the very best gardens of England that could be given or left to the Trust. There are thousands of English people who love gardens even more than buildings, and would willingly subscribe to such a fund. I tried, and think succeeded, in guiding the discussion along the right lines. At least I knew the constitution of the Trust better than the others.

Wednesday, 26th November

Today went to Harewood. Took the train to Leeds and arrived at one o'clock. Was met by a nice, old-fashioned chauffeur, not in livery, and a brand new small Daimler limousine with a large silver owl on the bonnet, and driven to Harewood village. Immediately on leaving Leeds one enters the Harewood estate, on either side of the road. God, what England owes to the landed gentry for the trim appearance of their estates. Harewood village is a fine specimen of a planned eighteenth-century community. The little houses are uniform, for they were all built of a piece by John Carr. I lunched with Mr. FitzRoy, the Agent. He is a hunchback, with protuberant, pointed chest; his wife young and pretty. It is very cold up here, frosty, clear and beautiful. After luncheon I talked in Mr. FitzRoy's office. He told me the estate was faced with 75 per cent death duties, but the family were resolved to remain at Harewood notwithstanding. During conversation I suggested that the family might approach the Treasury and ask for the house, some 4,000 acres of land around it, and also the chief objects of art to be taken in lieu of duties and handed over to the Trust. Mr. F. was interested. Then he took me in his car down the Leeds road, and through the lodge gates to look at the house across the valley towards the Wharfdale and high ridge of hills beyond it. At once saw how important it was that a large area should pass with the house which is visible from such long distances.

We drove back through the main entrance, past the stable block by Chambers, to the house. Were shown into the old library to the left of the hall, and stood before a fire. While I was debating with myself how I ought to make my first obeisance, suddenly H.R.H. ran swiftly into the room and shook me by the hand without saying a word. When I realised who she was I just had time to incline my head. My first impression was how good looking she is, far more so than photographs suggest. She has a beautiful complexion, neat greyish hair, cropped but wavy at the back. She wore a grey tweed skirt, thick mesh wool stockings, dark leather indoor shoes, a grey jumper and one string of pearls. The effect not dowdy, but simple country dress. She is extremely shy, but dignified; sensible and natural in manner. Rather abrupt and has little small talk. When interested in a subject she becormes vivacious and communicative. It was now 3.30 and already getting dark. She took us round the state rooms until 5 o'clock. The hospital which occupied the state rooms has recently gone, and the rooms are being cleaned and put back. There were men working on the floor boards with a machine like a tennis court marker, sandpapering them. The Princess picked her way through, opening shutters, removing dust-sheets and talking affably to the workmen. In the centre library one workman was relaying boards by the glass door, wearing his hat and smoking. When he spoke to the Princess he neither removed his hat nor his cigarette. When we left him H.R.H. was very worried lest he might set fire to the house. I thought his behaviour abominable.

Tea was in the breakfast-room, as were all meals. I always sat on the Princess's right. She kept jumping up to fill the teapot from an electric kettle. She has a smooth-haired dachshund called Bruna, to which she is devoted and with whom she keeps up a flow of banter. It sleeps in a basket in her bedroom. The other day she upset milk on the silver tray and let the dog lick it up, then, for fear of what the butler might think, washed the tray herself. Miss Lloyd and Mrs. Balfour, ladies-in-waiting, were in attendance. The younger son, Gerald, came in from shooting. He is stocky, with large chin, slightly oafish, a mixture of David Lloyd and Auberon Herbert in appearance only. Has drooping, sensual mouth. He is very jolly with his mother, whom he teases.

The Princess has a remarkably beautiful, deep voice, and rolls her 'r's slightly. She has fine white teeth and a curious mark on the upper lip, as of a scald.

After tea she took FitzRoy and me to her private sitting-room where some of the best Chippendale satinwood tables and commodes are; also a pair of Sèvres inlaid cabinets. I then explained my ideas about the Treasury scheme and she asked many questions quietly and intelligently about domestic arrangements under the National Trust. Asked if she might have a small strip of the terrace to herself and dog on opening days, and proposed providing teas for the public in the stable block. 'One can get used to anything,' she observed rather pathetically. We talked until 7.40 when the Agent left us together.

My bedroom was in the semi-basement. It had a coal fire. There was no time for a bath. In fear of being late I changed quickly and dashed up to the old library just as it struck eight. At dinner there was no waiting, the Princess going first to the sideboard, helping herself, the rest following. There was plenty of banter during dinner. The P. having rung the bell for coffee said, 'Now what is the betting that they won't answer it,' and two minutes later, 'I thought so.' The son then said, 'I will try, Mummie,' and his peals brought a response. The P. had changed with inordinate speed into a black dress, very plain, with black shiny belt and velveteen coatee, for she is still in mourning. After dinner, sitting till nearly twelve in the old library, stifling yawns, was a bit of a trial. Talk was about the crowds in the buses and tubes during rush hour, the smell of human beings on a muggy, rainy day (things which she can never have experienced), and then politics, and keen, anxious speculation over the Gravesend election. She says a little naively that, whatever happens, we mustn't emigrate or desert this country, however much we are tempted. I thought to myself, royalty never emigrates. It either stays put or is pushed out.

Thursday, 27th November

Breakfast at nine. I was up at 8.50 in case the Princess should arrive first. The ladies assembled in the breakfast-room. H. R. H. then came in. The two ladies curtseyed and I bowed. This was all the ceremony. Every sentence has a Ma'am in it, a slightly denaturalising suffix. And reference to her presence or absence is to Her Royal Highness. I like this. After breakfast I was allowed to walk outside on the terrace and round the house by myself. Was specially commanded to examine the small group of playing children in a painting by Baurscheit, dated 1725. I could not admire these insipidly mischievous children as much as the urns the Princess has bought at the Clumber sale and put in the Barry parterre garden. At 10.30 the Princess reappeared and until 12.20 conducted me round the house again. She takes great pride in and has considerable knowledge of the contents. Her taste too struck me as very good. Indeed the rooms are superb and the long gallery one of the noblest apartments I have seen in an English house. It is amazing how convincing the wooden curtain boxes are, carved to resemble drapery. The quality of the French-style Chippendale furniture the finest possible. Together we pulled off covers, compared the suites of furniture, examined ceilings, pier-glasses, door-locks and handles, chimneypieces, carpets and pictures, about which she knows a great deal. We went into every bedroom and bathroom, deploring the effects of last winter's damp on many ceilings. Went into H.R.H.'s bedroom, with large, brown, modern mahogany

double-bed, dog's basket and dozens of photographs of Queen Mary, the
late King, present monarch and family. Rather wistfully she kept saying,
'I do hope I shall not have to sell this, or that.' We even descended to the
cellar to examine the china. At the end I was asked if I was tired. Valiantly
I denied it, although nearly dropping, and expressed the same anxiety
about her. She said she never was tired showing the house to people who
appreciated it.

I was motored back to Leeds to catch the 12.45 to London, and went
to a party at Kew given by Mark Ogilvie-Grant, at which a Greek pianist
played while the guests sipped flat champagne in a large chilly chamber.
Papa is staying with me.

Saturday, 29th November

Unsatisfactory day. Worked at interrupted intervals. Lunched with
Patrick Kinross at the St. James's Club. He is finally back from Egypt after
seven years and is to retire to Devon where he intends writing a novel
about his past and all his friends. God help us all. This will be no contribution to literature. I was delighted to see dear old Patrick who has grown
enormous in length and breadth. He sprawls over chairs and tables and
puffs a great deal. He is not notably chic or clean, but otherwise
unchanged. The same, good-humoured, quizzical, gently cynical, kind
individual. We went to the Wallace Collection to look at the upstairs furniture which I wanted to compare with the Frenchified Chippendale at
Harewood while it was still fresh in my mind. But you can't compare the
French and English for the quality of each is so distinctive, and the
English better finished in fact. I had tea with Ralph Edwards and his
family at Chiswick Mall. Ralph was deploring present day amorality and
said that only a religious revival could restore western civilization, the
eastern having already gone.

Sunday, 30th November

I love having a Sunday to myself. A rare thing. Worked all day, finishing
M. Jourdain's *English Decoration and Furniture* and began Hall's *Life of
Henry VIII*. Then dined cosily alone with Colin Agnew who deplored the
cleaning of the National Gallery pictures. Philip Hendy is a great friend
of his. Nevertheless he thinks he has acted very unwisely and is entirely
in the hands of a crook German scientist scraper of paintings. He says
picture restoration has to be in the blood of families like the Drowns,
whose fathers have for generations cleaned with turpentine and no
chemicals and who understand the feel of varnish and dirt and can tell
which layer of paint beneath is the true one.

Tuesday, 2nd December

Michael [Rosse] and I motored to Polesden Lacey. He was delighted with the arrangement of the house, which is Robin's doing and is a credit to him. We both liked too the railings designed by Professor Richardson to separate Mrs Greville's grave from the garden.

I dined with Ivy and Margaret. Charlotte Bonham-Carter and Soame Jenyns the other guests. It was the greatest fun, although there was only cider to drink, and it was perishing cold. Ivy and Margaret were at their best, playing up to each other and making strikingly pertinent and lively observations. I brought some lace from Brockhampton for Margaret's expert opinion. She found a number of pieces that are quite good and valuable, particularly two large pieces of Charles II date in excellent condition.

Sunday, 7th December

Took Sarah Churchill to the Charlie Chaplin film, *Monsieur Verdoux*, not up to standard, but there were flashes of the old humour and genius. The last dock scene makes an appeal to the world not to use the atom bomb, which is far crueller than Bluebeard's murder of his seven wives – no overstatement. Afterwards I dined in Sarah's flat, she having cooked the dinner. I did not leave till long after midnight. She is going on Wednesday to Morocco with her father. The King sent Prince Philip to lunch with her father in order to learn about the Constitution. Churchill liked him, finding him very intelligent.

Monday, 8th December

Had tea with the Eshers in their small Chelsea house. There was an iced cake made for one of the grandchildren which he insisted on eating, to Antoinette's concern. He nearly devoured the whole of it. We discussed Harewood and he agreed that we should ask the Treasury if they would in fact take it in part payment of death duties and let the Princess Royal continue to live there.

Tuesday, 9th December

Eardley and I trained to Reading, picked up his car and motored to Stourhead where from 12 till dark, now 4.30, we worked in the house. This we continued the following day, and Thursday, I staying at Long Crichel for two nights. Stourhead in turmoil. We had to start from scratch, sorting, rejecting, with the minimum of help, carrying heavy furniture and busts together, back-breaking, yet giggling work. We sold a collection of sheer junk for £75 to the local antique dealer in Mere, who took it all away on Thursday, for which I hope the Trust will be pleased. We tried to trace all the younger Chippendale's pieces of furniture scattered about the house to put them in those show rooms to which they rightly belong. But we did no sort of arranging. It was the greatest fun, and oh how I enjoy Eardley's companionship. We think we make a splendid team, because we never spare criticism, neither taking offence; on the contrary each relishing outright condemnation of the other's efforts. I know we shall eventually succeed in making this house look splendid, we having picked the brains of all the experts, sifted, endorsed or rejected their several pieces of advice. The late Alda, Lady Hoare, has become a great mythical figure at Long Crichel. Eddy deplores our eradication of her appalling bad taste, and is going to write a novel about her. Desmond calls us the despoilers.

Friday, 12th December

At the Finance Committee I was appointed the Trust's representative on the Osterley Park Committee. Lord Esher said there was no one who knew more about Osterley than I, which is, I suppose true, after the years I have spent conferring with Jersey. Harold Nicolson said to me, 'Oh dear, I cannot get down to writing books for the constant interruptions. But I do not intend to abandon my other interests for a purely literary existence until I am seventy.' Eddie Marsh at luncheon at Brooks's told me three little stories in his clipped, Edwardian manner. Someone congratulated Lady Tree on the colour of her hair which he supposed she had recently dyed. 'How sweet of you,' she replied, 'to say, *my* hair.' Winston Churchill when told that Mr. Attlee had decided not to visit Australia, remarked, 'he feared that when the mouse was away the cats would play,' and described Socialism as 'Government of the duds, by the duds, for the duds.'

Monday, 15th December

In talking to Doreen this evening I was overcome by an urgent desire to leave and get home to my work, and be alone. Doreen very shaken because last evening a burglar broke into her house, stole nothing, but left large footprints everywhere. Or so Doreen maintained, for sometimes I think she invents these dramas just to bring incident into her placid life.

Tuesday, 16th December

Sam Carr lunched and brought me the proposed jacket of the National Trust *Guide*, showing a pretty, fanciful coloured view of the Knole gatehouse. He said he thought the book would bring me in a steady income.

I much doubt it, for it will soon be out of date. Lady Crewe had a party for Miss Ruth Draper to which I went out of politeness, but a horrid, heavy affair it was. I stayed twenty minutes and left with James who said, 'I only go to these parties for Peggy's sake.' I said, 'You mean you only go to Peggy's parties for Peggy's sake.' He said she loathed her own as much as she loathed other people's parties.

Wednesday, 17th December

Worked the whole day at the Stourhead guidebook. Malcolm Bullock dined at Brooks's and came back here afterwards. He would not go home but sat like Juggernaut telling funny stories about the Baldwins. Someone called at Downing Street. Mrs. Baldwin opened the door dressed as Madam Butterfly. She said, 'This is a surprise for Stan when he returns. I often do this. Last week I was a Turkish soldier.'

Thursday, 18th December

A harrowing visit this afternoon to see an old woman, Mrs. Walter Tibbitts, in a private residential hotel in Inverness Terrace, Bayswater. She had offered her 'collections' to the Trust. From her description of the Benares ware, Poona brass, marquetry furniture and from the photograph she produced of a Hindu carved screen, it sounded appalling and unsuitable. Yet she had not a flicker of doubt that it was important and insisted that the collection be kept together. She is seventy-eight and must find a home for it before she dies. I left her feeling more depressed than words can describe. When the old have to live in soulless drabness, which this hotel is, alone, ridiculous and unwanted, they are pitiable. When they are slightly truculent, to keep their end up, it moves me beyond compassion to a sadness which haunts me for days. The agony of it.

Tea at Sibyl Colefax's. Harold Nicolson said that Eddie Marsh's new book was of schoolgirl badness. He and I left together. In the tube, in which we had to stand, Harold said to me: 'I find myself constantly touching my hat and offering my seat to tough middle-aged men until I realise that they are twenty years younger than I am.'

Friday, 19th December

This afternoon, after the dentist, I called at Batsford's and collected five advance copies of *The Age of Adam*, of which the jacket is the prettiest I have ever seen. Met Mr. Harry in the shop. He made me talk with him upstairs, and promise, rather against my will, that I would help in the editing of some guidebooks. I could not quite understand because of the coughing and spluttering whether it was the same old Methuen guidebooks on which he is so keen, or not. 'Now then, Jim darling,' he went on and subsided into catarrhal chuckles. The house telephone rang: 'God damn the bloody swine,' he shouted. 'Is that you, Sam darling?' without a break between the two ejaculations.

Saturday, 20th December

Bridget took me to Covent Garden. Three ballets, *Les Patineurs*, *The Three-Cornered Hat* and the new Lecoque one, very gay with Derain scenery. On the way to the Ivy – the best food I have had since my return from Italy – a man accosted me and I, so Bridget said, was very snubbing. Indeed I did not recognize him until we had passed on. Then I suddenly remembered the sad, second-rate, hopelessly unpractical member of the A.R.P. who was in my platoon at the beginning of the war. The last person in the world I would wish to be unkind to. I left B. – angrily stumping the pavement – and tore after him. Alas, he had gone. Now for ever he will remember me as a cad, a man too proud while with a beautiful woman, to acknowledge him. He looked so thin, yellow, crinkled and *dégringolé*, which makes my behaviour worse. Perhaps he is starving and would have welcomed 5s. Instead B. and I continued to her flat in Mount Street where we drank whisky, were warm and happy.

Sunday, 21st December

Ugly hangover this morning. Worked all day. In the evening James dined here. After dinner we giggled so much over my book that we nearly choked. Then went to see Paul Wallraf who had Heinz Dietmar dining. Heinz said it was terribly depressing coming over to England from Germany. This annoyed James who observed tartly: 'Then I wonder you bother to come here at all,' Heinz having been a refugee from Germany all the war. Paul was cross with J. for his rudeness. I thought Dietmar a bore. Then France was discussed. James was angry with me for criticising the French before two Germans (who were after all his friends) and so the party broke up.

Wednesday, 24th December

I motored this morning early to Bibury. When not beset by angst I am happy motoring, for I can relax and assess my actions and tell my beads. I have given thirty-seven Christmas presents and, so far, received one, a wireless set from my parents. Financially, I am utterly broke. Most of my presents go to servants and friends like old Mrs. Strong, the caretaker of Carlyle's House. I suppose it is always the way.

Had a look at the Mill House at Bibury, which Eardley does not recommend, but which I favour on the whole. I like its great, stalwart buttresses. Then to Fossebridge to lunch with the dear Fairfax-Lucys, who are sweet friends and always give me a welcome – and a delicious luncheon. Called for Deenie at Stow and motored her home for Christmas, just the four of us staying.

Thursday, Christmas Day

Immediately after luncheon I drove to Brockhampton to fetch eight velvet cushions, then back to Worcester and had tea with the Matley Moores in The Tything. The first thing I saw was a beautiful leather screen, which I admired. He said, 'Yes, we have just bought that at the Brockhampton sale.' Then I realised it was the screen I had bid for and did not even know whether or not I had been successful. Miss Matley Moore is already repairing it. It is leather, painted with birds and rabbits, date about 1695 they think; a lovely thing. She is one of the leading restorers of mural paintings in England. She has ascertained that those at Harvington Hall were done by four different men, one of whom was left-handed. M.M., gruff but kind and very well informed antiquarian, is the Ministry of Works representative of Worcestershire and Diocesan Adviser. By profession a dentist. They let me join their Christmas tea with their old mother of eighty and another old woman. Earnest and genuine people. I like them. She has a tame magpie which eats off her shoulder.

Friday, 26th December

The family went to Wolverhampton Races in the extreme cold wind. Papa's horse was third and Mama says it is a dud. All morning I read Virginia Woolf's latest essays. I really believe she is the best prose writer of this century. In the afternoon walked to see Maggie [my old nursery maid]. Her little boy, aged five, has fair hair and the most beautiful and patrician face, yet he hardly speaks. His eyes are melancholy, and beseeching. Maggie says she is forty-nine but looks as pretty and young as when I first knew her. They have thirty acres of fruit trees.

Saturday, 27th December

This morning took Deenie back to Stow, then on to Charlecote where I spent the day with Hollyoak, the agent, fussing around with a view to improvements. Have an idea of making the morning room into a kind of state bedroom. Shall also get Kaynes-Smith to vet the pictures for me. Then to tea with Lady Throckmorton, that immortal woman whom I so deeply respect and admire. She asked if she might call me by my Christian name, which coming from someone of her age and generation is a compliment. She is very unhappy about the situation at Coughton [Court]. Her son has to renounce his lease and we discussed how she could continue to live there. It is imperative that we help her to do so.

Upon that I am resolutely determined. She said a little poignantly, 'You and I alone must work upon it.'

Sunday, 28th December

Motored to Stoneleigh [Abbey] this morning at 10.30 to talk to Lord Leigh about the showing of this house. He is rather annoyed that the Trust is taking so long to consider his offer. Indeed here is a house of first-rate quality, one we simply must save.

Monday, 29th December

I went to Burford Priory. The Southbys were away but I went round the house with the caretaker, and this evening wrote a long report for the Historic Buildings Committee. There are only three rooms of interest, Speaker Lenthall's Chapel of 1660, much restored, the 1583 great chamber with ribbed ceiling, and the Queen Anne staircase. The situation of the house in relation to the town is important, and its general appearance is attractive. It has been very much altered.

Tuesday, 30th December

At Stratford-on-Avon I visited Shakespeare's Birthplace. Last year they had 100,000 visitors at 1s. each. For so small a house I am surprised the trustees do not collect better furniture. The oak pieces I saw all looked fakes without exception. The birth-room, having been a shrine since Isaac Walton's day – his name scratched on a windowpane survives – is affecting. On comparing the building of today with early photographs taken in 1858 and still earlier prints, one sees how much it has been restored and altered.

Lunched at The George Inn, Shipston-on-Stour. The Cotswolds sprinkled gently with snow under a leaden sky, the roads deserted and dead and wild. At Oxford I tried to sell two huge volumes of William Nicholson plates of the colleges to Blackwells but they would make no offer. Strolled to the Divinity Schools. The weird roof is of Henry VI's time, heavy and base I think. The perspective Jacobean panels of the Convocation Room are quite classical. The guide was an awful old man whose ignorance was supreme. Moreover he was proud of it. In the Sheldonian Theatre the guide pointed out, what I should long ago have realised, that Streater's ceiling is meant to imitate the open sky as seen in his day from the Roman Theatre of Marcellus. Wren was responsible for this translation. The awning depicted above the cornice and the gold ribs representing the ropes that would pull it across are in every sense baroque. He said all the carving was Grinling Gibbons's. I seriously question this.

Wednesday, 31st December

Dined at Brooks's with Dick Girouard whom I met there. Walked home to bed at 10.30 and read *Dombey and Son* contentedly. Party-lust seldom irks me nowadays. That is one consolation. Heard the distant cacophony and catcall of sirens, and the cretinous shouting at midnight.

1948

Saw Lord Bearsted today. He assures me the catalogue of pictures at Upton is nearly ready. I fear this poor man will not last long, for he is very tired, slow and shaky. He is of my father's generation (the Kaiser's War and all) and they seem to age badly.

After 6 o'clock went, at their invitation, to see the Wyndham Clarks' house, 44 Berkeley Square, and the way Shearsby has repaired the painted ceiling of the great room. I introduced him to them and had forgotten I did so. What a wonderful house it is, but the Clarks, who seem to have money but no servants, keep it like a vast jumble heap, which, servants or no, is not necessary, I think.

Friday, 2nd January

To the British Museum. Soame Jenyns introduced me to Collins of the Manuscripts Department, to whom I showed some Charlecote mss. I brought up. He liked the Cromwell writ of summons and the Edmund Waller passport, but was not so keen on Sir Thomas Lucy's Wages Book. I am. I consider it romantic that here in his own writing are Justice Shallow's detailed accounts kept over the precise years when the Shakespeare incident is supposed to have taken place.

Saturday, 3rd January

Paul Hyslop lunched. He explained to me that the word 'rag' was coined by Eddy [Sackville-West] to mean a cagey queer, the opposite of a 'tearing' queer, the term rag applying to pages of children's books made of that material. A 'billiard ball' is the smart, dandified, smooth, City type of queer, who tries to appear otherwise. Well, one lives and learns.

Sunday, 4th January

Met Eddie Marsh in the bus, both of us bound for Brooks's and luncheon. He said he was busy correcting Winston Churchill's page proofs of the famous War History.

I gave a dinner party, without meaning to, for Riette Lamington, Lady George Cholmondeley, a banker friend of hers, and Jamesey [Pope-Hennessy]. After dinner we tried table-turning. Nothing stirred.

Monday, 5th January

Drove down to Long Crichel. Lunched excellently at my favourite eating place, the Wheatsheaf Inn, and stopped at Winchester. In the Cathedral choir were one old man reading the New Testament to himself, very loudly in an affected voice, and two ladies discussing hats, each party oblivious of the other. I enjoyed this odd little scene on a dull afternoon in January. The three had evidently sought refuge in the warmth rather than spiritual consolation. At the bookshop I was lucky to buy the architectural book I saw there last July and always meant to go back for – 'Some Designs of Mr Inigo Jones and Mr William Kent, by John Vardy 1744'.

Tuesday, 6th–Friday, 9th January

Each day Eardley [Knollys] and I went to Stourhead, arriving at 10 every morning. We worked like blacks. There is hardly one piece of furniture in the state rooms that we have not shifted ourselves. At last we broke the back of our difficulties and assembled all the furniture in the rooms allotted to them. It is astonishing the amount of stuff left over which we cannot place. Nearly every day it has rained and the rooms are pitch dark. But we have enjoyed ourselves.

Raymond Mortimer is staying at Long Crichel. A wise man. He warned Eardley and me against looking up all the words we did not know in the dictionary when reading French books, advising us to look up only a word that recurs frequently. Talking about some silly-billy, he observed that most of us have our own censor that prevents our uttering all the foolish thoughts that tumble into our minds. I returned to London on Friday afternoon. All the inmates at Long C., Eddy, Raymond, Desmond [Shawe-Taylor] and Eardley are angelic to me and this house has become a sort of second home.

On my return I dined at B.S.'s. There was present another man, Archie Colquhoun, whom I had met years back. B.S. terribly tied up and adolescent. At 10.15 Harold Nicolson arrived and ate a sandwich supper. He had come from Croydon where he was adopted as Labour candidate. He was rather silly and bumble-beeish. *Memo.* Not to be bumble-beeish with younger persons in twenty-five years' time.

Saturday, 10th January

Tonight I went, cursing, in the rain, to dine with the Barry Craigs. She was Theodosia Cropper whom I came to know and like well – she has a dreamy, abstracted manner which appeals to me – when I was on sick leave in 1941. There was a sweetness in her welcome and spontaneity that won my heart instantly. I liked him too; a good-looking, friendly and competent artist.

Monday, 12th January

At 6 went to Doreen [Colston-Baynes] in Ovington Square. She was very kind about my book, but has not read it, which shows that her

appetite has not been whetted. Says her brother has taken and is reading
it. I told her of Sachie Sitwell's charming letter of congratulation I
received this morning. It was unsolicited for I had not sent him a copy.
Evenings at Doreen's are a bit of a strain at times for she can be goosey,
dear thing that she is. She has been introduced to Chips Channon by
Peter Coats, and is thrilled to the marrow. Theirs seems to be no more
her *monde* than the Bing Boys' or the Crazy Gang's would be Queen
Mary's. Then I went to the Dorchester Ordinary. I had thought dinner
was to be at Sibyl [Colefax]'s house, but this is a habit she has of inviting
one and then at the last moment letting on that dinner is at the
Dorchester, for which one pays. But I felt sorry and my heart melted,
because she was just out of a sick-bed, looking bent, crumpled, ill and so
old. I sat next to Harold and Mrs [Eny] Strutt, whom I found rather
formidable. She talked of class and breeding and the necessity for both.
After the Ordinary I walked away with Harold, Ben [Nicolson] and Noel
Annan to Brooks's. The last very affable and, though young, coot bald, a
don at Cambridge who reviews for the *Statesman*. He was modest and
polite which is rare in a don and an intellectual. I liked him. He spoke
admiringly of James's writing and forecast that his *Lord Houghton* would
be *the* book of the decade. We drank whisky upstairs in the Subscription
Room. Harold in excellent form. He reminded us of Croker drinking at
Brooks's with Colonel Stanhope who was decrying the Duke of
Wellington at the moment when the mob poured past the windows with
the news of the victory of Waterloo. Sir Edmund Gosse related to H. the
following story: Lord John Manners told Gosse that he remembered
attending a Belvoir Hunt dinner at Belvoir Castle. A footman handed the
Duke of Rutland a letter. The Duke broke the seal, read and exclaimed,
'Oh, how terrible!' Rose to his feet, and said: 'Gentlemen, I think we must
discontinue our festivities. I have received bad news. Lord Byron is dead.'

   Doreen confessed to me this evening that she preferred the company
of stupid, well-bred people to that of intelligent, ill-bred or common
people. I think I do too, on the whole. Certainly I would on a desert
island. She complained how dirty were the hands of the bus conductors
– worse than those of the conductresses – so that she tries to avoid their
touching her gloved hand when they give her change. In consequence
she is apt to drop her coins on the floor of the bus. I said it would be surprising if at the end of a long day their hands were clean, poor things.

Tuesday, 13th January

Went to see Sibyl Colefax in bed today and brought her my book as a
present. Anything to give the kind old woman slight pleasure; this sounds
horribly condescending. Lady Anderson came in before I left in such a

cloud of scent that I smelt it on me all the way back on the tube to South Kensington. Bowler-hatted commuters sniffed me suspiciously.

Thursday, 15th January

Dined with Helen Dashwood who had asked Nancy [Mitford]. Just the three of us, very agreeable, until Francis [Dashwood] and friend arrived from Switzerland which interrupted the intimate flow. Nancy looking very beautiful indeed in lovely black dress, flounced and long, about one foot above the ankles, small waist, padded hips, and thick black petticoat of silk, and muff. As she says, never have women's fashions been prettier.

Friday, 16th January

I have seen a good deal of Michael [Rosse] these few days, he being very important and taking the chair at numerous meetings. A trifle too gracious. I was pleased to be able to reprove him for ordering Anthony Martineau [National Trust solicitor] to get in touch with the Princess Royal's solicitor without her authority. 'How could *you* do such a thing? Such an unwonted lapse by you of all correct people.' M. was for the first time in his life abashed, and actually blushed.

Saturday, 17th January

Quite a profitable day. Spent the morning at the National Portrait Gallery looking at the pre-Restoration portraits, of which at present there are only two rooms shown, so it does not take long. There ought to be more of these earlier people. I don't think the Gallery is very well hung. All this weekend I have worked on French Renaissance architecture.

Tuesday, 20th January

At breakfast this morning it snowed heavily and I wondered whether to put off my visit to Gunby. Decided to persevere. Luckily I did so for it stopped snowing by 10 o'clock. I motored off and passing by Wrest Park, drove up to the house, now under requisition. Rather an attractive big house of *c.* 1830, but I could see nothing of the famous gardens; the days are so short that there is no time for loitering. Then to Houghton, Bunyan's place, superbly situated on a hill, now a complete ruin. It is of red brick with stone dressings; in shape and general style Jacobean. Can just see how it might be by Inigo Jones. The windows are mullioned and pedimented and the over-lights are oval; the doorways are classical and on one front between the wings is a classical screen. Bunyan called it the House Beautiful, I believe, and Walpole, 'picturesque . . . but bad and inconvenient within'.

At Peterborough had a quick walk round the Cathedral to refresh my memory of the glorious Perpendicular ambulatory with fan roof. The cast-iron stoves in the Cathedral I always admire for their Early English Gothic design. There are no mural monuments in this Cathedral. Then I called at the Red Hall, Bourne, which the LNER have offered to the Trust. It is a nice Jacobean house, seductive from a distance, but unfortunately at the very edge of the railroad and indeed part of the station. It is divided into two tenements, inhabited by a railway labourer and a tailor. Both these people were very kind in showing me over. I was astonished at the deplorable condition of the insides and the friendliness of the inhabitants. The wife of the railwayman inveighed against the LNER for never improving, but the tailor was cheerful and made allowance for his landlords. The wallpapers in both houses were hanging in festoons; damp everywhere; many square panes missing and the holes stuffed with rags. Red Hall is square, of red brick and stone quoins, pointed gables, a central projecting porch with Orders. In one dwelling is the original oak staircase, balustered, and newels bearing obelisks. Upstairs under the roof one large room with gypsum floor called the ballroom; exposed braced timbers overhead.

I arrived after tea at Gunby, the car having gone very well. Lady Massingberd, only recently widowed after fifty years' bliss, was extremely cheerful and just like her old self. I do admire her. No complaints and she is making the best of her situation. She says that so long as the Whartons stay, she can remain at Gunby. The Field Marshal's pension of £1,700 p.a. is now gone and there is a big drop. She tells me that he died quietly, having had his first seizure nine months before. A tired heart finished him off. Wharton gave me some more particulars with the relish servants always indulge in. He confirmed that the FM suffered no pain, just declined; ate nothing towards the end, adding that 'not a drop came out of his body anywhere, after his death'. The Whartons were much moved and are erecting an iron gate, chosen by Lady M., with an inscription 'To the memory of our beloved Field Marshal', which is touching. Lady M. worried a bit who would live at Gunby when she was gone. She said the FM's last wish was that the Trust should give back the two portraits by Oswald Birley, for he did not want lumself and his wife to go down to posterity as portrayed by this artist. During the visit I read one volume of Peregrine Massingberd's diary, enjoying it immensely. I told Lady M. that it ought to be edited and published.

Saturday, 24th January

Tonight I went at 4.30 to Wayland Hilton Young's wedding at St George's, Hanover Square where my parents were married in 1904. Keith Miller-Jones persuaded me to go in act of friendship. Dosia Cropper was in the church and walked away with me to the reception with her left hand clasped in mine in my topcoat pocket. I love her spontaneous affection. She acts and speaks what is in her mind without forethought or afterthought. I knew no one else at the reception.

Had Nancy [Mitford], Bridget Parsons and Tony Gandarillas to dinner. Emily gave us a lovely spread, with partridges. I did not much enjoy it for Nancy's scintillations dry me up, and talk – which she hogged – was mainly Parisian scandal, which means nothing to me. She also mentioned Gerald Berners's stroke, a slight one. He is very depressed. This highly sophisticated man is unhappy because he cannot find God, according to N., and doesn't know where to begin looking for him. She gave us an outline of her new book, a funny story ending with the uncle, who had married his deceased wife's niece, greatly to the rage of the niece's parents, falling in love with a young man. N. longs to *épater* the public.

Monday, 26th January

Motored to Montacute arriving in time to lunch with the Yateses (pouring rain all day). Eardley already there. We spent a long afternoon rearranging the parlour, putting out the needlework furniture, and hanging Michael Peto's tapestry. Then to Long Crichel for the night.

Tuesday, 27th January

In pouring rain still E. and I in my car motored to Higher Bockhampton. Looked at Hardy's birthplace. The little house and surroundings are just as Hardy must have known them; the rising heath behind the property surely unchanged. The cottage of brick and thatch is of the simplest. The two nice elderly lady tenants are very anxious to stay on and willing to show visitors round. Educated women yet content to live without a bath and with oil lamps. We lunched at Exeter. Called at Bradley Manor and saw Mrs Woolner. The place tidied up since our last visit, the lodge painted and the neat NT notice board in place. Outside of house newly harled.

We stayed with Patrick Kinross at Easton Court Hotel, Chagford. Charming and friendly; greatly improved in health and looks since I saw him on his first return from Egypt – less gross and yellow. We were shown photographs of all of us, Patrick, Christopher Hobhouse, Alan Pryce-Jones and me – all quite nice-looking too – when we were here in 1932.

Wednesday, 28th January

Again in pouring rain motored to Cotehele, losing our way as usual down deep and narrow lanes. We started arranging the show rooms. Cook, ingenious man, clerk-of-works acting for us on the estate, most helpful, eager to clean the armour in the great hall and do anything we want. A sort of super-*bricoleur*. We made strides and felt quite pleased with ourselves.

Thursday, 29th January

Again poured heavily the entire day. I worried about my car standing in the rain lest water got into some vital parts of its anatomy. Cotehele has a peculiar melancholy and beauty of its own, especially at this season, for the state rooms are heated by large wood fires that fill the stuffy air with blue smoke. Eardley and I finished our arrangements. Every room is hung with tapestry treated like wallpaper over the plaster walls. No regard was had for the merit of the panels which were cut ruthlessly to fit over doorways, beds and cupboards.

On our return to Tavistock we combed the antique dealers. I bought a glass candlestick for the centre of my marble table, a strip of red and blue matting and a pink case lined with tortoiseshell and covered with leather. Very pretty and cost 3s. What it is exactly I don't know. The dealer and his son were 'characters'. The son said to the father in front of us, 'What are they?' and the father answered, 'Artists or something', and turning to us, 'What are you really?' 'Did you get any money out of them?' asked the son. Then the father became friendly and showed us everything he had. E. and I went to the cinema last night and tonight.

Friday, 30th January

Off we went this morning, glad to leave the gloomy Bedford Hotel. It was pouring again and I was in ill humour until the sun came out at Tintagel; but E. is patient and sweet, and helps dispel my ill humours. There is no one in the world with whom I have shared more cherished moments of giggling, *vide* yesterday carrying the grandfather clock down the stairs at Cotehele, clankings coming from the mechanism. I thought I would have a stroke we laughed so much, and yet could not put it down. This morning we looked at the Old Post Office, Tintagel, a dreadful Hans Andersen gingerbread witch's house. It was streaming with damp. I hated it. Such a sweet old caretaker took us round, a toothless hag with a beautiful voice and the manners of Lady Desborough. I warmed to her at once. A poor sad old thing. We wanted to embrace her. We lunched at Okehampton – no *antiquaires* here; an anti-*anti* town in fact. Then looked at Burrow Mump, a good new property, a landmark in the middle of Athelney on a mound. The ruined church late eighteenth century, very pretty. Tea at Wincanton. E. left my map behind in the Antelope. We found muff Raymond at Crichel, still with a cold, and Eddy back from broadcasting a record of his *Le Grand Meaulnes* for tomorrow night.

Saturday, 31st January

I left Crichel this morning, collecting my map at Wincanton. (Oldeworlde Eddy pronounces it *Win*canton, with accent on first syllable.) Then called at Stourhead to make a few more notes for the guidebook. Lunched at Amesbury very badly after passing through a vehement hail storm by Stonehenge. On my return B.S. telephoned and dined with me at Brooks's. He is a strange, unbalanced youth, with whom the world should be careful for he is sensitive and neurotic, torn between religious mysticism and the usual lusts of the flesh which he sublimates to his own unhappiness. Since he is handsome and engaging and intelligent I am tempted to advise him to make discreet hay while the sun of youth still smiles upon him, yet I don't want to influence him. He left at midnight, then early Sunday morning dropped a note through the letter-box at breakfast time. Note conveyed that he did not wish to 'hurt' me who am anyway unhurtable nowadays. I gathered from the strange effusion that he meant he could not fall in love with me who have not the slightest inclination to fall in love with him. How puerile, and pathetic, and vain.

Sunday, 1st February

Listened to a Covent Garden concert this afternoon, of contemporary English composers, Vaughan Williams and Walton. Enjoyed the first moderately, and the last's symphony a lot. What two years ago would have been cacophony was today melody. One must be prepared to undergo persistent torture to arrive at this blessed state of receptiveness. But were the *gondalieri* faced with this intellectual exercise before they positively enjoyed singing arias from Verdi, I ask myself? At 6 heard Eddy's excellent broadcast on *Le Grand Meaulnes*, and then B.S. called to explain away his note, poor youth. So I tackled his problem at once and counselled him thus – remain celibate provided you lead a truly saintly life and can maintain it: otherwise, live life to the full without restraint. The first path is undoubtedly preferable if you really mean to enter the priesthood. And please let me hear no more about it.

Had a dinner party of Viva King, Janet Leeper and Burnet Pavitt. Janet L. is in a wild sort of way intelligent and earnest. Viva so different, is more intelligent, not at all earnest. On the contrary is wicked and amusing. I prefer the latter's intelligence. I thought they would never go. They left at 11.40 but B. stayed on for half an hour. He confided that he could have done without either lady, I having invited them for his benefit. B. a very sympathetic man, extremely musical. Tells me he plays duets with Joan Moore who is a great friend.

Tuesday, 3rd February

Refreshed, I take the two brass horns from Cotehele to the British Museum and hand them over to the eminent expert, Kendrick, a dusty, vigorous man with a wooden leg and grey hair. I tell him that all the experts have given conflicting pronouncements, and he only can now judge whether the horns are genuine. He answers: 'Balls!' Then, 'Of course they are; value £50 a piece.' I say aghast, 'Is that all?' Anyway they are hideous things. I dine in and work but at 11 p.m. go to a party Hamish [St Clair-Erskine] and Jennifer Heber-Percy give in the next street to mine. In spite of the number of 'old friends' I hate it. I believe my generation to be, for the most part, 'unreal'; cliquey, dated, prejudiced, out of touch with the new world and preposterously exclusive – arrogant, arrogant, with few redeeming qualities of any kind. They have nothing original to impart. At any rate nothing to me. I do have one conversation with Roy Harrod and Sachie Sitwell on Roy's broadcast about Keynes. Roy says he has been all through Lytton Strachey's correspondence with his brother James written before 1914; a lot of it is purely – I don't know why I write 'purely' – 'about pieces of human organs!' I return home, not depressed, for Burnet rings me up and we have a jolly chat, but intensely irritated by pretence. I don't truly care if I never see these people again. They are only tolerable singly or in very small groups. In a mass they are detestable and contemptible. Am I one of them?

Wednesday, 4th February

Accompanied Admiral Bevir to the Public Record Office. We lunched with Colonel Malet, Keeper of the Archives, and Atkinson, and made liaison. They promised to give us the names of all local and county archivists to whom we might transfer deeds and papers that the National Trust inherits. They took us to the Rolls Museum afterwards and I saw Dr Young's tomb from the Rolls Chapel. I must say the figure, presumably not by Torrigiano (indeed it is Gothic) is far finer than the monument, and the heads of Christ and two angels in the lunette quite conventional and insipid. I was glad to see this tomb; also an illuminated portrait of the young red-headed Henry VIII positively looking pretty.

This evening took John Fowler to a box lent to Grace Davenport in Covent Garden for the *Meistersinger*. English performance. What a cock-teasing opera. Only the prize song is moving. Too many repeats. Bad voices except that of Frank Sale as Walter von Stolzing. John and I, seated at the back, being men, could see nothing. Thence we took Grace D. and Mrs de Freville to the Savoy. John was angelic and lent me money.

The whole evening cost us about £4.10s each. Agreed later, as we sat here after midnight, what *hell* affected, rich, smart, spoilt society women could be. Asked each other why we ever did these things? He is a kind, cosy, good-natured man to have put up with the evening I landed him in.

Thursday, 5th February

In rather good form today, and for once genial in the office in spite of a late night, for John talked till 2 a.m. In the afternoon came home and began upon my guidebook to Cotehele. Received from poor B.S. a long letter of a very compromising nature about himself, complaining of his hopeless effeminacy, and confessing that he wanted love to be made to him the other night; that his Sunday letter was all nonsense – which I suspected. There is nothing I can do to help him for he is ineducable.

Friday, 6th February

An old retired craftsman from the Wallace Collection called on me. He told me that very few young were attracted to his profession because they got bigger wages for mechanical, unskilled work in factories; that although he needed no extra money he regarded it as his sacred duty to impart his craft to those younger men and women who were anxious to learn it. I told him he was a noble man.

Tonight I dined at Mrs Carnegie's in Lennox Gardens. She has been ill but is now recovered, and as upright and sprightly as ever. The party was to meet the American Ambassadress, a good-looking, charming woman. There were three old butlers waiting in the hall in evening dress as I arrived five minutes late – the last to come – rather off-hand, but if one arrived on the dot to dine with one's contemporaries there would be no servants, hostess or guests assembled. At dinner I sat next to Frances Peto's sister, Cathleen, whom I mistook for Frances, and Diane Maxwell, Austen Chamberlain's daughter. She is not handsome but very agreeable. The large dining-table covered with a huge snow-white cloth and sprinkled with silver candlesticks, cups and bric-à-brac. A substantial sight. Dinner meagre compared with those of the old days here; a little fish, a little hot ham, deemed a luxury and American no doubt, a tiny savoury, and desert of one tangerine; a little red wine and a little port. Yet I had no appetite and ate sparingly of this sparse fare. During port I talked to old Lord Courtauld-Thomson who expressed a wish to read my book. I said there was nothing to prevent him. After dinner I talked to an American woman accompanying the Ambassadress. She spoke in that low Boston voice which I find the loveliest of the English-speaking voices. I could easily become enamoured of her. She said thousands of Americans will visit England this summer and she hoped they would not stay in the smart hotels but the lesser ones, in order to see how little the English still have to eat today.

Saturday, 7th February

A profitable day reading morning and afternoon in the British Museum library. Called on Francis Dashwood who told me he quite definitely intended to live at West Wycombe in no matter how small a way, and blamed his father for giving up the contest. Had an early supper with Bridget and went to the Anna Karenina film. The best photography I have seen and the clothes designed by Cecil Beaton. Vivien Leigh reminded Bridget and me of Anne [Rosse]. She has the same proud little way of walking, tossing the head and pouting. An exquisite creature.

Sunday, 8th February

Work at home all day while listening this afternoon to a concert of Bloch and, more interesting, the Brazilian composer, Villa-Lobos. Fate, or the god of Love, is extraordinarily mercurial. It is as though he has turned his back on me. I am loveless.

Sarah [Churchill] to whom I spoke yesterday on the telephone attracts me much. The sound of her voice again, mocking, independent and gay, quite made my heart jump to hear. I am to see her this week. I have only one trouble just now – money – or, like love, lack of it. Bills fly in and I have nothing with which to meet them. I suppose I am extravagant, yet I consider I live very simply, and have so little to show for it. And I work very hard. I just don't earn enough. It is all very sad.

Tuesday, 10th February

Diane Abdy had a party before dinner. B.N. was there, sitting starchly upright, nagging about the NT. How tiresome and dislikeable she is on social occasions. Maureen Dufferin I talked to about Ava and how well I knew him at our private school, less well at Eton, and hardly at all at Oxford. When I spoke of him her eyes, hitherto listless, sparkled and her whole body tautened with interest. She vibrated with memories. She said her son, Sheridan, is just like Basil. Freddie Birkenhead intends to edit a book of essays by different friends of Ava. Would I be a contributor? Could I write? I said I didn't know. She was wearing a dress bare above the breasts and elbows with no straps over the shoulders, and the effect was *inquiétant*. In talking to her I found myself stammering out of nerves. Burnet dined at Brooks's.

Thursday, 12th February

Had a hangover this morning. Burnet feels just as I do about parties. We telephone nearly every day. Young Lord Lothian lunched with me at

Brooks's. He is very shy and blinks and twitches. But he is very charming and handsome. Has three children already and is a passionate Papist. Professor Richardson telephoned me this morning and we arranged to meet at 2.30 at Brooks's. He said, 'I have read your book. It is superb. It is an important work.' All of which was very kind and heartfelt, but utter nonsense. I saw Doreen and she complained that she dreads James's visits nowadays. He sits drinking her sherry and never utters, looking bored to death. This must be very noticeable for she speaks ill of no one. We talked of highbrows. Agreed we were middlebrows and not intellectuals. She consoled herself by believing that what she wrote was sometimes thought well of by highbrows.

Friday, 13th February

Sarah dined with me alone and brought me one of Mr Churchill's Havana cigars as a present. Alas, I do not smoke cigars. We talked and talked. She told me that to leave Vic Oliver she had to adopt a sudden, cruel course – and just bolt. There was no other way. She is curiously ignorant of books and painting and music. Just not interested. Only knows about the stage. This is odd for she is bright, quick with an answer, and naturally intelligent. I like her very much.

Saturday, 14th February

At 12 I went to see Grandy Jersey and meet his new Italian wife, Bianca, not a beauty but attractive. Grandy said that Mr Aneurin Bevan had told him he wanted to nationalize the N. Trust because he thought the old families enjoyed too many privileges; that I must take cognizance of this attitude among the left-wing members of the Cabinet – damn them. I shall tell Lord Esher.

. Harold chucked our Blickling tour as I expected because of his beastly by-election impending. So I asked Burnet to come instead, and he accepted. Burnet and Ben lunched at Brooks's and we set off. We had tea at the Rutland Arms, Newmarket, and found Eardley at the Royal Hotel – a commercial, vulgar hotel – Norwich. We had the greatest fun nevertheless and went to *The Ideal Husband*, an excellent film.

Sunday, 15th February

The four of us motored to Blickling and spent the happiest day: weather sunny and mild. Miss O'Sullivan, the late Lord Lothian's old secretary, lunched with us at the Blickling Arms. Ben selected the best pictures to hang in the South Drawing-room. Burnet found a piano and played for an hour. We were all occupied. We hated the Norwich hotel, large, ugly, grim, no cheer, indifferent food. After dinner we walked round the town looking for drink or life. Found only coffee, like mud.

Monday, 16th February

Dropped Burnet at his factory in Welwyn and cast a quick eye over it. A pre-war building, light, cheerful and in parts beautiful. Clinically clean; drugs and pills being made by people in white overalls like dispensers; I thought how agreeable to work there.

At luncheon at Brooks's Woodbine Parish came up and said, 'You know I have decided to stay on at Batemans after all?' 'Why, yes,' I replied, for he had already announced that he was breaking his lease. 'It was because you told me how sorry you were to hear it the other day and said such kind things.' Ben, who was with me and overheard, said that one could be paid no greater compliment than that. Yes, but I don't know how pleased my colleagues will be about the 'kind things' I said.

Tuesday, 17th February

Lunched with Margaret Jourdain] and Ivy [Compton-Burnett]. The latter in a malaprop mood; referred to Vita having been made a CB and to a Cona coffee machine as a 'costermonger' machine. Margaret read me a transcription of letters from the Adam brothers to Lord Dalkeith in 1751, at which early date they apparently designed Dalkeith House.

Wednesday, 18th February

Had an excellent luncheon at Baldwin's with John Wilton, then drove to Merton where with Robin Fedden we looked at the Abbey wall which the NT owns, a ridiculous bit of flint wall in the middle of a paper factory yard, and quite pointless. Then drove to tea with Sibyl Colefax. Talked to Lady Anderson who told me Sir Stafford Cripps was devoted to the arts, yet had only once been to the opera, and that was in Russia. So she took him to Sadler's Wells. He hates private ownership of anything and gives all his possessions away.

Thursday, 19th February

Mrs Esdaile lunched at the Allies Club. Poor old thing, she looked very wild and odd and complained that she could not work as she used. She must have had a stroke. She asked eagerly to come to Stourhead and Charlecote and I told Eardley, who was there, that we must get all the information we can from her without delay. She told us there was a bust at Stourhead of Alderman Beckford. She was looking like an old rag-and-bone woman with the blackest handkerchief you ever saw; yet was so grateful for a nasty meal. She is a very great woman.

Friday, 20th February

A Reports Committee this morning. Lord Esher, back from America, in the chair, wearing his fur coat, and bright as a button. He teased Hubert Smith and the agriculturists who, he said, were wishing to hold agricultural estates within a ring fence inalienably, and pounced upon the immorality of this. Of course he was right and I found myself in entire agreement with him. So it was that as usual we were fighting together against the others.

I lunched with Alan Pryce-Jones at the Caprice restaurant to meet Princess Marthe Bibesco. Lys Connolly was the fourth. Princess B. in black with a toque slipping off her head, first this side, then the other after she adjusted it too vehemently. She told stories in English but spoke to Alan in French. She wanted us to meet in the near future to discuss George Lloyd and his Catholicism. She is quite unpolitical and got into trouble in both wars for entertaining the enemy. Personalities, not principles, are her concern.

Saturday, 21st February

I went out this morning; otherwise at home, huddled by the fireside, perished. The grip of winter has descended and the snow is thick outside. My pipes are frozen and I cannot have a bath. Heywood Hill told me my book is now his best seller.

Tuesday, 24th February

Called on Bill Astor at 12. He is always very friendly. I persuaded him to write and ask his father to agree to Cliveden house being opened at least one afternoon this season. I stressed that the public could not be expected to understand how Lord Astor found it impossible. Then I lunched with Lord Braybrooke who is most kind and thanked me for what the N. Trust had done in persuading the Government to buy Audley End from him. I *am* sorry that the NT has not got it all the same, because I am convinced that they will present houses better than the tasteless Ministry of Works. Alec Penrose called at my office to offer St George's Hall at King's Lynn.

Dined tonight at Dick Girouard's. The Eshers were there. We talked about the seven deadly sins which Lord Esher thinks are mostly misnamed. Gluttony and sloth he called 'perfectly divine sins'. He said that class feeling today is infinitely less strong than during the eighties. He remembers how as a child he, and the grown-ups, were in living terror of the East End marching to the West End. His mother could not drive to Buckingham Palace with the windows of her carriage down for fear of the 'mob' spitting into it. He said the poverty and rags were deplorable and terrifying. 'Things get better every day,' he finally said – and he meant it too.

Finished my Cotehele guidebook this morning. Lunched with the Admiral at the United Services Club. It is a fine building – by Burton? – with a beautiful and vast stairwell, the single first flight spreading into two.

Lord Esher at Brooks's said the Admiral never failed to write a letter that caused offence. He said, 'I know I worry you at meetings by always agreeing with you, to your embarrassment vis-à-vis the agents.'

Alex Moulton has come to stay with me. He tells me he has invented a new steam-, paraffin-driven motor car and hopes to have the first model on the road this year. He is certain it will be a success, but says he can make no money out of it, such a thing these days being impossible. It is his means of creation. He is earnest and intelligent, with a forceful, positive and inquiring mind. No philistine, and a reader of poetry and highbrow books. Human beings never fail to surprise me. Hitherto scientists and inventors have been enigmas to me. We drank wine and talked till midnight.

Oh, the dreariness of society with a large S. Went to a cocktail party given by Diane in her 'twee' little flat as Anne would call it. He! he! he! and giggles and preciousness. Would I sign my book and would I put 'from the author', for how could posterity know who Jim was? How indeed? But I would not, and that was the end of it. I hadn't *given* it.

Resold two tyres, the tractor ones, to the garage at Mortlake. Then went to the Chagall exhibition at the Tate which I was prepared to hate. On the contrary found the surrealist pictures gay, inspiriting and dreamlike. Jamesey dined with me here, and we had a gossip. He says that when he finds himself in bed with someone incompatible he prays all the time to St Teresa, who sympathizes. Harold is very shocking about his by-election. In the coldest weather he fears to wear his fur-lined coat. He dissuades Ben from visiting the constituency because his voice sounds too patrician; expresses the hope that the Communists, and not De Gaulle, will get to power in France. James had a row with him and told him he was unprincipled and defeatist.

Saturday, 28th February

Worked in the British Museum reading-room morning and afternoon. This vast domed room with galleries of bookshelves ought to be a national monument, if it isn't already. In the evening I had B.S. to dine and insisted on going to a film, *Cry Havoc*. Very bad film but I could not face an evening alone with this young man who bores me, with his unhealthy odour of sanctity and bottled-up lechery. I am trying to get him a job with *Country Life*.

Sunday, 29th February

Mass at the Oratory and work at home. After luncheon walked to the Tate to see the Chagalls for the last time – but this time far less impressed. I tire of the nursery bathroom fantasies and babyishness, and absence of all form and dignity. Certainly some of the silly fantasies are pretty, but they are pre-adolescent.

Monday, 1st March

Lunched at the Dorchester with Sibyil Colefax in a very overheated little room on the top floor overlooking the park, the sun shining directly upon us. A curious party and one wonders why it was given. There were the Hartingtons T. S. Eliot, Ava Anderson, Georgia Sitwell, Peter Quennell, Alan Pryce-Jones. I sat between Alan and Lady Anderson. T. S. Eliot dark, swarthy, professorial, retiring, quizzical, diffident – a medical practitioner or undertaker's clerk. Alas, I had no chance of talking with him. Lady Anderson, rather blowzy, resembled the Hayter portrait of Queen Caroline at Battersea House. She said she could hardly bear to look at her reflection in the glass. I made no comment. Very pleased to see Debo H. again. She said she would ask me to stay at Chatsworth in June. Wants to take me round the big house, now empty. She was pale, with no make-up at all. Beautiful and melancholy-merry.

Wednesday, 3rd March

Office in the morning, and after a quick luncheon drove to Olney, Bucks. Called at Lord Denham's house in Weston Underwood village. It was indeed Diana and Greville Worthington's house where I so often stayed before the war, and which the Denhams bought after the tragedy of their deaths. Lord D. was away but Lady Denham, a very pretty woman with grey hair, blue eyes and pink complexion, accompanied me in the car to Cowper's Alcove. She is a sister of Lord Redesdale and aunt of Tom and Nancy, etc., but my reference to them was unfortunate. I do not think she cares for the Mitfords. This will make Nancy chortle with wicked glee. She is a friendly, but stupid, philistine woman. The Alcove stands on a mound at the end of a field overlooking Olney, and is just as Cowper knew it, save for the wooden struts under the arches and the lime trees in the foreground which have now gone. I also saw the Gothic temple in the Wilderness and the urns and monuments to the poet's hare and the Throckmortons' dogs. The Denham boy showed me the blue ceiling of the Gothic temple painted by poor little Diana. They have removed all her pretty wallpapers from the house and substituted boring distemper, saying what awful taste the Worthingtons had.

Motored to Wickhamford in time for dinner.

Thursday, 4th March

Took Mama to Packwood today. We lunched adequately at the Swan's Nest in Stratford. Darling Mama has an increasingly tiresome habit of not listening to what I say, and repeating the same question three or four times during one meal. This cannot be age so much as lack of concentration. She now confuses everyone's names. We walked around Packwood, she being very sweet and friendly with the gardener Weaver and his wife, both old friends, and enjoying herself no end. Joshua [Rowley] has got an excellent couple who, by strenuous polishing, have made the rooms and furniture shine and sparkle. I think the place will be a success when opened.

Friday, 5th March

This morning left early for Charlecote, meeting Hollyoak (agent) and the Lucys. Alice is suffering from heart trouble, or nerves. Like Packwood, Charlecote is beautifully kept, and I approve of the introduction of the bed into the Morning-room. All here seemed well. I continued to Worcester and met John Wilton, returned from Croome, and motored him back to London. We dined at Henley. John very companionable, gay and gossipy. Much laughter.

Saturday, 6th March

Very fuggy and foggy. Burnet, back from staying with the Bowes-Lyons, lunched, and we set off for Slough. Had a look at Gray's monument at Stoke Poges, and entered the church. The monument is a singularly pleasing piece of classical architecture, or sculpture, not however in accord with Gray's sombre Gothic ethos. Then we walked round Eton. I was cross that we couldn't get into the Chapel at 4.45. The same denial at Windsor; St George's Chapel closed. We reached Englefield Green at teatime to stay with Garrett and Joan [Moore]. Carmen Gandarillas, also staying, has scarcely altered. Drank and ate too much. Burnet and Joan are closely united by a bubbling humour as well as great piano-playing proficiency. I have never heard two people enjoy playing duets with such gusto and giggling.

Tuesday, 9th March

An awful meeting at the Ministry of Works on the subject of Ham House. The Admiral presiding over a baker's dozen (I being the vantage loaf) of dreary subfusc civil servants and attorneys. How I hate their guts. Little achieved owing to huffing, puffing, um-ing and er-ing. Left at midday and met Eardley and the Curator of the Ashmolean who very kindly has offered to help us improve the museum at Chedworth Roman Villa. Lunched with Aunt Puss [Milnes-Gaskell], then rejoined Eardley in hunting for fabrics for the William Kent chairs at Stourhead. Suicidally depressed by the international situation and my own.

Thursday, 11th March

To the Albert Hall in Bridget's box to hear Furtwängler conducting. His movements are sharp, jagged, sure and Gothic, and he conducts with his long legs as well as arms. But a dull programme and the Sibelius very irritating. Bridget came back to dine. She has just returned from France. Brought me a black bow tie for a present. She has asked me to go to Monk Hopton for a week at Easter, to begin my new book, if I do not go to Belgium, which I now think I shall not do.

Friday, 12th March

Had a drink with Sheila Plunkett. Lady Coke said that she and her husband are moving into one wing of Holkham. Lord Bridport, who is younger than me, has not even *one* hair on his pate, which is smooth as a boiled suet pudding. He thinks Communism will not come to Italy in April, by a pip. He owns 30,000 acres in Sicily, he tells me.

Saturday, 13th March

Ted Lister, round as a ball, spectacles on the tip of his nose, dined with me alone and stayed till nearly midnight, knitting and gossiping. When he gave these two recreations a rest he practised on an imaginary harp, twanging non-existent strings with stumpy fingers, and humming execrably.

Monday, 15th March

Went to the theatre with Ted Lister – *The Hidden Years* – all about a romantic schoolboy friendship and its implications. Very bad, sentimental, toshy play, in the *Young Woodley* tradition, only the subject even today rather bold. Ted brought a pair of old-fashioned mother-of-pearl opera glasses through which to quiz the young ladies and gentlemen, much to my embarrassment, so that I was constrained to prevent him using them. He carefully put under the seat his square, semi-bowler, semi-tall hat. Theatre practically empty but for a sprinkling of old queens. A horrifying experience really.

Tuesday, 16th March

Went this afternoon with the Admiral and Lord Esher to the Treasury for a meeting with the permanent official, Sir Bernard Gilbert, and the Ministry of Works official, Sir Eric de Normann, two smug, obstinate, unimaginative civil servants. The meeting was about Harewood House. In spite of Esher's ably presented case these men implied that they might advise the Chancellor to let the Government hold the house and estate, if they were asked to take them in part payment of death duties, and not hand them on to the NT. A dangerous precedent indeed. Nothing we could say would convince them that we were the qualified body to hold and run country houses inhabited by their previous owners. Esher and I were distinctly depressed by the interview. The two brushed aside our argument that in an imperfect and disintegrating world country house owners disliked the NT far less than the Government.

Burnet and I met for tea at Brooks's and then went to the Opera at Covent Garden – *Tristan and Isolde*. We cut the second act, and dined at Rules. Both of us terribly tired. I could hardly speak for fatigue. I find the whole Wagner sentiment, the Heine-Nazi ethic most unappetizing. Yet I am glad I heard Madame Flagstad as Isolde, for she is one of the great singers of our time. Her massive mastery of her theme, and her discipline beyond criticism.

Wednesday, 17th March

Esher telephoned me this morning very depressed about yesterday's meeting, and came to the office at 12.15. We walked to Brooks's and discussed how best to bring pressure upon the Princess Royal's agent. I am to go up there and explain matters to her, if permitted, and the implications of the estate falling into the Government's maw.

Dined at 7 with Rick [Stewart-Jones] for John Summerson's lecture on eighteenth-century London architects.

Thursday, 18th March

Lunched with the Aspinall-Oglanders in their flat in Carrington House. Mrs Fleming, Ian and Peter's mother, once a great beauty, and the Eshers present. Lord E. took me into the passage the moment I arrived and said,

'I sat next to Sir Stafford Cripps last night at dinner and he remarked, "You are taking a long time to spend the £50m we have put aside for the Nat. Trust." ' Esher replied that he had had a set-back, describing the sour fruits of our recent Treasury meeting. Cripps brushed it aside and went on, 'You can spend as much of the reserve as you like so long as it is spent on the NT and not on the previous owners.' Esher feels that the two officials we saw were talking through their hats, and we must go over their heads (what a funny juxtaposition of similes). This is encouraging. I drove away with him to the SPAB [Society for the Protection of Ancient Buildings] meeting and he remarked, 'How Joan does talk. One cannot get a word in edgeways.' What a silly-billy of a woman she is, but goodhearted. During luncheon E. said rather acidly to Antoinette, 'Are you telling this story, or am I? For it is a mistake that we should both be telling the same story at the same time.'

Went to see Mr Harry Batsford who rather depressed me about my new book and seemed to want me to tackle another subject altogether, the Palladians. I said I had always wanted to write about them but Charles [Fry] had counselled me not to; that after one year's reading on the Renaissance I really could not throw over all the work so far done. I am always being depressed by something or other, and must stop it.

Saturday, 20th March

Yesterday motored to Cliveden, met Bill Astor and measured up the rooms for the ropes and drugget we shall need. Today motored to Woolbeding and lunched with the Edward Lascelleses and daughter, nice people who own this house. It is a disappointing house after the tantalizing photographs of it in last year's *Country Life*. It is near Midhurst in lush, wooded country off the Downs. It belonged to Lord Robert Spencer whose great friend, C. J. Fox, frequently stayed there. In 1875 Lord Lannerton spoilt it by converting the centre courtyard into a wretched stairwell and adding a wing in unsuitable style. None of the old rooms has any quality, but all the books, many pictures and some excellent inlaid furniture belonged to Lord Robert. The Lascelleses are hard up and the house is rather forlorn. They consider asking the Treasury to take it in lieu of death duties on Mr Lascelles's death and hand over to us.

This afternoon I also looked at the Cowdray ruins, and in particular for Renaissance detail, viz. the cherubs' heads in the spandrels of the fan vaulting of the hall porch. Then to Chichester Cathedral to see Bishop Sherbourne's monument which to my surprise turned out to be completely Gothic, not Renaissance at all – coloured alabaster.

Sunday, 21st March

Dined with Diana Selby-Lowndes who told me that she married two months ago a man called Charlton because she was starting a baby, that he has already left her, her father has washed his hands of her, she has no money and is selling her clothes to live on the proceeds. I am extremely sorry for her; but what a hash she has made. I wrote to Patrick [Kinross] to suggest that he should see her father, whom he knows, and tell him he must provide for her. Patrick is the best friend she has and is always ready to help those of us in distress.

Monday, 22nd March

Went to a lecture at the SPAB this evening by Sir Sydney Cockerell on William Morris, whose secretary he was and whom he knew intimately. He did not disclose anything new about Morris, but to listen to Sir S. talking of him, Ruskin, Burne-Jones, Philip Webb as his close companions conjured up the past vividly. Morris had fits of violent rage, once tearing his own clothes to ribbons; then immediately subsided and was penitent like a spoilt child.

Tuesday, 23rd March

The first meeting of the National Trust Gardens Committee. Vita, whom I had persuaded to sit on it, attended. She asked me to lunch and it was sad I could not go for I had Martyn Beckett lunching at Brooks's. The small committee are enthusiastic and not dampened by the silly Admiral's misgivings about inadequate funds. Sir M. Beckett a nice young man who turns out to have been Diana Worthington's half-brother. He cannot act for us as architect in Yorkshire, he says, because he is so seldom there.

Wednesday, 24th March

Trained to Leeds and back today. Lunched at Harewood with the agent, Mr FitzRoy, then after a talk went to the big house. H.R.H. was opening something, but young Lord Harewood received us, and we talked for an hour in the library. He is shy and bashful. Has a head shaped like his father's, but a large Hanoverian mouth, and the same resonant, deep voice as his mother's. Looks away from one while speaking, like H.R.H., but when he warms up and smiles, is engaging. Is hopelessly defeatist about the future of Harewood. Nevertheless is definitely opposed to the Government holding it and practically insisted that if not held by the NT then it must be held by no other body.

Being semi-royal must be tormenting, for one is neither fish, flesh nor good red herring, and to have one's mother in one's own house, with two ladies-in-waiting at every meal, curtseying and Ma'aming, yet oneself to be an ordinary human subject to the kicks and pricks of this mortal life, most unsatisfactory. In the train at dinner on my way home a seedy, black frock-coated individual sat opposite me. He looked the typical civil servant of an unimportant sort, with ill-fitting false teeth and a starched winged collar. He ate and drank little, choosing precisely different courses to mine. Yet I was struck by his intelligent face and his extraordinary courtesy to the waiters. When he got up and left, the attendant told me he was Sir Norman Birkett. I got home at 10 o'clock, rather tired but not exhausted, having had a satisfactory day.

Thursday, 25th March

Rather a rushed morning, packing, getting the car out and going to the office where I was bad-tempered. At noon called for Bridget [Parsons] and motored to Shropshire – glorious, clear, sunny day and the hedges bursting with shoots, life and spring. We lunched at Amersham, called at Charlecote, where the brew-house with its new labels looked very smart indeed. We reached Monk Hopton at 6 where we stay over Easter with Lord and Lady de Vesci. House very well 'appointed' and comfortable; delicious plain English food with yellow butter, home-made bread, eggs and everything the hungry but not over-fastidious stomach requires.

Friday (Good), 26th March

A gorgeous day. I already feel better. Sit in a summer-house reading books for my review in the *Spectator*. This afternoon we motor with the dogs to Wilderhope Manor, I informing Bridget and Lady de V. that it is a model of what a youth hostel should be. Indeed it used to be before the war. To my horror the place was untidy, filthy and unkempt; a positive disgrace and discredit. My companions, naturally hostile to the NT, were tacitly cock-a-hoop. I wrote a strongly worded protest which I shall circulate on my return to the office. We also called at Lutwyche Hall, now empty, but soon to be a school. Once a good Jacobean house, I guess about 1615, it was altered in 1861. All the windowpanes taken out and plate glass substituted. Nasty additions made. But the Queen Anne staircase is very good with twisted balusters sharply cut. The hall is a remarkable room with ceiling divided by thick plastered ribs and walls of Rococo stucco. The small library has early eighteenth-century carved Corinthian pilasters. The front of the house of the Bramshill type, only in miniature, but spoilt in Victorian times.

Saturday, 27th March

The sore place I have mysteriously developed on my leg will not heal. I cover it with boric acid but the constant rubbing through walking irritates it so that no scab will form. Interesting. Today we motored to Attingham and there met George Trevelyan and a grim-visaged companion. He is a self-confident man, talking of the wonderful things he is going to achieve at Attingham as curator of the Adult College. A little folk-dancing, some social economy and Fabianism for the miners and their wives. We felt quite sick from the nonsense of it all. At a time when this country is supposed to be bankrupt they spend (our) money on semi-education of the lower classes who will merely learn from it to be dissatisfied. The house looked very forlorn and down at heel which worried me a good deal. Then we visited Buildwas Abbey, well cared for by the Ministry of Works, I am bound to admit – Norman and Early English remains, and nearly the whole body of the church intact. We had tea at Wenlock Priory with the Motleys. Mary is a dear and very domesticated with her four sons whom conversation can barely range beyond.

Easter Sunday, 28th March

Beautiful sunny day, but still a cold wind. I drove the two little Irish maids two miles to Mass at the top of an old farmhouse, where a family called Bell have a chapel, decked with forsythia and daffodils. It was under the roof and might have been a recusants' place of worship in the bad times. From far and near about thirty people assembled. This was at 9 o'clock. We waited ages while they all went to confession, including myself. A romantic and bucolic little ceremony, miles away in Shropshire for a small community of proud and devout people. After Mass they offered the congregation tea. I gave ten shillings to the priest's collection.

Monday, 29th March

I left Monk Hopton after luncheon today, Bridget staying on for a week. As usual I was glad to leave, although I have enjoyed myself and am grateful for the kindness received. I suffer from *gêne* in other people's houses and from guilt in that I do not pull my weight, i.e. don't garden, which is always a welcome assistance from guests these days. The other three gardened all the time. Not once did I offer to do so. I hate it. Stooping makes me giddy. Yet the delicious food, deep sleep and the long lies in the mornings did me good. In spite of the nearly complete relaxation was obliged to take one Epanutin pill per day. Back in London shall be obliged to take three a day. One admitted drawback here is the dreadful, inescapable proximity of Lord de Vesci, with whom I repeatedly find myself alone, being the only other male. He is an arch-bore, who never stops talking and grumbling about the decline of the country, the incompetence of the Government, and the menace of Communism – what I am fairly apt to do myself. In another it is intolerable. He is the most reactionary man, bar none, I have ever met. On the other hand there is something rather likeable about him – that truculent bewilderment as of a spavined horse. And it cannot be agreeable to be despised by both your wife and stepdaughter.

On the way home I stopped at Harvington Hall and Coughton where I had tea with that angelic Lady Throckmorton, who looked thinner and not too well. She is all alone in this house, and has a struggle to keep going and make both ends meet. She is a noble and splendid woman.

Thursday, 1st April

At the Connaught Hotel this evening met Archie Gordon and Blewitt of the Television BBC who are organizing a broadcast – if that is what it is termed – on the television about the National Trust. They invited me to cooperate in finding suitable performers and to attend the performance, which I certainly shall do on the 16th. I declined to play a part on the screen because I cannot speak impromptu. Lord Vansittart talked to us – a nice, genial man, with smooth face and simple manners, about sixty-eight.

Friday, 2nd April

This week has been very bad. Terrible depression. Pierre Lansel says I am to go away and stop my pills and take others in their place. Michael and Anne have pressed me to go to Birr, which is noble and sweet of them.

Wednesday, 7th April

Flew this morning to Jersey. Left Victoria at 11 o'clock – departure was scheduled for 10.30 – and reached Jersey at 1.15. Grandy and his wife Bianca there to meet me. She is very appealing, pretty and vivacious. Elegant legs and feet. Pregnant. Has lovely dark brown hair, which she wears in a tail knot drawn across the nape of her neck and partly over one shoulder. Very smartly dressed with much gold and some good jewellery, which I like. But I don't like Jersey – the island. It is over-built with villas, over-cultivated, over-prosperous and middle-class with puny little coombes and slopes. There is always a wind. The Jerseys' house, Radier Manor, is a plain farmhouse Georgianized: all fresh painted, for here labour is abundant. Grandy has some few pieces of furniture from Osterley, one very 'Louis Seize' piece from the library, which he says is by Robert Adam, and several French Impressionists.

After luncheon we had a long talk of three hours, and again next morning. At first he told me he was making arrangements to sell Osterley, house and contents, in the open market. I almost fell on my knees and begged him to reconsider this lamentable decision. Eventually we reached the following arrangement. He definitely withdraws his unconditional offer of the complete property to the National Trust (a) because he is incensed with the Middlesex County Council going back on the settlement of 1944 and has no confidence in them at all, and (b) because as a landowner he feels the country persecutes him, and the Budget capital levy of yesterday has determined him to *give* nothing away to the Government. Instead he now agrees that if the Council will *buy* that part of the estate which they were to have rented from the Trust free of payment, and if the Government will buy the furniture and keep it in the house, then he will give the house and pleasure grounds to the Trust. Beyond this he will not go and, even so, he is removing all the pictures, including the Rubenses, to Jersey where he will build a gallery for them. I cannot blame him.

Thursday, 8th April

We lunched at St Helier and I was glad to get away. It was very windy indeed, so we flew high, 10,000 feet, and this affected my ears. It took 1¼ hours from Jersey to Northolt. I noticed that from the air the fields of pasture showed distinct brown streaks of the old medieval strip system.

Grandy looks very young still, has all his straight brown hair and very fair complexion: has a small, nervous mouth.

I dined with the Eshers alone at a club they belong to on the Chelsea Embankment and we returned to drink coffee at their house, and talk. I told them about Osterley, and Lord E. did not think Grandy's attitude blameworthy. Also discussed the NT generally, and the Admiral. I told E. that although I did not dislike the Admiral, he was a disastrous secretary, and left it at that.

Friday, 9th April

Lord Crawford came to the office at 5 and stayed till 6 talking about his tour, and I was late getting away to St Paul's, Waldenbury. Arrived at 7.30 to stay with Burnet whose fortieth birthday it is. He has taken a little red brick farmhouse next door to the Bowes-Lyons, called Bury Farm, and just moved in. It is not yet furnished; only the small dining-room in commission. We lived in the kitchen; cooked our own dinner, or rather heated what had been prepared for us by the daily char-woman. Bedrooms with no carpets down, etc. B. is rather depressed by the whole business, the loneliness, the expense of the move, but he will make it pretty and comfortable. He is not really a countryman. The house is on a corner of one of the finest landscape gardens of England. On Saturday we whitewashed the ceiling of the servants' hall and distempered the walls, as we thought, beautifully, but the following day revealed a very indifferent performance.

Sunday, 11th April

I left B. at 10.30 for London. After luncheon at Brooks's I drove – a glorious day – to Faringdon for the night. Arrived teatime. Was disconcerted to find Eddy S.-W. sitting at the table but later was glad he was there. Compton Mackenzie at tea, middle-aged, stout and undistinguished. Boisterous and verbose.

I enjoyed this visit. Faringdon is one of the most elegant country houses on the small scale, yet with large, grand rooms on the *piano nobile*. Wide horizoned views from one front, the town upon the other; as perfect a house as can be. I liked Gerald Berners more than I had done before. He was wearing a knitted green skull-cap. He is chronically depressed ever since his illness a year ago. For an ageing man he ought to be contented: possessor of the most coveted house in England, Robert Heber-Percy as it were, a son, with Robert's daughter Victoria, aged eight, living with him; art, music, books, beauty, civilization, excellent food and wine, and friends circumambulating.

Before dinner I wandered round the garden and lake with Eddy and Hugh Cruddas; then talked to Gerald and Robert about the place. Robert will not allow G. to make over any land, only the gardens, but suggests an endowment in cash to bring in £1,000 p.a. The NT ought to accept this even if the endowment is not enough on account of the lettableness (or is it 'lettability'?) of the house. They ask for opening days to be for two fortnights on end, spring and summer. After dinner talk of Catholicism. Gerald would like to become a Papist if only he could believe. A very amusing and not unedifying conversation ensued. Eddy said even he might be a convert one day. Robert too has inclinations. Penelope Betjeman has become one and worries Berners with proselytizing letters, taking the ecstatic's line of persuasion.

Monday, 12th April

After breakfast I motored Eddy to Salisbury and then, parting with him regretfully, continued to Wilton. Picked up Mrs Esdaile waiting for me on a bench in the sun, and drove her to Stourhead. Never have I been in closer contact with a more unkempt female; yet she is an old pet. Her stockings hang in folds, covered with stains; her face and fingers are yellow from cigarettes which she inhales. Her clothes are a nightmare of cobwebs and must. She is rather vague now and walks with difficulty. Yet at Stourhead she plodded gallantly round the house and told us what she knew about each piece of sculpture, which was everything. I took notes as we went round. Eardley was there for the day, and Bob Gathorne-Hardy came for tea to start cataloguing the books in the library. Mrs Esdaile kept prattling about a monument she wished to see in a church three miles from Stourton, at Silton. 'A stunner,' she called it. It was by Van Nost, she assured me, of a Windham. We took a look at it. I admit it was a splendid affair, dated 1684, full-blooded Charles II Baroque, standing in face of the open door. We got to London at 9.15.

Wednesday, 14th April

This morning called for Mrs Esdaile and motored her to Charlecote. A somewhat muggy day and, my goodness, the old lady and her chain-smoking in the car. I have never met any expert at a science (tombs) so dense about practical things. She cannot recognize a street, or a car. She could not even use the lighter in my car even after I had worked it ten times for her. At Wroxton she took me into the church. In the chancel is a magnificent Jacobean monument to Lord Downe, and she showed me how it was obviously by the same mason who executed the Sandys monument at Wickhamford; one by Wilton; one by Flaxman; and another, she positively avers, by Grinling Gibbons. An interesting lesson. At Charlecote she explained at once how Queen Elizabeth's bust was a cast of Colt's effigy of the Queen in the Abbey; the busts of the Lucys were plaster casts of the effigies in Charlecote church. Joshua Rowley met us and Kaines-Smith who talked volubly about the portraits.

I dropped the old lady at Oxford and dined late with John Fowler in his King's Road house.

Thursday, 15th April

George Howard of Castle Howard lunched at Brooks's: an odd, portly figure very like his cousin Carlisle, sweating although the day was cold. Exceedingly intelligent. He is willing to act as our representative in Yorkshire. He is knowledgeable about buildings, knows every landowner within the area and beyond, and would, I fancy, be a great help to the Trust.

Tonight I had a dinner party of Burnet Pavitt, Harold Nicolson and Malcolm Bullock. Party would have been better without Malcolm who all dinner kept up a running commentary about politics and mutual friends. This did not however dam Harold's flow except when H. went to the lavatory which he did three times after dinner. Once there was a crash. I rushed to see what had happened, mindful of Gerry's lament that Harold always broke works of art. He had knocked down my Ethel Walker picture, smashing the glass to smithereens. Without Malcolm he would have talked more about Byron, for M. is bored by literary talk at which H. excels. H. told us he was convinced the reason for the Byron separation was not the incest – for Lady B. had been told of this before she married – but B. trying tricks on her. She complained that he was mad. Gosse told Harold that he had advised Polidori's niece to destroy Polidori's diary, which she did. Silly old prudish Gosse.

Saturday, 17th April

In the Abbey this morning. How I adore this fane. The Henry III tomb and Confessor's shrine are the earliest classical revival (or proto-Classical) work in England, I suppose, thirteenth century. I thought I might have made a discovery in supposing the weeping figures round the D. of Buckingham's tomb to be by Le Sueur, the dragon helmet of the nearest one resembling Le Sueur's helmet of Charles I at Stourhead. After luncheon drove to South Mimms church. It was locked. I was nettled, and rang the rectory bell. A head appeared at a window and asked gruffly: 'Who are you?' I replied: 'Just an ordinary person. I want to see the tombs please,' crossly. Then was filled with remorse for the old clergyman, whose head it was, was pathetic, longing for someone to talk to, and offering me tea. He wasted my time all right showing me things I had not come to see – a window and font by Comper, very good – but I saw the Frowyk monument curiously classical for 1527, if the Roy. Hist. Monuments book for Middlesex is correct, which I doubt.

Arrived in time for tea at Clouds Hill with Blanche Lloyd who was so sweet, kind and pleased to see me. She is greatly mellowed, madly keen on Christianity, and against the Government and Communism of course. Also always losing her spectacles, her thimbles as of old, and terrified of having no money to live on. Still speaks of George with tears in her eyes and pride in her heart. I worshipped her.

Lord Lloyd called this house – which I think was the Rectory – after his friend T. E. Lawrence's cottage in Dorset.

Sunday, 18th April

Sat about, sometimes indoors under the sun through glass, sometimes out when warm enough, and agreeably wasting time, till 6 o'clock when I left. Stopped at St Ippolitt's church on the hill and saw the memorial to George Lloyd by Hugh Easton, tiny but pleasing. I liked the inscription: 'Remember George 1st Baron Lloyd of Dolobran', but not the Esmond Burton altar so much. Also liked George's tombstone in the churchyard, with the Eric Gill lettering and coat of arms with supporters and coronet. Stayed the night with Burnet at Bury Farm.

Monday, 19th April

Ran slap into a car in front of me in London, injuring one of my springs. The other car, having a buffer, was quite unharmed. Today had an interview with Sir Henry Hake and C. J. Adams at the National Portrait Gallery. Sir Henry, rather pompous, indicated that the Gallery must not be quoted in any advice it gives the Trust about pictures. He is an unattractive old man – vindictive, Ben Nicolson tells me. He quite sensibly suggested Ellis Waterhouse joining the Historic Buildings Committee. He would, I imagine, be an asset. After luncheon went to my first meeting as a member of the National Buildings Record, of which Sir Eric Maclagan is chairman. Not very interesting perhaps, but I am proud to be on the Council for I approve of what it is doing and make much use of its photographs.

Tuesday, 20th April

I am garaging my motor at a new place for 30s a week – fearfully expensive but it includes service. It is just behind the V & A Museum. I shall try it out. The man motored me in my own car to the Air Terminus which was rather nice, at 9 o'clock, half an hour too early actually. At the airport I met Alan Lennox-Boyd, also going to Dublin for a Guinness Brewery ball tonight. We took off at 11.15 but when in sight of the Irish Sea turned back because we were told we could not land at Dublin owing to ground mist. Went back to London again, and at the Service's expense ate an excellent cold luncheon. I was glad to be with Alan whom I like. We set off again at 3.30 and landed safely at Dublin, seeing little en route because of the clouds. We were in a 4-engine Constellation and sat in the navigator's cabin. These very large planes alarm me for they are so heavy I cannot understand how they leave the ground. It was too late to catch the last train to Roscrea, so I went with Alan to Farmleigh and stayed the night with the Iveaghs, his in-laws. Patsy and the three children were there and Chips Channon's son, Paul, a curiously sophisticated, plump little boy, perhaps cunning. There was a ball in the house and, had I not had a lot to drink, I should have been most unhappy. Farmleigh is a large Georgian house, the inside ugly and Edwardianized, but luxurious. Lord and Lady Iveagh paid little attention, but seemed not the least surprised to see me. Late at night Alan said what a tiresome necessity of life dissimulation was. He kept saying, 'Isn't Patsy a wonderful wife?' I could not deny it. Lady Iveagh once complained to Alan, 'Can't you change your friends a little more often?'

Wednesday, 21st April

Left Farmleigh at 8 with Alan, from whom I parted at Dublin airport, one of the best modern buildings I know. Its horizontal lines and tower give it a Picturesque quality. From Kingsbridge station to Roscrea the journey quiet and uneventful, through low-lying fields without a labourer in sight and stations with no one on the platform. A dead land-scape, all the trees looking as though they were part of the earth and a thousand years old in spite of the green buds. The faces of the inhabitants express no surprise and, as they stare, are utterly vacant. When they are animated they are the faces of demons. Arrived Birr Castle in time for luncheon. Alan [Pryce-Jones] and Poppy staying for the night. She talks a lot and to the point; and has greatly improved in looks. In the after-noon Michael had us driven (he cannot drive himself) to see the Jacobean ruin that belongs to the Harewoods: very melancholy but complete. I feel terribly tired.

Sunday, 25th April

So far I have not done a stroke of work. I have breakfast in bed, rise at 10.30 and am down at 11.30. I read a certain amount, eat a lot, but care-fully, wander into the town and buy handkerchiefs and shoes. The weather is superb and the air scented with peat. The shop assistants are polite and send whatever one buys round to the Castle; this never happens in England now. In the Castle are a butler, footman, four house-maids, besides a cook and kitchenmaids. Michael and Anne leave tomor-row but are allowing me to stay on for a week; and I have simply *got* to make a beginning of my new book. They are angels of generosity and understanding.

Sunday, 2nd May

Michael and Anne left on Monday last – I miss them – on which day I felt deathlike. I immediately drank at St Brendan's Well in the garden and wished that I might be enabled to begin my book. In the afternoon I could do nothing but lie in the sun feeling wretched. That evening the rector and his wife dined with Susan [Armstrong-Jones] and me. But I could eat nothing at all. Suddenly after dessert I made a bolt from the room and was sick with greater vehemence than I ever remember. It gushed with the propulsion of an engine rather than of a human stomach. I felt better, and ashamed.

All this week however I have not felt well. Have been without appetite and pursued by attacks of nausea. What is it, if not just Ireland? I do not like Ireland. I do not like the country here. It is horizonless and dead.

One cannot see further than one's hand. I wish I could define precisely what it is I do not like about the climate, the people and the scenery. My dislike is almost intuitive, certainly temperamental and racial. I fear the native hostility under the mask of deceit. At Mass the church here is so crowded that one cannot worship. Irish Catholicism is like a vice, crushing the congregation like nuts. The Irish God is not loving. He is a tyrant. The people are tight within his grasp. Unlike Latins they are subdued by their Church, not elevated by it. They derive from it no inspiration, recreation or romance. Here it is grey and puritanical. In the church the men herd on the Epistle side, the women on the Gospel side like battery hens. One senses that their appalling mendacity and untrustworthiness are the consequence of their age-long abortive attempts to escape the clutch of the priests. Oh, I do hate the whole island.

Things here strike me forcibly: a cart gallops through Birr town, with a line of three horses, unbridled, following at a trot obediently behind, in and out of the traffic through the streets. Why do they follow obediently without a rein? The lodgekeeper never fails to open the big double gates to the drive just at the very moment when the car comes into sight, as though by magic, the chauffeur not having hooted this time. Creepy! On other days, when many people are about the chauffeur keeps his hand on the horn, winnowing them aside, in warning. The family are treated like royalty and Michael is indeed a small king; or like a German princeling. One must realize this before understanding him. The town take the greatest interest in his coming and going, and Anne knows this and plays up to it. She is respected in consequence. There is too a sanctity about Desmond's memory. If you mention his name there is no respectful hush, but eyes sparkle and he is referred to as though still alive. The Irish are all eyes, and nothing else. No compassion, and I doubt whether there is any love, except for the dead. Much hate for the living.

Since the Rosses left I have got down to my new book – The Classical Revival shall I call it? – and worked about seven hours a day with short intervals for walking into the town and round the demesne. To this extent I have at any rate succeeded. I have begun the beginning. The plunge has been taken but I have hit, and shall hit again, my head against a few hard rocks.

Monday, 3rd May

Left Birr this morning at 9 o'clock; quite glad to get away though more grateful than any words can express to Michael and Anne who are my guardian angels. Travelled to Dublin in a first-class compartment, very old-fashioned and cosy, with an eccentric old peer wearing a scarf over his head under a homburg hat and a shawl over his knees. In Dublin met

Morogh Barnard at the Shelburne Rooms. He gave me a solid luncheon at the Russell Hotel, entrecôte and strawberry ice adorned with young strawberries. Had no time to sight-see, and caught the afternoon aeroplane to London.

Tuesday, 4th May

Cannot say I feel at all well; on the contrary in a highly nervous condition. I met Lord Esher at luncheon. He told me he had rented Iford from the Michael Petos on a fourteen-year lease; so this is the result of his abortive visit there to try and acquire the house for the Trust. He thought this a very funny joke and laughed heartily. This afternoon I went to the Annual Meeting of the SPAB held at the Apothecaries' Hall, near Ludgate Circus, a charming late seventeenth-century building, which has happily survived the blitzes. Esher made an excellent and witty speech, Harold Nicolson, the chief speaker, a not so good one. I took Harold off to Brooks's afterwards where we had a long talk. He told me Vita was not at all cross, but amused, to find that I had forgotten I asked her to lunch last Thursday. Michael had told her not to be cross with me because I was in a bad way and tired after my last book! A curious reason for forgetfulness. Harold told me the story of a German friend, a long-distance runner, whom he met in Berlin and who pursued him for ten years with a hopeless passion which very much bored Harold. However, the story had a tragic ending for the young man was finally shot by his own countrymen in a concentration camp. Harold remembers urging him, as a good German, to oppose and resist the Nazis at all costs. Harold said he thought and hoped Ben was in love with a friend he had met at Oxford.

Wednesday, 5th May

Went to the opening by Dr Trevelyan of K. Kennet's collected sculpture at Heal's shop. Trevelyan said K. was a woman whose life was dedicated, primarily, to the arts – which is true – that she hated fraud, sentiment and lack of courage; that she loved beauty and the young; and that it was not true she was among the dead.

Dined with the Chileans, Léon and Paz Subercaseaux. A very enjoyable party. Guests were the Aspinall-Oglanders, Barbara Moray, Riette Lamington and Leigh Ashton. Leigh told us about the burglary at the V & A of two of Gerry Wellington's swords. The burglars were professionals. They climbed a 40-ft wall, cut the electric wires behind them; smashed a plate glass case, wrenched off the jewelled hilts, left the scabbards and escaped while the watchman's back was turned. Gerry heard the news on the wireless when in Spain and wrote Leigh a very pompous letter beginning: 'These swords have been safe for over a hundred years in my family.' I sat next to Joan Oglander and Barbara. Barbara told me that staying at Windsor Castle she found beside her bed my Adam book and Peter Cheyney; it was the room occupied by Mrs Roosevelt the weekend before. Joan Oglander was far less twitchy, jumpy and talkative, and consequently nicer. After dinner Paz spoke very understandingly of James's romanticism. She said he lived in a dream world and fabricated dream theories about people; that his romanticism was incorrigible and attractive; that he had enough curiosity to make a great novelist; and that his friends should overlook his tiresome behaviour.

Thursday, 6th May

Hubert Worthington, the architect, called to see me about the mill at Alderley [Cheshire] – a nice, intelligent, rather vague man. Hubert Smith and Christopher Gibbs lunched with me at Brooks's to discuss Harewood. At the Reports Committee only Lord Esher turned up. He told the Admiral as plainly as possible that he was a fool: a most embarrassing moment. It was over Buscot discussions and the old Admiral just did not know what he was talking about.

Tony Gandarillas took me and Daisy Fellowes to the Palladium. We had champagne in Daisy's flat at the Dorchester and drove in her huge black limousine. Her lifted face is beginning to assume the taut, mask-like grimace which is so frightening. We dined at the Ritz, with more champagne, and were joined by Lord Sherwood who got very drunk. He is a foolish little man who looks like a rat, which is what Daisy calls him behind his back. He is fifty, worships Daisy who is fifty-eight and clings to him nevertheless, being lucky to have a lover at all. She is still quick as lightning, sharp as a packet of needles and capable of seducing God. She is going to invite me to stay at Donnington, which I rather dread and much look forward to.

Tuesday, 11th May

Went to see Pierre Lansel who insists that I go next week to the medical clinic to have another blood test. Sugar content far below normal.

To a cocktail party given by Mrs Foley in Eaton Square to see the Stoke Edith needlework hangings in her drawing-room. Magnificent they are on first sight, because of the size of the panels. But the subjects being domestic and horticultural give them almost a cottagey flavour. Mr Hobson of Sotheby's told me that he was in favour of works of art being sold abroad, for art was international and, besides, the museums in England were overflowing. Dined with the Alfred Beits at the Savoy. I fainted at the beginning of dinner, but soon recovered. Maud Russell told me she was thinking of selling Mottisfont which was too big for her.

Alfred and Clementine suggested my going to South Africa to help them influence the Boers to preserve their seventeenth-century Dutch houses.

Thursday, 13th May

Helen Dashwood, Billa Harrod and Pam Chichester lunched at Thurloe Square. A curious little party. I sensed that all three hated each other. Yet they called each other 'darling' and behaved like good pussy cats that rub against a table leg, purring.

The Admiral and I had a talk with Lord Crawford at the Travellers'. Lord C. told us of his interview with Sir Stafford Cripps who was quite ready to ask Parliament to buy the contents of both Harewood and Osterley, and indeed realized he would have to do this sort of thing increasingly in the future. He proposed having a list drawn up of the 100 greatest houses with collections. How often have similar lists not been drawn up? Cripps said he recognized the Trust to be the fitting body to hold them. This opens up a vast question as to how the Trust is to administer them. A limitation of great houses, with contents, to 100 is going to cause trouble in the future. What is considered bad architecture and bad art today may be considered good tomorrow. Besides, how many experts will agree on what is the best today?

Friday, 14th May

This glorious morning I motored to Rousham. On the way stopped at Quainton church near Waddesdon to look at two monuments, one to Winwood, husband and wife, erected by the wife in 1689; the figures very alive and Baroque, resting on their elbows. The second a strict Palladian affair with a broken pediment to Sir Richard Piggott of Doddershall, 1735, and signed 'I. Leoni'. I have written to ask Mrs Esdaile if this is the architect, Giacomo. Arrived Rousham at 1 o'clock and met by Mr Cottrell-Dormer, very gentle, intelligent, unassuming man. House itself disappointing, for it was added to and spoilt in the last century, and the Kent wings have been interfered with, or rather the connecting colonnades. There are only two rooms by Kent left, the dining-room with painted canvas ceiling in arabesques and great chimneypiece, gilded, and a surprisingly low ceiling; and the saloon, with ribbed ceiling and strikingly deep compartments. The stucco-work of picture frames and walls done by Roberts of Oxford about 1764. Some of the chairs are by Kent, but their quality is not outstanding.

The gardens are very important as the only Kent layout to survive, apart from the mess left by the urban authorities at Chiswick. There are statues, in a distressing condition, a seven-arched portico (Praeneste), grottoes, glades, a cascade, bath, pools, temples and straight and serpentine rides. The gardens are miraculously intact after 200 years. We had an *al fresco* luncheon below Praeneste, close to the Cherwell, and watched the mayfly hatching and flying off the river. Saw the kestrel.

At Banbury found the Reindeer Inn and called, only to discover that the fine ceiling and wainscot had been sold to America before the war. Arrived Upton at 5 o'clock and had tea alone with Lord Bearsted, she being ill upstairs. He informed me that on the Riviera Lady Kitty Lambton told him that Mrs Puleston left her some rare French medieval manuscripts; and that she had many other treasures from Emral. Lady Kitty had no idea who had inherited them. Lord B. showed not the least interest when I told him Mrs Puleston, wretched woman, was my aunt who on my uncle's death in 1936 informed me that she was leaving all these things to me as the rightful heir. I suppose it is boring for the very rich when the very poor lament their ill fortune. In any case I should remember that the rich at worst hate the poor and, at best, are embarrassed by them.

On my way to Wickhamford stopped at Weston-Sub-Edge church to see if there was any memorial to, or mention of William Latimer. Found nothing.

Monday, 17th May

Weather these holidays ideal – cloudless skies and a strong wind; even so sun too hot for sitting out of doors in the middle of the day. This evening after tea motored to Woollas Hall to talk to the Whitworths, but I knew before arrival that they would do nothing. She vaguely dallies with the idea; he is opposed to it since his son, he says, will not want to live there anyway. It is a most romantic house, perched on Bredon Hill. In the bad times the family of this Papist stronghold used to hang white sheets from the windows when Mass was to be said. The faithful from miles around would see the sheets and flock to Woollas. The Whitworths are upset by the new reservoir to supply Coventry with water which is to be made on their land. Their consent was never asked, nor have they been paid a penny in compensation. Is this sort of totalitarian measure what we fought the war for?

Visited Little Comberton, Great Comberton and Eckington churches, looking for other tombs by the mason of the Wickhamford ones, but in vain. At the last is a tomb to the Hanfords who built Woollas; his effigy exactly resembles his portrait at Woollas, of a thickset man with no neck. I dined at Overbury with the Holland-Martins. Old Mrs H.-M., Ruby and Christopher, all most friendly. To think how terrified I was, when a child, of the mother sitting on the top of a high step-ladder umpiring at tennis tournaments and shouting reprimands whenever I missed an easy shot, especially when partnering one of her sons. Rayner-Wood (and Julia, his wife) over from Colwall. I find this ex-Eton beak supercilious, snobbish and antipathetic. He complained about the condition of our old house at Tenby, as usual. Told us that the Provost of Eton now eats daily at a British restaurant. Horrors! That the Eton 'boys' maid' is extinct, and the boys make their own beds; and the housemaster's wife cooks for them. Times have indeed changed.

Tuesday, 18th May

Stopped at Burford church. What superb tombs; the Tanfields' might be by Epiphanius Evesham. A very good de Vries-type one, dated 1569. Then stopped at Christ Church, Oxford, to look at the Renaissance design under the oriel between the twin towers at the SW corner, and the hall which has no Gothic detail that I could find. Lunched at Henley. Stopped at Langley Marish and saw the Kederminster pew, but could not get into the library. The pew is a pretty example of painted Jacobean joinery. Went to a lecture at the Courtauld Institute given by Count Metternich on preservation of works of art and buildings in Germany.

Wednesday, 19th May

Enjoyable dinner at Barbara Moray's. I sat next to Elizabeth Glenconner. Conversation turned upon age and death. I suggested that the mere physical effort of attaining ripe years should entitle one to veneration, almost worship, as in the East. Agreed that of all the highbrows we knew John Pope-Hennessy was the least tolerant of silly people.

Thursday, 20th May

All morning sat in a clinic having a blood test. Had had no breakfast at all and nothing to drink until I got to the clinic where I was given one glass of sugared water. At half-hourly intervals I had blood extracted and urinated into a tin can, making a pretty tinkle up the scale, and not down, which seemed strange. What with a little hangover from champagne last night and an empty stomach this morning I felt rotten.

To tea with Lady Mander. A Pre-Raphaelite tea party – Sir Sydney Cockerell with whom I had a long talk about Ruskin whom he knew intimately; Miss Lushington about Rossetti (she has his willow pattern dinner service to sell), Mrs Angeli, William Rossetti's daughter, and Mrs Joseph (Holman Hunt's daughter). It was fun. Sir Sydney is very spry and on the spot. He said the pity about Dr Trevelyan was that he had no sense of beauty and was totally ignorant of art. These disqualifications prevented him from being a really great historian. Of Kathleen Kennet, whom he had loved, he said she was no artist and knew that he was aware of it.

I told Sir Sydney that because I was more interested in the Classical than in the Gothic it did not make me despise the latter, whereas Ruskin who loved the latter denigrated the former. Why did he do this? He said Ruskin favoured the Gothic because it was the individual expression of man's creative ability, whereas Classical motifs were mechanical and expressive of nothing. 'There is no scope,' he said, 'for individual expression in a succession of egg and tongue.'

Friday, 21st May

Last night dined with the Eshers. The other guests were Lady Gosport and the Harold Bowens. I sat next to Vera Bowen and was overheard by Lord Esher, who, although deaf, never misses anything he wants to hear, telling her that I suffered from remorse. Esher joined in: 'Now that is a flagrant untruth. Young people *never* suffer from remorse. It is simply because he knows he can indulge in sentimental confidences with Vera who is an emotional Muscovite.' He told us that there were actually people who hated him. One was Princess Marie Louise who overheard him say to his hostess at a dinner party when told to take her into the dining-room, 'Must I?' He spent the whole of dinner explaining to the Princess that he meant it differently, for his card told him he was to take in somebody else. His protests were in vain. He said that the late Lord Willingdon felled all and sundry with his charm, which was the only quality he possessed.

Today went to Swakeleys. Met Carew Wallace and Walter Godfrey's architect son. Walked over this house and inspected the alterations the Foreign Office are making inside. The hall fireplace and Restoration screen are very interesting. The plaster ceiling of the Great Chamber is coarse in execution, not in design. The floor over it had been taken out. We looked straight into the great hollow ribs of the plaster compartments which do not cover the beams as one might suppose. The exterior dressings of the house, instead of being in stone, are of composition. This gives a flimsy appearance.

At West Wycombe Carew and I visited all the temples. We punted over to the island and examined the Temple of Music. Then went to the house and met Helen, Johnnie and Francis [Dashwood], and the Eshers. Walked round outside and inside, listing all the improvements we would like to carry out, regardless of expense. Then had tea in the Brown Drawing-room. Lord E. and I teased Helen by observing that everything on the outside of the house was sham: imitation stone, wood, porphyry, etc. But we admitted that the interior had substantial, and exquisite, features, notably marble chimneypieces, ceilings, and the staircase of red mahogany with an inlaid star on each riser.

Saturday, 22nd May

To Westminster Abbey this morning. In spite of the perpetual crowds I never fail to be transported by aesthetic and historical emotions as soon as I set foot in this building. As for Henry VII's tomb the more I look at it the more moved I am by its abiding Tuscan beauty.

Caught a train to Denham at 2.10. Travelled with Dick Girouard and his daughter to visit Denham Place, open to the Georgian Group. A lovely William and Mary house of red brick overgrown with wistaria. House has a rich wooden cornice that gives a dignity and purpose, and relieves it from dullness. But the surroundings are dull, and indifferent. There should be a formal garden and a canal or some such feature. The interior is pretty good: two panelled rooms of the date, most richly carved. In the larger a great cupid suspended with bow from the ceiling. The plaster cove of fishing scenes in the Brown Tapestry Room is exceedingly bold and unusual; that of the next room, the colour of gingerbread, is astonishing in a peasant-like way, but too like a Walt Disney picture.

Got back for tea bringing Francis Watson, who was at Denham: a very entertaining, intelligent man, working at the Wallace Collection.

Monday, 24th May

Left by road to stay at Long Crichel. Stopped at Basingstoke. Inquired where was the Chapel of the Holy Ghost. No one knew. Finally a local antiquarian, proprietor of a jeweller's shop, told me the ruins of the Chapel survived in the cemetery. But the Chapel had been ruinous since the Civil War. Went to have a look but could find none of the Renaissance woodwork that Gotch talks of. Then to Winchester. Saw the classical screen of delicately carved woodwork erected by Bishop Fox in St Cross church. Then to the Cathedral. Looked at cathedral screen and Bishop Gardiner's Chantry, and the Le Sueur effigies of James I and Charles I. Don't think Le Sueur can be called a great artist. These chantry chapels were often built by grand personages long before their deaths. Hence a difficulty in dating them. At Long Crichel Eardley, Eddy and Desmond ran around, greeting me like three big affectionate dogs.

Tuesday, 25th May

Eddy left this morning for Bristol. E.K. and I off to Stourhead which depressed us. The house is still in muddle and chaos. We could see no daylight.

Wednesday, 26th May

At Stourhead today we suddenly saw daylight, and made great strides. Bob Gathorne-Hardy joined us at luncheon in the pub and was encouraging and inspiring. E. spent hours hanging pictures, I arranging china, furniture, statuary and busts. I felt better. We listened to Verdi's *Otello* all evening, very loud for they have the wireless blaring at Long Crichel, Desmond, Bob and E.K. following the score throughout while I read Sydney Cockerell's correspondence with the great over sixty years. Desmond suggests our going to Rome together in September.

Later tonight Bob talked to me about Logan Pearsall Smith, whom he hated at the end. He has finished his Life of Logan. I cannot but think he has made a mistake in writing it, and in particular in setting out to prove Logan's insanity. It can only do Bob harm, for his readers will assume he is getting his own back on Logan for having cut him out of his will. Bob is a charming person with a thirst for all forms of knowledge and bald truth. He has quenchless curiosity, disarming frankness, and great volubility. He told me how before Logan died he slept in Logan's room on the sofa, kept awake by Logan's coughing; how two nights after his death he slept, no less unhappily, in Logan's bed, Logan lying on the sofa in his coffin. Bob is not exactly fastidious in mind or body.

Thursday, 27th May

Today we called for the Anthony Wests and motored them to Stourhead, Kitty intending to paint in the garden. Anthony West is the natural son of H. G. Wells and Rebecca West. He has the profile of his father. His eyes and the lower part of his face are caricatures of his mother's. He has dark hair and eyes, sallow skin, a heavy, slack chin. Oafish. Is said to be clever; and is quirky, contradictory. He is a contributor to the *New Statesman*. Rennie Hoare greeted us at Stourhead with much gush which E. and I received without enthusiasm. In fact E. was very cold. I tried to appear warm but firm. Rennie made several preposterous suggestions regarding furniture arrangement that we could not adopt. I distrust him profoundly. This afternoon we finished arranging all the state rooms on the front. There are three behind which we have not yet tackled. They must wait for our next visit.

On our return the Wests took us to Fonthill. Of Beckford's Abbey there still remains one tower, into which we went. The complete Abbey must have been beautiful as well as striking. The quality of the surviving ashlar is good. Situation high and very remote. Tisbury church has good brasses and some stones to the Arundel family in the chancel. Then to Wardour Castle round which we walked. We were not allowed inside because there is to be a sale of all contents next week. Ted Lister once took me to luncheon before the war. The son and heir was present and told us how much he adored the place. He became a prisoner of war and, being a badly wounded case, was exchanged for a German prisoner. On his way from Liverpool to Wardour he died. The exterior is dignified and clean-cut; simple and severe. Much of the stonework now broken and the cornice of the front perished. The Jesuits have bought it. It is much neglected. I bet they won't repair it.

Friday, 28th May

Left on a lovely morning after breakfast, having much enjoyed this visit to Long Crichel, as usual. Drove to Wimborne. Looked inside the Norman minster; liked the Georgian painted grenadier outside the clock tower. Continued to Christchurch. Spent an hour in this minster which is singularly beautiful. Under the west tower is a 'Pietà' group of Mary Shelley holding the drowned poet in her arms, dated 1851 when I presume Mary died, though why it is here I don't understand. Carefully examined the Countess of Salisbury's chantry, Perpendicular with well-carved Classical arabesques. Observed the intersecting arcades of the north transept, a barbaric Classical. Drove on to Alresford, lunching there. To Miss Lushington's at Kingsley near Bordon. She is a dear lady but a great talker. Her house is awful. Built by her aunts in 1870 as a school, it is huge, rambling, and of flimsiest material. She showed me all the pictures given to her father by the Pre-Raphaelites. Her mother originated the Rossetti neck. She has some oils by Lord Carlisle which are creditable. She offers to sell us her china. Mrs Gaunt, wife of William Gaunt, author of *The Pre-Raphaelite Tragedy* and one of her tenants, came to tea. Talk was about the interest of our age in the sexual lives of distinguished men. Miss Lushington expressed disapproval, but not too forcibly. I hedged because I knew she has inherited many papers relating to the Byron scandal and Queen Caroline's trial which she threatens to destroy. How to discourage her from carrying out the threat?

In London dined with John Macdonell, Australian, who is too dull for words. His other guest was Count Metternich whom I took to. Like most Germanic aristocrats he has an urbane cosmopolitan manner. Nothing provincial. A well-bred, cultivated man, with considerable knowledge of British art. His uncle was Ambassador in London before 1914. He remembers London in 1903, and says the streets were more congested with horse traffic, and noisier, then than they are with cars today. From a distance, say, in the middle of Hyde Park in 1903 there was a thunderous rumble of horse traffic that was unique to London.

Sunday, 30th May

After Mass motored to Cambridge. Entered King's Chapel. All scrubbed as to roof and walls and glistening with soapy cleanliness. The windows mostly reinstated. The sun shining through them like jewels. I gasped at the exquisite beauty of this building. Wandered in the sun to Caius gateways and the bridge over the Cam at Clare. Then continued to Ryston Hall for tea with Colonel Pratt and family. I had written asking if I might look at Ryston. You can barely discern the vestiges of Sir Roger Pratt's house which Soane altered by adding two wings, and cementing over brickwork, and which Colonel Pratt's father altered again fifty years ago. The Colonel has made the architect's library into a kitchen. The portrait of the first Roger Pratt by Lely survives. So do two chimneypieces of this date. The others are eighteenth-century like the staircase. Some of Pratt's books lie loose about the untidy house. On my way to Bradenham I stopped at Oxburgh. By some miracle the Renaissance terra cotta Bedingfeld tombs survive, although when the tower fell the whole of the nave collapsed, and only the chancel escaped. How this fragile terracotta did not crumble I cannot imagine.

Alec Penrose's brother Beakers and his new wife staying at Bradenham [Hall]. At first I did not take to her but by the end of my visit succumbed to her extreme friendliness. I wish intelligent women were less affected and less familiar.

Monday, 31st May

Motored to Wisbech with Alec [Penrose] in the morning and went round Bank House, deciding how we could divide it up, letting the large library to the Wisbech Society, the basement to the Archivists, the balancing 1860 wing as a separate house, and keeping the main block for show. I visited the Wisbech Museum and was taken round by Rudsdale. A charming building of 1840 but hardly suitable for the Trust. We all lunched at the Crown. Alec showed me Beaupré Hall (red brick, diaper work, Elizabethan heraldic glass) which is in the most woeful state and only fit for a ruin. To Wallington Hall for a drink with the Luddingtons. A much restored house of the early fifteenth century. Best feature the gate tower with terra cotta panels and Gothic cusping. Luddington's father took out many of the Georgian sash windows, substituting bad casement lights.

Tuesday, 1st June

To Blickling where we had a fairly profitable day. Wyndham Ketton-Cremer lunched at the Buckinghamshire Arms, also Lord

Lothian whom I allowed to take away some engraved glass, golf clubs, etc., I trust acting correctly. Alec said of Wyndham he is the sort of man who has found contentment of mind by cutting off all limbs that offended him. Alec, I find, has aged mentally; is less elastic; slower, rather dogmatic, almost pompous and, I suspect, selfish.★ Frances seems to be on edge with him. He is not very nice to his boys – very schoolmaster-ish. Yet he is a dear man. I admire his taste and I am impressed by his profound faith. He peers bewildered through owlish spectacles in the way, I imagine, Edward Lear did.

I motored after tea to St Paul's, Waldenbury to stay with Burnet. We discussed the cussedness of inclinations beyond one's control. Something inside one may whisper futility, and caution against the inevitable back-fire of passion. Affairs of the heart mean not a fig more than the grip of momentary drunkenness, rendering one rudderless and unreliable. Civilized beings must rise above the distractions of lust. Pious thoughts which tomorrow may wither beneath the sun of a new love.

Saturday, 5th June

Have seen no one these last few days. Refused a tempting invitation from Joan Moore to a huge dinner party and then, too late, regretted refusal. I have stayed in of an evening working very hard, and reading Osbert Sitwell's *Great Morning*. I wish my judgements were not so easily influ-enced. I recall Desmond [Shawe-Taylor]'s animadversions upon the man's style. He is right. It is not so pure as I thought. Perhaps this book falls short of its predecessors. They were surely magnificent. The style flowed like a clear river in spate.

Bobo Mitford has died which I find very sad. How Tom teased her the last time I – and I believe, he – saw her at Swinbrook like the big child she had become again.

Today Count Metternich and John Summerson lunched. The Count is a delightful man. He is as much at home in this country as in his own. John Summerson has a mildly deprecating, cynical manner, combined with disarming diffidence. He took us to the Soane Museum.

Sunday, 6th June

Stuart Preston comes to stay here for a week. How shall I find him?

Stuart has come. I met him at Victoria station. He looks well, is brown, not fat but stalwart, and has become very bald, with a tonsure. I invited the Cyril Connollys to meet him at dinner since Cyril expressed the wish. C. is a lumpish, bad-mannered man and was as bored with me as I

★He was, I was to learn only too soon, already very ill.

was bored with him. His puny little wife is quite sweet and at any rate polite.

Monday, 7th June

Went to Covent Garden with Stuart – *Giselle* and *Les Patineurs*. I like Second Empire music. Stuart already in the opera house when I arrived. We dined late at the Ritz grill where Alvilde Chaplin joined us. Stuart said that she grumbled too much. I suspect that he thinks I do too. Grumbling is not at all a bad thing if, like literary criticism, it is constructive.

Tuesday, 8th June

Met Lord Gainsborough at 6 o'clock at the Marlborough Club and discussed Chipping Campden. He says he may offer his whole property including the Court House on condition that his family have a right of residence in perpetuity. He is a tubby little boy, very young, a sort of *Schoolboy's Annual* hero, with a distinct look of his handsome mother about the mouth. Very polite he is, earnest, Catholic, but physically a suet pudding.

I dined with the Harold Bowens in York Terrace and there met Midi [Gascoigne] whom I had not seen for nearly a year. She looks very thin, frail, delicate and beautiful. I have never seen her look more beautiful. But she is an invalid. At first I was shocked by her frailty and the smallness of her wrists. She has today seen a new doctor who says she has colon trouble, not ulcers, and has been starving herself for over nine months. She says her mother is now dying of cancer. She watched her mother come out of a coma and asked her if she had had nightmares. Her mother answered that they were not nightmares, but worrying dreams about little things she had neglected to do and others she ought not to have done. This is more frightening than sheer oblivion in the circumstances. Perhaps afterlife will be like this – worrying – for all eternity.

Thursday, 10th June

Lunched with Mr Harry Batsford and Sam Carr at the Connaught Hotel. This entertainment was intended as a kind assurance that they still wanted me to continue with my book. I asked if Batsford's would send me to Italy again this year and Mr B. said, 'Yes,' he thought so.

Dined at Dick Girouard's house with him and Alan Pryce-Jones alone. Very enjoyable. Alan very amusing in that sweet way he underestimates everything, including his own brilliance. Told us that he might become a Catholic one day. When a boy of seventeen he went to the Cathedral to be received. Had a formidable interview with several Fathers who sent him away with a flea in his ear.

Friday, 11th June

Stuart is staying till Monday. I have been nicer to him this visit. He and I dined with Bridget and Lady de Vesci who gave us champagne at the Ritz. We went to *Hamlet*; disappointing film. The play, an intellectual exchange between characters without action, does not work on the film where action seems to be required. The producer was evidently aware of this phenomenon and made Hamlet walk continuously up and down stairs like a restless fly. Very irritating. Olivier gave a fine performance, yet he is not my idea of Hamlet. He made the part too straightforward and was actuated exclusively by revenge, and nothing else. He has dyed his hair yellow which makes him look older instead of younger.

Saturday, 12th June

To the Royal Academy this morning. The standard of indifference is undeviating. The standard of the architectural drawings plumbs the depths. Summerson warned me of this. This evening Alec [Clifton-Taylor], who had written most kindly giving me a long list of *errata* to *Adam*, called.

Monday, 14th June

Vita [Sackville-West] and Doreen [Baynes] lunched. Vita was wearing the same old terra cotta dress she wore every day last August on our tour, and smoking from her long holder. Doreen said after V. left that she had the most beautiful features and eyes D. had ever seen. Was much impressed too by V.'s 'kindliness'. Though V. was here little over a quarter of an hour, for she had a dentist's appointment, Doreen studied her appearance and manner intently. She sees so few people and goes about so little that she manages to absorb impressions that wash over the rest of us.

Tuesday, 15th June

Lunched with the publisher Lindsay Drummond and his assistant, Miss Matheson, at the Escargot. They pumped me for information about the National Trust. I repeated that I did not wish to discourage them from issuing their series of books. Yet I did not encourage a venture which I believe to be incongruous. This evening Papa came to stay after his first day at Ascot. He looks well.

Wednesday, 16th June

Today gave a luncheon party of five and was quite nervous beforehand, my table being very small and my guests rather grand. But it was a success. Guests were Michael Goodwin, editor of *The Nineteenth Century*, Diane Abdy, Sibyl Colefax and Gerry Wellington. Gerry had to come to London unexpectedly for a meeting called by Lord Esher to discuss the Blickling Tower alterations this afternoon. Excellent meal, lots of drink, ending with Cointreau and brandy. G. again rattled off the names of every marble inlay of my round table.

To Hatfield as a tourist. Escorted round the house. This palatial mass less fussy than I remembered it to be. The north front quite plain and more austere than Blickling. Brick darker. Few fanciful windows. Condition still a little dusty and unkempt from the hospital having been there all the war. It is not the architecture so much as the relics that interest me – Queen Elizabeth's garden hat and stockings, her jewel case, and those three astonishing portraits.

Stayed the night with Burnet at Bury Farm. After dinner David Bowes-Lyon walked round from St Paul's. He was alone, his wife being in London. He was wearing a blue collarless shirt under his coat, his neck bare, suede shoes and tight trousers. Has strong, crisp brown hair and regular white teeth. Very youthful; good complexion in spite of some sharp, haggard lines on one side of his face. He is a charmer. Took us round his garden in the twilight, and into the house.

Thursday, 17th June

Drove Bowes-Lyon up to London, leaving 8 o'clock. Pouring with rain and no windscreen wiper working. His conversation very strange. Did I not think women's thighs ugly? Men's figures more aesthetic? Did I like wearing shorts? He did not disapprove of any sexual practices – and so on. Trying not to be too distant, I did not commit myself to any opinions. He must have found me either a dolt or a prude.

Friday, 18th June

Went to Covent Garden. The Sadler's Wells Company dancing *Coppélia*. Pamela May in this role good but has common mannerisms and facial tricks that make one want to smack her. Hunter in the *Tricorne* in Massine's wonderful part as the miller was feeble. I am tired of this ballet and the thumping of de Falla.

Saturday, 19th June

Antique Dealers' Fair. There is too much to see. This is a fault of exhibitions these days. Some wonderful pieces of furniture, of course. Indeed I am amazed at the high-quality furniture still left in this country. Much must be faked. Prices exorbitant. I noticed six ordinary Chippendale chairs priced at £700.

After luncheon motored Dame Una Pope-Hennessy to Petersham. I had a down on this lady today. Her vanity is o'er-reaching. She talked of nothing but her successes in Paris and how much more intellectual she is than anyone else. Told me she has sold over 150,000 copies of her *Dickens*, which I can hardly believe, and this year had a capital levy on the earnings. Most gracious to me about the favourable reviews of my book by the ignorant, and pitying over the bad ones. When I said humbly that it made no pretensions to be a contribution to literature, 'Of course it isn't,' she snorted. Now she was quite right but she could have kept her views to herself, or snorted with less vehemence. We joined a party of Richmond Georgian Groupers and went over Montrose House (very rich, very bad taste indeed), Rutland Lodge, Petersham Manor, and other houses, the names of which already escape me, as they say. Dame Una inquisitive and caustic. Would not allow me to have tea when offered – I was dying of thirst – because she wanted to return home for tea; and when I dropped her at 5.30 did not invite me in.

Sunday, 20th June

Patrick Kinross telephoned. He is back from Scotland, and came to dinner. Henry Reed, my American architectural historian, came too. Patrick very nice. He has finished his novel, which he has already rewritten once. It is about his wife, Angela, and is to be called *Ruthless Innocence* – not a good title. John Heygate is reading the manuscript.

Monday, 21st June

Drove to Stourhead, leaving at 9 o'clock. I stopped at the big church, St Michael's, Basingstoke and the verger told me all the glass from the Holy Ghost Chapel, moved to this church twenty years ago, was destroyed by bomb blast in the war. So that is that. Then called at Wilton. David Herbert not at home, but I saw the Holbein temple. Much of the detail resembles that on the gatehouse at Charlecote. An important textbook building. Reached Stourhead in time for luncheon and spent the afternoon with Eardley. At present the house is musty, dusty, drab and lacking charm. We made little headway and felt depressed. I fetched Eddy from Gillingham station. Both he and Desmond are at Long Crichel where I stay.

Tuesday, 22nd June

E. and I called on a Colonel Goodden at Compton near Yeovil. He owns a large Victorian version of Barrington Court built of Ham stone. The

Gooddens have been here since the eighteenth century. In the church are many memorials to them. One excellent statue of Robert Goodden, *c.* 1822, a kind of Coke of Norfolk personage, robust and John Bullish. The house is now empty but was occupied all the war by Lord Aberconway's Air Company who messed it up and decline to give the old man proper compensation. The Colonel offered to lend us several things for Montacute. We agreed to take a sedan chair and much oriental porcelain looted by the aforesaid Robert Goodden from the imperial palace, Pekin. We fetched the Yateses and motored them to Dillington House to view the contents to be sold tomorrow by auction. E. and I both rashly made some bids for various objects and I am terrified lest I get some and can't afford to pay for them. Then tea at Montacute. Round the house with E., rearranging furniture in our usual way.

Wednesday, 23rd June

Muggy, sulky day, the sun somewhere, but not penetrating. E. and I motor to Crichel House and were received by the headmistress, Miss Galston. Napier Alington's daughter, the owner, has let the house as a girls' school. Wonderful too the school must be for hardly any of the Alington contents have been put away. They are used by the girls and not spoiled, even carpets and curtains. Pretty, sweet girls they seemed, all out of doors reading, walking or playing musical instruments. The house outside is stuccoed, a grey texture – some dull nineteenth-century additions. Only the south colonnade, imposed in 1774 upon a George II wing, is noteworthy on the outside. But the interior is very fine indeed with some rooms of high quality. Wyatt must have been the architect for I notice several of his tricks – fan pendentives, ellipses, etc. The dining-room ceiling beautiful, like the Heveningham one, blues and greens and plasterwork clear and not over-fussy, all white, the walls biscuit. The school tables are certainly not ornamental. I see no reason why they should not be so, yet simple. The drawing-room ceiling reminds me of Adam's at no. 20 St James's Square; green silk walls (modern), crimson upholstered gilt of chairs. The mirrors throughout the house are fine. We walked round the grounds; lovely lake and woods.

Drove on to St Giles. Entered the church, too well kept up and over-restored. Every wall tablet to a member of the Ashley Cooper family. The exterior is early Georgian. Then tea at St Giles's House with Lady Shaftesbury. 'Shaftesbury', as she referred to him, was away. She is old, rather fat, bandy legs for she is lame, and *maquillée* in the Queen Alexandra fashion. Eyes very made up. Must once have been pretty, and has enchanting manners. Is a sister of the Duke of Westminster. Clips every 'g'. 'G-clippin'' has become a favourite joke at Long Crichel. After tea she showed us round the state rooms. They are *superb*; late seven-teenth-century and early eighteenth-century. One drawing-room of greeny-gold silk, striped; all the frames of pictures and glasses of unbeliev-able delicacy and beauty. The dining-room perhaps the best room of all with Chippendale suite carved in finest detail. Library is Regency. A good terracotta bust of the 1st Earl, Dryden's Earl. A magnificent house. Pray God the contents are never dispersed. Lady Shaftesbury told us that, their son having died last year, they are faced with £250,000 death duties. Presumably they had rashly made over the estate to him. Her exquisite personality impressed me strongly.

Thursday, 24th June

Eardley and I spent the day at Stourhead, again putting finishing touches to the state rooms. At last we completed all we had set out to do. There is still room for improvements of a lesser kind and some rehanging of pic-tures. This evening we discussed with Desmond plans for going to Italy, just the three of us, in September.

Friday, 25th June

Our great day at Stourhead. We met Paul Hyslop for luncheon at the Spread Eagle. Then the Eshers, Rennie Hoare and Paul Methuen joined us at the house. Rennie and Paul were somewhat in a camp apart. Lord E. cordially disliked R.H., thought him a bore and a philistine. He approved wholeheartedly Eardley's and my arrangements. He is the staunchest ally. He suggested a few minor alterations, really to appease Hoare and Methuen. We showed Esher the surplus furniture in the base-ment and attics. He decided that after Rennie Hoare had made a pick of what he wanted to rent from the Trust, we could take the rest to other houses, where needed, provided it was carefully catalogued as belonging to Stourhead, and sell the indifferent stuff. This will present a problem. We shall have to decide what may in the future be considered of inter-est to Stourhead that today we dismiss as rubbish.

After tea E., Simon Buxton [the NT agent] and I walked in the gardens along the lake. All the azaleas now over. Some of the old beeches have got to be felled for they are dangerous. It will be a tragic day when the great tulip trees by the water have to go. I motored home, dining at the King's Head, Cirencester en route. I was overcome by an attack of unaccountable melancholy in the dining-room. Life seemed to stand still. The room became claustrophobic. I could scarcely finish my meal for longing to get outside, and away. At Wickhamford I sat in Mama's bedroom, talking to her in bed. Told her of my strange experience at Cirencester. She explained to me that it was in the King's Head that her mother died in 1894 while waiting for the carriage to drive her home to Coates. Mama, a little girl at the time, was alone with her. My grandmother was driven nearly mad by the violent ringing of the Abbey church bells opposite. Ever since my mother has loathed church bells.

I called on Audrey at Prestbury and sat on a bench in her little garden under a rose tree and next to a mock orange of wonderful fragrance. In my imagination it seemed to conjure all the marvels of the East where I have never been.

Saturday, 26th June

Away at 9.30 to Hidcote. Walked round the garden with Lawrence Johnston who, apart from absent mindedness and some loss of memory, is otherwise sane and hale. He said he was incensed by a letter he had received from the Trust and had now decided no longer to 'give' us Hidcote. After much discussion and persuasion he agreed to leave it by will, if I would witness his codicil. The garden is a dream of beauty. The old-fashioned rose garden smelled as fragrant as I have always imagined a garden in a French Gothic tapestry might smell. Lawrie Johnston was very nice to me.

I stopped at Chipping Campden church to look at the Noel tombs. The two alabaster shrouded figures standing within their tomb are very moving. Then to Oxford. Left the car in the Roy Harrods' yard and joined my party of National Trust members in the charabanc. Drove to Ditchley. Mrs Tree received us smilingly and charmingly. She is handsome and natural and attractive. The butler came into the big hall and asked if I would go upstairs to Ronnie Tree, in bed with an injured back. He was very friendly and asked me to come again alone, and stay. While we were talking a tall, dark figure, a trifle bent, with long black hair, looking like the late Mr Winant, but more romantic, entered quietly. He was introduced to me as Peter Beatty. I said, 'You will not remember me. We were at school together and once swapped, you a beautiful pencil and I some trashy object. I got the better of the bargain and have ever since felt guilty. We must have been nine or ten at the time.' His reply was, 'I remember it well and I remember thinking I had got the better of you. You must excuse me for not having recognized you. I am quite blind at present; only temporarily of course.' But he will, I understand, never see again.

Ditchley inside is perfection. Exquisite furniture and fabrics, many original to the house. I have never seen better taste. Nothing jars. Nothing is too sumptuous, or new. The grounds, laid out by Ronnie Tree, are suitable to the house, the outside of which is a little austere, and I regret that the two cupolas and pediment were not carried out according to Gibbs's design. Our party had high tea at the Marlborough Arms,

Woodstock. Only eleven members came, but we enjoyed ourselves. I talked to them all in turn and on parting we all shook hands and everyone thanked everyone else.

I fetched my car from the Harrods' house and motored to South Wraxall Manor to stay with Lady Glyn. She is the mother of David Long who was killed in the war and the grandmother of the heiress of this beautiful house. David Long came to see me at the beginning of September 1939 in a great hurry for he was drafted abroad with his regiment. He begged me to devise some scheme whereby South Wraxall, which he loved, might be preserved by the National Trust. As far as I remember his solicitors raised difficulties and objections during his absence. The Eshers are staying here and they got me invited in order to talk over the future of the place. Lady G. is old now with a face like parchment, and painted parchment at that. Also staying Lady Marjorie Beckett, Diana Worthington's mother. She knew I was a friend of Diana and spoke sadly of her. Said she had no idea how desperate poor Diana was before her suicide. She was sweet to me because I loved Diana and asked me to stay with her in Yorkshire at any time. She must have been prettier than Diana who had a huge frog-like mouth that was, strangely enough, seductive. When smiling and lowering her eyes in the same poignant way she reminded me of Diana.

Sunday, 27th June

This house is not one I should care to live in. Lady Glyn has furnished it entirely by herself with what she bought from Thornton Smith's sale. The furniture is pretty, but not exactly good. All the floors are covered with rush matting. The various fireplaces of 1598 are interesting, particularly the gigantic Flemish one in the big room which gets uglier the longer you look at it: the loathsome caryatides with cruel boxes round their fat shapeless bodies. Lord Esher is restless during weekends. Likes to talk. Never reads. Nevertheless is bubbling with fun and jokes; counting the cakes on the tea-table and calculating how many he may eat; and then gorging. Never walks a yard, saying we should hold Sir Edgar Bonham-Carter, who was a rugger blue and is now a cripple, as a warning not on any account to take exercise. Says he would rather remain in England and be atom-bombed into a jelly than emigrate to the colonies, blaze trails through the bushvelt and be eaten by scorpions.

In the morning I drove the party in the Eshers' Buick to Corsham. Paul and Norah [Methuen] showed us over the house which I must say they have arranged well. It has been cleaned and repainted under their direction with infinite care. I motored back to London in 3¼ hours, arriving 9 o'clock.

Tuesday, 29th June

Yesterday and today I have suffered from loss of voice, owing to tiredness, Miss Paterson says, but I have had a sore throat for several days. I am distressed by Maud Mosley's death. She talked to me the last time I stayed with her in November about death and her indifference to it with cold detachment. I am indeed sorry for Aunt Dorothy. The two sisters wrote to each other every single day of the year, and had done so since my uncle's death in 1931.

Went to Shrewsbury for the day by train. To my surprise am not tired tonight, for I had a comfortable seat each way, good meals and read several things I needed to get through, on the journey. Walked home from Paddington. Keeble the decorator and I spent the day at Attingham. We went round the rooms estimating the work to be done in the state rooms. He means to start in a fortnight. This is satisfactory. The quality of the doors, friezes and ceilings of this house is pretty good.

Wednesday, 30th June

MacLeod Matheson lunched and gave some useful criticisms of National Trust properties he visited on a recent tour of Somerset. It is odd how an intelligent man can be an inverted snob – his consciousness of class distinctions is too acute for a left-winger.

Betty Hussey, whom I went to see this evening, urged me to ask David Bowes-Lyon to persuade the Queen to intimate that she would favour the surplus funds of the Queen's District Institute going to our Gardens Fund. This sentence reads like a minute from a subcommittee of an urban district council.

Thursday, 1st July

The Admiral picked me up at 8.25 with Ruby Holland-Martin and Colonel Vane, MP, of Hutton Vane. We drove to Fairford. I sat in the back with Vane, a nice man about my age. It is frightening how unfailingly disagreeable I am at this hour of the morning. Later I improved and kept the sombre party together, I like to think. I set out to be civil to Captain John Hill, the odious agent who was entertaining us. We got to Fairford before 11 o'clock and had time to look at the glass in the church. It is a medley of mellow colours, but lacks design. Dates from *c.* 1490. The handguides are most inadequate, giving descriptions of the subjects, i.e. Christ in the Temple, which one can make out for oneself (admittedly with difficulty), but no information about the workmanship or the artists. We inspected Fairford Park and estate. I was glad that Ruby H.-M. and Vane agreed with me that this property is unacceptable. We saw from Badbury Hill the Buscot and Coleshill estates. Drove to Great Coxwell and went inside the barn. It is really grand. I felt proud to be in it. Could any building be more serviceable, beautiful, robust, simple, religious and uplifting? It represents paganism and Christianity and is a shrine to Flora, Poma, Nature, what you will. Then to Boarstall Tower. Looked over the building. Then Hartwell House, where we had tea. This place greatly improved since I was last here, as regards the gardens. The interior is now being reconditioned, but all the walls still bare. The fake Jacobean staircase has been set in a new position so as to entail three flights instead of one central flight. It has involved some newly reproduced balusters, which do not matter. To think of Louis XVIII's court here, so densely packed that several members of the household were obliged to camp on the roof tiles.

Dined with Sibyl Colefax upstairs at the Dorchester. I sat between Cynthia Jebb and Mrs Hore-Belisha, who is outspoken. Both friendly, easy, rattling women. Left with Harold [Nicolson] who came home and drank brandy with me – to my distress next day – till midnight. Harold's affection for his old friends is demonstrated by a persistent desire to help them. Quite touching.

Friday, 2nd July

Dined at Kew with Mark Ogilvie-Grant, taking Malcolm Bullock and George Dix. A very hilarious, male, witty-smutty, funny party, at which disclosures and confidences poured out faster than the drink. Even Malcolm was embarrassed by certain idiosyncratic disclosures. The more outrageous they became the more harmless. Nearly choked with laughter. Oh, lust *is* a jest! How *would* we laugh without it?

Saturday, 3rd July

With courage opened Papa's letter in reply to mine telling him I was more than £600 overdrawn. He wrote kindly that we must have a financial talk next time I go home. No recriminations which was very unlike him.

Spent morning and afternoon at the Soane Museum, looking through du Cerceau's drawings of French châteaux, and talking to John Summerson and Dorothy Stroud. J.S. who is engaged upon Henry VIII is in despair. He is also about to edit Thorpe for the Walpole Society and confesses he cannot penetrate that mystery.

Sunday, 4th July

Dined alone with Puss Milnes-Gaskell in her flat. She talked of Queen Mary's astonishing activity. She said that Kenneth de Courcy actually sent

Queen Mary a telegram inviting her to luncheon. Q.M. was furious. Aunt Puss says that Princess Mary is a person of the greatest sweetness of character. Her one fault is talking far into the night. At Sandringham Aunt P. dragooned her to her bedroom where they discovered a bat on her bed. For one hour, amid giggles, they tried without avail to remove it. Instead they had to remove the Princess to another bedroom, the bat remaining asleep on the pillow.

Monday, 5th July

Dined at Barbara Moray's. I hope she likes me as much as I like her, but one never knows. Other guests were the Hugo Pitmans, he large, deaf, agreeable, and slightly tight; she, soft and inaudible: Lord Revelstoke who is distinguished and Lady Worsley, grey-haired and widowed in 1914. Barbara has struck up a warm friendship with this nice but ordinary woman who apparently asked to meet me. Strange I thought.

Wednesday, 7th July

Today had Sir Sydney Cockerell, Alan Pryce-Jones and Bob Gathorne-Hardy to luncheon. Bob thoroughly enjoyed himself, talking nineteen to the dozen. Sir Sydney, dear old man, very spry, not without a touch of – not malice – but impishness. He talked of Charlotte Mew as a great minor poet, whom Hardy admired. He seemed delighted that the three of us spoke with warmth of Ruskin, as though expecting a younger generation to decry that great man. He told us that Ruskin read aloud parts of *Praeterita* to him before publication. Ruskin spoke, as he wrote, in occasional passages of deep purple.

George Dix took me to Vanbrugh's *Relapse* with which I was deeply disappointed. Seventeenth-century bawdy unlike ours at Kew, not at all funny, and Colonel Blimp and his family crashing bores. Then went to a supper party given by the Eric Dugdales which was hellish.

At 4.30 (I have got my chronology wrong) Lord Crawford, Lord Esher, the Admiral and I went to the Treasury to discuss with Sir Edward Bridges, Sir Bernard Gilbert, and Proctor, arising from receipt of Treasury's letter announcing the Chancellor's intention to set up a Commission to deal with the problem of large country houses with collections. I am much concerned with this subject because my memorandum on the very problem was written before receipt of Bridges's letter, and is to be circulated to the Executive Committee. In it I have urged very strongly that the Trust ought to come to terms with the Government and indeed ask for, and accept, Government subvention, in spite of our hitherto having set our faces against the risk of state interference. The alternative, I submit, is for the Trust to sink, for we cannot

compete with Government competition and Treasury resources. I think
I have convinced Crawford and Esher, both clever men, but the Admiral
and Hubert Smith [Chief Agent] do not yet see the necessity. The Trust
is at a critical juncture and I seem to be playing a backstair role in guiding
its affairs. Backstair is the word.

Goodwin asked me to write an article on gardens for the *Nineteenth
Century*. After due consideration I declined. I want, before going to Italy,
to finish the synopsis of my book, and to begin writing it in the autumn.

Saturday, 10th July

Was to have gone to stay with the Oglanders at Nunwell in the Isle of
Wight. All the week did not want to go. Braced myself to go and got to
Waterloo at 9.15 this morning. Such an enormous queue on the platform that I could not even reach the ticket office. Returned home and
telephoned Joan Oglander. Went to the Soane Museum in the afternoon
and looked carefully through the Thorpe drawings, the whole book of
them. John Summerson is baffled but he considers Thorpe immensely
important, and undoubtedly a designer. Where Thorpe has written, 'per-
fected by me' or 'altered by me' John S. thinks he refers, not to the building, but to the design.

I went to tea with the Rosses in Stafford Terrace. This house is stifling,
choc-a-bloc and pitch-dark with late-Victorian furniture and Linley
Samborne *Punch* drawings. Interesting it undoubtedly is, but I could not
myself live in it. I feel it would induce asthma or some allergy. It is not
even comfortable. They told me that Emerald Cunard really is dying now,
which is very depressing.

Sunday, 11th July

On my way to the bathroom saw Emily's [my housekeeper] *Sunday
Express* with large headline: 'Fabulous Lady Cunard dies at 71'. This has
indeed made me sad. My day quite overclouded by it. Cannot get the
thought out of my head or concentrate on a book. I telephoned Tony
Gandarillas to condole with him. He was in tears. Said he was with her
while she died; she had no pain at the end, being kept under drugs. I met
little Diane [Abdy] in Bennet Street after luncheon. She said Bertie also
was with her when she died and feels as though he has lost his mother.
Yesterday morning Emerald tried desperately to say something important but was unable to speak. This worries Bertie. Gordon, her maid,
became a saint at the end, slept in her room, waited on her hand and foot,
and never left her. Apparently it was cancer that killed her. I remarked to
Diane that in walking to Brooks's this morning I kept saying to myself,
'Why do all these people I pass, live? They are so ugly and so stupid, and
yet Emerald dies.' She had been saying the same to herself.

My sorrow for Emerald is different to what I felt when Kathleen Kennet died. That was a dear friend going. Emerald's death means the end of an age, of a legend. I regret that I did not see her more often these past two years, but hers was a world not mine. I admired her more than I admired most women, for her lightning perception, her wide reading, her brilliant repartee, her sense of fun, and sparkling, delicious, wonderful nonsense. If only I could have attended her dinner parties like, say, a dumb servitor, the awkwardness of trying to contribute to the conversation and failing in the endeavour would not have arisen. I would have been content to listen to her, and watch her deft manipulation of the conversation until eternity. She seemed always to like me and was charming, but I knew I could never entertain her, and so I avoided her too often. That was the true reason. Yet I am glad I knew her for no one will ever take her place. No ordinary mortal can afford to be so detached from the chores of everyday life. Hers was entirely artificial, or rather unreal for these days, uncontaminated by worldly duties. What a loss she will be to society. It is hard to estimate it.

Monday, 12th July

John Summerson and I, by a process of slow and combined analysis, agreed that the ballroom at no. 4 St James's Square was perhaps from Burlington's design as regards surviving ceiling and cornice, but the heraldic achievements upheld by *putti*, the chimneypiece and tapestry panels could be dated 1860. This decision was reached at the party Philip James gave in the Arts Council office for the exhibition of Lord Leicester's drawings from Holkham. Had a talk with Philip Hendy who said with a snarl that, when Lord Crawford ceased to be chairman of the National Gallery trustees, then he might lend pictures to Osterley. He is a rude, disagreeable man and I dislike him for disliking Crawford.

Tuesday, 13th July

Sisson lunched. He said the reason why he disliked modernistic architecture was that it was puritanical and eschewed all embellishment, in fact everything that might delight the eyes and senses.

Bridget and Tony Gandarillas dined. He talked of little else but Emerald's death, having this morning taken her to Golders Green for cremation. He described how, lying on her bed last night, her little hands manicured, pretty white hair brushed and curled, with no lines on her face, she looked sweet and ethereal. (I wonder why death gives back a person a fleeting youth which is of no use to him or her. It is a dirty trick.) Only Tony and Bertie Abdy were in the room when she died, which she did so peacefully that Tony did not realize she had ceased breathing. He said that Lady Diana Cooper looked in at 5.30 a.m. after a ball, glanced at Emerald, and left by air for Paris in the afternoon. E. died at 6 o'clock. Numbers of people, who were never great friends, pushed their way to front pews of the church for the service.

Thursday, 15th July

Motored after dinner last night to Polesden Lacey and stayed the night with the Feddens. This morning at 9.30 Midi came. I motored her and Robin to Brighton, to the Regency Exhibition. No one could honestly say, although most people pretend, that the Pavilion is not hideous. The outside is tawdry. Clifford Musgrave had arranged the Banqueting Room very well. Curtains drawn; candelabra lit with candles, table-cloth Nelson's, dinner service Derby, with gold knives and forks; fruits and sweetmeats in dishes, hock and port glasses, and so on. The Dolphin furniture from the Admiralty very magnificent. The Duchess of Kent paraded round. She is tall and upright, extremely chic. Effect altogether splendid. Lovely skin, her mouth curiously drawn to one side. Then we motored to Bramber Castle, much tidied since I was last there. Then to Amberley Castle where we were shown by the owner panels of the Nine Worthy Women by the Bernardi, mentioned by Walpole in his *Anecdotes*, on wood. By no means works of art. Their ground colour a lacquer-red, enriched with gold; all the women wearing armour like Amazons. This house is pretty and uncouth like most castles that aren't bogus ones. The gatehouse with Richard II towers circular and cylindrical. Then we called at Goodwood and were shown over by the housekeeper in a charming manner, as one would have been in the eighteenth century if one's carriage had been respectable. The house is not striking outside, the texture ugly. It is of unfinished octagonal plan, more strange than beautiful, with round towers at the angles, by Wyatt. The double portico resembles the one at Crichel. The inside is extremely plain and pleasing; 'chaste', Horace Walpole would have called it. The dining-room has a suite of rosewood furniture, inlaid with ebony. The sarcophagi chaste too. Several portraits of the Duchess of Portsmouth, progenitrix of the Dukes of Richmond. Not a pretty woman, and bad-tempered. Grey granite pillars from Guernsey in the hall. In the drawing-room the two famous Canaletti and a fine collection of Sèvres in wall cabinets.

Friday, 16th July

Somewhat to my surprise my Memorandum passed through both Committees with hardly a dissentient voice raised. True, Lord Crawford added his account of the last meeting with the Treasury which thus made my Memo a little out of date. However, the Executive Committee agreed that if the Chairman were asked by the Chancellor of the Exchequer to accept a grant, it should be taken, provided it was attached to the maintenance of a specific building only, and was not a contribution to general funds.

Charles Fry back from America telephoned that he needed to see me at once. I called this evening. He is unchanged – detestable. I really dislike him unreservedly. He is utterly untrustworthy, without conscience, moral scruple, or decency. I shall have to see him once more as my publisher, and that is the end.

Saturday, 17th July

Sibyl made me take a friend of hers, assistant librarian to the hateful B.B., to Syon. Keith Miller-Jones very kindly gave us luncheon. The whole Georgian Group membership rallied there. It was like a royal garden party. It struck me during this visit, the last of so many, that after all the furniture was not up to much. But I was impressed by the early sixteenth-century portraits in the Fowler wing – a French picture of Protector Somerset with a red beard, a double portrait of Sir Philip Sidney and his sister Mary Pembroke.

This evening went to *Ambassador Extraordinary* with the Gandarillas and Bridget and dined at the Ritz. An indifferent play and the skit on atom bombs cuts too close to the bone to be in good taste. I suppose on that account it was hissed the first night. The Ambassador from Mars, a Frenchman, aged thirty-five, almost completely naked, a beautiful object.

Sunday, 18th July

Lunched with that fiend Charles Fry at the Ritz. He launched into paeans of praise of himself and his business successes, and when I asked if Batsford would send me to Italy this September, gave no encouragement and advised me to write to Mr Batsford. Conversation then lapsed into his drink and sex prowess, which disgusts and bores. During the hour and a half I was with him today he consumed five gins and tonic.

Monday, 19th July

This morning the Admiral talked to Smith, Gibbs and L.-M. about the Memo on office reorganization, which we presented to him on Friday. As usual he was generous and grateful to us for our criticisms. A good but foolish man.

At 3.45 I motored homewards. Called at Bisham Abbey, now leased to a physical jerks college. Sweaty young men and women, black and white, doing exercises on the browned lawns. A gruesome spectacle. The whole place looked horrible. The lady warden showed me the hall chimneypiece, on which I took notes. I suspect it may, after all, not be 1560 but Jacobean because of the cabochon ornament on the base of the capitals. Then called at West Wycombe to see how Shearsby has progressed with the colonnade. He has done it very well and Helen is well satisfied. She, her mother and aunt, were having tea in the colonnade. Very affectionate greetings. Continued straight to Broadway where I met the family at the Alexanders' golden wedding party. Lots of friendly old faces. Mama looking very bright and pretty, her complexion fresh and youthful. On seeing me her dear face lit up in its radiant manner as of old; suffused with childlike joy.

Tuesday, 20th July

Lunched at Madresfield [Court]. Lord Beauchamp is fat, with a great paunch, looking like God knows what, wearing an old blue shirt, open at the frayed neck, and a tight pair of brown Army shorts, baby socks and sandshoes. Lady B. plump, but pretty. Both kind and welcoming. A lovely warm day. The house is not in my eyes beautiful. The situation, however, is made beautiful by the Malvern Hills looming over it. You approach it by a straight drive of more than a mile, but the actual estate is on flat and dull ground. The gardens (there are ten gardeners) are delicious, especially the long avenues and paths, and the arboretum. Busts of Roman Emperors under arches of yew close to the house which is moated. The contents are marvellous pictures and sixteenth-century portraits. As for the miniatures, of which there are a great number, they are superlative. Also some good French furniture and many bibelots, snuff boxes, gold, silver, bejewelled, etc. One could spend hours here enjoying these things which by themselves make Madresfield worthy of preservation for all time.

We lunched in the great hall – again much altered eighty years ago. It faces a little central court, half-timbered in a Nürnberg manner. Lady Beauchamp is a Dane and her two stepdaughters and old mother, who does not speak and to whom one does not speak, were staying. Lord and Lady B. spent all afternoon conducting and explaining. A picnic tea was had at the swimming pool. Then he took me to look at two half-timbered lesser houses on the estate, one Prior's Court on the Severn, round a square central court with seventeenth-century staircase and panelling. The rich tenants from the Black Country most obsequious and apologetic to the Earl for not being in their best clothes, whereas the Earl was dressed as I have described. Earls with sores on their legs and knees should not parade them exposed to their villeins. In spite of his fatness and unshaven porky face his manner is patrician and stiff.

Wednesday, 21st July

Took Deenie to Chedworth Roman Villa. Went round with the caretakers, Irvine and wife, a keen young couple, and suggested improvements.

Thursday, 22nd July

Left Wickhamford at 10 o'clock. I have not been a success this visit. To Charlecote and met Joshua Rowley there. On my return to London looked at the Dormer monument in Wing church, the largest purely classical monument of the mid-sixteenth century I have yet seen. Then to Chenies church where I was able only to glimpse through a window at the tomb of the 1st Duke or Earl of Bedford of the same style and period. A cocktail party at the Osbert Lancasters. Champagne to drink.

Sunday, 25th July

Very hot. Walked in the Park at 7 o'clock. Had an uneasy feeling that the proletariat, sunning themselves so happily, truly believe that all is well with the world and themselves just because they are richer than ever before and work less than ever before.

Margaret Jourdain, Ken Davison and Osbert Lancaster dined. Margaret quite overshadowed by Osbert who talked ceaselessly. He catalogued every British monarch from William the Conqueror down to the present in a few pungent words Richard Coeur de Lion, the hearty Bullingdon bore, given to sodomy: Edward VII, the Jew-loving, lecherous philistine, etc. This doesn't sound as funny as it was.

Tuesday, 27th July

Dined at Sibyl's Ordinary and sat next to Godfrey Winn, who is more absurd than words can say. Still the eternal glamour boy and every mother's darling. He has snow-white hair where he is not totally bald and minces like a harlot. He has an inordinate opinion of himself. Notwithstanding all his follies there is something engaging about him. He is simple at heart, and wants everyone to be as happy and loved as he is himself. I went and had a drink with him in Ebury Street before he and his chauffeur drove off to his country house.

Gladwyn Jebb told me at the Ordinary that he saw a lot of George Mallaby who is the ideal secretary to a committee of Generals – a strange propensity.

Wednesday, 28th July

Today as hot as ever I remember it in England. Leigh Ashton and I drove together to the aerodrome and flew to Jersey, arriving at 1.20. The heat of the plane on the sizzling tarmac when we entered it was so intense I thought I should die. I was wedged between Leigh and a stranger. Leigh started to melt like a monstrous lump of butter. On arrival we drove to Radier Manor. Grandy [Jersey] received us, dressed in a canary aertex shirt and khaki trousers; looking distinguished and handsome. Pompously Leigh produced a list of figures which the Treasury is prepared to offer for the contents of each room at Osterley, making a total of £120,000. Grandy, keeping perfect control, said he would take the list and compare the figures offered with what he hoped to receive from an antique dealer in two weeks' time, and then let us know. In other words the Treasury has made an ass of itself in not putting a value on each individual item. To lump all the contents of Osterley together under a round sum is unacceptable to an owner. I suspect that Grandy was disappointed with the Government offer, and felt insulted. I don't blame him, and I don't view the outcome with optimism. He is a good businessman and no fool. I think our journey was a complete waste of time and money.

Grandy's wife is very pretty and big with child. Leigh Ashton is companionable but slightly too pleased with himself now he is a knight. Everyone in the aeroplane on the return journey sweating and stinking. Oh, the smell of the English. I even notice it in the open Park.

Thursday, 29th July

Took Countess Borromeo and Mrs Vaughan to Knole. State rooms stiflingly hot. Nearly died. This evening Burnet took me to the Caribbean dancers. They dance barefooted, with great *élan*. Beautiful brown creatures with gay coloured clothes and turbans. But the music to my ears is monotonous, and the *élan* itself too barbaric to be endured patiently for three hours.

Friday, 30th July

Lunched with Michael and Anne at Stafford Terrace. They are about to leave this afternoon for Womersley with all the children. The house consequently in some chaos. The Borromeos there too. They asked me to stay with them when I am in Milan. Countess B. complained to me yesterday that Susan, Anne's daughter, aged twenty, wrote to her as 'Darling Orietta', whereas Susan is no relation and she is a woman of sixty-one. She asked if all the young in England were so familiar. I said they were becoming so; and they meant no harm. All she said was 'Um!'

This evening I motored Malcolm Bullock to his house near Cambridge. Middlefield, it is called, built by Lutyens in 1910, on the grand scale in miniature. Of small, regular bricks very trimly laid. Nothing ingle-nooky about it. Perfect size for a widower. Pretty formal sweep of garden between yews. We had a delicious cold supper at 9.30 with pâté de foie gras and hock. Then sat till after midnight on the verandah drinking kümmel and gossiping about Edwardian society, a speciality of Malcolm's. It is so seldom one can sit out like this in England, and keep warm.

Lutyens evidently played a joke on the bachelor for whom he built this house. The staircase ceiling is supported by one stout twisted column, so fashioned to reproduce the outlines of the female bosom and buttocks, always there as you move round the newel post, either ascending or descending. Had palpitations during the night, presumably indigestion, or kümmel. Otherwise a perfect visit.

Saturday, 31st July

Left at 10 o'clock. Drove to Cambridge and looked at repairs in progress to roof of the Abbey House. Then to Stamford and had the filthiest lunch at the George I have ever eaten. Left the car at the drive gates of Burghley and walked to the house. Park open but house shut today unfortunately. Lord Exeter drove up and swept through to the forecourt where an old man wearing a bowler had been standing for half an hour to open the gate for him. So funny considering the Exeters have no indoor servants. Then I drove through Nottingham to Wollaton and spent an hour there. A thoroughly vulgar but well constructed palace. My conclusion today was that the *nouveaux riches* owners of these Tudor houses themselves designed them, Smythson at Wollaton being merely foreman of the workers; but I don't know. I looked at Smythson's mural monument in the church where the epitaph describes him as 'Architector and Surveyor unto the most worthy house of Wollaton, with divers others of great account'. This certainly suggests a status higher than a mere foreman's; but what exactly was an *architector* in Elizabethan times?

The interior of Wollaton is filled with glass cases of stuffed animals and fish. It doesn't much matter. The grounds are quite well kept up, but Nissen huts still cling like barnacles to one side of the house. Visited Winster to see the NT's little market house. Arrived Edensor House at 7 to stay with the Hartingtons. Their house built by Paxton as is the whole village of Edensor.

Sunday, 1st August

Debo and Andrew [Hartington] drove me to Chatsworth this morning. The site of house, the surroundings unsurpassed. The grass emerald green as in Ireland. The Derwent river, although so far below the house, which it reflects, seems to dominate it. Black and white cattle in great herds. All the hills have trees along their ridges. Neatness and order are the rule although, Andrew says, there are fourteen gardeners instead of forty before the last war. The inordinate length of the house undeniably impressive, and the 6th Duke's extensions do not make it lopsided, as I had been led to suppose. The limitless landscape can absorb it. The uniform yellow sandstone helps link old block to Wyattville's towered colonnade, which might be taken out of a Claude painting. We wandered through the gardens, the greyhounds streaming across the lawns. Andrew turned on the fountain from the willow tree. Water not only drips from the tree but jets from nozzles all round. The cascade not working this morning, but will be turned on for the public this afternoon.

At present the great house is empty, under covers and dustsheets. Next year the state rooms are to be shown. We entered the house from the west door, let in by Mr Thompson, the librarian. The state rooms are all on the second floor, reminiscent of Hampton Court, one leading to the next without passages. All pictures taken off the walls. Interior terribly hot and stuffy. Andrew let me look through two volumes of Inigo Jones drawings of masque costumes. Henry VII's prayer book, with illuminations. Given by the King to his daughter who was asked to pray for him, as well she might. Inscription in his kingly hand.

The scale of Chatsworth is gigantic, beyond comprehension (like St Peter's, Rome) until experienced. The detail of outside stonework of high quality, notably the antlers over windows, frostwork in the central courtyard, the panels of trophies, by Watson presumably. The Tijou ironwork easily identifiable. The Hartingtons, eager to know their possessions, intend to spend several hours each day systematically looking through papers in the library – like schoolchildren at a holiday task.

This afternoon we drove to Haddon. The D. of Rutland does not live in the house at all. It is open most days to visitors. Thousands flock. Today it was shut, so we had it to ourselves. Very romantically situated upon the Wye river, with hills all round. Beautiful lichened grey walls. Yet I would not care to live in it. It is a haphazard, uncomfortable house. We were shown the late Duke and Duchess's bedrooms, approached by a spiral newel stair. Small bedroom windows which barely open. Garden filled with hollyhocks, rambler roses, and the courtyards recently planted with roses trained to climb the walls. The long gallery is the most spectacular room. Panelling of walnut fields, arcading of oak inlaid with bog oak in very elaborate designs. In the dining-room too are Henry VIII panels and a frieze of plasterwork.

When it comes to working on Inigo Jones Andrew says I may have full access to all the Chatsworth library papers. As a couple the Hs seem perfection – both young, handsome, and inspired to accomplish great things. He has a splendid war record and won the MC. Has contested one constituency and is now nursing Chesterfield, a very Socialist seat. All the more reason, he thinks, for contesting it. Believing it unlikely to win does not deter him. Both full of faith in themselves and their responsibilities. She has all the Mitford virtues and none of the profanity. I admire them very much.

Monday, 2nd August

Hardwick is a different affair altogether. We motored there this morning. The old Duchess received us amid a mass of grandchildren. She is tall, imposing, imperious, gracious and seventy-eight. The park is sombre and the trees are black and stag-headed. From a distance the house rises above the trees on its knoll like a fairy palace. How romantic and beautiful it is. Its pretty yellow stone is sooty and crumbling. It seems to be slowly dis-integrating. The inside puts me in mind of Cotehele on the grand scale. There are few servants. Since the house is open to the public on two days a week the rooms are arranged for their benefit. Ropes tied from chair to chair and any old posts that are available. All floors covered with rush matting which being irreplaceable is today protected by old cloths and rugs where the public tread. All walls below the deep bold plaster friezes are lined with sixteenth-century tapestries. Unlike Cotehele where the tapestries have been cut ruthlessly, here they fit exactly because, the Duchess asserts, the house was built for them. The primary colours greens and blues, now faded, are heraldic. I suppose the Elizabethan furniture here is the most splendid in the world, inlaid and delicate, not coarse and clumsy. Not the usual old oak stuff. The height of the great windows is stupendous. The cold in the winter must be intense. The grandchildren say it is insupportable. The Duchess showed us round. She is rather slow and talks a great deal. Her knowledge is very wide but she muddles things up a good deal. Hardwick has become her life task and she serves it faith-fully. She enjoys conducting the public round the house, so when I arrived, she came to the front door and as she shook hands, said: 'I have always wanted you to come here' – which, Andrew observed, was very flattering. When we left however she neglected to say goodbye to me altogether, and I had to chase her in order to thank her and shake hands again.

Tuesday, 3rd August

This morning it poured, but slackened a bit at 11 o'clock. Andrew had to write letters, but Debo and I rode – the first time I have ridden for quite ten years and probably more. We went through the great Wyattville entrance and into the gardens of Chatsworth below the terrace. The wooden surrounds of the west front windows are still coloured gold, now rather faint, but the sash-bars have not been gilded that one can see. We went up the hill to look at the Cascade Temple and back again, then across the main road to the far side of the valley to see the Russian Lodge, built by the Bachelor Duke. His spirit at Chatsworth is very prevalent.

I left after luncheon for Bolsover where I went round as a tourist. Proudly set on its hill with far, misty, smoky views of open country and a few mines. The little castle has some unusual Jacobean apartments, notably the panelled room with paintings by Francis Cleyn, the tapestry weaver or designer, so the guide said. I carefully examined the castle which marks a transition from Jacobean to Classical, of which the doorways and some windows are absolutely pure. Yet the building as a whole is Mannerist. Went to the church and transcribed the Huntingdon Smythson tomb slab. It stands against the wall just outside the Cavendish chapel. These Smythsons are far more real than the Thorpes, it seems to me. The deserted houses hereabouts are rendered tragic by their past glory and present decay. I stopped at Sutton Scarsdale again. Am told that Osbert Sitwell has bought the ruin. Classical ruins in England are not as satisfactory architecturally as Gothic ruins. They lack the picturesque gloomth of the northern medieval and the sunset pallor of their Mediterranean prototypes.

From here to Buxton the country is beautiful; luxuriant dales. Between Buxton and Macclesfield it is hard and cruel, the awful Peaks. I stay with Charlie Brocklehurst these two nights in his horrid little Lodge (Hare Hill), so uncomfortable. This little man is becoming pompous, conventional, buttoned up, and more and more snobbish. I think I do not like him, and therefore should not stay with him another time.

Wednesday, 4th August

Charles and I went early to Lyme [Park] which looks dried up and worn down. The impact of countless masses is telling on the place. It is also becoming slightly vulgarized – Walls' ice cream notices, etc. The furniture is too sparse and regimented and not, I find, very attractively arranged. The Hartingtons came over for two hours and were appreciative and encouraging. I introduced Charlie who was delighted to meet them. This afternoon he and I decided what colours to paint the chapel and dining-room. We walked up to the lantern tower for the first time. On our way back to Hare Hill looked at Alderley Mill, a wretched Trust acquisition.

Thursday, 5th August

Glad to leave this morning for Little Moreton Hall which is looking very well. At Mow Cop saw Charlie's new stone to commemorate the

Primitives, and reached Attingham for luncheon with Lady Berwick, one
of whose eyes is very bad. I believe she is really suffering, poor thing. Met
Keeble and George Trevelyan and settled some colours for the
ante-library. Then drove to Wickhamford for supper with my mother, my
poor father ill in bed with lumbago, which she likes to think is gallstones,
and is worrying herself unnecessarily.

Friday, 6th August

This morning went to see Mr Wade at Snowshill to talk about the old
carriages he offers the Trust. Also persuaded him to leave us his fine
collection of clothes which he had suggested bequeathing to some
museum. He is the weirdest little man, looking far older than when I
saw him ten years ago. His thick dark hair parted in the middle almost
reaches the shoulders. He was wearing knickerbockers, a Norfolk jacket
and stiff winged collar. He lives retired from the world, lamenting the
old days when grass grew on the road to Snowshill and there were three
gates to open between it and Broadway. I well remember these things
and having to open the gates on my pony after leaving hounds at Spring
Hill, an 8-mile hack home from hunting with the groom when I was
about ten. Moreover the pony would invariably shy and make a scene
on approaching the spinney at the foot of the hill. It was supposed to
be haunted.

Sitting in Charlie Wade's bakehouse where he lives and sleeps is like
being in an alchemist's cell, except that here all the implements, anvils,
cogs, gyroscopes are spotlessly cleaned and brightly burnished.

At Oxford I looked at the portrait of old Bishop Fox at Corpus Christi
in the hall. A kind scout showed me his gold chalice, beautifully chased,
the earliest at Oxford, dating from the late fifteenth century.

I am forty today. The shock is not too great because during the past
year I had been telling people that I was forty, in anticipation. But I am
rather less good-looking and very bald now. My figure is as slender as
ever. Only occasionally does my stomach swell, owing to the bad bread,
but this is not serious. It soon flattens itself. I have lately found that the
skin of my jaw and chest is slacker than formerly. It used to be tight and
resilient. I am less stirred by desire than I used to be. It is the forms of
physical falling-off that I most resent: the fact that the life-line only
reaches an angle of 89.9 instead of 90 degrees. Oh dear, to say nothing
of the decay of teeth, eyesight and hair. When in another twenty years
I am too old to work I shall retire to a monastery and pray, for I shall
presumably no longer see to read. This is my one consolation: that when
my active life must cease I can still do good by praying. I am sure this

should be the occupation of old age. One need never be idle. The prayer
wheel when all else fails. At present my mental faculties, never first-rate,
are better than they have ever been. All my life I have been a slow devel-
oper.

Sunday, 8th August

Worked very steadily this weekend. My notes swell to enormous pro-
portions. Late this evening Rick [Stewart-Jones] and I walked in
Battersea Park in the drizzling rain and looked at the open-air sculpture. The setting very beautiful in Lord Redesdale's lovely garden of
umbrageous trees. This exhibition is an excellent idea and for England
the only sort of outdoor show possible. The weather is hellish, cold and
raining persistently. I told Rick I had hardly any true friends; but this
was an untruth. He said I was too fickle to deserve any. I don't believe
this is true either. I now think with affection of James Pope-Hennessy,
Ben Nicolson, Mark Ogilvie-Grant, Patrick Kinross, Johnnie Churchill,
Michael and Anne Rosse, Bridget Parsons, Harold and Vita, besides A,
B and C. I have however no lovers and with folded hands await some
devastating romance.

Tuesday, 10th August

Mrs James, widow of Henry James junior, the novelist's nephew, lately
deceased, came to the office this morning all the way from America to
offer us Henry James senior's house at Rye, which I am to go and inspect
with her next week. A perfectly charming, elderly, sensible woman, with
no affectations, and not rich. In the afternoon young Lord Rea came to
suggest our asking the Treasury for his father's estate in Eskdale. The
Treasury has now written that the Chancellor of the Exchequer is hesitating to let the Trust have Harewood. I take this gravely.

Wednesday, 11th August

Lunched with Ben Nicolson at Brooks's. He took me round St James's
Palace afterwards. I wanted to see the so-called Holbein ceiling of the
Chapel Royal. I find it too Italian for Holbein and prefer to think it may
be by Rovezzano who left England in 1540. There are only two chimneypieces left of Henry VIII's reign – in the Tapestry Room and the one
adjoining, which was redecorated by William Morris in the 1870s with
sunflower patterns, very pretty and interesting, to Queen Victoria's
express order. Patrick Kinross dined with me last night and he is really as
confidential and engaging and as fun to talk to as ever before. I am glad
we have returned to our old intimacy and mutual sympathy, only broken
by his long absence abroad during the war.

Motored Florence Paterson this afternoon to Ham, Cliveden and Hughenden; a fine day too. At Ham saw two hideous brick pillboxes which the Ministry of Works have erected as fire appliance shelters, without informing us. We shall certainly insist upon their removal. I found Ralph Edwards seated on a sort of throne, hanging pictures, moving furniture (by proxy of course) and directing an army of slaves. With his beady eyes, raucous voice, little moustache he looked like a seedy sergeant-major, cane in hand instead of under the arm on the parade ground. At Cliveden went over the state rooms, since it was opening day and I wished to see the ropes and posts. They looked all right. I said 'state rooms' as though there was an enfilade. In this vast palace there are in fact about three to which the public are vouchsafed access. Miss P. very interested in the gardens. The herbaceous borders nearly over. At Hughenden the rooms have been arranged by Mr Langley-Taylor's mother-in-law, and I was surprised how many contents there were: several portraits of Victorian politicians and statesmen.

I then met James Pope-Hennessy at Heathrow aerodrome. He is ill and had to fly swiftly home, from somewhere or other. He has a slightly sinister smell and complains of fever, inability to pass water and spots that discharge. I suspect the worst and J. fears it may be, dirty little thing, but doesn't seem unduly worried.

Batsford's have given me some advance copies of my guidebook to Trust buildings, about to be issued in a fortnight. The cover is a hideous green; the jacket rather vulgar; the chapter headings inadequate. They never sent me proofs of the foreword or the format, which was annoying, for although there are no howlers I could have improved the appearance of the production.

Motored to stay the weekend with the Sitwells at Weston. It took me a little over two hours. Sachie is like a child in his enthusiasms and impulsiveness, his simple and direct humour and readiness to laugh like a sensitive trigger. Lord Hesketh and a lady he fancies, very common American, lunched. Lord H. is contorted with shyness and repressions, and drinks too much port wine. After they left the Sitwells persuaded me by sheer force of charm to motor them to Kimbolton. On arrival we could not get in but the reluctant agent gave his consent to our seeing the outside only. It was profoundly disappointing, grim and unsympathetic. Through the windows we spied furniture in heaps, untidy and in disarray. The place is to be sold as a school. It is sad. Then drove to Easton

Neston, where the Heskeths gave us champagne on the lawn. The mother had had a seizure indoors, but is an imbecile in any case. I thought the house impressive and liked the late lord's improvements. His new forecourt and pool are excellent. The quality of the stucco-work indoors is very high. Staircase too narrow, with single returned flight. Like a large town house. The Hesketh family are ungainly to look upon.

Sunday, 15th August

Sachie is a voluble talker. His mind flits from houses, paintings, music, poetry, birds, nuns, flowers to jewellery and strawberries within one breath. He is infinitely sympathetic and inspiriting. The sweetest of men. Yet he is outspoken and likes giving advice. He warned me (a) to have more self-confidence in my writing and set aside more time for it, (b) to take steps to save what hair I have left – he recommends some infallible lotion the Duke of Westminster uses – and (c) not to dwell upon cancer. We talked for hours about writing. He has written fifty books, has seven more coming out this year. Yet writing is a terrible effort for him and for weeks he cannot put pen to paper. Georgia is charming in her own home. She is also very pretty. So is her old mother who is staying with them. Reresby a nice, good-natured boy, lively and intelligent.

This afternoon we motored to Chicheley and went round the house. Sachie delighted with what he saw. It is sad that the Chesters have left their wonderful looking-glasses to be ruined by a boys' school. Then to Gayhurst and looked at the Roubiliac tomb to Sir Nathan Wright and his son in the Wren church. The stucco books, open and shut on the frieze, curious.

Tuesday, 17th August

Motored at 8.30 to Polesden, picking up Robin Fedden. On to Rye where we found Mrs James, her niece and solicitor at the Mermaid Inn. Walked round to Lamb House which she offers with the garden to the National Trust. A delightful George I house in a narrow back street, on a corner. A great tragedy is the complete destruction of the garden house wherein Henry James wrote from 1898-1916. It was a simple structure judging from photographs and I would have it rebuilt. E. F. Benson rented Lamb House after Henry James's death until he died in 1941 or thereabouts. All the windows remain blown out. Hardboard has been temporarily substituted, so the rooms are pitch dark. They are nearly all panelled. The stair balusters are twisted and the treads shallow and broad, beautiful to walk up and down. The house is in bad condition but can be repaired easily. It is fully furnished with much furniture that belonged to the novelist. His pictures still hanging on the walls. Mrs Henry James told me that the most intimate belongings, including writing-table and piano, were destroyed with the garden house. Much of the rest had been removed to America by the family on the novelist's death. She is unable to 'give' what furniture is left in the house but we have the option to buy it. So Robin is going to pick out what he thinks ought to remain, with the assistance of Henry James's old secretary who is still alive.

On return we visited Bletchingley church and the huge monument to the Claydons which is early eighteenth century, very fine. Sachie thinks highly of it. Jamesey dines with me. He is better, but has contracted distressing complaints and told me how he had caught them. Is penitent and determined to be positively good for ever more, so he says.

Wednesday, 18th August

Drove to the south-west, lunching filthily again at the Cricketers' Inn, Bagshot, and reaching The Vyne at 3 o'clock. Mr and Mrs Chute received me most kindly for I had written asking if I might study the Renaissance windows in The Vyne chapel. This I did, and on hands and knees also took notes of the maiolica tiles on the floor in front of the altar. Mr C. kept interrupting by discussing the terms of his will. People adore reading one extracts from their wills, I notice, breathlessly and without pauses just as those idiots, solicitors, draft them without punctuation. I persuaded him to insert a clause whereby the National Trust might control the actual use to which the clergy tenants wish to put particular rooms. Otherwise we shall find abominable bad taste 'bon-dieuserie' disfiguring the Palladian staircase and the early Tudor gallery. Then he showed me a pile of books in the library which he had set aside for sale for, he said, the clergy would not want them. They were Wood's *Palmyra* and other eighteenth-century architectural volumes, the sort I would give my eyes for, and I can't think how to persuade him not to part with them. Damn the clergy! For a scholar, Oppidan head of Eton, who spouts Latin tags without cessation, Mr Chute is singularly unimaginative and philistine. He and his wife gave me tea and I left, arriving Long Crichel for dinner. Found Eardley there, very pleased to see me. Desmond at a concert.

Thursday, 19th August

Eardley and I motored to Montacute and did good work arranging Colonel Goodden's oriental china and some furniture brought from Stourhead, notably a new dining-room table and 1662 buffet inlaid with bone and mother-of-pearl. Crowds of visitors and everything here looking fine.

In the evening we motored to Cranborne Manor, taking Desmond. A dream house. Interior not very *commode*, but a number of large Jacobean chimneypieces *à la* Knole and Blickling, one with a wooden bust of a pope wearing triple tiara. Great Hall not good and stair up to great hall gallery bad. We were perplexed by the west wing, *c.* 1650, the windows of which on the outside looked renewed. Ancient grey walls very harmonious, notably colonnade of north side. Three stages of twin pilasters upon buttresses bizarre. Did not like grotesque gargoyle heads on colonnade, nor brick chimneystacks against grey stone walls. The green ride from the north front leading through iron gates between stone piers to a rise of ground, most effective. Enticing meadows beyond as though promising a world of the spirit somewhere out of sight. The garden simple and sweet with orchard trees amongst herbaceous borders. Many roses we noted and one François Juranville pink with a golden sunset sheen and an ineffably mellow smell. I had written asking Lord Salisbury if we might go over, and he called in to the office last week in a friendly way to say how glad he would be for me to see the house and that he had already written to his housekeeper notifying her to expect us. Altogether a dear, romantic, isolated English manor house. Church disappointing; a few pretentious and ugly monuments.

Friday, 20th August

A not so profitable day at Montacute for a meeting of the little Committee, consisting this afternoon of Sir Geoffrey [Hippisley-Cox] only. He brought his wife and the two of them had a few rather silly ideas of rearrangement to which E. and I listened politely, but acted not upon. After tea we left for Holnest Park on our way to Dorchester. Up the drive we encountered a tall, old-fashioned figure whom we took for the family butler hobbling with a stick. It was Mr Chafy, the owner, whom we had come to see. Poor man, he has a real grudge against fate. He complained that he is taxed out of existence and is obliged to sell the place, that he broke his leg fourteen months ago, that his wife died and that life for him is finished. And indeed it seems to be so. E. liked the house, but I did not. It is a dull early-Victorianized house of which there are so many. Grass is growing up to the windows. Dead flies lie in heaps within the windows. All is dirt, decay and desolation. House full of unsuitable furniture – mostly fake oak – some of which he offers to lend to Montacute. But we really have little room for more unless it be of extremely good quality.

Tonight stayed at the Bear, Wincanton, a pretty uncouth sort of inn. Wallpaper stained and peeling; but a kind welcome – which is a change – and excellent dinner of duck with Graves wine. After dinner we made friends with a nice young man called Michael Alvis, looking like Heywood Hill, with a sad voice. He is becoming a market gardener. Told us he was a navigator in the war and went out on sixty-eight operations. Pray to God he prospers.

Dear Uncle Robert's birthday. I looked at his mural plaque in Eton College chapel the other day – a joint one with William Leveson-Gower – 'and in their deaths they were not divided', it reads. Both were scholars and men of the utmost probity. This morning we motored to Longleat. The long straight avenue has been clear-felled. Miss Coates, Lord Bath's secretary-librarian, received us and conducted us round the house. I made several notes. Only the great hall, painted a healthy brown excrement colour, remains unchanged. The hall fireplace however is wholly Flemish. One cannot claim that this house is Italian. Indeed what sixteenth-century English country houses are? Grotesque terms and Persians linking arms, the free hands prinking their hair. I found upstairs in what may have been the long gallery a vast fireplace fairly classical, but earlier than the others, it may have been by Chapman. Otherwise the interior was much altered by Wyattville, and again in the 1860s by Italians in a very expensive manner. The library rooms are charming with inlaid doors of exquisite quality. Several interesting early portraits, notably of the Cobham family in the mid-sixteenth century, the children at table with apples, cherries, and marmoset and pet parrot. The orangery and stables by Wyattville we admired. Miss Coates has a flat being made for her in the stable clock tower.

At Stourton we found young Alvis had come on his Corghi to join us. We showed him the house. All day it has poured with rain. The inside of the house is now looking well. It merely needs flowers and small attentions to make it less lifeless.

Meant to stop at Taunton where I left my car at the garage, but the hotel looked so frightful we continued to Honiton, staying at the Dolphin. This inn pretty primitive too, dirty, but persons agreeable.

At 11.30 to Sheafhayne House to meet Mr Meyrick, a young man about to be married. He told us that, subject to his trustees' consent, he would lend Drake's Drum to Buckland Abbey for the summer months only. We liked him much. He was as sympathetic as his house, an over-grown early seventeenth-century farmhouse with exquisite furniture, chiefly eighteenth century. Bowls full of flowers, Meissen china figures and elegant knickknacks found a surprisingly happy background in gloomy panelling. Meyrick is a descendant of Drake and possesses the navigator's ivory seal given him by Queen Elizabeth, and his pocket map of the world engraved on a round silver disk. He has a small Adam inlaid commode he wishes to sell.

Then we lunched with Carol and Eric Dugdale at Yarty Farm nearby. Very good food and claret. All their small children present. Situated in a very luxuriant valley, Yarty is an enlarged farmhouse with John Fowler wallpapers and some pretty Regency furniture.

In Exeter Cathedral I saw a mural monument to Bishop Harvey, dated 1564, with much Renaissance decoration and candelabra. I don't greatly care for this cathedral. Liked the painter Northcote's monument, by Chantrey I presume – lifesize, seated.

Then motored to Buckland Abbey which I had never penetrated before. The combe in which it is set is nostalgic. Brings back Ribbesford to me with its rooks cawing, its deep belt of trees. But *qua* house it is awful. A mess. Uneven floor levels, broken arches, and not one decent liveable room. The only passable room is the great hall with mid-Elizabethan plaster ceiling and pendants, grotesque figures supporting the cove; ornate panelling with arcades in top stages and frieze inlaid with holly strapwork; in the end lunettes over the panelling are plaster scenes, somewhat Hilliardish in conception, i.e. trophies hanging on trees and reclining figures. Overmantel has Grenville arms displayed. One chimneypiece upstairs displays the Drake coat in stucco. But the house is literally carved out of the medieval Abbey church, of which the central tower and parts of the transept survive. There is a pleasant early Georgian back staircase. A fire gutted one wing. It has been renovated. Three long, low rooms with iron girder supports. E. and I agreed we could think of no old house we would less like to live in.

Monday, 23rd August

Stay at the Bedford Hotel, Tavistock, which we are growing to like. The proprietor and staff all friendly. Today spent entirely at Cotehele with which we were well satisfied. It is beautifully kept by the angelic Mrs Downes. Two old craftsmen from Harris & Sons, the furniture repairers at Plymouth, met us. They were joyfully enthusiastic with craftsmen's true love of old furniture. Although totally ignorant of dates they knew instinctively what furniture was genuine, recognizing good workmanship when they saw it, appreciating that no nails had been used on one piece and certain dovetails on another. For years they have renewed broken pieces and reproduced others so expertly that they have become guileless fakers. I suppose this does not matter.

Tuesday, 24th August

We went to a silly film, *Uncle Silas*, last night in Tavistock, which gave me
the creeps and frightened me. In the night I had a 'mare, but not about
the subject of the film. I dreamt that an old woman was pulling out my
toenails one by one. E. and I motored to Montacute and saw Bob
[Gathorne-Hardy] there. He has practically finished arranging the
library, and splendid it looks too. I trained back to London from Yeovil,
first-class single, 42 shillings.

Wednesday, 25th August

Carol Dugdale and I had an interview with the Ministry of Planning
about Matson House [Glos]. To start with I was apprehensive and embarrassed. Carol swept in and was very curt and imperious. Relations began
stickily. But I was immensely impressed by the very masterful way in
which she handled the case. She never faltered or used a wrong word;
held her ground and floored all counter-argument. In the end she got
her way, much to my surprise. What confidence the woman has. She
ought to be Prime Minister. She and Eric lunched with me at the Allies
Club.
    Dined with Alec Clifton-Taylor in Neville Terrace. He lives in a
modernistic flat where everything is white. He is a gentle and intelligent
man who knows his stuff, which is architecture, domestic and ecclesias-
tic. He says we are 'dedicants' to the arts.

Thursday, 26th August

At 4 Lord Esher came to the office. I motored him to Iford [Manor,
Wilts], the Petos' house near Bradford-on-Avon which he has just rented.
We called at Chelsea for innumerable parcels and oddments to take
down. He is *par excellence* the ideal travelling companion, humorous and
interested. He is however always a little too much in a fidget, anxious to
stop, or move on; and of course in an emergency he would be less than
useless, being totally unpractical and butter-fingered. Iford is romantic
outside; indifferent within. I do not greatly admire the Eshers' furniture.
He says he does not mind whether it is genuine or fake.

Friday, 27th August

We set off at 10.30. A lovely day rinsed in autumnal melancholy, the early
sun slanting through the Iford trees upon the dew and the tranquil doves'
notes soothing. We drove without stop to Hidcote. Found Lawrence
Johnston and lawyer, and Nancy Lindsay, Norah L.'s daughter. Lawrie J.
signed the deed of gift like a lamb so, since he leaves for abroad in a fort-

night, the place may be said to be saved. This has been a struggle but it is accomplished. We were conducted round the gardens by the usual route. How often must the old man have done this tour? I think it is a sad occasion for him and I wondered how far he understood that he was giving away his precious treasure of a garden. 'I have another Hidcote,' he murmured, presumably referring to his garden at Mentone. Miss Lindsay is like an old witch, very predatory and interfering. She maintains that she has been deputed by L.J. to supervise these gardens in his absence abroad. We were not overcome with gratitude. Anyway no mention of this condition was made either by L.J. or his solicitors before the signing. Sibyl Colefax will be delighted that the deed she worked so hard to bring about has been done. The Eshers always being in a hurry we did not linger at Hidcote. They kept buying things in antique shops at Broadway, and stopped for tea and cakes and jam at Winchcombe. Lord E. eats at tea with the relish of a child.

I enjoyed this visit and tour with the Es immensely. I arrived 7.30 at the Dower House, Bradford-on-Avon, to stay the night with Alex Moulton. It is his mother's house. Mrs M. is a sweet and saintly lady.

Saturday, 28th August

Alex and I talked till after midnight, drinking whisky. In some respects he resembles the earnest, high-minded pre-1914 generation, for there is an Edwardian air about him. Yet he has more sense of humour and none of the aggressive superiority and chauvinism which one associates with that generation. In his particular line he is creative. He showed me the design of his steam car. This morning he took me round his factory, old and new buildings, and the gardens of The Hall which Mr Cook has interested himself in. Though a bit over-restored 100 years ago by Alex's great-grandfather, The Hall is a textbook Elizabethan house. The two downstairs rooms are fine of their kind, with massive double-tier chimneypieces. How much restored I can't decide. I motored back to London, arriving teatime.

B.S. dined. I gave him a tremendous talking to for being sanctimonious and dishonest. I told him that if he were genuinely ascetic and spiritual I would not reprimand him, but that he was, on his own admission, craving sexual pleasures. His strictures on the subject were therefore most unattractive. Having adopted this schoolmastery line I have now written to three different people asking for a job for the poor youth. If I could be bothered – and knew how to set about it – I would hire some decent body to seduce him.

Sunday, 29th August

Mama's birthday, but she is away in Scotland. Worked all day till the evening. Went to Doreen at 6 o'clock, my head full of other matters than Doreen. But she talked me into interest on the subject of remarkable women we have known, or known about. She says that in Edwardian days to be successful women had only to be beautiful. Today they have to be intelligent. That is certainly some improvement.

Patrick O'Donovan dined. He goes to Singapore on Tuesday. He has made a success on the *Observer*, but little money. He is very funny about himself, a huge joke he considers, yet ponders over life and death, and sex. Has never yet slept with a woman, he so natural and hearty. He is a strong Catholic by temperament, but not by faith, like many of us, including James. Says the Greek Communists are fanatics and die bravely; but Communism must be extirpated. How?

Monday, 30th August

To Knole this morning by train. Robin and Mason [Lord Sackville's agent] and I went round the furniture, sizing up what has been done to date and what must still be done. All rather worried that so much necessary deworming has not yet been tackled and only 1/5th of the fabrics have been taken in hand whereas we have already spent £500 out of the £1,000 allotted by the Government for reparations. Looked over Quebec House, Westerham. A dull house with little visible reminders of General Wolfe.

Wednesday, 1st September

Audrey came to stay here last night and leaves Thursday. She is very sweet and pretty and a charming guest for she is happy doing anything, or nothing. Today Baron Ash and Sibyl Colefax lunched. Audrey thought Sibyl full of charm – I would not say she had charm – and was mightily struck by her personality, which I suppose is strong. Sibyl had returned this morning from Stratford where she went yesterday for *Hamlet*. Speaking to me she said, 'You and I are happy.' I said, 'I am not happy, Sibyl. Are you really?' She went on, 'I haven't finished my sentence – I was going to say happy in having been born with no possessions. No, I am not happy. Old people are not happy. But I was happy. Now I am only interested in the young.' This is the one occasion when I have heard her speak of her inmost self. I believe I am rather fond of this old woman, if only because she is so invariably kind to me. She said she would write by airmail tomorrow to that horrible old Berenson giving him my Rome address. And she will too. Now as to possessions the fewer one possesses, and of course I have a very few, the more one loves them. People like the Hartingtons who own priceless works of art are not so fond of their Inigo Jones drawings, their Rembrandts and William Kent furniture as I am of my one little watercolour by Ethel Walker.

Thursday, 2nd September

A meeting at the Treasury this morning attended by Lord Esher, the Admiral, Hubert Smith and myself: also by FitzRoy, the Princess Royal's agent, and solicitor, and accountant. To our dismay Lord Esher urged the Princess to accept the Treasury's terms to take Harewood and hand it to the Trust for five years, with the right for herself and son to live there during their lifetimes. After the five years it is to be a gamble who holds the property. Esher is so confident that it will be the National Trust that he is eager to take the risk, and for the present owners to take the risk. The rest of the staff and myself very uncertain. I was prevailed upon to tell Lord Esher so. Accordingly I drafted a letter from him to FitzRoy toning down his actual words at the meeting. I don't know how he will react to this. Perhaps he will be displeased.

Friday, 3rd September

I managed to clear up all outstanding letters and work at the office, this being my last day. Am determined in going abroad to give my work no further thought and anxiety. Went for a drink with Riette Lamington, who was alone. She is not unintelligent, but I don't want to see a lot of her. She can't relax without becoming coquettish. Very stormy day and returning on foot across the park a violent cloudburst of rain descended, so I sheltered in a temple alcove. In it were two working-class men talking disrespectfully of the Royal Family. Some women driven in by the rain joined in the conversation, and agreed that the Royal Family were an unnecessary expense. All spoke without vitriol and quite dispassionately. I was surprised, and merely said that I totally disagreed. Wished them good-day and ostentatiously walked off. Got soaked.

Saturday, 4th September

Set off with Desmond Shawe-Taylor at 9 o'clock for Victoria. We travel together as far as Rome, first class. Uneventful journey till Calais. In the corridor of the French train I see what I shortsightedly mistake to be a pink blancmange crawling along the floor. It is Oggy Lynn's hat with Oggy beneath it somewhere below my knees. Much embracing. We have her company in the next sleeper to ours as far as Milan. In Paris D. and I leave the train for a three-hour break; drink at a café on the pavement and drive in a horse-cab to the Place de l'Université where we dine, only fairly well, at Marius restaurant. A delightful ninetyish atmosphere. It is a beautiful square and when I come back to Paris I shall stay here.

The night full of disturbances but comfortable. Our sleepers are adjacent so we throw open the door and have one compartment of adequate size entirely to ourselves.

Sunday, 5th September

We wake up in the mountains in pouring, cataclysmic rain. All day it rains which dampens our spirits. Has the weather changed, we ask in great distress and fear. We sleep on and off. One cannot read for long stretches in a train. We reach Rome at 12.45 a.m. Lucky Desmond is met by his host, John Somers Cocks at the Vatican Ministry, who drives me to the Hôtel de Ville and takes D. onwards. Curiously enough I am given exactly the same room as I had last year, no. 88. It is not very nice, but fairly quiet.

Monday, 6th September

My first impression of Rome is that the whole city, and certainly the hotel, are slightly shabbier than last year; also the inhabitants. That bloom of expectancy has gone; and just the faintest disillusion prevails. Is it because in a foolish way the Romans expected an eldorado before the ensuing elections last year, and that now they are over and the same Government is in power, they are bored and disappointed? I pray not. On leaving the hotel my steps automatically take me past the Villa Medici to the Pincio. I then sit on the balustrade overlooking the Piazza del Popolo. It is a bright, cool day, ideal for sightseeing, with a breeze. I descend and look at both sides, Vignola's and Bernini's, of the great arch (the Porta del Popolo). Then immerse myself in the church of Santa Maria with its superb collection of Florentine sculptural tombs and screens. Then cash a cheque at the American Express for nearly 2,000 lire for each £1, and walk to lunch at a favourite *trattoria* close to the Piazza Navona.

Desmond calls for me at 5 o'clock and we walk to the Vatican City. I notice how much Bramante's Palazzo Giraud evolves from Alberti's Palazzo Ruccellai in Florence; the same thin pilaster strips to each floor. The approach to St Peter's very squalid at present with barricades everywhere, and the Borgo up and cranes working. I hope they do not mean to fill up the vista that Mussolini cleared. Rome is crammed with the Catholic girls from all over Italy wearing red berets, who smell very strong and acrid. 'What we now want,' said Desmond, 'is some Protestant boys.' More impressed than ever before by the unassertive splendour of the interior of the basilica, so vast and clear of all pews and seats. People complain of the arrogance and coldness of St Peter's. I do not agree. I find the interior, when empty, humbly offering shelter, asking to be filled and loved, offering faith and understanding. The predominant blue-grey is restful and effuses a misty tone through which the sharper colours of mosaic and gilding glow. Walked up to San Onofrio but could not enter the church. Enjoyed the western view in the sunset.

In the evening Guido Ferrari called at the hotel. Has improved in mind and body. Is now a very beautiful young man with raven hair and white teeth and eyes of bear-like brown, a Michelangelo ephebe. Is less discontented with his lot, which is a relief, no longer wishing to adopt British nationality. I expect he has a girl but do not inquire. Italians don't like familiarity. He says my Italian is worse than ever and it is a waste of his time giving me lessons.

Tuesday, 7th September

Walk straight to San Onofrio, via the Borghese Palace, and enter the cloister, timeless and tranquil and composed of ancient and modern (which is to say fifteenth-century) columns. Wall fountains with Persians carrying baskets on their heads, the alcoves with elaborate plasterwork of trees, etc., extremely pretty. Sat here meditating for an hour. Walked past the Villa Farnesina, the Porticus Octavianus, dull, and the Theatre of Marcellus. The two restored bays give a helpful understanding of the purity of Roman architecture from which Palladio profited. Climbed to Ara Coeli and took note of the Cosmati pulpits. I love this period and its oriental display of coloured mosaic and un-Gothic architecture – Proto-Renaissance the art historians call it. Trevi fountain is again dry, which is maddening. Why do the fountains not play?

Desmond called for me and we lunched with the Somers Cockses. He is an intelligent man; she very English and nice. He says that, deputizing for the Minister, he will ask for an audience for me at Castel Gandolfo, but that I must hold myself ready to go there – twenty miles off – at the very last minute.

This evening walked to the Gesù church with its Baroque ceiling, the clouds painted over the compartments just like the spreading waves of dry-rot fungus. The *giallo antico* pilasters of Vignola are shiny green as though erected yesterday. Then to Sant' Andrea della Valle and with Letarouilly in hand to the Massimo and Linotte palaces. Peruzzi is my architect for he has a strong sense of the Picturesque without licence.

Dined with Roger Hinks, or rather we went Dutch, I paying the larger share. He is not a modest man and boasts of his conquests in Venice where – so he says – young men rush at him like flies to fly-paper.

Wednesday, 8th September

Met Desmond sitting outside the Villa Giulia which we looked at together. He admired it much. Letarouilly revealed to me that many of the stucco panels by Udine on the outside of the hemicycle are now gone. This is sad and accounts for the present over-austere surface of that side. Such a pity the water not playing and the garden ornaments in such a mess. San Prassede: the mosaics in the Orto del Paradiso glow with red and gold. I am confused by the dates of the mosaics here. Those upon the spandrels of the arch in front of the apse have faded to a heather colour. The floor is of Cosmati mosaic. Desmond has no reverence in a church and talks loudly as though he were in the drawing-room at Long Crichel while devout pilgrims are bowed and prostrate in devotion before the holy column.

There are many anti-Government chalk *graffiti* on walls and pavements, such as 'Il popolo ha fame', and abuse of De Gasperi's Black Government. Guido tells me there is much Communism even in Rome and Somers Cocks says there are 2 million unemployed. Things certainly look to me worse this year than last. 'Il Christo è morto per i poveri. Che fa Gasperi?'

One should take stock of the alterations made by time when one asks why contemporaries thought more highly of such and such a monument than we do. Usually the answer is that depreciation of a sort has subsequently taken place. On the whole it is amazing how little buildings have altered in Rome. My Letarouilly drawings done in 1810 with extreme accuracy reveal how slight are the alterations since that date.

Tonight met a charming friend of Roger Hinks, called Kop, a Pole, drinking with Desmond. Then walked to the Via Giulia to a cocktail party given by the Taffy Rodds, to which Peter [Rodd] had invited us. I met Peter while lunching in a *trattoria*. Gavin Faringdon was with him. D. and I dined in the Piazza Navona watching the children playing with balloons around the fountains. On my return to the hotel I found Guy who had turned up without an appointment. Sent him away. A man at the Rodds' party who lives in the Palazzo Sacchetti told me that families of dwarfs occupy the mezzanine floor of the palace. They are very agreeable people.

Thursday, 9th September

Walked miles this morning for quite three hours. Left notes on Gavin Faringdon and D'Arcy Osborne. Then looked at Bernini's Triton fountain. Walked into the Barberini Palace courtyard and admired the corkscrew staircase of twin Doric columns, a marvel of engineering.

Then Santa Chiara something and San Bernardino, a baby Pantheon; then Sta Maria degli Angeli with vast transept, in fact the transformation of the great hall of Diocletian's Baths. The San Bruno by Houdon very pensive. Then San Lorenzo fuori le Mura, through the Porta of that name. This church was bombed by us in the war and, alas, the Cosmati work of the choir destroyed although the tabernacle remains; the ambones much injured. Restoration is in progress but by no means complete, and no admission to the nave. Some columns replaced very skilfully.

I lunched with Colonel Fothergill, a fat Colonel of fifty, whom Cuthbert Acland wants as assistant in the Lake District. No intellectual but extremely jolly. He has offered to take Desmond and me to Hadrian's villa on Saturday. D. and I looked at more churches in the evening.

I went to Sir D'Arcy Osborne's apartment in the Via Giulia at 7.30 and we dined out. He is a charming but shy man who suffers from periods of acute depression. He talked of the Pope (Pius XII) whom he sees at least twice a year and to whom he is devoted. The Pope told him the other day that he listens to the BBC course of English lessons. He loves England, speaks the language fairly well but does not understand a great deal. He seldom relaxes but works all day long, living extremely ascetically. His recreations are occasional music and talking to his half dozen friends among the Cardinals while strolling in the Vatican garden. Sir D. thinks the inner cabinet of the Cardinals should always be Italians for otherwise agreement would be impossible, and furthermore Italians are more level-headed than most nations in politics. This surprises me. He says that notwithstanding the Pope's sanctity things happen in Vatican backstairs departments that are far from edifying, such as black-marketing. The Vatican lately bought a great deal of wheat from Canada on this basis. Sir D. has invited me to attend the St Peter's ceremony on Sunday when the Pope addresses the Catholic youth gathered in Rome this week.

Friday, 10th September

Walked this morning to St John Lateran. Appraised Galilei's façade. It has a severe tightness like Gibbs's church in the Strand, and Easton Neston, which make me want to pick them up and shake them looser. Again failed to find a way into the cloisters. Then sat inside San Clemente; strolled through the Colosseum and noticed some fragmentary remains of Roman stucco on two archways.

Lunched at the Taffy Rodds in Via Giulia 167. She is his second wife and very pretty, fair Angle-angel type. Sat at a large circular table, five children and Peter. Agreeable talk about Communism which Peter thinks will destroy itself if only war can be avoided long enough; that the Tito break is more significant than people in England realize.

It seems that one can drink local wine in Italy with impunity. In the church of S.M. sopra Minerva it was revealed to me that the Tudor masons in England were only influenced by the earlier Florentine monuments of about 1480, and by nothing Roman. I suppose Rome was politically a dangerous city for Englishmen to frequent in Elizabeth's reign. Dined with Desmond and Roger Hinks in Piazza del Popolo. Desmond departed for the Piazza Colonna and I retired early to bed.

Saturday, 11th September

Went this morning to Palazzo Venezia, an exceedingly interesting building in its transition from Gothic to Renaissance. Thought that Sharington may have been influenced by it in building up Lacock Abbey. Possible? The collection of furniture, pictures and porcelain upstairs is admirably displayed. Quite exemplary. The pretty paving of old brown and green tiles makes lack of carpets not felt at all. In fact Roman palaces seldom have carpets.

At 12.30 Colonel Fothergill called for me and drove me to Tivoli, but we had a puncture and got no further than Hadrian's Villa. Here we lunched and spent the whole afternoon in exceeding heat, slowly walking over this remarkable acreage. Much is left. I was particularly interested in the remains of a plaster ceiling in the vaulted Baths. This ceiling was exactly copied by Robert Adam. The Colonel asked me if I had read a Batsford book – quite good, he thought – on Adam. The Colonel's spare tyres are made of synthetic rubber so we drove home at 15 mph, and burst a second. Never got to Tivoli.

At night the huge cemetery outside Rome is lit up, a light in each niche wherein the coffins are kept for seven years. Then the body, having disintegrated, is taken out and buried in a smaller space.

Sunday, 12th September

To Mass at the Trinità church at the top of the Spanish Steps. Hearing female voices issuing from persons unseen I recalled Mendelssohn's passage about his attending Mass in this church and noticing the same phenomenon. Sweet sisters of the Sacré Coeur they are. Then walked to the Farnese Palace, open Sunday mornings only. The Caracci room is a poem of beauty, an elegy rather than a lyric. Rich Renaissance, the flat of the ceiling contains the painted panels within ornate ribs. Paintings by Caracci against grey and gold. I can think of few rooms more beautiful. Every architectural detail of this palace is massive, strong and superlatively self-confident.

Somers Cocks in his car, with Desmond, met me at the Pal. Farnese, and we drove down the Via Appia. No words can describe how for miles around the Campagna has been utterly ruined. The mess and untidiness, aerodromes and, above all, pylons and wires, and revolting buildings have made a wilderness out of this historic pastoral landscape renowned throughout the ages, and painted by every artist visiting Rome. After this little tour we looked at San Stefano Rotondo. A circular aisle with central choir, enclosed by a ring of inner columns. On the walls indifferent frescoes of unspeakable martyrdoms and tortures. Against the church in the colonnade outside, at a long table, Catholic neophytes were eating their simple midday meal. With the columns as a background the scene resembled a Last Supper.

At 5.15 D'Arcy Osborne in the Chancery car motored me to the Vatican to watch Pope Pius address the Catholic Youths. We had a stance on top of the Bernini colonnade. From here I enjoyed the extraordinary medieval spectacle of nuns in a row sitting, apparently comfortably, on the sloping brown corrugate roof of a very high house with deep drop below, to watch the St Peter's ceremony. The nuns were quite unconcerned by their vertiginous perch. I liked the Pope's quiet, determined, unpulpity voice. Saw him carried in his Chair through a central gangway to a throne and *baldacchino* placed on the steps The cries of 'Viva, viva!' the waving of dark green caps in the air like the heads of daisies without the petals, the blues and greens of the shirts, and orange of the banners, wonderfully pictorial. The crowd stretched from the piazza further than the eye could see. That these hundreds of thousands of youths should look to the Pope as their leader is in these irreligious days astounding. A slightly disturbing element was the Fascist tinge of the meeting. The *vivas* were rather too well drilled, the demagogic voice of the Master of Ceremonies relayed from a dozen loudspeakers was reminiscent of a Nürnberg rally. Does this mean that in the Pope these youths are clinging to the next best substitute for a totalitarian dictator? For they are disillusioned with democracy. Desmond said cynically that he felt the crowd would have cheered Stalin just as enthusiastically.

I dined in a restaurant with D'Arcy Osborne. From the top of the Spanish Steps we watched the fireworks and a gathering thunder storm. The lightning lit up the dome of St Peter's. After each flash had subsided the dome remained a perceptible second as a grey ghost of itself against the deep purple sky. This seems a curious phenomenon. D. Osborne more sympathetic than ever. He confided that the Queen was the past love of his life, and he speaks of her with emotion.

Monday, 13th September

I have a bad cold in my head and chest and do not feel well. Moreover it is horrid weather, raining heavily at intervals. In the morning I looked at more palaces by myself, lunched alone and slept. Desmond joined me at 5 o'clock. We went to Trastevere where we agreed that the people, though grubbier, were better looking. Both immensely impressed by Bramante's Tempietto, but no view from the Janiculum on account of the rain. We sat in the square of S.M. in Trastevere which is like the scene in an opera, the noisiest square I have ever been in. Then we went to hear Alfredo play his guitar and sing Neapolitan songs to us in George's Café off the Via Veneto. D. considers him a remarkable artist, his art being of an intimate kind for it is difficult to hear him unless he plays close to one. It was sad for him having to perform in such noisy, unsympathetic sur-roundings, like expecting the late Mrs Gordon Woodhouse to play her clavichord in the middle of Paddington station. On returning to the hotel I was handed a letter from the Holy See through the Legation, announc-ing that I am granted a 'special' audience at Castel Gandolfo tomorrow morning at 10.45.

Tuesday, 14th September

My cold very much worse. Am feverish and my nose pours. All day without any intermission the rain also pours and pours. After a bad night I get up early and catch a tram – over one hour – to Castel Gandolfo. Am feeling very nervous because I can think of nothing special to say to the Pontiff. Arrive at the village at 10 and first look at the lake in a crater below and, over its bank, more extraordinary, at the Roman Campagna at a still lower level. A very classical situation. There are no buildings on the shores of the lake except on the Castel Gandolfo side. I go to Bernini's round church in the village to shelter from the rain, and to compose and prepare myself. A Mass is in progress. Then at 10.30 I walk to the Palace, a shapeless building of yellow wash towering above the village. At the gate are a crowd of boy scouts and the Catholic Youth. I edge my way through and wave my official invitation to the handsome Swiss guard in his fantastic Michelangelo uniform of yellow and blue stripes. I am passed from one guard to another, from one officer with a red plume to another, from one gentleman usher to a cosy butler, or majordomo, and left in the fourth chamber hung with crimson brocade and, over a table, one large crucifix. The green marble doorheads have 'Pius XI. Pont. Max. A.V.' carved on them. So this suite is fairly contem-porary. It is all right but not outstandingly opulent. I sit on one of the gold chairs with crimson brocade upholstery, and wait. Presently a very distinguished old lady in black, with black veil, and wearing pearls and a few good jewels, comes in. She has what was once a beautiful face with deep black shadows under her eyes. I rise from my seat and make a gesture of politeness. She does not recognize my presence but, grasping her rosary and muttering prayers, prostrates herself with utmost reverence before the crucifix. When I next look up I hear her say, 'Giovan signore, ho grand fame', which surprises me. She dives into a capacious bag, extracts a biscuit and nibbles it. She tells me that the Pope has suddenly had to see several cardinals just arrived from South America, and our audience will be postponed indefinitely. She draws me to the window and looks out upon the lake which she supposes is the sea. She is Brazilian and says, 'An English Catholic, what a contradictory thing to be.' She speaks with great volubility about the splendid qualities and strength of the English. Then she discourses very knowledgeably on religion. All our troubles today are due to our divorcing religion from everyday life, and even the pious only give lip-service to God. She directs me never to neglect the Holy Ghost in my prayers and thoughts, admitting that it is difficult to distinguish Him from the other Two. She assures me that through years of unhappiness she has reached absolute contentment through her religion. I admire and like her, but wish she would offer me a biscuit. We are then joined by a superior young Italian Monsignore carrying a precious parcel wrapped in tissue paper and an uncouth young American from Texas. For one hour we four are together, shunted by the majordomo from room to room in a sort of silent musical chairs. It is what I suppose the immediate after-life may be, namely thrown among the same people who have died the very moment as oneself, and moving through the mansions of Purgatory towards Heaven. We pass other people without making any contact. However a young priest in a wheelchair, in a deathlike apathy and presumably the last stages of consumption, is pushed past us. I saw his face on returning from his audience wreathed in ghastly smiles. It was an expression of resigned beatitude.

The Texan, much to my surprise, produced from a trouser pocket a gold wristwatch, a gold pocket-watch, a gold pencil and chain, and a gold cigarette case. He asked me if I supposed the Holy Father would accept them as a souvenir. I said I was sure he would not, but advised him to consult the Brazilian lady whose fourth audience with a different Pope this was to be. The American said, 'I don't think a cheque would be quite the same thing. I could not afford 100,000 dollars and I daresay he has enough money to go on with.' After a pause he said, 'I am going to be quite homely with the Pope. What are you?' And finally when we had reached the last state room and the Brazilian had complained of hunger pains and asked him for a biscuit, the Texan produced a Chesterfield cigarette and invited her to smoke.

By this time purple Monsignores were running in all directions. Whenever His Holiness was ready for the audience a vicious little bell rang and cassocked liverymen fairly scampered to open and shut doors. We were constantly moved along, now from chair to chair, the pace gradually slackening. The drill was very effective. First the Brazilian lady disappeared, and returned radiant, her hands full of parcels, saying, 'He is wonderful. He is so good and kind. May you all have every happiness and blessing from this visit. Arrivederci.' Suddenly, instead of the three of us who remained being called singly into the next room the door opened and in stepped swiftly a tall, erect, brisk figure, all in white, wearing a white biretta. Until I saw an attendant Cardinal genuflect I did not realize it was the Pope. He went straight to the Texan ahead of me – this was prearranged for the three of us were spaced on our chairs at intervals. The Pope without wasting a second talked to him with much affability. With one nervous movement the Texan fumbled in his trouser pocket, but mercifully thought better of it. The Pope turned, the Texan left, and the Holy Father approached me. I walked towards him and fell on both knees. The next one and a half minutes remain but vaguely registered. He held out his hand for me to take and I just noticed the ring, as I kissed it, to have a large dark stone encircled with lesser gems, not diamonds. His presence radiated a benignity, calm and sanctity that I have certainly never before sensed in any human being. All the while he smiled in the sweetest, kindliest way so that I immediately fell head over heels in love with him. I was so affected I could scarcely speak without tears and was conscious that my legs were trembling. His face was strong and healthy, not handsome, but made beautiful by his extraordinary charm. I noticed his nice strong teeth like old ivory. He spoke a gentle, hesitating English. Asked me where I lived and when I said London, said something of it being a 'dear place'. I told him I had witnessed the ceremony at St Peter's with Sir D'Arcy Osborne and had been immensely impressed by the crowd of Catholic Youth. He said, 'Did you see how beautiful it was. I am so glad. I want to bless you and all those dear to you,' and beyond a few other polite, but trite, remarks I can recollect nothing. He then handed me a little blue envelope embossed with the papal arms. It contained a not very expensive medal with his head on one side and his arms (heraldic) on the other. I knelt for his blessing and passed on. In turning to leave I noticed a Cardinal slip into his hand, held out behind with desperately waggling fingers, another little envelope for the next guest. I walked back through the state rooms now filled with groups of young men carrying some large images and awaiting their turn for the papal audience.

Got back to Rome in time to lunch with the Colonel and Desmond. The heavy rain made us postpone our Caprarola visit till tomorrow. Instead D. and I were lent the Colonel's car for the afternoon. So we drove to St Peter's, then to San Andrea al Quirinale, a splendid Baroque oval church by Bernini with beautiful inlaid marble floors, notably the arms and supporters in *giallo antico* of a Cardinal. Then to S. Agnese fuori le Mura where a friendly old priest took us and a small group of children into the catacombs. We were given thin tapers to hold. The children's faces of wonder and fear in the candlelight were very picturesque. There were ledges in the rock cut out for bodies of the earliest Christians, and remains of tombstones in alabaster giving the names of husbands and wives and their approximate ages in Latin.

Wednesday, 15th September

Raining still. Visited Keats's House and introduced myself to the lady custodian. Looked around and read that most moving letter, unfinished, from Severn to Brown the morning Keats died. Met Desmond at 12.30 and had a hectic time procuring supplementary tickets to Ischia and booking train seats. Colonel Fothergill called and motored us to Caprarola. The way out of Rome by the Porta del Popolo is the least congested of any. The surrounding country is comparatively unspoilt and the Campagna undulating. The situation of Caprarola is very fine indeed, on a hill with a panoramic view in three compasses. But ingenious though its pentagonal planning may be the building is grim and heavy. I was frankly disappointed. The palace is also very dilapidated and empty of all furniture. German troops were billeted here during the war. I admit that the circular colonnade inside with *treillage* work painted on the barrel vaulting is good – so, too, is the splendid twisted staircase of stone, all painted, a vastly improved version of the Barberini one which has a lift shaft in the middle of it. The dome of this staircase is painted. The rooms of the palace on the *piano nobile* are vast and likewise painted. The predominating yellow, blue and green of these frescoes produce a soft and rich tone that we associate with faded tapestries. Yet the individual scenes in large central panels of Francis I and the Farnese family are very poor when you look into them.

Unfortunately the visit was cut short and spoilt by a disagreeable incident. We wanted to walk through the garden up to the Casino but were forbidden by the custodian. Desmond and the Colonel disregarded him and persisted, pursued by the expostulating guardian and hesitant me. I was made cross both by the officious custodian and by the other two who were making his position difficult. I was so put out that I turned and walked straight back to the car.

John Bayley telephoned and dined with me. He is a tall, thin, bespectacled American of thirty-six, very bald, ascetic, yet puffy about the face. He talks non-stop about architecture. He has taken 3,000 photographs of

Roman palaces which are his speciality. He thrusts a way into private palaces which no foreigner has ever penetrated before. He intends ultimately to publish the photographs with a text, in the manner of Letarouilly or Piranesi.

Thursday, 16th September

Set off from Rome at 8 o'clock. Met Desmond on the train. Both gloomy because at Naples the weather still overcast and even drizzling. We hated Naples. Began with a terrible scene in the taxi with a porter over exorbitant tip demanded. We almost came to blows, but gave way. The same trouble was repeated on the boat where another porter dumped our luggage and started raving. Instead of giving the money demanded so bloodily, we threw the coins *at* him.

The sea passage to Ischia became increasingly beautiful. We passed Prócida island on the way. A long row of small houses of oriental appearance painted lemon, yellow, pink or blue. Each house has a curious half arch in the front. Within it hang tomatoes to dry, making a splash of red. The effect one of the prettiest things I have ever seen. The little round church is staring white. The sea almost a mill pond. Occasionally the boat gave a gentle heave. Whereupon a travelling priest clutching his beads, frantically crossed himself, exclaiming, 'Mama mia!' Desmond much amused and referred to him as Padre Muff Pozzi, having heard me frequently refer to the ceiling painter of S. Ignazio as Padre Andrea Pozzi.

Tuesday, 21st September

Ischia. Until today I have been alone with Desmond. The interlude after intensive Roman sightseeing has been a restorative. Rising about 9 we sit at breakfast, when the sun is not too strong, on the terrace overlooking the bay and Prócida beyond, and Vesuvius beyond Prócida. I have no shorts unfortunately, and wear my thin brown trousers and open-neck shirt with short sleeves. At 11.15 we sally to the shore and bathe in the delicious balmy sea. Lunch at 1.30. Desmond sleeps, I read in the hotel garden which overlooks Ischia Porto and town. Food not very good, but sweet servants. One evening we walked to the Castle, which is situated as romantically as St Michael's Mount. It is ruinous and has a Baroque and Renaissance chapel. Another day we took the steamer to Feria and back for dinner. Sitting in the street drinking innocuous aperitifs at sunset we watch the parade of youth and beauty. The boys and girls wear brilliant colours and are burnt nutmeg brown. Diminutive *carrozze* ply up and down. They are painted yellow with Edwardian pram sunshade hoods over them. There is a public garden with cut water melons for sale. The houses, clothes, human skin and fruit make a kaleidoscope, forever changing and forever new.

I left at 6 o'clock this morning and reached Rome at midday. Lunched with John Bayley and a tiresome party of American friends. After luncheon Bayley took me to the Villa Medici where we walked in the famous garden that Velasquez painted and, they say, Michelangelo designed. The back of the Villa is encrusted with panels and reliefs of ancient Rome. Bayley has some blind spots notwithstanding his long sojourn in Italy. For instance, knows nothing of Brunelleschi. Speaks disparagingly of his own countrymen. He is designing a palace for the Emperor of Ethiopia.

Dined with D'Arcy Osborne who has asked me to stay with him next year, if there will be one, and suggested we might motor to the south together. When amused he laughs till he cries. Yet he has a slightly abrupt manner that disconcerts. He wrote me a note, saying, 'If you are later than 8.30 I refuse to wait.' I arrived on time. He was charming.

Wednesday, 22nd September

At 10 o'clock Barbara Rothschild and Rex Warner drove up. They packed me into their car. Regretfully I kissed goodbye to Rome, as we dashed out of the Popolo gate. A perfectly beautiful day, hot indeed. Our first stop was a mountain town called Narni high above the valley of the Nar. We strolled into the Duomo. It was quite empty. There were no guides and no other sightseers. A most beautiful old church with columns of travertine, an ornamented font (early Renaissance) and curious white marble screen against the south wall. Barbara remarked how unlike a museum and like a church this Duomo was, compared to the Roman ones, a very Protestant observation.

Drove on to Spoleto and lunched. The Duomo here is Romanesque. Although altered by Bernini the interior is surprisingly dull. The outside portico below the rose window is early Renaissance. It incorporates two outdoor pulpits by Milano and thirteenth-century mosaics overhead. A simply splendid Renaissance tomb to an Orsini by Milano and another opposite to Fra Lippo Lippi. In the apse are Lippi's frescoes, very sweet, gentle and appealing. The soffit of the apse has been restored and is too gaudy. The stalls of a side chapel, dated 1550, are of intarsia, a form of art which is I think underrated. This seems to be the region of choir stalls and inlaid woods.

Drove to Spello through the loveliest Italian country. Trevi, literally tumbling down a steep hill in a stream of grey walls, is from the distance the most romantic village imaginable. Spello is a small town where we stopped to look at the Pintoricchio chapel, dated 1501. After the Lippi frescoes there is no insipidity here. How moving and divine Pintoricchio is.

Then Assisi. I had never been here before. It must surely be the loveliest town in all Italy. I had no idea how beautiful. By now tired (and I have not felt well all day) we saw only San Francesco and examined the Giottos. These childlike pictures must have been repainted for there is much crudity of outline. Yet the silence and motionlessness of the seated nuns, their backs turned to the spectator, is very solemn. Rex Warner and I walked along the outside cloister, high above the valley. Women are not allowed there. It is reserved for contemplation from which they are held to distract. No allowance is made for women's contemplation from which men distract. What a view from this city! We watched two women, who had slipped in, being turned out by a young Franciscan very politely. They evidently supposed we were enjoying pornographic pictures. Another Franciscan was playing the organ in the church with an air of tranquil distinction. All the while Barbara waited for us outside, seated with a book on the floor in a tumble of flounced skirt, totally unaware of the beautiful picture she made.

On our way to Perugia we stopped in the dusk outside Sta Maria degli Angeli and looked at the Golden Madonna over the portico. I fancied she was bowing, but the others said not. Drove on to Perugia where I stayed at the Hotel Brufani and they left me.

This afternoon, all three of us feeling languid, we decided to have a *piccola siesta* at the source of the Clitumnus, a romantic spot where the water bubbles up from the earth. It is crystal clear and pure to the taste. In the pool to which it runs it lies green as emerald. The grass is lush beside it. Barbara was amused as I hung my blue coat solemnly on a tree, propping myself uncomfortably against it, my body stretched upon my topcoat for the damp. In a Hilliard-like attitude, head on elbow, I remained for ten minutes in great discomfort, wondering how the Elizabethans managed to look so happy and natural in such awkward circumstances. The truth is that anything done comfortably indoors is always uncomfortable out of doors.

Barbara is enchanting. She refers to the Sibyls on the ceiling of the Spello chapel as 'those Colefaxes on the roof'.

Thursday, 23rd September

A very full morning sightseeing for I was out at 9.30. Determined first of all to visit the thing I had come to see, the choir stalls in San Pietro. So trotted down the hill, but on the way went into San Domenico. A large open church, a funeral Mass in progress, one small draped coffin in the middle of the nave, much incense, a priest before it and only two veiled women mourners. So I knelt and prayed for the poor lonely corpse at a discreet distance. Prayer can never do any harm. It may not do good. The fact that for more than two millennia human beings have prayed without thereby doing the slightest harm to anyone speaks well for it. Indeed to my way of reckoning it proves that it must be a positively beneficial thing. We can't have enough of it, and we can all do it when we are too infirm to do anything else. Then I wandered into the choir where the intarsia stalls are of great beauty: inlaid arabesques between little pilasters. I soon came to San Pietro where I was rewarded by a golden hour, and was uplifted. There was a rehearsal of Mozart's Grand Mass in D Minor, with full orchestra and choir. No one stopped me walking into the presbytery. I spent a long time among the incomparable stalls by Zambelli, carved about 1535, the most exquisite of their kind I have anywhere seen. They surpass in delicacy those in King's College Chapel. I was lost in amazement and delight. All the while the rehearsal was in progress. I then heard the loveliest voice in the world singing solo. It was Elizabeth Schwarzkopf's. I was much taken by her appearance, short, almost stocky, fair hair and complexion, unaffected, earnest little face. Could hardly tear myself away. Have been haunted by her all the day. A blue patch of heaven through white clouds.

Met Barbara and Rex coming out of the Perugino place – name forgotten – where are more stalls, again very fine but later work I take it, who persuaded me to go inside. After luncheon I took a bus for 800 lire across Umbria into Tuscany. Like all Italian drivers the bus driver galloped, his finger permanently on the horn. Reached Florence worn out, with emotion and fear.

I drove in a *carrozza*, which made me feel self-conscious – idiotic – from the bus station to the Grand Hotel. All I did this evening was to look at Ghiberti's door, now back at the Baptistery where it belongs. Far from being gold it is bronze covered with a veneer of gold leaf that in parts has quite worn away. I cannot see how it will endure the rain and dust, not to mention the exhaust fumes from motors and buses.

Saturday, 25th September

Siena – I lunched in the Campo overlooking the grotesque palace and its toy tower of vertiginous height. In the Duomo baptistery two babies were being christened, the priest holding a candle and the parents and friends all very jovial and good-tempered. More like a family party than religious ceremony, the sort of conduct that shocks Protestants.

A funeral procession passed outside. One of those black and gold motor hearses preceded by figures – paid mourners I presume – wearing black masks completely covering the face, allowing slits for eyes, and falling in a peak over the chest.

I returned to Florence by bus and stood for half an hour, which was agonizing. We passed over the grey hills, the brown earth bearing grey olive trees with incredible green berries, and vines bent down with purple grapes. The cypress trees on these hills like snuffed candles. This terraced Tuscan landscape unchanged since the days of Pintoricchio.

Sunday, 26th September

An unsuccessful day. Went to the bus station preparatory to going to Pisa, but the crowd was so overwhelming that I funked another long journey, possibly standing and certainly fighting for a place. It seems that one can book seats only for long journeys. So I came away. A pity. Instead I idled around Florence. A most beautiful autumnal day and rather hot. Walked to San Lorenzo and studied Brunelleschi's sacristy which is most moving. Geoffrey Scott has taught me not to suppose that Bramante's generation was necessarily an 'improvement' upon Brunelleschi's, an absurd assumption which the Victorians maintained. This conventional argument is a complete fallacy. Once again I found myself by chance with Barbara Rothschild and Rex Warner, meeting in a café at midday. What joy! So together we visited the Bargello. Barbara lost in admiration of Michelangelo's Brutus, which is indeed the quintessence of masculinity, and may be the greatest bust in the world. I can think of none greater. Then we lunched in the Piazza della Signoria. I had a siesta in the afternoon and then returned to San Lorenzo.

Monday, 27th September

Cashed my last cheque at the Grand Hotel and paid the bill. I much like this hotel and cannot speak too highly of it. Everything done for one's comfort, and the bill not exorbitant. This morning said farewell to Botticelli's St Augustine in SS Ognissanti next door, and went shopping. Bought pants, ties, socks, a belt, handkerchiefs and more photographs. Now wonder if I have enough money left. Arrived at Milan at 4 o'clock and went straight to no. 41 via Manzoni which is the Palazzo Borromeo. Orietta Borromeo, the mother, met me and showed me the palace which Carlo [Borromeo] has had repaired. It received a bomb during the war, one of ours I daresay. Orietta is a very seductive woman – her flashing eyes, her floating hair, dark, romantic, ruthless I guess. She is half-Italian (*née* Doria) and half-English (her mother a Pelham-Clinton). We went shopping together and wandered through the Cathedral. Much of the glass has been put back since last year, so there is more light. If ever Gothic embellishment needed justification it has it here. The splashes of colour upon pavement and monument are stupendous. Interior impressive, but I do not like the monstrous capitals. Carlo joined us at 6 o'clock and motored us out to Senago, the Borromeo villa which was bought by the Saint's nephew at the end of

the sixteenth century. It is a very large country house. Appears to have
been modernized about forty years ago. Carlo is quite unlike his mother
in appearance and temperament. More the phlegmatic Englishman than
the mercurial Italian. Resembles his cousin, Michael Rosse, good,
dutiful and chaste. More than can be said for his Fascist brother who, I
am told, takes after his mother in looks and character.

Tuesday, 28th September

This morning out at 10.30. No one else about. It is a fine autumn
morning with just a little dew, but no yellow leaf on the trees. Carlo
appears and conducts me round the garden which consists of a long, wide
vista made by himself, not very successful because too wide for its length,
and ends in nothing but some scrubby little trees. It is lined with small
statues between each of which is a terracotta oil pot. Ignoble and too
small in scale. There should be cypress trees. Nothing inside the house is
visibly old except some cinquecento ceilings, the soffits and rough beams
painted in monochrome. But in two rooms on the first floor are a suite
of gold console tables, shaped like tree branches, and mirrors and wall
sconces of elaborate gold ribbons in knots, made of wood. Very Baroque
and ornamental. There are few pictures of any consequence.

    After luncheon we motored into Milan. The old lady, Maddalène
Cotta, a notable gossip, and I looked at San Satiro church. The perspective
eastern apse is a successful piece of make-believe. Deplorable additions
in the last century, notably the pulpit, and ceiling of nave.

Wednesday, 29th September

Today the four of us – Carlo's wife Baby always stays behind with the
children – motored to Pavia. Spent two hours at the Certosa di Pavia.
Delightful setting, away in the country, remote and splendid. There are
no monks here at present. It is deserted. I like the panels of Luini in the
gatehouse. The façade of the church is horrible, bedecked with minute
carvings. As a museum screen of late-Gothic-early-Renaissance sculpture
it is unrivalled. The inside is mostly Baroque but of a boring, restless,
dreary kind. Did Geoffrey Scott really like this stuff?

    We lunched in Pavia town excellently. Soup with a raw egg in it – *strac-
ciatelli*, a speciality of Pavia – and marrow meat with saffroned rice. After
luncheon looked at three early Lombardy churches, one containing relics
of St Augustine.

Thursday, 30th September

The loveliest day imaginable. We motored down the *autostrada* to
Lakes Varese and Maggiore. Took the ferry to – not Pallanza – but

the town next to it where we lunched very well on the pavement. What I have greatly missed during my visit is wine, for my kind host is very abstemious in this respect. Motored to Stresa and took a rowing-boat across to Isola Bella. This is a little paradise. I could find nothing wrong with it – rare for me. The mist dispersed and the sun came through, serene in a cloudless sky. The island still belongs to the Borromeos and the palace is inhabited by them. The present owner is the father of Carlo's wife, Carlo having married his cousin. The father of Baby Borromeo is the son of a husband and niece who married each other, with papal dispensation, in order to keep the island in the family. So sensible. The situation is of course ideal and well-known. The palace built about 1650 by Fontana and other architects in living Baroque. The central portion was never completed and is a vast shell. The state rooms are remarkable for their white stucco in deep relief against blue, buff and pink walls and ceilings. The staircase has panels in stucco of the arms of the noble families who have married Borromeos. Most of the rooms are pretty. A few are over-ornate. I like the big Persians upholding the ceiling of the Throne Room painted to resemble terracotta, but actually made of wood. The bedrooms for Queen Caroline of Brunswick and Napoleon are shown; also the chamber in which the Stresa Conference was held by Mussolini. At the end of every passage or vista is the blue lake, with yellow villas dotted against the hills, and Isola Madre. Through a long gallery ranged with Flemish tapestries of wild animals fighting each other you walk into the garden. This to my mind is perfection. It is set upon six tiers of terraces, of which the last is built on piles over the water. You approach a theatre, formed of grotto work, the terraces adorned with obelisks bearing copper tufts of fruit, statues crowned with copper wreaths and the great central unicorn, which every Good Friday leaves his pedestal and descends into the lake. The view from these terraces is unsurpassed. The flower borders and urns filled with plants beautifully kept by the Borromeos. We did not see the owners who were away in Milan. Two little garden houses are set at the end of the lowest terrace over the water. An enormous camphor tree dominates the entrance to the garden, exhaling a strong and sweet smell.

We motored into the mountain above Stresa to tea with some friends of Orietta in a small house like a chalet overlooking the lake. Christopher and Betty Hussey were staying next door with a sister of Joan Haslip, married to an Italian. Christopher surprised me by saying he did not care for the garden at Isola Bella because there was not enough green. But there is enough of everything else, it seems to me.

Friday, 1st October

This morning I had a poke around Senago by myself. There are several relics of San Carlo, including bits of bones and his biretta. But what an ugly man with his great nose and huge mouth like a slice of water melon. Carlo motored me to Milan. At the station I was only allowed to buy a supplement to my second-class ticket as far as the Swiss frontier. Consequently was unsure whether I had enough money for the rest of the journey. Nevertheless rashly bought more ties and handkerchiefs in the town. Left at 3.30 and had a hideous journey, fraught with *angst*, all the way to Paris. Desperately uncomfortable and dirty. Unable to wash for over twenty-four hours until my return to blessed Thurloe Square, on

Saturday, 2nd October

at tea time. It is pleasant to be home amongst one's own things. How I love them and the cosiness of my flat, small and insignificant though it be. I look back upon the Italian tour with satisfaction and much happiness.

Monday, 4th October

Saw with joy that Elizabeth Schwarzkopf was singing in *Traviata* tonight at Covent Garden, so bought an expensive ticket for myself and went full of expectation. To my dismay it was announced from the footlights that she was ill and not performing. Her understudy, Blanche Turner, had a little reedlike voice. The words were in English and the whole performance disappointing.

Friday, 8th October

Left at 9 o'clock with Robin and his wife, Renée, in their car to Hughenden where we spent a busy morning putting finishing touches to the house which is to be opened next week. Robin extremely good at this sort of arrangement and under his hands the house resumes its Victorian flavour, helped by the Disraeli relics and association. The portraits of statesmen who were Dizzy's contemporaries are fascinating. Then back to London and caught a train to Bradford-on-Avon to stay the weekend with Ted Lister. He has had an operation for prostate but is little the worse, only rather bent which worries him. But he is seventy-four now, rising seventy-five. He is rather deaf and dense. Secretly I find the house *incommode* these days with its upright chairs, oil lamps and no alcohol at all, though it is heresy to say so. Ted allows no relief for reading, but talks ceaselessly without hearing what one says in reply. Christo is a perfect servant, attentive to all Ted's needs yet under no illusion as to his selfishness. His politics are amazingly sensible. He regards

Churchill with the utmost disfavour for landing us in the present mess with Russia. When I asked him how Churchill could have avoided the alliance with Russia in 1941 he said he should never have supplied her with arms but should have let the Germans exhaust themselves in defeating Russia, as the Kaiser did in 1917. Then we should have had the two Powers at our feet. He is not a Balkan for nothing. There is a good deal of the intelligence and cunning of his compatriot and former sovereign Foxy Ferdinand in Christo.

Saturday, 9th October

Ted insisted on driving me, instead of me him, in his dreadful old car to Norrington Manor, the other side of Shaftesbury. The car broke down en route but we reached the house. Its merit is that it is perhaps the last Gothic house in Wiltshire still to be unrestored. It might of course be made into another Westwood, but never as good, for it has no plaster ceilings or panelling of the date. It is at present in the most awful state. Is inhabited by an old man called Parham, aged eighty, and his horsey daughter. The Parhams have rented it for 120 years from the Wyndhams, to whom it still belongs. It has an interesting porch, late fourteenth-century, with central vault boss of a monster's head baring its teeth, and protruding a great tongue. The hall has been ceiled over but could probably be put back for it has, Ted tells me, a good open roof now hidden. Beneath the hall is a vaulted undercroft. There are two wings of Elizabethan date and in the ruinous 'banqueting hall' on the first floor can be seen a late Elizabethan stone fireplace. The Parhams gave us tea. Seldom have I witnessed gentry living in such squalor even in these post-war days.

Monday, 11th October

Luncheon at Sibyl Colefax's – Vita Sackville-West, James P.-H. and myself only. Sibyl so monopolized the conversation, shouting us all down, that discussion was out of the question. James tried once or twice to speak to Vita, gave up and merely giggled. Vita smiled when Sibyl aimed a sharp reproof at her because she made one spirited attempt to open her mouth. 'Just let me finish what I was saying.' Sibyl is not at all well, and the whole charade was piteous. It is inconceivable that the poor old thing can live long.

Tuesday, 12th October

Anthony Blunt lunched. He now asks to be appointed to the Historic Buildings Committee and says that where he is deficient, i.e. in English portraiture, he will get young Oliver Millar to deputize for him. My fear is that he will be too busy and not answer letters. But he has an agreeable manner, though distant. He told me in confidence that Ben [Nicolson] is 'no good at pictures'. One must discount this a little. All art experts are notoriously uncharitable about each other, especially if they are friends. He says someone must warn Ben who has made himself the laughing-stock of Europe over Carritt with whom he is madly in love. After luncheon I tubed to Blackheath, walked across the heath and inspected no. 32 Dartmouth Row, a pleasant little late eighteenth-century house in a terrace over which we are offered covenants.

Went through a gruelling drilling of a wisdom tooth by McKechnie who warned that next time I must lose that tooth. Barbara Moray, Midi and Colin Agnew dined. Midi arrived, wearing a black hat tee'd on her head like an eighteenth-century headdress which made her look like the Eiffel Tower. She's evidently lost a sense of scale. She has novel theories such as this one: children must not be thwarted by learning good manners, but must be rude if they are to become witty. Colin complained that he suffered violent diarrhoea again this year from the first day he arrived at Calais until he returned to Dover six weeks later. He seems to think diarrhoea is a germ in the foreign atmosphere. He is certainly thin as a wafer. He was a little put out that I had not suffered the same complaint in Italy. I regretted later that I had not pretended I had.

Wednesday, 13th October

Historic Buildings Committee this morning of inordinate length, but satisfactory. Lunched at the Ritz with Michael, Bridget and young Princess Doria. She is a giant of a girl, but gentle and genial. Is heiress to immense riches, possessions and position. Yet she cares only for horses and cats, hates society and intellectuals, and her spiritual home is Birchington-on-Sea.

Eardley greeted me sheepishly in disclosing that he is going to Rome on Saturday with Raymond Mortimer and Paul Hyslop. I told him straight out what a cad he was. There was laughter and forgiveness. He took me to tea at The Brook, Stamford, with Madame Lucien Pissarro, aged seventy-eight, an old bent Jewess, and her hideous daughter Miss P. who likewise paints, but E. says is no good. The mother wants to leave the place, overgrown, ramshackle, cottagey house and weed-infested garden, with what remain to her of Lucien's and Camille's pictures. She makes a condition that the daughter must retain the rents during her lifetime. It is remarkable that such a rural property remains in what is now London. Mother and daughter kept sparring in French *argot*. The daughter is a sort of monster with black, greasy face, and rather bald; fat elbows like rolling pins. I am so envious of E. going to Rome that I can hardly bear it.

This evening dined with the John Wyndhams. A young marrieds' party. I sat next to Mrs Alaric Russell and Miss Elizabeth Winn, a niece of Nostell. Venetia Montagu's daughter there – a tall, rather plain but commanding girl, with her mother's sharp Stanley intellect. Jock Colville greeted me by my Christian name as an old friend, but I scarcely know him. He is Princess Elizabeth's secretary and is marrying her lady-in-waiting next week. He worked under Churchill during the war. Very intelligent. Much charm. I liked him. Royal servants are trained to be come-hitherish. It must be a ghastly effort at times. After dinner, when the women left, talk was about how little we knew of the everyday life of our ancestors in spite of George Trevelyan's history. Jock Colville suggested we ought to go home tonight and write down in minutest detail how we drove to the Wyndhams' door, left our car at the kerb, its doors firmly locked, rang the bell, were kept waiting on the doorstep; how we were received by a butler wearing a black bow tie instead of a white one, what the hall smelt like, how the man took our coats and hats, putting them on the chest downstairs, and how he preceded us upstairs, one step at a time, etc., etc. He said that Princess Elizabeth's child would be the first heir to the throne born without the Home Secretary being in the room; that Chuter Ede was to stand in the passage. Said there is no record left of how Asquith treated George V when threatening him with the creation of 500 peers in 1911; but that the King told his mother Lady Cynthia Colville, at 9 o'clock one morning, when she had a splitting headache, the whole story which she felt too ill to record and has now forgotten. Thus does history pass into the shadows. He spoke of Churchill with great affection. I left at a quarter to 1 o'clock, having drunk too much champagne and port. A fatal mistake.

Thursday, 14th October

Eardley and I visited the Victoria & Albert cellars, looking for surplus pictures for Montacute. Graham Reynolds showed us such awful Victorian trash that I signalled E. a suggestion not to accept more than three small pictures. We don't want the N. Trust's houses to be dumps for rubbish not good enough for a roadside pub. Talk of looking a gift horse in the mouth. Polite Mr Reynolds did not know what was going through our minds or behind his back.

Friday, 15th October

Committee meetings today and the Trust's Annual Meeting at Goldsmiths' Hall at 4.30. The Bishop of London the chief speaker. He said that the social revolution we were going through would prove disastrous if this country did not preserve for the masses the culture which had been lost to France during the French Revolution. Mrs Hugh Dalton was present, smiling blandly like a crocodile, and I hope took it all in. The Goldsmiths exhibited for our benefit some of their choice plate. There was one salt dated 1522 that was absolutely classical. I took the 6.30 train to Taunton, but could not get a seat till after Reading. Then had to buy a first-class single supplementary ticket for which I was charged 52 shillings! On arrival at the Castle Hotel could not get a pot of tea or a biscuit, far less dinner which I missed on the train owing to all the restaurant car seats being taken.

Saturday, 16th October

Stinking day – pouring without intermission. Collected my car from the garage. It has been rebored, whatever that means. Pray God it behaves itself in future. Had a filthy luncheon at The George, Frome where I am staying tonight with Alex, and drove to Longleat. Kind Miss Coates received me and gave me tea. I looked through one of three volumes of the letters of Sir John Thynne on the building of Longleat. Fortunately nearly all had been transcribed fairly accurately by Canon Jackson in 1888, or I should have made little headway. Miss Coates lives with her sister in the Stables, not in a loose box, but a charming flat. They are nice, cosy, sweet-tempered women. They keep a dog, and a pleasant life theirs must be. Returned to Frome at 7. These country inns are hellishly uncomfortable, but we had a fairly good mixed grill and half a bottle of red wine for 9/-, which in Italy would have cost 9d.

Sunday, 17th October

Alex and I motored to Longleat in the morning. Miss Coates took us on to the roof which is fascinating. Here you see Chapman's pointed gables and carved beasts just like the Lacock Abbey ones, and the scale-capp'd towers with little lanterns like Bramante's on San Satiro, Milan, and the balustrade brattishing of great acanthus leaves. Today I finished the other two volumes of Sir J. Thynne's letters. Alex left in the morning. I motored to Wickhamford without my headlights which have fused. Mercifully the sidelights worked and in spite of tempestuous rain I managed to see by keeping close behind the cars ahead.

Monday, 18th October

Spent the whole day at Charlecote endeavouring once and for all to compile a list and description of every portrait for inclusion in a new edition of the guidebook. There is always a lot to do at Charlecote. I had tea with Alianore [Fairfax-Lucy] at The Malt House. She is an eccentric. Hollyoak the agent, who is very loyal to the Lucys, told me that yesterday she fell off her bicycle, grazing her ankle. To relieve her feelings, she silently walked to the newly painted stable door and kicked it out of all recognition.

Tuesday, 19th October

To Charlecote again all morning, trying to finish off. The portrait of Queen Elizabeth is too big to get into my car even without her frame. Drat the lady. Walked into Wellesbourne church, saw nothing but several tablets to the Granville family who, I now remember, lived here, but I think have gone. Anyway an aerodrome is right in front of the Hall, rather a nice red brick William and Mary building. I suppose the old Fairfax-Lucys would have looked down on the Granvilles, themselves an ancient family whose house, a mere mile away from Charlecote, was small by comparison with their large seat. How funny it all is or, rather, was. In Alcester church I saw a recumbent effigy of a Lord Hertford by Chantrey – what a prolific man! – and, under the tower, a seated effigy of a later Seymour in the Chantrey manner, signed Gleichen, that semi-royal person, and half-niece of Queen Victoria. It is good in a realistic fashion.

On leaving Alcester I drove to Ragley up the Worcester drive, not the Arrow drive. Arrived 3 o'clock. The house stands on an eminence and the ground slopes from all four sides. This is unusual. Consequently there are distant views from each front. Moreover there are no modern annexes to mar the house which was built in 1683 by a Seymour. My hostess told me the architect is thought to be Robert Hooke. I should have guessed Talman or Francis Smith for it has affinities with Dyrham and Sutton Scarsdale. The material is blue lias stone, of the off-Cotswold, Bidford-on-Avon variety, and some sandstone, which has perished, notably the dentils of the cornice. The great columned portico may be of later date than the house. You enter by an opening below the perron, (added by Wyatt) and, as at Kedleston, pass into an undercroft.

Lady Helen Seymour was awaiting me in the library. She is tall, about fifty-eight, with lovely blue eyes, and must have been a beauty. *Très grande dame.* Was the youngest daughter of the 1st Duke of Westminster. Her son, Lord Hertford, the owner of Ragley, is only eighteen, and has just left Eton. She showed me over house and grounds. The great hall magnificent, now quite empty. The stucco-work might be by Gibbs's Italians, or even the Italian who worked at Ragley, called Vassali. The other rooms on this floor have rococo plaster ceilings of 1740 or thereabouts, which Lady H. believes to be original, and later ceilings in a thin

Adamish style with small round grisaille cameos, perhaps by Holland,
but this is all guesswork. I have as yet read nothing about the house. In
the library is a large Reynolds of Horace Walpole as a young man. He
was cousin of Marshal Conway, a Seymour, to whom he was devoted.
There is a Reynolds of him too. Altogether some eight Reynoldses.
There are magnificent Chippendale hall benches, the finest I have seen;
two panels of carved fruit in the library that might be by Gibbons; some
Louis XV marquetry commodes; a huge bed under a dust-sheet or,
rather, very pretty chintz curtain, so that I could not see it, in the Royal
Bedroom that once had lacquer wallpaper. The woodwork is still
painted black and gold. Doorcases and dados are nearly all 1683. There
are excellent Moorlands and a huge Wootton of three packs of hounds
meeting at Ragley. I think it is one of the most interesting great houses
I have seen. The stables are enchanting, built round two courtyards. The
laundry yard has a colonnade. The lower courtyard is elliptical. Lady
Helen fears they will have to leave the house and move to a smaller one
on the estate. Heating is a great problem and they have only two servants, one Swiss. I liked her much.

I dined at Bretforton Manor with Harry Ashwin who showed me
photographs of the Ashwin family and us as children when we played
Red Indians, which we did in the shrubbery there for days on end.

Wednesday, 20th October

Got to Attingham at 3 o'clock but Charlie Brocklehurst not arrived and
Lady Berwick still out. So I walked in the deer park. They came in to tea
and so did Lady de Vesci to say goodbye for she leaves Monk Hopton
next week. She grumbled a good deal about leaving and having to live
in Ireland. Lady B. very tired and worried about everything. Two most
melancholy ladies. Charlie and I stayed the night at the Mytton and
Mermaid at Atcham. We agreed that Lady Berwick's moans and tragedy
queen acts are a trifle overdone, and she needs just a little shaking.

Thursday, 21st October

God, these English hotels! The food, too little of it and that barely eatable.
This morning Charlie and I looked over all the Attingham pictures.
Interesting, chiefly on account of the Neapolitan connection. The Picture
Gallery and Blue Drawing-room, now cleaned, are very splendid rooms.
George Trevelyan, who runs the Adult Education College, tackled me
about the hall walls which he finds gloomy. I said perhaps they were but
no consideration would persuade me to have them touched. Charlie and
I planned how to hang the pictures. When this is done and the furniture
and the bibelots are put out then I shall go there again with Charlie.

After luncheon motored to Dudmaston, 4 miles south of Bridgnorth on my road home. Very pretty, lush, green Shropshire country with blue hills in the distance. The house is typical English squirearchical – not grand like Ragley, but of the same date. The main block William and Mary, or Queen Anne, red brick with stone dressings, a provincial rendering of Wren with parapet added about 1830. The windows, alas, on two of three sides have plate glass. To the fourth side is attached an older Jacobean wing, overlaid with a harder brick. The house has been inherited since the twelfth century. Mr and Mrs Wolryche-Whitmore are my parents' age and delightful. Both very deaf, with instruments. She is a little slower than he and, like all couples who live together and see few outsiders, they think the same thoughts at the same time. Consequence is she repeats word for word what he has just said and she has not heard.

The best room is a long central hall with contemporary oak wainscot and a plain ceiling but for one oval band of acanthus or oak leaves and fruit. Many family portraits here and throughout the house, all in pretty carved wood frames. In this room two unusual portraits, one of a seventeenth-century gamekeeper with a rugged, square, unforgettable face, another of a gentleman in a large crimson hat, smoking a long church-warden pipe and holding up his foot in a crimson shoe. Behind this room is another long room (double pile) of less interest, facing west, and the garden with 17-acre pool at the foot of a slope. Views of a church, village and the Wrekin in the distance. Heart of England. A spacious staircase of *c.* 1800 of white painted, thin, iron balusters and wooden handrail. Doorways of the simplest description with stalwart surrounds and big brass locks and handles. I saw little furniture of great account, though most of it decent old country house stuff. The Wolryche-Whitmores say their niece and heir Mrs Labouchère has some very good Coalport china and Chippendale chairs which she will bring to the house when she lives here. The estate is 3,000 acres. He talks of handing over in his lifetime so as to avoid death duties on his demise. Dudmaston is not grade 1, but a charming old family home. Mrs W.-W. wearing a neat tweed made from the wool of the black breed of sheep which were kept here until quite lately when they had to be slaughtered for lack of foodstuffs. They have made two flats in the house which is big and rambling. They have only two servants. Yet these elderly people are cheerful and content; a typical squire and his lady of whom no man high or low could speak ill.

Friday, 22nd October

This morning Papa and I motored to Ombersley, the first time I have ever been inside the house. We were asked to go by the new Lord Sandys who has just succeeded his cousin, dead at the age of ninety. The present lord is seventy-two and as Colonel Hill was a friend of my father. He and his wife charming and hospitable. In return for asking me to wander round the house and assess the contents (a curious request) he gave me a present of four pots of honey, some pears and a box of cigars. The front of the house facing the road is dull Grecian, *c.* 1810, with plain portico, added in stone by the Marchioness of Downshire, the last Sandys in her own right, to a William and Mary house behind. The old house consists of a central hall comprising two storeys, a gallery connecting the upstairs bedrooms, and a ponderous ceiling of the *c.* 1810 period. The bedrooms all wainscoted in oak of William and Mary time with nice panelled doors and brass locks and handles. Handsome staircase of three balusters to each tread. One corner room contains elaborately raised door cases with small pediments. It is a treasure house, full of good, but not exceptional, and some junky, things. Many portraits of Sandyses, one mid-sixteenth-century portrait of Sir John Cheek, a good Jansens of George Sandys, poet and traveller, a charming Dobson of a Sandys and Prince Rupert at a junketing, Sandys dipping the ribbon of a third disaffected friend's hat in the Prince's glass of claret. A delightful portrait of Lady Downshire, her little foot peeping out of her skirts and resting on a footstool. There is some nice Regency furniture in the bedrooms, the remains of a George II state bed, of splendid red Genoa velvet, but mutilated. Several gilt gesso mirrors with gilt gesso tables of Queen Anne date, very good indeed.

We were given a picnic luncheon with sherry and white wine. Lord and Lady S. have not moved in yet.

Sunday, 24th October

Indoors all weekend. Made some further discoveries about Smythson having worked at Wardour Old Castle. This evening went with Geoffrey [Houghton-Brown] to Curzon Cinema to see *Monsieur Vincent*, one of the best films, and one of the best actors in Pierre Fresnay as the saint. The society ladies were bad indeed. They always are bad on stage and screen for, with all their tiresomeness, real society ladies are not common. The poor folk admirable; but what a depressing affair.

Monday, 25th October

To an exhibition at the Arcade Gallery of Italian late Renaissance pictures, over-restored I thought, and very chalky faces. One excellent portrait by Gentileschi of a young woman.

Tuesday, 26th October

Rather ghastly meeting of the Keats-Shelley committee at Lady Crewe's house. She makes acid remarks which she instantly corrects with something worse in a low voice which mercifully can seldom be heard by the victim. Has a great sense of malice, which is entertaining.

To *La Traviata* with John Fowler. It was excellent. Schwarzkopf has a beautiful face as well as incomparable voice, sure and impeccable. A bell-like tone that is uniquely hers. Also she acts well. Silveri, the father, a sound bass, and Neate the tenor singing better than the last time I heard him.

Wednesday, 27th October

Sir Francis Rose with his pretty wife at Lady Mander's this evening. He is a patient of Pierre Lansel who told him only yesterday that he had one other patient (me) suffering from the same complaint as his – what Lansel calls counter-diabetes. I think Lansel invents complaints as he goes along. Sir F. Rose lisps and is rather unctuous; and clasps his hands before his stomach like a curate.

Thursday, 28th October

At Osterley this morning I walked round the gardens for the first time for ages, never having done so with Grandy. Accompanied by Carew Wallace and old Mr Little, Grandy's agent. Behind the cedars to the west of the house is a circuit of trees. It is sad to think what the place is bound to become when made over to the public. The temples are all dilapidated, beds overgrown. Before the war they were immaculate, possibly too immaculate. This afternoon I went to a meeting with Sir Walter Jenner's lawyer and trustees. Eardley and I will have much work to do at Lytes Cary [Somerset] sorting contents, for the Trust may choose anything it wants.

Friday, 29th October

Riette Lamington took me to hear Rubinstein at the Albert Hall. The old man's hair is grizzled grey now. He played the piano with utmost vigour for two hours with only ten minutes' interval. He never gives one a moment's anxiety. Extremely impressive. We dined at the Ritz with the Denis Ricketts. This was the first time I ever talked to them properly. Liked them. She is very shy and very clever.

Saturday, 30th October

Walked this morning from Thurloe Square to Portland Place. In the RIBA library looked through three box files of Smythson drawings. They are more exact than Thorpe's, which are scratches in comparison.

A lovely weekend. A slight yellow fog, the sun occasionally filtering through; no wind or rain. Nothing. Utmost cosiness of approaching winter, and no desire to be out of London or anywhere else on wings.

Monday, 1st November

Patrick Kinross had a few people to drinks, amongst them Fitzroy Maclean, the MP and abrasive hero. A very tall man. Patrick's house is upside-down, he living in one rather bare room. Old pullovers and shirts scarcely hidden having been thrust under the window seat. He gave me dinner at a bistro kept by a tiresome, rather drunken old Norwegian woman who spoke affectionately of Nancy.

Tuesday, 2nd November

George Wingfield-Digby lunched to talk about how to clean tapestries. The information imparted was too technical to be helpful to me. A matter for the experts. I said I would consult him before having valuable Trust tapestries cleaned. A rather interesting lecture at the Courtauld Institute on Medicean patronage of sculptors.

Wednesday, 3rd November

The Devonshire collection of pictures at Agnew's is noteworthy. There are three Rembrandts. Lunched Alec and Frances Penrose to discuss Blickling problems. Then went to talk to Mr Harry [Batsford] about my books generally. Had tea with Lady Binning at Fenton House. She asked me to get Cliffy [Clifford Smith] to do an inventory of her collections. I promised her I would make him settle question of fee with me; I would act as intermediary because he is very tiresome over money matters.

    John Summerson gave a brilliant lecture this evening in Chelsea on Victorian church architecture in London.

Thursday, 4th November

Margaret Jourdain lunched in order to talk about her prospective book on National Trust works of art. We agreed it was a bad idea, and a better would be for her to write a booklet on each collection which could be sold at its particular house. Drinks with Dig Yorke and dined with Malcolm Bullock at the Turf. Excellent dinner as usual, grouse and Burgundy. Have finished my review for the *Spectator* on George Lloyd's Life.

Friday, 5th November

Sibyl Colefax lunched with me alone. She has a slight grievance against the Nicolsons. She says Vita is selfish and that neither she nor Harold does anything to get the boys married. It was bad for them to live with their

father all the week and both parents every weekend. Then she discussed
Ben's new love, Carritt, so I thought it best to change the subject. She
also wants to join the Keats-Shelley Committee, but James says Lady
Crewe will not hear of this.

Philippe Jullian dined with me at Brooks's, a little, dark, bespectacled
Frenchman, very serious and very mischievous. Tells me he designs
modern tapestries and book jackets.

Saturday, 6th November

At the Soane Museum all day. John Summerson told me of his new discoveries concerning John Thorpe. He knows the dates of his birth and
death and details of his whole professional life which was that of a Crown
Surveyor. All the old theories about Thorpe the architect are thus
exploded. I find my interest in Thorpe and his drawings dissolved
immediately now there is no longer mystery about him. What a clever
man is Summerson. He is generous too in imparting his immense knowledge. He is sure that the classical influence upon design in
sixteenth-century England came from France before any other country.
James dined and gossiped. He told me he had slept with a woman 'of our
acquaintance'. He has got the subject on the brain.

Monday, 8th November

Motored the Eshers to Knole to see the state rooms and the furniture.
They were delighted. He says he always has good weather on NT expeditions. I tell him he brings it. In the afternoon we went to Wierton and
Boughton, two adjoining estates bought by Mr Cook. The Eshers do not
consider them beautiful enough to be held by the Trust.

Wednesday, 10th November

Lord Esher told me at luncheon that he had seen Jack Rathbone and
liked him immensely – he was so cheerful – and would have appointed
him (to the Secretaryship) straight away if it had been in his power to do
so. But he says the Admiral who saw him did not think him suitable. As
it happens Hubert Smith, Christopher Gibbs and I had already written
a memorandum on the qualifications we thought the new secretary
ought to have. After a good deal of altering Smith's draft I agreed with
his points, it being essential that we three should be in unity. We did this
lest the Admiral might interview and select a candidate of his own choice
without consulting us. We have this evening presented our memorandum
to Lord Esher, who told me we might do so.

Christopher Gibbs and I then took a train to Leeds, staying the night at
Bramham Park. I was last here in 1937 on the same errand. Now our hostess

is the late Lord Bingley's daughter. Her husband has taken the name, Lane-Fox. Old Lady Bingley still lives in a wing, a dear old lady, very bent but active, a sister of Lord Halifax. Charming family they all are.

Thursday, 11th November

Foggy, calm and not cold. It is too late in the year properly to appreciate this place. Even in this season it is very beautiful. I find the pre-Palladian house lovely. The gardens have deteriorated since my last visit. We walked round them carefully. I made notes on the conditions of the temples, garden statuary and ornaments, and the ponds. We think about £3,000 p.a. is needed to keep them in order.

Friday, 12th November

Anthony Martineau with whom I lunched told me that the Admiral had warned him he ought to look for another job. I told Anthony I thought it an outrage and would speak to Lord Esher, which I did before the Executive Committee meeting. Esher said, 'Tell Martineau to do nothing whatever for the Admiral will soon go and I will support him through thick and thin.'

Saturday, 13th November

This morning paid my first visit to the Public Record Office reading room. After a long wait I was brought several long parchment rolls of accounts of royal building works, dated 1585. When I had unrolled them I endeavoured to anchor them with a heavy book. But they have a habit of releasing themselves, rolling themselves smartly up again and covering one with a shower of Tudor dust. The separate sheets also get entangled. Both sides are written upon. They are devilish things. Noel Blakiston came and read through some of them for me. With his help I became almost expert. With practice one's eye becomes accustomed to the script. The Elizabethan scribe abbreviated his script far more than we do ours. Hence *Ye* for *the*, and a squirl (˜) for *ion*.

Looked at da Rovezzano's sarcophagus made for Wolsey's tomb, which now adorns Nelson's in the crypt of St Paul's.

Sunday, 14th November

Newman, the hall porter at Brooks's, told me I would be surprised if I knew which members, to his knowledge, stole newspapers out of the Club. I said, 'You must not tell me,' so he promptly did. Queen Mary's equerry, Coke, he says, an old member, steals the *Sporting and Dramatic* the very morning it comes out. He does it every week and Newman has often watched him.

Soaking in my bath this morning I decided I should not have such hot baths for my body is becoming horribly soft. Of course if one has no features or bone structure one cannot remain handsome after forty. So is it worth bothering about?

Noel and Giana Blakiston dined. An enlightened, humorous couple with whom one can talk of absolutely anything. Both highly civilized and fun to be with.

Monday, 15th November

Went to the Leicester Galleries to see Oliver Messel's exhibition of designs for the *Queen of Spades*. Extremely pretty. I suppose connoisseurs would call them meretricious because they are pastiche, but I don't know, I'm sure. At the gallery some pleasing pictures by Paul Maitland (who died in 1909) in Sickert manner, but calm and well bred, of Hyde Park and London square scenes. Also some gay, sparkling pictures by Barbara Gillighan of domestic, nursery, nanny scenes, very colourful.

Dined with the Eric Dugdales to talk to Carol's old mother and Philip Frere, her solicitor, about Matson House. Delicious meal with champagne. Mrs Frere was the former wife of Toby Glanusk, pretty and sweet. When I reminded her that we met when the Glanusks rented Benmore Forest from my uncle in 1930 she tried to change the subject, which I thought foolish. She must have to make a blank in her memory of some thirty years, a difficult task. Eric D., heated with wine, became very funny. Is he a *faux sage homme*?

Tuesday, 16th November

A terrible meeting at the SPAB when it was revealed that poor old Mr Horne had spent £10,000 on restoring one of their lesser houses at Goudhurst and still wanted to spend a further £1,000. No one on the committee had an inkling of this. I suggested a subcommittee of inquiry should be set up; and so they put Rick and me on to this committee. Horne was sent out of the room like a disgraced schoolboy and much embarrassment ensued. I notice that although decent people profess to be saddened by another's discomfiture on such occasions they derive a nasty kick out of it (*Schadenfreude*, in other words).

Wednesday, 17th November

Lunched with the Eshers to meet Mrs Wyndham, John's mother, who cannot raise her head since she broke her neck hunting. Then to the Tate Gallery with Sir Geoffrey Mander to choose Pre-Raphaelite paintings for Wightwick from Mrs Angeli's collection. Tea with a Mr Bryant in a large block of flats in Putney. He has a card index of some 50,000 country houses of England, Scotland, Wales and Ireland, with detailed particulars of the architecture and previous owner. It knocks my list into a cocked hat. I have never seen such an achievement.

Thursday, 18th November

Motored today to Attingham, making first of all for Astley, Warwickshire. This adjoins Arbury and belongs to the Newdigate family. Called on the Vicar who took me to the Castle, now deserted and empty since the war. It is where Lady Jane Grey's father lived and is not of much architectural merit. Is partially moated and surrounded by a curtain wall of Severn sandstone. The exterior is embattled. It has one early front of 1554 with cusped windows. Nothing much inside but a wide oak staircase with very ordinary balusters. The house has dry rot and is quite empty. I fear doomed. The fine, tall church has painted stalls of the fifteenth century which the Vicar tells me are unique in this part of England. He is a dear, unworldly old creature, wearing a wide-awake, his talk full of genealogy. The church is threatened with subsidence if the Bishop of Coventry sells to the Coal Board the remaining pillar of coal on which it stands. I stop at Wall where the Museum had been freshly painted. Arrive Attingham after tea and find Charlie there. The drawing-room has been beautifully arranged by Lady Berwick.

Friday, 19th November

This morning walk with Lady B. into the park and she shows me the site for her husband's cenotaph where his ashes are to be buried. The spot is disappointing at present because it is close to a wire fence, but the plan is to remove this when the army camp leaves the park. Then the site will be more romantic. Her idea is that the deer should roam up to it as they do in Constable's painting. I left after luncheon and stopped at Coughton Court to look at two bedrooms which Lady Throckmorton means to make into one sitting-room for her new tenants. Terrible drive in dark and rain.

Monday, 22nd November

This evening called on Doreen Baynes, looking very delicate and frail. She thinks all laws against sexual offences should be abolished. I said, 'Even if cruelty against children is involved?' Her head shook and she said after a pause, 'Yes.' She wanted a detailed account of my Saturday in London from dawn till bedtime, in detail, nothing omitted. I said, 'Nothing, Doreen darling?' 'Oh well, you know what I don't need to hear.' She has the novelist's curiosity. She writes in bed every day till 1 o'clock, lunches alone, then walks at breakneck speed, she says often running; returns for tea to receive some friend or other; reads at dinner alone and retires to bed immediately. She says happiness consists in finding the right rut and never leaving it.

Tuesday, 23rd November

Lunched with Sibyl Colefax. Oriental incense from joss-sticks in the hall. Rather highbrow party consisting of the Ronald Trees (perhaps not very highbrow), Vita Sackville-West, Willie Maugham, Desmond MacCarthy, Ruth Draper and me. I sat between pretty Mrs Tree and Ruth Draper. Latter is an enchanting woman, with great perception. She misses no nuances, has a low, modulated, seductive voice, like her sister, Mrs James. They belong to the aristocracy of American women who are exceedingly gentle in manner. She told me that her performances tire her, but she *loves* them. Only once in her life has she missed one through illness. At present she has a cold and this makes work a great strain. She thinks she ought to stop acting soon or she will make the same mistake of most actors and actresses who do not know when to retire from the stage. She senses the kind of audience she has in front of her at once and always knows whether they have seen her before or not. She loves England. Towards the end of luncheon conversation turned to the Russian temperament. MacCarthy said all Russians were children, with children's sense of fun and cruelty. He is very entertaining and laughs a lot himself like a child for the sheer fun of being alive.

Wednesday, 24th November

The new Lord Bearsted came to see me. He said that several of the pictures his father gave us at Upton were not his to give. Would we please strike them off our list. I am always willing to oblige donors but I can't very well do this without my committee's consent. I have had a victory in getting authority for Lady Berwick to be paid £5.10s per week for her servant's wages as from the date of her husband's death. I was asked by the Henry Yorkes to a party to celebrate publication of Henry's new novel *Concluding*, but couldn't manage it.

Thursday, 25th November

Lunched at Mrs Wyndham's in Portman Square. Then met Rick at Trinity College of Music where the interview I had been dreading took place. It went well. The NT got what it wanted, namely control of the instruments. Having met Ruth Draper I thought I should see her on the stage. So went this evening by myself. Her monologues may not be, are not, I think, great art, but they amount to great virtuosity. It is a remarkable physical and mental feat for one woman to hold crowded audiences night after night, with matinées too. She is amusing as well as moving in the role of the Irish mother of a son killed in the 1914 War, and that of the village postmistress in *The Return of the Soldier* in 1945. This role was astonishingly evocative of a poignant subject.

Friday, 26th November

Called on Eddie Marsh this evening. He lives in a rather down-at-heel house in Walton Street. Old food from previous meals still lying upon the table at which he sits. A sweet black and white cat, which he adores, curled on his knees. This cat follows him everywhere. His picture collection a delight. There is scarcely one among the lot that I do not covet. Ninety per cent are moderns. He repeated many current witticisms about the Belcher Case.* People say, 'After all this Government is not so bad. It is the best money can buy.' And 'There is to be a new pantomime called Ali Baba and the Board of Trade.'

Dined with Sheila Plunkett, her husband and Lady Forres (white hair) in the little house Sheila has taken in Montpelier Walk. Lady Forres left and I stayed till 12.15 drinking brandy, which kept me awake during the ensuing night and gave me such palpitations that I thought I was going to have a heart attack. This was at 4 o'clock. We talked of her brother Johnnie Philipps. Sheila, who was in excellent form, said he was settling down and becoming more serious, working at his film and drinking less. Laughed over a story of him play-acting with their father, who was mad and when dying imagined he was in a railway carriage. Johnnie had to coax his father back to bed in the middle of the night on the pretence that the train was about to leave the station. Now while we were sitting and laughing about Johnnie he was dying in his bath in Albany a mile away. He was found drowned early next morning by the night watchman who had heard the overflow of his bath water. The papers say he had a heart attack. He was thirty-three. An erratic, whizzy creature, he had charm. He led a pre-war sort of life of dotty irresponsibility which was rare and only fairly acceptable. This death has upset me without moving me to tears. I am terribly sorry for poor Sheila who loved him very dearly.

Saturday, 27th November

At the British Museum all day looking at photostats of architectural drawings from Hatfield and old tomes in the reading room. A dense fog has lasted several days. I like it.

*J. M. Belcher (1905–1964) was Parliamentary Secretary to the Board of Trade (1946-8). A judicial inquiry was instituted by the Prime Minister, Mr Attlee, to examine charges of bribery against Mr Belcher, who resigned on 15 December. The tribunal reported adversely on Mr Belcher on 25 January 1949 but no criminal proceedings were taken against him owing to the comparative triviality of his misdemeanours.

Tuesday, 30th November

I dined with Malcolm Bullock after he had taken me to the *Prodigal Returned*, a play of little substance, but décor and dresses by Cecil Beaton extremely pretty. Also acting thoroughly good. John Gielgud as the young man of twenty-nine looked the part in spite of his forty-five years. Sybil Thorndike excellent too. At dinner at the Savoy I felt my heart racing and talked to Malcolm about it. He advised me to see Pierre Lansel at once. So I walked there this afternoon, in black fog and cold. However the walk heated me and Pierre was rather shocked that I was hot. He gave me three different sorts of pill to take three times a day. I decided that this sort of treatment was out of the question and threw the prescription into the wastepaper basket when I got home.

Wednesday, 1st December

Lunched with Tony Pawson at a restaurant in Duke Street; Loelia Westminster and Margaret Sweeny. The last was the great beauty of my generation, and is still so. Loelia took me to a picture-framer in Blue Boar Yard. Wearing extremely chic clothes and wrapped in furs. Not once or twice, but three times she asked for my picture to be framed in the *very cheapest* possible manner. Kind of her, but I caught the old aproned crafts-man casting a glance of amazement at her expensive presence.

Thursday, 2nd December

At 9.30 to the Aberconways' house, no. 12 North Audley Street, into which they have just moved. It was the Courtaulds' and has a gallery at the back with central coffered dome of Lord Burlington's time. Indeed might be a gallery at Chiswick House. The Aberconways' furniture is of the Knole settee type and they will decorate the house in, I suspect, a conventional cream.

Harold [Nicolson] having dined with me at Brooks's took me across the way to Pratt's. Talk was of the appointment of the new National Trust secretary and the pains the small committee were taking to choose a man who would not interfere with Hubert Smith's and my work. Harold observed that all scandals derived from written indiscre-tions. He told me that the Philip Trotters, the toads, brought a libel action against him when he was Parliamentary Secretary at the Ministry of Information during the war, and how Duff Cooper and Monckton made them drop it. Harold spoke too openly at Pratt's of his being ignored by the Socialist party who persistently overlook his very existence except when they make him stand for Croydon, and then do not thank him afterwards.

Saturday, 4th December

Last night I motored to Upton. Stayed with Richard and Heather Bearsted at Sun Rising. All day we spent sorting out pictures, there being no little embarrassment over the father's having given away some that he also left by will to his widow. Unlike the father the son cares little for art. Fortunately all the pictures he wants reserved for himself amount to a handful of horse paintings by Sartorius.

Yesterday before leaving I lunched with Loelia W. at her flat in Grosvenor Square. Hamish [St Clair-Erskine], back from Italy, was there. He made us rock with laughter over his war stories, some exaggerated no doubt but all extremely funny. Loelia laughed till the tears coursed down her cheeks.

Sunday, 5th December

Trained to Lancashire to spend two nights with Roger Hesketh. Meols Hall is a little red brick house in a tiny park on the fringe of Southport which practically surrounds it. The garden front faces a flat, mossy, soggy landscape, dotted with blackened and stunted copses. The house has been so altered that it belongs to no period. Some good taste early Georgian pastiche has been applied by the Heskeths. But the house contains beautiful things – Breughels, Sandbys, besides family portraits, and nice Georgian furniture inherited. I do not see how the place could be accepted by the Trust. However Roger sees it through argent- and gules-tinted spectacles because it is what remains of an ancient family estate round Southport. His father sold practically all the land. Roger bought back what he could, namely about 400 acres. He lives a secluded life as King of Southport, devoted to chairing local committees and doing his duty very conscientiously.

Tuesday, 7th December

Came back in time for the Handel *Messiah* in St Paul's Cathedral. Had a glass of sherry with the Dean – Matthews – then sat in the Dean's Gallery under the dome. Mounted a beautiful stone twisting staircase. Very high up, we had a fine view, but it was cold and draughty. The *Messiah* is a bit too long for sitting on a hard chair at such a vertiginous height. But it was glorious to gaze at close range at the illuminated Thornhill ceiling. I admire the Alfred Stevens mosaics. The later ones by Sir William Richmond are horrid.

Wednesday, 8th December

Historic Buildings Committee today. Peter Hesketh who attended for the first time said he was immensely impressed. Eardley and I later lunched with Ronnie Brocket at the Marlborough Club. His geniality is perplexing and a little unconvincing like an ingratiating spaniel's. Then I left for Belgrave Square at Lady Crewe's invitation to attend a concert given for the Keats-Shelley Committee, of which the Queen is patron. Those of us on the committee were aligned in a small room. Lady Crewe said to Jamesey in her sepulchral voice, 'I shall pass the Queen round from left to right like the port.' The Queen arrived dressed in red velvet. When my turn came to be presented Lady Crewe said, 'And you won't know Mr L.-M. of course,' which was not calcu-lated to put either of us at ease. But the Queen replied, 'Yes indeed,' with marked emphasis on the last syllable. For this I gave her the highest marks for she did not know me from Adam. She speaks in a clear, soft voice, is sweet and abounds in charm. Her voice is her secret weapon. It could disarm the most hostile adversary. She looked pale and would, I thought, have been improved by a little colour or rouge. We followed her upstairs to our seats. I was close to Quentin Crewe and just behind Midi. Vita recited two odes of Keats but was nervous and a little halting. Silveri sang Neapolitan songs in a huge, resonant voice far too big for the room, but I liked his singing. Finally Cecil Day-Lewis recited the last seventeen stanzas from *Adonais* in a measured, rhythmical voice, emotional enough and yet so firm that I don't remember being more moved by a poetry reading in my life.

This evening Sarah Churchill invited me to a party given by her sister Diana Sandys, that sweet, chirpy little creature. Two men, one called Bunny Austin (not the tennis player), and Anthony Beauchamp, a dark gigolo with a scar (I take it that he is going to marry Sarah), and Mrs Winston Churchill. I sat next to Mrs Winston at the theatre, a new review called *Oranges and Lemons*. I don't really like her, and never did in the old days. She is jerky and precise in manner, and yet miauly; laughs and speaks as though she feared to touch or swallow dirt. She is, I suspect, *au fond* snobbish, exclusive and disapproving. With her white hair she is still a beautiful woman. We had nothing to say to each other and at dinner at Sarah's flat later, all perching on chairs and sofas, I avoided her. I was very tired this evening and did not like the company at all. Don't suppose they cared for me.

Thursday, 9th December

Clifford Smith lunched and we went to Fenton House, to Lady Binning's. Tiresome, because there was nothing for me to do and I am overwhelmed with work. Dear Lady B. said she would feel safer if I were present – safe from old Cliffy! I am feeling very unwell, doped with the Luminal Pierre Lansel is giving me, over and above the pills which I have not admitted to him I threw away. Went with Michael Rosse to Anthony Wagner's party at the College of Heralds, a curiously academic, dry assembly of desiccated, hirsute pedants, but lots of drink and quite enjoyable. Am terribly put out that the bill for work on my motor this autumn has come to £150.

Friday, 10th December

Had a talk with Lord Crawford after today's meetings about various things. I asked if he would raise at the Fine Arts Commission the projected removal of Onslow Ford's Shelley monument by the dons of University College – a monstrous proposal; also discussed the Bearsted pictures. He was disturbed to learn that so many were to be withdrawn, and felt sure old Lord B. never intended such a thing.

Burnet Pavitt took me to Sadler's Wells to see and hear Verdi's *Simone Boccanegra*. Quite well done and some pretty arias but the audience ugly and unwashed. Smelly.

Sunday, 12th December

Worked over whole weekend: Saturday morning in the Public Record Office on Henry VIII's accounts of the building of Hanworth Manor, the script of this reign being Gothic and difficult to decipher. Last night Henry Henry dined. He is like some big, floppy sunflower with a radiant face which one watches slowly unfold when recognition of what one is endeavouring to impart slowly dawns upon him. He is not clever and rather backward. Is a gentle child. Tells me he is extremely in love with someone who inadequately requites his sad passion; that he is very undersexed, is seldom aroused and when he has had his pleasure takes two whole days to recover his senses. A poor look-out.

Had a dinner party tonight of Riette Lamington and Johnnie and Mary Churchill. Johnnie unchanged, also (like H.H.) a child in his approach to life, sweet and funny. Every person and thing is a rollicking joke to him. He loves giggling with me as we used to do at our crammers at Stanway. Mary seems a perfect wife whom I hope the volatile Johnnie will retain.

Monday, 13th December

Charlotte Bonham-Carter gave what she calls a fork dinner at 7 o'clock and then took me to the Albert Hall. She is an extraordinary character, flitting to and fro, from one idea and one place to another. Clever, charitable and engaging. I mean she can boast of possessing faith, hope and charity. The Vere Pilkingtons, Patrick Kinross and the Lennox Berkeleys there. Lennox had his new concerto for two pianos and orchestra played for the first time, Malcolm Sargent conducting. It was enjoyable, full of melodies and vigour. I watched Lennox sitting in profile with his long nose turned to the orchestra like a serious salmon, in his tense, shy, modest manner. At the end there was much applause. He appeared on the platform three times and bowed sweetly as though wondering why he was there. He is another childlike person. Charlotte insisted on dragging reluctant Patrick and me behind the stage to shake hands with Malcolm Sargent. Such visits to green rooms always embarrass me. I dislike seeming to be on the lion prowl.

Tuesday, 14th December

Lady Anderson asked me to lunch with her alone today. She has been appointed by Stafford Cripps to the Royal Commission which is investigating the future of historic country houses, and wants to learn about the Nat. Trust of which she is abysmally ignorant. She does not even know the terms of reference of her Commission. She fancies it is to take away from the Trust the houses it already possesses. She made herself out to be very uninformed and foolish. Yet she is well disposed to the Trust.

This afternoon in pouring rain I motor Sisson to Godmanchester. I stay the night at Farm Hall.

Wednesday, 15th December

I motored Sisson from his house – it is awfully dirty and too big for him – via Houghton to Wisbech where we looked at a farmhouse offered to the Trust. Sisson, of whom and his wife I am dearly fond, was intolerable. He practically told Penrose and Mrs Munday, the gentle and enthusiastic Wisbech Society lady, that he was not going to cooperate in getting the house repaired. I think he is overworked and on the verge of a breakdown. At the Penroses after dinner he became drunk and his bitterness and morbidity were frightening and distasteful. He gave a graphic description of a blow-fly alighting upon his father's corpse. He gloated over the prospect of worms devouring not merely his body, but mine, and was behaving like a cannibal. 'Nature *will* get you in the end,' he kept repeating. 'The worms *will* have you,' all the while looking like a death's-head himself. 'No, they certainly won't,' I replied. Poor Sisson went black with rage at this contradiction. 'I said, "They will",' he repeated. 'They won't,' I said again, 'because I am going to be cremated.'

Thursday, 16th December

To Blickling where I suppose I did some good going round the house suggesting improvements with Alec Penrose who was most helpful and quite charming. It was a clear, sunny day. The house and grounds in their sleep-

ing beauty I know and love so well. I am sure many of the Hatfield artific-
ers went to Blickling, for more and more affinities in the architecture strike
my eye, viz. the putti on the gable apexes on the south front resemble those
wooden ones on the stair newels at Hatfield. We motored back to
Godmanchester where Sisson retired to bed and was seen no more.

Friday, 17th December

Motored back to London after much trouble getting the car to start. The
battery had not been charged by that blighter, Druce, and I had to be
towed. Dined with Patrick Kinross and sat next to Dig Yorke and Peter
Derwent. Peter D. who is newly engaged to marry Carmen Gandarillas
is not easy at all and casts a supercilious gloom. Dig told me that Henry
[Green] her husband, writes his novels in the drawing-room with people
about and never retires into seclusion. Prefers writing with distractions
around him.

Sunday, 19th December

Work over weekend. Have now finished note-taking and by the New
Year shall begin writing book. I want to call it *Classical Tudor*. My notes
are so full I fear the book will be far too long and too crammed with
facts. Weeding will be a serious difficulty and a hard task.

Leigh Ashton, Olga Lynn and Loelia Westminster dined with me
tonight. Very successful party. I love Oggie and Loelia. Leigh, consumed
by jealousies and touchiness, is of course a common man.

Monday, 20th December

Lunched with Captain Hill who told me that Mr [Ernest] Cook was very
worried about the Commission. He feared the Government would seize
his houses on his death and they would never come to the Trust after all.

Tuesday, 21st December

Motored Lord Esher to Ham House to approve plans for a curator's flat,
which we did after examining every detail in our fussiest manner. Ralph
Edwards was there and showed us the rooms he is arranging. I told him
I disapproved of his wish to delete the perspective views under the front
colonnades, and also to remove the Edwardian radiator protectors.
Lunched with Margaret Jourdain and Ivy Compton-Burnett. Rose
Macaulay there. She becomes more and more like a wizened damson and
her voice sets my teeth on edge. But I like her. Then a friendly meeting
over Matson House with the Ministry of Planning, Philip Frere repre-
senting Carol Dugdale. Cocktail party at *Architectural Review* office.
Malcolm Bullock and Mark Ogilvie-Grant dined.

Thursday, 23rd December

Today worked slackly for there is a distinct Christmas feeling in the air. All the girls and women in the office are agog. Women revel in Christmas. My Mama is a genuine exception. I gave the girls some chocolates but, generally speaking, am cutting down presents this year because I am so very poor. Went to the exhibition of David portraits at the Tate. The famous *Madame Récamier* a poor thing; the self-portrait is fine. Also went to Danish exhibition which bored me very much; early stuff dull, the late stuff jejune.

Friday, 24th December

Motored home and stopped at Oxford to look at the Merton, Wadham and Bodleian frontispieces. At home this evening wondered how I could possibly survive Christmas: Deenie, Mama and Papa. My father's thin jokes, my mother's fuss about the cooking, Deenie's fuss lest the robin might not return to its bird-bath and her radiators freeze during her absence from home, made me irritable and snappy. Of course I am an absolute beast.

Christmas Day 1948

At least I was devout at Mass in Broadway. It was a bright sunny day and after church I motored up Willersey Hill and walked to Dover's Hill along the edge of the Cotswolds overlooking the Vale. It is a fine sweep of a hemi-cycle, like a Greek amphitheatre in terraces, a curious, primitive, isolated formation with distant views towards the Malvern, Bredon and Dumbleton hills. This Christmas I have visited Campden Market Hall, Hidcote, Charlecote, Packwood and the Dial House at Knowle, which a solicitor named Parr wants to leave to the Trust.

Thursday, 30th December

To an exhibition at the Arts Council of Constable drawings and sketches belonging to a Mr Gregory who, Philip James tells me, is a Ukrainian refugee. Two practically thumbnail sketches coloured, of ships in full sail on a rough sea, tiny specks on the horizon, drew the soul out of my body. Constable is *very* great.

Friday, 31st December

So soon after my return from several days' rest I find my nerves a jangle in the office, with nothing to account for it. It is in the mornings that I feel so ill. This evening Alvilde took me to *Scott of the Antarctic*. John Mills as Scott looked very like Peter [Scott]. Diana Churchill played the young wife, Kathleen. How strange to see featured in a film a woman whom I had known so intimately as K. How strange. She played the part quite well and K. would not have objected, I fancy. No sentiment she would have been ashamed of. It is a good film and the frostbitten heroes in their tent just as I imagined. The horror of it. How foolish I was not to have learned more about this epic story from Kathleen when she was alive. Returned and changed, and went to Savoy with Alvilde and her child Clarissa to join the Kenneth Clarks' party for New Year's Eve. It was horrid. Such a noise, with people whistling, pulling crackers and blowing streamers, that I could not hear a word anyone spoke. How can people enjoy this form of entertainment? I hate the New Year anyway.

1949

Helen and Johnnie Dashwood and Alvilde Chaplin dined. Johnnie embarrassed Helen by *risqué*, schoolboy stories, and Alvilde looked unamused. Yet next day I received from Alvilde a note of warm thanks and invitation to dine Monday week. I began, with the New Year, writing my Renaissance book this weekend, but was disconsolate.

Lunched with Loelia and the editor of her paper, *House and Gardens*, to discuss my doing an article on the Nat. Trust. Loelia says that if they publish the article in the States I may receive £40. Since I am overdrawn more than £600 a £40 reduction will be one drop less in my ocean of debt.

Called on Sibyl Colefax who was lying in her bed, coughing. Yet she talked and made plans for the future and was interested in everything. She is a courageous woman. She looked like a tiny dried leaf that is crumpling at both ends. I asked her about Kathleen Kennet who always told me that she disliked Sibyl for her lion-hunting. Just a slight case of pot and kettle. Sibyl told me she knew K. very well when she was engaged to Scott who was always unhappy with K. on account of her 'cheapness'. Said Sibyl, 'She was a self-advertiser. She dramatized her widowhood, seeking publicity at all turns.' Sibyl told a mutual friend that Peter, then aged three, would die of pneumonia if K. allowed him to walk about London in winter stark naked. When this unwelcome piece of advice was conveyed by the mutual friend to Hilton Young he repeated it to his wife and charged Sibyl with malicious intent. Sibyl also told me that K. was a snob who tried to vamp all distinguished men. I told Sibyl that it saddened me to hear this. How odd it is to hear conflicting explanations of mutual dislike from two women at different times, both women of more than normal intelligence and integrity.

Lord Esher at luncheon at Brooks's said that the present Lord Methuen had refused to allow his neighbours, the Hobhouses, to publish love letters between John Cam Hobhouse and a Lady Methuen written in Hobhouse's extreme youth, presumably 130 years ago now. Esher gave this as an example of an intelligent man's silliness.

I trained down to Salisbury and was met by Eardley. I stayed two nights at Long Crichel. Only E. and Desmond Shawe-Taylor there, Eddy and Raymond being away, for which in all the circumstances I was glad.

Wednesday, 5th January

E. and I motor to Lytes Cary, look round house and garden, and discuss questions of liability for death duties on the furniture with Sir Walter Jenner's agent, old Major Hodgson, whom we think a silly old pet. He told us he was tearing up letters and papers of the deceased Sir Walter as fast as he could go. He added, 'Thank goodness I have already thrown all the music away. You of course will get rid of that piano; good for nothing. People no longer play the piano these days.' Presumably when he hears music on the wireless he imagines it is never *live* but was recorded once and for all years ago.

Thursday, 6th January

I have a bad tooth. I knew this would happen. My face is swollen on one side. I telephoned Mary Kearney [my secretary] to fix an appointment for me tomorrow with McKechnie [my dentist]. I am terrified at the prospect of it being pulled out. E. and I motored to Montacute and discussed the proposed new flat for the Yateses [custodians]; then to Stourhead and looked around.

The day I left I received another communication from the Bank which threw me into such a panic that I wrote at once to Papa imploring him to sell for me the few shares that are in trust.

Friday, 7th January

This morning went to the dentist who gave my swollen face one look and in his heartiest manner said he knew the old tooth was on its last legs and must now come out. *His* face was wreathed with sadistic jubilation. I who am a perfect funk begged for a reprieve. He said it could not remain a minute longer and must be extracted at once and, what was more, with an anaesthetic. When I begged for it not to be gas which I hate because of the mask he said I could have an injection. He accordingly telephoned the anaesthetist who came into the room as though he had been waiting next door at the key-hole. What a strange experience to be awake and alive, and within sixty seconds as it were dead, in a different world. Scarcely had the needle come out of my arm when I was off, but not before they put a sponge of gas before my mouth, which was cruel and deceitful of them. Accordingly I had a moment's agony, only a moment's, but to me an eternity's. I was under for thirty minutes and the first thing I remember on coming round was a sensation of acute regret at leaving an elysium and returning to a real and less agreeable world. My eyes were literally pouring tears, although I was not sobbing. How dull an experience for the dentist and his assistant, yet what a thrilling one for me. It was proof beyond all measure that time does not exist and is a figment of the imagination.

I talked this over with Doreen Baynes this evening. She was convinced that my experience had been of the other world and the fact that I recall it as elysium proved her point. Of course I was not actually dead this morning, but was still alive, because my heart was beating. So in what world was I? On the threshold of another? Doreen was perplexed and could not give a satisfactory answer. No one ever can. We talked a lot about death of which she has no fears. She looks forward to it. As for gas, she loves it, and says she and Noël Coward are the only two people who do.

Sunday, 9th January

I made a little more progress with my book this weekend, but no 'through leaves' as I should like. Laboured, factual and stodgy stuff churned itself out. Essentially dull it is because my skeleton is too big. The word skeleton in this context does not relate to yesterday's preoccupation with death. There is a young man called Giles Eyre staying in this house who is bright and jolly and has probably never heard of death.

Tonight Paz Subercaseaux, Rose Macaulay and Roger Senhouse dined. Paz, whom I like, is a well-educated, cultivated, rather earnest Chilean. Miss Macaulay is very spirited in spite of her desiccated appearance to which Stuart [Preston] took such exception. She can and will talk of anything. She is wizened in feature and her lower jaw – false teeth, ill-fitting – juts out at you in speaking. But do not be alarmed. She has no airs of any kind and fills her intellectual inferiors with enthusiasms that flatter their mean understanding.

Monday, 10th January

Called on Sibyl still in bed. There were present when I arrived Bogey Harris and Lady Anderson, who was the first to leave. After her withdrawal the other two started gossiping about her, supposing that she had only called in order to verify that the orchids she had sent Sibyl, and for which Sibyl had already written to thank her, were still there and had not been given away. Sibyl talked fairly sensibly about the Chancellor's Committee on Historic Houses and suggested that we sent it a list of those houses that have disappeared within the last year.

Then dined with the Chaplins who have rented Cecil Beaton's house in Pelham Place. Amongst others were Paz again, Eddie Marsh and a new young man, called Christopher Warner who has taken John Philipps's flat in Albany. He is tall, dark and handsome, a tea-leaf fortune-teller's delight. Eddie Marsh tells countless stories of people he has known in the dim past and recites reams of poetry whenever conversation touches one hair's breadth upon a quotation. He must have been the perfect Edwardian house party guest. He told us how he saw Sarah Bernhardt act in 1887. No actress in his opinion has ever eclipsed her. It was an experience he can never forget. He saw her frequently but the first impression was the indelible one. Anthony C. teased a lot in pretending to be pro-Russian. He asked who would not prefer to live under Bolshevism than not live at all. I said I would.

Wednesday, 12th January

Somerset de Chair who lunched with me said he had found at Blickling all the original building accounts and the names of Thomas Thorpe and Lyminge referred to. He read that the gallery plaster ceiling cost £60 to erect. He said that his boy aged eleven went before a medical board for the Navy entrance examination. They ploughed him because he has incipient varicose veins of the testicles.

Thursday, 13th January

Went to Bourlet's to check which of the Pre-Raphaelites belonging to Mrs Angeli were to go to Wightwick [Manor]. Then to Batsford's where Mr Harry had some rare books to show me; then to Holder's and Drown's, the picture restorers, and then the dentist. My extracted tooth, or rather the cavity, still aches furiously. The dentist said he had to tear the jawbone a bit in taking the tooth out. Hence the pain.

   Malcolm Bullock telephoned that Peter Derwent died today in Paris. He had just returned with Carmen and Tony [Gandarillas] from Switzerland and was very fit. He had been shopping in the afternoon with Carmen, buying her wedding dress and presents, went to lie down because he was a little tired, fell into a coma and never regained consciousness. An abscess on his lung suddenly burst. He had been very ill towards the end of last year, I knew, and presumably caught tuberculosis from Sabine, his first wife. Poor Peter, I sat next to him at dinner with Patrick a month ago and thought him rather morose. I congratulated him on his engagement and he said, 'Yes, Carmen is a splendid person,' which I thought lacked enthusiasm. I noticed how white his hair had suddenly become. He was a pernickety, touchy, sensitive man, often taking and causing umbrage. He was more French than English in culture and tastes. He looked more like Byron than any man I have seen. I liked him without ever knowing him well. I first met him in 1937 when he and Robert [Byron] first conceived the Georgian

Group, and I well remember going with Robert to stay with him and Sabine at Hackness [Hall]. What with the Louis XVI decoration, the French furniture, French conversation and overheated rooms, Hackness was like the Ritz Hotel dumped in the Yorkshire dales.

Dined with Cyril Connolly and Lys [Lubbock]. Alan Pryce-Jones and Alan Ross there. Alan P.-J. likes to pretend that he is sodden with middle-age defeatism and gloom whereas he is the soul of youthful gaiety and charm. Cyril is the most brilliant talker I have listened to. He surprised me by saying he had read no Trollope, no Dickens and only one Jane Austen novel. After dinner a lot of people dribbled in for champagne. I believe Cyril and Lys frequently entertain like this. I left at 12.30 without saying goodbye. Must write.

Sunday, 16th January

Eardley, Alvilde Chaplin and Loelia Westminster dined. Eardley pronounced Loelia 'brave' in the French sense, and Alvilde beautiful.

Wednesday, 19th January

Dined with Alvilde and Anthony Chaplin; the Sachie Sitwells there. Anthony, who is sensitive about such things, was furious with Georgia for scolding him for not wearing a dinner jacket. Anthony claimed that he had worthier things to spend his money on, and I agreed with him, having no money of my own to spend on anything. Accordingly I got back into Anthony's good graces, so I was told later, without realizing that I had been out of them.

Thursday, 20th January

To the theatre with Alvilde — Ibsen's *Wild Duck* — most lugubrious but excellent, particularly the girl and Fay Compton. The latter had no words to speak but acted in most telling silence. Saw the Bearsteds at the theatre, he and his wife having been robbed of £23,000 worth of jewels the previous evening by a cat burglar.

Friday, 21st January

Lunched with Christopher Hussey at the Garrick Club in order to talk about my discoveries amongst the Longleat papers. It transpired that I was unable to impart much that he did not know already.

Dined Sibyl Colefax at her house. She was dressed and up, and though bent more than ever, was quite bright. A most excellent meal, the best I have had in England for years. I knew everyone there but the Angleseys, and sat next to her. Nigel [Nicolson], who is devoted and wished to marry her, and Diane Abdy present. Also John Sparrow, Paz Subercaseaux and Alvilde, with whom I went. Sitting with Sibyl after dinner we discussed sanctity and S. said quite seriously that I was probably a saint. Felt obliged to disabuse her.

Saturday, 22nd January

At 11 went to Peter Derwent's memorial service at St Mark's North Audley Street. The choir sang well and the music was beautifully chosen. I was moved by the hymn, 'Lord of our Life, and God of our Salvation'. Alvilde was present, wearing a snood over her hair, looking very romantic like a nun. We walked away from the service together and there, ahead of us was Nancy, not walking but running along the pavement to Heywood Hill's shop. We took a taxi to Cook's to inquire about fares to Portofino where she has asked me to stay in mid-February. I fear I cannot afford to go. The editor of *House and Gardens* lunched and asked me to write an article for him on country houses.

Sunday, 23rd January

Today I finished Chapter 1 of the book and sent it to Mary Kearney to type out. Sheila Plunkett dined. She told me Lord Milford had offered to purchase Picton Castle from her and she wanted my advice. I advised selling to him since he was a Philipps, descendant of those who had owned it since the twelfth century and her brother was anyway about to sell it to him before he died. Moreover Lord M. undertakes to leave it to the National Trust if his grandson on coming of age declines to live there himself. Sheila is determined to do the best thing for Picton as she thinks Johnnie would have done. I regard her piety greater than was his. S. is carrying on with his film companies in the hope that she will not lose money and may improve the quality of British films.

Monday, 24th January

Eardley and I set off in my car at 9.30 in pouring rain to Upton where we arrived at 11.30. We watched Kiddell and his assistant, Clark, from Sotheby's listing and valuing the porcelain that belongs to the NT. It was fascinating. He valued some pieces at £500 each, i.e. Chelsea figures, Sèvres *jardinières*, and the Gold Anchor set of the Muses, eight figures, at £4,000. Kiddell, modest and kind, very ready to teach. We were favourably impressed. We lunched in the house with Dorothea Lady B. and the young Bs. Easy to see they think the mother bossy; she thinks them feckless. Who is right?

We motored to Warwick and Hollyoak took us to the Castle where we found Happ, the middle-European, in process of restoring the Batoni portrait of George Lucy from Charlecote. He has stripped off all the overpainting, leaving a lot of injuries which had been badly restored and overpainted a hundred years ago. These he will himself paint over. He was very self-confident and E. gave him bad marks for boasting how *he* knew how to remove overpaint without touching the original underpaint. We stayed at the Shakespeare Hotel, Stratford and went to a British film, *The House of Darkness*, about a family *c.* 1902 who were either killed or driven away from their home by the evil machinations of a young, handsome brother. Finally this brother, left in possession, died of fear brought about by one of his dead brothers' ghosts accompanying on a ghostly violin his piano playing. An involved story. We liked the film very much.

Tuesday, 25th January

To Charlecote. Brian and Alice Lucy there. We all succeeded in choosing the final position of each picture. A great feat. E. far and away the expert at this task. It means that when the walls of the great hall have been cleaned down and the picture-hangers have done their work, I can attach my labels to the pictures and all will be finished. The Lucys having motored over gave us sandwiches in the little dining-room and were, as usual, generous and charming. Brian confided that until today Alice had not left home for eight months. Even so he feared she might not start until the last minute. She gave birth to two babies within one year late in life. E. stayed with a cousin in Broadway; I went home. Both parents very good to me.

Wednesday, 26th January

Picked up Mr Clouting (of the Ministry of Works) who stayed last night at the Crown, Evesham, and Eardley at Broadway. The three of us motored to Chedworth Roman Villa. Clouting reassured us about the condition of the stone capping he has put on the Roman walls. Their restoration and the rearrangement of the museum and redressing of the lawns show that progress is being made at this property. We lunched at the King's Head, Cirencester, leaving Clouting there after a visit to the Abbey church. E. and I drove to Horton Court and were horrified by the damp. Then to tea with Mr Cook at Bath whom we found an affable old man instead of the foxy old thing we imagined. E. even admired many of his pictures which he considers quite good – English school mostly – and I gave him a copy of my NT guidebook. We stayed with Mrs Knollys at Richmond Lodge.

Thursday, 27th January

Left for Lytes Cary, spending whole day there. We practically completed our selection of furniture, but have yet to arrange the rooms and sort the books. A successful day. Old Major Hodgson, who is one of Sir W. Jenner's executors, is a character. He shouts and yells at the servants and is loved by them all as a bluff, warm-hearted creature. He makes E. and me shake with laughter, for he is Colonel Blimp incarnate. At 5 o'clock we left for Exeter, staying two nights at the Clarence Hotel.

Friday, 28th January

Senior [Area Agent] called for Eardley at The Clarence early and took him to Plymouth. I motored to Lindridge to look at the house offered by Sir Edward Benthall. Was greeted by a Miss Reynolds, acting as lady housekeeper. I think her father was Rector of Stanton near Broadway. She remembers playing tennis with me. I pretended I remembered playing tennis with her. My committee accepted this property last month on E.'s recommendation, but I don't think it is good enough. The outside has been refaced with red brick. It has a modern projecting porch and dining-room window. I question the cornice's claim to being seventeenth-century. The staircase is early eighteenth-century. Great Chamber ceiling of copper wreaths painted a uniform cream. One other plaster ceiling of *c.* 1720. Unsightly additions.

I motored over Dartmoor, lunching at Two Bridges. Reached Cotehele. An exquisite day, strong winter sun slanting so as to penetrate the hearts of things and so warm that I drove without a coat. There were tortoiseshell butterflies on the wing which for January is unprecedented. Met Eardley there. We went round the house with the Ministry of Works letter of objections to our proposed alterations in hand. Back to Exeter for the night. Had a tyre puncture in Exeter last night; and on return from Cotehele this evening just missed by a bee's knee a head-on collision with a lorry. E. said it was the most miraculous escape from sudden death he has ever had. I kept my head but nearly died of shock when it was over.

Saturday, 29th January

Left in thick fog which cleared when we reached the heights. So we turned north to the Wellington Monument and examined [John] MacGregor's work there. We thought the spilling of cement down the obelisk and the substitution of cement blocks for stone a mistake. Called at Montacute and were pleased to find the garden beds had been dug. I dropped E. at Salisbury. Hesitated whether to give a lift to a sailor bound for London. Luckily I did so for at Staines we were plunged into dense fog as far as Osterley and by leaning out of the window he guided me until it cleared again. I could not see the kerb on the sailor's side and only the white central line of the road from mine.

Sunday, 30th January

Finished chapter on the French Renaissance. This evening dined at Alex Beattie's studio in Fulham Road very late, with Alan Lennox-Boyd and Gerald du Gouray. The latter told me he is writing the history of Meccan pilgrimages. He returns to Iraq in two days time. He does not want to live in England. Says he can only be happy in the East. I can't make out whether he is a second Lawrence of Arabia or a complete fraud. Wish somebody would tell me. Beattie is a good-looking and amiable ass. He asked me if I had ever been in love, and when I said 'Yes, of course', seemed surprised. He vouchsafed that he liked sleeping in one bed with people he was fond of, but did not care much for sex. It left him cold. Is, I suspect, a Narcissus. 'As for women,' he said, 'they are so damned soft. Their bodies have no firmness. That is what I dislike.' He is confident that the Conservatives will be returned at the next election. How can he possibly know beyond what he has gleaned from high quarters?

Tuesday, 1st February

Dined alone with Barbara Moray who spoke of her deep friendship with Tom Mitford, of how devoted she was to him, and how she deplored his attitude to women, whom at bottom he despised. I feel sure that after the war, if he had survived, he would have married her, for she was one of the few women whom he didn't despise. We became extremely confidential as we drank whisky. I left at 1 a.m.

Wednesday, 2nd February

X. dined with me here and we drank Beaujolais over the fire. Became very tipsy. I had the greatest difficulty in getting her away for she wished to stay the night – a thing absolutely out of the question. This sounds as though I were as virtuous as St Anthony and like him desired by every female I encounter. Both assumptions are very, very far from being the case. When one is a foot away from X. her cat-grey eyes dilate like those of a film star in a close-up. She is very bewitching and seductive, is always gay, loves the ludicrous and makes me laugh. Above all she is genuinely affectionate.

Friday, 4th February

Stayed last night at Long Crichel alone with my dear Eardley. Thank God, with him my relations are absolutely straightforward. The relief of it. We motored early to Lytes Cary on a still, clear, frosty and beautiful morning. We got through a lot of work and made our final selection of furniture, even arranging the rooms except for pictures and ornamental china. We were pleased with ourselves, no doubt too pleased. We feel sure that a great deal of Sir Walter's furniture supplied by Angel of Bath is made up. We kept what we thought best and most suitable, rejecting the rest. We like to believe we make a perfect combination for we criticize each other mercilessly, usually laughing like mad, for alone we are very funny. A third person overhearing us might not think so.

Saturday, 5th February

Corrected my chapter on the French Renaissance, now ready for typing, and dined with Riette Lamington. She was rather *distraite*. I really don't like her very much. She is too selfconscious, prim and disapproving. Nature's governess, yet amorous. I always remember Jamesey deliberately setting fire to her sofa with his cigarette in order to effect an escape. The Ivor Churchills were the other guests. She is a new wife, young and pretty. Lord Ivor says he has given up collecting pictures and is selling what he can in order to live – good enough reason – in the Ritz Hotel – which seems a bad one. He is an affable man, not stupid and not arrogant like many Churchills. He said Lady Anderson has cultivated an unerring gift of flattering men who like her. This explains why women hate her. She has a caressing, insinuating voice like the serpent of old Nile.

Monday, 7th February

Took Bridget to see Doreen Baynes at 6 o'clock. Doreen liked her very much. Conversation flowed along as it always does with this darling woman who told us that she often reads her own books, putting herself in the place of an admirer, in order to discover what in her writing it can possibly be that they enjoy. I said I never re-read my own writings, a thing I likened to a dog returning to its vomit. Bridget dined with me afterwards. We always have much to pick over.

Tuesday, 8th February

A long special meeting of the Finance Committee to discuss the Memorandum to be submitted to the Gowers Committee. It is agreed that our points are of the utmost importance. We have reached a crisis in the Trust's affairs. [Sir Ernest] Gowers is taking the matter most seriously. I strongly deprecated a proposal that we should surrender to the Government all 'museum' houses, i.e. those which the families have left and which may not be inhabited again, because I foresee all families leaving these anachronistic white elephants in time. And then what will be left to us?

At SPAB meetings I find myself listened to now for Esher (the Chairman) always appeals to me for help. This sounds to me conceited.

I hope it doesn't to anyone who may read these words. They have put me on to a subcommittee to work out the Society's evidence to be submitted to the Gowers Committee.

Dinner party given by Y. When the other guests left I stayed behind, thinking no evil, fearing no evil. Silly fool. I had put my head into a noose, and soon scented danger, too late. My hostess expected me to make love to her. How insatiable these women are. Any youngish man in a calm, it seems. Inventing an urgent excuse – one cannot have a committee meeting at midnight – I bolted, and heard the clang of the front door behind me. It made a terrible sound which echoed down the street. 'Heaven has no rage like love to hatred turned. Nor hell a fury like a woman scorned,' it seemed to shout at me. With my tail between my legs I shouted back, 'Damn, damn!' for neither heaven nor hell was of my seeking. Passionless friendship is all I need these days.

Wednesday, 9th February

Historic Buildings Committee this morning. Nearly all the area representatives present. Had my time full talking to them before and after the meeting about various problems. The Feddens gave me luncheon at Prunier's. I had oysters and *moules* and chocolate cream, and felt rather sick.

Thursday, 10th February

At 4.30 to the Society of Antiquaries as a guest of Clifford Smith. Cliffy's wife, that sweet, simpering old dear, and Lady Catherine Ashburnham of Ashburnham Place, also invited. The last, a simple, shy lady to whom Cliffy deferred in the most subservient fashion. His snobbishness and sense of class is Austenian. [Tom] Kendrick lectured with verve on English Renaissance antiquaries, a dull subject enough. The lecture room filled with the dreariest old crones imaginable, just what the ordinary person supposes archaeologists to look like – dry as dust. Rather splendid formality here, the Chairman with mace welcoming John Harvey as a new Fellow.

Friday, 11th February

Long discussion again today at both Committee meetings about the draft Memorandum for the Chancellor's Committee. Our people are now seriously concerned. Esher, to my surprise, read to the Committee my letter to him suggesting that a third body be set up to hold historic houses. Committee did not much like it but the result was, as is so often the case, that they modified their previous decision to surrender quite so many houses to the Ministry of Works. Lord Crawford and George

Howard lunched with me at Brooks's. Crawford said that at the party given by the National Art Collections Fund one old woman came up and thanked him personally for having bought for the nation all the beautiful pictures at the exhibition – the Chantrey Bequest!

Saturday, 12th February

This morning motored the Eshers to Steventon in pouring rain. Later it cleared. We were given coffee by Walter Godfrey who conducted us to the Priory Buildings. Esher modified some of MacGregor's proposals for restoration. Then on to Faringdon to lunch with Gerald Berners who looked very ill, shaky, twitchy. He shuffles rather than walks, a bad sign. He told me he suffered from acute, unrelieved melancholia and can neither write nor compose; an awful predicament for a creative man. Robert Heber-Percy came straight from the farm to the table in corduroys, covered with chaff and straw in his hair.

Sunday, 13th February

Worked all day finishing chapter on English humanists, now fit for typing. Rick [Stewart-Jones] called at 7.30 and drank with me. I had to drive him away, or he would have stayed till dawn talking. Anyway I was dining with Rory Cameron at Claridge's at 9.30. The Sachie Sitwells there. Sachie never sticks to the same subject for any length of time. Flits like a swallow and like a swallow never perches. Georgia said he lectured to a school the other day for one hour, having prepared no speech in advance. Instead, after his introduction by the headmaster he asked his audience what they wanted him to speak about, and then spoke. I was dog-tired before dinner began.

Monday, 14th February

To see Sibyl this evening; she up and much better. Victor Pritchett, Alan Pryce-Jones and Eddie Marsh present. Talk about there being far too many writers. You can't of course prevent people writing any more than copulating, but there ought to be some sort of contraception to prevent publication. When I was left alone with Sibyl she said how important it was that friends should be possessed of human feelings for intellect was not enough. This woman, regarded by strangers as worldly, has great warmth underneath. When I got home I wrote a brochure for the National Trust, thus at once contravening my view expressed above.

Tuesday, 15th February

Stayed at home this morning and wrote an introduction to the catalogue of the Attingham Park collection. Then lunched with Hubert Smith and

Christopher Gibbs, discussing agenda for Lord Esher's subcommittee on the new Secretary's duties. A sticky meeting with Barker of the Ministry of Works about the lease of Osterley, the Ministry strongly objecting to our imposing onerous terms. I began by adopting a stiff front on the general principle, then giving way over details. These were my tactics.

On Sunday Alvilde telephoned me from Amalfi urging me to join them in Rome. This evening I consulted Rick who instantly offered to pay for my ticket there and back, which is angelic and typical of him. He said he preferred it to be a gift to a loan. So now I shall fly to Rome on Saturday. I dined with Paz Subercaseaux who gave me 7,000 lire for my journey which was equally angelic. Jamesey, who was present, talked in raptures about Norway. Of course he is in love with a Norwegian, as he confessed to me after dinner. Tony Gandarillas's wife, hitherto kept in purdah, and married daughter there and a Chilean composer just arrived from Chile. Several different wines to drink which always disagrees with me.

Wednesday, 16th February

Dined with the Aberconways in their new house left to Christabel by Samuel Courtauld, in North Audley Street. A splendid house of Burlington date and style, with gallery on the grand-miniature scale; a central coffered dome. Many well-known French Impressionist pictures (Courtauld). Opposite my place at dinner a ravishing Renoir of women with parasols in a punt on blue, sunlit water. I sat next to Betty Hussey to whom I am devoted for she is gay and buxom, natural and forthright, and Lady Elizabeth Hofmannsthal who is a great beauty with the soft, peony skin of all Pagets. The David Bowes-Lyons, he insinuating all sorts of forbidden things in veiled terms and proposing a trip with me in the spring. He is an extraordinary, complicated, buttoned, perhaps not so buttoned-up man who cannot call a spade a spade and is a walking riddle. Anthony Blunt and Christopher Hussey with whom I had Tudor talk. Hussey is sure that Longleat is of French inspiration. His articles on this great house appear in April. Lady Aberconway, with her milk complexion, wants to appear a pretty goose, but is as clever and calculating as a monkey. He affability and big business. He holds up a hand as a dog holds out a paw to be taken. But one is not disposed to stroke him.

Thursday, 17th February

To the theatre with Lady de Vesci (Bridget being ill in bed), Rory [Cameron] and Helen Dashwood. Rattigan's play The *Browning Version*. Did not care for the first set but liked the second, called *Harlequinade*. They dined here after. Sticky.

Friday, 18th February

Lunched at the White Tower with Rose Macaulay, Roger Senhouse and Jamesey. Rose M. is writing a book on ruins and wants to be told where to go. James gave me another book to review for the *Spectator*, on the architect Godwin, a tormented aesthete.

Saturday, 19th February

Called very early and breakfasted. Druce motored me at 7 o'clock to the air station at Kensington where I straightway put my bag on what I mistook for a ledge and was in fact air. It tumbled down a staircase and emptied itself of all my precious luggage at the bottom. Found John Lehmann on my bus going to Rome likewise. This very agreeable although I know him but slightly. He is about my age, was at Eton with me although we never overlapped and is, like me, suffering from sciatica, seeking relief from the Mediterranean. Journey very easy. Within half an hour we were over the Isle of Wight, then across the Channel, Le Havre and all the way down France under-populated. Weather very fine in England, in mid-France cloudy, at Marseilles where we halted for half an hour extremely warm. I was told it might be cold so took my fur-lined coat. Over Riviera, Corsica, Elba, and Rome itself. Landed at 3.30. I am less scared of flying than I used to be, yet I do not think it any less unsafe. Even a little flying experience inculcates humility and a capacity to view the earth and life thereon as insignificant and transitory.

It is heaven being in Rome again after so short an interval. I drove in an old *carozza* round the Pincio to the Hotel de Ville where I supposed the Chaplins would be staying. But no, they were at the Inghilterra. Having engaged a room and unpacked I shall stay here until we move on Tuesday.

Went at 7 o'clock to the Chaplins' room at the Inghilterra which is Henry Jamesean, not unlike Brown's Hotel, Dover Street, with prints of Chantrey Bequest pictures in maplewood frames. In a pretty big double bedroom Alvilde has a white pekinese called Foo. Anthony asked if I wished to see his toad found at Paestum. I said yes. Whereupon he fetched a chamber pot covered with a face towel. In it lives the toad which he says is over sixty years old, possibly eighty, and has all its life been in the same garden avoiding the peasants and death, since all primitive people kill toads for being evil, which they are not. Anthony also has several lizards and frogs in cardboard boxes. They seem to be given nothing to eat yet thrive. Toads can live three months without food. We dined sumptuously at Alberotti's restaurant where D'Arcy Osborne once took me. I am so happy to be here – lovely Frascati wine, scampi and chocolate cake. It is warm tonight. No topcoat needed.

Sun shining. I dress with the double window wide open. Walk up the steps of Charles VIII's and Mendelssohn's church to hear the very end of a Mass, the nuns behind the grille. Then via the Corso to San Lorenzo in Lucina, and hear a complete Mass. An old monk takes the alms-basket round. He wears an expression of contemptuous boredom. Called at the Inghilterra where Anthony and Alvilde are furious because their car, left outside the hotel, had the lock broken during the night and many things stolen. However this morning they left it where it was and it was broken into again, and more things were stolen. They are both very anti-Rome on this account and on that of the noise and dirt round their hotel, which are appalling. The dustmen are on strike and the streets ankle-deep in garbage. A. and I walked towards St Peter's where Il Papa was speaking at 11 o'clock. There were great crowds so we diverged into the Castle of St Angelo. I was glad to go over Hadrian's great cylinder, never done before. The rooms painted by del Vaga in Raphaelesque arabesques are enchanting.

Geoffrey Gilmour met us at luncheon and motored us in his large Lincoln to Tivoli and the Villa d'Este. None of us had seen it for years. I was not disappointed though the others were. The rooms painted *c.* 1550 by Zucchero are beautiful just as a jumble of medieval glass may be beautiful, not for their composition (which is poor) but their kaleidoscopic quality. It is atrocious how Italians carve their names and write them with indelible ink on the wall paintings. In the Ara Coeli church I noticed a name and date '1907' in pencil upon a monument at chest height. One wipe of a sponge by a verger would have eliminated it in a second. But no. Italians have little aesthetic sense and are unobservant. They find sculpture irresistible to their biros. David Crawford wrote a respectful protest to the Pope but received no acknowledgement. Pirro Ligorio's frontispiece of the Villa d'Este is noble. The pencil-thin jets and fan-like gushes of musical water are a delight. The noble arch on the terrace framing a vast pink sky and expanse of mountain horizon is like a Panini painting. Architecture in Italy is painting, not the other way about. The Chaplins found the Villa d'Este melancholy.

At the Scotch Tea House at teatime Simon Harcourt-Smith approached and spoke. The others hid their faces in the table cloth and groaned which embarrassed me. Later John Lehmann called for me and we drank in the hotel. Graham Greene, like a raddled Noël Coward with a bad colour, talked to John. I made myself scarce. With the Chaplins dined at Nino's not too well. The sour red wine upset me in the night. Talk was of animals not having souls, and of humans being morally super-

ior to animals. Anthony maintains this a nonsense, for even the most ferocious wild beasts are not actuated by intentional cruelty. He says that birds
are just as capable of art and architecture as men.

Monday, 21st February

A wonderful day. Full sun and able to sit and drink on the pavement
before luncheon. John Bayley called at 10.15 with his camera and tripod
in a satchel. He is a strange man of few affections I would guess, devoted
to his studies and consumed by anxiety because he has no formulated
purpose in them, and absolutely no money. We walked for miles past the
Colonna church, up the Campidoglio, into the Ara Coeli church, he
taking photographs unconcernedly in the middle of the Corso and in
churches. Then down into the Gesù which is too lavish and in the decorating of which too many pains were taken. Into the Piazza Navona,
past the Farnese and Sacchetti palaces, over the Tiber, up to the American
Academy on the Janiculum. John Bayley is an indefatigable talker and
sightseer. He knows every building in Rome, yet he does not bother
about historic facts, or names of architects, or dates. He has a studio filled
with thousands and thousands of photographs that he does not know
what to do with. We lunched at a long table in a vast, whitewashed room.
The American Academy was built in the Renaissance palace style in
1913, and is very *bien*. Full of earnest, friendly students, with a magnificent library packed with tomes on Roman subjects and all the arts. John
Bayley says I could arrange to stay here as a guest in the summer. I was
attracted by the claustral atmosphere.

I took John Bayley to Keats's house and we talked to Signora
Cacciatore. We concluded that between the window and back wall facing
the fireplace Keats's bed must have stood. A poignant room. There is a
tin – the original one – from which remains of the aromatic gums were
thrown by Leigh Hunt upon Shelley's pyre and which, Signora
Cacciatore affirms, preserves quite a strong smell. In a tiny porphyry urn
repose some of Shelley's ashes snatched from the pyre by Trelawny.

Tuesday, 22nd February

This morning Alvilde and I motored to the Vatican Museum and walked
down the long galleries to the Sistine Chapel, straining our necks and
eyes towards the ceiling which she assured me had faded since she last
saw it twenty years ago. Again I thought the marble screen as fine as anything there. We were horrified by the damage done to the Loggie walls
by pencilled and incised names within recent years. The lower part of
these famous arabesques is totally obliterated, both paint and plaster
work. Even the Raphael walls of the Stanze have been mutilated. They

could so easily be protected by glass panels. These Stanze always leave something to be desired. True, they are much faded and cracked. But the scale of the murals is too big for the low rooms. We went into St Peter's. The overall grey marble makes a peculiarly fitting background to the opulent golds and reds and greens. I made Alvilde kiss St Peter's toe which she did with a reluctant grace, not to mention a positive grimace.

After a vast luncheon at Alberotti's I sat in the sun in the Pincio gardens and corrected typescript. The noise of motor scooters a distraction. But what noise does not distract in Rome now the fountains are silent, or inaudible? John Leslie dined with us. A dear man, and a fount of Roman gossip. He will never dry up.

Wednesday, 23rd February

I am constipated, as usual here. At 9.30 we left for Florence. I got awful sciatica in the tiny motor. Alvilde is a perfect travelling companion. Anthony is fun but one has to play up to him continuously. Sun dazzling, slightly cold, with wind on the hills. An exhausting drive for the road winds and winds and the hills are very steep. We passed Caprarola without stopping. Memories of Desmond [Shawe-Taylor] and the Colonel ranting against the custodian. We bought sandwiches and wine and grapes, and ate and drank on the roadside, our feet on the dusty surface. Stopped in Siena for coffee. A. and I visited the cathedral and admired the floor paving, or what we could see of it. Anthony refuses to look at any buildings or pictures. He will stop only to look for frogs in ponds. This affectation is silly especially since he claims to be a cultivated man; and it is maddening for A. The road between Siena and Florence covers beautiful country. In other words – not to underline the word 'beautiful' too faintly – Tuscany with its gentle hills and little towns, large villas, vine terraces and cypresses, *is* Paradise, Classical not Picturesque like the country round Assisi and Perugia. We stay at the Grand Hotel, Florence, in great comfort, overlooking the Arno. The view from our bedrooms, each with a terrace, on the top floor is exquisite, a rushing fall of Arno water below, the campanile and cupola of Santo Spirito and the bulk of the Carmine opposite us; and the cypress- and umbrella-clad rise of Bellosguardo beyond.

Thursday, 24th February

What a day! The sun so hot that I sat on my terrace without a coat, yet inside the churches icy cold. Alvilde and I sightsaw in the morning, first the Botticelli of St Augustine in the Ognissanti church next door, then to the Uffizi to feast on Lorenzo Credi and Bronzino. In the entrance there is an Etruscan torso of a man two centuries BC, massive and powerful just like one of the rowers of a skiff on the Arno this afternoon. Yet who were the Etruscans? And were they the ancestors of the Florentines? Then we ate *zabaione* in the piazza before plunging into the sombre Duomo.

Harold Acton lunched with us at the hotel. Was wickedly funny reviling the English *literati* whom he dislikes, including poor Raymond Mortimer who gave his book [*Memoirs of an Aesthete*, 1948] a filthy review. He said he was a Jew, which R. hotly denies, being connected with Meyer & Mortimer, the military outfitters; that as a young Bohemian in Paris he sported a cloak and broad brimmed floppy hat. One day a, passerby shouted at him, 'Va-t'en, folle bergère!'

I admire Anthony for the independence of his views, if I do not admire all his views. He dresses well and is always spruce. When at luncheon the waiters made A. take her pekinese out of the dining-room Anthony said to me, 'I wonder what they would say if they knew I had two toads in my pockets.' This afternoon instead of going out he sat on his terrace reading the Shakespeare sonnets.

We dined at Buca Lapi restaurant in the basement of an ancient palace, drinking delicious Orvieto white wine. A guitarist and violinist were playing Cimarosa, who was Napoleon's favourite composer, Anthony says.

Friday, 25th February

We left Florence after I had said farewell to St Augustine, for Pisa, a dull route, houses all the way. Looked at Pisano's ugily Gothic pulpit with classical cornice in the Baptistery. The Campo Santo completely destroyed in the War. What with Dresden we have much to answer for. The Tower would be very beautiful if only it would not lean. This it must have done since 1500 at latest for it is depicted leaning on an intarsia panel in the choir of the Duomo. We lunched in Pisa. How sad the gaps from bombing along the Arno. Then to Portofino across the mountains, a beautiful route. We arrived at 5.30 to find the Cliffords had come and moved into their Castello which they had in fact lent to the Chaplins. This quite naturally made the Chaplins rather cross. We had to stay at the Hotel Nazionale, primitive, but food excellent. Cliffords dined with us. Him we did not much like, a dark, smooth, saturnine newspaper correspondent, like a schoolmaster who does not look his pupils in the eye. She the daughter of Robert Graves, very talkative and bright.

Saturday, 26th February

Still fine and sunny but fearfully cold. None of us like Portofino. It is too *mignon* and shut in. We crave open space. All morning I wrote on my window terrace while the Chaplins took their pekinese who is ill with enteritis to the vet. This afternoon we again packed up and moved to Santa Margherita to stay at the Miramare, a more luxurious hotel.

Sunday, 27th February

Wrote most of the morning in the sun but behind glass doors because of piercing winds. In the afternoon we visited the Cliffords in the Castello, the site of which is extremely romantic. There are views from the terrace in every direction, a rare thing, over the fishing village of Portofino behind, over the outward sea towards Genoa and Sestri in front. Furthermore the place is on a promontory as well as a hill.

Monday, 28th February

I had sudden but acute toothache in the night and was only saved from madness by the kind night watchman finding me some aspirin. In the morning A. took me to a dentist in Rapallo who painted the tooth with medicament and refused to accept a fee. This is typical of one of the extremes, rapacity and generosity, to be met with in the Italian character. In the afternoon A. and I left Santa Margherita for the Castelletto, Portofino, the Cliffords having left it this morning. An old gardener, Pipo, carried our heavy bags up the hill. Paola the cook walks from the village every day, carrying provisions bought in the shops. It is divine up here. Much wind but burning sun. I sat in an arbour overlooking the sea and wrote at a table Pipo improvised for me. A. and I dined at the Nazionale, the best food we have had in Italy.

Tuesday, 1st March

I worked in the tower room till 4.30. Anthony arrived at luncheon time. His love of Shakespeare is deep and passionate. He quotes at great length and is moved to ecstasies of veneration. Music and ornithology are his prime interests, yet he says Shakespeare transcends everything, even Mozart. A. and I drove to Rapallo in the evening to deliver a letter of introduction from Eddie Marsh to Max Beerbohm. We three dined at the Nazionale. Such laughter we have. They say I must come and live with them in Paris. Alvilde is incredibly generous and I notice that she pays for everything. It is Mardi Gras today and all the young in Rapallo are dressed up and making much din.

Wednesday, 2nd March

Terrible gale during the night and all day blowing relentlessly and noisily. From my window I see snow on the mountain tops beyond Genoa. Paola brings up a tiny pot of flowers on my coffee tray. Worked all day. Anthony

says all great men have been preoccupied with death. Shakespeare never
overcame his awe and fear of death, so how should we endeavour to do
so? The smell of the fires that burn olive tree wood and roots is sweet and
not a little intoxicating. I burn it in the stove of my bedroom, which is
in a detached tower.

Saturday, 5th March

We leave Portofino this morning, the Chaplins glad to go for they have
not liked it and truthfully I would not care to have the Castelletto as my
only home because of exposure to the fearsome *tramontana* we have been
having. Apart from the bitter cold it brings, it is extremely tiring to listen
to. Besides, on this eyrie there is nowhere to walk, except down to the
village and up again.

We motor to Genoa where the climate completely changes to mid-
winter. It is snowing hard. The Chaplins drop me at the station. We
are all sad at parting. Left alone I wander down the Via Balbi, looking
at the massive palaces one after another, and the University with the
marble lions descending the stairs into the courtyard.

Shared a sleeper with a decent, inarticulate South American.

Sunday, 6th March

How rude and surly the French are after the outgiving Italians. I found
myself sitting next to the Duke of St Albans in the train from Paris. He
is a non-stop talker about nothing, but very funny. Hitherto I had only
met him casually in Brooks's. I was furious that at Dover he paid no duty
on two bottles of brandy and six of champagne whereas I had to pay 32/-
duty on one bottle of liqueur. He was delighted and said it was because
he was wearing a hat and I was not, but I believe it was because he is a
Duke and I am not. In the carriage to London he spoke about King
Edward VII's petty nature and his awful behaviour with women, as
though his own was impeccable. He said that whenever the King saw a
pretty woman he sent his equerries to fetch and present her to him; then
would invite her to tea while commanding her not to come wearing a
hat, or veiled. He said, quite irrelevantly, 'Oliver Messel is a pervert, isn't
he?' I said, 'I don't think so.' I will not subscribe to the notion of old
brutes that homosexuality is wicked or disgraceful.

Monday, 14th March

I have been back a week. My mind in turmoil. A fire has been lit. How
absurdly coy and genteel one is, even to oneself, about one's emotions, when
they are serious. Here the weather has been bitterly cold, unrelieved by sun.
A sore throat turned to a cold, so I retired to bed on Saturday until today.

Jack Rathbone, our new Secretary, has started work. We were friends at Oxford. He is going to be a success with my colleagues. Have received several post cards from Alvilde who arrives in London tomorrow.

Tuesday, 15th March

I lunched with Harold at the Travellers'. He ordered a bottle of white wine of which I foolishly partook, for I had vowed on my return from Italy, never to drink in the middle of the day. The old men at the Travellers' look askance at Harold, the Socialist, surrounded by young men whom he corrupts with wine and seditious talk, the fools. But Harold is as dear as ever and enhances the lives of his friends, young and old. I drove him to Knole and we looked at the garden wall. He was deeply shocked. He thought it had been repaired in a way an urban corporation would have done it and is going to complain to the Committee. I hope, since he thinks we cannot undo the work, there will be no need for me to see Lord Sackville on the matter. I would hate this, for I am very fond of Lord Sackville who, I believe, trusts me. He might be hurt and angry.

Back in London I told Harold I was going to meet Alvilde on the Golden Arrow and wanted to buy flowers for her. He dissuaded me, saying it was a continental and *bedint* thing to do. I met her and she dined here, bringing me some ham and liqueur as a present – not *bedint*.

Wednesday, 16th March

Sam Carr [of Batsford's] lunched and warned me that my book must be popular, short, and not too factual. As it happens everything he said it should be it isn't, and everything it should not be, it is.

Went to tea with Lady Binning at Fenton House, Hampstead to approve the colours she has chosen for her two front rooms. The kind woman, who really likes me very much, insisted upon my accepting the present of a sixteenth-century book of Roman palaces, which I am delighted to have. I could not refuse (didn't want to of course). She promised she would never give me another present. I wanted to embrace her, but refrained.

I took Bridget to the Hills' cocktail party. We could hardly move for the crowd.

Thursday, 17th March

Lunched with Sibyl Colefax at the Dorchester in a fearfully overheated room. I thought I should die and sweated like those spongy water ferns met with in Italian grottoes. My cold is now feverish. Sat next to Juliet Duff and Lys Connolly. Alvilde there but we could not speak. Walked away with James who told me his mother is to have a serious abdominal operation. Tonight Alvilde took me to the French Ballet – *Carmen* vigorous and sexy – and we dined at the Dorchester. Her beauty is proud, guarded, even shrouded. Rather Pre-Raphaelite in manner, not in substance. She has had a sad married life, if it can be called married. Cecil Beaton invited us both to meet Nancy for dinner, but we decided we would be happier alone.

Friday, 18th March

Drove the Eshers to Upton [House, Warwickshire] for the day. It was too long an outing, and with my cold I felt rotten. Bridget took me to a film première of Oliver Messel's *Queen of Spades*; beautiful décor by him; Louis Quinze dresses superb. Edith Evans as the raddled old countess in her element. I sat next to Rose Macaulay who talked throughout the performance.

Saturday, 19th March

Stayed in all day on account of my cold. Alvilde called with a bottle of champagne for our dinner here tonight. Sent a car for me and we went to *The Heiress*, an absolutely splendid production with Ralph Richardson and Peggy Ashcroft. He is invariably natural which few English actors seem to be. Her performance is unforgettable. A great actress when she sheds the affected, suburban delivery. Alvilde and I dined at home over her champagne. I took her back to the Dorchester and left her there. My cold is still very bad. I am in a daze. I do not quite realize what has happened to me. This is the first time that a woman I have loved has loved me. I say 'loved' which is totally different to 'lusted after'. I have had plenty of reciprocal lust of one kind and another. I want to be with her all the time. My cold makes the situation even more unreal, and me surely unappetizing. Which goes to show . . . What? Her nobility and sincerity.

Sunday, 20th March

Stay indoors all day except to go to Mass. Still feel ill. Try to write fitfully. The reality of this love dawns on me slowly like creeping paralysis. One becomes a victim to a great power that is irresistible. How selfish I have been hitherto, all the stony way to middle age, in full control of my emotions, and probably cruel at times. I meet A. this evening. We tried Soho and could get in nowhere, so ended at the Mirabelle where we had a very expensive and perfectly filthy meal. Then returned home and talked and made plans for the summer. We are very happy.

Monday, 21st March

A. and I lunched at the oyster bar, Wilton's. This evening she came round here and we ate honey sandwiches and drank tea, sitting on the floor in front of the fire. She left to dine with Anthony who came over from Paris this evening.

Tuesday, 22nd March

Motored Alvilde from the Dorchester to Victoria. Put her into the Golden Arrow, and left. I sent her a telegram and posted her a long letter. Then went to the ballet – Danilova in *Coppélia* – with Sheila Plunkett. Very enjoyable. Although S. said Danilova's neck and back showed age I did not notice it. Danilova's precision is wonderful. It is the steadiness and sureness of the older dancers that convey necessary confidence to the spectator. A lifetime's arrival at perfection. The young ones will dance as well in time. Dined at the Lyric. S. is a dear, so gay and laughing, and very pretty and distinguished.

Wednesday, 23rd March

This morning we had a Reorganization Committee in the office. Satisfactory for it laid down general principles. We, the staff, now know where we stand. Esher of course always says that general principles are arrived at only to be disregarded. Jack Rathbone is very sensible and understanding, and grasps the situation of our peculiar, sensitive, dedicated staff, which must be totally unlike the staff of most organizations, and maddening to an outsider. In the luncheon interval went to the Abbey to look at Ben Jonson's stone with the four words, 'O Rare Ben Jonson', which moved A. so much. In the afternoon to Dr Johnson's House in Gough Square. It has a handful of important relics compared with the quantity of Carlyliana in our Carlyle's House. It is however more attractively furnished than the other because it has carpets and curtains. Rick means to enliven Carlyle's.

Thursday, 24th March

Depressed because no letter from A. today and as yet – 9 p.m. – no telephone call.

This morning I went on a small deputation with Crawford, Esher, [Ruby] Holland-Martin and the Admiral [Bevir] to give evidence before the Gowers Committee set up by the Chancellor of the Exchequer, at the Treasury, a fine early Georgian room. It was an interesting and enjoyable experience, conducted informally. I sat between Esher and Anthony Blunt. All very nice people and I was greeted by

Ansell and Sir Cyril Fox. Crawford launched the discussion. He was very nervous and repetitive and was sweating. This surprised me. But dear Lord Esher, who never lets one down, contributed wise and weighty interpolations. How excellent he is in dealing with civil service minds. The chairman and others raised a number of questions which we answered adequately. I found myself speaking up rather a lot. After all I do know a good deal about this subject. The issue lies between us and the Ministry of Works. I felt that general sympathy was with us, and believed that we made a good case. Lady Anderson asked one or two pertinent questions – and me to the ballet next week.

Jamesey came at 6 o'clock. I told him about Alvilde. At first he made wild and preposterous guesses. When I disclosed, he was amazed and delighted, and encouraged unreservedly. When he left I got worried, but at 11 o'clock she rang up. Line as clear as though she were in the room. Her usual firm, take-it-or-leave-it, fierce little voice. I knew she was pleased really, and I went to bed happy.

Friday, 25th March

That beloved man Lord Esher accompanied Rick and me to Carlyle's House, and endorsed all our ideas for improving the place, and the conditions of poor, wretched Mrs Strong, the caretaker, and her husband.

Saturday, 26th March

A fine, bright, sunshiny day, everything singing. I motored in a clean car to Stratfield Saye, arriving luncheon time. The Willy Kings and a Commander Thwaite staying. Gerry [Wellington] at his most entertaining and charming, although fussy. For example, he came into the drawing-room and saw me with my feet, in perfectly clean evening shoes, poised lightly on an ordinary footstool. He rushed up with newspapers, seized my feet, arranged the papers on the stool, and banged down the said feet, exclaiming, 'It never occurred to me that anyone would. actually put a foot on a footstool.' There were similar protests from time to time. He made a considerable fuss because Viva, on going to bed, took upstairs a tumbler of water. G. confided to me in a desperate air that this would mean the tumbler never returned to its allotted place downstairs. Henceforth it would for ever belong to the housemaids' pantry where the glasses were of a different pattern. Food bad and little to drink. Thwaite a dull man, also G.'s librarian; and the party not gay. I did not on the whole much enjoy it, although I usually enjoy G.'s company and anecdotes. We motored to a distant antique shop where I bought a small oil sketch, which G. said might be by Poussin, for £2. He was rather put out, pretending that he had seen it first.

I went to Mass on Sunday morning at Heckfield House. Willy King has no manners and his appearance is grotesque – face blue all over like a parakeet. At first he is taciturn but after a bit warms up and is funny but caustic.

Monday, 28th March

At 10.30 picked up Jack Rathbone at Reading station and drove to Banbury where we lunched. On to Upton and showed him the house and garden. He was very impressed by the condition of both. Then to Charlecote which was looking perfectly beastly. He remarked on the deplorable state of the garden. We stayed at Stratford-on-Avon and went to an excellent English film with Zimmerlin, the divine Austrian girl I saw in *The Wild Duck*, as heroine of a displaced persons' camp. Went to Evensong in Shakespeare's church and were accosted by the vicar, an old queen and friend of Noël Coward.

Tuesday, 29th March

This morning to Hidcote in impenetrable mist. Nothing out for it is not exactly a spring garden; even so, tidy, and Jack admired the layout; also appreciated Albert the head gardener. Then to Packwood looking magnificently polished and shining. Then Coughton and dear Lady Throckmorton. Had tea with her. I had written explaining that I was bringing the new Secretary to make her acquaintance. She drew me aside afterwards and said, 'Jim, who is this nice little man?' Then to Malvern, and stayed at the Abbey Hotel.

Wednesday, 30th March

With Colin Jones [the Area Agent] we motored over the Malvern properties, ending with Colwall and Rayner Wood. J. has a habit of taking a person's arm, Lady T.'s, Rayner Wood's and in a confidential whisper begging them when in difficulties to communicate with him at once. Too affable, this. He is a good companion, gay and understanding, with acute sense of humour. But lacking *gravitas*.

Got home before 6 o'clock to find a note from my father. He has seen a specialist who reports a growth on his bladder. He is to go to a home in Queen's Gate next Monday to have bladder opened up and diagnosed lest it be malignant. This worries me a good deal. Mama is to stay here for a week at least. A. telephoned as arranged at 6 o'clock. She writes every day, as do I.

Went to *Coppélia* again, with Lady Anderson in the Royal Box. Danilova ill and Swanelia taken by Moyra Shearer who is far better, with beautiful legs and arms and hands. It is a pretty ballet indeed. We ate, in the little room behind the box, a course during each interval, a most civilized manner of dining. The box and room so elegant and Edwardian. I sat next to a very young Princess Murat who is in London to learn typewriting, and Susan Lowndes that was, now married to a Portuguese and living in Lisbon, charming. Was driven back to Belgrave Square in Chips Channon's Rolls. Had a drink with him and Peter Coats in Peter's bedroom, he being ill in bed. Chips imparted some astounding information not to be recorded alas, but which will be remembered.

Thursday, 31st March

Helen Dashwood lunched at the Allies Club to meet Robin Fedden. She was in a gay mood and liked Robin who is to go to West Wycombe [Park] and try to unravel those ghastly knots. This evening went to a cocktail party given by Mrs Carr and the Lothians. It was the usual hellish squash and agony. I literally fought my way in and out. I don't believe either the hosts or guests enjoy these entertainments. Then why are they given and attended? I then called for Garrett Moore and drove him to Hampstead to dine with the Kenneth Clarks. Admirable hosts. One other guest only, an Australian woman, artist and swimmer, pretty and rather bitchy. Talked a lot with Jane Clark who is very easy. Her husband's gracious manner – I don't think he cares for men one bit – frightens me. Yet he arouses my fervent admiration. He is a sort of Jupiter in intellect.

Friday, 1st April

No letter from A. either yesterday or this morning. Drove to luncheon at St Clere, a house belonging to Mr [Ronnie] Norman's eldest son Hugh. Mr Norman called in my office this morning to consult about painting the pine panelling of the hall and asked who might advise. I said I was going to Penshurst this afternoon and offered my services, if he wanted them. So he telephoned the son and I went. Nice, large red brick early Georgian house somewhat spoilt by a rich grandfather in Victorian times.

Penshurst had a reopening of state rooms ceremony. Bill de Lisle invited me which was kind. He has greatly improved the place since I was there ten years ago. Some of the furniture is superb. Crowds of people from the museum world, Leigh Ashton, Summerson, Gerry Wellington, etc.

In the hall at Penshurst Gerry W. drew me aside and pointing at the screen said, 'Look at that classical entablature. The whole thing is pure Batty Langley and not medieval at all.' I am always ready to be convinced, and was. Then I told John Summerson who said, 'Nonsense. It is not eighteenth-century, but pure Jacobean.' I was convinced again. Now I am not sure and think it is made up.

On return to London no letter from A. today. Was worried and unhappy, so telephoned her at Jouy. She said she had written every day.

Saturday, 2nd April

Felt quite calm and content this morning having spoken to A. last night. By the first post received two letters from her. While reading them Emily handed me a telegram asking me to ring again tonight because she was anxious. So I again fell into a state of *angst*. Goodness, the absurdities of love. Just before luncheon came a letter from Dr Astley, my father's doctor at Wickhamford, announcing that he had received a report from the London specialist of 'exceedingly grave' news. The tumour on the bladder was almost certainly malignant. I telephoned the nursing clinic where Papa is to go on Monday and spoke to the matron. She confirmed that the specialist was right in his diagnosis. She advised that we should await the chemical examination of the piece of tumour to be extracted on Monday before telling Mama, who as yet knows nothing; not till then will they be sure they can operate properly and remove the whole tumour. Everything will depend upon how bad it is. If bad, I gather nothing can be done. I telephoned Dick [my brother] at Shaw. He is a great comfort and help and strongly advised against telling any member of the family until the diagnosis is known.

I telephoned Wickhamford this evening and both parents spoke to me from their beds, sounding quite cheerful and cosy, which made me feel how pathetic they were in their ignorance. I telephoned Paris and spoke to A. who was unhappy because she had received no letter today and would not now have one until Monday. Heavens, what mixed emotions!

Sunday, 3rd April

Worked at my book, correcting rather than composing, my mind concentrated upon Papa's illness. Dined with Alex Beattie and Ivor Newton, the pianist, an old pussy cat not attractive and rather common. He played a little Chopin after dinner.

Monday, 4th April

Met Mama and Papa at Paddington at 11.30 and motored him to the Queen's Gate Clinic. Took her to lunch at the Allies Club. At 4.30 she and I went back to the Clinic and found him coming round after his operation. The specialist removed two small growths in the bladder through the penis, which is almost unbelievable. Mama is staying with me in the flat, she having my room, I sleeping in the back of Geoffrey

[Houghton-Brown]'s drawing-room. She insisted on meeting, with me, the specialist's assistant, who told her Papa would have to return every three to six months for observation, which alarmed her, but nothing further. I made an appointment to see Millin, the specialist who did the operation.

Tuesday, 5th April

I lunched with Sibyl, sat next to Leigh Ashton and Lady Salter. Lady Hudson, widow of Lord Northcliffe, a rather jolly old lady, slightly deaf, was there.

At 6 o'clock I saw the specialist who told me that he had indeed removed two malignant growths. He assured me my father could only live two years at most, that the growths were bound to return. He advised against telling either him or my mother the truth unless the analysis next week reveals something even more serious than what he has already discovered.

Wednesday, 6th April

Historic Buildings Committee this morning very long and dull. Nothing of interest beyond designs of memorial plaques. One controversial question arose over the restoration of the Roman remains at Housesteads Camp. I consider that there is no conflict between aestheticism and Ministry of Works restoration of these archaeological remains whose interest is exclusively historical. I except of course the Roman wall itself which is undeniably beautiful and romantic, serpentining across the Northumbrian hills.

Went to see Lady Berwick at 5.30. She begged there should be no opening ceremony at Attingham until the end of the summer. My father looks so well and has such a good colour that it is difficult to believe he can be seriously ill. He eats well. Mama has, thank God, accepted my equivocations. Alvilde telephoned from Paris this evening while she was in the room. A. suspected she was present and asked me. I said yes, and she rang off. Then I told Mama our story, sent her to bed, and rang up A. again after 11 o'clock. Woke her up. Mama said Clara Mitchell – foolish woman – told her today that I was handsome. My dear mother told Clara she was talking rot; and as she (Mama) had given birth to me she knew I was nothing of the sort. Rather sweet of her.

Thursday, 7th April

Received a letter from John Betj[eman] in which he mentioned that Basil Champneys died in April 1935 and would, if alive, be 107. Did I remember taking him to dinner with the Champneys in Church Row,

Hampstead? Architecture was never mentioned, as though to be a professional architect was not quite the thing socially, although the old man
did talk about 'my friend Mr [Coventry] Patmore' and less enthusiastically about 'that Father Gerard Hopkins'. What I do well recall is our
having to go into the dining-room arm-in-arm. I was to take in the
daughter, and J.B. Mrs Champneys, who was very grand and correct. She
had greying hair brushed back and wore a gown with train. John could
not remember which arm to proffer. She gave him no help and stood up
motionless like a statue, waiting. John jazzed around, caught my eye, in
which anxiety and embarrassment were blended, and dissolved into
giggles.

Jamesey lunched at the Allies Club and was *distrait* and inattentive, but
we ended by laughing like mad over some Algerian wine. I bought some
shoes for him and went to the dentist who took three-quarters of an hour
extracting a nerve. This operation left me in pain and very exhausted.
Then Dick came to Brooks's where we had a long talk. I was relieved to
see him. He approved of what I had so far done and is sure that withholding the truth is right. I am so glad.

At 6 o'clock to Miss Ethel Sands. She is charming, the most charming
ugly woman I have met. She has a delightful soft, sincere laugh, a running
laugh with a lilt that misleads a little, making one suspect she may not be
simpler than she appears. I was perished by the cold wind. She was kind
and asked me to come again. Clive Bell there, very affable and talkative.
He said Desmond MacCarthy does a wonderful imitation of Henry
James recounting with much earnestness the appalling treatment Ethel
Sands received, when a girl, from her mother who was a noted beauty
and a cruel woman. Dick dined with Ma and me at Thurloe Square.

Friday, 8th April

Lunched at 5 Belgrave Square with Peter Coats and Chips Channon. Sat
next Sylvia Compton. She told me she was fifty. She is great fun with her
stories. She said George Lloyd would always ask penetrating questions
about matters of world importance and expect immediate answers. He
liked her company so long as she gave quick retorts, no matter whether
sensible or silly.

Went to see Doreen and had a gossip.

Monday, 11th April

Papa and Mama went home today. They seemed so pleased and I pray
that by some miracle he may be all right. Mama very sweet and considerate yet I find her a little tiring because she cannot concentrate upon one
topic at a time. She says she will not come to London this summer to

meet Hugh Macdonell because he upsets her so much and she is now determined to do nothing to distress Papa. Evidently at the age of sixty-five she is still moved to love. She advised me to love Alvilde while I could, adding that this was perhaps not the advice a mother should give a son. James called last night while I was with Papa. They got on like a house on fire.

Tuesday, 12th April

I lunched with Giles Eyre at the Travellers', a happy, mundane youth, and a little *affairé*. At 6 o'clock sat in the Travellers' with David Crawford and the Admiral talking over the Gowers Committee evidence. Crawford is so vague I wonder how he gets any work done. Dined with the Kings. A very enjoyable, giggly dinner. Ruth Lowinsky and Robert Cecil from the Wallace Collection, whom I liked. He too was immensely amused by Willy who was rather tipsy and beetroot-coloured. Viva shouted at him, 'Willy, do keep your mouth shut when you are eating. Nobody wants to see what you have got inside it.' And after dinner, 'Willy, don't sit so close to Robert, and Robert don't let Willy tickle your face with his beard.' Alvilde telephoned at 10.30 and I gave way and said I would fly to Paris on Thursday to stay with her. Weakness, for I ought to stay at home and work.

Wednesday, 13th April

Dined tonight with John Lehmann at his covetable house in Egerton Crescent. Guests were Sibyl Colefax, Miss Ethel Sands, Peter Quennell and an unknown woman. Much Sibyl talk of famous people she had known, such as Robbie Ross. John Lehmann and Peter Q. complained that there were in England no young authors with any style; that in their young days their elders, like Lytton Strachey, kept them up to the mark. How often have not these sorts of complaint been exchanged by the middle-aged? Peter's wit and brilliance always impress me but his malice is without any limit. I relish it because, so far, it has not been directed at my face, and what is directed at my back I cannot mind, so long as a kind friend does not repeat it.

Thursday, 14th April

The office shut at noon for the holidays. I, who had decided after all to go to Jouy-en-Josas, collected my ticket and, having worked in the afternoon, bought A. an Easter egg made of Sèvres porcelain and another smaller one for Clarissa [Chaplin] and left by the 5 o'clock plane for Paris. A wonderful day but I felt so full of misgivings that I was nearly sick. Fortified myself in the air with brandy and water.

Landed at Le Bourget and was met by A. looking beautiful and radiant at the Invalides. She took me to a restaurant for dinner, I consuming a whole bottle of white wine and a liqueur with the result that, although blissfully happy to be with her, I was reduced to a state of nervous idiocy. We drove to Jouy-en-Josas. Her house Le Mé Chaplin most picturesquely set on a hill with Turneresque view over a valley, crossed by a Louis XIV aqueduct in the background. The village of Jouy hidden by misty trees below. The moon was shining like day, the nightingales singing like sopranos, everything as romantic as could be desired while, arm-in-arm, we walked into the garden and into the house where Anthony was playing Mozart on the piano.

Friday, Good Friday, 15th April

The actual house is modern and unbeautiful but filled with A.'s pretty things. Doors of glass and huge windows open upon a garden of enchantment. It is a summer retreat. We went in the morning to the village. The church all shut and dark and dead, the tabernacle door wide open, the dove flown as though God were deliberately withholding himself from me. This evening the four of us (Clarissa is here) motored to Dampière and looked at the outside of the Luynes château, most impressive, Mansard's work, with detached wings and forecourt and, on the far side of the road, a stone balustraded 'lay-by' as it is called today in Great North Road jargon. We dined and drank Suze which tastes of gentian. Anthony behaves wonderfully to me. We are a sort of blood brothers. His conversation with Clarissa, aged fifteen, about his love affairs and sex life makes my hair stand on end, but not hers evidently. How much, I wonder, should one believe?

Tuesday, 19th April

I return today, A. having motored me to Paris. This visit has been unsurpassed. It exceeded my dreams. Perfect weather, sun shining every day and moon at night. The eyes of God did not blink for one single second. Perhaps it would have been better if they had. The country at its zenith, the hyacinths and tulips out by day, the nightingales and tree frogs by night. Like little green toys or jade jewels they look so pretty, until they croak when their chests expand hideously like a monstrous goitre or a balloon one wants to prick. Anthony took us to a marsh where these creatures on warm nights congregate and sing in thousands, so that the chorus is like a cannonade. He says their voices were the first animal voices heard on earth – a very impressive thought. I sat on the terrace of my room writing, or in the garden reading, talking and laughing. Anthony is delighted because A. is made happy. Was there ever a more topsy-turvy business?

One morning we walked about Versailles, round the Trianon and the Temple d'Amour. Another day we took a picnic luncheon and drove to Chartres, never seen by me before. Surely no blue glass like this exists anywhere else in the world. It has a particular cerulean, jewel-like quality. The solemn grey cathedral is untouched by time and accident.

Thursday, 21st April

Motored today to Biddlesden Park, close to Stowe, in well-wooded Buckinghamshire country. It was in 1937 I went to see this house for the National Trust and recommended acceptance. Now the same owner Colonel Badger and his wife, very nice people, entertained me again to luncheon and showed me round. I had forgotten it entirely and after this second visit read my first report made twelve years ago and was surprised at the things I had noticed. I then motored to Wickhamford and stayed the night. It was Papa's sixty-ninth birthday. He is thinner and does not eat much. Deenie and Colonel Sidney, lately widowered, dined and we drank champagne in celebration of this most melancholy little event. Colonel Sidney is seventy today and is absolutely miserable.

Friday, 22nd April

Spent all day happily at Charlecote on ladders, sticking labels on the pictures or walls, the sort of occupation I most love, with the new caretaker, a nice man, having had to say goodbye to Wickers, the late caretaker and wife who were practically in tears. I felt so sorry for them. Dear people. On my return I found two letters from A., one depressed, so I telephoned her.

Monday, 25th April

After a National Buildings Record meeting I met Alvilde at Kensington air station and motored her to the Dorchester. The Bearsteds had travelled over in the same plane. As I said to A. one can never get away with any secret, however much one tries. Therefore it is better not to try. We went to the ballet at Covent Garden, Prokofiev's *Cinderella*. A little too pantomimey, but Freddie Ashton and Bobby Helpmann as the ugly sisters were extremely funny. The Queen attended but since she sat right above us we saw her not. We went for a drink of champagne in the Clarks' box in the interval and dined afterwards in the restaurant of the Dorchester.

Tuesday, 26th April

Went to A. at the Dorchester at 4.30. Then to the Courtauld Institute to hear the first of Count Metternich's lectures – this one excellent – on German architecture of the seventeenth century. Returned to A. at the

Dorchester but dined alone since she had to go to the ballet again with Clarissa and the Clarks.

Wednesday, 27th April

To the Goldsmiths' Hall this morning to look at their Renaissance silver, the Bowes Cup being very Holbeinesque; and an exquisite little salt dated 1522 quite classical by comparison, although about fifty years earlier. Lunched at the Allies Club with A. and Anthony and Oggy Lynn.

Thursday, 28th April

A. and I went by air to Paris this afternoon, I having to make untruthful excuses to the office, and feeling guilty and unhappy. She gave me a little gold toothpick as a present. We dined at Albert's again and motored to Jouy. We stopped at the same corner of the road near the village to listen to the same nightingale that we heard singing on my first evening a fortnight ago exactly. Anthony remains in London and Clarissa away. Terrible black moments of despair are mercifully redeemed by moments of unadulterated bliss. I suppose this is often the case. Neither can be described.

On Friday morning we were taken round Versailles by the curator, a young man called Van der Kemp, previously arranged by A. I was so shy about my bad French that I could not converse intelligently. I feel desperately ashamed because when I left Grenoble University in 1927 I spoke like a bird. Van der Kemp took us not only into the state rooms but into the *petits appartements* of the Pompadour and du Barry, not seen by the public. *Petits* they are, and enchanting. In Marie Antoinette's boudoir her own clock played tunes for us, little airs specially composed for it by Mozart, Glück and others. The pathos of it. These rooms must be the most exquisite in the world. In my youth I used to despise French architecture for being effeminate and effete. How I dared, contemptible fool that I was. The prejudices of adolescence make one blush in remembrance. We walked upon the lead roof of the palace and admired the formal rides and parterres.

We went to George Chavchavadze's concert of Mozart and Schumann concerti, lovely works which A. said he played badly – he had a horribly inflamed eye; then to a party the Chavchavadzes gave in Noël Coward's flat in the Place Vendôme. Awful, it was. A. says French society is less intellectual and more superficial than English. It is certainly more sophisticated and alarming.

Saturday we went to Chantilly. Had the most excellent luncheon I ever ate, and then round the castle, looking at the pictures – the Clouet drawings and Fouquet illuminations. To tea at the Duff Coopers', a delightful

Louis XV villa with an English garden lolling down to a lake with weeping willows and a cascade. The Walter Elliots staying. She a red-faced, horsey-looking English woman, yet clever and non-horsey, but plain and badly dressed. He speaks with a broad Scotch accent. Lady Diana wearing trousers and cowboy jacket with large silver buttons and cowboy hat. She is very offhand. When I left she was lounging across a chair, did not get up or proffer a hand, so I mumbled goodbye and followed A. out.

We are ecstatically happy alone, and dined at home. All Sunday spent at Jouy in the sun. A. is considered one of the best-dressed women in France, which for an English woman is some compliment.

Tuesday, 3rd May

I flew back from Paris yesterday morning. Today left at 9 o'clock for Barnstaple. Was met at the station by Eardley wearing corduroys and a French beret and Raymond Mortimer, with his black, now greying, but thick curly hair, always hatless, chain-smoking, dusty, talkative and enthusiastic. Typical Bloomsbury in his disregard of clothes. Do they consider sartorial elegance synonymous with mental degeneracy? R.'s exaggerated voice is like a raven's croak. We spent the afternoon at Arlington Court, a forbidding, gloomy, neo-Grecian house, stacked with some 200 cases of old ship models and chests and chests of shells and other bric-à-brac. The trees all over-mature, intergrown and 'gone back'; the park a jungle. Miss Chichester who left us Arlington was very eccentric and during her last eighteen months spent £35,000 buying whatever junk she could get hold of. She must have been cheated by agents she employed to buy these things at sales and auctions. It was wicked of her solicitors not to restrain the poor old lady. Surrounding country very beautiful and remote. We stay the night at Lyndale Hotel, Lynmouth.

Wednesday, 4th May

Walked up Watersmeet this morning. Then drove back to Arlington, worked there, picnicked on terrace and drove to Exeter. E. and I to the Cathedral. A young verger showed us the tomb effigies repainted by Tristram. One I approved of for it was a judicious restoration, the old colours having been lightly touched up, a Siena patina predominating. The others were too gaudy. The fifteenth-century chantry tombs are very fine. Then we motored to Long Crichel for the night, stopping at Lyme Regis where at 7.45 we failed to get a meal at any hotel and finally had beastly, greasy fish and chips at a lorry-drivers' café. Raymond very indignant. Found Eddy [Sackville-West] in his crotchety, querulous and spiky mood.

Friday, 6th May

Motored Jack Rathbone to Polesden Lacey and Hatchlands. At Hatchlands where Goodhart-Rendel took us round gardens and house I was deeply impressed by the learnedness of the man. There is nothing he cannot talk about wittily and to the point. His trouble is that he speaks too much and with such rapidity that persons like me have difficulty keeping pace with the trend of his thoughts. I like him and we have many subjects in common.

Went to a poor play (Alec Guinness, that great actor) about Dr Simpson who discovered chloroform.

Sunday, 8th May

All this weekend at home working fairly well. Had besides time for reflection. No letter from A. this morning – Saturday, I mean – and great difficulty getting through to her on the telephone. Have felt very lonely.

Monday, 9th May

To the National Gallery to see the Munich pictures. Only managed three rooms within an hour, chiefly of Flemish and German painting. Colours of the Dirk Bouts startling. A Guardi of a concert in Venice and a Botticelli Pietà detained me. The Grünewald mocking of Christ very terrible.

To Ockwells with Carew Wallace to approve a site for a Dutch barn. Went for quarter of an hour to St George's Chapel. Wonderful though this Perpendicular fan vaulting is, it is never tenuous enough. I like the theatrical monument to Princess Charlotte, her soul flying skywards leaving her shrouded body on the ground. The Reid Dick effigy of George V is pretty awful. On my way back I stopped at Cranford. The house has been swept away as has every single one of the pleasant Georgian villas of the village, now a wreck of its former self. Only some broken-down garden walls and gate-piers to the big house remain, a shocking commentary. The church very pretty seventeenth-century, with several fine tombs and mural monuments. The Berkeley family has associations with this place.

Tuesday, 10th May

Whereas there were two letters from A. yesterday there are none today. The unpredictability of the post is disturbing. I prefer to have one letter a day to two every other day. I bought two seats for *Das Rheingold* for ourselves on Thursday and ordered a table for supper at the Savoy. I ought to have asked the Clarks but want to have A. to myself. Went to the

Munich pictures again and looked at the later ones, two lovely Claudes in early morning light, Rembrandts and two Poussins. Murillo fine.

Jamie Caffery dined with me at Brooks's. I drank too much – 2 glasses of sherry, ½ bottle of Burgundy and 1 glass port – and felt ill next day. When shall I ever learn? Caffery is a handsome-ugly young tough of twenty-nine, with fine straight hair like powdered gold. Face cruel in repose and mouth of no shape. Comes from the American upper crust, whatever that means. He told me he has a great-grandmother alive. His sister has a child of ten, so the old lady is a great-great-grandmother. Unusual.

Wednesday, 11th May

Went to Munich pictures again, to look at Rubens and Vandyke. Then to Sotheby's with Robin Fedden and checked the condition of the tapestries to be lent to Little Moreton Hall. Then to tea with Lady Binning who, dear woman, is becoming another cross. She is so lonely that my heart bleeds, whereas hers melts.

Thursday, 12th May

Count and Countess Metternich and the Eshers lunched here. Then I met Alvilde at Kensington Air Terminal. Took her to *Das Rheingold* at Covent Garden which bored me fiercely. I only enjoyed the clever way the Rhinemaidens swam round the rock upon thin wires. We dined at the Savoy.

Friday, 13th May

This evening after my committees I met A. at Thurloe Square where Jamesey came to say goodbye. She and I motored off for the weekend. We stayed the night at Harleyford Manor on the Thames. This was the best night's lodging we were to have, for the food was excellent and the beds comfortable. Otherwise a squalid, adulterous place run by peroxide blondes. Nothing dusted, tooth tumblers unwashed. Yet still a country house with Clayton family pictures on the walls, a lovely house once, a true riverside villa built by Sir Robert Taylor. We were told the proprietor was a Clayton, a curious déclassé sort of man, as much gone to seed as his house, only less handsome.

Saturday, 14th May

Poor A. trying to choke down a bad cold. We motored to Bibury and stayed at the Swan, she spending the day at Hatherop Castle school with Clarissa whose confirmation took place today.

Sunday, 15th May

We took Clarissa and Barbara Moray's daughter Arabella Stuart out from
school for the day, starting with a drink before luncheon with David
Stuart at his house in Coln St Aldwyns. He looks a sweet, pretty little boy
of eighteen, whereas he is already a widower, aged I don't know what,
for his wife, Mrs Fyfe's daughter, died giving birth to a son. David lives
here with the baby and his wife's ten-year-old daughter by a former
husband. After lunching at Bibury we drove to Newark Park for me to
see the house offered to the Trust. It is of little importance and the most
desolate and gloomy place imaginable, miles from anywhere. The house,
basically a mid-sixteenth-century hunting-box, has one window of that
date with pediment over Corinthian columns. Otherwise done over in
the late eighteenth cent. with stucco composition and fake battlements.
Interior of simple, classical decoration. The site overlooking a Cotswold
coomb with overgrown view towards the Severn estuary unsurpassed.
We left this Wagnerian haunt for Nether Lypiatt. During tea a sudden
storm arose out of a blue sky. Lightning struck the water tank at the top
of the house, burst a main pipe and flooded the drawing-room, ruining
the ceiling. Our hosts were desperately searching for buckets and in their
panic producing tea cups to stem the devastating tide. What a bore children are! The two girls giggled over the disaster like zanies. I never know
how one should treat them. I adopt the jocular attitude until I, and they,
grow tired.

A. and I stayed the night at Cricklade. We find country hotels and
narrow beds and paper-thin walls, and unbrushed carpets, and baths with
rusted enamel and soap dishes with extinguished cigarette stubs in them,
unpalatable. The church here has a tower of 1550 in Perpendicular style
built by John Dudley. The tower is carved with Elizabethan conceits,
banners coming out of hearts and playing-cards in stone. The Tudors
were given to emblems, riddles, divination and subterfuge. They liked
nothing straightforward and composed in allegories and mystical termi-
nology.

Monday, 16th May

A. and I to Chedworth Roman Villa where we met both Eshers, Eardley,
Smith, Jones and Clouting the Ministry of Works expert, whom we
severely chastised for his pedantic treatment of the remains. A. very bored
with them, preferring ruins above to below ground, and longed to move
me on. We picnicked at the Villa which was fun.

After dinner in London I took A. to Victoria and saw her off in the
ferry. Both full of red wine and tears.

Friday, 20th May

By train to Llandudno yesterday, and at Bodnant met Hubert Smith who arrived by car. We stayed the night with the Aberconways. I like Lady A. with her lovely skin and blue eyes, all pearly. She purses her mouth and is very affected. Nevertheless I don't understand why people laugh at her so much. He is incredibly stiff yet genial in an old-fashioned keep-your-distance manner. I find this famous garden frankly ugly and lacking taste. I don't like conifers and rhododendrons. The layout has no symmetry, and is over-packed with trees and shrubs. There are no vistas, glades or open spaces. It is not picturesque. I am not interested in rare shrubs. The garden is merely an expensive nursery arboretum. All the urns and architectural adjuncts are likewise ugly and the house the most graceless I have ever beheld. I admire the Aberconways, however, and they are both charming to me. Yet I could never love either of them. She showed me a long passage O. Sitwell has written about her in his new book which could not be more complimentary, and is a tribute to her intellect. I am suffering from terrible sciatica from much recent motoring, and sitting in the train; the worst for years.

Sunday, 22nd May

Some fiend impels me to go on writing this diary which no one will want to read, not even my great-great-nephews and nieces. I used to keep it at the end of each day. Now I allow intervals to elapse, sometimes as long as a week when I forget the salient events to record. It is a vice, an indulgence. Now that I write every day to Alvilde and tell her my days, it is a case of duplication.

Tonight I dined with Bridget in her new house in Eaton Terrace, which was, and maybe still is, Anne's. B. has made it not pretty exactly, which it definitely was in Anne's time, but conventional. Then I went to join Anne and Harold Acton at Oliver Messel's. When I arrived they were still seated round the table lit from silver candlesticks, and drinking champagne at 10.30. Harold, rather intoxicated, saying outrageous things in front of Susan, Anne's child, whose presence nevertheless somewhat cramped the adult style. Van the Dane, tiresome in boasting how he quarrelled with all Oliver's friends whom he suspected of trying 'to get things out of' Oliver for nothing. Disingenuous, I thought. In any case what gossipy, fatuous conversation this is.

Tuesday, 24th May

Went to the Chelsea Flower Show for the first time and straightway met Bridget, Diane Abdy and Lady Sibell Rowley. Diane and I made ·

for the Aberconways' tent and had a scrumptious tea and iced coffee. Then both looked at some of the show. I never knew flowers could be forced into such size: delphiniums 12ft high, begonias like dishes and everything too big and unnatural. David Bowes-Lyon dragged me off to see the Hidcote stall of common geraniums which we thought *quelconque*. He came back here for two minutes and seemed keen that we should go on a motor tour in August. A curious man he is. Then went to a sherry party given by Margaret Jourdain and Ivy C.-B., both of whom have made so much money from their respective books lately that they admit to being rich. This is rather touching. I am glad. Ivy's novel is coming out next month.

Wednesday, 25th May

Motored to West Wycombe and looked around. The grounds far tidier. Johnnie Dashwood there wearing a blue beret and carrying a huge axe. He took me to watch six men blow up a tree trunk with gunpowder. Then [Captain John] Hill took me to Bradenham House, now a school for very young children. It is the house which Disraeli's father rented, a very homely red brick William and Mary building, with terraced garden. In spite of quantities of children the gathering was more like a large family party than an institutional half holiday, in fact what a pause in a school curriculum ought to be.

As time goes by I miss A. more and more. After a month I yearn to see her and be with her. Yet what can be done? I do not know. I am longing for next Friday with great desire. Mama has written me a long letter telling me to put A. before my religion and marry her. But would A. agree to this? It would mean altering her life completely, selling Jouy in order to live in England with me, and be tied to London which she would not like. The alternative is for me to throw up my job and live altogether in France, on her money. This I could not do. So what? I cannot help looking ahead to the time when she may not love me any longer. Then where would we both be, with me an incubus round her neck? I should not look ahead perhaps. It is strange how love unfolds itself like a gigantic scroll of which only the lettering immediately under the eyes is clearly readable, the rest being lost in misty lines. Now the last time I saw my father he said that he was sorry about the condition I had got myself into; that of course there was no predicament, for being a Papist I could not possibly contemplate marriage. He spoke nicely, but knowing his loathing of Catholicism I detected in his eye a glint of *Schadenfreude*. 'I told you so,' and 'You are reaping what you have sown,' and other reproachful expressions were hovering about his lips.

Tuesday, 31st May

Bridget and I went to *The Snake Pit*, the film about a woman who had a breakdown and was put into an American asylum. Not very convincing although acted extremely well. It was not as harrowing as it ought to have been. I don't believe nurses behave with the callousness evinced in this film.

Thursday, 2nd June

To the opera with the Andersons in the Royal Box – *Siegfried* which I enjoyed, especially the last act with Flagstad whose voice rolls over one like gigantic waves on shingle. Cecil Beaton in the box for two acts. He giggled with me in the lavatory during the second interval over Sir John's bossiness, for he orders everyone about and spars with his wife, but, I think, good-humouredly really. He is a dour Scot and resembles a disapproving family butler. Lady A. remarked that Daisy Fellowes was looking ill. 'I didn't notice it,' he retorted downright, 'I thought she was looking old.' Caroline Paget there too. Such a whimsical twisted face she has. Ineffably attractive.

Friday, 3rd June

Motored to Knole this morning in pouring rain to meet members of the Gowers Committee on their jaunt to various country houses. They all turned up except Sir Cyril Fox, and were enthusiastic. Lady Anderson much in evidence, asking fatuous questions. I don't find her rebarbative. On the contrary she is always forthcoming. Anthony Blunt made a number of discoveries among the pictures, the only things in the house he was interested in. Lord Sackville, distinguished and patrician in a tidy blue suit and yellow waistcoat, conducted them round the house very graciously.

At 6 o'clock I flew to Paris. Arrived an hour late. Poor A. waiting at Le Bourget. She motored me to the Venezia restaurant where we dined happily. On to Jouy where we were happier still.

Saturday, 4th June

We are a curious party *à quatre*, for Rosemary Lyttelton is staying. Rosemary is very pretty and very slight, too thin perhaps for some tastes, but evidently not for others'. As A. says, she is *racée*. Her little face is dead-white, her hair auburn which glitters in the sunlight. She reminds me of the young Queen Elizabeth. She is musical, talented and extremely intelligent, well read for her age, and much in love with Anthony who pretends to us to be tired of her because she is too clinging. This is nonsense, of course, and a pose. I fear Anthony is determined by a concatenation of paradoxes and contradictions not to disclose what are his intentions. He treats her very sweetly, however. Anthony has breakfast with A. in her bedroom always, plying her with outrageous questions about us. He is a very strange man. His buffooning becomes irritating after a surfeit.

A. and I motored this morning to Versailles. We walked in the gardens looking at the statuary. This afternoon we motored to Fontainebleau where we went round the apartments which display a wonderful sequence of decoration and furnishing from the time of François Premier to that of Napoleon. I find the F. Premier style slightly sickening, like the monarch himself, a bounder, who was also straitlaced and lascivious. At Fontainebleau is the best of the genre to be found anywhere in France. I am possibly mistaken in despising it, for every style that is distinctive and earnest should be respected, if it cannot be liked. An architectural historian must learn to evaluate every style and not allow his judgements to be swayed by fashionable quirks and prejudices.

Monday, 6th June

Lovely hot day of brilliant sun. Lay in the garden till 5 o'clock when A. and I flew back to London. Were met by her Clarissa and dined here in Thurloe Square.

Tuesday, 7th June

Tonight I had a dinner party – A., of course, the Kenneth Clarks and Paz Subercaseaux. I was alarmed by the prospect of the Clarks and the evening was a strain. But A. came early; so did the Clarks before I expected them. K. walked straight round the room looking hard at everything and assessing everything. He rejected everything out of hand as rubbish beneath contempt except my Renaissance bronze of San Sebastian which he started to polish with the ball of his hand, saying it had silver in it and would brighten with this treatment. He was very agreeable and gracious, but does not put one at ease. I told Jane I was terrified of him and she said, 'Don't let him know.' He is for ever instructing. I admire him more than anyone of my generation for his universal learning. Talking of modern art he said there was only one contemporary English portrait painter, Lawrence Gowing. I don't know how unbiased his judgements of modern art are. I suspect he only recommends artists who are among his circle of friends. We talked of Hampton Court. He agreed that the grisaille of the Pope being stoned must be Flemish, certainly northern and not Italian. When the Clarks left the three of us sank back exhausted by the tension and discussed him. We all agreed in giving him unqualified praise for mind and scholarship, and prose. Paz said he was not as great as T. S. Eliot who is creative, and K. is not creative. We agreed too that he lacked the fine human instincts that make people sociable and beloved. Clarissa, aged fifteen, who formerly was frightened of him, told us that having stayed with the Clarks over the weekend, all her fears fled. 'You need not speak to him,' she told A. confidently, 'I have breakfast with him and never address a word to him. He is very easy and mild'!

Wednesday, 8th June

A. and I lunched at Wilton's, fearfully expensive and very little to eat. Agreed not to go there again when hungry. I motored her to Shalford (Surrey) to look at the Mill House, a National Trust property which I had never seen before and do not wish to see again. Then to Polesden Lacey. Went to *Daphne Laureola*, a very good play with Edith Evans, whose performance was brilliant. A joy to listen to diction which is always clear as a bell. She is as trained as a circus horse. Dined excellently at the Savoy Grill and back to the Dorchester at 11 o'clock. On arrival A. spied her mother-in-law on the doorstep and with utmost presence of mind told me to go on while she jumped out. I asked the cabbie to drive to Chesterfield House. Got out and walked back to Dorchester.

Thursday, 9th June

Trooping of the Colour this morning. The whole of London's traffic disorganized. I had a terrible time getting a new ticket for A. back to Paris. By a stupid mistake I tore hers up thinking it was my old, used one.

I dined with Harold [Nicolson] at the Travellers'. Over a bottle of champagne I told him I needed his advice how best I could work half-time for the National Trust in order to spend the other half with A. in France. Harold mumbled that love was a wonderful thing which must not be thrown away. That was not much help. Then he rambled off in talk about Vita who is ill with a weak heart. Consequently I did not press my point, seeing that I would get no sympathy if I did. I had told A. I would ask Harold for his advice. I failed.

Friday, 10th June

A. has gone. For five weeks I shall not see her, and already the agony has begun. After committee meetings all day I went home to change for the opera. Jamesey, returned from France, came in to talk. His advice is that I should do all in my power to marry by letting A. divorce Anthony, if she wants to. He says it is middle-class to have financial scruples because she has money and I have none, and ridiculous to have religious scruples about divorce; also needless to have moral scruples about Anthony who is a thoroughly selfish, if charming, cad. At least his advice is considered and direct, if expedient. He took his bus conductor friend to France and is taking him to Norway. The friend loves women and treats James with goodnatured but rough bonhomie which J. likes. J.'s last remark to me as he jumped into a taxi cab was: 'I am having boxing lessons now.'

In the Kenneth Clarks' box at Covent Garden heard the last performance of *Tristan* with Flagstad as Isolde. She surpassed all criticism. Everyone I spoke to agreed that she is the greatest singer of our age. I was extremely moved throughout. In the box were Christabel Aberconway, Leigh Ashton, the Italian Ambassador and Duchess Gallarotti-Scotti. Drove back to dine at the Clarks' beautiful house and sat next to the Duchess and Yvonne Hamilton who spoke high-speed Italian across me.

Monday, 13th June

A. writes that Oggy Lynn, Paz and the Duff Coopers know all about us. What does it matter, she asks? So now this is general knowledge and she doesn't mind I shall take no pains to conceal it. Took the train to Windermere arriving at 5.30. Stayed the night with the Bruce Thompsons. They are dears, particularly Bruce, but by no means exciting.

Tuesday, 14th June

Bruce motored me to Town End, the little yeoman's home of the Brown family of Troutbeck. He has in his meticulous way tidied it up and made it very neat. It is open daily to the public. The house is pitch-dark and crammed with black varnished oak settles, chests and lace. Then to Hill Top, Beatrix Potter's house, filled to the brim with her things. I cannot help wondering whether the public will be interested in her 100 years hence. Then to Wray Castle, a fascinating, castellated 1840 structure which the National Trust has contemplated pulling down. It has some period charm and a pictorial quality and, although not architecturally important, should be spared. From a distance it is an ornament to the shores of Windermere.

At Ambleside I was handed over to Cuthbert Acland. I now like this severe, censorious man. He took me to Sizergh Castle where we were given luncheon and tea by the Hornyold-Stricklands. Both the Hornyold (he) and the Strickland (she) come of Papist families which survived the bad times, indeed since the Reformation, without a break. Very nice, solid, worthy people too. He may be a bit of a bore with his family pride and genealogy talk. This castle is nothing like so good as nearby Levens, but it is an historic place and worth holding. There is some indifferent furniture, but there are several pictures of interest, notably the Rigaud portraits of the Stuart family. There are Jacobite relics, including diamond earrings given to a Strickland by Charles II. After a deal of talk Mr Hornyold-Strickland agreed to supply in cash the endowment for which we asked. So it was a successful visit and worth my going all this way. Returned to Cubby Acland's charming little plain white house, set at the foot of a wild moor up which we walked among the curlews and sea-gulls and snipe. Smells of peat bog and heather in the nostrils. Distant fringe of the Lake mountains. I was much struck by the isolated, bachelorish charm of this little establishment, so stark and pretty inside. What a curious fellow he is: very intelligent and quick, with proud craggy features, and deep-set quizzical eyes of a romantic cast. Puritanical, and exuding continence. I took a sleeper back to London.

Wednesday, 15th June

Found my father at Thurloe Square, he having come to stay yesterday. He is a bit thinner but looks extremely fit and feels it, I am glad to say. But he still passes a little blood, which is a worry to him, and to me a horrid prognostication of his fate. He goes to Ascot every day. This evening I went to Jamesey's flat. His new friend, a house painter, was there, wearing a battle-dress and rather grubby. Has a nice open face and laughs in raucous guffaws. I think this sort of association pathetic. What can J. get from it beyond the one thing which is not dispensed because the boy likes girls? Paul Wallraf who walked away with me deplores it very much. He says J. is becoming amoral about money and borrows from his mother and poor friends what they cannot afford in order to make frequent trips abroad, taking friend. Silly business.

Thursday, 16th June

Rather unhappy because I cannot communicate with A. There is a strike in France of telephonists and post offices. So no letters or telegrams, and no talks.

At Batsford's Sam Carr told me they were sacking Charles Fry who has become quite impossible. Their American branch has suffered badly from him. I am not surprised. Yet I am sorry for this clever and deplorable man losing his livelihood in his middle age.

Motored to St John's, Jerusalem to meet the Gowers Committee whom Sir Stephen Tallents showed round and entertained to tea. I can't quite fathom what is in their minds. St John's is merely a pretty little house, readily lettable, without problems. Then I went to Stoneacre which does look rather startling, like an ice cream. We have had it whitewashed over the timbers. Even the mullions and window heads have been so treated which is going a bit too far.

Friday, 17th June

Jack Rathbone and Mark Ogilvie-Grant dined. Odd little party but Midi, whom I had asked, chucked. Jack determined to subdue any exalted sense of importance as the new Secretary of the National Trust, and succeeding well. I have never met a man more eager to please and be liked. If he only knew, he has no need to try so hard.

Sunday, 19th June

Carmen Gandarillas dined. Much bereaved and pathetically talking of Peter Derwent without cease. Dressed in deep black with her jet-black hair she looked beautiful as the picture of woe. The unfulfilled wife and widow, and yet neither.

James called once yesterday, and once today. Reiterated his advice of the other day – marry A. at once, *come* what may. He says I am blessed beyond my deserts, that my weakness is indecision; that few men are vouchsafed such an opportunity; that if I drift it will peter out, for that is the nature of things. Then I shall become a dreary old failure and he will wash his hands of me. A little nettled, I said that that would save me money.

Monday, 20th June

To the Tate Gallery and an hour's revel in the Vienna collections. The jewelled boxes, the rock crystals fascinate me. Jack Rathbone dined with the Hugh Daltons and delighted me by saying that Mrs Dalton read him an extract from my preface to *Adam* as an example of my 'intransigence'. I always hoped it would reach her eyes, the bloody woman. Reflecting upon James's words I feel how skunkish I am even contemplating disregard of the Church's rules. I who have always been a noisy partisan of Papistry and whose profoundest principle has been to uphold it against the devil and all his ways, Communism, puritanism, etc., etc., while overlooking those other little ways that seem to me unharmful and even pleasurable.

Harold Acton had a dinner party of twenty at the Ritz. I knew everyone present and hated every moment. Harold is the least vulgar man I know. But this cannot be said of some of our mutual friends. Often my loyalty is severely strained.

Tuesday, 21st June

Vita has asked me to stay at Sissinghurst on Wednesday of next week. John Wilton dined and was charming and percipient. He has lost that marmoreal cast of feature which no man preserves after reaching his quarter-century. He told me he had definitely bought Ditchley from the Trees and, when all was settled, intended to make it over to the National Trust. That would be splendid but I shall not believe it until it has happened having had other disappointments of this nature before. James says Princess Margaret is high-spirited to the verge of indiscretion. She mimics lord mayors welcoming her on platforms and crooners on the wireless, in fact anyone you care to mention. A considerable gift. She has a good singing voice. In size she is a midget but perfectly made. She inadvertently attracts all the young eligibles to her feet, which doesn't endear her to the girls.

Wednesday, 22nd June

Took a morning train to Nottingham. Looked at the classical castle built in 1674 by one of the Smythsons, and made notes. It is an interesting building outside. Then was driven by the Town Clerk's people to Rufford Abbey and conducted all round. It is deserted and depressing. I cannot call it a first-class building but it is better in the stone than the illustration. Inside deplorable apart from the twelfth-century undercroft. Nothing old left otherwise. It is suffering cruelly from dry rot to the extent that all the floors and the ground storey of the Stuart wing have had to be ripped up and the earth is showing through. The property has been bought by Harry Clifton who is now anxious to demolish it. It seems a pity to let it go, but no use can be found for it. Myles Hildyard met me and motored me to Clumber. We looked at Bodley's chapel, a veritable small cathedral, noble both in- and outside. Then to Welbeck. Then to Flintham to stay the night with his elderly parents. Flintham Hall, *c.* 1850, is a sort of Venetian classical. Myles loves it. He is the perfect squire in embryo, the cultivated countryman in the still living tradition of Gyles Isham and Wyndham Ketton-Cremer, versed in their counties' history and culture.

Thursday, 23rd June

A letter from A. saying she cannot make up her mind to divorce Anthony and that anyway she thinks we had better live apart lest I get tired of her. I? Does she mean lest she gets tired of me? This has depressed me somewhat. Dined at old Mrs Carnegie's in Lennox Gardens. I and Sir Francis Humphreys were the only men wearing black ties, all the others wearing white. Too ridiculous. Sat next Lady Humphreys, now an old lined woman but friendly, and Diane Maxwell. The whole performance was over by 10.30. There was no flourish to this tail-end of Edwardian Kensington entertainment, which there was the last time I dined with this splendid old lady. She is still upright but her rapid deer-like movements have degenerated into the gait of a stricken hind.

Friday, 24th June

Luncheon party at Sibyl Colefax's house. Wonderful food, but so wedged was I between Cynthia Jebb and Hamish Hamilton that I could scarcely raise the fork to my mouth. John Gielgud is very shy and retiring on these occasions, which is strange. He is very bald now. Told me he has long since given up trying to stop his hair from falling out, and is resigned.

Gerry Wellington called at Thurloe Square for tea and we motored off to Stratfield Saye. John Steegmann, author of that inimitable *Rule of Taste*, Rupert Gunnis and Esmond Burton staying, all of us enlisted as guides to the party of National Trust members visiting the house tomorrow.

Saturday, 25th June

Everything went well and fortunately no one misbehaved. Each one of us was posted in a different room. Gerry, quite ruthless, would not allow a moment's relief. We were coached what to say and he took infinite pains labelling the exhibits and providing a printed brochure. The usual ignorant, dreary lot of members came. After a high tea we were driven, the five of us, in G.'s tiny Morris (the Rolls being away having its door mended which Harold [Nicolson] smashed off its hinges the previous week, greatly to G.'s annoyance) to Bradfield School to see a performance of *Agamemnon* in Greek in the outdoor theatre. This theatre is a disused chalkpit converted. Stone seats *à la grecque*. Trees surrounding. Very picturesque. The boys performed extremely well and Clytemnestra brilliant. I think boys prefer melodrama to less emotional forms of acting. I was a bit bored at times, but the seat was too uncomfortable to allow dozing off. As the night drew on, so lights were turned on to the stage. The beauty of the setting, birds and doves cooing from the trees, the coloured togas, the chorus of boys declaiming, certainly made a picture. The Duke and Lord Montgomery were the guests of honour. They walked in with the headmaster, Hills, late of Eton. I sat immediately behind Montgomery, now a little bent man, with small, mean hatchet face like a weasel's. He has ugly hands with crooked, gnarled fingers. The knuckles nearest the fingertips stick out like twigs from oak branches. I hated his little brown bald skull a foot below me.

Sunday, 26th June

Went with Esmond Burton to Mass at Heckfield Park family chapel, the doors wide open, the misty heat sizzling pale blue outside, blackbirds singing crisp, dewy bars, the butler in the pantry next door clattering breakfast cups and silver spoons. This kind of Mass makes me feel devout. After luncheon Gerry took us in my car to Silchester. We scrambled about the walls for he wished to show me how well the Ministry of Works had repaired them by cementing the top courses on which the lichen and moss were happily growing. Reluctantly I had to admit the Ministry's successful treatment.

Lady Hudson and Lady Granville came to tea, and Lady G. suddenly developed St Vitus's dance and jangled her cup in her saucer, spilling scalding tea through a thin silk dress on to her knees, and smashing the saucer to smithereens. Gerry leapt up, seized the table upon which a few drops of the tea had sprinkled and rushed away with it to have the surface repolished. He made not one gesture of help or sympathy to poor Lady Granville who was in considerable pain and distress. Typical Gerry behaviour! Oh I do love him. He never lets one down. His patent anxieties about his possessions bring these catastrophes about. I enjoy teasing him in a subtle way. Oblique references to sex make him bridle with a nasty covert leer. Now that he is a duke he thinks it unbecoming to let himself go.

Motored to Wickhamford after 5. In Oxford stopped at Wadham Chapel to look at the glass which is signed and dated 1622: a wonderful chapel with Jacobean screen and this glass amazingly colourful and clear. At home found a cocktail party on the lawn – hellish. Mama talked of Alvilde. I showed her my photographs of her. She looked at them very attentively and pronounced A. beautiful, which she is.

Monday, 27th June

Very hot day indeed. Motored to Castle Bromwich. Rich warm smells of hay, eglantine and elder now in full flower looking like side plates. A completely rural drive. Spent several hours making a survey of the late seventeenth-century Hall and gardens which are under a covenant with the N. Trust. The garden temples and piers, etc. in a poor way. The sphinxes on the end garden piers are noble. In the house the stucco ceilings are in very deep relief. Stopped at Kenilworth Castle; little to see beyond Leicester's building of 1570–5 which has remains of two fireplaces of a classical type, high up in moulding Severn stone.

Wednesday, 29th June

Motored to Sissinghurst to stay the night with Vita. When I arrived she and Mrs Lindsay Drummond were drinking sherry in the long room. I told them the story of the tea disaster at Stratfield Saye which amused them very much. The garden here is almost blowzy with bloom – an incredible spectacle. Surely no other county in England but Kent can be so lush and rich. No wonder it is called the Garden of England. I asked

Vita why she liked the old-fashioned roses so much. She said because
they reminded her of Tudor heraldic roses and Caroline stump-work.
The Sissinghurst garden enchants because it is both formal and informal.
The straight paths lined with yew and the pleached lime alleys lead to
orchards, their fruit trees swathed in ramblers and eglantines.

She and I sat down to dinner at 8 o'clock. A cold meal with white wine
which we drank and drank until 12.20 when we left the table. Vita is
adorable. I love her romantic disposition, her southern lethargy conceal-
ing unfathomable passions, her slow movements of grave dignity, her
fund of human kindness, understanding and desire to disentangle other
people's perplexities for them. I love her deep plum voice and chortle.
We talked of love and religion. She told me that she learnt only at
twenty-five that her tastes were homosexual. It was sad that homosexual
lovers were considered by the world to be slightly comical. She is worried
about Ben's love for Carritt who doesn't reciprocate and is perpetually
unfaithful. As for my predicament her advice was to marry if I had the
chance. She protested that it was nonsense for the Catholic Church to
discountenance a Catholic marrying a divorced Protestant whose previous marriage it has not regarded as a sacrament. Was very emphatic on
this point. The memory of this evening will be ineradicable.

Thursday, 30th June

Motored to Smallhythe. The 'Trouts' as Vita calls them very old. Miss
Atwood wearing trousers, a tight little brimless cap, from which her
white, man-cropped hair obtrudes upon her cheeks, and a white coat like
a waiter's. Their little old Priest's House pretty, and untidy, reminds me of
Madame de Navarro's house in minute miniature, I mean as regards
ninetyish Bohemian flavour. Mrs Chaplin, the curatrix, is Ellen Terry's
niece, a very beautiful woman with grey hair.

This evening Barbara Moray took me to the Hugo Pitmans' lovely
house, 16 Cheyne Walk, where Rossetti lived. Inside it is like a country
house, so large and quiet and filled with splendid pictures by John, Tonks
and others of the early years of this century.

Friday, 1st July

At 9.30 picked up A. E. L. Parnis [Secretary of the Gowers Committee]
and Mr Ansell and motored to Hughenden where we were joined by
the rest of the Gowers Committee. They all liked Hughenden and
thought it well kept. Then to West Wycombe, rather shabby by contrast,
but Helen [Dashwood] very sweet to them after a sticky start. Then to
Hatchlands. At the end of this trip I was dead tired. Called on Midi and
dined with her. On arrival the place teeming with children. Midi seem-

ingly insensitive to their clamour which would get on my nerves after half a day.

Sunday, 3rd July

Extremely tired after my week of dashing around. Tonight I motored to Send to dine with Loelia [Westminster]. The Hofmannsthals there. Dinner talk was of the awful austerities forthcoming as the result of Cripps's speech this week – more tax on tobacco, and less petrol. Everyone says we are in for a bad economic crisis and that America is already undergoing a slump.

Tuesday, 5th July

To Doreen Baynes for a talk. When I told Eddy West that I considered her nearly a saint he laughed me to scorn. He said she used to lock her sister up in a cupboard when her friends came to the house because she was so ashamed of her. Indeed I do recall a luncheon guest before the war going to the lavatory in her house, finding the door unlocked and the sister on the seat, a pekinese on her lap, reading a novel. But I attributed this to the sister's intense shyness and reluctance to meet Doreen's friends. Doreen talked of love, of King Edward walking into Queen Alexandra's ladies' room and asking one of them to go to bed with him, like picking out a whore in a brothel. Doreen does get hold of the most improbable tales. She is extremely credulous.

Wednesday, 6th July

John Russell lunched. He has recovered his young Shelley looks and is handsome again; and more mature. He and his wife now live in Essex where they have a farm. I cannot envisage John milking cows or cleaning pig stys or spreading manure. It is splendid how this young man, the son of a bicycle shop proprietor, became rich and established at the age of twenty-three.

Mama came to stay and went out with Hugh Macdonell, in spite of her pious avowal. This clever man is tremendously dull. I dined with Mark Ogilvie-Grant, and took the Rosses to Kew. It is curious how every human being believes the set he moves among is superior to every other.

Thursday, 7th July

Had a drink or two of champagne at Diane's. She is always affectionate and always sparkling like a nymph by a fountain in a landscape by Lancret. Anthony Devas, a sympathetic man, looked out of place listening to Diane and Bridget discussing what they should wear at Mrs

Hulton's ball. Mama and I dined alone. She is exceedingly worried about my father, who is not well: haemorrhage and clots in his urine.

Friday, 8th July–10th July

Weekend with the Eshers at Iford [Manor, Wilts]. I motored Sibyl Colefax there. She never ceased chattering for one instant and I could barely hear a word for my car is so noisy. In bending down my ear to listen my head was well below the dashboard and windscreen, a hazardous operation. Eddy Sackville-West and Lady St Germans the other guests. Eddy says outspoken things in a way I do not always like, my reason probably being that what he says is usually true. Weather hot. The deep blue sky over Iford with its terraces and statuary allows one to imagine one is in Italy.

Wednesday, 13th July

Had a sebaceous cyst cut out of my ear. No pain at all, but this day ill with fits of unconsciousness. Stayed at home.

Thursday, 14th July

Better today, but not very well. I went to Paris this evening. A. met me. We dined at Jouy with Anthony.

Friday, 15th July

A. and I left Jouy at 9.30 and motored to Chalon-sur-Saône, staying at the Royal Hotel. After dinner we walked in the moonlight. On the bridge I made a confession which greatly disconcerted A. Slept in a large bed, if sleep is the right word, for some demon kicked a tin can in the street below our window all night long. En route we had stopped at Sens Cathedral with twelfth-century façade. A renaissance tomb with stars and lime leaves sprinkled over the canopy in carved stone. A large handsome rococo tomb to Louis XV's son buried here. Auxerre Cathedral very fine. Saulieu has remarkable Romanesque capitals.

Saturday, 16th July

Weather gets very hot indeed after Lyons. With the wonderful Roman triumphal arch at Orange Provence begins. I like to think the arch was expressly built by the Romans as the entry to the exquisite, mysterious South. A. drove nearly all the time, I only occasionally for her car is new, a Hillman. It has steering wheel gear change. A. is a fussing car owner who shouts directions all the time and gets rather impatient with me. In fact she is impatient with inefficiency, hesitancy and hopelessness, which are among my many failings. We arrived at the Riviera Hotel in Aix in time for the first of the Festival's concerts, chiefly Mozart given by Casadesus in the Bishop's Palace. The courtyard of the palace has been made into an open air theatre, the stage contrived by Cassandre. Pretty in a Rex Whistlerish way. An adjoining exhibition of his designs for the stage and dresses for the Don Giovanni opera. Casadesus, A. says, is the best Mozart player she has ever heard. Rory Cameron, George Chavchavadze and a large party all in rich, huge American limousines, with chauffeurs and valets, arrived from Paris last night. A. and I have adjoining rooms, a bathroom each. Rory guessed all and in fact everyone now knows. A. doesn't care at all. So why should I? The hotel very comfortable and food excellent.

Sunday, 17th July

Aix is a ravishing little town set like a jewel in the open country. It has rows of very old palaces in a sort of Florentine late Renaissance style, but with a character Provençal rather than provincial. The Cours Mirabeau is completely over-arched with planes which form a vault of shade. A. adores Provence and is determined to buy a house here or nearby, but I am a little depressed by this thought for I would prefer to live in Italy. Our idea is to live together, married or not, dependent upon whether she and Anthony divorce and upon money arrangements, for I could not have a job in England if we were married owing to her domicile abroad. That raises a major problem. This evening a Haydn concert in the Cathedral, we having first dined with Rory's party.

Monday, 18th July

I visit George Chavchavadze and Rory in the morning, they sharing a room, *faute de mieux* I gather. George was lying in bed having his toes pared by a valet and reading to me the whole of *The Young Visiters* amid shouts of laughter. He is such a sweet fellow, unchanged by opulence since his Kensington bedsitter days. We motored to St Cannat, lunched, and continued to Arles. Squinted at the Cathedral, the Roman theatre and amphitheatre, then drove through the Camargue looking for birds. Saw a roller which flies in a rolling motion and a bevy of white aigrets. Back to Aix to find Nancy Mitford and Mogens (pronounced *Moans*) Tvede, a Dane with whom she is staying in Marseilles, a friendly man. We went to *Don Giovanni*, beautifully performed in the courtyard of the Bishop's Palace. The Don a young baritone of twenty-two who really assumed wickedness. The stage effects deliberately contrived on a small scale in the eighteenth-century fashion. A blackbird accompanied the sopranos at the top of his darling voice. The louder they sang the louder he followed suit.

Tuesday, 19th July

Motored to the aqueduct of Roquefavour and lunched there. Then lay
in the sun a little beyond. A. is determined to make me brown and fatter,
for she says I am a white Gandhi-like skeleton, which must be very unbecoming.

Wednesday, 20th July

Motored through Marseilles to 157 Avenue de Montredon to spend the
day and bathe with Tvede and his wife Princess [Dolly] Radziwill, an old
witch, intelligent, witty and gossipy. Nancy very well and happy; her new
book just out. She told me she enjoyed life to distraction.

Thursday, 21st July

This morning stayed late in my room trying to burn myself for A.'s sake
at my window. I don't really like it. Sunbathing is a modern craze. The
Ancients would never have done it. At midday we met Mérode de
Guevara at a very bohemian cafe in Aix. We followed her in her jeep,
containing herself, daughter, friend, cook, dog, casks of wine, bread and
sundries, to her house. The road became so bad that we left our car in
the shade of a bush and climbed into Merode's jeep, I sitting over the
wheel, my legs in great danger of being amputated by passing rocks and
trees. We arrived at a barn-like structure up a hill. There under some
scruffy trees we ate a truly bohemian luncheon, the remains of our fish
being thrown to the cats and dogs hovering in droves. We left for Les
Baux, stopping at the Pont du Gard on the way, and staying at the
Beaumanière Hotel the most luxurious of all the hotels so far. The bill
for dinner came to over £5.

Friday, 22nd July

The drive from Les Baux to Saint-Rémy covers the most beautiful area
of Provence to my mind. It is low-lying and fertile, intensively cultivated.
It is partitioned into rectangular sections between high cypress hedges.
As we flash past in the car we see a peasant in blue trousers driving an
ox, then an old woman with wide straw hat tending a vine, then a
mahogany-brown body on a ladder mending a roof. The Roman mausoleum at Saint-Rémy, standing in a clearance of olives, must be the most
complete Roman monument in existence. Avignon disappointed me. It
is a poor version of Florence. Unsympathetic texture of stone, and architecture mediocre. The Cathedral has little to recommend it. A. is more
keen than ever to buy a house in these parts. She says she could not live
in Italy because of the Italians' cruelty to their animals. It is so frequently

the case that people who care so vehemently for animals do not care for humans. Both Chaplins and my mother are like this. We stayed the night at the Beau Rivage inn at Doudieu on the right bank of the rushing green Rhône – a quiet little place. But owing to relentless mosquitoes did not sleep a wink. We do not book rooms ahead. We just turn up and are never sent away.

Saturday, 23rd July

A very tiring day indeed. A. exhausted by sleepless night allowed me to drive most of the journey. The long straight roads and chequered light and shade under the plane trees have a mesmeric effect. Terribly hot driving. We covered nearly 300 miles and on arrival at Jouy for dinner I felt quite sick, to be revived by the flat champagne we drank. Then sat up late with Anthony discussing our affairs. It was settled that in September he and A. would consult a lawyer in London as to whether it would be advantageous for them to divorce, or have a legal separation. Anthony says he wants a job in London where Rosemary will be, but doesn't wish to marry her, or she him, which I doubt being true. A. does not necessarily wish to marry me but wants me to leave the Nat. Trust if they will not give me a half-time job. If they will, I can live half the year in England and half with her in Provence. She will definitely not surrender her French domicile. With this decision I sympathize. It is difficult for me to know what to do. I am in great confusion.

Monday, 25th July

I am back in the London office. Eardley dined and I told him all. He is so patient with me and listens to all my problems. We drove to Fulham at midnight, walked along the river and drank coca cola from a night shelter, which he considered very paintable. It was on wheels beside some bollards on the embankment. E., who is incurably romantic, said that he would chuck up Long Crichel and his perfect life there for love and give all he possessed to the loved one. And he would too. The heat in London is as oppressive as lead.

Tuesday, 26th July

Lunched with Lord and Lady Ilchester at their house in Montagu Square, filled with lovely and historic possessions from Holland House: portraits of Foxes, a lovely Hogarth group including Butcher Cumberland, paintings of all sorts, a commode by Cobb. Sat between Lady Ilchester and Mrs Kendrick, plain, Viennese wife of Kendrick of the British Museum, not a distinguished man in appearance. Eddie Marsh, Freda Lady Listowel and Mrs [Muriel] Warde present.

Raymond Mortimer and Paul Hyslop gave an evening party. The heat was so great that every time I turned my head I broke into a sweat. Drank lime juice to keep cool. Hundreds of people I knew as friends or acquaintances. Eventually I sat out on the roof talking to Paz Subercaseaux. David Carritt was trying unsuccessfully to vamp Garrett Moore when Joan came up to them quizzically. Carritt asked G., 'Who is that glamorous female?' 'My wife,' said Garrett.

Thursday, 28th July

Dined at Alan Lennox-Boyd's punctually at 8.30 to meet the Regent of Iraq and his new wife. They came at 9.15. Then dinner at separate tables. I hated the evening and talked to Gerald du Gouray and Alex Beattie and Svelode of Russia and Mamie Pavlovsky. The party did not break up till 1.30 so I was obliged to stay on, drinking more and more and getting more and more tired. Mamie resolutely refused to go on to a night club with the silly Iraquis, and I did too. They went to the Four Hundred and we stayed behind. Mrs Iraqui only interested in film stars, horses and night clubs, so I was not a great success with her. She is a pretty little thing, plastered with jewels. How people like Gerald can be bothered with them I don't understand. He dances attendance. For what reasons? He is *éminence grise*. Is he a spy, and if so, for whom?

Sunday, 31st July

I took Papa to Paddington station this morning. He had had no operation. They looked at his growth and cauterized it a little, although he declared they did not touch it for he felt no pain. The doctor told me there was nothing they could possibly do and that he might live eighteen months to two years at most. Dined with Ivy and Margaret. Ivy, talking of the uneducated English masses, said that hitherto England had come out on top because she had been pushed along by the educated few. Hence her success in the world. Now that there was open competition between nations England must go down owing to her standard of education being lower than that of every other European country. I agreed, adding that the situation seemed to me even more serious in that the educated few were being pushed around by the uneducated many.

A. keeps on writing me letters nobly offering to do anything I ask, even to live with me in England in spite of losing money. I am in a quandary. I dined with Burnet at St Paul's, Waldenbury, motoring there and back.

Friday, 5th August

Lunched with A. E. L. Parnis at La Coquille to meet the editor of *Vogue* who asks the favour of the National Trust to photograph women models in front of its country houses. Next to our table sat Herbert Morrison, napkin tucked under his chin, with two tarty elderly ladies on either side and a pot-bellied gentleman, all eating voraciously and drinking two sorts of wine.

Monday, 8th August

Lunched with Countess Borromeo who had lunched with me yesterday. The Italian Ambassador and Peter Tunnard the other guests.

At Mass yesterday in the Oratory, while kneeling before the Gospel at one of my favourite stances in the west transept, it came to me that of course God alone was worthwhile because enduring; that nothing human, animal or vegetable endures, neither love, sex, friendship, hatred, oneself, one's ideas, ideals, nor anything man-made, even by Pheidias, Michelangelo, Shakespeare or Mozart. Only God remains immutable, unchangeable. A very commonplace revelation certainly which dawned upon me extremely forcefully in a new, clear under-standing. Then I qualified the satisfaction the revelation gave me by asking myself if God was not merely a fiction, made by each man in his own image. I decided perhaps not, because in thinking of, or wor-shipping God I do not picture him as possessing all the particular virtues which I venerate. Instead I purposely keep him rather vague and woolly, wholly beneficent, perfect certainly, and of course omnipotent. I don't investigate his ingredients. I don't inquire of myself if he is handsome, ugly, has a sense of fun (this would be a sur-prise), is gloomy, likes art or horse racing, is normal or queer, nice or nasty. In fact I can't believe in a personal God the Father. I do believe in the divinity of Christ, a human being wholly possessed of God. Thus I accept the Father and Son. The Holy Ghost perplexes me. Must get to grips with, and the Logos.

I have just finished Ivy's book [*Two Worlds and their Ways*]. Now this novel really is worthwhile, is literature after the tosh some of our friends write, for which they receive acclaim. Yet it will never be popular.

Tuesday, 9th August

Motored to Stratfield Saye and took Gerry Wellington to Selborne Hill. Getting into the car I fell over the bumper and badly cut and bruised my leg and hand. All Gerry said was, 'Some people make a terrible fuss over a scratch. Now the other day I fell, cut my head open to the skull, bled, was dreadfully messed about, and never turned a hair.' Neither had I turned much of a hair, nor uttered one word. I merely sucked the wound in my hand and limped. G. was very good at Selborne though ducal with the local people. He came to an instantaneous decision about the watch-tower, dismissing the design they proudly showed him with the wave of a hand. I lunched at Stratfield Saye with him. In the afternoon we went round the disused bedrooms of the house. He showed me the Great Duke's Garter robes unpacked for the first time since his death and in perfect preservation, even the long brown curl with the wigmaker's name attached to the label. Gerry held up the Great Duke's underpants to the light, looked intently at the fork and said solemnly, 'I am glad to see no signs of sweat – or anything else,' as though this were occasion for personal congratulation.

On returning to London I called at Bramshill. Ronnie Brocket was away but his daughter aged eleven, a fat little dumpling, showed me round. A disappointing house because too much restored, too stockbrokery. No antique spirit left; no good furniture. Bad taste pile carpets and curtains. The long gallery with dappled panelling is the only good room left. The garden done in poor taste, inappropriate Italian well-heads and urns introduced, and looking forlorn and homesick for Italy. Not so long ago this great house was shabby and romantic, with its continuity unbroken since James I's reign and the breath of hereditary lunacy still heavy on the stagnant air.

Wednesday, 10th August

Dined at Colin Agnew's. Bogey Harris there, talking of Edwardian days, said that when he stayed at a great house he always took in addition to his valet, a man to shave him and do nothing else. He and Colin told me Berenson was an old pansy in spite of kissing in the garden every pretty woman who came to the place.

Thursday, 11th August

Tom Driberg, reeking of a very adhesive scent, called to tell me he must sell Bradwell, his eighteenth-century villa in Essex, which he had left by will to the National Trust. Dined alone with Jack Rathbone. Before and after dinner Raymond Mortimer, Paul Hyslop and Desmond Shawe-Taylor came in. A good deal of puppyish embracing which I take in good part, but don't really care for. Like Berenson I prefer to kiss women and even in amity or affection don't relish kissing men as a form of salutation, though it is becoming common. The embracing of women has even got out of hand. Once you give way you can never stop it. And there are times when I sense that women friends, however intimate, are not in the mood to be mauled. Nor can one always be in the mood to maul them, poor things.

Friday, 12th August

Drove away at 11 o'clock to the west. In a bad, bad mood, feeling ill and miserable. Called at Longford Castle. Lord Radnor conducted me round the grounds and principal rooms of the house. This house is interesting on account of its triangular plan, a Tudor conceit. Salvin's alterations did not improve its beauty. He added too many towers and turrets. They began in the nineteenth century to turn it into a hexagon but got nowhere beyond one extra round tower and one square tower. The three inner turrets that figure in Thorpe's drawing survive. The main elevation was rebuilt in three parts, the upper recessed. I wonder if Smythson had a hand in it after Wardour and before Wollaton.

Called on a man Tibbits in the grounds of Wilton to talk about his house at Warwick. Then motored to Iford to stay with the Eshers.

Saturday, 13th August

We drove in slow stages to Attingham. My car was simply packed with the Eshers' luggage, he squashed in the back seat, she in front with me. We stopped at Gloucester, lunching vilely at the New Inn. Visited the Cathedral and I showed them Edward II's tomb and Duke Robert of Normandy's which I think particularly impressive because of its simplicity; the crossed Crusader leg and pointed toe in a recumbent ballet dancer's pose. The marvellous cloisters too we saw, deprecating the opaque glass in the walk lights. We stopped at Tewkesbury to look at the Abbey and canopied tombs. A pretty wedding was in progress, the bride and groom coming out into the full sunlight. Then Worcester Cathedral, King John's tomb, the Cathedral so grossly over-restored. These three cities horribly crowded with people and cars. One couldn't put a pin between them. We turned off the main road, proceeding via Stourport and Ribbesford to show them the house, and glanced at Bewdley. Dined at Lady Berwick's. Charlie Brocklehurst there. Delicious dinner with champagne from her cellar, the Eshers drinking nothing. Lady B.'s sighs and tragedy queen gestures irritated him, and in consequence he talked to me on his other side throughout the meal, which was rather rude.

During the drive I told him that I wanted to retire from the Trust, or work part-time. This announcement caused quite extraordinary concern. He said that nobody else could do my job but me, whereas hundreds of people could write books better than me. I said yes, I was sure of that, but my health was not good and I was tired. His last comment was, 'Well, we must find you a very rich deputy,' presumably so that he needn't be paid anything. Alvilde's fortieth birthday and she away from Jouy, somewhere in mid-France, I don't know where. Oh, lack-a-day.

Sunday, 14th August

Rather a ghastly day motoring Lord Esher round the estate and showing him the house. In the afternoon the opening ceremony took place and he delivered the speech I had drafted for him. Of course he altered and embellished it so that it turned out inimitably his. Tiring, hanging about, talking to people unknown. I left at 5.30 and arrived at Wickhamford at 7.30. Found my mother in the kitchen worn to death and my father looking, at first sight, well. But his haemorrhage worse than ever. In fact he is not at all well. He is always languid, gets up late, goes to bed at 5.30 and when up lies on his sofa. I saw his doctor who is much worried; gives him six months at most and told me he is now probably dying.

Monday, 15th August

Mama terribly worried. It is awful leaving her in this predicament. I had to tell her that everything depended upon her. Until he becomes bedridden I don't think we should tell her the truth, or go there too often, or do anything to arouse suspicion. Haines [the old chauffeur] took me aside this morning to say he was certain Papa is failing and moved me greatly by adding that he could think of little else. 'When he does not come to talk to me in the morning then I knows how ill he is.' I left exceedingly depressed for Bath, calling for Eardley who was with his mother in a nursing home. We motored to Wells, lunched there and visited the Cathedral. Early English is not my favourite style. Arrived at Arlington Court at dinnertime. A most glorious drive, the fields peopled with corn stooks. We stay till Friday at the Lodge with Woodrow, the clerk of works. Ensuing days with Eardley very happy, we working like blacks arranging Miss Chichester's collection of ships as best we can. The ship expert from Greenwich Maritime Museum, Mace; the pewter expert, Michaelis; the agent, Reeks, all came over at different times. Only one letter from A. has followed me. This house is awful outside but inside there are four very pretty 1825 rooms. These, alas, we cannot arrange as furnished but must cram with ships and show-cases, save one exquisite little boudoir. There we shall put all the china, of which some is good. The boudoir has beautiful yellow curtains and the walls are hung with rose silk.

One evening we called at East Down Manor a mile away belonging to an old family called Pyne. An enchanting Queen Anne House. Several nice rooms with coved ceilings, panelling and watercolours by W. H. Pyne, founder of the Watercolour Society in 1804. I have a tiny picture by him, of peasants round a camp fire.

Saturday, 20th August

At 6 o'clock went to Carmen Gandarillas's house to meet Jamesey who is broken-hearted, Dame Una [Pope-Hennessy] having died. James admirably brave and sensible. He says his mother had a fulfilled life, had written many good books and several first-rate ones. More important than these were her astringent mind and capacious intellect. She was one of the most important women of her day. I told him she was the best debunker of the second-rate. On Tuesday evening she was remarkably collected, and seemed filled with renewed energy. She gave him detailed instructions how he was to finish her book on Lamartine and how to put her collated notes together. Having settled these and other matters she announced that she was going to die the following afternoon. But at 7 o'clock the following morning she failed and J. said the ten minutes of her death were an experience he would never free his memory from. It was awful. He never thought such a noise could be emitted from a human frame. Her face became a skull with a veil of torment drawn across it. She was unrecognizable except for her hair. He held both her hands and tried to help her to die. Meanwhile she was kept conscious while extreme unction was administered by a clumsy, fumbling priest. Otherwise there was nothing terrifying about her death, James said. What he described sounds terrifying enough to me. He oversaw everything, dressed her head with her favourite lace veil and surrounded her with piles of all the books she had written. Then he broke down utterly. Poor James, as sensitive as a film on which every impression is registered. John returned too late, and James is glad he did not have to witness what he did.

Monday, 22nd August

Carmen took me to Dame Una's Requiem Mass in the little chapel of Saints John and Elizabeth. Not many people there, and it was extremely hot. James and John in dignified distress. I sat next to Rose Macaulay who looked terribly thin and unhappy The old nanny sat at the back and looked broken and ill. Her poor old hunched shoulders, worn navy blue coat and skirt and frozen grief very poignant. I shall not quickly forget the spectacle. A sight to rend the heart-strings.

Tuesday, 23rd August

I motored to Bexleyheath for an interview with the town clerk and several councillors, all extremely amiable, sensible and conscientious. They wish to vest Hall Place in the Trust if we can help them to raise the money for upkeep. Ivan Hills, our nice agent, and I went to the house later. It is in far worse state than it was in 1938 when Archie Gordon took me to see it. But it is very fine, set in a beautiful old walled garden and enclosed by green fields. It might be in the depth of the country instead of the middle of suburbia. I drove to Midi's for dinner. Stopped en route to look at Nonesuch House. Well kept by the Ewell Council, and now a show place. Gardens not urbanized. There are no disfiguring notices, no wire litter-baskets. The house was shut. It is not the least like what one pictures the famous Nonesuch Palace which Henry VIII built. It is a plain neo-Gothick, cement-rendered edifice. In discussing my problems Midi declined to give advice. She has never met A. She merely said, 'You have to bear in mind that you may be sacrificing your country, your religion, your career and your independence.' That was food enough for thought.

Monday, 19th September

I got back from my three weeks' holiday in Italy today. During this time I did not keep my day-to-day diary, and I have now little doubt it is high time I stopped it altogether. Anyway, a diary of travel to the continent is of little interest unless it is a learned disquisition on the arts and manners, containing profound and stimulating thoughts. Nevertheless . . .

On the 26th August I flew to Paris (this sounds as if I am contradicting the gist of my previous paragraph), stayed that night at Jouy and next day motored alone with Alvilde in her new car, a Plymouth, which is a treat to drive and runs smoothly like the wind after my lumbering old Rolls. We stayed the night at the Grand Hotel, Nancy, that wonderful city. We wandered in the *place* and down the street leading to the elegant palace by Emanuel Héré. Indeed the architecture here is superbly elegant. Elegance may not be the foremost quality of great architecture, yet no country in the west has eclipsed the French manifestation. The ironwork by Jean Lamour is grander and more elaborate by far than Tijou's at Hampton Court. Next day we stayed in Zurich at the Belle Rive au Lac, clean and well-appointed after the French hotels we experienced. On the 29th we reached San Vigilio on Lake Garda, staying at the Locanda, picturesquely situated on a small quay projecting into the lake, and run by Walshe, an old English horror who is the best cook on the south side of the Alps. Mosquitoes, however, were appalling and the rooms so hot that we were only free from torment when bathing. So we soon moved to the Ermitagio, an annexe away from the lake. Some embarrassment caused by Sir Eric de Normann and wife staying. He is head of the Ministry of Works and knows me. Since A. and I were sharing a room we had to be on our guard and pretend we were not together.

Thereafter Verona (the thirteenth-century statue of the black Bishop

San Zeno 'che ride', with face of radiant benignity), Milan (while A. shopped I visited San Satiro baptistery – life-size medallion heads in bronze). On the 7th to Venice, staying at the Danieli (two rooms with a bathroom between). Weather here cooler. Too many English people about. To my amazement Cyril Connolly meeting us in the Piazza solemnly congratulated A. on becoming a viscountess on the death of her father-in-law. He should have known better. K. Clark accompanied us one day to Padua, conducting us to his chosen monuments. A signal honour. Bergamo and Vicenza visited. At the former the intarsia choir stalls in the presbytery of S. Maria Maggiore of Old Testament scenes to the designs of Lorenzo Lotto, about the loveliest things seen this visit. In the latter city the streets are more crammed with masterpieces and less messed about than those of any other I can think of. As for the Palladian palaces words are superfluous. In Venice we visited all the architect's churches with Hiram Winterbottom, a great Palladio enthusiast.

We lunched one day with Bertie Lansberg at the Villa Malcontenta. I was disappointed. The elevations are grim and that not facing the Brenta positively ugly. The planning most ingenious, for the rooms fit skilfully one above the other, though of varying heights. The lack of a staircase is conspicuous. The same afternoon we motored to the Villa Maser which is over-restored. The church is exquisite. On our return to France we stayed a night at Vicenza to see the exhibition of Palladio drawings in the Palazzo Chiericati. We also visited the Villa Capra which eclipses all the Palladio villas I have so far seen. The lesser rooms like satellites revolving round the great sun of the central domed hall are all pretty. Even so the quality of the interior decoration is clumsy compared to that of Chiswick, when looked into closely. We were shown the kitchen by a charming, handsome son of the house, Count Valmarana, aged about twenty. It was whizzing with peasant women, with scarves over their heads, singing, and scouring pots and pans.

Our Italian tour was punctuated by some unforgettable little scenes and incidents that make me love Italy. 1. The small urchins, to one of whom, the leader, we gave a few lire for guarding the car while we visited the Villa Capra, waving and cheering us as we drove away. 2. After horrible difficulties in the garage in Venice, when we were driven to exasperation, the lift boy kept lighting Hiram's cigarette which for some reason refused to take flame, while bubbling with laughter. 3. Three extremely well-bred old ladies drifting in a superbly groomed gondola to the steps of the Danieli and being helped to land by a pair of gorgeously liveried gondoliers. 4. At a restaurant a mother and daughter licking their handkerchiefs and scrubbing with all their might the lapel of a man's coat which had been stained by food. 5. Women and men with their hands on St Anthony's tomb in Padua cathedral, wishing, as they prayed with the utmost fervour and faith, for what? A new pair of shoes? A new carpet sweeper? Renewed faith? Or new lovers? 6. The night on Lake Garda when I left A. in the garden in anger, and walked by myself under the moon along the shore, and sat on the shingle hoping for help from the lapping waves. When I returned A. was in tears. I was all penitence. I was forgiven. The relief and bliss ineffable. Perhaps not concerned with Italy, and could have happened anywhere else. But did happen in Italy and will always be registered with it.

Now my relations with A. have entered a new phase, undergone a sea change from the first fine careless raptures into something certainly richer and possibly stranger.

Tuesday, 20th September

A. and I returned by the ferry boat on Sunday night, reaching London at 9.30 yesterday. I am glad to be out of France. I hate the beastly country and its ferocious, mean, cruel inhabitants. I lunched with A. today. This evening she left for Scotland with Anthony and her mother-in-law to attend Lord Chaplin's memorial service at Dornoch. A. did not telephone me before leaving so at 6.55 I scribbled a note, hailed a cab, rushed to Euston station and gave a porter half a crown to deliver it in the two minutes before the train left.

Wednesday, 21st September

Alec Penrose lunched to discuss how we could save Holkham now Lord Leicester had died. We concocted plans for him to put to the new peer. At 4 o'clock I trained to Manchester and stayed the night with Dick and Elaine at Park Cottage. We deliberated how best to tell Mama the truth about Papa's illness and agreed that on the next occasion when he was taken worse whichever one of us was present should tell her, with Astley the doctor present. D. and E. are devoted to each other. Their little house is bright and comfortable and they are, I believe, perfectly happy. But oh! what a district of solid rain like stair rods, black tearing clouds across the blacker moors and scarlet cottages, and tall chimneys like prison warders at every corner one tries to escape from.

Thursday, 22nd September

To Lyme Park this morning with Charlie Brocklehurst. Back to London and joined Bridget [Parsons], Lady de Vesci, the Dorias, and Orietta Borromeo at the musical comedy, *Tough at the Top*. Dined at Bridget's afterwards.

Friday, 23rd September

Lunched A. and Anthony and Mr Harry Batsford, to whom I introduced Anthony, and upon whom Anthony exercised all his charm. We want him to write a book on reptiles for Batsford's. On leaving I walked with Anthony who said he could not think why I hesitated to live permanently with A. A. tells me that Anthony says to her she is a fool to be cross with me. Poor A., it is as much my fault as hers. I should be stronger and capable of helping her instead of throwing up my hands in despair and running away. She dined with me at Thurloe Square and is very sad indeed that we separate tomorrow.

Saturday, 24th September

Lunched with A. I believe and trust I left her happy. I motor home this afternoon and send her a devoted telegram from Oxford. Call upon Deenie at Stow-on-the-Wold and talk about my father. She wants him to have a nurse in order to spare my mother, but I am against that. Twenty nurses would not spare her and it is better for her to be occupied now she is so wretched. She would be more wretched if she had nothing to do but be irritated by the nurses. However the situation at Wickhamford is very sad. Papa remarkably cheerful and getting up again after a strangulated hernia trouble of a fortnight ago. Yet he passes water every hour, some days and nights every quarter of an hour, and during the nights Mama wakes too. To pass water (terrible doctors' phrase) gives him much pain. After a talk to Astley on Sunday morning it became clear to me that she should now be told the truth. It fell to me to tell her.

I took her for a stroll along 'the donkey patch' in the sun and said that Astley took the gravest view and wished to speak to us both at a convenient moment. Thus I tried to break the news to her gradually. She said at once that she knew what it was to be and did not wish to be told by the doctor. She wanted him to tell me so that I could pass it on to her. Her courage was wonderful. She did not weep. At one moment only I thought she might break down when she said she could not imagine life without him after forty-five years. (I marvelled that she seemed to have forgotten those long wretched years when they were on the worst possible terms. God is sometimes merciful to the afflicted.) Then she pulled herself together and said he must have no suspicions of what we knew. While we were talking old Mason called to speak to her from the road. She called back to him cheerfully, answering his inquiries about Papa as though nothing were the matter. In the house Papa was up and dressed and she joined him and laughed and joked with him. When I confirmed later in the day that Astley pronounced the bladder growth to be malig-

nant and gave him three months to live at longest she took it calmly. How
I admired her.

Monday morning I left Wickhamford for Bath, collected Eardley in my
car and drove to Arlington Court, where we worked hard all the week
sorting the desultory collections. We stayed at the Lyndale Hotel,
Lynmouth. Weather divinely beautiful. Autumnal sun every day. E. and I
made a great discovery. One morning we spent clearing away old rubbish.
There were a few broken frames, fragments of glass and trashy Pears Annual
illustrations in a dusty heap on top of a wardrobe in the housemaid's pantry.
We debated whether to tell Newman, the custodian, to throw away the
lot; then decided we might as well complete the work ourselves. So I
climbed on to a chair and handed the junk down to Eardley. I held out one
picture and said, 'I do believe this is the reproduction of a Blake drawing.'
It proved to be better than that; a large watercolour drawing, typical Old
Testament scene, signed and dated 1821. The frame was contemporary and
the name of Blake's framer, Linnell, known to Eardley, written on the back
in the handwriting of Miss Chichester's grandfather, Colonel Chichester,
the builder of Arlington Court. Furthermore when we took the back off
some newspaper stuffing was dated 1820.

In Lynmouth we went to the *Fallen Idol*, that splendid film I always
wished to see but missed in London, with Ralph Richardson and the
little French boy. It was excellent and the child most moving. He never
cried once; that is why he was so moving.

On our return on Saturday I bought at Porlock in an antique shop for
£2 a small portrait of a man on a panel by Samuel Lawrence, quite a good
bargain.

Jamesey amused me by telephoning: 'You know that picture of an
eighteenth-century house which I am leaving to you in my will?' 'Yes,'
I answered, 'I can't wait for it.' 'Well, I am ringing you up to say that I
have sold it and it is in Appleby's shop window if you want to buy it.'

Ivy and Margaret lunched with me in the Cromwell Road and later
Margaret returned me the second half of my book with her corrections.
Prudence [my niece] came at teatime from Paris to stay. I took her for a
walk in the Park and tried to show her buildings of interest and tell her
the history of Hyde Park. But she was not interested and is, I fear, an
incurious girl. 'Heavy,' Alvilde calls her. She may improve, but I like children to ask questions. Then I met A. and Anthony on the Golden Arrow
and brought her to dine here.

Monday, 3rd October

Went this evening to see Dr Spira, the Chaplins' doctor, at their urgent request. He was certain my trouble was the old complaint persisting, and the sugar content disability was nonsense. He said it was very wrong that I should be in pain part of every day and this must be stopped. He made me write to Pierre Lansel before he would consider taking me in hand. This I did, and of course Pierre will be furious. So I have certainly lost him as my doctor without definitely gaining a new one.

Tuesday, 4th October

Went to see a Miss Sketchley in Kensington who offers to leave some decent pieces of family furniture to the Trust, not museum stuff but the sort to be found on the second bedroom floor of a grand country house. She lives on the ground floor of a beastly house in Baron's Court, her sister having just died. She is sad, old, lonely and resigned in a bitter way. What indeed is the purpose of life for someone like this? My heart bled.

A. and I went to the Cimarosa opera *Il Matrimonio Segreto*. Very pretty Mozartian music never rising to great heights, and repetitive.

Inspired by A. I have begun the study of wild flowers. Having acquired a few books from Barnstaple I picked what flowers I could from the roadside on Salisbury plain and looked them up on my return. This is a new fascination which promises to be more dangerous than architecture in so far as turning the eye from the wheel is concerned. How shocking that I, country-bred, never learned about wild flowers in childhood.

Margaret Jourdain's corrections of my book have depressed me. I agree with nearly all of them. Nonetheless they shake my unstable confidence. She has rightly suggested my cutting out certain passages that are irrelevant, but she also suggests cutting out the little light touches which I hoped would enliven the book. After all, her own books are deadly dull.

No true and enduring love affair ever runs entirely smoothly. How can two individuals, composed of different and often warring elements, who decide to coalesce, not clash fairly frequently? The triumph of love consists, not in winning, but enduring. Marriage is a very unnatural state. But then so are logic and art unnatural. All the most worthwhile and glorious things achieved by mankind are unnatural. To be natural is to be animal. Only fly-by-night lovers may expect to have no ups and downs – for six weeks at most. Jamie Caffery, a Papist, once told me that in the eyes of the Church marriage with a divorced person was a worse sin than adultery. For adultery has no permanent purpose whereas the other means permanent excommunication, a state one cannot but shudder at being put into. Bosh, I am inclined to think.

Thursday, 6th October

A. and I went to a bad performance of *The Magic Flute* at Covent Garden; but what heavenly, transporting music.

Saturday, 8th October

All my meals are with A. when I am in London. Today I motored to Ascott, Leighton Buzzard. This is another case of a rich man's collection of treasures housed in an unworthy building – half-timber of the 1870s – and set in poor surroundings. House and gardens spick and span. The owner, Mr Anthony de Rothschild, is a very nice man indeed, and so is his pretty wife a sweet woman (Colin Agnew told me that after their marriage she ran away but after much woe was received back magnanimously and rehabilitated). I arrived at midday and stayed till 5 o'clock. French furniture particularly good. Dutch paintings, Lawrence sketches, two full-length Gainsboroughs, one head and shoulder Gainsborough of a young man, a Lorenzo Lotto of a dark young man, two Rubenses, one of mother and child and one of Hélène Fourment, very seductive. A collection not to be sniffed at. It is sad that the rich so often have indifferent houses.

I dined with A. and stayed the night at Olga Lynn's flat which she has been lent.

Sunday, 9th October

I was amused and rather flattered that Anthony Chaplin telephoned asking me to ring up Rosemary Lyttelton on his behalf.

Tuesday, 11th October

Tonight Rose Macaulay dined, for Anthony particularly wished to meet her. She is to him a goddess. I invited Jamesey, thinking he would improve the party, but James talked incessant 'shop' to her and Anthony became more and more visibly annoyed. However after dinner he found that she knew about green tree frogs and was delighted. Talking of religion, Rose said she was an Anglo-Agnostic, explaining that she had great affection for the Church of England, in which faith she had been brought up, yet was a non-believer.

Wednesday, 12th October

At the Historic Buildings Committee there was much excitement over the Blake drawing discovery. If either of us had an exclusive claim to the discovery it was Eardley. Leigh Ashton was anxious to have the drawing for the V & A. We said *no* to this; it must stay at Arlington Court. On the other hand we promised to let him have the four Beauvais tapestry panels of the Four Continents from Arlington Court for Osterley. A very good idea.

Friday, 14th October

A. and I went to Marlow, staying at the Compleat Angler. Over dinner I said I saw no prospect whatever of my being able to leave England and the National Trust for half the year. The Trust could not be expected to approve such an arrangement. I am rather tormented by this problem.

Monday, 17th October

Dick telephoned from Wickhamford that they were bringing Papa up by car to the nursing home tomorrow, Mama to stay with me, Dick and Elaine in Ronald Fleming's flat.

After dinner with A. and me at the Allies Club William McKie and Nadia Boulanger played the organ in Westminster Abbey. The Abbey incredibly romantic lit only by the organ loft lamp, deserted by the thousand pairs of feet of daytime, full of deep shadows and of ghosts of the great and famous, and now possessed by us two; such a rare and extraordinary privilege, as A. and I wandered, to the strains of Bach, among the royal tombs.

Tuesday, 18th October

A. left this morning. My family arrived after a terrible journey, Papa suffering agonies. I had a glimpse of him lying in bed at the nursing home looking like a corpse. To me it is inconceivable that he can survive another operation, now fixed for Friday. This prolongation of life is a cruel and unnecessary business.

Wednesday, 19th October

I have put off my plans for going away this week. Audrey has come up from the country to join us. We all sit around doing and saying nothing but the same fatuous things. It is a great strain. It is terrible how far I feel from them all. A bad day, this. Dentist in the morning. Luckily the X-ray shows no abscesses so again I am reprieved from having several teeth out. In the afternoon an X-ray at St Thomas's Hospital of my back. Apparently nothing is wrong with the spine, but Spira, the doctor, says I must always take Luminal, the very drug that Lansel spent years gradually reducing until he put me on to something more innocuous. Worst of all Margaret Jourdain returned the first part of my book with a letter that has properly put me in my place. She says that the book does not hang together, a third of it must be cut, and my style is atrocious. In short I am flattened. Can she be quite right, I ask myself?

I am not being as nice to Mama as I should be, and it is wicked to allow her to get on my nerves at a time like this when she is so worried. Her love for my father nowadays is absolutely wholehearted and unreserved.

Thursday, 20th October

I say to myself this morning that all this moaning and groaning and self-pity must cease instantly. Circumstances may be bad at the moment but the world is not wholly unendurable, and the sun is shining. Then I meet poor Keith Miller-Jones at Brooks's who tells me his engagement is not going well. *She* is very emotional and worried that she cannot reciprocate his passion for her. She also has grave misgivings about marrying a third time; and besides is subject to recurrent depressions. Oh Lord! I was very sympathetic with Keith and inwardly cheered that others have their ups and downs as well as myself. *Schadenfreude* again. We went to an exhibition of Adrian Ryan, a young painter-protégé of Eardley, his medium in the Van Gogh manner, very forceful and sharp; also to see pictures at the Redfern Gallery by Tom Carr in a soft Corot style, which pleased me more. On parting I said to Keith, 'Do you now feel better?' 'Not much,' he said. The truth is that love makes people lunatic. No man or woman ought to be appointed to any position of authority if he or she is in love. Just imagine in time of great crisis, or war, a Prime Minister being head over heels in love.★

I asked Jack Rathbone (who is always sympathetic and patient with his maddening subordinates) over a drink if he thought it feasible for me to have a half-time job with the National Trust. He strongly counselled me to wait until the Gowers Committee Report comes out at the end of the year, for it may affect the composition of the Nat. Trust and my job in particular.

I called at the nursing home in Queen's Gate at 7.10, ten minutes later than arranged. Went to Papa's room, he sitting up eating and very cross that I was late. He said he had seen enough people and I had better go back to the others in the flat. I felt like a whipped puppy and slunk away, tail between legs.

Friday, 21st October

Papa had his operation this evening and it passed successfully. We were all sitting round the tea table at no. 20 when Astley, the doctor, arrived long before we expected him. He told us the news for he had been in the theatre. Mama saw him through the window. There was an awful silence

---

★At the time of writing this I was unaware that during the First World War Asquith had been deeply in love with Venetia Stanley and Lloyd George with Frances Stevenson.

because we all feared his arrival so soon must mean that Papa had died under the anaesthetic. Dr Astley's kindness overwhelms us.

Monday, 24th October

I had the best of luncheons at the White Tower with Rose Macaulay and John Pope-Hennessy. They talked so learnedly of Latin medieval authors they had actually read, Josephus, Aeneas Silvius, etc. that I felt very ignorant. John spoke indignantly about Bob Gathorne-Hardy's book on Logan Pearsall Smith which he considers scandalously depreciatory; and condescendingly about K. Clark's new book on landscape painting which, while admitting the excellent style, he thinks twists facts to bear out the author's preconceived theories on the progression of the subject throughout the ages. I have already read Bob's book about which I am inclined to agree with John, for it suggests that the author had a grievance against Logan. But I have assumed that K. Clark's book must be excellent for the likes of me and ordered it from Heywood Hill's shop at once. John approved the little Millais of Effie Gray which I brought with me and had just shown to Harry Leggatt. Having taken much trouble in consulting several experts I told Sir Ralph Millais it was not worth more than £200. He, very trusting, agreed to sell it to the National Trust for that sum. So I have purchased it for Wightwick Manor. Hope to God we haven't swindled the poor man.

Thursday, 27th October

I motored to Buscot. A most lovely autumnal day after violent storms and rain, yesterday being non-stop torrential. Along the road verges I noticed toad-flax, dandelions and vetch still in flower. Am glad to get away from no. 20 and poor Mama, whom I have told to stay on in my bedroom until the end of next week, if not longer. At close quarters she gets fearfully on my nerves. She is interested in nothing I say and her insincerity amounts to positive dishonesty and an inability to be straightforward and even truthful. Yet I am so deeply sorry for her and filled with admiration of her bravery. Why can't I be demonstrative? What a stinking beast I am.

I went round the Buscot rooms with an exclusive eye upon the pictures for the very tiresome chapter on the NT picture collections which I have been asked to write for A. Blunt's volume.* Gavin [Faringdon]'s pictures, as well as his Deepdene furniture, make a very fine collection indeed. Two Rembrandts and some rather boring Sir Joshuas were bought by the grandfather.

---

*The Nation's Pictures: A Guide to the Chief National Galleries of England, Scotland and Wales, edited by Anthony Blunt and Margaret Whinney, 1950.

Stayed last night with Ted Lister and talked long with him till late into the night about the future of Westwood. I think I convinced him that his best hope of preserving the place was in leaving it to the N. Trust with the expressed wish that his nephew might have the right to rent it. Ted is determined to do all he can to prevent the nephew selling a single stick of the furniture, even if he leaves the house to him out-right. The old man is well, less deaf and in good form. He sits huddled in his armchair before the stove in the dining-room downstairs, with one oil lamp, knitting in hand. He has just bought a new sheepdog puppy.

Today I went to Stourhead and made some notes on the pictures. This is a difficult task for me because I am an ignoramus about painting. Motored to Longbridge Deverill church looking for and finding Sir John Thynne [builder of Longleat]'s tomb slab with inscription, quoted by Hussey. But of course it was put up quite 100 years after his death, to judge by the design and lettering. So the wording, from which I deduced he was his own architect, is valueless. This shows the importance of seeing *everything* one is writing about for oneself.

Monday, 31st October

I am terribly disheartened about my new book. Am still carefully pruning and rewriting and improving (I hope), but realize that it is definitely bad – damn M. Jourdain – and there is no other word for it. If ever I write another I must on getting to the end, put it aside for two months at least, then re-read it with a fresh and highly critical eye. I think the failure of this Tudor book is depressing me more than Papa's illness, which is a wicked thing to say and a proof of irredeemable self-centredness. How, I ask myself, can a person honestly feel more concerned for others than himself? He may say he does, and may try hard to do so; he will certainly pretend that he does, but can he? Is it humanly possible? Superhumanly possible, yes. Subhumanly no. I am still subhuman.

Tuesday, 1st November (All Saints Day)

My poor mother. All her tiresomenesses are dissipated by her abundant sweetness and charm. I said goodbye to her for she is taking Papa home to Worcestershire in an ambulance on Friday. Doctors can do no more for him. The tumour in his bladder continues to discharge pus. This is a terrible disappointment to him and to her who realizes what it means. I would definitely do anything within my power and deprive myself of what I hold most dear (which is A.) if I could thus prolong his life free from pain and distress. But this is not saying that I would want to. One must be honest with oneself.

I took the 7 o'clock evening train to York, writing in the carriage. Was met by Christian Howard at York station and driven to Castle Howard. She is a plain-spoken, frank girl who has let her appearance go in favour of diocesan work. George is not back from Scotland. He does not live in the big house but in one half of the gate-house, rather uncomfortably and untidily. His wife is away in Scotland burying an aunt.

Wednesday, 2nd November (All Souls Day)

Whereas the Saints can look after themselves, the Souls need all the help we who are still on this earth can give them. Christian Howard motored me to York. I spent three-quarters of an hour in the Minster. Inside disappointing, a jumble of Gothic periods and too few monuments. Much of the famous glass is back, rearranged by the Dean in some sort of design. I am right in having written that English medieval glass lacks design and artistry, which the French can claim. It has splendid splashes of colour – I had forgotten how much bottle green and twilight violet. Before I had made any progress back came Miss Howard and bustled me off. One must not be hounded when sightseeing.

A filthy wet November day. George Howard arrived for luncheon. He is stout and uncouth; sometimes forthright to rudeness. Perhaps his heart is kind. How can one tell? He took me over Castle Howard, now empty, the school having gone. Its aspect is exceedingly forlorn. It is not in bad condition, but very unkempt. It looks sad with the dome and the best rooms burnt out, but there is enough space left for a country house these days in all conscience. The lack of symmetry in Castle Howard has always worried me. The sculpture of the stonework, cornices, columns, etc., is crisp. George intends to move himself into the East Wing and open the rest to the public. We drove to the Temple of the Four Winds, now in a state of dereliction, but a very elegant building, more Palladian than Baroque. The monopteral, Doric Mausoleum is a splendid affair and the bastioned retaining wall forms an impressively massive base. In fact it is a composition of grandeur and genius. We went into the vaults where are many gaping niches unused. No one buried there since the eighteenth century. George intends to be buried there, he told me. And so he should be for he will be the second creator, or more correctly the re-creator of Castle Howard. The rotunda chapel above is faultless. The quality of workmanship is far superior to Palladio's chapel at Maser or elsewhere in Venetia. The English Georgians were better craftsmen than Palladio's men. George much distressed because hooligans have thrown bricks through the windows, breaking panes of original glass. The Kentian reading-desks, the marble inlaid pavement are of superb quality. What a wonderful building. Its condition is better than the Temple's because its construction is more stalwart.

Today George motored me to East Riddlesden Hall where we met Cubby Acland. For I suppose the sixth time in my life I went round this depressing building in vain endeavour to improve its neglected condition. I was handed over to C. Acland who drove me to Gawthorpe Hall through an endless hedge of hideous industrialism. We arrived at 5 o'clock in the dark for tea and were greeted by pretty Lady Shuttleworth in the drawing-room, one of the best Elizabethan rooms I have ever been inside. Nice small wall panels with deep fields, an interior porch and really pretty ceiling of vine patterns, the bunches of grapes like fir cones in the round. It is a very cold house. Young Lord S. is a rather stiff, too serious, but extremely gallant young man who lost both legs in the war, and is filled with a sense of duty to the locality. He sits on committees, dispenses patronage and does what is required of him, yet speaks of the inhabitants of Burnley and the neighbouring towns as one would of Hottentots. I notice that this view is commonly held by England's aristocracy and I think they, the aristocracy, are right on the whole, although I must admit it is the unwise who reveal these sentiments in public. I am sure Lord S. never would.

Friday, 4th November

A horrid day up here of drizzle and smog, blackness and gloom. The ring of industrialism has to be penetrated to reach this property. When Gawthorpe is reached one feels hemmed in and isolated from the wide world. A drive and belt of smoke-ridden trees separate one side of the house from Padiham and Burnley. The other side faces a noble sweep of orange-green fields with pits and cranes on the skyline. The Shuttleworths fear that open-cast mining may be realized at any moment so as to make their continued residence at Gawthorpe impossible.

Gawthorpe is a charming house, not large but tall and compact, built by the Shuttleworths in 1605. It reminds me of Wootton Lodge in Staffordshire. Barry made alterations in 1849, heightened the central tower – now riddled with dry rot – and put a parapet round the house and added a porch and terrace. Barry's exterior alterations lend character and interest. His interior staircase is not so good, but the warm patterned wallpapers, the mahogany-topped baths are cosy and *gemütlich*. There are many family portraits and some very nice furniture. The house is the typical home of a distinguished long line of squires. Lord S. was not too pleased when I pointed out that he had dry rot in the tower. I meant to be helpful. He would have had reason to be annoyed if I said he had bad breath which, I feel sure, he hasn't.

The Shuttleworths left early next morning and I not till midday. I had the opportunity of a good pry around by myself when they had gone off in their beautiful Rolls with less beautiful baby boy and nurse.

Got back to London by dinnertime to find that Mama had left with Papa in the ambulance for Wickhamford. He managed the journey all right but was desperately tired. Alvilde arrived in London the day before. Tonight she sent Clarissa to dine with her grandmother. She and I went to the Greek restaurant.

Wednesday, 9th November

Alvilde left for Paris this morning. Every evening we met and dined and nearly every day lunched together. This visit was a great success. There were no crises or difficulties, and all was sunshine. I am happy and at ease. I left early this morning for Newport, Monmouthshire. Was met at the station by John Morgan flying his personal flag on the radiator of his motor, and driven to Tredegar. He has already become another Shuttleworth but absurdly pompous and puffed up with self-import-ance. Ridiculous as this may be he has a sense of duty, genuine, and his religion means everything to him. We spent the afternoon going round the house. Now *it* is important, and probably the best in Wales. Nevertheless I was a trifle disappointed by the coarse, unrefined quality of the craftsmanship. The famous wainscot is very rough indeed, notably the staircase. The red brick exterior is attractive, and so are the heraldic supporters of lion and unicorn in porous stone over the window pedi-ments. It is a great pity that the cupola and roof balustrade of this Restoration house are missing. The iron railing put round the roof during the war to prevent fire-watchers falling off is unsightly. Some of the contents are superb, notably the French furniture and in particular the Adam bureau-cum-harpsichord all in one, with a clock in the pedi-ment. John showed me the figures of his estimated income after he has paid death duties, which amount to 80 per cent. His gross income is £40,000. After paying tax it will be reduced to £3,700 and he cannot spend his capital because it is all in trust. Avis Gurney [his sister] came to stay in the evening, having travelled from Edinburgh. She is just as ugly to look upon as she was when a girl, but is very affected and amusing. One laughs with her a lot. Both siblings are devoted to Aunt Dorothy whom they call 'Ma'. I slept in the panelled room in the bed said to be Mary Queen of Scots', but I wonder. John is very dogmatic about his belongings and at the same time ignorant, like many owners. A sciolist no less. He told me that on clearing his cousin Evan's bedroom cupboard he came upon 'instruments of the most blood-curdling nature'. He took them gingerly between finger and thumb and threw them in the dustbin. I said that in doing this he gave the dustmen ample opportunity of circulating scandalous gossip about his family. John forebore to tell me what the 'instruments' were.

Thursday, 10th November

This fine morning we motored to Ruperra Castle which the Welsh want to buy from John as a memorial to Welshmen killed in the war and vest in the Nat. Trust. I could not see any point in it at all. The castle was burnt out during the war by British troops. From vestiges of remains it must have had rather nice Adam decoration. It is rendered all over with grey pebble-dash. The windows are nearly all nineteenth-century. There remains one Jacobean two-storeyed porch which is all right. Some unsightly outbuildings, the walled garden gone to seed and deer park to thistles and nettles.

When I left Avis kissed me most fondly, pressing me to stay with her in Edinburgh and go with her on a visit to Aunt Dorothy. She is a kind soul. She wears a turban on her head as if trying to resemble Lady Hester Stanhope. John motored me to Newport and got out of the car at the YMCA branch office which he is to open this afternoon. On his express orders the chauffeur immediately furled the flag on the radiator covering it with a leather sheath. He then drove me 100 yards to the station, to return to pick up his master and, presumably, unfurl the flag. I thought only Field Marshals indulged in this state and ceremony.

Got back in time to dine with the Aberconways in North Audley Street. Not fun, but stuffy. I sat between Lady Anderson and Lady Berwick. Sweet compliments were bandied between us three.

Friday, 11th November

All today meetings. I very irritable. Is it champagne of the previous evening and of the one before — a drink that disagrees with me horribly? Or my quandaries? Or just nerves and that accursed office? We had our annual meeting in the great hall of Lincoln's Inn. I went with Harold [Nicolson] to the Travellers' where he gave me a drink. About to leave the club we ran into Crawford who called out, 'Jim, I have something to say to you,' and spoke to me. I could not very well ignore my chairman when he called. Harold walked on to fetch a cab. When we were in it he said, 'You are such a dear and old friend and I always find the failings of my old friends invariable and endearing. You dawdle today in the same way you have always dawdled since I first met you.' Until he said this I never had the slightest idea that I was a dawdler at all.

Saturday, 12th November

Patrick Kinross dined. He is back from Cyprus, Turkey and Greece. He says Greece and the Greeks are heaven. They are warm-hearted, human and more intelligent than other Europeans. They are all sensual without being sentimental, and every Greek man is homosexual. They go to bed with a laugh just as they would sneeze and laugh. I said I would not care to go to bed with anyone who sneezed and laughed. Patrick in his funny pontifical manner which I love says that true love can only exist between man and woman, true sex between man and man; that women know and hate this without understanding it, just as the Ancient Greek women did. Accordingly they resent all men's relationships, fearing them to be such that they can never attain. I think this notion is probably far-fetched.

Sunday, 13th November

David Carritt dined with me at Brooks's and came back here afterwards. He is brilliant and sophisticated and not entirely without feelings or scruples, but nearly so. To me he is not an attractive being. I do not like that little pinched face, over-confident eye and bad complexion. He tells me he has quite broken with poor Ben [Nicolson] who behaved in a very hysterical fashion. Ben, he maintained, and I could not disagree with him, is immature and has no *savoir-faire*. In other respects he spoke nicely of Ben – of his innocence – for which I gave him marks. Carritt told me that he [Carritt] was entirely unemotional in all his relationships. I can well believe it.

Monday, 14th November

Dining with the Johnnie Churchills I noticed how Mary has J. firmly under her little thumb. He showed me after dinner the frieze on black Welsh slate of the Battle of Blenheim which he has just incised for his uncle Winston's ornamental temple at Chartwell. I thought it far better than any painting he has ever done and told him he had perhaps found his true medium. It is entirely linear. I am going to see it put up next week. He has decided to paint the figures, which I deprecate.

Tuesday, 15th November

Lunched with George Wingfield-Digby and wife, a Viennese. Robin Darwin, the other guest, said he was renting Coleshill from Captain Hill for his art school. George Digby told me he was treated like an outcast by his parents because he took up art, although he was quite good at most sports. Now he is the youngest keeper of a department at the Vict. and Alb. Museum.

Wednesday, 16th November

I had arranged to motor to Henham Hall, Suffolk, for the day with Rick [Stewart-Jones] and start at 8.30. I arrived at his house punctually and he was still in bed. So I drove off without him. At Regent's Park the fog was so thick that I turned back. Fog cleared. In the afternoon I went to Osterley. Was conducted to a turret room and presented with a key on which was a large label addressed to me. A cupboard was sealed with a label and my name on it. All this was done by Grandy Jersey. Inside the cupboard was a mass of bills and accounts of the Child family in the eighteenth century concerning the building of the house and the making of the furniture. I told Ralph Edwards who was very excited and wanted to lay his hands on them; to which I said no, not until I had read them myself first, and then asked Grandy's permission. Presumably G. has some good reason for wanting me to look through them before any of the V & A officials [who ran, and still run Osterley for the National Trust].

Thursday, 17th November

Luncheon party at Sibyl Colefax's. Guests: the Italian Ambassador, Lord and Lady Camrose, Harold Macmillan, Harold Nicolson, Sir Arthur and Lady Salter, Thelma Cazalet, me. Sibyl so thin that it hurts to look at her. Her old maid told me as I left that Sibyl becomes thinner every day and that when she is not at a party she is in bed resting; that only within the past two months has she heard her confess to feeling unwell. I sat next to Lady Salter and Harold who reproached me for telling Christopher Hussey about the Blake discovery and allowing him to publish the story in *Country Life*, instead of giving it to Ben for the *Burlington Magazine*. I said to Harold, 'Ben's attitude is that of an editor of a parish magazine who is too proud to refer to news that has previously appeared in *The Times*.' The silly talk of politicians. H. Macmillan a pompous, inflated man full of self-importance. Sir A. Salter and Harold told fairly funny stories about Mr Gladstone and that tiresome Winston Churchill's constant allusions to Gladstone having become Prime Minister again at eighty-three. Lust for power is what it is. I liked the Camroses. He struck me as good and sincere and Lady Camrose as an intelligent, whimsical and cosy old lady, with no airs.

Friday, 18th November

At dinner at Jack Rathbone's Duff Dunbar said that Bob's life of Logan Pearsall Smith was brilliant, well-composed, honest and direct, and makes Logan, with all his warts, a kind of Dr Johnson, dedicated to upholding the English literary style.

Monday, 21st November

I stayed the weekend with Deenie at Stow, very comfortable. She is easier to be with than my mother. Twice I went to Wickhamford, yesterday and today and saw my father, the first day sitting in his chair, this morning in bed. He is pitiably thin, but his colour good. He gets extremely tired after twenty minutes of talk. Elaine says that he cannot live two months and that the cancer in his bladder has grown to the size of a grapefruit. In fact this terrible thing literally eats its victim who appreciably diminishes as it increases in bulk. There is something evil and damnable about this. Yet here is my poor father talking about his plans for next spring, how he intends to buy a racehorse if he can afford it, and go to Deauville or somewhere abroad in order to gamble. Is this put on in order to deceive us, or himself? Does such talk keep his poor spirits up? He surely must know. Perhaps God is good to one in such condition in allowing one not to despair, despair.

This morning I talked to Heather Muir at Kiftsgate. She will help us at Hidcote but says we must try and get rid of Nancy Lindsay. I looked at Quainton church where the mural tablets are all to Corbets of Adlington. At Charlecote I fetched a rare book of Erasmus, possibly illuminated by Holbein, to take to the British Museum, and the Isaac Oliver of Sir Thomas Lucy to show to the National Portrait Gallery.

At 6.15 had my first Italian lesson from an old Polish refugee, a pathetic old lady who teaches Anne Hill. She is a better teacher than that flibbertigibbet, Guido Ferrari in Rome.

Wednesday, 23rd November

Motored Johnnie Churchill to Chartwell this morning. Mr and Mrs Winston were in London so we were able to go wherever we wanted. It must once have been a nice Queen Anne house, but Mr C. has altered it out of all recognition, and it is now quite ugly; but of course bears W.C.'s strong impress. We saw his study and adjoining bedroom. If all the photographs and pictures and framed letters from Marlborough, and from himself to General Alexander and others remain, Chartwell will be interesting to posterity. His bedroom is rather austere in spite of windows on all sides and three telephones by the bed. The view from it is splendid – the great lake made by him and the dam, which I remember him constructing when I stayed here twenty years ago, and the chain of pools to the topmost of which water is pumped by a machine from the bottom lake! What a to-do went on during these operations, Mr C., clad in waders, standing up to his chest in mud and shouting directions like Napoleon before Austerlitz. The long downstairs room is now full of his paintings, of which the earlier ones in the style of Sickert, without the later ubiquitous blue, are not too bad. We looked at Johnnie's slate frieze being installed in the loggia. Johnnie is a dear old friend and we had a great gossip about his family. He says he doesn't care for Christopher Soames, but does like Duncan Sandys. Mr C. has cultivated a deafness which he turns on like a tap when he is bored: an excellent form of defence and one adopted by many old people to whom time is precious. Chartwell is fascinating as the shrine of a great man, just as Hughenden is. The moment I set foot in the house I said to Johnnie, 'I have not been here since Oxford days and I vividly remember the smell of the house. What is it?' 'Cigars and brandy,' he said. Of course. It is far from disagreeable, rather like cedar wood. Agreeable, I suppose, because his cigars are expensive ones.

Friday, 25th November

Robin Fedden took me to Clandon this afternoon. The poor Onslows find they cannot afford to live in it any longer. They offer the house and garden, without further land, and will lend the contents of the state rooms. All these are on the *piano nobile* and are splendid, with some of the best Palladian ceilings in England. I last saw the house when the Blakistons were living here during the war and the rooms were piled with wooden crates of deeds and papers stored by the Public Record Office. Lady Onslow is a personage, slim and delicate, while something in the eyes and mouth denote strength of character. She has excellent taste in dress and decoration, to judge by her appearance and the way she has reanimated Clandon after the mess she found it in. He is a curious-looking man with a large mouth, capricious and 'an original', so Robin described him. He was wearing attractively bizarre clothes, check tweed trousers getting tubular towards the bottoms like the pilasters of Mannerist architects. At tea I, who normally don't eat, wolfed away; so did Robin, the Onslows eating nothing. Robin later remarked on the embarrassment of our behaviour, to which I was totally insensitive: the bloody bureaucrats from London come to take over their house and gorging on the victims' victuals.

Monday, 28th November

I accompanied Audrey, Dale and Prudence to Woolwich to see Audrey and the child Dale off to the Bahamas. Prue and I, not allowed on board ship, left Audrey and Dale after a long wait at a barrier. I last saw Audrey's pathetic and taut little face, so thin and tired it looked, but smiling, in her extraordinarily courageous way: a sort of *The Last of England* scene. These past few days I have been with her a lot and overcome by that mingling flood of exasperation and pity. In the move she lost her pearl necklace and ruby ring – the only jewellery she has not had to sell. She left them on her dressing-table. Oh dear. And then her sorrow at leaving England which has always treated her abominably and worry about Papa. Now tearing off, in abject poverty, in pursuit of this husband she knows so little about. Will he be kind to her? And will she still love him?

Tuesday, 29th November

This morning at 8 o'clock I was woken by Emily telling me Mrs Dick wanted me on the telephone. I guessed what it meant. She said my father was worse, was almost certainly dying. I said I would leave at once. Within one and a half hours I had packed, put off arrangements and left in the car. Arrived at Wickhamford at 12 o'clock. Found Mama walking in the garden, very quiet and composed. Papa unconscious. Deenie was there and before luncheon Dick arrived from Lancashire. The nurse was with my father all day and Mama went up at intervals but was so overcome that she couldn't bear it and went downstairs. Elaine also sat with him. By the evening I steeled myself and went upstairs and into his room. He was lying on Mama's bed, curled up on his side, his head twisted, almost unrecognizable. His head had wizened to a skull with skin stretched tightly across it, so shrunk and taut it was. His mouth seemed to have slipped to one side of his face and his tongue lolled out. The breathing was deep, wracked and intermittent. How he would have hated me seeing him in this condition. I felt a trespasser, uncomfortable, apologetic. I felt infinite compassion because of the indignity he was put to. Perhaps for the first time in my life I loved him unreservedly.

There he lay all through the night. At 4 o'clock I went to bed at the doctor's cottage across the road.

Wednesday, 30th November

When I got back at 9 he was in precisely the same condition. At 10 o'clock the nurse ran downstairs and told us to telephone Dr Astley at his surgery. I went up with Mama. The breathing seemed to me louder and more laboured. Otherwise I noticed little change. There ensued a terrible hour, poor Mama on her knees at his bedside, talking to him who understood not a word and beseeching him to give up the struggle. This he did a little before 11 o'clock. The nurse, M. and I were present. The breathing became a little easier, stopped, his mouth moved, then his throat, and then nothing. Swiftly the nurse with great dexterity, her hand over his heart, pulled the sheet over his head, and I led Mama away, prostrate with grief. It was a terrible, harrowing experience, yet one which nearly every human being has to undergo, once if not twice in a lifetime.

I hope never again to go through another like it. The very worst things about death are the disrespect, the vulgarity, the meanness. God should have arranged for dying people to disintegrate and disappear like a puff of smoke into the air. There are many other scraps of advice I could have given him.

Dick has been wonderful throughout, a tower of strength, so gentle, efficient and controlled unlike me who was constantly moved to tears. We acted at once; got the undertakers from Cavendish House, Cheltenham, visited the *Evesham Journal* for insertion of the announcement in *The Times*, and registered the death.

Friday, 2nd December

Dick and I motored to Cheltenham. Went to an employment agency looking for a servant for Mama, without success. Then to the cremation ceremony at the crematorium just outside the town. We were punctual to the minute, 3.45, for we had been warned not to be early or we would run into the congregation of the previous funeral service. I suppose these services go on every day from morning till night, one after the other, bodies like sausages passing down a factory belt. Behind the chapel was a round building with large central chimney. I pointed out to Dick that it was belching black smoke. We giggled. Dick and I sat alone in a hideous late Victorian chapel without ornamentation, strictly non-denominational. Behind us the black mutes of the undertakers' party. The coffin on a slab in front of us. Sympathetic C of E clergyman officiating, but the service short and devoid of the devotional and spiritual. We were completely unmoved even when the clergyman pressed a button and the coffin slid away and the tatty velvet curtains opened, and a cheap, cracked gramophone record struck up *Abide with Me*, and faded out. This disgusted us. There was nothing to be seen when the curtains were drawn open. I believe the coffin is taken off the conveyor belt and does not go to the crematorium until a number of others have been collected. And oh, the unctuousness of the chief undertaker, with his faultless manner, greased hair and black kid gloves! Enough to make one sick.

Saturday, 3rd December

Yet the memorial service in Wickhamford church was far worse. All morning the villagers were decorating the church with chrysanthemums and taking infinite pains. Mama remained in the house with Clara Mitchell. Deenie, Elaine, Dick and I went. The church was packed. We went to our pew, the manor pew, and I sat in Papa's place beside the pew door. Felt an interloper. I managed somehow to get through without making a fool of myself, not without effort. Dick, who sat next to me, and was far closer to my father than I was, sang throughout most lustily. The parson gave an excellent address, not embarrassing in any sense. He praised Papa's wisdom, courtesy and charm. Said he never refused to respond to a good village cause and was a typical country gentleman. It was rather strange that the first service for which the choir gallery (which my father gave and which it was his great ambition to see finished) should be used was for his own memorial service. I noticed no one in the church. One is made insensate on such occasions, luckily. Was upset when all was over. Was full of remorse for not having been more understanding and kinder, for until recently my father and I did not get on. He never liked me from the start, for which I do not blame him, although I think he should have tried to be nice to me first. Ours was a case of biological incompatibility. Our hackles rose on the mere approach of the other. Yet within his limitations he was a good man, respected by strangers and loved by his friends and other people's children.

Wednesday, 7th December

Went to see Father d'Arcy to ask him if it would be appropriate to have a mass said for my father's soul. I explained it was a thing which I would never have dared mention to him were he alive, for he hated Catholicism and all it stood for. I didn't want to take an unfair advantage of him, so to speak, he being in no position to answer back. Father d'Arcy's reply was 'Certainly, yes. If your father is in heaven, it can do no harm; if in purgatory, he will now be glad of it.' I doubted that. Then I asked if I might be cremated, please. His answer unsatisfactory. He said it was a difficult concession and I must regard the Church's dislike of cremation as an etiquette, not a dogma, to be respected. I said it seemed to me good manners and socially considerate in view of the appalling increase in the population. If everyone insisted upon having a grave there would before long be little room left for any other purpose. To this remark Father d'Arcy turned a deaf ear in the way of priests who have been floored. Then I told him I wanted to marry. He said that if A. and A. could establish that their marriage had never been taken seriously, an annulment was possible, notwithstanding that a child was born of their union. I don't like Father d'Arcy very much. He is artful, as one would expect the Provincial of the Jesuits to be.

Tuesday, 13th December

Lunched with Midi at her club to meet George Chavchavadze who turned up with Malcolm Sargent. The meal was about the most hilarious I ever sat through. Conversation was sheer nonsense from beginning to end so that I laughed till it hurt. None of the talk bears recording. In

fact it was inconsecutive and quite unrecordable. Malcolm is a splendid
foil to George. Each eggs the other on to inconceivable follies.

I have slight nightmares about corpses and coffins, which trouble me.
Mama was so pleased with Papa after death that she wanted to show him
to people. Very extraordinary, for it is just what she laughed at the village
people for doing. She thought he looked young and serene. I thought he
looked fearsome – emaciated, stern and a travesty of his former self, like
an unsuccessful waxwork at Madame Tussaud's.

Thursday, 15th December

Alvilde has come back. I met her at Victoria.

Thursday, 22nd December

At Ethel Sands's this evening Prince Antoine Bibesco came in. He is
oldish, with straight, thick grey hair. He is the man Proust loved and the
widower of Elizabeth Asquith. Abounding in charm and I would guess
the cause of havoc in many hearts of yore. John Lehmann was present.
Talk was of publishers. John says only the old and established firms can
make a profit and survive today.

Sunday, 25th December

Christmas Day spent at Stow-on-the-Wold with darling old Deenie and
Mama. No one else. Dick telephoned from Lancashire and Audrey sent
a cable from Nassau. Alone with D. it would have been easy and restful,
but with Mama present it was not. She became vague, argumentative and
cantankerous. Abused Elaine until I could hardly bear it and not too nice
about Dick. I wrote to Dick and begged him not to pay too much heed
to what she might repeat about me, for I should not pay any to what she
says about him.

I walked in the afternoon down to Swell, looked in at the little
Norman church and at the manor with its Tuscan-Jacobean porch; then
across to Nether Swell and on to Lower Slaughter, and back to Stow. Very
northern, dark, cloudy afternoon, the distant hills cold and watercolour-
ful. How snug England is in the winter, with the cottage windows lit up,
warm fires blazing and Christmas decorations hanging from the beams.
So pretty all the rooms were, while outside grim and dusky. This is
England in the distant heart of the sweeping Cotswolds, with the sweet
aromatic smell of log fires unchanged since my childhood.

During the walk I reflected upon my relations with my poor mother
and the sad change that has come about. It may be due partly to having
witnessed her perpetual nagging of my father ever since I can remember
anything. In my boyhood I took her side. Years passed before I realized

my mistake and cruelty in so doing. I should not have taken her side, or
his. Now I must never forget that until I was about thirty my mother
meant everything to me. We were as one. All things change and relationships turn topsy-turvy. Perhaps in the next world they right themselves,
I mean the good ones become good again and the bad ones are totally
forgotten, as they can be partially overlooked in this.

Thursday, 29th December

Went to see Sibyl Colefax in bed, looking bright-eyed but slighter than
ever. This woman who has known thousands of people in her time is now
near death and is content, or should I say compelled for lack of anyone
better, to call upon me, who am younger than she and outside her intimate circle, to her bedside. We talked of the wickedness of mothers for
being possessive, something I can never accuse my poor mother of. Then
T. S. Eliot came. He is remarkably youthful in appearance, with smooth,
unlined, tight skin behind the ears and on the neck. He has a mischievous
manner of speaking which is attractive. He talked of his play's success at
Brighton and said he feared for its reception among the wolves and tigers
of America. Said the Americans owe their figures to the starch and sweets
they eat. We talked of Einstein whom he had supposed, until today's discovery of the new equation, to be long ago finished. He said that Einstein
plays the fiddle interminably and badly and rows with his wife on a small
lake, known as Lake Listerine, given him by the millionaire manufacturer
of that lotion.

Saturday, 31st December

Such an odd luncheon today with Anthony Chaplin alone at the
Berkeley to discuss our mutual plans. A. wanted me to talk to him and
find out what precisely was in his mind. The occasion was as happy as
could be. Anthony definitely wants A. to divorce him, but he will not
marry Rosemary, he assures me. He merely wants to be free: of what, I
asked him? Not of A., for he has been free from her ever since he married
her. He agrees with me that I would make a great mistake to abandon
the Nat. Trust altogether. I told him that A. was depressed by the thought
of a divorce. He said this was pure sentiment for, once the divorce was
over, he would see as much of A. as before it; and that I must try and make
her happy. This should be the first objective of the years that remain to
me. We parted in mutual piety.

In the evening she and I went to the theatre and the Savoy. I promised
her that if Anthony goes I will live with her and marry her when I get
the Church's consent. We went home to her flat before midnight and
were together when the New Year came in.

Index

438 INDEX